Great
American Naval
Battles

Great American Naval Battles

Edited by

Jack Sweetman

Naval Institute Press
Annapolis, Maryland

Naval Institute Press
291 Wood Road
Annapolis, MD 21402

First Naval Institute Press paperback edition published in 2016.
ISBN: 978-1-59114-634-6 (paperback)
ISBN: 978-1-61251-734-6 (eBook)

The Library of Congress has cataloged the hardcover edition as follows:

Great American naval battles / edited by Jack Sweetman.

    p. cm.

   Includes bibliographical references and index.

   ISBN 1-55750-794-5 (alk. paper)

    1. United States—History, Naval. 2. Naval battles—United States—History. I. Sweetman, Jack, 1940–.

E182.G76 1998

359'.00973–dc21   98-38021

♾ Print editions meet the requirements of ANSI/NISO z39.48-1992 (Permanence of Paper).

Printed in the United States of America.

24 23 22 21 20 19 18 17 16   9 8 7 6 5 4 3 2 1

FIRST PRINTING

In Memoriam

Dr. W. M. P. Dunne

Professor Emeritus E. B. Potter
United States Naval Academy

Commodore Kostis Varfis
Hellenic Navy (Retired)

Contents

Maps

Tables

Acknowledgments

I am greatly indebted to the distinguished team of historians who participated in this work. Its members not only contributed essays of their own, but, with the lamented exceptions of Dr. Dunne and Professor Emeritus Potter, also read my introduction, offering helpful comments and suggestions. The responsibility for its content is, however, mine alone.

It was, as always, a pleasure to work with the staff of the Naval Institute Press. Dr. Paul Wilderson, executive editor, furnished encouragement and sound advice. Mr. J. Randall Baldini, managing editor, Ms. Rebecca Hinds, production editor, Ms. Sandy D. Adams, design and production manager, and Ms. Karen White, senior designer, saw to it that the manuscript moved smoothly through the press. Ms. Sara Elder, photo editor, and Ms. Dawn Stitzel, manager, library services, and photo archivist, helped to assemble the illustrations.

I am also grateful to Ms. Dory Meister, who patiently put the manuscript on disk, and to Ms. Kim Cretors, who painstakingly copy-edited it.

Convention dictates that the closing lines of a book's acknowledgments should be devoted to an expression of thanks to one's wife or husband; but when I record that my greatest debt is to my wife Gisela, it is not a matter of convention. It is a matter of fact.

Introduction

This is a book about battles—nineteen of them, altogether—fought by American naval forces from the War of the Revolution to the recent past. At a time when much of the work being done in military history centers on its social and institutional aspects, it seems well to remember that, much as one would wish otherwise, fighting battles is the most essential function of armed forces. This is obviously the case in time of war, but even in time of peace the utility of armed forces as instruments of national policy depends on the perception that they are prepared to fight effectively if required. Indeed, subject to the occasional aberrations to which none are immune, all of their organic activities, from weapons development to public relations, are directly or indirectly intended to promote "combat readiness"—that is, the ability to give battle. To these generalizations, the U.S. Navy is no exception. The history of how the navy has fought its great battles is therefore an examination of how it has fulfilled its fundamental reason for being.

Whether such an examination can possess more than purely historical interest is a matter of opinion. Today a substantial portion of the academic community would deny that the discipline of history has any value other than to nourish an understanding of the past, a value sufficient unto itself. In contrast, as the historical studies that figure in the curricula of the world's war colleges attest, the military profession retains the conviction formed more than a century ago that, despite the recurrent changes technology dictates in tactics, an understanding of past conflicts can be of direct, practical benefit in future ones: not by furnishing prescriptions for action, but by providing bases for judgment. To readers, civilian or military, who share this conviction, the history of the navy's battles, even those fought under sail, must be a rich source of lessons in leadership and illustrations of the application of the principles of war.

Of the battles treated in this volume, two took place during the War of the Revolution—Valcour Island and Flamborough Head; three during the War of 1812—the *Constitution*'s battles, Lake Erie, and Lake Champlain; three during the Civil War—Hampton Roads, New Orleans, and Mobile Bay; two during the Spanish-American War—Manila Bay and Santiago; eight during World War II—the attack on Pearl Harbor, the Battles of the Coral Sea and Midway, the Battleship Night Action in the Naval Battle of Guadalcanal, the Battles of the Atlantic, the Philippine Sea, and Leyte Gulf, and the Battle for Okinawa; and one during the postwar period—Operation Praying Mantis. In seeking to identify what constituted a great battle, the key consideration seemed to me that it must have had major historical consequences—political, military, or moral, or a combination thereof. All save one of those named above arguably satisfy that criterion. The exception is Operation Praying Mantis, an engagement with no current claim to having much affected the flow of history, but which appears great in interest as an example of the changes that have occurred in the nature of naval combat since World War II. To explain why these particular battles were chosen, however, it will be best to place them in the context of American naval history; and while it is too much to hope that every reader will agree with every selection, I believe that the majority will agree with most.

There are basically two offensive naval strategies: commerce raiding (which seventeenth-century French strategists called cruiser warfare, *guerre de course*), the aim of which is to destroy the enemy's merchant marine; and fleet operations (which the French called squadron warfare, *guerre d'escadre*), the aim of which is to destroy the enemy's battle fleet and assert the overall maritime supremacy known as command of the sea. These strategies are not mutually exclusive. Historically, navies strong enough to undertake fleet operations have usually been able to detach sufficient cruiser types—or in the case of the U.S. Navy's war against Japan, submarines—to conduct a simultaneous war on trade; but for a navy lacking the number or type of ships required to fight for command of the sea, commerce raiding (coupled with coast defense) is the only regularly available option. Although on occasion the weaker navy may attempt to attain local and temporary sea control for an ulterior purpose—to cover a landing or screen a convoy, for example—such operations are by their nature infrequent. For roughly the first hundred years of its existence, the U.S. Navy professed—though it did not always practice—the strategy of *guerre de course*. Its conversion to *guerre d'escadre* forms the watershed of American naval history.

In the War of the Revolution, American naval forces had no choice but to pursue a *guerre de course*. In January 1775, four months before the outbreak of hostilities, the Royal Navy numbered 131 ships of the line—the capital ships of the day—mounting from 60 to 100 guns, and 98 cruiser types mounting from 20 to 50 guns, and it was reinforced until by January 1782 it included 161 ships of the line and 183 cruisers. The Continental Navy, on the other hand, did not even exist until six months after the war began, and of the fifty-four vessels, all cruisers, it eventually commissioned, only two remained in service as of 1782. Fortunately, the need to maintain a powerful fleet in British home waters and lesser commitments elsewhere made it impossible for the Royal Navy to bring its full strength to bear in the North American theater; but the forces it could deploy there were ample to exercise undisputed command of the sea until France entered the war.

The American war on trade was carried out by both public and private vessels. The former were the commissioned warships of the Continental Navy. The latter, far more numerous, were privateers, privately owned vessels licensed by governmental authority to prey on enemy (only) shipping. This license, called a letter of marque, represented a mutually beneficial, centuries-old arrangement that entitled a government to a share of its privateers' profits and privateersmen, if captured, to be treated as prisoners of war rather than hung from the nearest yardarm. How many American privateers put to sea is unknown. The Continental Congress issued 1,697 letters of marque, and state governments and diplomats abroad granted hundreds more. How many prizes the privateers made is also uncertain, the usual estimate being about 2,200, or roughly ten times the number taken by the Continental Navy.

Two other, minor American maritime forces may be mentioned in passing. Between 1775 and 1777 George Washington, commander in chief of the Continental Army, chartered eleven armed merchantmen that took fifty-five prizes, and a few of the home-defense navies established by most states included blue-water vessels that attacked British shipping.

The American *guerre de course* sent British shipping insurance soaring, obliged the Royal Navy to detach cruisers to serve as convoy escorts, and on several occasions garnered military material greatly appreciated by Washington's army, but there is no evidence that it seriously inconvenienced Britain's prosecution of the war. The most positive outcome of the *course* was to give America its first and still its best-known naval hero, John Paul Jones, victor of the Battle of Flamborough Head (23 September 1779). The action, which pitted three frigates and a corvette forming a little squadron nominally under Jones's command against a frigate and a sloop of war escorting a British merchant convoy, should have been no contest. In the event, one of the frigates and the corvette avoided harm's way, and the second frigate found her hands full dealing with the British sloop, leaving Jones in the *Bonhomme Richard*, a rotten old ex–East Indiaman, to win an unlikely victory over HMS *Serapis*, a swifter, more heavily armed, and in every respect superior ship.

Strategically the battle was of little consequence. The Royal Navy could easily afford the loss of two cruisers, and the fight they put up enabled their convoy to escape, but morally, Jones had achieved the Continental Navy's greatest triumph. To have captured one of His Britannic Majesty's frigates in her home waters made him an international celebrity, the recipient of a French knighthood, and the subject of pop songs. In addition and most important of all, John Paul Jones had set an example of courage, skill, and fortitude that would be a source of inspiration to future generations of American naval officers.

The Continental Navy's contribution to coast defense proved unavailing. Six of its ships and the entire Pennsylvania State Navy were lost in a futile attempt to prevent the British from seizing control of the Delaware River in 1777; three more, plus sixteen state and chartered ships, when a British squadron interrupted an amphibious operation in progress against a British outpost on Penobscot Bay, Maine, in 1779; and another four in the unsuccessful defense of Charleston, South Carolina, in 1780. Years before these disasters, however, a scratch force improvised by an army officer whose name would become synonymous with "traitor" to defend a waterway more than a hundred miles from the sea had won a crucial strategic victory in a battle in which it was destroyed.

The officer was Brig. Gen. Benedict Arnold, one of the ablest patriot leaders before he turned his coat, and the waterway was Lake Champlain, a link in the almost unbroken chain of rivers and lakes extending from Montreal to New York. In the late summer of 1776, a British army began to advance south from Canada along this invasion avenue. Arnold's mission was to contest control of the lake until a defensive front could be organized around Fort Ticonderoga near its southern extremity. After more than a month's sparring, his command was for practical purposes annihilated by a stronger British squadron at the hard-fought Battle of Valcour Island (11–13 October 1776).

Tactical defeat notwithstanding, Arnold had achieved his objective. By the time of the action it had grown so late in the campaigning season that afterwards the British retired to winter quarters in Canada. The following summer "Gentleman Johnny" Burgoyne's attempt to renew the advance along the same route ended in his battered army's capitulation at Saratoga, New York, in October. This event, for which Arnold's delaying action set the stage, marked the turning point of the Revolution, for it moved France, already covertly aiding the colonists, to enter the war on their side.

French intervention proved decisive. There were almost as many French as American troops in Washington's forces when they closed around Cornwallis's army at Yorktown, Virginia, late in September 1781. Earlier that month a French fleet of two dozen ships of the line under Count de Grasse had accomplished something American cruisers never could, fending off a British fleet's attempt to enter the Chesapeake Bay and make contact with Cornwallis. Thwarted at the Battle of the Virginia Capes, the British withdrew to New York for reinforcements. When they returned to the Chesapeake on 24 October, it was too late. Cornwallis had surrendered five days earlier. Although the war sputtered on another eighteen months, America's independence had been won.

Congress ordered the sale of the Continental Navy's last vessel in June 1785. For the next nine years, the new nation had no navy. The feeble central government established by the Articles of Confederation could not afford one. Even after the ratification of the Constitution in 1789 specifically empowered Congress to "provide and maintain a Navy," an extended and passionate debate took place on the wisdom of acting upon that authority. The Federalist Party insisted that a navy was necessary to protect American trade; the Republicans countered that a navy would plunge the country ever deeper into debt and embroil it in needless foreign wars. In the end congressional hands were forced by the failure of U.S. diplomacy to reach an agreement with Algiers.

For centuries the Barbary Powers—Morocco, Algiers, Tunis, and Tripoli— had made a lucrative business of charging maritime nations an annual fee to refrain from attacking their shipping. As long as American vessels sailed under British colors, they had been covered by the arrangements the mother country made for the safe passage of its trade. Once they hoisted their own flag, they became fair game. The United States was not in principle opposed to paying tribute but balked at the sum Algiers was asking; and while negotiations languished, so did the American seamen being held for ransom in Algerian dungeons. The upshot was the passage of the Navy Act of 27 March 1794, which authorized the creation of a navy consisting of six ships, all frigates, four of forty-four guns and two of thirty-six.

The choice of frigates, the largest type of cruising vessel, ideally suited for commerce raiding and convoy escort, was significant. Earlier, the Federalist leader Alexander Hamilton had proposed building a small balanced fleet including ships of the line. Even though such a force could not, he conceded, compete with the navies of the European great powers, its alliance value would ensure that they respected American interests. Given the opposition that existed to building a navy at all, this idea did not go far. Later, Congress would approve the construction of a few ships of the line, but it did not expect them to engage in fleet operations. Their projected mission was to punch occasional holes in enemy blockades to allow cruisers and privateers to get to sea. The United States had purposely adopted the strategy of *guerre de course.*

Ironically, a treaty was negotiated with Algiers before the frigates could be finished, and the first vessels upon which the U.S. Navy fired belonged to its nation's oldest ally—France. Furthermore, the conflict took the form, not of a *guerre de course,* but of the closest single ships could come to a *guerre d'escadre.* Britain and France had gone to war again in 1793. Since then both sides, determined to disrupt neutral trade with the other, had inflicted injury and inconvenience on American commerce. In 1797 the swarm of French privateers and sprinkling of naval vessels based in the West Indies seized nearly three hundred U.S. merchantmen, some off the southeastern seaboard. That and other insults were more than a Federalist administration could stomach, and in May 1798, after the procurement of additional vessels, it instructed the navy to commence attacking French armed ships. An undeclared, naval-only Quasi-War ensued. In no need of additional enemies, France immediately opened negotiations, and the conflict was settled to American satisfaction in September 1800. During its course the new navy captured eighty-five French ships, including two government frigates, at the cost of a single schooner of its own.

Peace proved fleeting. Scarcely three months after its ratification, the pasha of Tripoli, dissatisfied with the amount of the annual tribute he was receiving, declared war on the United States. The struggle, which took the form chiefly of a naval blockade of the port of Tripoli, dragged on four years. Finally, in April 1805, an overland invasion of his domain by an American-sponsored army of six hundred Arab mercenaries (plus eight U.S. Marines) prompted the pasha to reconsider his options.

The U.S. Navy had performed well in its first two, albeit small, wars. If not of great historical significance, those contests gave the nation a trio of naval heroes in the tradition of John Paul Jones—Thomas Truxtun, captain of the frigate *Constellation* when she captured the French *Insurgente* and, a year later, defeated the *Vengeance;* Edward Preble, by far the most vigorous of the Mediterranean Squadron's commodores during the War with Tripoli; and Stephen Decatur, leader of the raid that destroyed the frigate *Philadelphia* after the Tripolitans captured and refloated her when she ran aground. The deeds of such men as these made Americans proud of their navy.

Nevertheless, as increasing friction with Britain foreshadowed the coming of an immensely greater war, the U.S. government, now controlled by the Republicans who had opposed establishing a navy, declined to add to the number of its major units. What the Republicans did build, and in profusion, were gunboats, small coastal craft carrying one or two guns, flotillas of which were to act in concert with shore fortifications to defend major seaports. Thus it came about that on 18 June 1812, the day Congress voted to declare war on Great Britain, the U.S. Navy had 18 oceangoing vessels in commission; the Royal Navy had 1,048. Once again, as in the Revolution, the navy's *guerre de course* was dwarfed by the activities of privateers, who captured 1,344 British merchantmen to its 165. These losses did nothing to popularize the war with the British mercantile community, but, also as in the Revolution, it took defeat in battle to convince Britain to bring the conflict to a close.

The difference, exemplified by the *Constitution's* battles, was that this time government cruisers aggressively sought and often as not won actions with equivalent classes of British warships. At a time when its innumerable victories over the navies of France and her allies had given the Royal Navy an aura of invincibility, the American successes created a sensation on both sides of the Atlantic. The fact that all except two of the twenty-five engagements fought on the high seas were won by the ship hurling the heaviest broadside did not diminish the U.S. Navy's achievement. It had proven itself to be as good as the best.

Yet for all that, American victories in thirteen cruiser actions could not alter the calculus of the war at sea. Confronted by the overwhelming strength of the Royal Navy, the U.S. Navy was unable to retain control of American waters. By 1814 a British blockade had buttoned up the Atlantic seaboard, reducing U.S. maritime trade to approximately 10 percent of its prewar level, and in 1814–15 British squadrons brushed aside gunboat flotillas to land armies outside Washington, Baltimore, and New Orleans. The resistance that repulsed the attacks on the last two cities occurred ashore, not afloat. Throughout the war, the Royal Navy enjoyed and exploited the advantages of command of the sea.

In contrast, American victories in two grueling, freshwater fleet actions fundamentally affected the course of the conflict. The clean sweep Commo. Oliver Hazard Perry made of the British squadron at the Battle of Lake Erie (10 September 1813) and the subsequent destruction of the enemy's ground forces at the Battle of the Thames blasted British hopes of establishing an Indian buffer state to block American expansion into the Ohio Valley. A year later, at the Battle of Lake Champlain (11 September 1814), Commo. Thomas Macdonough frustrated the most formidable British offensive of the war, an advance from Canada using the same invasion avenue the British had followed in 1776 and 1777 by a ten thousand–man army including many battle-hardened veterans of the Napoleonic wars. Stunned by this setback, the British cabinet sought the advice of the country's greatest soldier, the Duke of Wellington. His gloomy counsel ("that which appears to me to be wanting in America is not a General, . . . but a naval superiority on the lakes") was instrumental in its decision to make peace. Had Perry or Macdonough been defeated, a considerable portion of what is now the northeastern United States might well be southeastern Canada.

In the decades after the return of peace the navy undertook a wide range of activities in support of the mission for which it had been created—the protection and promotion of American trade. Salient among those activities were collaboration with the Royal Navy in the suppression of West Indian piracy (1819–26), the establishment of six small but permanent overseas squadrons to show the flag and safeguard American interests around the world (1815–35), and the conduct of a number of scientific expeditions and diplomatic missions intended to facilitate maritime commerce. The navy also played a significant part in the Mexican War (1846–48). The inability of Mexico's minuscule navy to oppose its operations made this the first major conflict in which it enjoyed command of the sea. The navy was quick to exploit the opportunity, blockading, raiding, and seizing ports on the Pacific and Gulf coasts of Mexico; furnishing naval brigades to assist in the conquest of California; and, in a flawlessly planned and executed amphibious operation, landing an army that marched inland from Veracruz to capture Mexico City and bring the war to an end. This exemplary application of sea power notwithstanding, the nation's naval policy remained unchanged.

Thus it seems almost ironic that in the great Civil War that broke out in 1861 the U.S. Navy should again enjoy command of the sea. It exercised that command against the Confederate States in much the same way as it had against Mexico—and, in earlier wars, the Royal Navy had against the United States—to blockade the southern seacoast, deliver armies where desired, and support inland offensives along navigable waterways, while the Confederate States Navy pursued the traditional American practice of commerce raiding and coast defense. Like the colonists during the Revolution, the Confederates had no choice in the matter. The agrarian South lacked the means to compete with the already industrializing North in construction and conversion programs that increased the U.S. Navy's strength from 90 vessels at the onset of hostilities to a wartime peak of 671.

The Confederacy's only hope of defying the blockade was therefore to overcome quantity with quality by capitalizing upon recent advances in naval technology. The most recent of those advances was the introduction of the ironclad warship, the first of which, the *Gloire*, had been completed by France in 1859. Accordingly, Confederate Secretary of the Navy Stephen R. Mallory enthusiastically approved plans to build an ironclad ram, later christened the CSS *Virginia*, on the hull of the former U.S. frigate *Merrimack*. Upon learning of this project, the U.S. Navy authorized the construction of three ironclads of differing designs. The outcome was almost a dead heat. The *Virginia* sortied from Norfolk in time to sink two wooden blockaders in the first day's Battle of Hampton Roads (8–9 March 1862), but when she returned to continue her work of destruction the next morning she found herself confronted by the USS *Monitor,* the first of the Union ironclads. Tactically, the ensuing action ended in a draw, but strategically the *Monitor* was clearly the winner. By showing that her opponent could be contained, she had ensured that the blockade would be preserved.

A month later, the Confederacy was staggered by the most potent demonstration to date of the capability of Union sea power. New Orleans, its biggest city and principal port, fell to forces commanded by Flag Officer David Glasgow Farragut after a wild night action (24 April 1862) that, in numbers of ships engaged, proved to be the war's largest naval battle. In addition to carrying the blockade ashore (and, incidentally, discouraging Britain and France from intervening to uphold southern independence), the capture of New Orleans contributed to another of the navy's missions—collaborating with the army to cut the Confederacy in two along the line of the Mississippi. That campaign concluded with the surrender of Vicksburg, Mississippi, and Port Hudson, Louisiana, in July 1863, and by July 1864 Mobile, Alabama, and Wilmington, North Carolina, were the only refuges left in the eastern Confederacy for the blockade runners that continued to slip through the cordon around its coast. Farragut's victory at the Battle of Mobile Bay (5 August 1864), the war's last major naval action, eliminated Mobile. When in January 1865 a Union amphibious assault overran the fort guarding the entrance to the Cape Fear River and thereby closed Wilmington, the navy's war was effectively over. Its ships would stay on station for another four months, but all of its objectives had been accomplished.

Following the Civil War the nation, absorbed in domestic concerns, allowed the powerful navy of 1865 to undergo a precipitous decline. By 1889, it ranked twelfth among the navies of the world, inferior to those of every major European power, not to mention Chile and China. Its missions remained the same as the antebellum navy's: in peace, championing commerce; in war with a great power, *guerre de course.* Faith in the latter had been reinforced by the depredations of the Confederate commerce raiders, the strategic sterility of which somehow escaped notice.

All this was soon to change. At least in hindsight, it became evident that Congress had initiated a naval renaissance in 1883 by funding the construction of the ABCDs—the "protected" (by armored decks shielding their engine spaces) steel cruisers *Atlanta, Boston,* and *Chicago,* and the dispatch-vessel *Dolphin*—the first state-of-the-art warships built for the navy since the Civil War. The first two American battleships, the *Maine* and the *Texas,* were authorized three years later. Other appropriations followed almost annually thereafter, until by the eve of the War with Spain the U.S. Navy ranked fifth in the world, with six battleships, six modern monitors, two powerful armored cruisers, and sixteen protected cruisers, plus a number of smaller units, in commission.

But the navy of the 1890s acquired more than new ships. It also adopted a new strategy, that of *guerre d'escadre:* fleet operations aimed at achieving command of the sea. Though many developments combined to create an intellectual climate receptive to such a reorientation, its proximate cause was the publication in 1890 of Capt. Alfred Thayer Mahan's study of *The Influence of Sea Power upon History, 1660–1783.* Six years earlier, Mahan had been serving in the Pacific Squadron when he received orders detailing him to teach a strategy course at the recently established Naval War College. At that time Mahan shared the conventional American belief in the efficacy of *guerre de course.* To prepare himself for his forthcoming assignment, he turned to naval history, using the seven wars Britain had fought with Holland and France between 1660 and 1783 as test studies to see whether he could discover any general principles of naval warfare. The result surprised him. After suspending fleet operations midway through her first war with Britain, France had consistently pursued a policy of *guerre de course,* reserving her battle fleets for ulterior operations, usually in support of the army; and, aside from the tie represented by the American Revolution, France had always lost. Britannia ruled the waves because she invariably sought to establish command of the sea. Commerce raiders might wreak havoc on enemy shipping, but they could not win a war.

These views, first propounded in the lectures that became the basis of the book, won the acclaim of government leaders, naval officers, editors, and academicians around the world. Their impact on the U.S. Navy was immense. In wars with other naval powers, it would no longer be content to send cruisers to cripple the enemy's merchant fleet, as it had in the Revolution and the War of 1812; it would send capital ships to crush the enemy's battle fleet. Once that had been accomplished, it could proceed to strangle his shipping, and much more, besides: to blockade his ports, isolate his overseas possessions, and, if necessary, transport armies to invade his homeland or occupied territories.

The demonstration it appeared to provide of Mahan's contention that command of the sea comprised the strategic equivalent of a universal solvent was among the many important consequences of the Spanish-American War. Barely a week after the U.S. declaration of war, Commo. George Dewey boldly led the Asiatic Squadron into Manila Bay, gave his flag captain the most famous order in American naval history—"You may fire when you are ready, Gridley"—and demolished Spain's decrepit Philippine squadron in a battle in which not a single American seaman was killed (1 May 1898). Little more than two months later, Rear Adm. William T. Sampson's North Atlantic Fleet gained an equally one-sided victory over another inferior Spanish squadron at the Battle of Santiago de Cuba (3 July 1898). These actions sealed the fate of Spain's insular empire, disconnecting it from the metropolis and depriving its garrisons of the prospect of outside assistance. Six weeks after the Battle of Santiago, the signing of an armistice through which Spain conceded defeat brought hostilities to an end. By then, the U.S. Navy was preparing to send a squadron to attack the Spanish seaboard.

The Spanish-American War marked the United States' debut on the world stage. For the first time, it had vanquished a European power, albeit a weak one, in an offensive war. That the victory had been won mainly at sea made the navy, nearly forgotten a few years earlier, an object of national pride. Furthermore, the United States emerged from the conflict with an empire of its own, acquiring the Philippines, Guam, and Puerto Rico, establishing an informal protectorate over Cuba, and, in an outburst of wartime exuberance, annexing the Hawaiian Islands—territories that, as the Spanish example showed, required a strong navy to defend them. Thus the U.S. Navy entered the new century committed to a policy of command of the sea and assured of the public support needed to build a fleet competent to pursue it.

More than forty years would pass before the navy fought another great battle. The peace the United States enjoyed throughout those years was broken only once, in April 1917, when it intervened in World War I. By that date the Imperial German Navy, abandoning hope of defeating Britain's Grand Fleet in detail, had suspended fleet operations in favor of a ruthless, undersea *guerre de course*. This decision preemptively defined the possibilities of American naval action. The navy made a vital contribution to victory, helping fight the Kaiser's U-boats and together with the Royal Navy escorting the American Expeditionary Forces across the Atlantic, but the battle squadron it sent to reinforce the Grand Fleet never fired a shot in anger.

From an institutional standpoint, however, the period was among the most eventful in the navy's history. Theodore Roosevelt, who succeeded to the presidency in 1901, established the goal of building a navy second only to that of Great Britain, for so long mistress of the seas. In 1916, acting under the stimulus of the Great War raging in Europe, Woodrow Wilson obtained congressional approval to build a navy second to none, and in 1922 the achievement of parity with Britain was recognized by the terms of the Washington Naval Treaty. This agreement, proposed by the United States to promote international stability, established a ceiling in capital-ship strength for the five foremost naval powers of 500,000 tons each for Britain and the United States, 300,000 for Japan, and 175,000 each for France and Italy.

Like the United States, Japan was a newcomer to the world stage. Its advent also had been heralded by the clash of arms, in its case what contemporaries found a startling victory in the Russo-Japanese War of 1904–5. The Imperial Japanese Navy had played a vital role in the conflict, which climaxed with its annihilation of a Russian fleet at the Battle of Tsushima, the largest fleet action fought in a century. Ever since Tsushima, the U.S. Navy had been convinced that sooner or later American interests in the Pacific—especially the Philippines, six thousand miles from San Francisco but only a thousand miles from Tokyo—would involve it in a great sea war with Japan.

Anticipation became a reality on Sunday, 7 December 1941, with the Japanese surprise attack on Pearl Harbor. Whether the action that took place that morning should be considered a battle is debatable since U.S. forces were at peace when the bombs began to fall, but certainly it constituted a military event of the first magnitude. The Japanese objective was to paralyze the U.S. Pacific Fleet, the only regional force capable of offering serious resistance to the conquest of the Southwestern Pacific and Southeast Asian territories intended to comprise a "Southern Resources Area" that would make Japan economically independent of the West. In an operational sense, the raid was a brilliant achievement. In a broader, political, psychological, and ultimately, strategic sense, it was a disaster. At one searing stroke, it extinguished the isolationism that had loomed so large on the American scene between the wars and united an outraged people in a determination to defeat Japan.

In the weeks and months following the attack, Japanese forces raced from victory to victory. An Allied attempt to hold the so-called Malay Barrier extending from Singapore through the Netherlands East Indies to New Guinea ended in the destruction of the hastily organized ABDA (American, British, Dutch, Australian) Strike Force at the Battle of the Java Sea in late February 1942. So swift, in fact, was the progress of its oceanic blitzkrieg that by early spring the Imperial Japanese Navy found itself running out of plans. Two views emerged as to what it should do next. The Naval General Staff favored driving still deeper into the South Pacific to interdict the vital sea lanes between Australia and the United States. The commander in chief of the Combined Fleet, Adm. Isoroku Yamamoto, who had sponsored the attack on Pearl Harbor, advocated returning to the Central Pacific to provoke a battle in which the American carriers that had been at sea at the time of the raid could be destroyed. The disagreement culminated in a ruinous compromise. The light carrier *Shoho* and fleet carriers *Shokaku* and *Zuikaku* would support an amphibious assault on Port Moresby, the base of supply of the Australian forces defending eastern New Guinea, in early May, and rejoin the Combined Fleet in time to take part in a Central Pacific offensive later that same month.

Alerted by code-breakers of the Japanese designs on Port Moresby, the commander in chief of the U.S. Pacific Fleet, Adm. Chester W. Nimitz, sent a two-carrier task force under Rear Adm. Frank Jack Fletcher to intercept the enemy off the Papuan peninsula. Its deployment eventuated in the Battle of the Coral Sea (4–8 May 1942), the first carrier air battle ever fought. In five days' deadly hide-and-seek, Fletcher's force sank the *Shoho*, the destroyer *Kikuzuki*, and several lesser units, damaged the *Shokaku*, and decimated the *Shokaku* and *Zuikaku* air groups at the cost of the fleet carrier *Lexington*, oiler *Neosho*, and destroyer *Sims*. With barely any aircraft left to cover an assault on Port Moresby, the Japanese withdrew.

The U.S. Navy had won a crucial moral and strategic victory. For the first time in five months of war, a major Japanese offensive had been stopped short of success. Tactical honors are often accorded the Imperial Navy, a view the statistics support. Though each side's score included an enemy carrier, the Japanese had come out much the better in the exchange of the 11,000-ton *Shoho* for the 37,000-ton *Lexington*, largely because of which they emerged from the battle having sunk more than twice as many tons as they lost. The statistics are misleading. At that moment, the permanent loss of the *Lexington* mattered less than the temporary loss of the *Shokaku* and *Zuikaku*, both of which had to be deleted from the Japanese order of battle for the Central Pacific offensive.

The Combined Fleet sortied from its base at Hashirajima on 27 May 1942 (Japanese Navy Day). Its territorial objective was Midway Atoll, eleven hundred miles west of Pearl Harbor. The seizure of this position was expected to compel the Pacific Fleet to come out and to fight the decisive battle Yamamoto desired.

Even without its two sidelined carriers, the Combined Fleet possessed a seemingly insurmountable material advantage over its adversary: 2.4 to 1 in all types of surface combatants and 8 to 3 in carriers. For the second time, however, cryptanalysts gave Nimitz advance notice of Japanese intentions. This intelligence enabled him to deploy his three carriers northeast of Midway to ambush the Japanese as they approached from the northwest. Further-more, the Imperial Navy's failing for the fanciful inspired an egregious disper-sion of force that reduced the odds in its favor at the point of contact to 4 to 3 in carriers, and, because U.S. carriers embarked bigger air groups, practical parity in aircraft. Bold decisions and extreme gallantry provided the final ingredients of a stunning American victory. At the Battle of Midway (4–6 June 1942), all four Japanese carriers were sunk at the cost of only one of their U.S. counterparts, which succumbed to a submarine a day later. Midway broke the momentum the Imperial Navy had sustained since Pearl Harbor and brought the strategic balance in the Pacific to a precarious equilibrium.

Both navies then turned their attention back to the South Pacific. The Japanese planned to strengthen the defensive perimeter being established around their conquests by ejecting the Allies from eastern New Guinea and instituting an air barrier over the Solomon Islands. The Americans prepared to launch an amphibious offensive leading to the capture of the Japanese fleet and air base at Rabaul, on New Britain.

These rival programs unexpectedly converged on Guadalcanal in the southern Solomons, where in early July 1942 Allied aerial reconnaissance dis-covered that the Japanese were constructing an airstrip. The American high command responded by landing the 1st Marine Division, which captured the unfinished airfield and two adjacent islets without undue difficulty on 7–8 August. Japanese General Headquarters promptly resolved to expel the invaders, precipitating a savage, six-month struggle on land, at sea, and in the air that included the most concentrated combat in the U.S. Navy's history. The climax came in the three actions comprising the Naval Battle of Guadal-canal (12–15 November 1942). The losses it suffered in those engagements convinced the Imperial Navy that it could not continue to endure such attri-tion. Accordingly, on 12 December it formally recommended abandoning the contest for Guadalcanal. General Headquarters concurred at year's end, and in February 1943 the Japanese evacuated the island.

Japan's admission of defeat at Guadalcanal marked the turning point of the Pacific War. At Coral Sea and Midway the United States had stopped los-ing; at Guadalcanal, it started winning. No longer would U.S. forces have to scramble to counter enemy initiatives. From now on, they would set the agenda.

Meanwhile, halfway around the world the Battle of the Atlantic was near-ing a climax. Unlike the others treated in this volume, the battle waged there could not be measured in days or weeks or months. It began in 1939, when the German navy launched a second undersea *guerre de course,* and, although the crisis was passed in 1943, it continued fitfully until the war's end. The U.S. Navy joined the struggle unofficially in September 1941 following President Roosevelt's order to attack any vessel threatening merchantmen, American or otherwise, under its escort, and officially on 11 December, when Germany and Italy honored their pact with Japan by declaring war on the United States.

Again unlike the other battles, the Battle of the Atlantic was not won by any particular action on any specific date. It was an endurance contest of technology, tactics, and intelligence, and the U.S. Navy, the Royal Navy, and the Royal Canadian Navy shared in the victory. The ingredients of their success included, among others, the work of the Ultra code-breakers in decrypting the *Kriegsmarine*'s top-secret transmissions, the allocation of adequate numbers of long-range aircraft equipped with microwave radar to antisubmarine patrols, the use of radio direction-finding and surface-search radar, and the deployment, beginning in early 1943, of increasing numbers of escort carriers in convoy escorts and the U.S. Navy's hunter-killer groups.

To achieve any degree of depth, a chapter-length treatment of this complex struggle must concentrate on one of its phases or aspects. That presented here focuses on the operations of the hunter-killer group headed by the escort carrier *Card*, whose destruction of five U-boats in a single cruise (25 September–9 November 1943) set a record never surpassed. In his history of *The Second World War* Sir Winston Churchill wrote, "The only thing that ever really frightened me . . . was the U-boat peril." The neutralization of that peril, to which the *Card* and her sister ships contributed, ensured that the Atlantic sea lanes remained open.

The outcome of the Atlantic battle still appeared uncertain in January 1943, when American leaders resolved to exercise the initiative won at Guadalcanal by mounting a great dual offensive against Japan. Admiral Nimitz would initiate a navy drive across the Central Pacific, while Gen. Douglas MacArthur pressed an army advance, already under way, westward along the coast of New Guinea. Originally the American agenda included capture of the Japanese base at Rabaul, but in August U.S. leaders decided that it could be bombed out and bypassed.

The navy's new campaign commenced with the seizure of the Gilbert Islands in November 1943, and continued to the Marshalls in January and February 1944. Neither of these operations was opposed by the Imperial Japanese Navy, which had yet to recover from the losses, especially of carrier pilots, it had sustained at Coral Sea, Midway, and in the Solomons. Its passivity ended in June 1944, when Pacific Fleet forces under Adm. Raymond A. Spruance leapfrogged seven hundred miles to the Marianas. For Japan an

American encroachment in the Marianas would be disastrous, breaching its inner defensive perimeter and bringing its highly flammable cities within range of big, land-based bombers. Imperatives both strategic and psychological obliged the Imperial Navy to act.

The ensuing Battle of the Philippine Sea (19–21 June 1944) was the war's largest carrier air action, involving almost fifteen hundred planes flying from twenty-four carriers—nine Japanese and fifteen American. U.S. pilots, who shot down ten of Japan's inadequately trained new airmen for every loss they suffered, called it the Marianas Turkey Shoot. Owing largely to Spruance's conservative tactics six Japanese carriers survived, an outcome that provoked considerable criticism from the aviation community; but by the time contact was broken, those surviving carriers had a total of thirty-five aircraft. Japanese carrier air power had been destroyed.

In October, the pincers of the dual advance closed on the Philippines, and once again the Imperial Navy attempted to repel the invaders. Its desperate plan called for a carrier force with less than half its full complement of aircraft to invite annihilation by luring the fast carriers and new battleships of Adm. William F. Halsey's Third Fleet away from the beachhead while two powerful surface-action groups converged on the assembled amphibious shipping of Vice Adm. Thomas C. Kinkaid's Seventh Fleet. The result was four interlocking actions collectively known as the Battle of Leyte Gulf (24–25 October 1944), the largest naval engagement in history, fought over an area of 110,000 square miles by 190,000 men onboard 282 ships. Although for a few hours the Japanese appeared to be on the verge of a suicidal semisuccess, the ultimate outcome was never in doubt. At the battle's end, the Imperial Navy had lost 47 percent of the big ships—cruisers, battleships, and carriers—that entered it. This constituted a defeat from which there could be no recovery. Leyte Gulf eliminated the Japanese fleet as a strategic factor in the war.

From the Philippines, the Allied offensive followed a single axis of advance northward toward Japan. Iwo Jima was secured in bloody fighting between 1 February and 22 March 1945, and on 1 April U.S. forces landed on Okinawa, just 340 miles from Kyushu, southernmost of the home islands. That the seizure of Okinawa would be succeeded by an assault on the Japanese homeland was obvious to all, and the Imperial Navy set out to help break up the invasion with the only means left it, land-based naval air fleets concentrated on Kyushu. Together with the Japanese Army Air Forces, it pinned its hopes primarily on the recently organized kamikaze Special Attack Corps, whose efforts to inflict unacceptable attrition on the U.S. fleet off Okinawa would be supported by conventional air units. The Battle for Okinawa was therefore a new kind of naval action, one in which ships at sea came under sustained attack by an enemy operating, not from naval platforms, but from unsinkable airfields ashore. During the Falklands War of 1982 the British task force found itself engaged in the same sort of contest when many of its ships had to operate within range of mainland-based Argentine aircraft; but the Argentine airmen were not kamikazes.

The struggle was probably the most grueling the U.S. Navy has ever experienced, especially for the brave destroyer pickets to which the kamikazes devoted disproportionate attention. It was definitely and by far the most bloody; before it ended, close to ten thousand American seamen had been killed or wounded. But it ended in victory. The Allied armada withstood the worst the kamikazes had to offer, and on 21 June Okinawa was declared secure. Two months later, the atomic bombing of Hiroshima and Nagasaki stunned Japan into surrender.

Since 1945 the U.S. Navy has participated in major wars in Korea (1950–53), Vietnam (1965–73), and the Persian Gulf (1991); conducted or collaborated in a number of police actions, some including the use of limited force; served as the key instrument of American diplomacy in several Cold War confrontations, most notably the Cuban Missile Crisis (1962); and, beginning with the deployment of atomic weapons at sea in the 1950s, contributed to the strategy of nuclear deterrence. Though the wars were fundamentally ground conflicts, the navy played a major supporting role. In all three, it ensured the uninterrupted flow of shipping without which American power could not have been projected thousands of miles around the globe. In all three, it provided carrier air and gunfire support, and in Vietnam, for the first time since the Civil War, it created a "Brown-water Navy" of small combatants for action on coastal and inland waters. In the Korean and Gulf wars, it blockaded the enemy homeland. In Vietnam, fears of the Sino-Soviet reaction caused Washington policy makers to reject such action until very late in the day, but in 1972 it was finally allowed to seal off the North from the sea by mining its ports. In Korea, the navy conducted the largest amphibious operation of the last fifty years, the Inchon invasion. In Vietnam, it staged a number of unopposed (though seldom very productive) landings in concert with overland advances against enemy coastal enclaves. In the Gulf, the threat it posed of an assault on Kuwait City immobilized several Iraqi divisions.

In none of these conflicts, however, did the navy fight a naval battle. It lacked the opportunity. North Korea had no navy; aside from two sunk during a night bombardment of Haiphong in August 1972, North Vietnam's handful of patrol-torpedo boats did not attempt to interfere with U.S. naval operations; and the units of the Iraqi navy that escaped destruction en route sought sanctuary in neutral Iran. American command of the sea was undisputed.

In contrast, two police actions have precipitated distinctly naval engagements. The first occurred on 24–25 March 1986, during Operation Attain Document III, one of the periodic freedom-of-navigation exercises held to demonstrate the U.S. rejection of Libya's pretension to sovereignty over the thirty thousand square miles of the Gulf of Sidra. After at least five land-based surface-to-air missiles were launched at the combat air patrol covering a small surface-action group that had crossed the Libyan "Line of Death" into the gulf, the Sixth Fleet commander, Vice Adm. Frank B. Kelso II, directed that all units exiting Libyan waters or air space should be considered hostile. Three warships—a fast attack craft and two guided-missile corvettes—subsequently qualified. The attack craft and a corvette were severely damaged and the second corvette was left sinking by carrier aircraft, which also attacked the missile site's target-acquisition radar. U.S. forces emerged unscathed.

The second engagement, the largest naval action the navy has fought since World War II, took place as a result of the U.S. agreement to escort Kuwaiti supertankers caught in the midst of the Persian Gulf "Tanker War" between Iran and Iraq. Staged in retaliation for the Iranian mining of the frigate *Samuel B. Roberts,* Operation Praying Mantis (18 April 1988) involved nine U.S. warships and aircraft from the carrier *Enterprise.* At the cost of a Marine light attack helicopter and its two crewmen, these forces destroyed or disabled four Iranian vessels, including two British-built frigates, damaged a fighter-attack aircraft, and demolished two offshore oil platforms being used to support attacks on merchant shipping.

Compared to the great battles of the Pacific War, Praying Mantis was scarcely a skirmish, but it illustrates some of the more striking changes that advanced technology has brought to naval warfare since 1945—from the possibility of real-time communications between commanders on the scene and policy makers in Washington to the use of air-to-surface, surface-to-surface, and surface-to-air missiles and laser-guided bombs. It also illustrates the constraints that rigid rules of engagement may place on commanders in "twilight war" situations, of which it seems unlikely that the U.S. Navy has seen the last.

The reader will note that in the following essays ships are referred to by the traditional feminine pronouns. For the uniform application of this usage the editor should be held accountable.

About the Contributors

JEFFREY G. BARLOW (*Okinawa*) completed his Ph.D. at the University of South Carolina. Formerly an analyst for the Heritage Foundation and the National Institute for Public Policy/National Security Research, he has been a member of the Contemporary History Branch at the Naval Historical Center in Washington, D.C., since 1987. His numerous articles on aspects of World War II include "The U.S. Navy's Fight against the Kamikazes" in Jack Sweetman et al., eds., *New Interpretations in Naval History: Selected Papers from the Tenth Naval History Symposium*. His book, *The "Revolt of the Admirals": The Fight for Naval Aviation, 1945–50*, was awarded the John Lyman Prize for U.S. naval history. He is in the process of writing an official history of the navy's role in national security affairs, 1945–63.

EDWARD L. BEACH, Captain, U.S. Navy (Ret.), (*Pearl Harbor*) graduated from the U.S. Naval Academy in 1939. During World War II he took part in twelve Pacific submarine patrols, progressing from assistant engineer to captain of his own boat and winning ten decorations for gallantry, including the Navy Cross. From 1953 to 1957 he was Naval Aide to President Eisenhower. In 1960 Captain Beach commanded the nuclear submarine *Triton* in the first submerged circumnavigation of the globe, a 41,000-mile voyage that still holds the record for submerged speed and endurance. His first book, the nonfiction *Submarine!*, appeared in 1952 and immediately appeared on the *New York Times* best-seller list. It was followed in 1955 by the novel *Run Silent, Run Deep*, which has been recognized as the classic account of the American undersea war against Japan. Since then he has written two more novels, also best-sellers, and four nonfiction works, including *Scapegoats: A Defense of Kimmel and Short at Pearl Harbor*, and has coauthored four other books. Captain Beach's contributions to naval literature have been honored by the Alfred Thayer Mahan Award for Literary Achievement of the Navy League of the United States and by numerous other awards.

JAMES C. BRADFORD (*Flamborough Head*) received his Ph.D. from the University of Virginia and teaches early American history and the history of American sea power at Texas A&M University. He has edited three volumes in the *Makers of the American Naval Tradition* series, *Crucible of Empire: The*

Spanish-American War and Its Aftermath, and *Quarterdeck and Bridge: Two Centuries of American Naval Leaders,* as well as a comprehensive microfilm edition of *The Papers of John Paul Jones.* At present he is working on a dictionary of American naval history, a letterpress edition of John Paul Jones's correspondence, and a biography of John Paul Jones.

THOMAS J. CUTLER, Lieutenant Commander, U.S. Navy (Ret.), *(Leyte Gulf)* joined the navy at the age of seventeen and retired after twenty years' service, including a tour as an advisor to South Vietnamese riverine forces. Currently Associate Director of Membership and Development at the U.S. Naval Institute, he has taught at the U.S. Naval Academy, the University of Maryland, and in the Naval War College extension program. Formerly an associate editor of the Naval Institute *Proceedings,* his publications include *Brown Water, Black Berets: Coastal and Riverine Warfare in Vietnam,* for which he received the Alfred Thayer Mahan Award for Literary Achievement, and *The Battle of Leyte Gulf, 23–26 October 1944.*

W. M. P. DUNNE (*Lake Champlain*) was a practicing naval architect and yacht broker before returning to academe to acquire his advanced degrees, including a doctorate from the State University of New York at Stony Brook. Still earlier, he had served in the U.S. Navy as a diver and demolitions expert. An adjunct professor of history and literature at Long Island University, Southampton, he authored *Thomas F. McManus and the American Fishing Schooners: An Irish-American Success Story,* as well as many articles and reviews, collaborated with Capt. Edward L. Beach on *The U.S. Navy: 200 Years,* and contributed to several television documentaries. Dr. Dunne died while this work was in progress.

JACK H. FRIEND (*Mobile Bay*) is a graduate of the Virginia Military Institute and the Amos Tuck School of Business Administration at Dartmouth University. During the Korean War he served as a tank company commander in the U.S. Army. Afterwards he formed John H. Friend, Inc., a market research firm from which he recently retired. A resident of Mobile and a member of the Alabama Historical Commission, he has a long-standing interest in the Battle of Mobile Bay, about which he is writing a book.

JOHN B. HATTENDORF (*Manila Bay*) is Ernest J. King Professor of Maritime History and Director of the Advanced Research Department at the Naval War College, Newport, Rhode Island. He holds degrees in history from

Kenyon College, Brown University, and the University of Oxford, and an honorary doctorate of humane letters from Kenyon College. His nearly eight years' active duty as a U.S. naval officer included service in destroyers in both the Atlantic and Pacific fleets. A Fellow of the Royal Historical Society, he has authored or edited twenty books and many articles on American and British naval and maritime history, among them *Sailors and Scholars: The Centennial History of the Naval War College,* and is general editor (with Wayne P. Hughes Jr.) of the *Classics of Naval Strategy* series.

MARK L. HAYES (*New Orleans*) served as an officer in the U.S. Navy from 1986 to 1990 and received his M.A. from Western Michigan University. He is now a historian in the Early History Branch of the Naval Historical Center, where he is an assistant editor of the series, *Naval Documents of the American Revolution.* He has presented several papers on naval topics in the American Revolution and the Civil War and has published a chapter on the Battle of Port Royal Sound in *Forgotten History: Hilton Head Island during the Civil War.*

LINDA M. MALONEY (*The* Constitution's *Battles*) holds two doctorates: a Ph.D. in American Studies from St. Louis University and a Th.D. in the New Testament from Eberhard-Karls-Universität, Tübingen, Germany. She is the author of four books and numerous articles, including *The Captain from Connecticut: The Life and Times of Isaac Hull* and "The War of 1812: What Role for Sea Power?" in Kenneth J. Hagan, ed., *In Peace and War: Interpretations of American Naval History, 1775–1984.*

JAMES KIRBY MARTIN (*Valcour Island*) is Distinguished University Professor of History at the University of Houston. He earned his Ph.D. from the University of Wisconsin and has also taught at Rutgers University. His fields of interest include early American military and social history. Among his publications are *A Respectable Army: The Military Origins of the Republic* (with Mark E. Lender) and *Ordinary Courage: The Revolutionary War Adventures of Joseph Plumb Martin.* His book-length study, *Benedict Arnold, Revolutionary Hero: An American Warrior Reconsidered,* appeared in 1997.

MICHAEL A. PALMER (*Praying Mantis*) earned his Ph.D. from Temple University. From 1983 to 1991 he served at the Naval Historical Center, for which he worked as a field historian in the Persian Gulf during the summer of 1988. At present he is an associate professor of history with the Program in Maritime History and Nautical Archeology at East Carolina University. A recipient of the Samuel Eliot Morison Award for Naval Literature, he is the author of six books, among them *On Course for Desert Storm: The U.S. Navy and the Persian Gulf* and *Guardians of the Gulf: The Growth of American Involvement in the Persian Gulf, 1833–1992*.

E. B. POTTER (*Coral Sea*) was Professor Emeritus of History at the U.S. Naval Academy, at which he taught for more than thirty years. A graduate of the University of Richmond and the University of Chicago, he served in the Pacific theater during World War II, attaining the rank of commander, U.S. Naval Reserve. He authored, coauthored, or edited seven books, including *Sea Power: A Naval History*, coedited with Fleet Adm. Chester W. Nimitz; the *Naval Academy Illustrated History of the United States Navy*; and biographies of Admirals Nimitz, William F. Halsey, and Arleigh Burke. For these works, he was honored by the Alfred Thayer Mahan Award for Literary Achievement and numerous other awards. Professor Potter died in 1997.

DAVID CURTIS SKAGGS (*Lake Erie*) is Professor Emeritus of History at Bowling Green State University where he taught from 1965 to 1998. He has written or edited eight books and more than thirty articles, among them *A Signal Victory: The Lake Erie Campaign, 1812–1813* (with Gerard T. Altoff), which was published in 1997. A U.S. Army Reserve colonel (retired) of field artillery, he is a graduate of the Army War College and has twice been a visiting professor of military history and strategy at the Air War College.

WILLIAM N. STILL JR. (*Hampton Roads*) recently retired as Professor of History and Codirector of the Program in Maritime History and Underwater Research at East Carolina University. The recipient of a Ph.D. from the University of Alabama, he has written extensively on American maritime and military history. Among his books are *Iron Afloat: The Story of the Confederate Armorclads, Confederate Shipbuilding* and *Odyssey in Grey*; as coauthor, *Why the South Lost the Civil War*; and as editor, *The Confederate Navy: The Ships, Men and Organization, 1861–1865*. He has been involved in a number of underwater archaeological projects, including the survey of the USS *Monitor*.

PAUL STILLWELL (*Guadalcanal*) is Director of the History Division of the U.S. Naval Institute. He has also served as managing editor of the Naval Institute *Proceedings* and editor-in-chief of *Naval History* magazine. His publications include *Air Raid: Pearl Harbor!*, *The Golden Thirteen*, and histories of the battleships *Arizona*, *Missouri*, and *New Jersey*. In 1994 he received the Alfred

Thayer Mahan Award for Literary Achievement. At present he is conducting research for a biography of Vice Adm. Willis A. Lee, the commander of the U.S. forces in the Battleship Night Action of the Naval Battle of Guadalcanal. A Vietnam veteran, Mr. Stillwell served in the tank landing ship *Washoe County* and the battleship *New Jersey* in the late 1960s. In 1992 he completed thirty years in the U.S. Naval Reserve, retiring as a commander.

JACK SWEETMAN (*Introduction*) graduated from Stetson University and served as a company commander in the U.S. Army before becoming a Ford Fellow at Emory University. He received his doctorate in 1973. He is the author or editor of a number of Naval Institute Press titles, including *The Landing at Veracruz: 1914, The U.S. Naval Acadamy: An Illustrated History, American Naval History: An Illustrated Chronology,* and *The Great Admirals: Centuries of Command at Sea, 1587–1945.* Retired from the history faculty of the U.S. Naval Academy, he serves as series editor for the press's Classics of Naval Literature collection, some forty volumes of which have appeared to date, and as consulting editor of the U.S. Naval Institute's bimonthly periodical, *Naval History.* In 1988 he received the Alfred Thayer Mahan Award for Literary Achievement.

BARRETT TILLMAN (*Midway*) has written more than twenty books, including four novels, on naval aviation subjects, for which he has been recognized by the Radford Award for Naval History and Literature and a number of other awards. His fascination with naval aviation began in childhood and developed to the point that he has logged more than five hundred hours at the controls of historic navy aircraft. A graduate of the University of Oregon, he has been active as an editor and publisher as well as an author and remains a contributing editor to *The Hook* and *Flight* magazines. Among his books are *The Dauntless Dive Bomber of World War Two* and *The Wildcat in WWII.*

DAVID F. TRASK (*Santiago*) received his Ph.D. from Harvard University. After teaching at several universities and the Naval War College, where he was Visiting Professor of Strategy in 1974–75, he became Director of the Office of the Historian in the U.S. State Department. At the time of his retirement he was Chief Historian at the U.S. Army Center of Military History. He has written numerous books and articles on naval and military history, including *The War with Spain in 1898.* His most recent work, *The AEF and Coalition Warfare, 1917–1918,* is the last in a series of four books devoted to political-military relations during World War I. He is a past president of the Society for History in the Federal Government.

H. P. WILLMOTT (*Philippine Sea*) holds an M.S. from the National Defense University, Washington, D.C., and a Ph.D. from King's College, University of London. From 1972 to 1979 he was a member of the British airborne reserve forces. A fellow of the Royal Historical Society and research fellow with the Institute for the Study of War and Society, De Montfort University, he has taught at the National War College and several American universities. Dr. Willmott has published thirteen books on modern naval and military subjects, including *The Great Crusade: A History of the Second World War*. His work in progress is entitled *When Men Lost Faith in Reason: Reflections on Warfare in the Twentieth Century*.

WILLIAM T. Y'BLOOD (*The Atlantic*) has served as an historian at the Air Force History Support Office (formerly the Office of Air Force History) since 1986. A graduate of the University of Oregon, he flew B-47s in the Strategic Air Command from 1960 to 1966 and then became an airline pilot, accumulating more than eleven thousand hours of flying time. In addition to studies written for the U.S. Air Force, he has authored five books on naval and military history, including *Hunter-Killer: U.S. Escort Carriers in the Battle of the Atlantic* and *The Little Giants: U.S. Escort Carriers Against Japan*, plus numerous articles and reviews. He is currently working on his sixth book.

*Great
American Naval
Battles*

I

The Battle of Valcour Island

JAMES KIRBY MARTIN

At dawn on 19 April 1775, a column of British regulars raised their muskets in reaction to a mysterious shot as they marched onto the village green in Lexington, Massachusetts. Eight patriot resisters lost their lives in the flurry of fire that followed. So began the War for American Independence. Once ignited, the conflagration spread quickly across the land. Before dawn on 10 May 1775, a band of rebels, mostly Green Mountain Boys from Vermont under Ethan Allen, with Benedict Arnold claiming joint command, overran a small British garrison at Fort Ticonderoga on Lake Champlain. The seizure of Ticonderoga and Crown Point, twelve miles to the north, two days later netted the rebels an invaluable cache of artillery pieces. The occupation of these points also drew attention to the prospect that Quebec Province might choose to become the fourteenth British North American colony in rebellion.

Col. Benedict Arnold wrote the Continental Congress in June about the possibility of invading Canada. The time for action, he vigorously argued, was now. The British had only a handful of regulars in Quebec, and "great numbers of the Canadians" could be expected "to join us whenever we appear in the country with any force to support them." Arnold's "plan of operations" envisioned an army of two thousand patriots. Half of them would seize Montreal while the other half captured the fortresses at St. Johns and Chambly along the Richelieu River to the southeast. Then the two detachments would proceed down the St. Lawrence River and take Quebec City, the provincial capital and the greatest prize of all. Arnold emphasized the need to act before Quebec's governor, Maj. Gen. Guy Carleton, an experienced soldier, could receive reinforcements from Britain. A preemptive invasion, Arnold concluded, would force the British to confront the Americans at Quebec City and deny them easy access to the Champlain region, from which

The northern theater in the War of the Revolution and the War of 1812.

they could strike at the backs of the rebellious colonists in New York and New England.[1]

From a strategic perspective, the idea of invading Canada had many merits. The members of the Continental Congress understood that if British forces gained control of the Hudson River/Lake Champlain water corridor, New England—then the epicenter of rebellion—would be effectively cut off from the remainder of the colonies. His Majesty's land forces could then sweep eastward to crush the rebels while the Royal Navy tightened the vise by blockading and threatening to bombard and possibly destroy New England's coastal communities. Thus on 27 June 1775, the delegates, after debating the thoughts of Arnold and others, approved the invasion.[2]

Congress gave the Canadian command to a wealthy New Yorker, Philip Schuyler, a veteran of the Seven Years' War whom they had recently named the fourth-ranking general officer in the Continental Army. As head of the army's Northern Department, Schuyler was to oversee preparations for the offensive, which Congress instructed him to launch as soon as sufficient troops and supplies were in place at Ticonderoga and Crown Point.[3]

The invasion that followed ultimately failed on the brink of success, at least in tactical terms. Two rebel armies spearheaded the attempted conquest. Brig. Gen. Richard Montgomery, a former British officer who had settled in

New York in the early 1770s, led twelve hundred men down Lake Champlain in late August. By mid-November Montgomery's troops had taken the fortresses at St. Johns and Chambly and captured Montreal. Meanwhile, Benedict Arnold, who had gained the favor of commander in chief George Washington, guided eleven hundred patriots on a harrowing march through the Maine wilderness. Their numbers depleted when they reached the gates of Quebec City in mid-November, Arnold's troops were in no condition to attack the walled Upper Town. In early December Montgomery, also with reduced numbers, joined Arnold. The assault they delivered under cover of a driving snowstorm early on the morning of 31 December 1775 was a debacle. Montgomery was killed; Arnold was badly wounded; and casualties were high. As events would demonstrate, any realistic expectation of conquering Canada ended that day.

Late in 1775 the king's ministers in London were in the process of reckoning with the patriots' rush to arms. Before Lexington and Concord, they had blithely dismissed the colonists as a "rude rabble without plan, without concert, and without conduct" who lacked the fortitude to resist for long the concentrated musket fire and gleaming bayonets of British regulars. Subsequent events had shown the ministers otherwise. Crushing the colonists' martial spirit would require the systematic display and application of massively superior military force.[4]

Once in motion, the ministry of Lord Frederick North acted vigorously. By late spring 1776 an invasion force of truly impressive proportions was getting ready to sail for New York City. By mid-August about thirty thousand soldiers, including many Hessians, and thirteen thousand sailors were present in New York Harbor and on Staten Island. In overall command was Maj. Gen. William Howe, whose older brother, Vice Adm. Richard Lord Howe, was in charge of naval forces.

In mounting the largest land and sea offensive of the eighteenth century—indeed, an overseas expedition not to be surpassed until the Allied invasion of North Africa in 1942—the British had demonstrated their seriousness about putting down the American rebellion. However, they had accomplished their initial objective without having clearly defined their strategy. Initially, the plan was to establish New York City as the primary base from which to reconquer the surrounding countryside. The rebel invasion of Canada skewed that intention. Rather than fully concentrating His Majesty's forces, Lord North and Lord George Germain, the American secretary, approved the diversion of some twelve thousand soldiers and sailors to Canada to relieve Quebec City and drive the rebels back into New York and New England.

This relief force began to debark at Quebec on 6 May 1776. With Governor Carleton in overall command, the king's minions moved up the St. Lawrence toward Montreal and into the Richelieu River Valley, pushing the rebels back to the northern shore of Lake Champlain. By late June the battered patriot army, riddled with smallpox and dissension, was retreating up the lake to Crown Point. The only question was how quickly Carleton would attempt to reclaim Lake Champlain.

Here British strategy, rendered more convoluted by the necessity of diverting forces to Canada, seemed to founder. For a host of reasons, among them sheer expense and the undesirable prospect of the Americans gaining material and financial support from France or other enemies of Britain, Lord Germain wanted the rebels broken by the end of the 1776 campaign season. He saw no reason why the Howes could not easily crush Washington's army, and he expected Carleton to retake Lake Champlain and press all the way south to Albany, in position for mopping-up operations in New England. Ideally, in Germain's scenario, the two British armies would seize control of the Hudson/Champlain water corridor, the worst of all prospects for the Americans, before winter weather interrupted operations. He had to settle for much less, in no small part because of the truculent stand of Benedict Arnold and the patriot fleet on Lake Champlain at Valcour Island.

Benedict Arnold, whose name comes down to posterity forever disfigured by the word "traitor," ranked among the most zealous of patriots when the rebellion broke out in 1775. He was from an old and once prominent New England family that had settled in Rhode Island during the 1630s. His great-great grandfather, Benedict Arnold I, had served with distinction as governor of Rhode Island, but succeeding generations fell on hard times and Arnold's father, Benedict IV, received an apprenticeship to a barrel maker as his inheritance. Dissatisfied with his humble station, he migrated to Norwich, Connecticut, married Hannah Waterman King (the well-to-do widow of a prosperous merchant), and soon became involved in the West Indies trade. Benedict V, the future Champlain commodore, was born to Benedict IV and Hannah on 14 January 1741 (new style).[5]

Looking backward through the prism of treason, nineteenth-century Americans embraced a host of fictional stories about Arnold's youth. These tales characterized him as a wanton lad, a show-off, and a bully who liked to climb trees to break the necks of baby birds—in short, the kind of perverse, egotistical youngster who, once convulsed by adult greed, had no compunctions about stabbing his comrades in the back.

Arnold recalled his childhood very differently. He described himself as "a

Benedict Arnold. An engraving published in England in 1783 from a drawing made in Philadelphia a few years earlier. *U.S. Naval Institute*

coward until . . . fifteen years of age." His "vaunted" courage was an "acquired" trait, forced on him by family difficulties. In 1753 a diphtheria epidemic swept through Norwich and snuffed out the lives of two of his sisters and his only surviving brother. Arnold's father never recovered emotionally from this devastating blow to his family. He buried his sorrow in alcohol, which eventually led to his ruin. Young Benedict had to give up his formal schooling and accept an apprenticeship with his mother's cousins, Daniel and Joshua Lathrop, men of substantial affluence in the apothecary and general merchandise trade. Impressed by Benedict's talents and determination, the Lathrops became his patrons in business, setting him up as an apothecary in New Haven.[6]

Arnold expanded on this base. As his father had done, he honed his nautical skills by sailing his own vessels back and forth to the West Indies. By 1774 he was among the most credit-worthy merchants in New Haven. During these years he also gained a favorable reputation among New Haven's ordinary citizens for his forthright stand against tightened imperial trading policies and taxation.

An ambitious man, Arnold hoped to restore his family name to its once exalted status. The outbreak of the rebellion gave him that opportunity. Late in 1774 he joined sixty-five New Havenites in forming a militia company—the Governor's Second Company of Guards. Many of these folk admired Arnold, and they elected him their captain. When word of the combat at Lexington and Concord reached New Haven, Arnold mustered the guards and marched them off to war. Now in his mid-thirties, he was an imposing figure, no more than average in height but broad-shouldered and powerfully built. Once in eastern Massachusetts, he met with the Massachusetts Committee of Safety about the stockpile of artillery at Ticonderoga and Crown Point. The committee gave him a colonel's commission, and off he rushed to the Lake Champlain region.

Despite his lack of military experience or formal training of any kind, Arnold demonstrated an unusual aptitude for command. He did have problems with Ethan Allen and the Massachusetts government, but he also came to the attention of Philip Schuyler, whose advocacy helped him secure George Washington's patronage, a colonel's commission in the Continental Army, and the detached Canadian command. Arnold acquitted himself with distinction in Quebec Province, coming to be called America's Hannibal for his grueling march through the Maine wilderness. Congress rewarded him with a brigadier generalship, the rank he held when British reinforcements drove the invaders out of Canada.

While the dispirited patriot force was in the final stages of retreat in June 1776, Arnold hurried south to Albany to discuss the situation with Schuyler. Arnold did not view Carleton as an aggressive, offensive-minded warrior. He expected the governor to move forward only in carefully planned steps. The Americans, he thought, would have ample time, perhaps as much as two months, to construct a respectable lake fleet. Arnold concluded his report by promising to strain "every nerve" in resisting the British advance out of Canada.[7]

Benedict Arnold was to have several months' worth of opportunity to display his multifold martial talents. He would serve directly under Gen. Horatio Gates, another retired British officer who had moved to the colonies and recently shown much ability as Washington's adjutant general. Gates had made a play for the northern command but settled for field duty under Schuyler, who placed him in charge of organizing patriot ground forces into a defensive front at Fort Ticonderoga. Because of Gates's admitted ignorance of naval matters, Arnold willingly accepted duty as the commodore of Lake Champlain.

Schuyler and Gates also asked Arnold to provide general supervision of the fleet's construction at Skenesborough, some thirty miles south of Ticonderoga at the base of the lake. Having asserted that it was "of the utmost importance" to construct "a large number (at least twenty or thirty) of gundalows, row galleys, and floating batteries," Arnold left the actual business of shipbuilding to David Waterbury, a militia general from Connecticut with extensive maritime experience. For his part, Arnold concentrated on sending appeals across the countryside in an attempt to overcome shortages of all kinds. Beside a paucity of shipwrights at Skenesborough, basic naval supplies—ranging from anchors and cordage to sailcloth and linseed oil—were very scarce. Other major shortages included skilled sailors and marines, artillery pieces, and various types of shot.[8]

Arnold again showed a capacity, as he had in Canada, for making brick with very little straw. By early August the Champlain fleet was taking shape. Once it was outfitted, Arnold had at his disposal three row galleys (the *Congress*, *Trumbull*, and *Washington*) and nine gundalows (the *Boston*, *Connecticut*, *Jersey*, *New Haven*, *New York*, *Philadelphia*, *Providence*, *Spitfire*, and *Success*), plus three schooners (the *Liberty*, *Revenge*, and *Royal Savage*), the sloop *Enterprise*, and the cutter *Lee*, the last five craft having been captured from the British in earlier actions on the lake and in the Richelieu River.[9]

The fleet's strength lay in its highly maneuverable row galleys. These were fairly sizable craft, seventy to eighty feet in length, with crews numbering up to eighty men. Their two short masts were lateen rigged, which enabled them to tack into the wind. The galleys also had rounded bottoms that made them better sailers in rough weather than the flat-bottomed gundalows. The latter were forty to fifty feet long and carried about forty-five men. Each had a single mast with a fixed square sail that caught the wind only as long it came from astern. For a gundalow to move against the wind, the crew had to take to the oars. Arnold would have liked to have more row galleys, but with time pressing to get a fleet on the lake he readily accepted the available craft.

Patriot lake operations occurred within a carefully constructed set of instructions, which Gates completed, no doubt with Arnold's advice and assistance, on 7 August. The "momentous" task at hand was to secure "the northern entrance into this side of the continent . . . from further invasion."

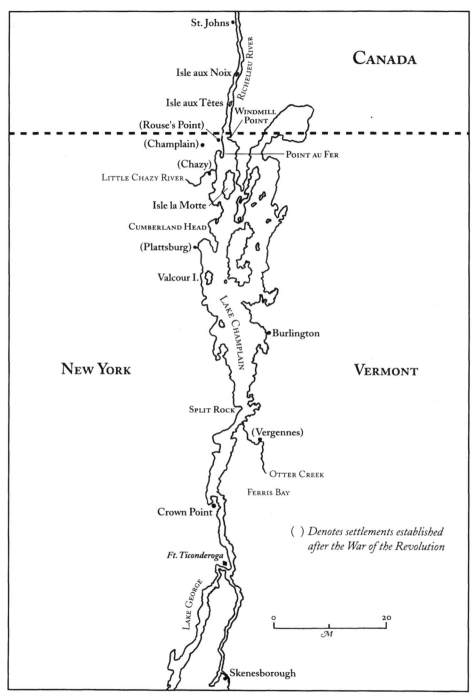

St. Johns

RICHELIEU RIVER

CANADA

Isle aux Noix

Isle aux Têtes

WINDMILL POINT

(Rouse's Point)

(Champlain)

POINT AU FER

(Chazy)

LITTLE CHAZY RIVER

Isle la Motte

CUMBERLAND HEAD

(Plattsburg)

Valcour I.

LAKE CHAMPLAIN

Burlington

NEW YORK

VERMONT

SPLIT ROCK

(Vergennes)

OTTER CREEK

FERRIS BAY

Crown Point

( ) *Denotes settlements established after the War of the Revolution*

Ft. Ticonderoga

LAKE GEORGE

0   20
ℳ

Skenesborough

The Lake Champlain area in the War of the Revolution and the War of 1812.

Enjoined against conducting offensive operations of any kind, Arnold could venture as far north as the Isle aux Têtes, just inside the Canadian border; but he was to take "no wanton risk" or engage in any "unnecessary display of the power of the fleet." Gates expected the commodore to employ his "courage and abilities" in "preventing the enemy's invasion of our country," which represented, he said, "the ultimate end of the important command with which you are now entrusted."

In the absence of useful intelligence about the size and strength of Carleton's fleet, it would be imperative for Arnold to maintain a defensive posture. At the same time, he was to do everything possible to delay or, optimally, deflect the expected invasion. Should Carleton's flotilla appear too strong to oppose, the commodore was to fall back on Ticonderoga. In the meantime, Gates would be busy trying to get the reinforcements he was receiving in shape to beat off an attack.[10]

To complicate matters further, it was at least equally imperative that Arnold avoid withdrawing prematurely, for Ticonderoga was desperately deficient in munitions, especially lead and powder. If Arnold failed to retard Carleton's advance, at least until Gates received sufficient munitions, Ticonderoga's defenders would be able to offer only token resistance. And if Carleton breached Gates's defenses and reached Albany before the campaign season ended, the consequences would be potentially catastrophic for the American cause, especially with the British already concentrating thousands of troops 150 miles south of Albany in the vicinity of New York City.

Arnold thus had to reckon with the additional responsibility of inviting battle should Ticonderoga remain in want of powder and ball. His underlying objective then would be to create so vivid an impression of rebel resolve that Carleton would think long and hard about proceeding with a full-scale assault on Ticonderoga. The prospect of fighting a pitched battle held little appeal for Arnold. His squadron had only a limited supply of ammunition—and virtually no grape or chain shot for shredding enemy sails and rigging and shattering masts. Worse yet, Arnold's crews, mostly drawn by lot from the soldiery at Ticonderoga, were largely ignorant of the art of sailing, and very few had training as gunners or marines.

Under these circumstances, the two American generals decided upon a ruse that exploited Arnold's aggressive reputation and his reading of Carleton's cautious temperament. The commodore did not disclose to anyone, not even his senior officers, that his orders forbade him from entering the Richelieu River or conducting any other offensive operation for that matter. In public, however, he bragged of his determination to attack St. Johns, where the

British were readying their fleet. Spies at Ticonderoga soon apprised Carleton of Arnold's swaggering words. The idea was to encourage the governor to remain at St. Johns in anticipation of easily routing the overly pugnacious rebel fleet. Meanwhile, if nothing else, Arnold could get his vessels out onto the lake, not only to give his green crews some training but to determine the most favorable location from which to offer battle in the event he was obliged to do so.

After many frustrating delays caused mostly by incessant supply shortages, Arnold finally had a portion of the Champlain fleet—but no row galleys— sailing northward from Crown Point on 24 August. Surviving a terrible storm, the vessels "arrived safe" on 3 September at Windmill Point, just south of the Canadian border. To advertise his presence to the British, Arnold ordered the flotilla to form a line extending across the lake.[11]

Carleton soon learned of the proximity of the rebel force. He had no way of knowing whether Arnold would actually proceed down the Richelieu to strike at St. Johns, as spurious intelligence reports had earlier indicated. Of course, Carleton might have moved his own sizable squadron upriver to challenge Arnold's less-than-brawny collection of ten craft. The governor refused to do so, even though a victory would have opened an unobstructed path to Ticonderoga. He was not going to take unnecessary risks against what he described to a friend as Arnold's "considerable naval force." Rebel initiative and bravado thus helped to keep the British fleet immobilized at St. Johns for what turned out to be a crucial month—a major tactical triumph.[12]

Back in May, Carleton had received instructions from Lord Germain to "endeavor to pass the lakes as early as possible, and in your future progress to contribute to the success of the army under General Howe." Germain expected the governor, at a minimum, to reconquer the Champlain region before the coming of winter. After so easily driving the rebels from Quebec Province, however, Carleton did not rush ahead with his assignment. The rebels could wait because he believed that time—and periodic applications of superior force—would ultimately convince these "unhappy subjects" to accept "the king's mercy and benevolence," which was "still open to them."[13]

Still, Carleton authorized a massive naval buildup at St. Johns. This river town lay above the Richelieu River rapids that blocked navigation between the St. Lawrence River and Lake Champlain for about twelve miles. By midsummer St. Johns was buzzing with construction work. In contrast to the Americans some 150 miles to the south at Skenesborough, the British were well provided with shipwrights and supplies. They also had a number of suitable vessels already afloat on the St. Lawrence. Their greatest challenge was

TABLE 1.1   The Battle of Valcour Island, 11–13 October 1776

Name	Type	Armament (approximate)
CONTINENTAL FORCES		
Brig. Gen. Benedict Arnold		
Congress (F)	Row galley	2 18-pdrs., 2 12-pdrs., 4 6-pdrs., 16 swivels
Trumbull	Row galley	1 18-pdr., 1 12-pdr., 2 9-pdrs., 4 6-pdrs., 16 swivels
Washington	Row galley	1 18-pdr., 1 12-pdr., 2 9-pdrs., 4 4-pdrs., 16 swivels
Boston	Gundalow	1 12-pdr., 2 9-pdrs. or 6-pdrs., 8 swivels
Connecticut	Gundalow	1 12-pdr., 2 9-pdrs. or 6-pdrs., 8 swivels
Jersey	Gundalow	1 12-pdr., 2 9-pdrs. or 6-pdrs., 8 swivels
New Haven	Gundalow	1 12-pdr., 2 9-pdrs. or 6-pdrs., 8 swivels
New York	Gundalow	1 12-pdr., 2 9-pdrs. or 6-pdrs., 8 swivels
Philadelphia	Gundalow	1 12-pdr., 2 9-pdrs. or 6-pdrs., 8 swivels
Providence	Gundalow	1 12-pdr., 2 9-pdrs. or 6-pdrs., 8 swivels
Spitfire	Gundalow	1 12-pdr., 2 9-pdrs. or 6-pdrs., 8 swivels
Success	Gundalow	1 12-pdr., 2 9-pdrs. or 6-pdrs., 8 swivels
Liberty	Schooner	2 4-pdrs., 4 2-pdrs., 8 swivels
Revenge	Schooner	4 4-pdrs., 4 2-pdrs., 10 swivels
Royal Savage	Schooner	4 6-pdrs., 8 4-pdrs., 10 swivels
Enterprise	Sloop	12 4-pdrs., 10 swivels
Lee	Cutter	1 12-pdr., 1 9-pdr., 4 4-pdrs., 10 swivels
BRITISH FORCES		
Capt. Thomas Pringle		
Inflexible	Sloop of war	18 12-pdrs., 10 swivels
Carleton	Schooner	12 6-pdrs., 6 swivels
Maria (F)	Schooner	14 6-pdrs., 6 swivels
Thunderer	Radeau	6 24-pdrs., 6 12-pdrs., 2 8-in. howitzers
Loyal Convert	Gundalow	7 9-pdrs.
Nos. 1–20	Gunboats	1 gun, from 24-pdr. to 8-in. howitzer

Note: (F) = flagship

the disassembly of these craft near Fort Chambly, where the rapids began, for transportation overland and reassembly at St. Johns.

By the time Arnold reached Windmill Point, Carleton had a formidable fleet virtually ready to sail. His force included four square-rigged vessels: two heavily-armed schooners, the *Carleton* and *Maria*; a bargelike *radeau* (raft) dubbed the *Thunderer*; and the refitted *Loyal Convert,* a gundalow built by Arnold's rebels during their siege of Quebec City. Supporting these vessels were twenty gunboats, ten of which had been prefabricated in England, and twenty-eight longboats to carry supplies and field pieces for shoreline duty.

Unlike Arnold, Carleton had well-trained naval officers, expert mariners, and seasoned gun crews and marines. His fleet already possessed superior firepower, especially in the form of a dozen or more 24-pounders; Arnold's green crews had no guns of this weight or firepower. Still, the governor hesitated, determined that his squadron should be indisputably more powerful than Arnold's. He therefore deferred action until the *Inflexible*, a three-masted, 180-ton sloop of war then in the process of being transported in pieces over-land from Chambly, could be assembled at St. Johns. This was a substantial vessel by inland water standards. Her keel was relaid on 6 September, and by 3 October her reconstruction was complete.

The next day the British squadron, twenty-five fighting vessels manned by about one thousand sailors, gunners, and marines, finally began moving up the Richelieu River. Already in motion were some four hundred Indian allies in birch-bark canoes. What was no longer in full motion was Carleton's com-mitment to executing Lord Germain's orders. While waiting for the *Inflexible*, the governor decided to enter the lake with only limited objectives. "Unfortu-nately the season is so far advanced," he wrote to Germain late in September, "that I dare not flatter myself we shall be able to do more . . . than to draw off their [the rebels'] attention and keep back part of their force from General Howe."[14]

In delaying his advance rather than embracing Arnold's challenge, Carleton had revealed his lack of commitment to retaking the Champlain region during the 1776 campaign season. Moreover, he had allowed the patriot fleet to gain considerable strength by the addition of the three row gal-leys and other craft. He had not widened his advantage in relative fleet power. Rather, he had put himself in a position where he could not accomplish his assigned objectives—unless, of course, the rebels refused to stand and fight. Arnold, however, was ready to give Carleton and his fleet plenty of action.

Arnold had long since withdrawn from the Canadian border in response to British/Indian scouting parties, which, under cover of darkness on 7 Septem-ber, placed batteries along the shoreline at Windmill Point. Dropping anchor near Isle la Motte and elsewhere, he kept thinking about how best to reckon with Carleton's flotilla. A running engagement in retreat, he was sure, would result in the annihilation of his vessels, since the gundalows lacked maneuver-ability, especially in rough water. To try to block the British by deploying his fleet in a thin line across the lake was also fraught with risk, especially if strong northerly winds allowed Carleton's vessels to come crashing down on his stationary craft. Deciding against these options, Arnold wrote to Gates on 15 September: "I design making a remove to the island Valcour, until joined by the three galleys." The island, he explained, has "a good harbor, and if the enemy venture up the lake, it will be impossible for them to take advantage of our situation."[15]

Valcour Island lay not quite midway between Ticonderoga and St. Johns. In the bay on the southwestern side of the island Arnold perceived a natural defensive position. Valcour's steep, wooded heights would prevent ships coming from the north from seeing into the bay, which opened to the south. Shoal water between the island and the shoreline would also prevent all except the smallest enemy vessels from attacking through the channel to the north.

Arnold then made a series of assumptions. The British would certainly follow the lake's main channel, which would take their fleet around the island's eastern side. With a brisk wind behind them, they would cruise past the island before spotting the rebel fleet. When they reversed course, even Carleton's experienced mariners would have trouble organizing a battle line while beating to the windward. Without a well-defined line, the British would not be able to take full advantage of their superior firepower. Further, so long as the patriot vessels held to a fixed position in the bay, they might be able to destroy enemy craft in detail, perhaps inflicting enough damage to send the cautious Carleton staggering back to Canada. Offering combat from a stationary position would also negate another of Arnold's disadvantages—his lack of trained mariners.

Nevertheless, Arnold would retire rather than fight, as he wrote to Gates at the end of September, unless the row galleys finally appeared. Two critical considerations kept Arnold waiting in Valcour Bay. Not only had Gates failed to receive the munitions needed to defend Ticonderoga, but news had reached the Champlain commodore of Washington's resounding defeat by General Howe on Long Island in late August. Having for so long appreciated the dire consequences of losing control of the Hudson River/Lake Champlain corridor, Arnold feared the worst. Even at this late date, with the weather turning sharply colder, an easy breakthrough by Carleton was unacceptable, especially if the triumphant Howe should move swiftly up the Hudson with substantial forces.

Arnold had no way of knowing how little interest Howe had in such operations or how uncertain Carleton had become about what he should accomplish that season. When all three row galleys were at last present in Valcour Bay on 6 October, Arnold committed himself to making a stand. He knew the British fleet would have to appear soon because of fast-approaching winter weather. Early on Friday morning, 11 October, when he spied one of his little lookouts cutting through the gap between Valcour Island and the New York shoreline, he showed scant surprise. The wind, blowing strongly out of the north, told the story. Carleton's flotilla would soon be at hand.

Arnold assembled his officers aboard his flagship, the *Congress,* and instructed them of their duty to offer a "resolute but judicious defense of the northern entrance" to the rebel colonies. They were not to retreat until having "discovered the insufficiency of every effort to retard" the enemy's "progress" toward Ticonderoga. Arnold then went over his battle plan. The fleet would fight in a compact, crescent-shaped formation positioned across the bay as the British vessels tried to attack into the wind.[16]

Only David Waterbury, Arnold's second in command, objected. He feared being caught in a trap since the British squadron was "so much superior to us in number and strength." Survival, Waterbury stated, depended on beating the enemy to Ticonderoga, where the flotilla would enjoy the support of Gates's land forces.[17]

It would be impossible to maintain an effective defensive formation while retreating, Arnold replied, especially with inexperienced crews. Moreover, there were not enough row galleys to screen the sluggish gundalows. Finally, should the wind change to the south, the gundalows would be practically locked in place, even under oars. But regardless of the wind direction, the British advantage in speed and firepower would allow them to overtake and overwhelm the rebel fleet. Retreat would be far more hazardous than an engagement at Valcour Island.

The Champlain commodore emphasized that officers must watch for his orders concerning the fleet as a whole. He would be in the *Congress* at the center of the line. Waterbury would command the fleet's right wing in the *Washington*, and Col. Edward Wigglesworth, "a good seaman" of "unimpeached character" from Massachusetts, would direct the left wing in the *Trumbull*. The officers then returned to their vessels, where with some 750 crew members they waited uneasily for the enemy to appear.[18]

The British did so just after 10:00 A.M. Carleton and Capt. Thomas Pringle, an aggressive young Royal Navy officer whom the governor had placed in command of the fleet, were aboard their flagship, the *Maria*. Having shown little interest in reports that the rebel fleet was lurking in the vicinity, they sailed well past the southern tip of Valcour Island before spotting Arnold's squadron. Pringle soon had his vessels hauling confusedly into the wind, at which point Arnold threw down the gauntlet. He had to make sure his adversary accepted battle before thinking twice, dropping anchor, and waiting patiently for a southerly breeze. The British could then have made an orderly advance into the bay and systematically obliterated the rebel fleet.

At 11:00 A.M., Arnold raised sail in the *Congress* and signaled the other row galleys and the schooner *Royal Savage* to follow his lead. Riding favorable winds, the four craft dashed headlong toward their disconcerted adversary, firing as they came. Arnold was counting on British impulsiveness and contempt for rebel fighting prowess to draw his adversaries into combat. If

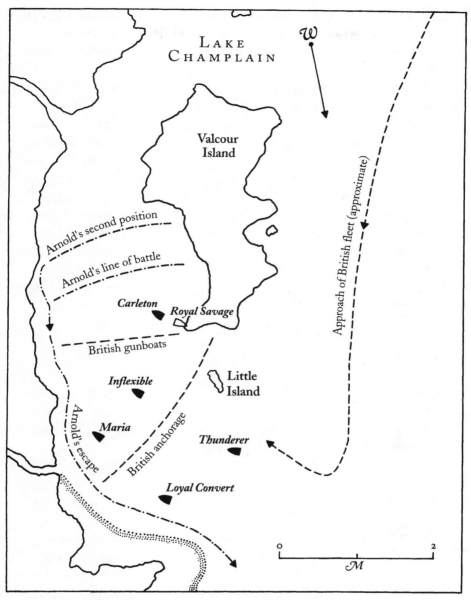

The Battle of Valcour Island. Action of 11 October 1776. *Based on a map published in London in 1779.*

Carleton had shown as much deliberation about entering action as he had about entering the lake, he would have told Pringle to wait for favorable winds. As for Pringle, he was eager to open a battle that he believed would end in a quick victory.

With the British acceptance of Arnold's challenge, the Battle of Valcour Island commenced. Arnold thereupon ordered the row galleys and the *Royal Savage* to rejoin the carefully aligned patriot fleet. The galleys had no problem retreating. The square-rigged *Royal Savage,* hauling awkwardly into the wind, suddenly staggered as British shot struck one of her masts and sliced through her rigging. As a result of what Arnold called "some bad management," the schooner fell away to the leeward and grounded on the southwest shore of Valcour Island. Some of Pringle's gunboats, a few mounting 24-pounders, soon rowed into effective range and took deadly aim at the stranded craft. The rebel crew had to abandon ship but reached Arnold's fleet almost without loss.[19]

Cheered by the fate of the *Royal Savage,* the British looked forward to what they believed more than ever would be an easy victory. The gunboats succeeded in forming a line of battle by the use of their sweeps, but four of the five bigger British vessels found their efforts to beat their way into the bay frustrated by the northerly wind. Their contribution to the engagement was for the most part limited to a relatively harmless, long-range fire.

The exception was the schooner *Carleton.* Her commanding officer, Lt. James R. Dacres, had successfully navigated to the windward and closed to within seven hundred yards of the American ships by a little after noon. The schooner then inched forward to about 350 yards, point-blank range for the ordnance of the day, where Dacres dropped anchor. By hauling on a spring line attached to the anchor cable, his trained seamen swung the *Carleton* broadside to the patriot fleet. Supported by several gunboats, Dacres quickly brought his battery of 6-pounders into action.

"The engagement," Arnold recorded, "became general, and very warm." Clouds of black-powder smoke settled over the bay, vessels shuddered from the impact of enemy shot, and the sharp splinters that ranked among the deadliest ingredients of battles between wooden ships flew at the combatants. Even though at this point the action was going in favor of the British, both fleets were taking casualties, and on the *Carleton* Dacres was knocked unconscious by flying debris.

Arnold ordered the American gun crews to direct their fire at the *Carleton.* His poorly trained men did their best, but, as he wrote, "we suffered much for want of seamen and gunners." Like Dacres, Arnold sought to inspire his crew by setting a fearless example. In the absence of skilled gun layers, Arnold was even "obliged . . . to point most of the guns on board the *Congress*." Unlike Dacres, he came through the fight unscathed.[20]

Arnold and his men shouted in triumph when one of their shots blew up the magazine of a gunboat manned by Hessians. The survivors were taken off by other gunboats before their burning vessel sank. Another rebel round cut the spring line holding the *Carleton* in place. The ship's bow swung toward the American line, and she went adrift. As shots fired by Arnold's exuberant gunners slammed into her hull, she heeled over so far that she appeared in danger of capsizing.

Noting the *Carleton*'s distress, Captain Pringle conferred with the governor and then signaled the schooner to disengage. That was more easily ordered than accomplished. Dacres remained unconscious, and his second in command had been badly wounded. But there was still a leader on board the *Carleton*, nineteen-year-old Midshipman Edward Pellew, who many years later would end a distinguished career as Admiral Lord Exmouth. Dashing through the shot sweeping his ship's deck, Pellew climbed out on the bowsprit and attempted to swing the jib to the windward. He failed, but his heroism encouraged the schooner's crew not to give up. Eventually, a pair of longboats managed to tow the seriously damaged vessel, now burdened by two feet of water in her hold, out of the line of fire.

Though the *Carleton* left the action, the British gunboats remained full of fight. These craft "continued a very hot fire," stated Arnold, until about 5:00 P.M., when they retired some seven hundred yards from the rebel fleet. Each of them had entered the action with about eighty rounds of ammunition— thirty of roundshot and fifty of grape. Most of the grape was gone, but they maintained a sporadic fire of roundshot. Meanwhile, the heavily armed *Thunderer* succeeded in working her way far enough forward to place the American line briefly under fire. She withdrew as darkness began to fall, and the day's battle came to an end.

Neither fleet had won a decisive advantage or suffered a disastrous reverse, although the patriots had sustained heavier casualties, about sixty to not quite forty, and many of their vessels were in bad shape. The gundalow *Philadelphia* had been hulled so often that she foundered about an hour after the firing ceased. The Americans also lost the *Royal Savage*, which both sides had boarded during the battle, only to be driven off by the other. Soon after nightfall a British force ended this side action by getting onto the vessel and putting her to the torch.

Arnold's tactics had been successful, insofar as they had kept the British from bringing their full strength to bear. On the other hand, the patriots had not inflicted enough damage on the enemy squadron to cause Carleton and Pringle to go slinking back to Canada. More immediate, the northerly breeze started to fade away at dusk. No one could be sure from which direction the wind would blow the next day. If it swung around to the south, the patriot fleet faced the prospect of a fiery end not unlike that of the *Royal Savage*. The only alternative would be surrender. In either case the British would acquire control of Lake Champlain.

Arnold was now in the very corner so feared by Waterbury. British regulars and Indian warriors had landed all around the patriot fleet, even on Valcour Island, and Carleton's squadron formed a floating barricade across the mouth of the bay. Carleton was also collecting bateaux to board the rebel craft. To make matters worse, Arnold wrote, the patriot ammunition supply was "nearly three-fourths spent," and the galleys *Congress* and *Washington* had sustained serious damage. The former had received seven hits "between wind and water" and been "hulled a dozen times," while the latter had her "mainmast shot through," beside being "hulled a number of times." Both were "very leaky and want repairing." Of the galleys, the *Trumbull* alone remained fairly intact.[21]

Something drastic had to be done to stave off disaster, as Arnold explained to Waterbury, Wigglesworth, and other officers sometime before 7:00 P.M. Fortunately, Pringle gave the patriots a way out, in the most literal sense. Apprehensive about the shoals that extended from the New York shoreline, he had left an open space beyond the western end of his line. With a heavy fog blanketing the bay, the Americans decided to exploit the lack of visibility to attempt a breakout. With muffled oars Arnold's ships slipped single file around the British line with the aim of making a run for Crown Point. Amazingly, the maneuver worked; by midnight, the patriot vessels were in open water beyond the enemy fleet.

The next morning as the fog burned off Valcour Bay, the British were shocked to see that Arnold's vessels had disappeared. After boats sent to scout north of the island returned with nothing to report, Carleton ordered Pringle to proceed southward. Once under full sail, the governor suddenly recalled that he had neglected to order his ground forces to move south, too. So the British fleet returned briefly to Valcour Bay before heading south a second time.

Arnold's fleet, meanwhile, had paused to assess damages. The situation was grim. Three of its gundalows had been battered beyond repair. Two were scuttled, and a work party tried to set fire to the third, the *Jersey*. This vessel was too waterlogged to burn and had to be left to the British. Before proceeding, Arnold instructed his officers to save what they could of the fleet. He ordered Wigglesworth in the *Trumbull* to sail immediately and shepherd the surviving craft to Crown Point. Although badly damaged, the *Congress* and *Washington* would act as a rear guard.

When the two galleys spied enemy sails on the horizon at about 2:00 P.M., Arnold and Waterbury got under way. A robust wind out of the south laced with recurrent squalls of sleet and rain held both sides to a snail's pace. Near sundown the wind subsided, and the Americans stayed ahead of their adversaries by rowing throughout the night. Still, by sunrise on 13 October Arnold's vessels had covered only a few miles, even though they had preserved their lead over the British.

Late in the morning the wind shifted in Carleton's favor. A brisk breeze from the northeast swelled his flotilla's sails precious minutes before it reached Arnold's two galleys and four gundalows that had been unable to keep up with the *Trumbull*. Soon, the British were bearing down on the six patriot craft. When Waterbury's battered galley fell behind, he asked permission "to run my vessel on shore, and blow her up." Arnold demurred, instructing Waterbury "to push forward to Split Rock," where the lake narrows. The commodore intended to give battle to buy time for the remaining vessels to catch the northerly breeze and make good their escape.[22]

Waterbury almost reached Split Rock but quickly surrendered "after receiving a few broadsides" from the British craft pressing in on him. His capture allowed the enemy to mass against the *Congress*. As the *Maria*, the partially repaired *Carleton*, and the sloop of war *Inflexible* swarmed toward the galley, Arnold brought her about into the wind. The time was around noon. For more than two hours, Arnold and his men put up a magnificent fight. Although the three British vessels possessed at least a five-to-one firepower advantage, Arnold refused to strike his colors. By shortly after 2:00 P.M. the *Congress* was on the verge of sinking.[23]

But Arnold still had a stratagem up his sleeve. Prewar experience in the West Indies trade had taught him a thing or two about shiphandling, as he was about to demonstrate to his opponents' chagrin. Throughout the action, Arnold had been casting keen glances toward the Vermont shoreline southeast of Split Rock hoping to discover an avenue of escape. He also kept track of the four crippled gundalows treading water nearby. The British paid no attention to these craft. There would be plenty of time to gobble them up after the *Congress* had been put out of action.

When all seemed lost, Arnold shouted for his men to seize their sweeps.

The Battle of Valcour Island, 11–13 October 1776. A print published in London a few months later compresses the climactic events of the third day. The three vessels nearest the viewer, all British, are from left to right, the *Maria, Carleton,* and *Inflexible.* At far left, in the distance, the *Congress* and the gundalows have run ashore and are being set afire; at left center, between the *Maria* and the *Carleton,* the *Washington* is striking her colors; and, at far right, a British gunboat comes into action. The American schooners whose masts appear between the *Carleton* and the *Inflexible* are products of artistic license. *U.S. Naval Institute*

He had found what he was searching for. Pivoting to the windward, the *Congress* cut between two enemy vessels and darted into Ferris Bay. Taking their cue, the gundalows scurried close behind. The British ships, caught off guard by this maneuver, had to haul into the wind, which slowed their pursuit.[24]

With a scattering of enemy shot striking around them, the Americans ran their craft aground. To keep the vessels out of British hands Arnold ordered powder trains laid to their magazines, after which they were set on fire. He then led their crews on a ten-mile southward march before crossing over to Crown Point. Carleton's Indians "waylaid the road" in hopes of staging an ambush. As Arnold wrote, his followers "very luckily escaped the savages" by going through the woods.[25]

Of the rebel vessels that challenged the British on Lake Champlain during the three dramatic days of 11–13 October 1776, only four now survived.

Beside the loss of at least one gunboat, the British admitted to somewhat fewer than forty men killed or wounded. Arnold calculated patriot losses at "eighty-odd," not counting an estimated 110 men made prisoner when Waterbury surrendered. Thus, the overall patriot casualty rate approached 25 percent.[26]

Down to our own time the question remains: What had Commodore Arnold gained, if anything, in expending the patriot fleet? Despite the Americans' gallant stand, Carleton's flotilla had swept away their squadron in three days' time, swiftly achieving control of Lake Champlain. By 15 October, British advance units were already debarking at Crown Point, the obvious assembly point from which to assault Ticonderoga and smash through the only remaining line of rebel resistance in the Champlain region.

Some contemporaries did not hesitate to bash Arnold for wasting the fleet. Among them was Brig. Gen. William Maxwell, a former British officer in command of New Jersey troops assigned to Ticonderoga. He characterized Arnold as "our evil genius to the north," who "has, with a good deal of industry, got us clear of all our fine fleet," which "by all impartial accounts, was by far the strongest." Arnold's was a "pretty piece of admiralship," concluded Maxwell sarcastically, that had put Ticonderoga in real jeopardy.[27]

David Waterbury agreed. Soon released by Carleton, he denounced Arnold in a blistering letter to the Continental Congress. His superior's defense of the lake was both "absurd and desperate." Waterbury also implied that a glory-hunting Arnold had willfully violated Gates's orders by not seeking, above all else, to avoid combat.[28]

Pioneering naval strategist Alfred Thayer Mahan challenged such commentary in his classic study, *The Major Operations of the Navies in the War of American Independence* (1913). As a vigorous advocate of naval expansion, Mahan wrote that "control of the water was the most determinative factor" in winning the Revolutionary War. He argued that Arnold's actions on Lake Champlain and Admiral de Grasse's at the mouth of the Chesapeake were "the two great decisive moments of the war." Mahan especially lauded Arnold's "recognition of the fact—implicit in deed, if unexpressed in word—that the one use of the navy was to contest the control of the water; to impose delay, even if it could not secure ultimate victory. No words could say more clearly than do his actions that, under the existing conditions, the navy was useless, except as it contributed to that end; valueless if buried in port." In sum, Mahan concluded, Arnold's vigorous defense of the lake caused Carleton to withdraw to Canada, bought the rebels several months to strengthen the northern theater, and set the stage for the defeat and surrender of "Gentleman Johnny" Burgoyne's army at Saratoga in October 1777—the key to a formal alliance with France and ultimate American victory.[29]

More recently, some historians, Paul David Nelson among them, have asserted that Mahan greatly overstated the importance of Valcour Island. Nelson looked at the contest for Lake Champlain from both the British and the American perspectives. He faulted Carleton for excessive caution and Arnold for undue aggressiveness. Since Carleton talked himself into accomplishing so little, Arnold should not have engaged at Valcour Island and lost the fleet. Rather, he should have kept closer to Ticonderoga where he could have offset the enemy fleet's advantages by scurrying under "the protection of the fort's guns."[30]

Nelson's argument goes full circle back to the contemporary denunciations of Arnold, none of which seemed to comprehend the necessity of employing a dynamic as opposed to static operational strategy on Lake Champlain. Arnold's purpose was to intimidate and delay Carleton while keeping the British fleet away from Ticonderoga for as long as possible. That is why Gates authorized Arnold to sail to the Canadian border, and that is why Arnold moved north with only a portion of his vessels. The fleet's appearance at Windmill Point was a critical factor in Carleton's decision to put off his invasion for a month while waiting for the *Inflexible* to be reassembled. Equally important, Arnold's tactical boldness at Valcour Island and raw courage off Split Rock helped convince Carleton that the defenders of Ticonderoga would also fight to the death, if need be. This was the impression that Arnold, above all else, wanted to create. In doing so, he deceived Carleton into thinking that Ticonderoga could not be taken without major bloodshed, an erroneous impression, indeed, in the absence of adequate munitions, but a product of Arnold's willingness to expend rather than conserve the rebel fleet.

By acting so resolutely, Arnold won the most important battle, the psychological contest with Carleton, who after a harmless probe of Ticonderoga's defenses on 28 October decided to pull back into Canada for the winter. His advisors, chief among them General Burgoyne, were furious. They wanted to initiate siege operations, at a minimum—ironically, when Ticonderoga's defenders finally were receiving shipments of the lead and powder they needed to defend themselves. Carleton, however, insisted that he had achieved his objectives. After all, he had devastated the rebel fleet and gained control of Lake Champlain, accomplishments he thought would easily satisfy his superiors in London.

Carleton's forces began their withdrawal on 2 November. No longer directly threatened, eight Continental regiments marched southward in early December to reinforce Washington's battered army west of the Delaware River. Some of these troops participated in Washington's vital turnabout victories at Trenton and Princeton, thereby keeping the flame of rebellion flickering in the face of Howe's superior strength. In reality, Carleton had not, even in the remotest sense, done anything "to contribute to the success of the army under General Howe," as prescribed by Lord Germain in March 1776. He had succumbed to the brazenness of such fighting rebels as Arnold. As at Valcour Island, by not pinning down the patriots and seizing the right moment to strike, he had afforded them an opportunity to offer combat another day. And some of them would do so at such places as Trenton, Princeton, and, when Burgoyne tried to complete Carleton's assignment, at Saratoga. Had Arnold and his fleet shown less tenacity on Lake Champlain, those opportunities might well have been lost, perhaps forever.[31]

NOTES

1. Benedict Arnold to Continental Congress, Crown Point, 13 June 1775, Peter Force, comp., *American Archives* (4th ser., 6 vols.; 5th ser., 3 vols., Washington, 1837–53), 4 ser., 2:976–77 (cited hereafter *AA*). In the interests of consistency and reading clarity, I have modernized spelling and capitalization in quoted materials Any use of the term "Canada" in this essay refers specifically to the British province of Quebec.

2. Worthington C. Ford et al., eds., *Journals of the Continental Congress, 1774–89* (34 vols., Washington, D.C., 1904–37), 2:108–10 (hereafter *JCC*)

3 After appointing George Washington as commander in chief on 16 June (ibid., 2:91–92), Congress chose four major generals and a number of brigadiers. Because of his influence in the Albany region, Schuyler was the natural choice to head the Northern Department. See *JCC* minutes for 17 and 19 June 1775, ibid., 2:96–100.

4. Lord Dartmouth to Thomas Gage, Whitehall, 27 January 1775, Clarence E. Carter, ed., *The Correspondence of General Thomas Gage, . . . 1763–1775* (2 vols., New Haven, 1931–1933), 2:179–83.

5. The materials on Arnold, as well as the interpretation, have been derived from my book, *Benedict Arnold, Revolutionary Hero: An American Warrior Reconsidered* (New York, 1997).

6. Arnold described his boyhood temperament to Benjamin Rush, most likely during the spring of 1777 when in Philadelphia attempting to persuade Congress to restore his seniority in military rank. See George W. Corner, ed., *The Autobiography of Benjamin Rush: His 'Travels Through Life' Together with his Commonplace Book for 1789–1813* (Princeton, 1948), 158.

7. Benedict Arnold to George Washington, Albany, 25 June 1776, Philander D. Chase et al., eds., *The Papers of George Washington: Revolutionary War Series* (7 vols. to date, Charlottesville, Va., 1985–), 5:96–97.

8. Ibid., 5:96.

9. There is a debate as to whether the patriot fleet at Valcour Island included eight or nine gundalows. The vessel in question was the *Success*. William M. Fowler Jr., in *Rebels under Sail: The American Navy during the Revolution* (New York, 1976), 183, 288 n40, concludes that the *Success* was not present. My reading of the sources suggests that she was. The *Success*'s presence or absence made little difference in the outcome of the battle. The schooner *Liberty* was in the midst of a supply run to Ticonderoga on 11 October so Arnold had a total of sixteen (or perhaps only fifteen) vessels at his disposal on the day of the battle.

10. Horatio Gates's orders to Benedict Arnold, Ticonderoga, 7 August 1776, William Bell Clark and William James Morgan et al., eds., *Naval Documents of the American Revolution* (10 vols. to date, Washington, D.C., 1964–), 6:95–96 (hereafter *NDAR*).

11. Benedict Arnold to Horatio Gates, Windmill Point, 7 September 1776, *AA,* 5th ser., 2:223–24.

12. Guy Carleton to [Henry] Caldwell, Pointe au Fer, 6 October 1776, Ernest Cruikshank, ed , *A History of the Organization, Development and Services of the Military and Naval Forces in Canada from . . . 1763, to the Present Time* (2 vols , Ottawa, n d), 2:193–94 (hereafter *HMNF*).

13. Lord George Germain to Guy Carleton, Whitehall, 28 March 1776, ibid., 2:150–51; Guy Carleton to Lord George Germain, Quebec, 10 August 1776, ibid., 2·184. As Carleton also stated, he believed that "valor and good conduct in time of action with humanity and friendly treatment to those who are subdued . . . at our mercy" was the best way to overcome rebel resistance and achieve an enduring reconciliation. Germain, in contrast, wanted decisive, definitive action. Stephen Conway, "To Subdue America: British Army Officers and the Conduct of the Revolutionary War," *William and Mary Quarterly,* 3d ser., 43 (1986): 381–407, divides the ranking British officers into conciliationists and hard-liners. Carleton clearly belonged in the former group.

14. Guy Carleton to Lord Germain, Chambly, 28 September 1776, *HMNF,* 2:290–91.

15. Benedict Arnold to Horatio Gates, Isle la Motte, 15 September 1776, *AA,* 5th ser., 2:531

16 Horatio Gates's Orders to Benedict Arnold, Ticonderoga, 7 August 1776, *NDAR,* 6·95–96

17. David Waterbury to John Hancock, President of Congress, Stamford, Conn , 24 October 1776, *AA,* 5th ser., 2:1224.

18. Horatio Gates to Benedict Arnold, Ticonderoga, 5 September 1776, ibid , 5th ser , 2:186–87.

19. Benedict Arnold to Horatio Gates, Schuyler's Island, 12 October 1776, ibid., 5th ser., 2:1038–39. In this hastily prepared after-action report, Arnold stated that he launched his attack around 11:00 A.M Joshua Pell, a British officer, recorded that the action opened at noon. See "Diary of Joshua Pell," 11 October 1776, *Magazine of American History* 2 (1878), 46. Both may have been correct; in the absence of a standard time, the British were likely keeping time an hour ahead of the Americans Because the battle occurred in so isolated a locale, eyewitness commentary is sparse. Beside those of Arnold and Pell, other useful descriptions include Thomas Pringle to Mr Stephens, *Maria* off Crown Point, 15 October 1776, *AA,* 5th ser., 2:1069–70; Elizabeth Cometti, ed., *The American Journals of Lt. John Enys,* 11–12 October 1776 (Syracuse, 1976), 18–22; Horatio Rogers, ed , *A Journal Kept in Canada and Upon Burgoyne's Campaign in 1776 and 1777, by Lieut. James M. Hadden, Roy. Art.,* 5–16 October 1776 (Albany, 1884; reprint, Boston, 1972), 18–30; "Journal of Captain George Pausch," 11–13 October 1776, *NDAR,* 6:1259–60; and "Journal of Bayze Wells of Farmington, [Conn ,] May 1775–February 1777, . . " 11–13 October 1776, *Collections of the Connecticut Historical Society* 7 (1899): 283–84.

20. Benedict Arnold to Horatio Gates, Schuyler's Island, 12 October 1776, *AA,* 5th ser., 2·1038.

21 Ibid., 5th ser., 2·1038

22 David Waterbury to John Hancock, President of Congress, Stamford, Conn , 24 October 1776, ibid., 5th ser , 2:1224.

23. Benedict Arnold to Philip Schuyler, Ticonderoga, 15 October 1776, ibid., 5th ser., 2:1079–80.

24 The long-standing mystery regarding where Arnold actually abandoned these vessels has been cleared up in Art Cohn, "An Incident Unknown to History. Squire Ferris and Benedict Arnold at Ferris Bay," *Vermont History* 55 (1987): 97–112.

25. Benedict Arnold to Philip Schuyler, Ticonderoga, 15 October 1776, *AA,* 5th ser , 2:1079–80.

26. Ibid., 5th ser., 2:1080; Howard Peckham, ed , *The Toll of Independence: Engagements and Battle Casualties of the American Revolution* (Chicago, 1974), 24, accepts Arnold's estimate but does not note the more than one hundred rebels on the *Washington* taken prisoner

27. William Maxwell to Gov. William Livingston, Ticonderoga, 20 October 1776, *AA,* 5th ser., 2:1143.

28. David Waterbury to John Hancock, President of Congress, Stamford, Conn., 24 October 1776, ibid., 5th ser., 2:1224.

29. The arguments contained in Mahan's *Major Operations* (Boston, 1913), 1–28, appeared earlier in Alfred Thayer Mahan, "The Naval Campaign of 1776 on Lake Champlain," *Scribner's Magazine* 23 (1898):147–60.

30. Paul David Nelson, "Guy Carleton versus Benedict Arnold The Campaign of 1776 in Canada and on Lake Champlain," *New York History* 57 (1976)· 339–66.

31. Lord George Germain to Guy Carleton, Whitehall, 28 March 1776, *HMNF,* 2:150–51.

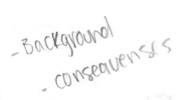

2

The Battle of Flamborough Head

JAMES C. BRADFORD

In the summer of 1779 Americans' morale reached a nadir in their then four-year-old struggle for independence. In 1775 and 1776 the colonists had launched their rebellion with visions of quick victory. Americans easily evicted royal governors from New Hampshire to Georgia and believed they had forced the British to evacuate Boston in March 1776. An invasion of Canada had failed, but by July 1776 the departure of British troops from all thirteen colonies emboldened the Continental Congress to declare independence from Great Britain. The summer and fall brought disappointment. British forces under Gen. Sir William Howe and his elder brother, Adm. Lord Richard Howe, easily occupied New York City and drove George Washington's army across New Jersey. A British invasion from Canada was stopped at Valcour Island but at the cost of Benedict Arnold's entire flotilla. Winter attacks on British outposts at Trenton and Princeton raised American hopes, but the British never lost confidence in their ability to deliver a knockout blow to the colonial upstarts in 1777. Britain's two-fold strategy called for capturing the American capital at Philadelphia and renewing the invasion from Canada to cut America in half along the Hudson River–Lake Champlain axis. General Howe achieved the first objective by using the Royal Navy to transport his army around Washington's position in New Jersey and attacking Philadelphia via the Chesapeake Bay. The second element of the British plan miscarried when Gen. John Burgoyne's army was forced to surrender at Saratoga, New York.

This capture of an entire British army buoyed American spirits. In February 1778 France signed an alliance with the United States and promised dispatch of a fleet that would combine with Washington's army to entrap British forces in New York and bring an end to the war within a year. Prospects of such a peace evaporated when Comte d'Estaing, commander of the French fleet, first refused to risk crossing the bar off Sandy Hook to attack the British fleet at New York, then abandoned the siege of the British outpost at Newport, Rhode Island, and fought an inconclusive battle with a British fleet. In November 1778 d'Estaing abandoned North America for the West Indies, leaving Americans to spend a cold winter trying to cobble together new plans to achieve their independence.

American fortunes followed a similar pattern of diminishing hope at sea. At the onset of hostilities George Washington leased a squadron of eleven ships to support his army. Between September 1775 and April 1776, converted trading vessels demonstrated the vulnerability of British shipping to commerce warfare by capturing fifty-five vessels.[1]

When Congress formed the Continental Navy in October 1775, it hoped the new service would be able to do more than raid enemy commerce. Contracts were let for the construction of thirteen frigates. While these were being built, officers of the new navy converted merchantmen into warships at Philadelphia, sailed to the Bahamas, captured the forts protecting Providence, and returned with fifty-eight cannon, fifteen mortars, and a quantity of shot and shell, though with none of the gunpowder so badly needed by Washington's army. The squadron was broken up following its return to New England and its ships were assigned to protect American trading vessels, support Washington's defense of New York City (where they were overwhelmed by the Royal Navy), and attack British commerce. In the latter role John Paul Jones achieved the most. During two cruises to the Grand Banks in 1776 he took twenty-three prizes, including the armed transport *Mellish*, and destroyed the local fishing fleets of Nova Scotia.

Construction of the thirteen frigates lagged, but in November 1776 Congress, confident of success, authorized construction of three ships of the line, five additional frigates, a brig, and a packetboat. Few of these vessels were ever completed, and fewer than half the original thirteen frigates even made it to sea. Those that did not were destroyed when the British captured New York and Philadelphia or lost attempting to slip through the British blockade. Thus 1777 was a year of disappointment for the Continental Navy, broken only by Lambert Wickes's capture of five prizes in the English Channel during January and another eighteen in the Irish Sea in May.

News of the alliance with France and anticipation of assistance from its fleet sent American hopes soaring in early 1778. Another successful attack on the Bahamas in January renewed Americans' confidence in their own naval forces, a feeling reinforced by stunning news of the cruise by John Paul Jones and the *Ranger* in the Irish Sea in April. Surpassing even Wickes in audacity, Jones landed parties at Whitehaven—the first enemy to set foot on English soil in more than a century—and spiked the guns of a fort protecting the harbor, crossed the Solway to St. Mary's Island, where he tried to kidnap the Earl of Selkirk, then crossed the Irish Sea to Ireland and captured the sloop of war *Drake.*

But the summer brought only disappointment, most notably the failure of the eagerly awaited French fleet to take decisive action, but also the loss of five Continental Navy ships—the *Randolph, Raleigh, Alfred, Columbus,* and *Independence*—within ninety days. Its resources exhausted, the Marine Committee, which supervised naval affairs for the Continental Congress, was forced to suspend most of its building program and to rely on privateers—privately owned ships licensed to prey on enemy commerce—to conduct the war at sea. During 1778 the number of such raiders rose to a wartime high of 115.

The year 1779 began equally as bad as the previous year for the Americans. During the last week of 1778 the British occupied Savannah, Georgia, and the single Franco-American operation of 1779 failed to dislodge them in October. Without naval support Washington could not attack the main British army, which remained at New York City, and in August 1779 an expedition attempting to oust a British force from the Penobscot River in Maine ended in disaster with the loss of nineteen ships.

Although the British appeared to be expanding their area of control in North America during 1779, their leaders feared for the outcome of the war. France's alliance with the United States in 1778, followed by Spain's entry into the war a year later as a partner of France (though not as an ally of the United States), had transformed the colonial rebellion in America into a worldwide struggle. Spanish strategists argued that the best way to force British concessions anywhere in the world was to attack Britain at home, and the French, though skeptical, agreed to preparations for invading the British Isles. Thus forces operating in European waters, not those in America, posed the greatest threat to Britain in 1779.[2]

While French and Spanish diplomats negotiated terms for an alliance and plotted strategy in late 1778 and early 1779, events were occurring in western France that would result in greater success than any operations being planned in Madrid or Paris. Few were aware of these developments, at the center of which stood John Paul Jones, a thirty-two-year-old Continental Navy captain.[3]

Jones, the son of a gardener, was born John Paul at Arbigland, near Kirkcudbright in Scotland, on 6 July 1747. He grew up within sight of the sea,

John Paul Jones sat for this bust by the noted French sculptor Jean-Antoine Houdon.
U.S. Naval Institute

received a rudimentary education at the Kirkbean Parish Church, and went to sea at age thirteen, apprenticed to a merchant from across the Solway Firth at Whitehaven in England. For the next decade he plied the trading routes that linked the British Isles with the West Indies, Chesapeake Bay, and the islands off the west coast of Africa. When the master and mate died aboard a ship in which John Paul had taken passage from Jamaica to Scotland, the twenty-one-year-old mariner took charge of the vessel, brought it safely to port in Kirkcudbright, and was rewarded by the owners by being made its commander. John Paul proved an exacting master. Five years later, part of his crew mutinied in Tobago, and he was forced to kill the ringleader in self defense. At the urging of friends, he decided to "retire incognito to the continent of America [and] remain there until an Admiralty Commission should arrive in the island [to hear his case], then to return."[4] But he never returned.

Instead, having made his way to the mainland, John Paul took the surname

"Jones" and settled in Fredericksburg, Virginia, where his older brother was a tailor. Soon after the outbreak of the Revolution Jones proceeded to the Continental capital at Philadelphia. There he met Joseph Hewes, a merchant from North Carolina whose partner Jones had known in Scotland. Hewes was representing his home state in the Continental Congress and used his influence to get Jones commissioned the senior lieutenant in the new Continental Navy on 7 December 1775. After serving as first lieutenant in the *Alfred,* flagship of the squadron that raided the Bahamas in early 1776, Jones received command of the sloop *Providence* on 10 May. Later that month he transported soldiers to New York for Washington's army as it prepared to defend the city from attack by the British, and in July he convoyed colliers from Boston to Delaware Bay. On 8 August, Jones was promoted to captain and six weeks later entered the harbors at Canso and Ile Madame, Nova Scotia, where he destroyed or captured several British fishing schooners. Returning to Newport, Rhode Island, after taking sixteen prizes, of which eight were burned and eight sent into port, he transferred to command of the larger *Alfred* and in November again sailed for the Grand Banks off Nova Scotia. On 16 November Jones captured the *Kitty,* and a week later he sent men ashore to burn a British supply ship, destroy a warehouse, and capture a small schooner. On 24 November, he took three colliers off Louisburg and on the following day captured the letter-of-marque *John.* Though now clearly the most successful officer in the Continental Navy, Jones was ordered to relinquish command of the *Alfred* and return to the *Providence.*

Frustrated by this demotion, Jones visited Philadelphia to lobby influential members of Congress. In June 1777 he obtained command of the 18-gun sloop of war *Ranger,* then under construction at Portsmouth, New Hampshire, with orders to oversee its completion and then to sail to Europe, where he would receive command of a frigate being built in Holland for the United States. When Jones reached France he learned that because of British protests the Dutch would not deliver the ship. The American commissioners at Paris issued Jones discretionary orders to cruise as "you shall judge best for distressing the enemies of the United States."[5]

After overhauling the *Ranger* in France, Jones sailed to the Irish Sea in April 1778. On 21 April he approached the harbor at Carrickfergus, where bad weather foiled his attempt to capture by boarding the British sloop of war *Drake.* The next day he crossed the Irish Sea and on the night of 22–23 April landed with thirty-one volunteers at Whitehaven, England, the port from which he first went to sea seventeen years before. Jones planned to spike the guns of the fort and burn the coal fleet lying in the harbor. A party under his

John Paul Jones's cruises in British waters.

personal leadership entered the fort by climbing on each other's shoulders, spiked the guns, and withdrew to the harbor, where Jones discovered that members of a second landing party had entered a pub and proceeded to make "very free with the liquor" rather than set any of the three hundred vessels in the harbor ablaze. Jones himself started a fire on the collier *Thompson*. Smaller fires were set on other ships, but townspeople, alerted by a turncoat from Jones's party, began gathering along the waterfront, forced the Americans to withdraw, and extinguished the flames. The total damage done was small in monetary terms, but the psychological impact was great on both sides of the Atlantic. No English town had suffered such an attack since the Dutch burned Sheerness in 1667. Coastal communities all over England pleaded for protection from the government, and Americans, who had little to cheer about in 1778, were heartened that the people of England had received treatment similar to that dispensed by the Royal Navy on the other side of the Atlantic.

Only hours after the Whitehaven raid, Jones crossed the Solway Firth and took a dozen men ashore on St. Mary's Isle to abduct the Earl of Selkirk. Jones hoped to trade the earl, a member of Parliament, for American naval prisoners held by the British. When he learned "from some inhabitants" that the earl was not at home, Jones ordered his men to return to their ship, but "disposed to pillage, burn, and plunder" they refused to follow his orders. Reluctantly Jones allowed a small party to go to the house and seize the family silver.[6] Jones would later write the Countess of Selkirk, who had handed over the silver to his men, explaining his actions: "It was my intention to have taken [the earl] on board the Ranger, and to have detained him till thro' his means, a general and fair Exchange of Prisoners . . . had been effected. . . . I have drawn my Sword in the present generous Struggle for the rights of Men; yet I am not in Arms as an American, nor am I in pursuit of Riches. . . . I profess myself a Citizen of the World."[7] These lofty sentiments have been discounted by many writers, but this is a mistake. Though not an American by birth, Jones shared the idealism of the struggle for independence, and the concept of world citizenship appealed to him as it did to others, including Edward Gibbon and Thomas Jefferson.

The frustrations of Whitehaven and St. Mary's Isle did not dampen Jones's spirits and after leaving the Solway he crossed the Irish Sea to Belfast Lough, where he challenged HMS *Drake* to battle. The two ships were evenly matched. The *Ranger* held a slight advantage in ordnance, with eighteen 9-pounders to the *Drake*'s twenty 6-pounders, but the *Drake* had a larger crew. Rather than risk pitting his mutinous crew against the British in hand-to-hand combat, Jones kept his distance from the *Drake* and, in an hour-long action that killed her captain and second in command, pounded her into submission. Knowing the psychological value of carrying a British warship into a French port, Jones risked capture by the ships sent in search of him by spending a day repairing the *Drake*'s masts and rigging so she could be taken to France. On 8 May the *Drake* sailed into Brest behind the *Ranger*. In her hold were two hundred prisoners who would be exchanged for mariners held in England. The cruise was a great success. "What was done," Jones said, "is sufficient to show that not all their boasted navy can protect their own coast, and that the scene of distress which they have occasioned in America may soon be brought home to their own shores."[8]

Though Jones was honored in Paris, the rest of 1778 brought him mainly frustration. Various enterprises were proposed by both French and American officials, and some by Jones himself, but all came to naught. Jones relinquished command of the *Ranger* because he was again promised the frigate under construction in Holland. When delivery was again delayed, he searched for a ship to command in the interim. In December he found the *Duc de Duras,* an old East Indiaman, in Lorient, renamed her the *Bonhomme Richard* in honor of Benjamin Franklin, and set about refitting—actually, more rebuilding—the vessel and locating cannon for her armament.

While work on the ship dragged on, plans were made, then abandoned, for its employment. The most ambitious proposal concerned an assault on Liverpool or some other port in northern England or Scotland. Jones would command the naval squadron and the Marquis Lafayette the landing force in an expedition intended to draw British forces away from the English Channel, the target of the Franco-Spanish invasion being planned for the summer of 1779. In May the undertaking was canceled and, after a cruise in the Bay of Biscay protecting merchant ships, Jones returned to Lorient to ready the *Bonhomme Richard,* the Continental Navy frigate *Alliance* (thirty-six guns), the French frigate *Pallas* (thirty-two), the corvette *Vengeance* (twelve), and the cutter *Cerf* (eighteen) for an extended voyage.[9]

On 14 August, the five ships put to sea from Lorient accompanied by two privateers. Jones had carte blanche to set his own course of action, subject only to the requirement that he arrive at the Texel in Holland by 1 October to receive further instructions. He originally proposed to hover off the west coast of Ireland near Limerick and intercept eight ships expected from India, but he had to abandon this intention when Pierre Landais, French captain of the *Alliance,* refused to follow his orders. He next planned to sail clockwise around the British Isles, taking whatever prizes presented themselves, then to lay Leith, the port city of Edinburgh, under contribution (i.e., to require it to pay a ransom to escape being burned), and finally to intercept a convoy expected from the Baltic carrying naval stores. For three weeks the operation proceeded generally according to plan, with the squadron taking seventeen prizes, two of which were sent to Bergen in neutral Norway. The two privateers, the *Cerf* and the *Vengeance,* abandoned Jones during the cruise, and the *Alliance* disappeared for several days.[10]

On 13 September, a month after leaving France, Jones and the *Bonhomme Richard, Alliance,* and *Pallas* stood off the Firth of Forth ready to threaten Leith. In a memoir written later, Jones explained his goals:

Though much weakened and embarrassed with prisoners, [I] was anxious to teach the enemy humanity, by some exemplary stroke of retaliation, and to relieve the remainder of the Americans from captivity in England, as well as to make a diversion in the north, to favor a formidable descent which [I] then expected would have been made on the south side of Great Britain, under cover of the combined [French and Spanish] fleet.[11]

Jones planned to sail up the Firth to Leith, where he would send a messenger ashore to demand payment of £200,000 or else the squadron would set fire to the town. Just as Jones was about to land the messenger, a "sudden storm rose and obliged [him] to run before the wind out of the gulf of Edinburgh."[12]

Jones next tried to convince his officers to attack Newcastle-on-Tyne, but their timidity forced him to settle for cruising along the Yorkshire coast in search of British shipping. On 22 September, Jones and the *Bonhomme Richard* passed Spurn Head, northern cape of the Humber estuary, and signaled for a pilot boat. Two sailed out, and he took both prisoner. When attempts to lure other ships failed, Jones turned north toward Flamborough Head, which he had designated as a rendezvous should his squadron become separated by bad weather or operational exigencies. At dawn on 23 September he met the *Pallas,* whose captain, Denis-Nicolas Cottineau, had taken her in pursuit of prizes, and the frigate *Alliance,* whose erratic captain, Pierre Landais, had deserted Jones north of the Orkneys. With the corvette *Vengeance,* Jones now had four warships under his tenuous command.

At virtually the same time Jones reformed his squadron, a British fleet of merchant ships escorted by two warships spied Whitby on the Yorkshire coast. Thankful to have crossed the North Sea without being attacked, several ships turned northward for Scottish ports, and the rest headed southeasterly. By noon the second group was strung out for several miles. A few were even ahead of the *Serapis,* commanded by Capt. Richard Pearson, the man responsible for defense of the convoy. As Pearson approached Flamborough Head, his lookouts spotted a red flag flying from Scarborough Castle, just north of the headland. Such a flag signaled that enemy warships were in the area, and a cutter soon brought a messenger to warn Pearson that John Paul Jones had tried to attack Leith a week before and that his squadron had been sighted off the Humber only a day earlier. Taking no chances, Pearson ordered the merchant vessels to reverse course and head northwest for the safety of the fort at Scarborough. His charges ignored his signals until they sighted strange sails to the south. Then the lead ships let fly their topgallant sheets, fired warning shots, and all but one frantically sought to come about. Fearing that the sails belonged to an enemy—probably John Paul Jones—Pearson placed *Serapis* and her consort, the *Countess of Scarborough,* between the fleeing merchantmen and the enemy and prepared for battle.

Informed of the merchantmen rounding the head at 2:00 P.M., Jones realized immediately that they must be part of the valuable Baltic convoy and set course to pursue. As he approached, the British warships turned seaward, and light winds prevented Jones from closing with them until almost dark. As the distance between the two British and four American warships narrowed, Jones hoisted flags signaling "Form Line of Battle." Denis-Nicolas Cottineau, Pierre Landais, and Philippe-Nicholas Ricot, the captains of Jones's squadron, all ignored the signal, but Richard Pearson of the *Serapis* could not know this and demonstrated his determination to fight to the death by ordering the ensign nailed to the flagstaff at the stern of his ship. At approximately 6:00 P.M., Pearson tacked to keep his ships between the Americans and the convoy.

Had Jones enjoyed the full support of his subordinates in the ensuing battle, the advantage might have been his; but he did not. The *Bonhomme Richard* would have to fight the *Serapis* without help from the *Alliance, Pallas,* or *Vengeance,* and in a single ship-to-ship engagement quantitative measures promised a mismatch. The *Serapis* was not a standard British frigate of the era. A "5th Rate 44," she had two gun decks, like a ship of the line, rather than a single gun deck like most frigates. Instead of carrying forty-four guns as implied by her rating, she carried fifty, including a main battery of twenty 18-pounders, a secondary battery of twenty 9-pounders, and ten 6-pounders on the quarterdeck. Less than seven months old, the *Serapis* was returning from her maiden voyage and, having a coppered hull, was more maneuverable than the aged *Bonhomme Richard,* which carried six 18-pounders, twenty-eight 12-pounders, and six 9-pounders. This gave the *Serapis* a broadside firepower of 300 pounds to only 229 for the *Bonhomme Richard.* The *Bon-*

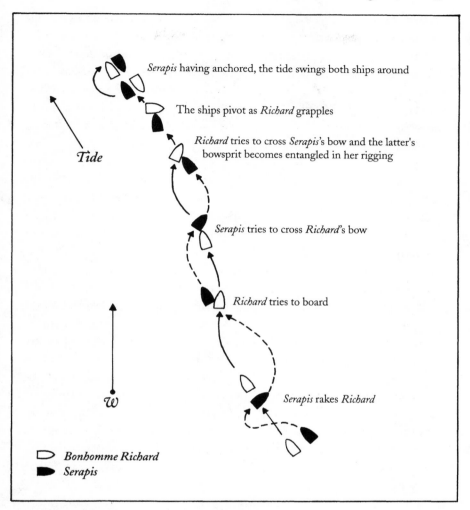

Serapis having anchored, the tide swings both ships around

The ships pivot as *Richard* grapples

Richard tries to cross *Serapis*'s bow and the latter's bowsprit becomes entangled in her rigging

Tide

Serapis tries to cross *Richard*'s bow

Richard tries to board

Serapis rakes *Richard*

W

▷ *Bonhomme Richard*
▶ *Serapis*

Bonhomme Richard vs. Serapis, 23 September 1779.

homme *Richard*'s crew, 380 strong at the start of the cruise, had been reduced by desertion and the manning of prizes to a motley assortment of 322 by the time of battle. This approximately equaled in number, if not quality, the 325-man crew of the newer, more heavily armed *Serapis*.[13]

At 6:30, the *Serapis* and *Bonhomme Richard* were steering parallel courses westward toward the land. Jones, sailing to windward, hauled up his lower sails to provide better visibility. When the two ships came within pistol shot,

Captain Pearson hailed the *Richard,* asking, "What ship is that?" Jones, flying British colors and hoping to close still further ordered his master, Samuel Stacey, to answer, "The *Princess Royal.*" "Where from?" inquired Pearson. When no reply was heard, he shouted, "Answer immediately, or I shall be under the necessity of firing into you." Jones responded by striking his British colors, replacing them with an American flag, and ordering his broadside to fire. Thus began one of the fiercest and most deadly ship-to-ship actions of the Age of Sail.[14]

For an hour the pair of ships maneuvered exchanging broadsides. During the first or second broadside two of the old 18-pounders on the *Richard's* lower deck exploded, killing several men and rendering the rest of the guns on that deck unusable. As the two ships jockeyed for position, Pearson in the *Serapis* directed his fire into the hull of the *Bonhomme Richard.* This was in keeping with usual British tactics of the era, which aimed at smashing the hull of the opponent. Though usually effective against the French who tended to favor firing into the sails of their opponent to cripple its ability to maneuver, the British were ill-served by Pearson's decision in this battle. True they were able to destroy large sections of the hull of the *Bonhomme Richard* and to knock out of action most of the cannon on her lower decks, but aiming low left the men on the *Richard's* quarterdeck and in its tops relatively unscathed. That would have disastrous results for the British as the battle progressed.

The greater maneuverability of the *Serapis* gave Pearson the advantage in a pure gun duel, so Jones, with his own main battery out of commission, decided to board the enemy. At one point he maneuvered the *Richard* against the starboard quarter of the *Serapis* and ordered "Boarders Away," but his men were driven back when they attempted to gain the enemy's deck. When the ships parted Pearson tried to steer the *Serapis* across the bow of the *Richard* to rake her while Jones tried to "lay the *Bon Homme Richard* athwart the enemy's bow."[15] Neither succeeded, but as the two ships jockeyed for position, the bowsprit of the *Serapis* became entangled in the *Richard's* mizzen rigging, and the two ships pivoted alongside one another, the bow of one against the stern of the other. Seizing the opportunity to force a boarding action, Jones ordered his men to lash the two ships together. He personally knotted a loose forestay from the *Serapis* to the *Richard's* mizzenmast.

Captain Pearson responded by ordering his men to let drop their anchor in the hope that the tide would jerk the *Richard* free from the *Serapis* once the anchor bit into the sandy bottom off Flamborough Head. Pearson probably feared that he faced a stronger force when he first sighted the Americans, but by now he knew that he had only to deal with one of the four ships and that, having the superior vessel, it was in his interest to stand off and fight an artillery duel. Fortunately for Jones, the two ships remained locked in their deadly embrace.

At 8:00 a full moon rose to light the seascape, revealing to Jones that he had only two cannon, quarterdeck 9-pounders, able to fire on the enemy. Purser Matthew Mease, who had been in charge of the guns, was seriously wounded, so Jones took personal command of them. Immediately, he gathered a group of men and trundled another 9-pounder into the battle by moving it across the quarterdeck from the ship's unengaged side to a position where it could fire on the *Serapis*. Selecting his targets shrewdly, Jones ordered two cannon loaded with grapeshot and canister to sweep the British vessel's upper deck and the third to fire barshot at her mainmast, whose yellow paint rendered it clearly visible in the moonlight. French Marines in the tops supported the cannon with musket fire, grenades, and swivel guns, but the rest of the *Bonhomme Richard* was silent, the *Serapis*'s 18-pounders having rendered the *Richard*'s 12-pounders useless. During the next hour the Americans destroyed the bulwarks lining the enemy's quarterdeck and swept clear his quarterdeck, forecastle, and tops.

While this was going on, the erratic Pierre Landais sailed the *Alliance* past the clenched pair and fired a broadside that struck both ships, doing more damage to the *Richard*, which had crewmen on deck, than to the *Serapis*, whose personnel had been driven to relative safety below. Pearson did not realize how seriously the *Richard* was damaged, nor possibly that cannon on his maindeck were continuing to pour fire into her hull, cannonballs entering one side and exiting the other. Seeing only the carnage on his upper decks and personally observing the fire of the three cannon directed by Jones, Pearson discussed surrender with his officers. Jones later charged that at this critical juncture three of his petty officers, afraid the *Richard* would sink beneath them, called out to the enemy for quarter. Taking heart, Pearson hailed Jones, asking, "Do you ask for quarter? Do you ask for quarter?" to which Jones is reputed to have replied, "I have not yet begun to fight."[16]

Thus the battle resumed, the British again hammering the *Bonhomme Richard* "with the fury of vengeance and despair."[17] Jones described the results:

The bulwarks of the *Serapis* were damaged or burned, and the mainmast was gradually cut down by the grapeshot of the *Bon Homme Richard*, while the much superior artillery of the *Serapis*'s two batteries struck one side of the *Bon Homme Richard* and blew out the other so that during the last hour of combat the shot passed through both sides of the *Bon Homme Richard* meeting little or no resistance. The rudder was

The Battle off Flamborough Head, 23 September 1779. This engraving of a painting by Richard Paton was published in England in 1781. It illustrates the final phase of the action, with the *Bonhomme Richard* and *Serapis* grappled bow to stern. At right center, the *Alliance* pours one of her indiscriminate broadsides into both vessels, while at far right the *Pallas* and *Vengeance* take possession of the *Countess of Scarborough*. *U.S. Naval Institute*

shattered and only an old timber here and there kept the poop from crashing down on the gundeck.[18]

For a second time, Pierre Landais sailed the *Alliance* past the two ships, sending another broadside into the bow of the *Serapis* and stern of the *Richard*. Jones and others on board the *Richard* shouted to the *Alliance* to cease fire and to send men to aid the *Richard,* but Landais ignored their requests, circled to the other side of the ships, and fired a third broadside into them, this time striking the *Serapis* in the stern and the *Richard* in the bow. "After this the *Alliance* kept at a respectful distance and took great care not to expose herself either to receive a blow or to have a single man killed or wounded."[19]

The reasons for Landais's irresponsible actions remain a matter of conjecture, but whatever the explanation, his firing into the *Richard* certainly added to the consternation of its officers and crew. Fearing the ship was about to founder, master-at-arms John Burbank opened the hatches to release the hundred British prisoners taken from prizes and until then held below deck. Thinking quickly, Jones ordered the prisoners to man the pumps as they emerged on deck. Probably stunned by the chaos about them, the men obeyed.[20]

As the desperate struggle continued, the *Serapis*'s fire drove the *Richard*'s gun crews from her gun deck to the upper deck, where they reinforced the marines and sailors who were firing muskets and swivel guns at the *Serapis*. For a time neither side held an advantage, then the balance began to shift. William Hamilton, a sailor posted in the fighting tops of the *Richard*'s mainmast, took a basket of grenades and a lighted match and edged his way out the main yard until he was directly above the *Serapis*. From there he began lobbing grenades at every group of enemy sailors he could see. One of his grenades dropped through a hatchway and set fire to powder charges on the deck below. The chain reaction that ensued set off charges the length of the ship, killing or wounding dozens of men.

At the same time, conditions aboard the *Richard* reached a critical point. The carpenter reported to Jones that the ship was about to sink. Fearing for his life, the gunner screamed that they had to surrender and headed aft to lower the American flag. In a stroke, Jones knocked the gunner out with the butt of his pistol. All at once, the *Serapis*'s mainmast, then held in place only by the *Richard*'s rigging, began to quiver. This was the last straw for Captain Pearson, who was in the process of striking his colors as the mainmast fell into the sea. At 10:30, the fighting ceased. Half an hour later Richard Dale, senior lieutenant in the *Richard*, went on board the *Serapis* as prize master. Officers of the *Serapis* who remained able to walk crossed to the *Richard*, where Pearson surrendered his sword to Jones. In a gesture typical of the era, Jones invited his foe to his cabin for a glass of wine.

What of the rest of the squadron? While Jones in the *Bon Homme Richard* was defeating the *Serapis*, Captain Cottineau and the *Pallas* captured the *Countess of Scarborough*. Pierre Landais and the *Alliance* contributed nothing to the American victory, except perhaps to cause Pearson to fear they might assist the *Bonhomme Richard*. In fact, the *Alliance* probably inflicted greater damage on the *Bonhomme Richard* than on the *Serapis*. The corvette *Vengeance* and the pilot boat captured on 22 September may have been too weak to engage either of the British warships, but their failure to pursue the fleeing merchantmen casts doubts on the ability or courage of their commanders.

The escape of the Baltic convoy and its safe arrival in port led many in Britain to consider the Battle of Flamborough Head a strategic victory for Pearson even if the loss of its escorts, the *Serapis* and *Countess of Scarborough*, constituted a tactical defeat. The convoy's insurers agreed and presented Pearson and Thomas Piercy, captain of the *Countess of Scarborough,* with silver services. The courts-martial required of every officer who lost his ship judged that Pearson and Piercy "had not only acquitted themselves of their duty to the country, but had, in the execution of such, done infinite credit to themselves by a very obstinate defense against a superior force," and George III knighted Pearson for his conduct. Members of the court can be forgiven for shading the truth when they called Jones's force superior. It was wartime, and the Royal Navy was not accustomed to losing warships to the enemy. When informed of Pearson's knighthood at a dinner some months later, Jones responded, "Let me fight him again . . . and I'll make him a lord."[21]

Pearson's surrender to Jones brought rest to neither side. For the remainder of the night, all the following day, and on through the night of 24–25 September the damaged ships half drifted and half sailed slowly to the eastward. Casualties had been high. Each ship lost between seventy and eighty men killed, and about as many wounded. Years later, Midshipman Nathaniel Fanning remembered the "shocking sight" of "the dead lying in heaps . . . the groans of the wounded and dying . . . the entrails of the dead scattered promiscuously around, [and] the blood over ones shoes. . . ."[22] The survivors worked to save their ships, first extinguishing fires, then patching holes and replacing rigging, but by the morning of 25 September Jones had to accept that the *Bonhomme Richard* could not be saved. Transferring the wounded and his flag to the *Serapis,* he ordered the men at the pumps to cease their losing battle. At 10:00 A.M. the last seamen left the *Bonhomme Richard,* and an hour later Jones watched "with inexpressible grief, the last glimpse of the *Bon Homme Richard*[,] mangled beyond my power of description," as she slipped bow first below the surface.

Jones hoped to take the battered ships to Dunkirk, the nearest French port, but his subordinates, Landais, Cottineau, and Ricot, refused to obey his signals and headed for the Texel, directly across the North Sea in Holland. Jones, in the *Serapis,* had little choice but to accompany them. Foul weather combined with good luck allowed the squadron to elude the dozen British warships searching for it and to enter the Texel on 3 October.

News of the American victory at Flamborough Head traveled quickly to Amsterdam and The Hague, then to Paris, London, and America. The Dutch gave Jones a hero's welcome, mobbed him in the streets, and applauded him at the theater.[23] In Britain, Jones was both feared and admired. "Paul Jones resembled a Jack O'Lantern, to mislead our marines and terrify our coasts," said London's *Morning Post.* He is "still the most general topic of conversation," the paper reported a month later. Poems and ballads extolled his victory and attacked his character.[24] Sir Joseph Yorke, Britain's ambassador to the Netherlands, was outraged by the reception Jones received there and demanded that he be expelled from the country and that the *Serapis* and *Countess of Scarborough* be turned over to the British navy.

Dutch officials debated what to do. The ruling House of Orange wished to maintain close ties with Britain, but the Patriot Party favored France and was sympathetic to the United States. A number of Dutch officials suspected that Jones had been ordered to Holland specifically to try to drag their country into the war against Britain. Though Jones undoubtedly enjoyed the celebrity accorded him ashore, he had no wish to remain in the Texel longer than absolutely necessary. He asked the Dutch only for permission to land his sick and wounded, to temporarily confine his 504 prisoners ashore, and to purchase materials for repair of his ships.

After failing to negotiate an exchange of his prisoners for Americans held in Britain, Jones was forced to relinquish both the prisoners and the captured British ships to French officials. Jones shifted to the *Alliance* and on 27 December departed the Texel. Perhaps through luck he eluded the British ships laying in wait for him and sailed first to Corunna, Spain, then across the Bay of Biscay to Lorient, which he reached on 19 February 1780. For the next two months Jones set his men to making alterations in the *Alliance* in preparation for another cruise. The ship's crewmen had received neither wages nor prize money since leaving America. Jones lacked resources to pay them, so in April he traveled to Paris, where he hoped either French or American officials would provide assistance.

When Jones arrived in Paris, French society, starved for signs of success in the war with Britain, greeted him with open arms. Benjamin Franklin presented Jones to the French court, where Louis XVI awarded him a gold-hilted sword and conferred the Order of Military Merit upon him. Jones attended dinners held in his honor, went to the theater with Marie Antoinette, and was inducted into the Masonic Lodge of the Nine Sisters, which commissioned a bust of Jones by Jean-Antoine Houdon.[25]

Jones had reached the pinnacle of his fame. His capture of the *Serapis* stood in stark contrast to the dismal record of French arms elsewhere that year. On 3 June the main French fleet sailed from Brest, cruised off the Iberian coast until rendezvousing with the Spanish fleet on 26 July, then headed for England. The Allied fleet reached the Lizard on 14 August, the same day that Jones set out from France. While Jones's squadron of five ships circled the British Isles, the combined Franco-Spanish fleet of sixty-four ships of the line sailed along England's south coast. On 31 August the French commander spotted the British fleet off the Scilly Isles and for two days gave chase. Having only thirty-eight ships of the line, the British admiral wisely kept his distance until the French admiral d'Orvilliers received orders to return to port. A week later his ships reached Brest, where he landed seven thousand sick seamen. The Spanish fleet returned home, and the campaign of 1779 collapsed.[26] The abject failure of operations in the Channel was compounded by setbacks in the West Indies, where the British reestablished naval supremacy in January 1779, in India where Mahé, the last French post on the subcontinent, fell to the British in March, and in North America, where d'Estaing's siege of Savannah failed in November. In January 1780 a British fleet defeated a Spanish fleet off Cape St. Vincent and delivered a large convoy to Gibraltar, thereby rendering the siege of that fortress ineffectual.[27]

American arms fared no better at home. Britain followed its capture of Savannah, Georgia, on 29 December 1778 with the seizure of Augusta a month later. In May 1779 naval parties captured and burned Portsmouth and Norfolk in Virginia. Two months later raiding parties put Norwalk and Fairfield, Connecticut, to the torch. In August an expedition organized by the state of Massachusetts ended in disaster at Penobscot, Maine, with the loss of three Continental Navy ships, a New Hampshire State Navy brig, three Massachusetts Navy brigantines, and thirteen leased privateers. Jones's victory over the *Serapis* provided one of the few glimmers of hope in an otherwise dark year for the young United States.

It proved also to be one of the last achievements of the Continental Navy. The British capture of Charleston, South Carolina, in May 1780 resulted in the loss of four Continental Navy ships, three frigates and a sloop. By year's end the Continental Navy retained only six ships, three of which were lost in 1781. No other action approached the Battle of Flamborough Head for drama or success.

To combat the British at sea, the United States was again forced to depend on privateers. Indeed 1781 saw a new high of 449 in the number of ships licensed by Congress and the states to prey on enemy commerce. During the entire eight years of war, American privateers captured about 2,200 British merchant ships, more than ten times the 196 taken or destroyed by the Continental Navy. Great Britain also employed commerce raiders, which captured about fifteen hundred American ships. Thus, neither side emerged the clear victor in destroying the other's shipping. Although commerce raiding did not determine the outcome of the conflict, it was one of the most active, if underappreciated, aspects of warfare during the Revolution.[28]

The action at sea that led to peace involved neither the Continental Navy nor commerce raiding, but was fought by French and British fleets at the Battle of the Virginia Capes on 5 September 1781. Tactically inconclusive, the engagement proved strategically decisive, in that it prevented the British from entering the Chesapeake, leaving Lord Cornwallis's army isolated at Yorktown, where it surrendered six weeks later. By then, two years had passed since the Battle of Flamborough Head. In the hour of victory, few Americans gave any thought to John Paul Jones or his capture of the *Serapis*, but over the decades the memory of both grew in the American mind.

Finally, in 1905, a century after Jones died and was buried in Paris, ships of the U.S. Navy transported his body to Annapolis, where it was laid to rest in the crypt beneath the chapel at the Naval Academy. The inscription on his tomb reads: "He gave to our navy its earliest traditions of heroism and victory." Those traditions, determination in the face of overwhelming odds, cool judgment under fire, bravery, and victory, are the true legacy of the Battle of Flamborough Head.

NOTES

1. Several books trace the maritime history of the American Revolution. William M. Fowler Jr., *Rebels Under Sail* (New York, 1976), and Nathan Miller, *Sea of Glory* (New York, 1974) are among the best modern surveys.

2. Jonathan Dull, *The French Navy and American Independence* (Princeton, 1975), 125–35, examines French negotiations with Spain as well as the role of the French Navy in the war.

3 The best Jones biographies are Samuel Eliot Morison, *John Paul Jones: A Sailor's Biography* (Boston, 1959); Lincoln Lorenz, *John Paul Jones, Fighter for Freedom and Glory* (Annapolis, 1941); and Mrs. Reginald (Anna) DeKoven, *The Life and Letters of John Paul Jones*, 2 vols. (New York, 1913).

4. John Paul Jones to Benjamin Franklin, 6 March 1779, in James C. Bradford, ed., *The Papers of John Paul Jones* (Alexandria, 1986), document 550.

5. American Commissioners to Jones, 16 January 1778, Bradford, *Jones*, 234.

6 Gerald W. Gawalt, trans. and ed , *John Paul Jones' Memoir of the American Revolution* (Washington, D.C., 1979), 19.

7. Jones to Lady Selkirk, 8 May 1778, Bradford, *Jones*, 287.

8. Gawalt, *Jones' Memoir*, 21.

9. For the Jones-Lafayette expedition, see Lafayette to Vergennes, 1 April 1779; Lafayette to Jones, 27 April 1779; Benjamin Franklin to Jones, 27 April 1779; Lafayette to Jones, 22 May 1779; Stanley J. Idzerda, ed., *Lafayette in the Age of the American Revolution: Selected Letters and Papers, 1776–1790* (Ithaca, 1977–), 2:251–53, 258–63, 267–68. Sartine to Franklin, 27 April 1779, Franklin Collection, Library of Congress.

10. Jones described the entire voyage in virtually identical letters to Benjamin Franklin, the president of the Continental Congress, Lafayette, and French minister of marine, Antoine Sartine, all dated 3 October 1779. Bradford, *Jones*, 749–51, 753.

11. From the lost English-language version of Jones's "Memoir of the American Revolution" quoted in Robert Sands, *Life and Correspondence of John Paul Jones* (New York, 1830), 171.

12. Gawalt, *Jones' Memoir*, 31.

13. Jean Boudriot, *John Paul Jones and the Bonhomme Richard* (Annapolis, 1987). Jones estimated the crew of the *Serapis* at four hundred. Gawalt, *Jones' Memoir*, 39.

14. This account on the battle relies most closely on Jones's description of it in the eighteen-page letter he wrote to Benjamin Franklin from Holland on 3 October 1779 (Bradford, *Jones*, 749) and his accounts of the battle in the memoir he sent to the King of France (Gawalt, *Jones' Memoir*, 31–41), as well as in *Memoirs of Rear-Admiral Paul Jones* (Edinburgh, 1830), 1:177–99 (hereafter, *Memoirs of Jones*), Louis F. Middlebrook, ed., *The Log of the Bonhomme Richard* (Mystic, 1936), and John S. Barnes, ed., *The Logs of the Serapis—Alliance—Ariel Under the Command of John Paul Jones, 1779–1780* (New York, 1911). Captain Pearson of the *Serapis* and Thomas Piercy of the *Countess of Scarborough* described the battle in letters to the Admiralty dated 4 and 6 October 1779, which are printed in Don C. Seitz, *Paul Jones: His Exploits in English Seas during 1778–1780* (New York, 1917), 93–99. The battle has been the subject of two books. John Evangelish Walsh, *Night on Fire: The First Complete Account of John Paul Jones's Greatest Battle* (New York, 1978), and Thomas J Schaeper, *John Paul Jones and the Battle off Flamborough Head: A Reconsideration* (New York, 1989). The latter summarizes previous accounts of the battle, assesses all contemporary sources concerning it, and prints transcriptions of the most important documents. All the documents can be examined in facsimile and transcription in Bradford, *Jones*. Every Jones biography cited above describes the battle, as does Peter Reavely in Boudriot, *The Bonhomme Richard*, 64–91.

All these authors differ with one another in chronology and details. From his study of the log of the *Bonhomme Richard*, Schaeper makes a plausible case that the battle took place on the twenty-fourth rather than the twenty-third of September even though "nearly every firsthand summary of the battle [including those by Jones and Pearson] that gives a precise date gives the 23rd." Schaeper, *Jones*, 7–16.

15. Gawalt, *Jones' Memoir*, 182.

16. In one account Jones reported that, "I having answered him in the most determined negative, they renewed the battle with double fury" (Gawalt, *Jones' Memoir*, 185). In the account he presented to the King of France, Jones reported replying, "Je ne songe point à me rendre, mais je suis déterminé à vous faire demander quartier" (Ibid., *Memoir*, 35). This translates, "I give no thought at all to surrendering, but I am determined to make you ask for quarter." Another contemporary account says that Jones cried, "I may sink, but I'll be damed if I'll surrender." The shorter version, "I have not yet begun to fight," first appears almost half a century later in John Henry Sherburne, *Life and Character of the Chevalier John Paul Jones* (Washington, D.C , 1825). Sherburne cites as his source Richard Dale, first lieutenant in the *Bonhomme Richard*, who first recorded his memory of the battle around 1814, but later expanded upon it at Sherburne's request. The most thorough analysis of contemporary versions of the reply is Charles Lee Lewis, "'I Have Not Yet Begun to Fight,'" *The Mississippi Valley Historical Review* 29 (September 1942): 229–37.

17. Gawalt, *Jones' Memoir*, 35.

18. Ibid., 37

19. This assessment by Jones (Gawalt, *Jones' Memoir*, 37) is supported by affidavits of four midshipmen on the *Richard*. Bradford, *Jones*, 2047–49, 2054.

20. Morison, *Jones*, 189–90, 194, 228, 234–35, believed that Landais acted with malice aforethought, clearly knowing what he was doing. Others are slightly kinder, judging his actions to have resulted from incompetence, cowardliness, or even insanity, the last judgment resting more on Landais's bizarre behavior during a transatlantic voyage in the *Alliance* in 1780. Alfred Thayer Mahan, "John Paul Jones in the Revolution," *Scribner's Magazine* 24 (1898): 212, says Landais "was not only unfit by temper and professional ability to command a ship, but [also suffered from] excessive timidity"; Charles Oscar Paullin, "A Forgotten Rival of John Paul Jones," *Army and Navy Life* 13 (1908): 68; André Lasseray, *Les Français sous les treize étoiles (1775–1783)*, 2 vols. (Macon, France, 1935), 1:255–63; Lorenz, *Jones*, 293, 301; Walsh, *Night on Fire*, 104–5; William Gilkerson, *The Ships of John Paul Jones* (Annapolis, 1987), 39, called Landais "clinically insane." For the 1780 voyage, during which his crew placed Landais under arrest and at the end of which marines had to drag him from his cabin, see Richard B. Morris, "The Revolution's Caine Mutiny," *American Heritage* 9 (April 1960): 10–13, 88–92. Only Schaeper, *Jones*, 35–54, is sympathetic to Landais, finding him "innocent of   . cowardice or treachery" (44).

21. From the diary of M. Bachaumont, 20 May 1780, quoted in Morison, *Jones*, 289.

22. John S. Barnes, *Fanning's Narrative* (New York, 1912), 53

23. Jones's activities in Holland, Dutch politics, and speculation about his motives are described in Jan Willen Schulte Nordholt, *The Dutch Republic and American Independence* (Chapel Hill, 1982), "Here Comes Paul Jones!," 70–91.

24. Morison, *Jones,* 247–49, quotes several; Seitz, *Paul Jones,* provides transcriptions of virtually everything printed about Jones in London during the war.

25. For Jones's activities, see the letters he received from Sarsfield, 27 April; from Murray de Nichson, May; from Angelique, May; from Barbantane Hunolstein, May; from Castille, 2 May; from Velye, 10 May; from Michelle de Bonneuil, 10 May; from Nassau-Siegen, 10 May; from Monplaisir, 10 May; from Madame La Présidente de D'Ormoy, 16 and 23 May; from Madame de St. Julien, 17 and 28 May; and from Girardot de Marigny, 22 May. Bradford, *Jones,* 1057–60, 1062, 1067–70, 1075, 1077–78, 1782–83, 1091. Also see M. Bachaumont, *Mémoires Secrets* (London, 1781), 15:181–82; Gawalt, *Jones' Memoir,* 47–50; *The* [London] *General Advertiser and Morning Intelligencer,* 10 May 1780; and F. de la Dixmerie [La Loge des Neuf-Soeurs], *Discours adresse par le premier orateur . . . à l'illustre F.: Paul Jones* ([Paris, 1779]).

26. Dull, *French Navy,* 150–58, 163–65.

27. S. P. Sen, *The French in India, 1763–1816* (Calcutta, 1958), 71ff; Alexander A. Lawrence, *Storm Over Savannah: The Story of Count d'Estaing and the Siege of the Town in 1779* (Athens, Ga., 1951), 113ff; Ernle Bradford, *Gibraltar: The History of a Fortress* (New York, 1971), 75–89.

28. James C. Bradford, "French and American Privateers," in David Cordingly, ed., *Pirates* (London, 1996), 169–75.

3

The Constitution's *Battles*

LINDA M. MALONEY

In the course of American history it sometimes happens that the election of a new Congress leads to a flurry of action on matters long debated. So it was in 1812. The arrival of the "Class of 1810," many of them first-term representatives from the South and West, was a significant factor in the vote of Congress to declare war on Great Britain in June 1812. It was an unpopular war, particularly in New England, and the epithet "war hawks," attached to Congressional militants by the opposition press, would be echoed in the rhetoric attending an unpopular war in the twentieth century.

These were, in fact, the final years—as some might suspect, but none could know—of the military and economic struggle between Great Britain and France that had formed the immediate or distant background of the life of everyone in the northern and, increasingly, in the southern hemisphere for six or seven generations. After the American Revolution, combat on the North American continent had ceased, but citizens of the new nation continued to be caught up in the war at sea. As neutral carriers their ships were prey to both sides, and there had even been a period of purely naval hostilities between the United States and France, in 1798–1801, over the American right to trade freely in the Caribbean.

On the whole, however, the Royal Navy was the more annoying, for British warships not only seized neutral vessels and cargoes but impressed seamen from them as well. Still, as postrevolutionary American commerce resumed its accustomed patterns the merchants of the eastern seaboard preferred to resent these minor disruptions as little as possible and to carry on with business as usual. They were particularly contemptuous of Republican measures short of war, the series of embargoes and nonintercourse acts that only did harm to American trade. For a long time it seemed that war, if declared, would be with France. One U.S. Navy captain wrote to another in 1808: "Mr. B[onaparte] appears to dictate to us in high style. Will not those communications change the minds of the people of this country very much? Shall we not have war with France, or shall we suffer them to go on with their insolence? You know the cloth has no politics, but I wish to see this country take a position and stick to it, let what will be the consequence."[1]

But the War of 1812 was fought against Great Britain, not France. The adamant and sustained opposition to the war on the part of the northeastern commercial barons—whose interests at sea it was ostensibly declared to defend—has long led historians to suspect that its real cause was the western representatives' desire to seize land in Canada and the southwest. The concentration of effort on the Great Lakes frontier and the relative feebleness of U.S. forces on the high seas seem to confirm this judgment. On the other hand, it is equally obvious that, given American geography and the state of the national resources, the Lakes frontier was the place where the best results could be anticipated for the smallest effort and investment.

As it turned out, the land war in the west was a series of disasters punctuated by minor successes (and two naval triumphs), while the war at sea yielded an immediate set of victories that sustained national morale during the first months of the conflict and preserved in the American mind a lasting impression of a victorious "second war of independence," despite the fact that the result was a restoration of the status quo *ante bellum*. Waterloo and the end to the long worldwide struggle between England and France brought stability and commercial expansion to America as well as to Europe: nevertheless, it was the exploits of the *Constitution* and other U.S. vessels that endured as the icons of American triumph.

It is now obvious that, in spite of the rhetoric about violations of American sovereignty on the high seas, war was declared against Great Britain because that nation had a flourishing commerce at sea and vulnerable territories on the North American continent. France had neither. As for the navy, the prospect of opposing the thousand ships of the Royal Navy with the American total of eighteen seagoing vessels was so ludicrous that some members of the Madison administration thought it best to moor the ships in major harbors as floating batteries rather than risk them at sea. The initial orders received by the *Constitution*'s captain from Secretary of the Navy Paul Hamilton advised him that "you are not to understand me as impelling you to battle . . . unless attacked, or with a reasonable prospect of success," and a second set warned that "[i]f . . . you should fall in with an enemy vessel, you will be guided in your proceeding by your own judgment, bearing in mind, however, that you are not voluntarily to encounter a force superior to your own."[2]

This was by no means the point of view of the naval officers themselves. Fearing the timidity of their own administration as much as the possibility of a British blockade, the commanders of the ships on active service sailed as soon as the declaration of war was in their hands. Four days after the 18 June declaration Secretary Hamilton ordered Commo. John Rodgers, commanding the concentration of U.S. warships at New York, to remain near the coast to protect American merchantmen returning from abroad. Rodgers, however, had written to Hamilton on 19 June that "should war be declared, & our vessels get to sea, in squadron, before the British are apprised of it; I think it not impossible that we may be able to cripple & reduce their force *in detail,*" and on 21 June he proceeded to act on his own advice, sailing with the frigates *President, United States,* and *Congress,* the sloop of war *Hornet,* and brig *Argus.* He narrowly missed meeting a squadron of similar makeup that had been hastily dispatched from Halifax under the command of Capt. Philip B. V. Broke, the most effective British commander on the American station throughout the war. Rodgers took his squadron eastward in pursuit of the Bermuda convoy. His only encounter with Broke's forces was a brush with the frigate *Belvidera,* which escaped unscathed; the rest of the cruise was equally frustrating.

One vessel that should have been part of Rodgers's squadron was absent. This was the *Constitution,* one of the three big, 44-gun frigates Joshua Humphreys had designed to outgun anything they could not outrun. On the date of the declaration of war she had just completed refitting and repairing her hull's copper sheathing at the Washington Navy Yard. Receiving a new crew and enough stores to take her to New York kept her in the Chesapeake for nearly a month; she cleared the capes on 12 July. Despite the raw crew Capt. Isaac Hull was optimistic. "In a few days," he assured the secretary on 2 July, "we shall have nothing to fear from any single deck Ship; indeed, unacquainted as we now are, we should I hope give a good account of any Frigate the enemy have."[3]

Isaac Hull was thirty-nine years old in the summer of 1812 and a native of Connecticut, the "land of steady habits." His had been a solid but not spectacular career. He had begun as a lieutenant in the *Constitution* in 1798, served three years in her in the Caribbean, then spent four years in the Mediterranean in the *Enterprize* and *Argus,* as lieutenant and master commandant, and was promoted to captain in 1806. He had commanded the *Constitution,* "that favorite frigate," as he called her, since 1810, having obtained her in exchange

This miniature portrait of Captain Isaac Hull was painted by an unknown artist circa 1807–12. *Courtesy of The New-York Historical Society, New York City*

for the *President* because Commodore Rodgers found the *Constitution* too slow. Indeed, after thirteen years of hard and almost constant service, the frigate was in bad condition when Hull took command. He worked for more than a year to clean her bottom and improve her sailing. Having completed a European cruise in the early spring of 1812, he had finally obtained permission to heave down the ship, scrape the bottom, and repair the copper. The *Constitution* was now in the best possible condition for sailing fast, with clean copper, an allotment of only eight weeks' provisions, and a commander who had known her "from her youth" and who had a reputation as the best ship-handler among all the navy's captains. He was also popular with his men, known for his concern for their welfare and his reluctance to flog offenders but also for insistence on a high standard of performance in sailing and gunnery. His officers were headed by the experienced and capable First Lt. Charles Morris. All in all, it was a formula for a happy and successful cruise.

That formula was put to the severest possible test within days of the *Constitution's* departure from Norfolk. She was approaching her New York rendezvous on 17 July when warships were spotted to the northward. Hull initially guessed that this was Rodgers's squadron, waiting at sea for him. Fortunately he delayed a closer approach until the next morning; by that time he knew that he had almost sailed into the arms of Broke. The ensuing three-day chase was one of the most exciting in navy annals; as one of the *Constitution's* officers observed, "nothing but superior management and unheard-of exertion preserved her."[4] It was an essential morale-builder for the ship's complement. Not only did they gain confidence in their ability to work together and succeed, but they observed the care of their captain and officers for everyone's safety: unlike the pursuing squadron, the *Constitution* did not cut loose any of her boats. No "Constitutions" were set adrift to fend for themselves or be captured by the enemy.

Cut off from New York, Hull decided to take his ship to Boston, where he anchored on 27 July. He *said* that he hoped to receive orders there from the Navy Department, but in the meantime he provisioned his ship for a long cruise and purchased charts of distant seas: the Gulf of Mexico, the Spanish Main, Demerara and Cayenne, Brazil, La Plata, and the coast of Africa.[5] He must have suspected that he was about to be ordered out of the *Constitution*— and if he did not suspect it, William Bainbridge told him. Bainbridge was commanding the Boston Navy Yard, but he was senior to Hull, he had applied for command of the *Constitution,* and he expected to get it. In fact, orders to Hull to turn over his ship to Bainbridge and return to Washington to assume command of the smaller frigate *Constellation* were sent from Washington on 28 July, and it remains one of history's small miracles that they did not reach Hull at Boston before he sailed on 2 August. Despite his many protestations to the secretary about his uneasiness in sailing without orders, and the need to get out of easily blockaded Boston before superior force arrived, it is not hard to imagine that Hull preferred to take his chances at sea rather than surrender his carefully prepared frigate to another man.

Hull's first plan was to follow Rodgers's course onto the Grand Banks and attempt to intercept British convoys outward bound from Canada. Without knowing it he was also following his old foes. An officer on board the *Shannon* dated a letter "Banks of Newfoundland" on 4 August.[6] Hull expected that sooner or later Broke would divide his squadron, and he did approximately a week thereafter, at about the time the *Constitution* was taking her first prize just south of the Grand Banks. Now detached from the squadron and shaping a course for Halifax to repair a damaged foremast was the frigate *Guerrière.*

On 15 August the *Constitution* recaptured some prizes from the British sloop of war *Avenger* off Cape Race, Newfoundland. Having learned from the officers of the prizes that the Banks were thick with British warships, Hull decided to change his cruising ground. The *Constitution* turned her head southwest. On the night of 17–18 August she ran down a privateer brig, the *Decatur* of Salem, and learned from her master that a lone British frigate had chased the *Decatur* the previous evening. Hull then directed the *Constitution* southeast in search of the enemy ship.

On the afternoon of 19 August, the *Constitution* was in latitude 41°42' north, longitude 55°48' west, running before a fresh northwest breeze, when a large vessel was discovered ahead, standing westward under easy sail. Hull had all hands called and made sail for the stranger; by 3:30 P.M. her black hull and the yellow stripe delineating her gun deck were visible, together with the thick, stubby spars that were the unmistakable mark of a British frigate. Hull edged the *Constitution*'s head southwest to prevent the quarry from escaping; an exchange of mutually unintelligible signals soon confirmed that this was an enemy.

The frigate that the *Constitution* was now approaching was HMS *Guerrière*. She was French-built and therefore large for her rate. Captured on 19 July 1806, she had sailed six years and one month in the British service. Officially rated at thirty-eight guns, she actually carried forty-nine, adding extra ordnance being common practice in the Age of Sail. For her part the *Constitution* had ten more than her nominal forty-four guns on board, and enjoyed a 25 percent superiority in weight of broadside.

The *Guerrière*'s captain, James Richard Dacres, was the son of an admiral. He had showered contempt on the U.S. Navy during the year or two previous to this encounter. After John Rodgers in the *President* had devastated the British sloop of war *Little Belt*, claiming he mistook her for a frigate, Dacres had patrolled the American coast sporting a topsail on which were boldly painted the words "Not the Little Belt." Only a few days before meeting the *Constitution*, Dacres had stopped an American merchant vessel bound from Liverpool to New York and written on her ship's register: "Captain Dacres, commander of His Britannic Majesty's frigate *Guerrière*, of 44 guns, presents his compliments to Commodore Rodgers, of the U. States frigate *President*, and will be very happy to meet him, or any other American frigate of equal force to the *President*, off Sandy Hook, for the purpose of having a few minutes tête-à-tête."[7] Dacres now summoned one of his American prisoners, Capt. William B. Orne, and asked him whether he thought the ship to the northward was American. Orne said he was certain she was, but Dacres's contemptuous opinion was that "she comes down too boldly for an American." Still, "the better he behaves, the more honor we shall gain by taking him." He told Orne that being the first to capture an American frigate would be the making of him; he would soon be an admiral, like his father.[8]

The two ships cleared for action and reduced sail. Topsails were reefed, decks sanded, supplies of shot and wads prepared for each of the great guns. Marines manned the fighting tops and mustered in the gangways: the *Guerrière's* wore bright-red coats, the *Constitution's* blue coats with red facings. The naval officers in both ships donned their blue uniform coats. Dacres allowed the ten impressed Americans in his crew to go below so they would not have to fight against their countrymen.

By 5:00 P.M. the *Constitution* had approached within long-gun range of the *Guerrière,* and the British frigate opened fire, first with a single shot, then with her entire starboard broadside. Most of the shot splashed just short. The *Guerrière* wore and fired her larboard broadside. This time most of her shot flew overhead, though two struck the *Constitution's* side. The *Constitution* responded by hoisting her fifteen-striped flag at masthead and mizzen peak to the cheers of her crew.

Dacres was trying to disable his opponent at long range, then close in and batter her from a safe angle. Hull's strategy was to close immediately with his opponent, use his superior firepower to cripple her, and then take advantage of his much larger crew by boarding. He therefore declined to return *Guerrière's* fire, except for a few shots from the bow guns. Nor did he attempt to maneuver, except to cause the *Constitution* to yaw slightly so as to receive the enemy's fire at an angle. The shot striking the American frigate at this range bounced off her heavy scantling, provoking a shout: "Her sides are made of iron!" So she became, and remains, "Old Ironsides."

After three-quarters of an hour Dacres abandoned his attempt to cripple the *Constitution* at long range and bore up before the wind. It was clear that neither ship could readily obtain the weather gage, the windward side of the battle. Having the weather gage enabled one combatant to maneuver much more freely than the other, but this fight would begin with both sides running free. After a few minutes' serious action things could change, and would.

To close the range as rapidly as possible, Hull ordered the *Constitution's* main topgallant sail set. By 6:00 P.M. the American frigate's bow began to come abreast the *Guerrière's* larboard quarter, and the British sailors commenced firing as their guns bore. The *Constitution* remained silent, reserving her fire. Captain Orne, below decks in the *Guerrière* where he could hear but not see, was worried at the American ship's failure to return fire. Would this

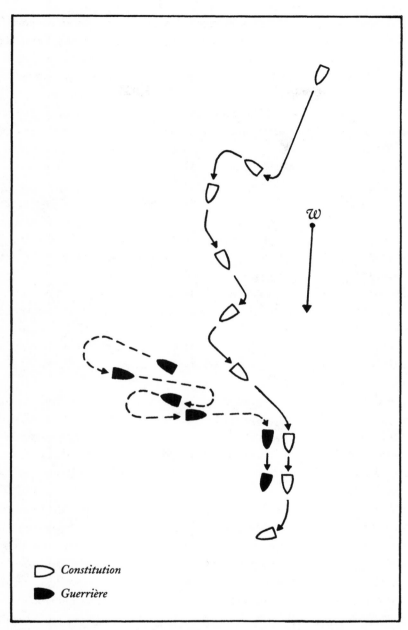

W

▷ *Constitution*

◆ *Guerrière*

Constitution vs. Guerrière, 19 August 1812. *Based on a sketch by Hull in the New-York Historical Society.*

be a repetition, he wondered, of the *Chesapeake* affair of 1807, when the American frigate had been unable to resist the attack of the *Leopard*? On the *Constitution's* deck First Lt. Morris asked Hull for permission to fire. "No, sir, not yet," said Hull. "Mr. Morris, I'll tell you when to fire. Stand ready, and see that not a shot is thrown away."

Five minutes more and the frigates were almost alongside. The *Guerrière* was firing rapidly and high, trying to disable the *Constitution's* propulsion system. Hull quickly ordered sail reduced to slow his ship: "Haul down the jib! Shiver the main topsail!" Then he shouted: "First division, fire! The next, sir! Pour in the whole broadside! Now, boys, pour it into them!"

Into this moment went the careful preparation not just of hours, but of years. The *Constitution's* starboard guns—fifteen 24-pounder long guns on the main deck, twelve 32-pounder carronades on the spar deck—were double-shotted with roundshot and grape. In one broadside they sent seven hundred pounds of iron into the *Guerrière's* side at close range—half-pistol shot. The *Constitution* fired as she rolled toward her opponent so that the shot cut close to the deck and into the hull itself. The *Guerrière* shuddered as if she had been wrenched by an earthquake, and a spray of deadly splinters leaped as high as her fighting tops. Reloading, the "Constitutions" fired again and again. Hull, standing on an arms chest for a better view of the action, cried, "By heaven, that ship is ours!"

The exchange of broadsides continued for fifteen minutes. Most of the damage to the *Constitution* was aloft. One ball cut the foremast's flag halyards, and as the American ensign swooped downward the British cheered in anticipation of surrender. Instead, seaman Daniel Hogan snatched up the bunting and carried it aloft again, knotting it firmly in place. Not long after this the course of the battle changed irrevocably as the *Guerrière's* mizzenmast, battered again and again by the *Constitution's* broadsides, gave way a few feet above the deck. With its entire weight of rigging and sails it swept down over the British frigate's starboard quarter. Another cheer arose from the "Constitutions," and Hull shouted, "Huzza, my boys! We've made a brig of her!" Someone added, "Give her another, and we'll make her a sloop!"

At this point reports of the action become less easy to follow, no doubt because the people involved were too busy to keep a careful account of what happened. However, all the American eyewitnesses agree in general terms with the sequence of events given by Isaac Hull in his official letters and depicted some years later in a diagram he had prepared and a series of four paintings done by Michel Corné under his direction.[9] The crippled *Guerrière* slowed and fell off to starboard. The *Constitution* shot ahead, and Hull ordered

The *Constitution* and the *Guerrière,* 19 August 1812. "In action," the second in a series of four views of the engagement painted for Hull by Michel F. Corné, shows the *Guerrière's* mizzenmast going by the board. *U.S. Naval Academy Museum*

the helm to port to bring his ship around on the *Guerrière's* bow. From that position he could rake his opponent and control the course of the battle.

The *Constitution* did rake the *Guerrière* twice, with deadly effect. But the loss of so much of the American frigate's rigging meant that her maneuvers could not be tightly controlled. Her turn to starboard continued until she shot up into the wind and was caught aback. As she lay dead in the water, the *Guerrière's* continued forward progress threatened to bring her across the *Constitution's* stern, in position to rake. There was a frantic struggle to bring the *Constitution* under control again. As she began to swing back to port, the oncoming *Guerrière* slammed into her stern. The British frigate's jibboom and bowsprit swept across the American quarterdeck, snapping the spanker boom and gaff and becoming tightly entangled in the rigging. The *Guerrière* fell into the *Constitution's* wake, with her bowsprit extending over the *Constitution's* larboard quarter and resting on the boat davit.

Trumpets blared in both ships, calling for boarders. Most of the mortal wounds on both sides were suffered during the few minutes that the ships were entangled, as the sharpshooters and marines aloft swept the enemy decks with deadly effect. On board the *Constitution,* First Lt. Charles Morris was shot through the abdomen as he stood on the taffrail, trying to lash the ships together. Lt. William Bush of the marines leaped to the rail crying, "Shall I board her?" and was shot through the head. Isaac Hull moved forward to lead the boarding party himself. According to legend a seaman begged him to take off the uniform coat that made him such a tempting target: the split in the portly captain's white breeches he could ignore, but not "them swabs"— the epaulets that marked a captain!

The attempt at boarding failed. With both ships rearing and plunging wildly in the heavy seas there was little hope of getting a large party of men across such a narrow bridge as the *Guerrière's* bowsprit. Only if the ships could be secured yardarm to yardarm could the "Constitutions" hope to board. Accordingly Hull made sail to pull away from the enemy frigate. The time was 6:30 P.M. As the ships parted, the *Guerrière's* bowsprit, freed from the tangle, snapped upward, releasing the tension on the foremast rigging. The foremast, wounded by a double-headed shot, wavered and fell, dragging the mainmast and the jib boom after it.[10] The *Guerrière* was left without a single spar aloft, an unmanageable hulk.

The *Constitution* stood off for half an hour to repair her rigging and tend her wounded, and to put out a fire in her cabin kindled by flaming wads from the *Guerrière's* bow guns while the ships were locked together. During this time the "Guerrières" attempted to set a spritsail on the bowsprit to give their frigate enough propulsion to keep her from falling into the trough of the sea. But no sooner had the sail been set than it carried away, and as the *Constitution,* scarcely the worse for wear, stood down in the twilight to cross her bow, the *Guerrière* signaled her surrender by firing a gun to leeward. She had no ensigns left to strike; the battle flag that Hull preserved was a jack found stuffed under the heel of her bowsprit.

Hull sent his boat, commanded by Third Lt. George C. Read, to ask whether the *Guerrière* surrendered. It was full dark by the time the boat returned twenty minutes later, bearing Captain Dacres. The two captains went through the ceremony of surrender, with Hull refusing his opponent's sword and inviting him to rest in the *Constitution's* mangled cabin.[11] The "Constitutions" worked all night, ferrying men from the *Guerrière* to the *Constitution,* while below decks the two ships' surgeons splinted and bandaged, amputated and cauterized. Those killed in the *Guerrière* numbered fifteen, including Second Lt. Henry Ready; among the sixty-two wounded were Captain Dacres and First Lt. Bartholomew Kent, both slashed by splinters. Another two dozen of the *Guerrière*'s complement of 302 were simply missing; they had probably been aloft when her masts went by the board. In the *Constitution* the surgeons counted seven dead and seven wounded. Among those dangerously hurt, beside Lieutenant Morris, was a seaman named Richard Dunn, whose leg had to be amputated. Captain Hull took a continuing interest in Dunn. He took up a collection for him and invested the funds; moreover, he managed to find a navy yard job for him at each of his shore stations for decades afterward until Dunn finally received his pension and retired.

By dawn the *Constitution* was so "shipshape" that she could have faced another enemy, if need be. It was far different with the *Guerrière*. Lieutenant Read reported that the *Constitution*'s broadsides had pierced her hull all along her larboard side and torn six feet of planking near the waterline completely away. The American prize crew had pumped all night, but the British prisoners remaining on board had refused to help, preferring to rifle the ship's liquor supply. Much as Hull would have liked to bring his prize into port, to attempt it would be to hazard his own ship as well as the men he sent into the prize. He decided to destroy the *Guerrière*. Read and his crew laid the powder train. As their boat pulled away from the wreck at 3:00 P.M. on 20 August the *Guerrière* was already wrapped in flames. At 3:15 P.M. the explosion of her magazine blew the British frigate in two. Her quarterdeck rose and shattered in the air, and the ruins of her hull soon disappeared into the sea.

Hull could have continued his cruise, but his ship now contained nearly three hundred prisoners. Moreover, he was aware of the sensation his news would create. It was important that the American people should know what their navy had done and could do. Ten days later he was in Boston. By chance, Rodgers's squadron arrived while the *Constitution* was still at Boston Light. After an early morning panic in which the *Constitution* cut her anchor cables and fled for the inner harbor, thinking that Broke had come in pursuit of her, the victorious frigate led the entire squadron in procession up to Long Wharf, the *Guerrière*'s jack flying below the American flag.

Boston went wild (or as wild as the stronghold of Federalism could go under the circumstances), and as the news swept southward and westward the whole country was agog. The ironic coincidence of the news of Isaac Hull's victory and of his uncle William Hull's surrender of Detroit could not be overlooked. One wag observed that "we have a Hull up and a Hull down." For Isaac Hull the day was more bitter than sweet because letters waiting for him at Boston informed him that his favorite brother William had died at New York two weeks earlier. William had been in charge of the financial and business affairs of the entire family. It seems to have been this loss, rather than any sentiment of magnanimity toward a brother officer, that led Hull to hand over the *Constitution* to William Bainbridge. Certainly no one would have dreamed of imposing on him the previous orders to that effect! Hull was, in every sense, the man of the hour.

The transfer of command on 15 September was not effected without some hard feelings because the "Constitutions" were loath to exchange their beloved captain for Bainbridge, a well-known martinet. The ship's surgeon, Dr. Amos Evans, noted in his journal that "[t]he scene altogether was affecting. This whole crew had a great affection for [Isaac Hull]. They urged him to remain: said they would go out with him and take the *Africa* [a 64-gun ship], and finally requested to be transferred on board any other vessel." Bainbridge, nettled, demanded to know whether there were men in the crew who had sailed with him before and were unwilling to go again, and indeed there were several with long memories, some going back to the war with Tripoli. The scene was tersely recorded in the log: "At 4:00 P.M. Commodore William Bainbridge superseded Captain Isaac Hull in the command of this ship . . . at which the crew expressed their dissatisfaction."

The *Constitution* again sailed from Boston in October, accompanied by the sloop of war *Hornet* and intending to rendezvous with a third member of Bainbridge's squadron, the small frigate *Essex,* off the coast of Brazil. That rendezvous was never kept because both the *Constitution* and the *Hornet,* operating separately, took British warships and returned to the United States to refit and spread the news. The *Essex,* under David Porter, proceeded to cruise alone, eventually entering the Pacific Ocean and wreaking havoc among the British whaling fleet before her eventual capture.

The *Constitution*'s encounter was with His Majesty's frigate *Java,* another large, French-built vessel. They met a little south of São Salvador (Bahia) on 29 December 1812. This time the action began about 2:00 P.M., and the actual fighting lasted almost two hours. The *Java* retained the weather gage, and her captain, Henry Lambert, was able to keep the *Constitution* at a distance of half a mile or more for at least thirty minutes while the ships exchanged broadsides. Early in the action the *Constitution*'s wheel was shot away, and from then on she had to be steered by a system of ropes attached to the rudder, according to orders relayed down the companionway from the quarterdeck. In spite of this Bainbridge managed to close with the *Java* at about 2:50 P.M. Once again the British frigate's bowsprit became entangled in the American's mizzen rigging. The *Java* soon lost her jib boom and part of her bowsprit, quickly followed, as in the case of the *Guerrière,* by her foremast. The *Constitution* then proceeded systematically to mow down the *Java*'s remaining masts.

At about 4:00 P.M. the *Java*'s fire slackened, and *Constitution* drew away to repair her rigging. While this was going on the remnant of the *Java*'s mainmast went overboard, and at 5:25 P.M., when the *Constitution* returned to the fray, the *Java* struck her colors.

This longer and more stubborn engagement brought with it more casualties: the *Constitution* lost nine killed and twenty-six wounded, the latter including Bainbridge and Lt. John Aylwin, the *Constitution*'s former sailing master who had been wounded in the action with the *Guerrière* and promoted to lieutenant for his gallantry. This time he died of his wound. The *Java*'s loss was fifty-seven killed and eighty-three wounded. Among the latter was Captain Lambert, who died on 3 January. The British ship, crowded with troops en route to the East Indies, was able to station extra men at her guns, but the *Constitution*'s shot did all the more execution on her teeming decks.

Again the *Constitution*'s prize was too badly mauled to be brought into an American port.[12] She was therefore blown up on 1 January 1813. Surgeon Evans, the chronicler of these pyrotechnics, noted that "The explosion was not so grand as that of the *Guerrière*."[13] The *Constitution* returned to Boston on 15 February.

The "favorite frigate" underwent a long overhaul at the Charlestown Navy Yard. Not until July 1813 did she receive her new commander, Charles Stewart, who had been chafing under blockade in the *Constellation* at Norfolk (which would have been Hull's fate if he had not sailed from Boston in the nick of time). He could now continue his chafing in Boston because the *Constitution*, although ready for sea, was short of men due to the demands of the Lakes squadrons. Then, in the fall of 1813, when operations slowed on the Lakes, the British began an intermittent blockade of Boston harbor. Stewart finally got to sea on the last day of the year. His cruise took him to the Caribbean and back, but by the time he returned to Boston in April he had encountered no warships of any size.

The *Constitution* remained blockaded in Boston again until winter drove the enemy off the coast. She sailed on her last war cruise in December 1814. Captain Stewart had good reason to believe that the war was over by early February 1815, when he spoke a merchant vessel with news of the Treaty of Ghent (24 December 1814), yet notification was not official, and he chose to continue cruising. On 20 February the *Constitution* fought her last battle. It was a night action off Madeira in which she outmaneuvered and captured two lesser British warships, the small frigate *Cyane* (twenty-four guns) and corvette *Levant* (eighteen guns). Stewart's handling of his ship was exemplary, but the overall advantage was his. He had the weather gage and he had long guns, while both his opponents were equipped almost exclusively with short-range carronades. As the loss of the frigate *Essex* had shown, a ship carrying only carronades was extremely vulnerable unless able to control the action and force fighting at close quarters—and that was rarely the case. The days of close fighting were nearly at an end; within the lifetime of this generation of officers the development of iron vessels and rifled guns ensured it.

Both the *Constitution* and *Cyane* got safely home; the *Levant* was recaptured. Although the Treaty of Ghent had been ratified on 17 February a thirty-day clause allowed the retention of prizes taken until mid-March, so the *Cyane* became the second of the war's "trophy ships" to join the U.S. Navy (the first being the frigate *Macedonian,* captured by Stephen Decatur in the *United States* in 1812).

This last victory of the *Constitution* came too late to give much more than a fillip to the war, which everyone was glad to see end. It was the early battles that were remembered and celebrated, particularly the first. It is because of that triumph that the *Constitution* herself has survived every effort at decommissioning, from the occasion of Oliver Wendell Holmes's "Old Ironsides" in the 1830s to the hard times of the early twentieth century. As her second century draws to a close, she is still in commission and underwent a refit to make her sparkle for the 1997 bicentennial of her launch, marked by her first sailing, under her own power, in more than a century. On a more mundane level, contradancers still step lively to the strains of "Hull's Victory," composed in 1812.

What did it all mean? On a world scale, scarcely anything; in the minds of Americans, almost everything. They were quick to note the unseemly haste with which the British admiralty and government produced excuses for the loss of the *Guerrière,* the *Macedonian,* the *Java.* It did not matter that in these engagements the American frigate had, on the average, enjoyed an advantage of approximately 25 percent in the weight of her broadside; British ships were accustomed to triumphing over heavier odds. An American paper gleefully reprinted the London *Times*'s lament:

We have been accused of sentiments unworthy of Englishmen, because we described what we saw and felt on the occasion of the capture of the *Guerrière* . . . it is the first time we have ever heard that the striking of the English flag on the high seas to anything like an equal force, should be regarded by Englishmen with complacency or satisfaction. . . . It is not merely that an English frigate has been taken, after what we are free to confess may be called a brave resistance; but that it has been taken by a new enemy, an enemy unaccustomed to such triumphs, and likely to be rendered insolent and confident by them. He must be a weak politician, who does not see how important the first triumph is in giving a tone and character to the war. Never before in the history of the world did an English frigate strike to an American. . . .[14]

Even though the writer blithely ignored the successes of John Paul Jones and other American revolutionary commanders, he was certainly accurate in emphasizing both the novelty of the event and the depth of the impression it left on people's minds. One frigate more or less was nothing in the British scheme of things, and yet the impact of first one such loss and then another and then still another—to an upstart navy that might well become "insolent and confident" to the point of conceiving itself the arm of a future world power—that was not to be taken lightly. Two results were immediately apparent: first, by the end of 1812 British warships were under orders not to meet the Americans in individual combat. The timorous advice issued to the American frigate commanders in June was now being imposed on the mighty "lords of the ocean." That, more than the coastal blockade, accounts for the decline in frigate actions after 1812. The *guerre de course* was continued mainly by the privateers and smaller warships, with a considerable, though diminishing effect.

The second obvious result was that the single combat that did occur in 1813, in which Philip B. V. Broke in the *Shannon* captured the American frigate *Chesapeake,* became a cause for national rejoicing in England comparable to the American delight in the *Constitution's* battles. From the amount of effort devoted to describing and celebrating that action one would think that it comprised a victory of the magnitude of Trafalgar not the capture of a single ship. On both sides it was *meaning* that was at issue—not so much the outcome of the war, for the British a remote annoyance during the final and crucial stages of the real struggle in Europe, but perceptions of the future.

In the long run it was a war about pride more than possessions. Certainly the Americans would have liked to possess themselves of Canada, but it became apparent fairly soon that they could not. At the same time when those ambitions were crumbling, however, a new set was appearing: the aspiration for a kind of stature in the eyes of the Europeans that would make them wary of interfering with America's future plans, wherever those might lead.

It is in this sense that the War of 1812 constituted a "second war of independence" for the United States. Particularly in the actions at sea it severed the last ties of dependence or deference that bound Americans to the old home. In summarizing his action with the *Guerrière*, Isaac Hull had written to the Navy Department that "from the smallest boy in the ship to the oldest seaman not a look of fear was seen."[15] Americans had shown themselves in that battle, and in the others, to be smart, stout, and unafraid. Nothing could stand in their way.

NOTES

1. Isaac Hull to William Bainbridge, 11 April 1808, New-York Historical Society (hereafter NYHS)

2. Hamilton to Hull, 18 June, 3 July 1812, Record Group 45 (hereafter RG 45), Area 7 File, National Archives (hereafter NA)

3. Hull to Hamilton, 2 July 1812, RG 45, Captains' Letters 1812, NA.

4 Thomas Chew to Thomas Turner, 26 July 1812, Letters Received by the Accountant of the Navy, RG 217, NA.

5. Bill for Charts furnished frigate *Constitution*, 29 July 1812, Fourth Auditor Accounts, Alphabetical Series: Bemis & Eddy to Amos Binney, RG 217, NA

6 *The War* (New York) 1:79, 24 October 1812.

7. *The War* (New York) 1:51, 12 September 1812. See also George Coggeshall, *History of the American Privateers, and Letters-of-Marque, During our War with England in the Years 1812, '13 and '14* (New York, 1856), 20 The merchant captain presented the register to Isaac Hull after the battle, and he kept it among his prized souvenirs.

8. Coggeshall, *American Privateers,* 26

9 Readers of Cdr. Tyrone G Martin's lively book, *A Most Fortunate Ship: A Narrative History of "Old Ironsides"* (Chester, Conn., 1980; rev. ed., Annapolis, 1997), will find a rather different version. Commander Martin's account rests on his own reasoning about the behavior of the ships, as well as Captain Dacres's letter describing the battle Dacres reversed the position of the ships, placing the *Constitution* on the *Guerrère*'s starboard side. This simplifies the ships' movements, but the complete agreement of the American accounts, as well as the wide publicity given to the paintings and the engravings made from them, leave little doubt in my mind that the action was substantially as Hull, Charles Morris, and other Americans described it. My sources include Hull's official letters (Hull to Hamilton, 28 and 30 August, 1 September 1812, RG 45, Captains' Letters 1812, NA); the *Constitution*'s log (RG 24, NA); Charles Morris, *The Autobiography of Commodore Charles Morris, U.S. Navy* (Annapolis, 1880); a letter of Lt John Contee, USMC, to Col. Franklin Wharton, USMC, 31 August 1812 (RG 45, Area 9 file, NA); a letter from Capt William B. Orne to Phineas Sprague (G H. Stuart Collection, Library of Congress), and Dacres's court-martial (Public Record Office, Admiralty 1/502). For more detail and additional sources, see Linda M. Maloney, *The Captain from Connecticut: The Life and Naval Times of Isaac Hull* (Boston, 1986), especially 183–95 and 498–503

10. The *Guerrère*'s captain and surviving officers attributed their defeat to the "accident" of losing the ship's masts, and the court-martial solemnly concurred: the loss of the frigate was attributable to "the accident of her masts going, which was occasioned more by their defective state than from the fire of the enemy, though so greatly superior in guns and men."

11 The legend that the two captains had a wager of a hat on the outcome is only that; it seems impossible that these men could have met before the war, and at any rate Hull was adamantly opposed to dueling in any form

12. Both Hull and Bainbridge had cause to complain afterward that Capt. Stephen Decatur was voted four times as much prize money for the capture of the *Macedonian* as they received for their feats "because he was not so *unfortunate* as to shoot away her masts and got her safe in " Isaac Hull to David Daggett, Senator from Connecticut, 24 November 1814, NYHS.

13. Amos A Evans, *Journal Kept on Board the United States Frigate Constitution, 1812* (n.p., 1928), quoted in Martin, *A Most Fortunate Ship,* 1st ed., 137

14. *The War* (New York) 1:114, 28 December 1812.

15 Hull to Paul Hamilton, 30 August 1812, RG 45, Captains' Letters 1812, NA.

4

The Battle of Lake Erie

DAVID CURTIS SKAGGS

The War Hawks—belligerent young congressmen from the South and the West who voted to declare war on Britain in June 1812—imagined that they were launching the conquest of Canada. The completion of this undertaking would not only extinguish British power in North America, a most attractive prospect in itself, but also isolate the Indian tribes which that power was rightly suspected of supporting as a buffer against American expansion. With fewer than six thousand British regulars garrisoning Canada, the campaign was expected to be, as Thomas Jefferson once forecast, "a mere matter of marching."

Such prognostications proved unfounded. Superannuated commanders, an enterprising enemy, and an inability to transform troops on paper into troops in the field combined to cause the three American invasions of Canada in 1812 to end ingloriously. The embarrassments began in the northwest. In July, Brig. Gen. William Hull, governor of the Michigan Territory, led an army of twenty-five hundred men across the Detroit River into Ontario. Upon learning that the British had captured the little fort on Mackinac Island, near the confluence of lakes Huron and Michigan, he fell back to Detroit, and there on 16 August Hull surrendered to a British and Indian force that he outnumbered almost two to one.

Hull's surrender was the wake-up call for the United States. The administration of President James Madison responded by resolving to win command of the Great Lakes and recapture Detroit. The army's effort failed with Brig. Gen. James Winchester's defeat at the River Raisin (in modern Monroe, Michigan) in January 1813, but naval operations on the Great Lakes began with considerable vigor.

To command on the lakes, Secretary of the Navy Paul Hamilton selected

Capt. Isaac Chauncey. The secretary placed special emphasis on asserting control of Lake Erie, going so far as to instruct Chauncey to assign approximately a third of his personnel to the squadron to be built there.

Several factors figured in the administration's thinking. In the first place, command of Lake Erie would facilitate the attempt to retake Detroit by a ground force being organized in the Ohio Valley. Second, it would shield the American settlements south of the lake from enemy incursions. Third, a quick victory in the Detroit–Lake Erie theater would permit the majority of the naval and military forces engaged there to be redeployed to take part in operations on and around Lake Ontario.

The strategic consequences of these decisions were far reaching. Secretary Hamilton's orders diverted attention from what should have been the primary focus on the St. Lawrence River Valley. It is possible that, had Chauncey shown the enterprise expected of him, the emphasis on Lake Erie would have proven productive; Detroit could have been retaken and the troops released for duty to the east before the British had time to react. Granted the advantages of good leadership, dependable troops, and interservice cooperation, the American strategy might have succeeded; but none of these prerequisites was present. Even so, the British operated on an extremely narrow margin for error.

Chauncey faced two major questions relative to Lake Erie: where should the squadron be constructed, and who should command it? The debate over the former was between Black Rock on the upper Niagara River, which had shipbuilding facilities but was vulnerable to attack from the British across the river, and Presque Isle Bay at Erie, Pennsylvania. The latter was less liable to attack but more difficult to support, and the sandbar at the harbor's mouth constituted an obstacle to large vessels seeking to exit the bay. Chauncey and his investigating subordinate, Lt. Jesse Duncan Elliott, urged construction at Black Rock, largely because it possessed more extensive facilities, it would be easier to support from Lake Ontario, and the British presence on the opposite bank was expected to be eliminated by U.S. land forces. They found their position undercut by a Great Lakes commercial ship captain named Daniel Dobbins, who made a direct appeal to Secretary Hamilton for Presque Isle Bay. Since the original plan was to construct only gunboats at Erie, the bar posed little problem. Subsequently, however, the army's failure to secure the opposite shore of the Niagara made Black Rock unsuitable as a building site for brigs, and their construction was shifted to Erie. Crossing the bar remained problematical, but Dobbins promised it could be done. Accordingly,

Commo. Oliver Hazard Perry, by an unknown artist. *U.S. Naval Academy Museum*

Chauncey contracted with Noah Brown, a New York City shipbuilder, to construct two 20-gun brigs there.

The quest for a commander ended in early 1813 when William Jones, the new secretary of the navy, selected twenty-seven-year-old Master Commandant Oliver Hazard Perry. Perry had entered the navy in April 1799. As a midshipman and acting lieutenant he took part in the Quasi-War with France and the War with Tripoli, but, much to his chagrin, had no opportunity to enter combat in either. In 1807 he was advanced to permanent lieutenant and assigned to build and command a gunboat flotilla based on his hometown of

Newport, Rhode Island. Two years later he assumed command of the 12-gun schooner *Revenge* which was lost as a result of pilot error in early 1811. A court of inquiry absolved Perry of blame, and he was ordered back to Newport to supervise the construction of still more gunboats. Promoted to his present rank in September 1812, Perry actively pursued the chance for combat. Service on the high seas was preferable to any other, but when lake service appeared the only alternative to gunboat duty at Newport, he eagerly sought the assignment.

Perry possessed great command presence. An expert seaman, his mastery of shiphandling was so impressive that subordinates often took him as a model. Perry was noted for his "calm collectedness & decisive Character." He nevertheless had an impetuous streak that sometimes affected his judgment. Both officers and men were attracted by his character and competence, but he "repelled the slightest approach at undue familiarity" and was "exacting of every etiquette from an equal or inferior in service." His ship's surgeon wrote: "Captains in those days kept their men at an awful distance, and none more so than Perry." Acquaintances found him a very private person with a dislike of display and "a severe conscience that set duty as the first law before him." A voracious reader, he had improved his education by diligent self-study of literature, mathematics, and composition.[1]

In view of his experience building gunboats at Newport, Perry seemed an excellent choice to superintend the construction under way at Presque Isle and Black Rock. Chauncey expected to win control of Lake Ontario that spring; Perry's task would be to build a squadron Chauncey would command. These expectations would be thwarted by the British reaction to Chauncey's activities of the previous autumn.[2]

Just before his death at the Battle of Queenston Heights (downriver from Niagara Falls) on 13 October 1812, Gen. Sir Isaac Brock cautioned his superior, Governor-General Sir George Prevost, that the Americans were "making every exertion to gain a naval Superiority on both lakes which if they accomplish I do not see how we can retain the country."[3] There was little the British could do that fall but await the arrival of Royal Navy officers and men the next spring. The capture of Mackinac Island and Detroit in 1812 provided them with a number of vessels they could use on the upper lakes: the U.S. Army supply vessel *Adams* was promptly renamed the *Detroit* in honor of Brock's victory, and the North West Company's brig *Caledonia* joined the Provincial Marine force on Lake Erie consisting of the *General Hunter*, *Lady Prevost*, and *Queen Charlotte*.

In October 1812, Lieutenant Elliott captured the *Caledonia* and burned the *Detroit* while they were at anchor in the Niagara River. Thus, by the time Perry arrived on the lake, the anchorage at Black Rock contained the *Caledonia* and four other former merchant vessels now in naval service—the sloops *Trippe* and *Somers* and the schooners *Ohio* and *Amelia*. British control of Fort Erie penned these ships in the Niagara River.

In late spring 1813, Capt. Sir James Lucas Yeo arrived at Kingston to command the Royal Navy and Provincial Marine forces on the Great Lakes. Yeo ordered Lt. Robert Heriot Barclay, a one-armed veteran of the Battle of Trafalgar, to assume command of the upper lakes. Barclay immediately found himself threatened by a growing American presence on Lake Erie and frustrated by the difficulties encountered in building a vessel to counter it.

Temporarily promoted to the rank of commander, Barclay's initial objective was to prevent Perry from uniting the Black Rock vessels with those being built at Presque Isle Bay. After American ground action forced the British to evacuate Fort Erie, Barclay sought to intercept Perry's flotilla during its trip from the Niagara River to Presque Isle. The effort failed when the U.S. ships slipped past him in a fog. Now Perry had both squadrons together at Erie. That fog is generally considered to be the first instance of "Perry's luck," which assisted him throughout the campaign.

Meanwhile, at the British base at Amherstburg, shipbuilder William Bell directed the construction of a vessel to be named HMS *Detroit* (not to be confused with the *Detroit, née Adams,* sunk by Elliott the previous October). The largest ship on the upper lakes, the *Detroit* was designed to carry sixteen 24-pounder carronades and four long 12-pounders. She never received her projected ordnance—the American raid on York (modern Toronto) on 27 April 1813 having resulted in the destruction or capture of the cannon, cordage, canvas, tools, and stores intended for the Amherstburg shipyard. Barclay soon realized that the loss of this equipment, coupled with the interruption of the supply line along the Niagara River (which made the transportation of large cargo impossible) meant that he and Bell were going to have to build and equip the *Detroit* with what was available at Amherstburg and Fort Malden. Bell was short of more than supplies; he also needed shipwrights and other skilled craftsmen. Although he laid the *Detroit*'s keel in January, by the time Barclay arrived in June she was still incomplete. In fact, she would not be ready until late August.

During these same months, Perry and Noah Brown continued construction of the ships under way at Erie. Benefiting from a superior supply line and numerous unemployed craftsmen from coastal ports, Brown quickly completed the vessels—two identical brigs, the *Lawrence* and *Niagara,* and the schooners *Ariel, Tigress, Scorpion,* and *Porcupine* (see Table 4.1).

Barclay's aim now was either to destroy Perry's squadron in Presque Isle Bay or bottle it up there. He could not accomplish the first objective because the British army commanders on the Niagara and the Detroit frontiers would not spare soldiers for an amphibious attack on Erie. He failed in the second because he briefly lifted his blockade of Erie to return to the Canadian shore for rest and resupply. In the interval, Perry, with some ingenious support from Noah Brown, raised his brigs enough to lift them over the sandbar at the bay's mouth. "Perry's luck" held for a second time, and the crossing was accomplished before Barclay returned on 4 August. Unaware that the two brigs he saw were not fully manned, loaded, or rearmed, he withdrew to Amherstburg to await the completion of the *Detroit.*

By breaking out of Presque Isle Bay, Perry overturned the strategic balance on Lake Erie. The Americans now held the naval advantage on the upper lakes. Yet Barclay had to contend with more than just the tactical inferiority that Yeo faced on Lake Ontario. Virtually all the supplies that reached the British at Amherstburg came up the lake. Perry's presence on its waters threatened their logistical lifeline. To make matters worse, several thousand of Britain's Indian allies had assembled at Amherstburg. These unruly warriors, Barclay reported, were "prone to quarrel and turn their Arms against their friends as well as foes if their wants were not Supplied and liberally too." Their demands, coupled with the needs of the British naval and military personnel and Canadian settlers, made it imperative for Barclay to keep the lake open to British shipping.[4]

Perry had his own problems. Desperately short of seamen to work his ves-

TABLE 4.1   Vessels Built on Lake Erie, 1813

Name	Type	Tonnage	Launched
AMERICAN			
Lawrence	Brig	480	25 June
Niagara	Brig	40	4 July
Ariel	Schooner	112	April
Tigress	Schooner	96	April
Scorpion	Schooner	86	April
Porcupine	Schooner	83	April
BRITISH			
Detroit	Ship	490	July

sels, he also lacked senior officers to captain them. Especially needed was an experienced officer to command his second brig, the *Niagara*. For weeks, no one of any rank reached him from Lake Ontario. Then on Sunday, 8 August, Perry learned that Jesse D. Elliott was on the way with another lieutenant, eight midshipmen, and eighty-nine men.

Perry was delighted. Elliott had demonstrated his intrepidity as commander of the raid on the Niagara River in October, and in April he had served as Commodore Chauncey's flag captain during the capture of York. Soon to receive early promotion to the rank of master commandant, he appeared to be just the man to captain the *Niagara*.

Perry's mood changed when Elliott arrived at Presque Isle bearing what Perry found to be an infuriating letter from Commodore Chauncey. Chauncey charged Perry with seeking to establish a *"separate command"* because of the delays in communication between Sackett's Harbor and Erie. Perry was also admonished for writing directly to Secretary of the Navy Jones about his manpower problems without regard for the chain of command. Chauncey's choler was not assuaged by the knowledge that Jones had authorized Perry to bypass him.[5]

Highly insulted, Perry wrote Secretary Jones offering to resign his command. He failed to perceive that Chauncey's letter conceded that Perry would command the squadron on Lake Erie, since, contrary to Chauncey's expectations, he would be unable to leave Lake Ontario. The secretary refused to accept Perry's resignation, informing him that the government regarded a change of command on Lake Erie as "inadmissible."[6] Under a direct order from the senior official in the Navy Department, Perry sailed on toward destiny.

In the days that followed, Perry made the final allocation of officers to his ships. Newly promoted Master Commandant Elliott was assigned command of the *Niagara*; Perry himself took that of the *Lawrence* (see Table 4.2 for the full list of principal officers). The Lake Erie officers were not a Nelsonian "band of brothers." Only two, Thomas Almy and Stephen Champlin, belonged to the group Perry had brought from Newport; Daniel Turner had served with the Lake Erie squadron since the spring; all the others arrived with Elliott just a month before the battle. They were woefully inexperienced. None had taken part in a fleet action. Only Perry and Elliott had commanded vessels; only Elliott had participated in squadron maneuvers and that on a rather limited scale; and only John Packet had ever been in ship-to-ship combat, having served as a midshipman on board the *Constitution* in her vic-

571 - 594 - 8302

tory over HMS *Java*. All were quite young; Elliott was thirty, Perry twenty-eight, and the remainder in their early twenties.

Such seasoned combat veterans as Barclay, Robert Finnis, George Bignell, and Edward Buchan gave the British squadron a distinct advantage in experienced officers to captain its major vessels. On the other hand, the American enlisted force included a much higher proportion of regular naval personnel.

Gen. William Henry Harrison agreed to call for volunteers from the Army of the North West to flesh out Perry's crews. About 130 men responded to his appeal. These joined the sixty-five militiamen serving as sailors and others as marines. Harrison's readiness to help Perry overcome his manpower shortage shows that the Lake Erie campaign was truly a joint operation. That summer the North West Army and the Virginia, Pennsylvania, and Kentucky militias provided more men to Perry's command than did the Lake Ontario squadron of the U.S. Navy.[7]

Perry's next need was for a good anchorage from which he could either engage the British squadron or escort the army across the lake. He followed Harrison's recommendation to use Put-in-Bay on South Bass Island. When it appeared that Barclay would not engage in open combat on the lake, Perry and Harrison agreed to carry out a long-contemplated amphibious assault on the Canadian shore regardless of the risk that Barclay might attack them in the midst of the movement. They intended to launch the operation about 15 September, and Harrison began moving his troops forward to the mouth of the Portage River on the mainland near Perry's anchorage at Put-in-Bay.

Advantageous as it was from a strategic standpoint, Put-in-Bay proved distinctly unhealthy. Shortly after the squadron's arrival, its personnel fell prey to a remittent fever that attacked twenty to thirty men daily, downing a total of more than two hundred. The illness usually persisted little more than twenty-four hours, but on occasion it progressed into a kind of typhus. At least one man succumbed to it before the battle began, and between 78 and 116 others, including the brigs' surgeons, were unfit for duty the day it was fought. Perry was seriously affected and spent most of a week in his berth aboard the *Lawrence*.

Whatever the intentions of Harrison and Perry, they went for naught when on 9 September the British squadron dropped down the Detroit River into Lake Erie. What prompted Barclay, out-gunned and ill-prepared, to hazard everything on the gage of battle? The logistical crisis at Amherstburg left him no choice. Possessing a fleet-in-being could not remedy the supply problems facing the British and their Indian allies along the Detroit River. He simply had to try to regain control of the lake.

TABLE 4.2 Lake Erie Senior Officers, 10 September 1813

Name	Type of Vessel	Commander	Subordinates
AMERICAN			
Lawrence	Brig	O. H. Perry	John Yarnall
			Dulany Forrest
			John Brooks, USMC
Niagara	Brig	J. D. Elliott	Joseph E. Smith
			John Edwards
			Henry Brevoort, USA
Caledonia[b]	Brig	Daniel Turner	
Ariel	Schooner	John Packet	
Scorpion	Schooner	Stephen Champlin	
Tigress	Schooner	Augustus H. M. Conkling	
Porcupine	Schooner	George Senat	
Trippe[c]	Sloop	Thomas Holdup	
Somers[c]	Sloop	Thomas Almy	
BRITISH			
Detroit	Ship	R. H. Barclay	John Garland
			George Inglis
			Francis Purvis
Queen Charlotte	Ship	Robert Finnis	Thomas Stoke
			Robert Irvine
General Hunter	Brig	George Bignell	
Lady Prevost	Schooner	Edward Buchan	
Chippawa[a]	Schooner	John Campbell	
Little Belt[a]	Sloop	John F. Breman	

[a] Captured American commercial vessel
[b] Captured British commercial vessel
[c] American commercial vessel

The British squadron carried 64 guns throwing 905 pounds' total weight of metal and 496 pounds in broadside. Barclay had 562 crewmen compared to Perry's 582 (including those on sick call). The U.S. squadron mounted 54 guns with a total weight of metal of 1,536 pounds and a broadside of 936. Barclay brought six vessels into his line of battle, Perry nine. Neither the British advantage in number of guns nor the American advantage in number of ships was decisive. What really mattered was the type and size of their guns. Barclay's squadron was armed principally with long guns, which, depending on their caliber, had an effective range of approximately a mile. Perry's two largest vessels carried shorter-barreled carronades with a range about a third of that of long guns.

The relative merits of carronades versus long guns was a matter of controversy. By mounting solely carronades a ship could triple the weight of her broadside without adding to the weight of her armament. In action against an enemy armed with long guns, however, such a vessel might be disabled before she could reach a position from which she could return fire.

Perry possessed a substantial superiority in both types of ordnance. Though the British squadron carried more long guns, they were mostly of smaller caliber. Furthermore, all the Americans' heavy long guns were mounted on pivots, which enabled them to fire in any direction. These circumstances gave the U.S. squadron a more than 3-to-2 broadside advantage of 264 to 196 pounds. In carronades the disparity was still more pronounced. Numerically, the Americans' advantage was not great, thirty-nine to thirty-one, but their pieces were of much heavier caliber. The result was a crushing carronade broadside superiority of 672 to 300 pounds (see Table 4.3).

Another critical tactical factor was the wind. Sailing ships of the period, especially square-riggers like Perry's two brigs, could not sail within an approximately 135 degree arc of the eye of the wind. Ships holding the weather gage—that is, the upwind position—could therefore dictate the range at which an engagement was fought. If it held the weather gage, a fleet with long guns could pulverize an adversary mounting carronades from a range at which the latter, regardless of the weight of its broadside, would be unable to reply.

In order for Perry to bring his squadron and particularly his two brigs into the close quarters that favored carronades, he needed the weather gage. Conversely it would be Barclay's advantage to hold the weather gage so that he could keep his distance from the U.S. squadron.

For Perry, victory depended upon placing his two big ships in close action with their counterparts. He intended to engage the British flagship with the *Lawrence*. Assuming that the *Queen Charlotte* would head the British line, he assigned the *Niagara* the corresponding position in his own line. The *Lawrence* would sail directly behind the *Niagara*, a station from which Perry could exercise command and control of the whole operation. The smaller vessels would, for the most part, play only a peripheral role. However, the three powerfully armed, long-gun schooners, the *Scorpion, Tigress,* and *Porcupine* with their 32-pounders, and the sloop *Trippe* with her 24-pounder, might batter the British ships from beyond reach of their smaller guns. To make this possible, these four relatively slow vessels needed wind enough to keep pace with the brigs that would precede them in the line of battle.

Beside establishing his line, Perry gave his captains two standing orders. The first stipulated that "[c]ommanding officers are particularly enjoined to pay attention in preserving their stations in the Line, and in all cases to keep as

TABLE 4.3   Lake Erie Squadron Armament

Name	Long Guns	Size and Type	Carronades	Size and Type
AMERICAN				
Lawrence	2	12 pdrs.	18	32 pdrs.
Niagara	2	12 pdrs.	18	32 pdrs.
Caledonia	2	24 pivot	1	32 pivot
Ariel	4	12 pivot		
Scorpion	1	32 pivot	1	32 pivot
Tigress	1	32 pivot		
Porcupine	1	32 pivot		
Trippe	1	24 pivot		
Somers	1	24 pivot	1	32 pivot
TOTAL				
Guns		54		
Broadside Firepower		936		
Weight of Metal		1,536		
BRITISH				
Detroit	2	24 pdrs.	1	24 pdr.
	1	18 pivot	1	18 pdr.
	6	12 pdrs.		
	8	9 pdrs.		
Queen Charlotte	3	12 pdrs. (1 pivot)	14	24 pdrs.
General Hunter	2	6 pdrs.	2	12 pdrs.
	4	4 pdrs.		
	2	2 pdrs.		
Lady Prevost	3	9 pdrs. (1 pivot)	10	12 pdrs.
Chippawa	1	12 pivot	1	12 pdr.
Little Belt	1	12 pivot	1	24 pdr.
			1	18 pdr.
TOTAL				
Guns		64		
Broadside Firepower		496		
Weight of Metal		905		

near the *Lawrence* as possible." The second instructed his commanders to "[e]ngage [their] designated adversary, in close action, at half cable's length." This distance—120 yards—was to be maintained between U.S. vessels, not between themselves and the British.

Barclay's ordnance problems did not end with a simple inferiority in weight of metal. All except two of the *Detroit*'s nineteen cannons were long guns. This meant that it would be to her advantage to fight a stand-off battle without coming within reach of the Americans' carronades. On the other hand, fourteen of the *Queen Charlotte*'s seventeen guns were carronades, which would be effective only at close quarters. In short, Barclay's two biggest ships were armed in such a manner that they could not engage to best advantage under the same circumstances.

The incompatible armament of these two vessels posed a problem no standard tactic could solve. Barclay's solution was to try to damage one of the American brigs at long range and then employ the *Queen Charlotte*'s carronades to destroy her while he engaged the other. This was a risky plan, but about the only one that offered any prospect of success. As Prof. Frederick C. Drake sums it up: "Barclay was damned if he fought a close action, damned if he ranged in a running fight, and damned if he had not fought at all."[8]

Before 10 September, Barclay's efforts to maintain control of Lake Erie had been thwarted by "Perry's luck." As the British squadron neared Put-in-Bay that morning, it seemed that the tables had finally turned. The wind was out of the southwest, giving Barclay the weather gage. This would enable him to engage the U.S. squadron beyond range of its carronades. "Perry's luck" appeared to have run out.

American lookouts spotted the enemy's sails on the horizon at dawn, and by 7:00 A.M. the U.S. squadron was outside its anchorage. To make the best use of their greater firepower, the Americans needed to possess the weather gage. But after nearly three hours of futile maneuvering, Perry conceded he could not attain it. A fighter by nature, he decided to engage regardless of the tactical disadvantage under which he would enter action. Reminded of that disadvantage, Perry exclaimed, "I don't care, to the windward or to the leeward, they shall fight today!"[9] His attitude differed from that of Commodore Chauncey, who invariably declined to accept battle on Lake Ontario unless the tactical situation was altogether in his favor.

Before the American squadron could change course, the wind faltered and died. Moments later, it picked up again, but it had backed 90 degrees to blow from the southeast. Perry's incredible luck had asserted itself again, for the new wind direction was ideal for the Americans. To Barclay it must have seemed as though fate was against him.

As the distance between the squadrons decreased, it became apparent that Barclay had not formed his line in the order Perry anticipated. Instead of placing the *Queen Charlotte* ahead of the *Detroit*, Barclay had put her to the rear of the flagship. The British line was headed by the *Chippawa* followed by the *Detroit*, *General Hunter*, *Queen Charlotte*, *Lady Prevost*, and *Little Belt*. Perry therefore reorganized his line with the *Ariel* and *Scorpion* on the *Lawrence*'s weather bow, and the *Caledonia*, *Niagara*, *Somers*, *Porcupine*, *Tigress*, and *Trippe* following in that order. No doubt this came as a severe disappointment to Jesse

Elliott. It deprived him of not only his prestigious place in the American van but the unexpected honor of engaging the British flagship. While Perry's dispositions seem normal, by stationing the *Lawrence* at the head of his line he impaired his ability to exercise command. Moreover, because the *Caledonia's* designated opponent, the *General Hunter,* was between the two larger British vessels, Perry placed the slow ex-merchantman between his two brigs. If Elliott were to maintain his position in the line of battle, the *Caledonia's* sailing characteristics in a light wind would keep him further from the U.S. flagship than Perry desired.

About 11:00 Perry climbed an amidships' gun carriage with a large, dark-blue banner in his arms. Stitched on it in crude white letters was the quotation "DONT GIVE UP THE SHIP," which was uttered by his dying friend James Lawrence during the *Chesapeake's* unsuccessful action with HMS *Shannon* in June. "My brave lads," Perry called, "this flag contains the last words of the brave Captain Lawrence. Shall I hoist it?" "Aye, Aye," they cried and gave three cheers. As the flag shot up the halyard, Perry shouted to the crew: "My Good Fellows, it is not to be hauled down again."[10]

The squadrons slowly converged in a gentle breeze that created a problem for Perry. Fore-and-aft rigged vessels were not at their best in light winds, and the schooner *Somers* began to fall behind the *Niagara.* The vessels following the *Somers* maintained station, with the result that Perry's first five ships gradually drew ahead of the others. By 11:30 the *Trippe,* at the tail of the American line, had dropped two miles astern.

By continuing to close with the British line while a gap opened in his own, Perry again evidenced his impetuosity. Of course he knew that between them the four vessels astern of the *Niagara* mounted only five guns. Furthermore, he was confident that simply by bringing his two brigs into action he would achieve a decisive fire superiority. Nonetheless the wise commander utilizes all the support and whatever diversions he can muster. Three of the cannons in the four vessels in the rear were long 32-pounders, and one was a long 24-pounder. All four could carry more than a mile. Barclay had come to offer battle. Intent as Perry was on fighting, he had no need to charge into action with only a portion of his available force. By doing so, he left 40 percent of his long-gun broadside armament behind. No wonder that some of his contemporaries said that "an officer seldom went into action worse, or got out of it better." At 11:45, with the U.S. line strung out and the British closely bunched, Barclay ordered the *Detroit* to fire one of her long guns at the *Lawrence.* The battle for Lake Erie had begun.

The *Detroit's* first shot fell well short of its mark. Perry ordered the *Scorpion* to reply, as her 24-pounder was the longest cannon at the head of his line. Soon the *Ariel* joined in with her 12-pounders, as did the *Lawrence* with her two 12-pounder bow chasers. At the same time, Perry signaled for all ships to engage their designated opponents.

Perry headed directly for the *Detroit*. He signaled for the other ships to follow, but slow-sailing, converted merchant vessels like the *Caledonia* and the trailing schooners and sloop continued to lag. This meant that Elliott's *Niagara*, positioned astern the *Caledonia*, also dropped behind. Meanwhile, the British flagship's long guns began to have a telling affect on the *Lawrence*. For nearly half an hour, the U.S. vessel withstood the *Detroit's* broadsides without being able to bring more than a fraction of her armament to bear. Finally, at 12:15 P.M., the *Lawrence* came into close range, and Perry ordered his 32-pounder carronades to commence fire. Their shots opened an exchange of broadsides that would continue for more than two hours. Considering that in the Age of Sail battles between two warships typically lasted less than an hour, the duration of their engagement is remarkable.

Up until the moment Perry fired his first broadside, Barclay could not help but be satisfied with the situation. Perry's impetuosity had played into his hands. His long guns were hammering the *Lawrence*, the gap between her and the other American brig was growing steadily greater, and half the American long guns remained out of action. If the *Lawrence* could be forced out of the battle before the American long guns and the *Niagara's* carronades entered it, Barclay could win the victory upon which so much depended.

It happened otherwise. By sailing almost straight at the *Detroit*, the *Lawrence* presented a much smaller target than if she had been on a parallel course. Despite the barrage to which she was subjected, none of her masts or yards went by the board, no holes punctured her hull. The *Lawrence* was hurt but not badly. Perry's luck had held again. All he needed now was the *Niagara*. With an additional broadside of 32-pounder carronades, the pendulum would inevitably swing to the American side, and the British would find themselves overcome by weight of metal.

But the *Niagara* did not come up. Instead, the *Lawrence*, supported only by the little *Ariel* and *Scorpion*, became engaged in an exceptionally brutal action at the apex of the opposing lines. After the first broadside both crews began firing at will, loading their guns as rapidly as possible. Soon the *Detroit* and *Lawrence* were so close together that gun captains had no need to aim; despite the dense smoke that made it impossible to see their opponent, they could not miss.

The *Lawrence's* deck quickly became the scene of terrible carnage. Seaman David Bunnell was momentarily blinded by a face full of brains when a shot shattered the skull of a sailor standing beside him. For a second Bunnell wondered whether he himself had been hit. Another shot tore a man's legs off and pierced him with splinters from the ship's bulwark. Still alive at the end of the battle, he responded to the report that the Americans had won by exclaiming, "I die in peace," and he did. Peas that had been boiling for dinner spilled to the deck, and a loose pig began eating them even though it had lost its hind legs. An officer's dog was wounded and ran back and forth howling "in a most dreadful manner." In a brief interlude, Bunnell looked around and saw "such a sight [as] at any other time would have made me shudder, but now in the height of action, I only thought to say to myself 'poor souls!' The deck was in a shocking predicament. Death had been very busy. It was one continued gore of blood and carnage—the dead and dying were strewed in every direction over it—for it was impossible to take the wounded below as fast as they fell." [11]

The ship suffered as well. Only a quarter hour into the action, Sailing Master William Taylor recorded in the *Lawrence's* log that "our braces, bowlines, sheets, and, in fact, almost every strand of rigging" was cut off. Masts and spars were also damaged.

Gradually, the *Lawrence's* battery was overpowered. One British shot went into the bore of a carronade, and the gun burst into metal shards that wounded the entire gun crew. Guns not disabled by enemy fire were damaged by prolonged firing. As the gunners became casualties, sailors were called out of the rigging, and marines pressed into service to man the guns. Perry himself helped fire the last gun left in action. By about 2:30, it was clear the *Lawrence* was incapable of continuing the fight.

The reason for this situation was that the *Niagara* had yet to become seriously engaged. Why was the *Niagara* not brought forward? This remains the most controversial aspect of the battle. Elliott kept his vessel behind the *Caledonia,* as though he expected Perry to cross the enemy "T." When the *Queen Charlotte's* commander noticed Elliott's reluctance to close, he brought her past the *General Hunter* and began blasting the *Lawrence* with his carronades. For more than two hours the *Lawrence* fought not only the *Detroit* but also the *Queen Charlotte* and *General Hunter.* Barclay's plan to destroy one American brig and then attack the other seemed about to bear fruit, even though he had lost the weather gage. But the British sustained heavy losses during their mauling of the *Lawrence.* Both the *Queen Charlotte* and *Detroit* were severely damaged. More important, the squadron lost the services of its senior officers. The captain and first lieutenant of the *Queen Charlotte* fell early in the en-

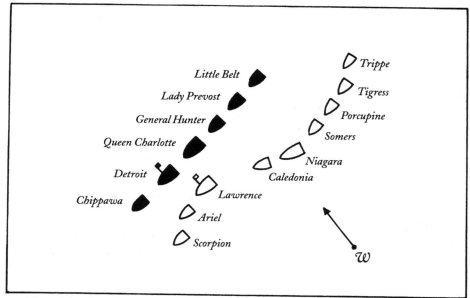

The Battle of Lake Erie, 10 September 1813: situation about 2:30 P.M., shortly before Perry decided to shift his flag to the *Niagara* and Elliott began to bring her forward.

gagement, and command of that vessel devolved to a young and inexperienced Provincial Marine lieutenant. The first lieutenant of the *Detroit* was mortally wounded, and Barclay had to go below because of two wounds. The captains of the *Lady Prevost* and *Chippawa* were also wounded. The British had lost their principal advantage—experienced officers—by 2:30.

At this time, both Perry and Elliott made critical decisions. Elliott, who had received no signal from Perry since noon, decided to leave the line and brought the *Niagara* forward to the windward of the flagship, which was now adrift. Meanwhile, Perry informed the *Lawrence's* thrice-wounded first lieutenant, John Yarnall, that he intended to take one of the ship's boats with four unwounded sailors and shift his flag to the *Niagara*. Yarnall was to continue resistance for only a short while before striking the *Lawrence's* colors.

The *Niagara* was making sail toward the head of the British line when Perry boarded her. He immediately ordered Elliott to take the boat that had brought him and bring the trailing vessels into closer action. Perry then steered the *Niagara* between the *Detroit* and *Lady Prevost*, which had moved ahead of the *Detroit*, pouring broadsides into both. With eighteen carronades firing at the Royal Navy squadron, the devastation was intense. The junior officers now commanding the two largest British vessels sought to bring them

The Battle of Lake Erie, 10 September 1813. This contemporary engraving depicts the decisive phase of the battle, when Perry brought the *Niagara* into close action with the British brigs. From extreme left to right, the vessels are the *Little Belt*, *Lady Prevost*, *Scorpion* (US), *Chippawa* (masts alone visible), *Ariel* (US), *Niagara* (US), *Detroit*, *Queen Charlotte*, *Hunter*, *Caledonia* (US), *Trippe* (US) (masts alone visible), *Tigress* (US) (masts alone visible), *Somers* (US), *Porcupine* (US), and *Lawrence* (US). *The Beverley R. Robinson Collection, U.S. Naval Academy Museum*

about so as to fire their undamaged, starboard batteries; but the inexperienced commander and depleted crew of the *Queen Charlotte* failed in their maneuver, and her rigging became entangled with that of the *Detroit*. Not only did the *Niagara* wreak havoc on the British vessels, but Elliott brought the gunboats forward and their long guns began to pepper the increasingly helpless enemy. In short order, all the British vessels were battered into submission. The *Scorpion*, which had fired the first American shot in the battle, fired the last when she compelled the fleeing *Little Belt* to haul down her colors.

The American victory was complete. Even though the *Lawrence* had lowered her flag to avert useless carnage aboard a vessel unable to resist, the British had not been able to board her. Every Royal Navy ship surrendered to Perry, who wrote one of the most succinct after-action reports in American history: "We have met the enemy and they are ours: Two Ships, two Brigs, one Schooner, & one Sloop."[12] This was one of the very few times in its long history that the Royal Navy lost an entire squadron. British dead numbered forty-one. All the survivors, including ninety-four wounded, were made prisoner. U.S. losses totaled twenty-seven killed and ninety-six wounded.

Perry's squadron returned to Put-in-Bay on 11 September and began the process of burying the dead officers of both sides (enlisted personnel had been buried in the lake), refurbishing the ships of both squadrons, and preparing to transport General Harrison's Army of the North West across the lake. The army's landing on the Canadian shore, 27 September, was the result of an extraordinary degree of army-navy cooperation. The endeavor was the largest joint operation in the history of the U.S. armed forces prior to the War with Mexico.

Barclay's defeat ended the British Army's ability to maintain control of the Detroit River region. Gen. Henry Procter, who had commanded at Amherstburg, slowly retreated up the Thames River Valley. Harrison's forces caught up with him, and, at the Battle of the Thames on 5 October, eliminated serious British resistance in the Western District of Upper Canada.

Strategically the delay imposed on American victory by Barclay and his crews was critical. The British, Canadians, and three Indians who fought bravely on Lake Erie helped bring about a stalemate on Lake Ontario. By the time of the Battle of the Thames, winter was too near for Perry to join Chauncey in an offensive on the lower lake. In the spring of 1814, Napoleon's first abdication allowed the British to reinforce Canada with veterans of the Peninsular War. U.S. hopes of annexing British North America had been disappointed. Even in defeat, the British campaign for Lake Erie saved Canada.

Although Perry initially sought to stifle criticism of Elliott's conduct, eventually their differences broke into the press and became quite bitter. Elliott tried to redeem his reputation, arguing that if Perry had wanted him to break the line and come forward, he should have so signaled. But he could never explain his failure to support Perry promptly to the satisfaction of the contemporary public or modern historians. Elliott continued on active duty for a quarter century after Perry died of yellow fever off the coast of Venezuela in 1819, eventually becoming a commodore. But he remains one of the Age of Sail's few commodores for whom the navy has never named a ship.

The Battle of Lake Erie made Perry a national hero. President Madison promoted him to the rank of captain with seniority from the date of the battle. Congress voted gold medals be struck honoring both Perry and Elliott. The prize money awarded the crews was the largest of the war, and Congress gave Perry an extra five thousand dollar bonus. "We have met the enemy and they are ours" became one of the U.S. Navy's cherished mottos. As one of the best known of the captains and commodores who made the War of 1812 a glorious page in the young navy's history, Perry became an inspiration to future U.S. Navy officers. Since 1843, five warships and an entire class of modern frigates have been named in his honor, and today his "DONT GIVE UP THE SHIP" flag is the first thing a visitor sees upon entering Memorial Hall at the U.S. Naval Academy. Impetuous as he may have been, Oliver Hazard Perry was a superb combat leader.

NOTES

1. The standard biographies are Charles J. Dutton, *Oliver Hazard Perry* (New York, 1935); Edwin P. Hoyt, *The Tragic Commodore: The Story of Oliver Hazard Perry* (London, 1966); and Alexander Slidell Mackenzie, *The Life of Commodore Oliver Hazard Perry*, 2 vols. (New York, 1840). For the quoted materials see, Sarah Wallace Perry, "A Sister's Reminiscences of Oliver Hazard Perry's Childhood," *The American Magazine and Historical Chronicle* 4 (Autumn–Winter 1988–89): 19–31; William V. Taylor, "Description of the Battle of Lake Erie," 23 June 1818, and Francis Vinton to Benson J. Lossing, 17 April 1860, Usher Parsons to Alexander S. Mackenzie, 24 January 1841, Perry Papers, William L. Clements Library, University of Michigan, Ann Arbor (hereafter WLCL).

The most valuable primary sources for the Battle of Lake Erie are the Perry Papers and the Chauncey Papers, WLCL; Samuel Hambleton's Diary, MS 983, Maryland Historical Society, Baltimore; Frank Allaben, ed., "The Log Book of the 'Lawrence,'" *Journal of American History* 8 (January 1914): 111–21; William S. Dudley, ed., *The Naval War of 1812: A Documentary History*, 2 vols. to date (Washington, D.C., 1985–); [Jesse Duncan Elliott], *A Review of a Pamphlet Purporting to be Documents in Relation to the Differences which Subsisted between the Late Commodore Oliver H. Perry, and Captain Jesse D. Elliott* (Boston, 1834); Elliott, *Speech of Com. Jesse Duncan Elliott, U.S.N., Delivered in Hagerstown, Md. on 14th November, 1843* (Philadelphia, 1844); William C. H. Wood, ed., *Select British Documents of the Canadian War of 1812* (Toronto, 1920–28); John C. Fredriksen, ed., "A Grand Moment for Our Beloved Commander: Sailing Master William V. Taylor's Account of the Battle of Lake Erie," *Journal of Erie Studies* 17 (Fall 1988): 113–22; Usher Parsons, *Battle of Lake Erie* (Providence, R.I., 1852); Parsons, *Brief Sketches of the Officers Who Were in the Battle of Lake Erie* (Albany, 1862); W. W. Dobbins, *History of the Battle of Lake Erie* (Erie, 1913); and David C. Bunnell, *The Travels and Adventures of David C. Bunnell* (Palmyra, N.Y., 1831).

Standard modern studies include Theodore Roosevelt, *The Naval War of 1812* (New York, 1893): 254–375; A. T. Mahan, *Sea Power in Its Relations to the War of 1812*, 2 vols. (Boston, 1905), 2:62–107; Leonard F. Guttridge and Jay D. Smith, *The Commodores* (Annapolis, 1986); William Jeffrey Welsh and David Curtis Skaggs, eds, *War on the Great Lakes: Essays Commemorating the 175th Anniversary of the Battle of Lake Erie* (Kent, Ohio, 1991); Michael A. Palmer, "A Failure of Command, Control and Communication: Oliver Hazard Perry and the Battle of Lake Erie," and Frederick C. Drake, "A Loss of Mastery: The British Squadron on Lake Erie, May–September 1813," *Journal of Erie Studies* 17 (Fall 1988): 7–26, 47–76; Thomas Malcomson and Robert Malcomson, *HMS Detroit: The Battle for Lake Erie* (Annapolis, 1990); and Lawrence J. Friedman and David Curtis Skaggs, "Jesse Duncan Elliott and the Battle of Lake Erie: The Issue of Mental Stability," *Journal of the Early Republic* 10 (Winter 1990): 493–516; Skaggs, "Creating Small Unit Cohesion: Oliver Hazard Perry at the Battle of Lake Erie," *Armed Forces and Society* 23 (Summer 1997): 633–68; Skaggs and Gerard T. Altoff, *A Signal Victory: The Lake Erie Campaign, 1812–1813* (Annapolis, 1997).

2. Chauncey to Perry, 15 March 1813, Dudley, ed., *Naval War of 1812*, 2:422–23.

3. Brock to Prevost, 11 October 1812, ibid., 2:321–22.

4. "Narrative of . . . the Command of Captain Barclay," Wood, ed., *Select British Documents*, 2:303–4.

5. Chauncey to Perry, 30 July 1813 (original emphasis), Dudley, ed., *Naval War of 1812*, 2:530–31. This letter was in reply to Perry to Chauncey, 27 July 1813, ibid., 2:529–30. Secretary Jones was pressuring Chauncey to support Perry. See Chauncey to Jones, 4 August 1813, ibid., 2:528–29. The idea of

a establishing a separate command had definitely occurred to some of Perry's subordinates.

6. Perry to Jones, 10 August 1813, Jones to Perry, 18 August 1813, Dudley, ed., *Naval War of 1812*, 2:532–33, Hambleton Diary, 12 August 1813.

7 Gerard T. Altoff, *Deep Water Sailors, Shallow Water Soldiers* (Put-in-Bay, Ohio, 1993).

8. Frederick C. Drake, "Artillery and Its Influence on Naval Tactics: Reflections on the Battle of Lake Erie," in Welsh and Skaggs, eds., *War on the Great Lakes*, 29. See also W. A. B. Douglas, "The Honor of the Flag Had Not Suffered· Robert Heriot Barclay and the Battle of Lake Erie," ibid., 30–37

9. Mackenzie, *Commodore Perry*, 1 225.

10. Hambleton Diary, 12 October 1813; Taylor to Mackenzie, 16 January 1841, Fredriksen, ed., "'A Grand Moment:'" 118–19.

11. Bunnell, *Travels*, 113–17, quote 115.

12. Perry to Harrison, 10 September 1813, Dudley, ed., *Naval War of 1812*, 2:553. Actually, the British squadron consisted of two ships (*Queen Charlotte* and *Detroit*), one brig (*General Hunter*), two schooners (*Lady Prevost* and *Chippawa*), and one sloop (*Little Belt*). The *Lady Prevost* was a two-masted schooner mistaken for a brig.

5

The Battle of Lake Champlain

W. M. P. DUNNE

The significance of the Battle of Lake Champlain is straightforward. Whether evaluated from a political, diplomatic, or military point of view, it stands as the most important engagement fought during the War of 1812. To achieve victory, the British government committed the largest combined army and navy force in its century-and-a-half history of military operations on the North American continent. The ground component included numerous Napoleonic War veterans, seasoned campaigners from what the Duke of Wellington called "an unrivalled army for fighting."[1]

On the American side, the muddled war aims of the Madison administration, particularly as interpreted by its egocentric secretary of war, John Armstrong Jr., blighted any chance of victory. Armstrong's benighted strategic posture, that in 1814 the U.S. forces should "carry the war as far westward as possible while we have the ascendancy on the Lakes," ensured a reduction of troops around Lake Champlain, the point of the British invasion.[2] But, even without Armstrong's bungling directives, his army possessed nothing like the military might necessary to withstand the enemy thrown against it at Plattsburg, New York, in September 1814.

The senior king's officer in Canada, Sir George Prevost, united the posts of governor-general and commander in chief. He thus controlled both civilian and military power within British North America. A cautious man, Prevost reported directly to Lord Bathurst, Secretary of War and the Colonies in the ministry of the Earl of Liverpool. Prevost's mandate since 1812 had been to defend Canada—not to launch an invasion of the United States. But in June 1814, a dissatisfied Bathurst, prompted by the defeat of Napoleon, wrote to Prevost saying: "If you shall allow the present campaign to close without having taken offensive measures, you will very seriously disappoint the expecta-

Commo. Thomas Macdonough by Gilbert Stuart. *National Gallery of Art, Mellon Collection*

tions of the Prince Regent and the country."[3] Bathurst's expectation that Prevost would suddenly acquire the mentality of an offensive campaigner bordered on the absurd.

The pivotal event in the Champlain Valley during the conflict occurred on 28 September 1812, when twenty-eight-year-old Lt. Thomas Macdonough was ordered to Lake Champlain to assume command of a nonexistent fleet.[4] A relatively unknown figure, Macdonough had been appointed a midshipman during the Quasi-War with France. Subsequently he served with the intrepid

Stephen Decatur in the War with Tripoli. Well before peace came to the Mediterranean, Macdonough, a man of deep religious convictions, had become a battle-scarred veteran. From 1805 to 1810, he served as first lieutenant in several ships and also had a spell of gunboat building. By age twenty-five, he had earned an enviable reputation, not only as a brave fighting sailor but also as a highly competent executive officer. Briefly assigned to the *Constellation* upon the outbreak of war, he soon received orders giving him command of the gunboat flotilla at Portland, Maine, where he arrived on 7 September 1812. Four weeks later, bearing his third change of orders in as many months, he left for Lake Champlain.[5] Through the autumn he converted a small fleet of lake traders into pseudofighting ships and made a war patrol before ice closed the lake. Over the following winter he improved his squadron and during 1813 gained, lost, and regained naval ascendancy over the British.

On 28 January of the crucial year 1814, Secretary of the Navy William Jones responded to reports of increasing enemy strength by authorizing Macdonough to build fifteen gunboats *or* a ship and three or four gunboats, the choice to be his. Jones emphasized that "[t]he object is to leave no doubt of your commanding the lake and the waters connected."[6] No sooner had this directive reached upstate New York than Macdonough learned that the British had a true warship, a potent brig, under construction at Isle aux Noix, their forward base in the Richelieu River at the northern end of the lake. Informed of this development, Jones contracted with the Brown brothers of New York City to build a larger warship for Macdonough. By 7 March, Macdonough could report that Noah Brown had laid the keel of a 26-gun ship at Vergennes, a Vermont village seven miles up Otter Creek from the lake.[7]

Early in April, after a spell of unusually mild weather cleared the lower lake ice, the enterprising British squadron commander, Daniel Pring, made the first sortie of 1814, entering the lake with several gunboats that he brought to anchor off Rouse's Point. Their appearance provoked apprehensions that, as soon as the ice would allow, the British might seize every suitable lake vessel, load them with stones, and sink them at the mouth of Otter Creek to bottle up the U.S. squadron. But with most of the lake icebound the threat failed to materialize, and Pring returned to Isle aux Noix.[8]

At Vergennes, the *Saratoga* splashed into the creek on 11 April, only forty days after the laying of her keel. To protect her and his other vessels, Macdonough met with Maj. Gen. James Wilkinson and Vermont governor Martin Chittenden to select a site for a 7-gun battery intended to keep the British away from the creek mouth.[9] On Wilkinson's suggestion, Chittenden also sent fifteen hundred militia to Otter Creek, an action that almost cost Macdonough's life. Naval headquarters in Vergennes occupied three second-story rooms directly above the Vermont troops' guardroom. One day a militiaman accidentally fired a musket ball through the ceiling. It missed Macdonough by inches. With exceptional self-control, he sought out the soldier's superior and suggested that, "if you will take your militia home I will take care of the fleet. I am in more danger from your men than from the enemy."[10]

On 30 April Macdonough sent a progress report informing Jones that the *Saratoga*'s outfitting was well under way.[11] Meanwhile, Noah Brown turned his attention to an unfinished steamboat hull the department had authorized Macdonough to purchase. The amazing shipwright promised to launch it as an armed schooner within two weeks, as well as constructing six 2-gun row galleys.

Fears that the British might sortie in force assumed serious proportions when Pring entered the lake on 9 May with *Linnet,* his new 16-gun brig, two sloops, several smaller vessels, a 180-man landing force, and two old merchant sloops that he did indeed intend to sink at the mouth of Otter Creek. The morning after the British squadron appeared on the lower lake, Brig. Gen. George Izard, who had succeeded Wilkinson at Plattsburg, reported its presence to Brig. Gen. Alexander Macomb, his opposite number at Burlington. Macomb in turn alerted Macdonough.[12]

The prevailing southerly breezes bought time for the Americans. Unable to sail into their teeth, Pring did not near his objective until the evening of 13 April, when he anchored a few miles below the creek. At daybreak on the fourteenth he sent the gunboats and cutter to bombard the American battery. A ninety-minute engagement convinced Pring of the impracticality of landing or sinking the block ships, and he returned down the lake, taking up station two miles north of the border on the sixteenth.[13]

Just before this skirmish, Noah Brown had sent the former steamboat hull, now converted to the 19-gun schooner *Ticonderoga,* down the ways at Vergennes. Macdonough hoisted his broad pendant in the *Saratoga* and gave command of the new schooner to his best officer, Stephen Cassin. The squadron sailed on 26 May, but personnel shortages caused Macdonough to leave two sloops and four older gunboats behind.[14] Even so, he once again enjoyed naval ascendancy, a situation that proved short-lived. In early June rumors of a powerful British frigate under construction at Isle aux Noix soured the tone of Macdonough's correspondence with Jones, striking the overburdened secretary the wrong way at the wrong time. As late as 6 May, he had confidentially advised the president that, "I do not anticipate anything to disturb our complete control on Lake Champlain."[15] But on 8 June Macdonough breached Jones's confidence by the first of a series of increasingly distraught letters. Given the supposed strength of the British frigate, he warned: "No time should therefore be lost in our either increasing our force on the Water or fortifying in the narrow part of the Lake."[16] Another letter dispatched on the eleventh relayed alarming reports from enemy deserters and declared, "Should it be ordered to increase our Naval force, it should be commenced without loss of time."[17]

Despite his disappointment that these pleas failed to elicit authorization to build another ship, Macdonough never ceased his efforts to make do with the vessels he had. He completed his manning and took on the last of his stores while the squadron lay in Plattsburg Bay. He also designed a manual of more than three hundred numerical signals to manage the squadron before he sailed from Plattsburg on the eleventh. The next day, as his ships approached the Richelieu, the British lookouts spotted them. As soon as Pring realized that the Americans were out in strength, he pulled farther back into the river, thereby frustrating Macdonough's desire for an engagement. Shortly afterward, Capt. Peter Fisher, RN, arrived to relieve Pring. The advent of the new frigate dictated that a more senior officer should command the British naval forces.

In comparison to the slow growth of British power on the lake, ashore their might blossomed swiftly. Toulouse, the final battle of the Peninsula War, took place on 10 April 1814. A month later, the abdication of Napoleon allowed the transfer of four of the Duke of Wellington's brigades to Canada. As soon as these troops reached him, Prevost stood ready to mount an irresistible invasion of the Champlain Valley, with the military depot at Plattsburg as his initial objective.[18] He realized that naval superiority was essential to his goal. The Champlain waterway allows direct access between the St. Lawrence and the Hudson Rivers, or between Quebec and Montreal to the north and Albany and New York City to the south. With forbidding mountains edging the lake on the New York side and friendly Vermonters whom he dared not disturb on the other, the lake waters offered Prevost his only highway to the south. An advance into the United States beyond Plattsburg would depend entirely on control of Lake Champlain.

General Izard, with no inkling of the thousands of enemy troops about to arrive in his theater, had begun preparations to invade Canada by mid-June 1814. At that date the British barely equaled his strength, but the first troopship had already reached Montreal, and sixty others had begun to enter the St.

Lawrence.[19] By the end of August, some thirteen thousand British veterans would have reached Lower Canada—many of them intended for Lake Champlain—giving Prevost an incontestable superiority over the Americans.

On the lakefront, Macdonough asked Izard on 17 June: "Will it not be advisable to have some guns on Cumberland Head or some other point for me to retire to in case I should be compelled to retire from so superior a force?" Izard concurred, advising Macdonough on the nineteenth: "Tomorrow, before night, a battery of four eighteen pounders shall be established on Cumberland Head. . . ."[20] That same day, Macdonough warned Jones: "The Enemy are preparing a large increase in their force. . . . My information from the Enemy is as late as yesterday—they were then raising the frames of a Vessel, intended to equal or surpass the *Saratoga*."[21] More bad news came on 26 June, when Macdonough's spies reported that the big ship building at Isle aux Noix would be completed by late August. "[T]he increase of our force," he told Jones, "will have to be so considerable, not less than an 18 Gun Brig."[22] But Macdonough's pleas met only silence from Washington. On 9 July he sent the secretary a thinly disguised demand: "I am daily expecting orders to build for the enemy will when he gets his force contemplated have one superior to ours."[23] Four days later, he reiterated, "If an increase of our force on this Lake is contemplated we should commence building without delay."[24] But if his correspondence had become increasingly frantic, Macdonough's handling of the squadron remained cool-headed and clear. Throughout the weeks his vessels lay off Point au Fer, he drilled their skippers in battle tactics and endlessly exercised their crews.

At first Jones stood fast in the face of this barrage of warnings and demands. In early July, after receiving Macdonough's first two missives, he gave Secretary of War Armstrong, "an explicit declaration that he would not add to the naval means on Lake Champlain." At that point, however, President Madison stepped in and for the only time in the war overturned one of the secretary's decisions. On 5 July, Jones authorized the Browns to return to Vergennes for the purpose of adding an 18-gun brig to Macdonough's fleet.[25]

On shore, General Izard, with reliable intelligence of burgeoning British strength, realized that the planned offensive into Canada had become impractical. Early in July, while unaware of the size of the British Army assembling on the Champlain front, he had suggested to Secretary Armstrong that he could support an invasion of the Niagara Peninsula by marching west to Lake Ontario. On 2 August, Armstrong, driven by his oft-repeated wish to mount an attack on Kingston, claimed Izard's idea as his own, adamantly refused to credit reports of a British buildup above Lake Champlain, and thus made the most monumental mistake of a career filled with arrogant errors. He ordered Izard to Sackett's Harbor. This egregious miscalculation stripped the Champlain Valley of 80 percent of its effective troops at the very moment the British were massing along the border.[26]

Armstrong's order arrived 10 August. Izard informed the secretary by return dispatch that a vastly superior enemy force stood poised to invade the United States. With keen foresight, he predicted "that everything in this Vicinity but the lately erected works at Plattsburg and on Cumberland Head will in less than three days after my Departure, be in the Possession of the Enemy."[27] As if to punctuate Izard's dilemma, Prevost chose this moment to move his headquarters from Montreal to Isle aux Noix and assume personal command of the coming invasion.

The naval balance of power improved for Macdonough when his new brig, the *Eagle,* joined the squadron on 27 August. While the *Eagle* augmented the U.S. fleet, ashore the army suffered a disastrous diminution when, with the greatest reluctance, Izard led his troops away to the westward on 29 August. The dust of his march had not settled before Prevost began the British invasion by pouring ten thousand men, the largest army ever to take the field in North America, across the border and occupying the town of Champlain. Gen. Thomas Brisbane led the advance. Along with Frederick Philipse Robinson and Manley Power, he was one of three brigade commanders, major generals all, whom Wellington had described as "the best of their rank in the army."[28]

South of the Canadian border, command of the American army devolved upon General Macomb, who, acting to fill the enormous gap left by the loss of four thousand regulars, concentrated his men at Plattsburg and set them to work to establish a defensive line along the heights on the south bank of the Saranac River. Macomb had a total of thirty-four hundred men at his disposal, only twelve hundred of whom he considered effective.

On 30 August, the British pushed forward from Champlain to Chazy, thus bypassing the U.S. squadron and putting it in jeopardy of being pincered between British artillery on land and their flotilla on the lake. Macdonough decided to withdraw to Plattsburg Bay, but in light southerly airs the squadron could only creep up the lake with the galleys towing the larger vessels. Every man in the fleet breathed a sigh of relief when the ships reached Plattsburg after sunset on 1 September following a blistering, two-day struggle with their oars.

As the Americans had begun to edge up the lake on 30 August, yet another British change of command occurred. Captain George Downie, who had come out from England that summer and briefly commanded the sloop of war *Montreal* on Lake Ontario, arrived to supersede Fisher, who had relieved Pring only five weeks earlier.[29] In the period of ninety days, therefore, the Royal Navy had three different commanding officers on Lake Champlain. This contrasts strikingly with Macdonough's experience as commodore of the U.S. squadron, which dated back to October 1812. Considering the importance of local knowledge on a tricky body of water like Lake Champlain, these indiscriminate personnel changes gave the Americans a distinct advantage.

The mountain ranges on either side of the lake control its sailing dynamics. Their narrow confines along the lake's entire 120-mile length predicate that the prevailing winds will usually come from the north or south, while the current sets steadily northward into the Richelieu River. Unlike oceangoing vessels, the warships of the opposing squadrons had uniformly flat and shallow hulls that could not work into the wind very well. Thus, against a strong south wind, the British had little chance of beating up to Cumberland Head from the mouth of the Richelieu. Furthermore, given the lateness of the season, the threat of sudden equinoctial squalls would make it dangerous for them to wait outside Plattsburg Bay until the wind swung in their favor to enter or the Americans chose to come out. The bay opens to the south. The tip of Cumberland Head lies on one side of its mouth and a large shoal extending eastward toward the lake from low-lying Crab Island on the other. The northerly wind the British needed to sail up the lake from the Richelieu would turn against them once they rounded the head and attempted to enter the bay.

Macdonough's superiority lay not only in his accumulation of local lore but also in the shrewd forethought he gave to the exigencies of the approaching battle. The defensive arrangement he decided upon showed that he had anticipated, and as far as possible overcome in advance, every conceivable mode of attack the British might adopt. Ultimately, he forced them to engage on his terms, not theirs.

Lacking knowledge that Bathurst had asked Prevost to do no more than to gain a foothold in New York that autumn, Macdonough had to assume that Plattsburg would be the initial, but not final, enemy objective. The town's location, just a few miles below the border, its attributes as a major lakeport, and the facilities constructed there by the U.S. Army made it an ideal forward base for a British offensive toward Ticonderoga, Lake George, and the Hudson River. Macdonough knew that the British would not only have to capture Plattsburg but also gain control of the lake to cover an advance to the south. Thus, he reasoned, strategic imperatives put the onus of attacking squarely on the enemy. If he was correct, the Royal Navy would have to conduct its assault in the arena of his choice. This concept became the keystone of Macdonough's strategy. He would await the enemy at anchor inside the bay.

On 3 September, Downie, who had been evaluating the situation since his arrival at Isle aux Noix two days earlier, made his first moves. He had James B. Robertson, his trusted first lieutenant from the *Montreal*, take over the outfitting of the frigate *Confiance*, which had been launched on 25 August. He then ordered Pring to turn the *Linnet* over to Lt. William Drew and take the sloops *Chub* and *Finch*, the gunboats, and a party of marines to capture the Isle la Motte. There Pring was to position a battery of three 18-pounders to protect the mouth of the Little Chazy River, the planned landing point for Prevost's supply vessels. With his usual determination, Pring took the island later that same day, paroled its garrison of American militiamen, and had the battery in place by Sunday, 4 September.[30]

About fifteen miles away, Macdonough, acting on the questionable intelligence that the British squadron would not leave the Richelieu until the middle of the month, decided not to establish his line of battle yet. During the weekend of 3–4 September, Joseph H. Dulles, a Yale divinity student touring Lakes George and Champlain, went on board the *Saratoga*. Dulles left a description of his visit to the flagship for posterity: "At noon Divine services were performed, the commander and officers being seated on the quarterdeck, the chaplain at the capstan, and the crew, about 300 men [*sic*], occupied the room from midships to the bow." After the service, he joined Macdonough, whom he found "of a light and agile frame, easy and graceful in his manners, with an expressive countenance, remarkably placid." He also observed that the commodore "conversed with singular simplicity and with the dignity of a Christian gentleman on whose shoulders rested the weightiest responsibility that bore on any man in that period of our history." Perhaps what most impressed the Yale man was the fact that "the confidence of his officers and men in him was unbounded, and such as great leaders only can secure."[31]

At sunrise on Monday the British army continued its marching seven miles beyond Chazy along the Little Chazy River to an encampment on the lake road about halfway to Plattsburg. Meanwhile, the U.S. soldiers on the heights to the south of the Saranac continued to work around the clock to finish their redoubts and blockhouses. The next morning, 6 September, the British moved toward Plattsburg in two columns. American skirmishers attempted to hinder their advance, but the seasoned British troopers simply ignored them. "So undaunted . . . was the enemy," Macomb reported "that he never deployed [during] his whole march[,] always pressing on in Column."[32] Facing an assault force by thousands of British regulars, Macomb ordered his vastly outnumbered skirmishers to fall back on Plattsburg.

The seventh was an event-filled day for both sides. The British took Plattsburg without serious opposition, and Prevost proceeded to erect some works intended to give him command of the Saranac, Plattsburg Bay, and the American forts and blockhouses south of the river. When Macdonough learned that the enemy had occupied the town, he assumed their squadron would soon put in its appearance. A signal from the *Saratoga* sent the squadron into its predetermined line of battle, which ran from northeast to southwest parallel to the mouth of the bay. The *Eagle* anchored perpendicular to and a little below the Saranac River mouth to secure the northern end. Then came the *Saratoga* and *Ticonderoga,* with the *Preble* at the southern end about a mile and a half north of Crab Island. Following his usual practice, Macdonough ordered his captains to attach spring lines to their anchor cables so that each vessel could be turned 180 degrees within its mooring lines. In apprehension of damage to the springs, he also had them position stern anchors. Finally, he directed that each ship's boats be lowered on their larboard, or unengaged, side. From his own ship, the commodore sent out a kedge anchor from each bow with a line leading aft to the stern on each side.

To the north Downie sailed from Isle aux Noix a week sooner than Macdonough anticipated, but his ships met the same adverse current and wind conditions the Americans had experienced on the first. After warping the *Confiance* into the stream, he set about hauling her up to the lake to the tune of saws, mallets, and adzes echoing about her decks as shipwrights worked to complete a myriad of last-minute jobs. After a hard day's pull, she reached the Ash Island anchorage that evening, where the *Linnet* joined her.

At Plattsburg, the ever-cautious Prevost spent the next four days—from the seventh to the eleventh—bringing up his artillery and supply trains. The first of several notes he sent Downie went off that morning; it asked whether the new commodore was familiar with Macdonough's fleet and, if so, was he willing to engage it? He closed by emphasizing that his movements would depend upon Downie, who received Prevost's inquiry in the midst of his struggle to get the *Confiance* out of the Richelieu. "I am aware of the Comparative force of the Enemy," he replied, "and am thus far on my way to find the Enemy; Conceiving that the moment I can put this Ship into a State for Action I shall be able to meet them."[33]

On 8 September the British ships worked their way up the lake as far as Chazy, where they united with the *Finch* and *Chub* and the gunboats. Another vexatious message from Prevost also awaited them: "[I]t is of the highest importance . . . your Command should commence a cooperation with the division of the Army now occupying Plattsburg. . . . I only wait for your arrival to proceed against General McCombe's last position."[34] Downie, who could have done without this pressure, replied: "I am advancing with the Squadron to Chazy as fast as wind and weather will allow," and he testily closed: "In the letter I did myself the Honor to address to you yesterday, I stated to you that this Ship was not ready. She is not ready now, and, until she is ready, it is my duty not to hazard the Squadron."[35]

The British force spent the ninth off Chazy preparing for battle. Prevost's aide-de-camp showed up during the morning bearing yet another dispatch. "In consequence of your communication of yesterday's date. I have postponed moving on the Enemy's position," Prevost wrote, sounding like a man constructing an alibi in advance, "I need not dwell with you on the Evils resulting to both Services from delay."[36] Between ducking Prevost's darts and living with the racket on board as the shipwrights worked to complete the *Confiance,* Downie exhibited exemplary patience. Instead of answering the commander in chief in kind, the commodore told him what he wanted to hear: "It is my intention to Weigh and proceed from this Anchorage about Midnight, in the Expectation of rounding into the Bay of Plattsburg about dawn of day, and commence an immediate action with the Enemy."[37]

Unfortunately for army-navy relations, the weather intervened. The squadron did not gain a fair wind until early 11 September, when Downie got his ships under sail before the sun rose over the Green Mountains. The aroma of strong, hot coffee pervaded the lower lake as the sun cleared the horizon. About 5:15 A.M., Downie had the *Confiance*'s guns fired with double-shotted blank charges to scale the bores and signal the army of his squadron's approach.[38]

Soon after firing these charges, Downie signaled his ships to heave to about three miles above Cumberland Head, lowered his gig, and went to assess the American line of battle. He determined his plan of action: *Confiance* to anchor between *Eagle* and *Saratoga* and rake them both with her powerful broadsides; *Linnet* and *Chub* to anchor at the north end of the American line and concentrate their fire on *Eagle*; *Finch* to head for the lower end and engage *Commodore Preble*; the gunboats to surround and board *Ticonderoga*. As his squadron cleared Cumberland Head about two hours later, Downie signaled a course change to the northwest. But the mass of the head broke up the north-northeast breeze he had enjoyed. The wind backed to light and variable from the northwest, right in his face. Nevertheless, Downie brought his fleet slowly onward. Fifteen warships ranging from the 37-gun *Confiance* down to the

TABLE 5.1 The Battle of Lake Champlain, 11 September 1814

Name	Type	Armament
AMERICAN		
Saratoga	Sloop of war	8 24-pdrs., 12 32-lb. carronades, 6 42-lb. carronades
Eagle	Brig	8 18-pdrs., 12 32-lb. carronades
Ticonderoga	Schooner	8 12-pdrs., 4 18-lb. columbiads, 5 32-lb. carronades
Preble	Conv. merchantman	7 9-pdrs.
Allen	Row galley	1 24-pdr., 1 18-lb. columbiad
Borer	Row galley	1 24-pdr., 1 18-lb. columbiad
Burrows	Row galley	1 24-pdr., 1 18-lb. columbiad
Centipede	Row galley	1 24-pdr., 1 18-lb. columbiad
Nettle	Row galley	1 24-pdr., 1 18-lb. columbiad
Viper	Gunboat	1 24-pdr., 1 18-lb. columbiad
Alwyn	Gunboat	1 12-pdr.
Ballard	Gunboat	1 12-pdr.
Ludlow	Gunboat	1 12-pdr.
Wilmer	Gunboat	1 12-pdr.
BRITISH		
Confiance	Frigate	27 24-pdrs., 6 24-lb. carronades, 4 32-lb. carronades
Linnet	Brig	16 12-pdrs.
Chub	Conv. merchantman	3 6-pdrs., 8 18-lb. carronades
Finch	Conv. merchantman	4 6-pdrs., 1 18-lb. columbiad, 6 18-lb. carronades
Yeo	Gunboat	1 24-pdr., 1 32-lb. carronade
Prevost	Gunboat	1 24-pdr., 1 32-lb. carronade
Blucher	Gunboat	1 18-pdr., 1 18-lb. carronade
Wellington	Gunboat	1 18-pdr., 1 18-lb. carronade
Murray	Gunboat	1 18-pdr.
Drummond	Gunboat	1 18-pdr.
Beckwith	Gunboat	1 18-pdr.[a]
Popham	Gunboat	1 32-lb. carronade
Beresford	Gunboat	1 32-lb. carronade
Simcoe	Gunboat	1 32-lb. carronade
Brock	Gunboat	1 32-lb. carronade[b]

[a] Formerly *Lord [Cockburn?]*.
[b] "Statement of British Squadron in Action with the American Squadron on Lake Champlain—11 Septr. 1814," in Wood, *British Documents*, 3:476.

smallest gunboats sailed into the bay side by side with their flagship's bow aimed straight at the *Saratoga*—the heart of the U.S. line.

When the masts of the British squadron appeared offshore, Prevost set his troops into motion. Robinson was ordered to move out with parts of his own brigade and some of Power's along the north bank of the Saranac River to a ford about three miles upstream. The defenders, New York militia and Vermont volunteers, broke and ran as hundreds of redcoats splashed across the stream. To cover Robinson's assault, Brisbane's brigade provided a diversion by attacking the two bridges near the river mouth. Here the British encountered stiff resistance from Macomb's regulars. Their musket fire, supported by artillery in the earthworks behind them, held the attackers on the north bank.

Macdonough watched the British squadron struggle toward his line. A man "who feared his foes not at all, but his God a great deal," he chose this moment to kneel on the quarterdeck with his officers and lead them in a prayer for victory.[39] When he stood up, he ordered his signal midshipman to break out a prepared hoist: "Impressed seamen call upon every man to do his duty." Perfect silence ensued while the men grimly waited for the enemy to come within range. Macdonough had merged his four row galley and gunboat divisions into two groups in order to seal off either end of his line. The *Allen, Centipede, Burrows, Alwyn,* and *Ballard* lay to the north of the *Eagle,* thus blocking an enemy attempt to pass between Henley's brig and the Cumberland peninsula. At the other end, the *Viper, Borer, Nettle, Wilmer,* and *Ludlow* lay between the *Commodore Preble* and the tip of the reef extending from Crab Island. For good measure, Macdonough had a 6-pounder cannon moved onto the north end of Crab Island and manned by ambulatory hospital patients. By stationing his force in this manner, he had closed the entire bay to the British—unless Downie's ships could break his line—thus denying Prevost the support of the Royal Navy's broadsides.

Thirty tension-filled minutes later, Robert Henley became the first ship commander on either side to crack under the strain. Shortly after 9:00 A.M. the *Eagle* opened fire prematurely, shattering the silence with a salvo that fell well short. A few minutes thereafter, as the *Linnet* came abreast of the *Saratoga* on her way to engage the *Eagle,* Pring loosed her broadside of long 12-pounders, but his barrage also failed to reach its mark—with a single exception. A spent ball ricocheted off the water, lazily looped over the *Saratoga's* hammock netting, bounced on her deck, and shattered the gamecock's coop. Unbowed, the indignant rooster sprang to the nearest carronade slide, crowed loudly, flapped his wings with furious energy, and flew up to the starboard fore yard, from where he gasconaded loudly throughout the battle. Watching his antics, the previously tight-lipped sailors broke their silence and cheered. The officers might kneel in prayer, but for the men, "a bird in the rigging was worth a dozen prayers on deck."[40]

Moments later, Macdonough fired the *Saratoga's* first shot from his favorite 24-pounder. The ball struck the *Confiance's* bow and blasted its way down the length of her gun deck, slaughtering several crewmen. As his shot echoed away, the American line opened a withering fusillade. The *Confiance,* which had outdistanced her consorts, became their primary target. Downie courageously stood the *Confiance* into the hail of cannonballs and grape without re-

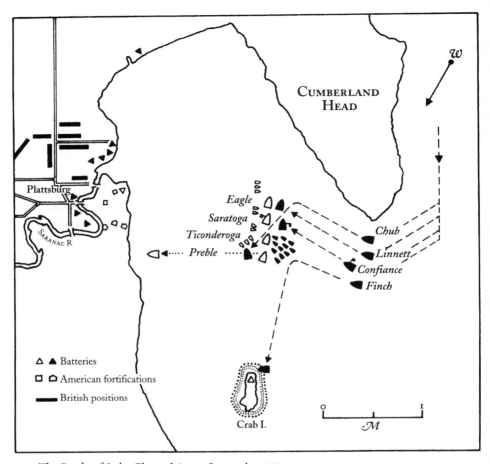

The Battle of Lake Champlain, 11 September 1814.

sponding. The American barrage shot away the cable and spring of her larboard bow anchor, sliced the spring of her starboard bow anchor in two, divested her of both larboard anchors, and cut up her rigging so badly that Downie had to give up any idea of driving between the *Saratoga* and *Eagle*. Instead he ordered the quartermaster to larboard her helm and come to an anchor while still a quarter of a mile from the *Saratoga*. Once moored fore and aft, and before he loosed so much as a single shot, he had his men scamper aloft and alow to furl the sails and secure everything on deck. Not until they finished did he unleash his first broadside. The result was stunning. Thirty-odd 24-pound balls—fired out of carefully aimed, double-shotted cannons at point-blank range from a stable platform lying in smooth water—smashed into the *Saratoga*'s hull. Macdonough's ship shuddered under their impact.

The blast hurled nearly half her crew to the deck. Although many had merely been thrown off their feet, the butcher's bill came to forty killed or wounded. Among the dead lay Peter Gamble, her first lieutenant.[41]

Macdonough quickly rallied his surviving crew, which numbered less than two hundred after the dead and wounded had been sent below. His lieutenants reorganized their gun crews while Macdonough himself pointed and fired his 24-pounder with ferocious concentration. Shortly after Gamble's death, a shot fractured the *Saratoga*'s bare spanker boom. The spar snapped in half, and, in falling, the inboard section grazed Macdonough's head as he bent over his cannon. The blow knocked him unconscious for a moment. Men rushed to his aid, but he waved them off, staggered to his feet, and returned to his gun-laying. Then a grisly incident occurred. An enemy projectile beheaded one of Lt. E. A. F. Vallette's gunners and drove the man's skull into Vallette's face with force enough to send him sprawling.[42] Like his commodore, he quickly returned to his station.

About fifteen minutes into the engagement, the British squadron suffered the loss of its commodore. Downie was standing behind one of the quarterdeck guns when a shot from the *Saratoga* struck its muzzle. The cast-iron monster, weighing nearly three tons, reared up off its carriage and slammed into his midsection. The jolt flattened the watch in his waistcoat pocket, leaving its hands pointing to the second the gun struck him. Downie died before he reached the sick bay. With his demise, command of the *Confiance* devolved upon Robertson, and that of the fleet should have passed to Pring, but the flagship's boats had been shot away and when Robertson "ordered the Signal [to the *Linnet*]," he found that "the Signal Book, in consequence of the Captain's Death, had been mislaid."[43] Thus he had no means to communicate with Pring.

Both squadrons were fully engaged by 9:40 A.M. The *Linnet*, with the *Chub* to her windward, successfully came to anchor at the north end of the U.S. line as Downie had ordered. She was the only British warship to reach and maintain her intended station—a measure of Pring's skill and fortitude. From her position forward of the *Eagle*'s beam, the *Linnet* concentrated a heavy fire at the American's bow. Things did not go so well for the *Linnet*'s consort. Before her skipper, Lt. James McGhie, could position the *Chub* to rake the *Eagle*'s bow, Henley's heavy guns engaged her. They had a shocking effect on the sloop's frail, sixty-one-foot hull. The former merchantman had never been intended to withstand the force of 32-pound carronades fired at half-musket-shot range. Their percussion literally drove her backward. Robertson reported that "*Chub* having never anchored[,] passed astern of the *Linnet*, and dropping between *Confiance* and the *Eagle* and then between that Ship and the *Saratoga* with her colours struck, prevented the *Confiance* for some time from firing on the Enemy, while she drifted slowly within the line of fire."[44] The *Chub* was a perfect wreck: her jib boom shot away, bowsprit shattered, forestay and fore halyard gone, foresail torn from its control lines and hanging over the leeward side in the water, her main boom fractured, throat and peak halyards gone, and her hammocks on fire. Among her nearly forty-man crew, she suffered six killed and sixteen wounded, including McGhie, who lost two fingertips and received a severe splinter wound in the thigh. Only six seamen remained at their stations. The rest, mainly soldiers and marines, fled below. The foresail, acting as a drogue, was tugging the *Chub* toward the *Eagle*'s starboard quarter battery. Midshipman James Bodell assumed command, got the errant canvas back onto the forecastle, and attempted to pull her away by manning the oars, but, as he recalled, "they were shot away nearly as fast as they were got out."[45] With no means of propulsion, the *Chub* drifted helplessly between the *Eagle* and *Saratoga*. From the sick bay, McGhie sent word to Bodell to strike her colors.

The action at the lower end of the line was equally torrid. When the British squadron formed into a line abreast after rounding the headland, Lt. William Hicks found that he could not sail the *Finch* close enough to the faltering breeze to maintain the squadron's course. Although his sloop fell off to leeward, he still managed to bring her into action against the *Commodore Preble* and *Ticonderoga* at about 9:20 A.M. with five British gunboats following a couple of cables' lengths behind. Around forty-five minutes later "when within Pistol Shot," he related, "[I] observed the Enemy's Sloop to slip her cable and haul down her Colours to me."[46] From the *Confiance*, Robertson also witnessed the *Preble* "cut and retire in shore with her colours struck, where however she afterwards rehoisted them."[47] She was the first ship to abandon the U.S. line. Macdonough later condemned her commander, Charles Budd, stating "he did not behave well on the 11th Septr."[48]

Hicks enjoyed but a fleeting moment of glory. After the *Preble* retreated, he turned his guns on the *Ticonderoga*, but this time he caught a tartar. Cassin had been blasting away at the leading British gunboats and sustaining a desultory fire on the *Finch* since about half-past nine, but now that the *Ticonderoga* had received Hicks's full attention, the American skipper promptly retaliated. Many of Cassin's gunners had worked together since they had driven off the attack on Otter Creek the previous May. They fired with lethal precision, a fact confirmed by the recipient of their largesse: "nearly every shot from the Schooner either cut away some of my Rigging or hulded [*sic*] me."[49] By five minutes after ten, the sloop had taken five shots below her waterline and the carpenter advised Hicks "that there was about 3′ Feet of Water in the Hold."[50] The *Ticonderoga* kept up a relentless fire as the sloop scudded toward the reef off Crab Island. Hicks attempted to tack away from that danger spot, but between her shot-torn sails and the baffling winds, the *Finch* fatally missed stays and now came under fire from the 6-pounder manned by the invalids. Unable to tack, he had the helm put to windward and attempted to wear ship, but at that moment she struck the reef. He straightaway ordered his crewmen to heave four of her carronades over the side and had a kedge anchor run out astern in a futile bid to get her off. The sloop's situation was hopeless, and Hicks eventually had to lower her flag. With Downie's death, the *Chub*'s surrender, and the *Finch*'s grounding, the British squadron had suffered the crippling loss of its commodore and two of its principal units very early in the battle.

The Americans' Lieutenant Budd was not the only officer to behave badly. On the British side, Lt. Mark Raynham demonstrated craven cowardice. He had been charged with leading the gunboat flotilla during its attack on the *Ticonderoga* and given instructions to board "the American Schooner . . . before she had fired the third broadside."[51] Trailing behind the *Finch* during the approach, Raynham in the *Yeo* led a line of gunboats that included the *Beresford, Drummond, Murray, Popham,* and *Blucher* to within three cables' length of the *Ticonderoga*. From that safe distance, he "made the Signal to board" to his consorts and then "instantly hauled it down and pulled out of the Action."[52] Reversing course, he rowed back to the *Icicle,* a tender for the British wounded and, although unhurt, vaulted on board her, leaving the *Yeo*'s crew to their own devices. (Days later, he went absent without leave to avoid the inevitable court-martial.) Given the desertion of their flotilla commander and the vacillating breezes, the remainder of the British gunboat force, the *Prevost, Simcoe, Beckwith, Brock,* and *Wellington,* milled around in confusion.

After Raynham fled and the *Ticonderoga* drove the *Finch* out of the battle, Lt. James Bell in the *Murray* gallantly took charge of the five steadfast British gunboats and stormed the *Ticonderoga*. Had he been able to drive her from the American line, he might have won the day, but Cassin fought his schooner too well for that. Unlike Raynham, he gave little thought of his own safety as he stalked about the *Ticonderoga*'s quarterdeck in a constant hail of musketry and grape, miraculously unscathed. On the forecastle, his first lieutenant, John Stansbury, was not so lucky. A cannonball cut him in two.[53]

Cassin carefully tracked each of Bell's probing attacks through the billowing smoke. Early on, he saw the *Drummond* veer off in pursuit of the *Com-*

modore *Preble*, then watched Bell close the other four alongside the *Ticonderoga*, obviously intending to board. He expected assistance from the other division of galleys and gunboats, but, with one exception, they failed to provide it, relying solely on their long guns to support the *Ticonderoga*. Midshipman Thomas Conover in the *Borer* would have none of this and drove forward to engage the British. Unfortunately they saw him coming as he rounded the *Ticonderoga*'s bow and fired a volley that killed three of his men, wounded another, and knocked the fight out of the *Borer*'s militia oarsmen. Macdonough later declared that Conover "bids fair to make a good officer."[54]

Conover's diversion gave Cassin time to load his guns with canister and musket balls, depress their barrels, and let fly. The hail of lead induced a part of the French-Canadian militiamen manning the British gunboats to desert their stations. Twenty-three of them refused to fight in the *Murray*, Bell's own command, and lay down in the bottom of the boat, leaving Bell only ten willing hands to press the attack. Despite these desertions, he led the British boats within a few feet of the schooner several times, but the *Ticonderoga* always beat them off. Bell himself suffered severely. A grapeshot painfully wounded him in the foot, but he propped himself up and carried on. Bell's day came to an end a little later when a round shot from the *Ticonderoga* shattered the *Murray*'s gunwale, and sliced the brave Briton's right leg off above the knee. His coxswain backed the *Murray* from the engagement and rowed Bell to the tender for surgery.

Had it not been for Macdonough's consummate seamanship, which ultimately saved the day, Cassin's stand might well have been the turning point of the battle. But, if his valiant performance against Bell's gunboats pointed toward an American victory, ninety minutes into the engagement an ill-advised move by Henley threatened any chance of achieving it. At 10:30 A.M., without orders from Macdonough, he took the *Eagle* out of the line of battle. "The starboard spring being shot away and the Brig laying exposed to the raking fire of the Enemy," he explained, he had her cables cut "and shifted our position and with a spring brought the Broadside to bear on the Enemy and opened our fire on them again."[55] But his succinct explanation, "shifted our position," did not clarify his actions or expose his true intention. When the *Linnet*'s guns shot the *Eagle*'s anchor spring line away, she swung head to the wind. Until this could be corrected, Henley had no means to answer Pring's raking broadsides. But Henley did not stop for repairs. He dropped astern on the *Saratoga*'s unengaged side and came to anchor between the flagship and the *Ticonderoga*. Macdonough was anything but pleased by Henley's maneuver. "As regards this act of this vessel," he declared, "I am decidedly of opinion her duty was to remain in the station assigned her as long as it was possible for her to maintain it."[56] In Henley's defense, his brig had absorbed a thorough pounding from the *Linnet,* and to his credit, when he gained his new location, he opened a damaging fire on the *Confiance.*

Before the *Eagle's* exodus, Pring had ignored the five galleys and gunboats at his end of the U.S. line, and the *Linnet* had suffered severely from their fire. Now her gunners turned on them with a vengeance. After driving off the pesky gunboats, the *Linnet* directed her broadside on the *Saratoga,* whose forecastle had been left exposed by the *Eagle's* departure.

Left to face the uninterrupted fire of the British frigate on her beam and the brig on her bow, the *Saratoga* suffered heavily. A fire was briskly burning on her deck and another smoldering in the brailed-up spanker. Gradually her guns fell silent, the result either of British broadsides or being unwittingly overcharged by their crews. Finally, Macdonough's last starboard carronade took a direct hit, leaving him without a weapon to oppose the few guns that the *Confiance* and *Linnet* still had firing.

In one of the great exploits of naval history, Macdonough now winded his ship. He began by ordering the kedge anchor suspended from the *Saratoga's* stern away, and then personally directed his sailors as they hauled in the hawser leading to the starboard quarter, and brought the ship's stern up to the kedge. To avoid unnecessarily exposing his gun crews, he ordered them to the forecastle as the ship swung around and exposed her stern to the remnants of the British line. Pring proved the efficacy of Macdonough's action. As soon as the *Saratoga* presented her stern, the *Linnet* raked it with her remaining broadside guns. But then, as the *Saratoga's* sailors hauled her around, one by one the previously unused guns of Lieutenant Vallette's larboard quarter division began to bear on the *Confiance.* He called his men back to their stations and opened fire on her, but before his second gun could engage, the *Saratoga's* swing slowed to a halt. She refused to budge any further. In masterful control of the evolution, Macdonough immediately had the hawser leading from the larboard quarter brought forward under the bow and then carried aft to the starboard quarter. Once the men took a strain on the hawser, the ship began to move again and continued around until all her previously unused larboard battery faced the *Confiance.*

In response, Robertson endeavored to bring the battered British flagship around to her unengaged side, but without the complex turning rig Macdonough had deployed and with the *Confiance's* larboard anchors shot away, he had only the starboard spring lines to employ. Lacking a fulcrum to wind his ship, Robertson's efforts simply forced her forward, and she soon hung there with her head to the wind. The *Saratoga* fired several broadsides with terrible effect, particularly from her three fresh carronades. On board the *Confiance,* "the Ship's Company declared they would stand no longer to their Quarters, nor could the Officers with their utmost determination rally them."[57] Reluctantly, Robertson lowered the British colors.

At the sight of the red ensign fluttering down on the *Confiance,* Macdonough had his men haul the starboard hawser further inboard until the *Saratoga*'s guns began to bear on the *Linnet.* In the pause before the *Saratoga* could resume fire, Pring sent his first lieutenant, William Drew, to the flagship for orders. When Drew returned, Pring learned for the first time of Downie's death. He had little time for sympathy, as by then Macdonough had opened a one-sided ship-to-ship duel with his brig. The Briton valiantly maintained this very unequal contest for fifteen minutes, but when the water in her hull reached a foot above her berth deck, he had to haul down the *Linnet*'s colors before she sank. At this point, none of the principal ships in either squadron possessed a spar worthy of bearing canvas. Most were in sinking condition. The *Saratoga* had been hulled 55 times and the *Confiance,* 105.

As the cannon fell silent, the British gunboats reformed at the south end of the line. Vallette boarded the *Confiance* to take possession of her; but, as he passed along the shambles of her gun deck, he accidentally trod upon the lock string of one of her cannon. The flint sparked, and the gun, which had been loaded before the end of the battle, went off. Apparently taking its blast as a signal to retreat, the British gunboats pulled toward Cumberland Head, with *Icicle* in company. The American gunboats went in pursuit, but Macdonough signaled a recall. The commodore desperately needed their crews to help keep his ships and their prizes afloat. With this incident, the Battle of Lake Champlain came to a close, a little more than two and a half hours after Henley had fired the opening gun.

Macdonough returned his personnel loss as fifty-two killed and fifty-eight wounded; but the wounded apparently only included those who had to enter the hospital. Another ninety men were more or less slightly wounded. British casualties totaled 54 dead and 116 wounded. When the captured British officers were assembled onboard the *Saratoga,* Macdonough returned their swords in honor of their bravery. As soon as word of the disaster reached his headquarters, Prevost, fearing that his supply lines would be cut by the American squadron, ordered a retreat. The British withdrawal was so precipitate that Wellington's legions were eight miles beyond Plattsburg before General Macomb realized what had happened. Before sunset, Macdonough dispatched a message to Secretary Jones: "The Almighty has been pleased to

Grant us a Signal Victory on Lake Champlain in the Capture of one Frigate, one Brig and two sloops of war of the enemy."[58]

With Prevost's withdrawal into Canada, the border remained safe for the balance of the war. But of far greater historical significance, the international picture changed dramatically with Macdonough's victory. The London *Times* bemoaned: "This is a lamentable event to the civilized world." At the peace conference in Ghent, Belgium, the British negotiating policy—predicated on the acquisition of territory—slowly collapsed. On 24 December 1814, peace was concluded on the basis of the prewar status quo.

NOTES

1. Rodney Macdonough, *Life of Commodore Thomas Macdonough, U.S. Navy* (Boston, 1909), 157.

2. Leonard F. Guttridge and Jay D. Smith, *The Commodores* (London, 1970), 257.

3. C. P. Lucas, *The Canadian War of 1812* (Oxford, [1906]), 196–97.

4. William S. Dudley, ed., *The Naval War of 1812, A Documentary History* (Washington, D C., 1985), 1.319–20.

5. "The Autobiography of Commodore Thomas Macdonough," in Macdonough, *Commodore Macdonough, 26*

6. Jones to Macdonough, 28 January 1814, Record Group 45 (hereafter RG 45), M-149, roll 11, pt. 2, 191, National Archives (hereafter NA).

7. Macdonough to Jones, 30 April 1814, RG 45, M-147, roll 5, pt. 2, no. 115, NA.

8. Macdonough, *Commodore Macdonough*, 137, 139.

9. Ibid , 139.

10. Henry P. Smith, ed., *History of Addison County, Vermont* (Syracuse, 1886), 231.

11. Macdonough to Jones, 30 April 1814, RG 45, M-147, roll 5, pt 2, no. 115, NA.

12. Dennis M. Lewis, "British Naval Activity on Lake Champlain during the War of 1812," unpublished manuscript, July 1982, New York State Library, #3662, and *Plattsburg Republican,* 14 May 1814, p. 3, c. 3; Russell P. Bellico, *Sails and Steam in the Mountains: A Maritime and Military History of Lake George and Lake Champlain* (Fleischmanns, N.Y., 1992), 216; Izard to Armstrong, 13 May 1814, RG 107, M-221, roll 7, NA.

13. Lewis, "British Naval Activities," 17; Macdonough to Jones, 14 May 1814, RG 45, M-147, roll 5, pt. 2, NA.

14. Macdonough, *Commodore Macdonough,* 146–47.

15. Jones to Madison, 6 May 1814, James Madison Papers, Library of Congress.

16 Macdonough to Jones, 8 June 1814, RG 45, M-147, roll 5, pt 2, no. 143, NA.

17 Macdonough to Jones, 11 June 1814, ibid, no. 145

18 Peter Burroughs, "Sir George Prevost," in *Dictionary of Canadian Biography* (Toronto, 1983), 5:696.

19. Benson J. Lossing, *The Pictorial Fieldbook of the War of 1812* (1869; reprint, Somersworth, N.H., 1976), 856; Major General R. H. Sheafe to Prevost, 5 June 1814, in William C. H. Wood, ed., *Select British Documents of the Canadian War of 1812* (Toronto, 1920–28), 2:227.

20. Macdonough, *Commodore Macdonough,* 148–50.

21. Macdonough to Jones, 19 June 1814, RG 45, M-147, roll 5, pt. 2, no. 146, NA

22. Macdonough to Jones, 26 June 1814, ibid., no. 152

23. Macdonough to Jones, 9 July 1814, ibid.

24. Macdonough to Jones, 13 July 1814, ibid., no 5.

25. Edward K. Eckert, *The Navy Department in the War of 1812* (Gainesville, Fla., 1973), 33; Irving Brant, *James Madison* (Indianapolis, 1961), 6:273; Jones to Bullus, 5 July 1814, RG 45, entry 441, roll 1, pt. 2, no. 121, NA.

26. Izard to Armstrong, 19 July and 7 August 1814, in James Pack, *The Man Who Burned the White House* (Annapolis, 1987), 196–97.

27. Izard to Armstrong, 11 August 1814, ibid. C. Edward Skeen, *John Armstrong, Jr., 1758–1843: A Biography* (Syracuse, 1981), 185.

28. Reginald Horsman, *The War of 1812* (New York, 1969), 187–88.

29. John Wilson Croker, MP, First Secretary to Their Lords Commissioners of the Admiralty, to Captain George Downie, RN, 1 March 1814, in Wood, *British Documents*, 3 334; Thomas Hooper, "The Royal Navy Station at Isle aux Noix (1812–1839)," unpublished manuscript, Fort Lennox National Historic Site, St. Paul de l'Ile aux Noix, Quebec, September 1967, 17.

30. Allan S. Everest, *The War of 1812 in the Champlain Valley* (Syracuse, 1891), 162

31. Macdonough, *Commodore Macdonough*, 153–56.

32. Macomb to Armstrong, 15 September 1814, RG 107, M-221, roll 64, NA

33 Downie to Prevost, 7 September 1814, in Wood, *British Documents*, 3:379.

34. Prevost to Downie, 8 September 1814, ibid., 3·379–80

35. Downie to Prevost, 8 September, ibid., 3:380.

36. Prevost to Downie, 9 September 1814, ibid , 3:381.

37. Downie to Prevost, 9 September 1814, ibid , 3:382.

38. Ibid , 1.124.

39. Theodore Roosevelt, *The Naval War of 1812* (New York, 1882), 389.

40. Waldo H. Heinrichs Jr , "The Battle of Plattsburg, 1814—The Losers," *The American Neptune* 21 (January 1961): 54.

41. Ibid.

42. Lossing, *Pictorial Fieldbook of the War of 1812*, 872.

43. Testimony of Lt James B. Robertson, "The Plattsburg Court Martial 18th to 21st August—1815," in Wood, *British Documents*, 3:374–75.

44. Ibid., 3:471

45. Testimony of Midshipman John Bodell, ibid., 3:425

46. Hicks to Pring, 12 September 1814, ibid., 3.483; "Narrative of the Proceedings of H M. Cutter *Finch* in Action with the American Squadron [*sic*]; on the 11th day of September, 1814 in Plattsburg Bay, Lake Champlain," ibid., 3:495–96.

47. Testimony of Lieutenant James B. Robertson, "The Plattsburg Court Martial 18th to 21st August—1815," ibid., 3:473.

48. Macdonough to Commo John Rodgers, President of the Board of Navy Commissioners, 6 May 1814, RG 45, Subject File NI, NA.

49. Hicks to Pring, 12 September 1814, "Narrative of the Proceedings of H.M. Cutter *Finch* in Action with the American Squadron [*sic*]; on the 11th day of September, 1814 in Plattsburg Bay, Lake Champlain," in Wood, *British Documents*, 3 495.

50. Ibid , 3:496.

51. Testimony of Lt Christopher James Bell, "The Plattsburg Court Martial 18th to 21st August—1815," ibid , 3:432.

52. Testimony of Lt. James B. Robertson, "The Plattsburg Court Martial 18th to 21st August—1815," ibid.

53. Lossing, *Pictorial Fieldbook of the War of 1812*, 872.

54. Ibid.

55. Kevin Hames Crisman, *The EAGLE, an American Brig on Lake Champlain during the War of 1812* (Shelburne, Vt., 1987), 226.

56. "The Autobiography of Commodore Thomas Macdonough," in Macdonough, *Life of Commodore Macdonough*, 30.

57. Robertson to Pring, 12 September 1814, "Narrative of the Proceedings of H.M. Cutter *Finch* in Action with the American Squadron [*sic*]; on the 11th day of September, 1814 in Plattsburg Bay, Lake Champlain," in Wood, *British Documents*, 3:374.

58. Macdonough to Jones, 11 September 1814, RG 45, M-125, reel 39, NA.

6

The Battle of Hampton Roads

WILLIAM N. STILL JR.

The first shots of the Civil War were fired by forces of the Confederate States of America at Fort Sumter, a Federal installation in the harbor of Charleston, South Carolina, on 12 April 1861. The election of Abraham Lincoln, the Republican candidate for president, in November 1860 had brought the decades-old differences between North and South to a head. Seven southern states seceded from the Union between December 1860 and February 1861, and in the latter month they organized their own government. The refusal of Sumter's commander, Maj. Robert Anderson, to surrender the post to Confederate authorities within the time specified by their ultimatum touched off the conflagration. When President Lincoln responded to the attack on the fort by calling out seventy-five thousand militia to put down the "insurrection," four more states adhered to the Confederacy. The four grueling years of war that followed cost both North and South more casualties than the entire nation would suffer in World War II.

In addition to raising troops, Lincoln proclaimed a blockade of the thirty-five hundred miles of Confederate coastline from the Potomac to the Rio Grande. To deny the cotton-exporting, agrarian South access to the markets and industry of Western Europe would deal it a devastating blow. The enforcement of the blockade, the primary task of Union sea power throughout the war, obviously required a sizeable navy. With only ninety ships in inventory and few more than half in commission, the navy of 1861 did not meet that definition, but by 1864 it had become the largest in the world, with nearly seven hundred vessels in service.

Although the South was significantly inferior to the North in virtually every quantifiable category of war-making potential, it had one great advantage. To reunite the country, the North would have to win the war; to uphold its independence, the South would simply have to avoid losing. Confederate strategy was therefore fundamentally defensive. Southern leaders compared the Confederacy's position in the Civil War to that of the thirteen colonies in the War of Independence. Ideally, Britain and/or France would intervene in its behalf; but even if that failed to happen, just by prolonging the struggle the Confederacy could wear out the Union's will to win.

The imposition of the blockade and the adoption of the "Anaconda Plan" proposed by Gen. Winfield Scott to subdue the South by occupying its ports and seizing control of the Mississippi forced the Confederate Navy to concentrate on defending home waters. It sent out commerce raiders in the American tradition of *guerre de course,* but it never contested Union command of the sea. Instead, it sought to collaborate with the army to stop the enemy from gaining access to the interior of the Confederacy via its waterways and to keep its ports open to foreign trade.[1]

The war was a milestone in the advance of military technology. Never before had rail transport, the telegraph, rifled guns, repeating small arms, underwater mines, and ironclad warships been so widely utilized. From a naval perspective, the most influential of these weapons and inventions was the ironclad. The Civil War was not the first conflict in which such ships entered action. Three French armored "floating batteries" had overcome the Russian fortress at Kinburn, on the Black Sea, late in the Crimean War (1853–56). But the Civil War provided the setting for the first battle between ironclads.

Both the Union and Confederate navies quickly decided to build armored ships. They clearly drew their inspiration from developments in Europe. Encouraged by the success of her floating batteries, France had begun laying down seagoing ironclads in 1858. The first of them, the *Gloire,* was launched the following year. Britain responded in kind, and by May 1861 the two foremost sea powers had a total of twenty-eight ironclads under construction or afloat.

The Confederacy hastened to follow their example. On 10 May 1861, Secretary of the Navy Stephen R. Mallory informed the chairman of the congressional Committee on Naval Affairs that "I regard the possession of an iron-armored ship as a matter of the first necessity. Such a vessel at this time could traverse the entire coast of the United States, prevent all blockades, and encounter, with a fair prospect of success, their entire Navy. . . . Should the committee deem it expedient to begin at once the construction of such a ship, not a moment should be lost."[2] The Confederate Congress promptly

The Confederate States of America.

appropriated $2 million for the acquisition of ironclads from European ship-yards.

Mallory also hoped that it would be possible to build such vessels in the Confederacy. On 10 June, three weeks after dispatching a purchasing agent to Europe, he directed Lt. John M. Brooke, one of the new navy's most talented officers, to design an ironclad. The plan for a casemated vessel with inclined sides was finalized on 23 June at a conference in Richmond between Mallory, Brooke, and two officials summoned from the Gosport Navy Yard at Norfolk, Naval Constructor John L. Porter and Chief Engineer William P. Williamson. In the following days, they discovered that no engines of the size the ship would require were available in the Confederacy. Williamson then suggested using the engines and hull of the screw frigate *Merrimack,* which had been partly burned and scuttled by Union forces during the evacuation of the Gosport Navy Yard in April. Upon investigation, Brooke and Porter endorsed his proposal, and on 11 July Mallory gave the project the go-ahead.[3]

Brooke was responsible for the ironclad's armor and ordnance, Porter supervised her construction, and Williamson overhauled the *Merrimack*'s two engines. Before the end of the year Porter had begun to claim exclusive credit for the ship's design, a claim he would press for three decades, but the evidence indicates that it belonged chiefly to Brooke. Work was supposed to have been finished in November, but problems arose in procuring armor. The Tredegar Iron Works in Richmond, which had undertaken to furnish the materials, had trouble obtaining the amount of iron required. A shortage of rolling stock to carry the plate to Norfolk made matters worse. Seven months passed before the ironclad was completed.[4]

On 17 February 1862, the ship was launched and commissioned the CSS *Virginia*. She was 262 feet in length and 51 feet abeam and had a 22-foot draft. Her hull had been cut down almost to the waterline and decked over to support a wooden casemate 194 feet, 8 inches long. The rounded ends and sides of this structure sloped outward at an angle of thirty-five degrees, the greatest inclination at which her guns could be worked, and were plated with two layers of armor, each two inches thick, rolled from scrap iron and railroad rails. The inner layer was bolted horizontally and the outer vertically. The casemate was topped by a two-inch-thick iron grating that formed the *Virginia*'s upper deck. Access was through three hatchways covered by pivoting shutters. Forward, a conical, cast-iron pilothouse with sides a foot thick was positioned at its edge. The decks fore and aft of the casemate and the sides of the hull were protected by a single inch of iron extending three feet below the projected waterline. The ends of the hull and the eaves of the casemate were to be submerged a depth of two feet. Beside shielding the thinly armored hull from enemy fire, this feature was intended to improve the vessel's buoyancy by means of ballast tanks built into her bow and stern. Brooke also believed it would increase her speed. A false bow was added to prevent water from banking in front of the casemate.[5]

The *Virginia* carried a total of ten guns. Two 7-inch rifled guns Lieutenant Brooke designed specifically for her were mounted on pivots at the ends of the casemate. Three gun ports allowed each of these pieces to fire ahead and to both sides. Two 6.4-inch Brooke rifles were placed in broadside along with six 9-inch smoothbore Dahlgren guns. One of the Dahlgrens in each broadside was capable of firing hot shot. Finally, a wedge-shaped, 1,500-pound cast-iron ram was bolted—none too securely—to the ship's bow.[6] The addition of this antique device reflected the latest trends in naval tactical thought. Bearing in mind the facts that at Kinburn the French floating batteries had been unharmed by enemy fire but that steamers often sank ships with which they collided, many officers reasoned that the ram might well replace the gun as the most effective naval weapon.

The *Virginia*'s complement numbered 320 officers and men, including 55 marines. Most of her crewmen were volunteers from the army. All except a few of her officers were veterans of the U.S. Navy. She was not assigned a captain. Secretary Mallory's choice for the post was Capt. Franklin Buchanan, at sixty-two a veteran of forty-seven years' naval service, but officers with even longer service applied for it. Mallory circumnavigated this difficulty by naming Buchanan flag officer in command of the naval defenses of the James River. The *Virginia* would be his flagship.[7]

The ship's executive officer was quiet, forty-one-year-old Lieutenant Catesby ap Roger Jones. Assigned to the vessel in November 1861, he had been in charge of fitting her out. He had hoped to obtain command himself but resolved to give Buchanan the best service he could render.[8] An ordnance specialist, Jones enjoyed the esteem of his contemporaries in both navies. Years later, David Dixon Porter, next to Farragut the Union's most prominent admiral, stated that there were only two U.S. naval officers whose resignations he had regretted: John M. Brooke and Catesby Jones.[9] The *Virginia's* surgeon, Dinwiddie B. Phillips, a veteran of the Old Navy, believed that Jones was "head and shoulders above Buchanan in ability"—but Phillips was not among Buchanan's admirers.[10]

When Buchanan reached Norfolk on 25 February 1862, he found that Jones had the *Virginia* almost ready for action. Jones was not altogether happy with her, however. Greatly to his consternation, Constructor Porter had miscalculated the ship's displacement. Neither her bow nor her stern nor the eaves of her casemate, all of which were to have been two feet underwater, did much more than break its surface. This was especially serious in the case of the eaves, below which the hull carried a bare inch of armor. Even after all the ballast the vessel's bottom would bear had been added, the exposed areas were not submerged more than a few inches. The knowledge that a shot striking at her waterline might perforate the *Virginia's* hull caused Jones concern throughout the vessel's career. An even worse flaw was her engines, which had been condemned at the end of the *Merrimack's* last cruise. They had not benefitted from weeks underwater and at best gave the *Virginia* a speed of only seven knots. Her helm was so sluggish that she needed at least half an hour to turn 180 degrees and often took more than half a mile to do so.[11] In addition, the armored shutters for her broadside gun ports had yet to be installed.[12]

Hampton Roads, the scene of the *Virginia's* forthcoming operations, is the basin into which the James, Nansemond, and Elizabeth Rivers empty before flowing into the Chesapeake Bay. At the widest, above the mouth of the Elizabeth River, the basin is some seven miles across, but the *Virginia's* draft would confine her to the channel inside the three-fathom line, never more than two miles wide and in part obstructed by the Middle Ground shoal. The

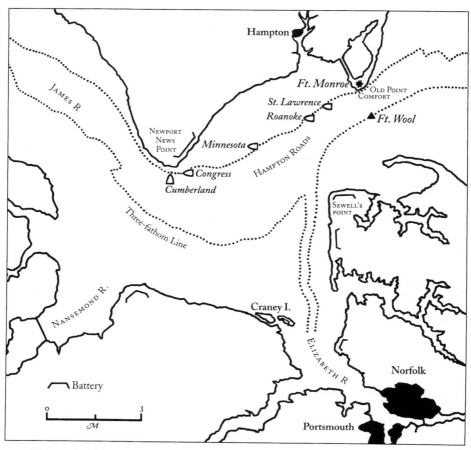

The Battle of Hampton Roads, 8–9 March 1862.

northern shore was occupied by Union troops; the southern, by Confederate. The two days' battle would therefore be witnessed by thousands of men in both armies as well as crowds of local residents. Some Confederates even went out in boats to get a closer look.[13]

Before leaving Richmond, Buchanan tried to interest Maj. Gen. John B. Magruder, commanding the Confederate forces north of the James, in a combined operation against the Union position at Newport News. While Magruder's troops assaulted the enemy lines, Buchanan's ships would attack the blockaders in Hampton Roads. When the army proved unreceptive, he decided to go ahead with the naval part of the program. His force would consist of the *Virginia, Beaufort,* and *Raleigh,* all based on Norfolk, and the three vessels comprising Cdr. John R. Tucker's James River Squadron, the *Patrick Henry, Jamestown,* and *Teaser.* All except the *Virginia* were wooden gunboats converted from civilian craft. The *Beaufort, Raleigh,* and *Teaser* were former tugs armed with one gun each; the side-wheelers *Jamestown,* with two guns, and *Patrick Henry,* with twelve, had been passenger steamers.

Buchanan planned to sortie on 6 March. Bad weather imposed a delay, but at 12:45 P.M. on Sunday, 8 March, Union lookouts spotted the *Virginia, Beaufort,* and *Raleigh* emerging from the Elizabeth River. At first glance, one observer thought the ironclad looked "like the roof a very big barn belching forth smoke as from a chimney on fire."[14] The Confederate gunboats in the James got under way as soon as the *Virginia* was seen coming out from behind Craney Island.

The portion of the North Atlantic Blockading Squadron anchored in Hampton Roads that morning constituted an impressive force. There were five big ships, the screw frigates *Minnesota* and *Roanoke,* both of fifty guns, the sailing frigates *St. Lawrence* and *Congress,* both of forty-four, and the sailing sloop of war *Cumberland,* twenty-four, plus a number of gunboats and armed tugs mounting from one to five guns. Northerners had been aware that the *Merrimack* was being converted into an ironclad for months. Nevertheless her sortie took the ships in the Roads by surprise. Several had laundry hanging in their rigging and boats at their booms. The two nearest the Elizabeth River channel, the *Congress* and *Cumberland,* would presumably be the first to be attacked. Because of the *Virginia's* slow speed, they had almost an hour to clear for action. The frigates anchored to the east, off Fortress Monroe, started forward to support them but ran aground on the shoals that extended from the northern shore of the Roads.

The ensuing battle affirmed that this war was truly a fratricidal conflict, for as Franklin Buchanan knew, his brother McKean was paymaster in the *Congress.* The *Virginia's* clerk believed that when Buchanan told the crew, "I intend to do my duty, men, and I expect you to do yours," he was alluding to that fact. Happily, McKean Buchanan passed through the engagement unharmed.[15]

Buchanan had decided to begin the action by ramming the *Cumberland,* which carried heavier guns than the *Congress.* The opening shot was fired by Lt. William Harwar Parker's little *Beaufort* at the *Congress* at exactly 2:00 P.M. Moments later, the *Virginia* hoisted the signal for "close action," the only one she made that day. While the *Virginia* proceeded toward the *Cumberland,* the *Beaufort* and *Raleigh* continued to annoy the *Congress.* With only two guns

TABLE 6.1 The Battle of Hampton Roads, 8–9 March 1862

	Commissioned	Displacement	Speed	Complement	Guns
U.S. NAVY[a]					
Capt. J. Marston[b]					
Ironclad					
Monitor	1862	987	7	53	2
Screw frigates					
Minnesota	1857	4,883	12.5	646	50[c]
Roanoke	1857	4,772	11	674	50[c]
Sailing frigates					
Congress	1842	1,867	—	480	44[c]
St. Lawrence	1848	1,726	—	400	44[c]
Sailing sloop					
Cumberland	1843	1,726[d]	—	376	24[c]
Gunboats					
Cambridge	1859/61[e]	?	10.5	96	4
Dragon	1861/62[e]	?	?	42	2
Whitehall	1850/61[e]	?	?	?	4
Armed tugs					
Young America	1857/61[e]	173	?	13	3
Zouave	1861/61[e]	127	10	25	2
C.S. NAVY					
Flag Officer F. Buchanan					
Ironclad ram					
Virginia (flagship)	1859/62[f]	4,636[g]	7	320	10
Gunboats					
Beaufort	1854/61[e]	85	?	35	1
Jamestown	1853/61[e]	1,300	?	+/−150	2
Patrick Henry	1853/61[e]	1,300	?	150	12
Raleigh	?/1861[e]	65	?	+/−25	1
Teaser	1855?/61[e]	64	?	25	1

[a] Only vessels directly involved in the battle are included

[b] Senior officer present afloat

[c] Rated totals, from which the number actually aboard usually varied

[d] As a frigate; cut down into a sloop of war in 1855–56

[e] Date completed/date taken into naval service

[f] Date commissioned as USS *Merrimack*/date commissioned as CSS *Virginia*

[g] Prior to conversion

between them, the gunboats could hardly hope to do the frigate much harm. Conscious of the ruin her broadside might inflict on them, they were careful to remain outside its reach.[16]

The *Cumberland* lay about eight hundred yards west of Newport News Point. The tide had pulled her athwart the channel, with her stern pointing out and her keel in line with her spring anchors, so she could not be swung to direct a broadside at her oncoming assailant. When a few guns could be brought to bear, their shot ricocheted off the *Virginia*'s greased armor. The response from the ironclad's bow pivot gun was deadly. Its first shell struck the *Cumberland*'s starboard quarter, killing or wounding nine marines. The second knocked out one of the guns that had come into action and cut down its entire sixteen-man crew with the exception of the powder boy.[17]

As she neared the *Cumberland*, the *Virginia* drew abreast the *Congress*. The Union ship, which had been firing the guns that would bear, greeted her with a broadside. Fortunately for the ironclad's crew, no shots entered her open gun ports, and those that struck her casemate bounced off. The broadside the *Virginia* returned dismounted one of the frigate's guns, killing or wounding its crew, and started serious fires in two places.

Closing at almost a right angle to her target's starboard side, the *Virginia* struck the *Cumberland* well forward, punching a great hole below her waterline. At once, the stricken vessel began to go down by the bow. She almost took the *Virginia* with her, the impact having embedded the ironclad's ram in her hull. It broke loose when the strain became too great, and the *Virginia* managed to back away. The movement brought her nearly parallel to the *Cumberland,* and Lt. Thomas O. Selfridge, commanding the sloop's forward gun division, recorded that "[t]hree solid broadsides in quick succession were pounded into the *Merrimac* at a distance of not more than one hundred yards."[18] The ironclad's armor deflected the shot, but two of her Dahlgren guns had their muzzles blown off. Both remained in use, although the barrel of one was so short that each discharge set the woodwork framing its gun port on fire. The *Cumberland*'s captain was absent, but her executive officer, Lt. George U. Morris, kept her in action to the end.

The Confederate ironclad continued to shell the *Cumberland* as she sank. Lt. John Taylor Wood, in command of the *Virginia*'s stern pivot gun, recalled, "The [Union] crew were driven by the advancing water to the spar-deck, and there worked her pivot-guns until she went down with a roar, her colors still flying. No ship was ever fought more gallantly."[19]

The *Virginia* was now ready to attack the *Congress*, anchored only a few hundred yards to the east. First, however, she would have to turn around. As a result of her poor handling characteristics and the restrictions her deep draft imposed on her movements, she required almost half an hour to accomplish this feat. The *Beaufort* and *Raleigh* were still banging away at the *Congress* when, at about 4:00 P.M., the *Virginia* lumbered toward her. Commander Tucker's gunboats reached the scene of the action about this time, having fought a brisk running battle with the Union batteries at Newport News as they emerged from the James.

In the meanwhile, the *Congress*'s young commander, Lt. Joseph B. Smith, had slipped her anchor, and, with the help of the armed tug *Zouave,* grounded her under cover of the batteries at Newport News Point. This was a shrewd move, but it had an unwelcome side effect. The tide swung the frigate's stern into the Roads so that only two guns could be trained on her adversary.

Still, Smith had succeeded in making it impossible for the *Virginia* to ram. The closest she could come to the *Congress* without running aground herself was about two hundred yards. Taking position under the frigate's exposed stern, the ironclad opened a relentless, raking fire. In a matter of minutes, the *Congress* lost nearly a quarter of her crew, more than a hundred men. The *Zouave* also took some hits, one of which disabled her rudder. The gunboat *Whitehall* towed her to safety.[20] Soon the *Patrick Henry* joined the *Virginia,* *Beaufort,* and *Raleigh* in pouring shells into the *Congress.* Although the frigate's two guns were soon knocked out, she stood the fire for nearly an hour before striking her flag. Lieutenant Smith had been decapitated by a shell fragment a few minutes earlier. When his father, a commodore on duty in Washington, heard that the *Congress* had surrendered, he said quietly, "Joe's dead."[21]

Buchanan directed the *Beaufort* and *Raleigh* to take the frigate's officers prisoner, rescue the wounded, allow the remainder of the crew to escape, and burn the ship. Lieutenant Parker received the *Congress*'s surrender from her executive officer. Minutes later, Union troops ashore opened a terrific fire on all three vessels, killing and wounding friend and foe. The Confederate gunboats quickly cast off. Unaware of the reason why Parker had not set fire to the *Congress,* Buchanan sent his flag lieutenant, Robert D. Minor, with eight men in an open boat to carry out his order. Two hundred and fifty yards from the *Congress* the party came under fire and turned back with Minor and two of his men wounded.[22]

This time Buchanan, standing on the *Virginia*'s upper deck, saw what had happened, but he assumed the shots came from the *Congress.* Being in Surgeon Phillips's words, "naturally high-tempered and easily excitable," Buchanan became furious. "Burn that damned ship, Mr. Jones," he shouted, "she is firing upon our boat under her flags of surrender."[23] Then, grabbing a rifle, the flag officer began shooting at the Union vessel. The *Virginia* backed close astern the *Congress* and commenced fire with hot shot and incendiary shell. Soon the frigate was in flames. In the course of these events, Buchanan was badly wounded in the left leg by a rifle ball from shore, and Catesby Jones assumed command.

Having disposed of the *Congress,* Jones turned his attention to the *Minnesota,* the nearest of the frigates that had grounded earlier in the day.

Together with the *Jamestown* and *Patrick Henry*, the *Virginia* steamed toward the enemy ship. Shoal water stopped her a mile away, and after what Jones called "a distant and unsatisfactory fire," he decided to withdraw. It was past 6:00 P.M. The light was already too dim for accurate gunnery, and the *Virginia*'s pilots were afraid of running aground in the dark. The Confederate squadron retired to anchor off Sewell's Point for the night.[24]

In less than five hours, two major Union warships had been destroyed, another damaged, and a minor vessel disabled. Union casualties amounted to about 250 dead and 75 wounded. Another twenty-six men who boarded the *Beaufort* from the *Congress* were captured. Of the Confederate vessels, the *Virginia* alone had sustained visible damage. She had been hit approximately one hundred times. Her casemate was scoured clean of boats, davits, railings, and flagstaffs, and as Phillips put it, "her smoke-stack would have permitted a flock of crows to fly through it without inconvenience."[25] Her ram remained in the *Cumberland*, she was leaking at the bow, two of her guns had been damaged, and some of her armor plates loosened. Two crewmen had been killed and eight others wounded seriously enough to be listed in Phillips's official report. Total Confederate casualties numbered about thirty.[26]

With the coming of darkness, the flames climbing over the *Congress* created a spectacle witnesses never forgot. A midshipman in the *Patrick Henry* related that "[t]he *Congress* presented a beautiful sight as she burned. . . . As her guns became heated they were discharged like signal guns of a ship in distress on a lee shore in a gale. Step by step the fire mounted until we had topsail, topgallant and royal seas of fire instead of canvas."[27]

That night, the Confederates carried out the repairs they could make with the materials at hand. Jones planned to resume the action at daybreak. At 6:00 A.M. the *Virginia* led the *Patrick Henry*, *Jamestown*, and *Teaser* into the Roads to destroy the still-stranded *Minnesota*. Beside the frigate the Confederates made out a small, odd-shaped craft that some took to be a boiler on a raft. The craft was the USS *Monitor*.

The *Monitor* was the creation of John Ericsson, a brilliant, cantankerous Swedish engineer who had migrated to the United States twenty-two years earlier. He had forwarded plans for a similar vessel to Napoleon III during the Crimean War, but the emperor had not considered them worth pursuing. In August 1861 Union Secretary of the Navy Gideon Welles had invited interested parties to submit proposals for ironclad warships to a board of three senior officers. Like the French emperor, the Ironclad Board initially rejected Ericsson's unorthodox design, but changed its mind after a masterful presentation by the inventor himself. In September it approved the construction of three ironclads, one of which became the *Monitor*.[28] The contract, signed on 4 October, required her to be delivered to the navy by 12 January 1862.

On 25 October 1861, the *Monitor's* keel was laid at the Continental Iron Works on Long Island, New York. In contrast to the delays the Confederacy's industrial inadequacy imposed on the construction of the *Virginia*, work on what skeptics called "Ericsson's Folly" proceeded at a rapid rate.[29] Even the indefatigable Ericsson was unable to meet the hundred-day deadline, but he succeeded in launching her on 30 January. By 19 February the *Monitor* was completed, fully loaded, and ready for trials.[30]

It is revealing of the way Ericsson thought about his creation that he customarily referred to the *Monitor* as a battery or steam battery rather than as a vessel or a ship. In place of a conventional hull, the *Monitor* had an armored "raft" 179 feet long and 41 feet abeam supported by an iron lower hull 122 feet long and 30 feet abeam. The raft, protected by 1 inch of armor on deck and 4 inches on the sides, overhung and shielded the hull to a depth of 3 feet, 6 inches all around. Amidships was a revolving, cylindrical turret weighing 120 tons. The pilothouse, which protruded 3 feet, 10 inches above the deck, was encased in wrought-iron beams 9 inches thick. The turret and the pilothouse were the extent of the *Monitor's* superstructure. Her freeboard was a mere 18 inches and her draft only 10 feet, 6 inches.[31] Ericsson designed her two engines to give her a speed of nine knots, about two more than she actually achieved.

The *Monitor's* numerous technological innovations included forced-draft ventilation of her interior and an armored well through which her anchor could be worked without coming under fire. One of her engineering officers calculated that she incorporated forty patentable inventions. Although (as Ericsson took pains to point out) the idea of a rotating gun platform was not new, what struck contemporaries as the ship's most revolutionary feature was her turret. Nine feet high and twenty feet in diameter, it housed two 11-inch Dahlgren smoothbores side by side behind eight layers of inch-thick wrought-iron plates.

Forty-three-year-old Lt. John L. Worden was selected to command the *Monitor*. Since receiving his midshipman's warrant in 1834, Worden had performed a quarter-century of creditable though by no means conspicuous service. He had, however, created a favorable impression on Commo. Joseph Smith (the father of the *Congress's* captain), who as chairman of the Ironclad Board was instrumental in his appointment to the *Monitor*. "This vessel is an experiment," he told Worden. "I believe you are the right sort of officer to put in command of her."[32] In an age when men were not embarrassed to admit a

John L. Worden. A portrait taken after his promotion to rear admiral in 1872. *U.S. Naval Institute*

thirst for glory, Worden confessed that his "greatest hope" was to become a hero.[33] Captured by Confederates while returning overland from a mission to Pensacola, Florida, in April 1861, he was exchanged in November. At the time he took command of the *Monitor* he had not fully recovered from the effects of seven months in prison. Paymaster William F. Keeler, whose letters to his wife Anna are an invaluable source of information on life aboard the *Monitor,* described Worden as "tall, thin & quite effeminate looking, notwithstanding a long beard hanging down his breast—he is white & delicate probably from long confinement & never was a lady the possessor of a smaller or more delicate hand. . . . He is a perfect gentleman in manner."[34]

Worden assumed command on 16 January. The *Monitor* was commissioned on 25 February. She carried a complement of ten officers and forty-seven petty officers and men. Both were a combination of prewar regulars and wartime volunteers.

The *Monitor* left New York for southern waters under tow of the tug *Seth Low* on 6 March. It had been hoped that she could set out the day after her commissioning, but a steering defect and bad weather delayed her departure. The two ships entered the Chesapeake Bay at noon on 8 March. Four hours later, the rumble of distant cannon became audible. Worden immediately had the *Monitor* cleared for action. Near Hampton Roads a pilot boat confirmed his suspicion that the *Virginia* had attacked the blockading squadron and informed him of the results.

By then, the screw gunboats *Cambridge* and *Dragon* and the armed tug *Young America* had pulled the *Roanoke* and *St. Lawrence* off the shoals. The *Monitor* came alongside the *Roanoke* about 9:00 P.M., and Worden went aboard to confer with her commander, Capt. John Marston, the senior officer present afloat. Three days earlier reports that the *Virginia* was almost operational had led Secretary Welles to send Marston an order instructing him to have the *Monitor* proceed directly to Washington upon reaching Hampton Roads. Welles wanted her on hand to protect the capital in the event the Confederate ironclad pushed up the Potomac. Disregarding the secretary's order, Marston directed Worden to defend the *Minnesota*.

About 1:00 A.M. the *Monitor* anchored beside the frigate. Not long thereafter the flames consuming the *Congress* reached her magazine, and she blew up. "[A]nd certainly a grander sight was never seen," wrote the *Monitor's* executive officer, Lt. Samuel Dana Greene, "but it went straight to the marrow of our bones."[35] According to Paymaster Keeler, no one aboard got any sleep that night.[36] At dawn, the *Monitor* raised steam and passed along the *Minnesota's* side. Keeler related, "Capt. Worden inquired of the *Minnesota* what he intended to do.—'If I cannot lighten my ship off I shall destroy her,' Capt. Van Brunt replied.—'I will stand by you to the last if I can help you,' said our Capt."[37]

Soon the Confederate ships off Sewell's Point could be seen getting under way. Battle was joined a little after 8:00 A.M., when the *Virginia* opened fire on the *Minnesota* at a range of a mile and a half. Keeler told Anna, "Capt. Worden, who was on deck, came up & said more sternly than I ever heard him speak before, 'Gentlemen, that is the *Merrimac*, you had better go below.'"[38] Worden then proceeded to the pilothouse, which he shared with the pilot and quartermaster. Lieutenant Greene occupied the turret and directed the ship's gunnery. Ericsson had installed a speaking tube to allow communication between the two stations. It soon broke, and Keeler and the captain's clerk were pressed into service to carry messages back and forth.

Worden steered straight for the *Virginia*. He had explicitly instructed Greene not to open fire until he sent word. Even after shells from the Confederate ironclad and the *Minnesota* began howling overhead, Worden waited. The position of her pilothouse prevented the *Monitor* from firing over her bow, in any case. Finally, when the range had fallen sufficiently for the *Monitor* to turn parallel to the *Virginia*, Worden gave the order "Commence Firing!"

Catesby Jones wrote later that he was not surprised to see the *Monitor*.[39] Civil War security was lax. Each side knew of the ironclads the other had under construction, and during the night one of the *Virginia*'s pilots had surmised that a strange-looking craft he saw briefly illuminated by the glare from the *Congress* was the "Ericsson Battery."

Initially, Jones planned simply to ignore the *Monitor* while he finished off the *Minnesota*. He told his pilots to place the *Virginia* half a mile from her target, but the depth of her draft made them unwilling to venture nearer than a mile. Meanwhile, the *Monitor* had closed to well within half a mile of the *Virginia*, firing as she came. Jones soon conceded that he would have to deal with her, and at about 8:45, the *Virginia* changed course toward the *Monitor*.

The gunboats that had followed the Confederate ironclad into the Roads did not attempt to intervene. As the *Patrick Henry*'s executive officer, Lt. John H. Rochelle, remarked, "No wooden vessel could have floated twenty minutes under the fire that the *Virginia* . . . [endured] from the *Monitor* and the *Minnesota*."[40]

The ironclads advanced toward each other at a slightly oblique angle. After closing to about fifty yards, they began circling at ranges that fluctuated from a hundred yards to a few feet. Both experienced problems with their gunnery. The *Monitor* could not fire more than one gun at a time at intervals of seven or eight minutes each since the massive iron shutter that shielded each gun port had to be raised in order to fire and lowered to reload. In addition, Lieutenant Greene, who personally fired every shot, found his position inside the *Monitor*'s turret disorienting. "The effect upon one shut up in a revolving drum is perplexing," he wrote, "and it is not a simple matter to keep the bearings."[41] He had the foresight to make chalk marks on the floor indicating the direction of the vessel's port and starboard, bow and stern, only to see them quickly rub off. Eventually he decided to leave the shutters open, stopping the turret to reload when the gun ports were facing away from the *Virginia* and firing "on the fly" as it rotated. The *Virginia*'s gunnery officers did not have

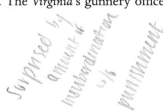

The second day's Battle of Hampton Roads, 9 March 1862. Though inaccurate in a number of details—for example, the *Virginia*'s ends were rounded and her sides did not come to a point—this 1862 lithograph by Currier & Ives provides a stirring overview of the action. From left to right, looking northeast: Newport News, with the masts of the sunken *Cumberland* visible above water; the frigate *Minnesota*, with the steamer *Dragon* at her side; in the distance, Union vessels clustered off Fortress Monroe; the *Monitor* and the *Virginia*; the gunboats *Jamestown* and *Patrick Henry*; and the Confederate position at Sewell's Point. *The Beverley R. Robinson Collection, U.S. Naval Academy Museum*

those kinds of problems, but the *Monitor*'s turret and pilothouse were very small targets.

Yet at such short range it was inevitable that both ships would score a number of hits. The *Monitor* struck the *Virginia* with about twenty of the forty-one rounds she fired and was struck twenty-three times in return. Neither ship was badly harmed. At the time she left Norfolk, the *Virginia* had not been expected to encounter another ironclad. Aside from a few hot shot and some canister, she was armed only with shell. Though deadly against a wooden ship, this was less damaging than solid shot to an armored one. The *Monitor* had 180-pound shot for her two Dahlgrens, but the big guns' effectiveness was limited by a regulation dating back to 1844. In that year a gun had burst during a demonstration firing on the corvette *Princeton*, killing two cabinet members and several other guests on board. The navy had reacted by forbidding any gun to be fired with a powder charge weighing more than half as much as that for which it had been designed. This regulation was canceled to allow the use of full-weight charges immediately after the action between the *Monitor* and the *Virginia*. Had it been canceled beforehand, the outcome of their engagement would undoubtedly have been very different. As it was, even at point-blank range, shot propelled by the *Monitor*'s weak, 15-pound charges rebounded off the *Virginia*.[42] Still, the *Monitor*'s hits were not entirely innocuous. Some cracked the *Virginia*'s armor, buckled its wood backing, and started new leaks in her hull. Jones felt sure that if two shots had struck the *Virginia* at exactly the same point, the result would have been "a large hole through everything."[43]

Making a quick tour of the *Virginia*'s gun deck midway through the engagement, Jones was surprised to see Lt. John R. Eggleston's division standing at ease.

"Why are you not firing, Mister Eggleston?" he asked.

"Why, our powder is very precious," came the reply, "and after two hours' incessant fire I find that I can do her about as much damage by snapping my thumb at her every two minutes."[44]

Jones then decided to try to ram the *Monitor*. The *Virginia* was a heavy ship, and even though she had lost her ram, he hoped that the impact of her wooden stem would crush her opponent. Despite the difficulties posed by her slow speed and sluggishness, the *Virginia* eventually struck the *Monitor* a glancing blow. The only result was a "heavy jar" noted by Paymaster Keeler.[45] The idea of boarding proved equally unproductive. The two ships were never in contact long enough for it to be put into practice. This saved some lives that would probably have been wasted since the men in the *Monitor*'s turret had hand grenades ready to toss out its gun ports.

Worden also thought of ramming. If he struck the *Virginia* at full speed from astern, he might wreck her rudder and propeller. The attempt resulted in a near miss. Such disappointments notwithstanding, the *Monitor* kept the Confederate ironclad from concentrating on the *Minnesota* until Worden had to disengage to take more ammunition into her turret. Jones seized the opportunity to turn back to the *Minnesota*. Once again, shoal water held the *Virginia* almost a mile away, but her bow pivot gun made some hits. One detonated two of the *Minnesota*'s powder charges, starting a short-lived fire. Another blew up the boiler of the little *Dragon*, which was trying to pull the frigate into deep water, putting an end to her activities that day. Before the *Virginia* could do more damage, the *Monitor* reentered the fight.

A few minutes past noon, a shell from the *Virginia*'s stern pivot gun struck the *Monitor*'s pilothouse outside the viewing slit through which Worden was peering, breaking one of the iron beams and driving tiny particles of iron and unburned powder into his face. Keeler wrote:

I was standing near, waiting an order, heard the report which was unusually heavy, a flash of light & a cloud of smoke filled the house. I noticed the Capt. stagger & put his hands to his eyes—I ran up to him & asked if he was hurt. "My eyes," says he, "I am blind." With the assistance of the Surgeon I got him down & called Lieut. Greene from the turret. A number of us collected around him, the blood was running from his face, which was blackened with the powder smoke. He said, "Gentlemen, I leave it with you, do what you think best. I cannot see, but do not mind me. Save the *Minnesota* if you can."[46]

Having spent the morning fighting in his first battle, Lieutenant Greene now found himself holding his first command. Just twenty-two, he was a graduate of the same Naval Academy class (1859) as Alfred Thayer Mahan. A lieutenant for less than a year, he had been assigned to the *Monitor* in December. Despite his youth, Greene quickly won his shipmates' respect. Worden consistently took his side in the postmortems concerning the accuracy of Greene's gunnery and his conduct after taking command.[47]

The shot that wounded Worden was the most important the *Virginia* fired that day. She had run hard aground, offering Greene the advantage of a stationary target, at the time Worden was disabled. During the resulting confusion, the *Monitor*'s quartermaster steered her into shoal water in the direction of Fortress Monroe, and the *Virginia*, the safety valves of her boilers tied shut, finally managed to get free.

A curious situation ensued in which the commander of each vessel interpreted his opposite's movements as an admission of defeat. Greene was among the party who led Worden to his cabin. Twenty to thirty minutes passed before he actually assumed command. By then, the two ships were nearly a mile apart, and Jones had concluded that the Union ironclad's apparent refusal to renew the engagement meant that she was beaten—a view to which Confederate veterans of the action always clung. Thus, when Greene took Worden's place in the *Monitor*'s damaged pilothouse he saw the *Virginia* steering toward Norfolk, evidently in retreat. He did not pursue her. "We had strict orders to act on the defensive and protect the *Minnesota*," he declared.[48]

For his part, Jones insisted, "Had there been any sign of the *Monitor*'s willingness to renew the contest we would have remained to fight her." Assuming that she intended to stay in the shallows, he considered making another attempt to reach effective range of the *Minnesota*. The *Virginia*'s pilots opposed the idea, reminding Jones that the tide was falling and that the water entering her leaks was increasing the vessel's already deep draft. Their objections moved him to consult the ship's officers. After all except one of them agreed on the wisdom of returning to port, Jones ordered the *Virginia* to proceed to Norfolk.[49]

The battle had lasted almost four hours, during which neither ship had suffered severe damage. Some of the *Virginia's* armor plates had been cracked, and she entered drydock to have them replaced, a new ram mounted, and other work done. Aside from her pilothouse, the *Monitor* was for practical purposes unscathed. Not a single man had been killed on either side, and Worden was the only one badly wounded.

Worden's dream of becoming a hero had come true. President Lincoln visited his bedside. Two congressional votes of thanks followed, and despite the permanent loss of sight in one eye, he returned to active duty late in 1862. His postwar assignments included a tour as Superintendent of the U.S. Naval Academy, during which he was promoted to the rank of rear admiral. But glory came at a high cost. Shortly before his death in 1897 Worden commented that since Hampton Roads, "I have never known the time when I wasn't suffering both physical and mental pain."[50]

Tactically the first day's battle of Hampton Roads was undeniably a southern victory. The indecisiveness of the second day's battle allowed both sides to claim victory. The northern claim is compelling. As the *Beaufort's* Lieutenant Parker wrote in his memoirs, the *Virginia* "went out to destroy the *Minnesota*. . . . The *Monitor* was there to save the *Minnesota*. The [*Virginia*] did not accomplish her purpose. The *Monitor* did."[51]

Strategically also, the honors were divided. Mallory's hope that the *Virginia* could singlehandedly break the blockade had been revealed to be an illusion. After being repaired, she reentered Hampton Roads on two occasions—11 April and 8 May—but the *Monitor's* orders to remain on the defensive prevented a new action from taking place. On 19 May, the approach of Union troops forced the Confederates to evacuate Norfolk. The *Virginia's* draft was too deep for her to ascend the James, and that night her crew blew her up. Until then, however, she had denied Union forces access to the river. The consequences were far reaching. Union plans for what became known as the "Peninsular Campaign" had included the use of the James River. In April, the decision was made to use the York, the next river to the north, instead. This change proved to be an important factor in the offensive's ultimate failure.

Many of the popular impressions to which the battle of Hampton Roads has given rise are untrue. For example, it did not spark a revolution in naval construction (the revolution was already underway); the *Monitor* did not save the Union (the *Virginia* was too unseaworthy to have lived long outside Hampton Roads); and the *Monitor* did not serve as a model for the modern warship (she was not especially seaworthy, either). Yet none of this means that the battle was unimportant.[52] The first clash of ironclads, gripped—and held—the public imagination on both sides of the Atlantic. It also exerted a major influence on Civil War shipbuilding. Less than a month later, the U.S. government awarded contracts for ten bigger, better monitors. The Union Navy favored the type throughout the war. Of the fifty-seven armorclads put under construction in the North after March 1862, fifty-five were some kind of monitor. The Confederate Navy also took note. Hampton Roads confirmed Secretary Mallory's faith in ironclads. In the course of the war, the Confederacy would lay down more than fifty and commission twenty-two. Finally, Hampton Roads heralded the passing of the wooden warship. Following the battle, the London *Times* observed: "Whereas we had available for immediate purposes one hundred and forty-nine first-class warships, we have now two, those being the [ironclads] *Warrior* and her sister *Ironside*. There is not now a ship in the English navy, apart from these two, that it would not be madness to trust to an engagement with that little *Monitor*."[53] Or, for that matter, the *Virginia*.

NOTES

1 William N. Still Jr., "The American Civil War," in Robert Gardiner, ed., *Steam, Steel and Shellfire: The Steam Warship, 1815–1905* (London, 1992), 69.

2. *Official Records of the Union and Confederate Navies in the War of the Rebellion* (Washington, D.C., 1894–1927), series 2, 2:67–69

3. John M. Brooke, "The Virginia, or Merrimac: Her Real Projector," *Southern Historical Society Papers* 19 (1891). 1–34 (hereafter *SHSP*); William N. Still Jr , *Iron Afloat: The Story of the Confederate Armorclads* (Columbia, 1986), 12–15.

4. John L. Porter, "The Plan and Construction of the 'Merrimac,' II," in Robert Underwood Johnson and Clarence C. Buel, eds., *Battles and Leaders of the Civil War*, 4 vols. (New York, 1884–87), 1:715–16 (hereafter *B&L*); Still, *Iron Afloat*, 19–23; Robert Holcombe Jr., "The Evolution of Confederate Ironclads" (M.A. thesis, East Carolina University, 1993), 17–21; and Alan B Flanders, *The Merrimac* (n.p. 1982).

5. Brooke, "The Virginia," *SHSP* 19 (1891): 4, 16, 24; Holcombe, "The Evolution of Confederate Ironclads," 17–21. Holcombe's study is the most accurate description of the *Virginia*.

6. Ibid., 18–19.

7. Still, *Iron Afloat*, 23–24; William C. Davis, *Duel between the First Ironclads* (Garden City, N.Y., 1975), 38–39.

8. Davis, *Duel between the First Ironclads*, 38–39.

9. William N. Still Jr., "Catesby Jones," in Richard N Current, ed., *Encyclopedia of the Confederacy*, 4 vols. (New York, 1993), 2 863, W. S. Mabry, *Brief Sketch of the Career of Captain Catesby Ap R. Jones* (Selma, Ala., 1912), and manuscripts on Jones in the Confederate Naval Museum, Columbus, Georgia.

10. Dinwiddie Brazier Phillips, "The Career of the Iron-Clad *Virginia*, Confederate States Navy," *Collections of the Virginia Historical Society*, New Series, 6 (1887): 204 (hereafter *CVHS*).

11. Flanders, *The Merrimac*, 5, 70.

12. Ibid., 66–67; Davis, *Duel between the First Ironclads*, 37–38. For the problems experienced obtaining powder, see Robert Minor to his wife, 5 March 1862, Minor Family Papers, Virginia Historical Society, Richmond, Virginia.

13. Davis, *Duel between the First Ironclads*, is the most detailed account of the battle. This action generated more eyewitness accounts than any other engagement in American naval history.

14. Henry Reaney, "How the Gun-Boat 'Zouave' Aided the 'Congress,'" *B&L*, 1:715.

15 Charles Lee Lewis, *Admiral Franklin Buchanan: Fearless Man of Action* (Baltimore, 1929), 188n; Arthur Sinclair, "How the 'Merrimac' Fought the 'Monitor,'" *Hearst's Magazine* 14 (December 1913): 887.

16. William Harwar Parker, *Recollections of a Naval Officer, 1841–1865*, Craig L. Symonds, ed. (Annapolis, 1985), 273–74.

17. Thomas O. Selfridge Jr., *What Finer Tradition: The Memoirs of Thomas O. Selfridge Jr., Rear Admiral, U.S.N.* (Columbia, 1987), 46–48.

18. Ibid., 50.

19. John Taylor Wood, "The First Fight of Iron-Clads," *B&L*, 1:707.

20. Reaney, "How the Gun-Boat 'Zouave' Aided the 'Congress,'" *B&L*, 1:715.

21. Wood, "The First Fight of Iron-Clads," *B&L*, 1:707.

22. Parker, *Recollections of a Naval Officer*, 276–77; Still, *Iron Afloat*, 31.

23 Phillips, "The Career of the Iron-Clad *Virginia*," *CVHS* 6 (1887): 204.

24. Catesby ap R. Jones, "Services of the 'Virginia' (Merrimac)," *SHSP* 9 (1883): 70.

25. Phillips, "The Career of the Iron-Clad *Virginia*," *CVHS* 6 (1887): 207.

26. Davis, *Duel between the First Ironclads*, 105.

27. W. F. Clayton, *A Narrative of the Confederate States Navy* (Weldon, N.C., 1910), 28.

28. Donald L. Canney, *The Old Steam Navy: The Ironclads, 1842–1885*, 2 vols. (Annapolis, 1990–93), 2:25.

29 Work was subcontracted with nine firms. William N. Still Jr., *Monitor Builders: A Historical Study of the Principal Firms and Individuals Involved in the Construction of the USS* Monitor (Washington, 1988) For building the *Monitor*, see Gordon P. Watts Jr., "Monitor of a New Age: The Construction of the U.S.S. *Monitor*" (M A. thesis, East Carolina University, 1975); and Stephen C. Thompson, "The Construction of the U.S.S. *Monitor*" (M.A. thesis, Old Dominion University, 1987).

30. Ernest Peterkin, "Building a Behemoth," *Civil War Times Illustrated* 20 (July 1981): 16–17; Davis, *Duel between the First Ironclads*, 47–48.

31. Canney, *The Old Steam Navy*, 2:25. Most authorities say that the raft's actual length was 172 feet. See, for example, the *Dictionary of American Naval Fighting Ships*, 8 vols. (Washington, D.C., 1959–81), 6:415, and Davis, *Duel between the First Ironclads*, 16. For details of the vessel, see Canney, *The Old Steam Navy*, 2:25–31; Edward M. Miller, *U.S.S. Monitor: The Ship that Launched a Modern Navy* (Annapolis, 1978), 26–33; *The Engineer* 16 (1863): 357; and Ernest Peterkin, *Drawings of the USS Monitor* (Raleigh, 1985).

32. William N Still Jr., *Ironclad Captains: The Commanding Officers of the USS* Monitor (Washington, D.C., 1988), 5.

33. Ibid., 4.

34. William Frederick Keeler, *Aboard the USS* Monitor, *1862: The Letters of Acting Paymaster William Frederick Keeler, U.S. Navy, to His Wife Anna*, Robert W Daly, ed. (Annapolis, 1964), 8.

35. S. Dana Greene, *An Eye-witness Account of the Battle between the U.S.S.* Monitor *and the C.S.S.* Virginia (Washington, D C., n.d.), 3.

36. Keeler, *Aboard the USS* Monitor, *1862*, 32

37. Ibid., 33

38. Ibid., 34.

39. Jones, "Services of the 'Virginia' (Merrimac)," *SHSP* 9 (1883): 70–71.

40. Quoted in J. Thomas Scharf, *A History of the Confederate States Navy* (reprint, New York, 1977), 197.

41 S. Dana Greene, "In the 'Monitor' Turret," *B&L*, 1 724–25

42. Ibid , 725

43 Jones, "Services of the 'Virginia' (Merrimac)," *SHSP* 9 (1883) 73

44. Wood, "The First Fight of Iron-Clads," *B&L*, 1 702

45. Keeler, *Aboard the USS* Monitor, *1862*, 37, Davis, *Duel between the First Ironclads*, 125–27.

46. Keeler, *Aboard the USS* Monitor, *1862*, 38

47. Still, *Ironclad Captains*, 17

48 Greene, *An Eye-witness Account*, 4

49 Jones, "Services of the 'Virginia' (Merrimac)," *SHSP* 11 (1883): 72, Davis, *Duel between the First Ironclads*, 133

50. Still, *Ironclad Captains*, 8

51 Parker, *Recollections of a Naval Officer,* 286

52 For the importance of the battle and ships involved, see James P. Delgado, *A Symbol of American Ingenuity: Assessing the Significance of the U.S.S.* Monitor (Washington, 1988), William N Still Jr , "The Historical Importance of the USS Monitor," in William B Cogar, ed , *Naval History: The Seventh Symposium of the U.S. Naval Academy* (Wilmington, 1988); Robert J Schneller Jr., "Adam Badeau's 'The Story of the *Merrimac* and the *Monitor,*'" *Syracuse University Library Associates Courier* 27 (Spring 1992)· 25–53; and Howard P Nash Jr , "A Civil War Legend Examined," *The American Neptune* 23 (1963): 197–203 Together these works cite what has been written on this subject

53 Quoted in Wood, "The First Fight of Iron-Clads," *B&L* 1·692

7

The Battle of New Orleans

MARK L. HAYES

"New Orleans gone—and with it the Confederacy. Are we not cut in two? The Mississippi ruins us if lost."[1] Mary Chestnut's diary entry for 27 April 1862 echoed the feelings of many southerners. The capture of the Confederacy's largest city delivered a tremendous blow to the young nation's morale. It was the most significant success in what one northern paper described as a "Deluge of Victories in the West." Between February and June 1862, Union forces won battles at Forts Henry and Donelson, Island Number 10, Shiloh, Memphis, and New Orleans, occupied fifty thousand square miles of Confederate territory, gained control of one thousand miles of navigable rivers, and captured two state capitals.[2]

Confederate authorities in Richmond must shoulder much of the blame for the loss of New Orleans. Secretary of the Navy Stephen R. Mallory and President Jefferson Davis believed that the greatest threat to the port came from Union forces on the upper Mississippi. They stripped New Orleans of troops and sent a large portion of the Confederate fleet to Memphis. The lack of urgency with which Richmond regarded the local defense of New Orleans also led to innumerable delays in the construction of the ironclads *Louisiana* and *Mississippi*.[3]

The tactical side of the action was summarized by the Confederate commander responsible for the defense of the city, Maj. Gen. Mansfield Lovell, with the words, "The battle . . . of New Orleans was fought and lost at Forts Jackson and Saint Philip."[4] Fort Jackson, a star-shaped work of stone and mortar, mounted seventy-four guns. It stood one hundred yards from the levee on the right or west bank of the Mississippi. Fort St. Philip stood on the opposite bank about half a mile upstream. Built of brick and stone covered with sod, it mounted fifty-two guns with a much longer field of fire than those in Fort

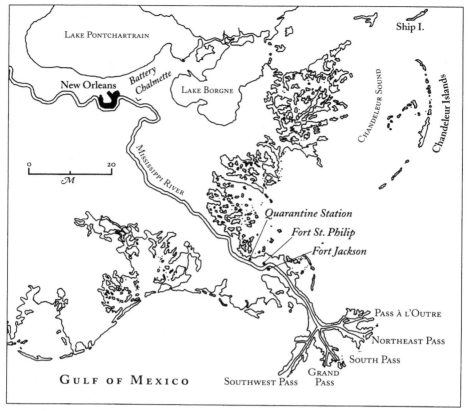

The New Orleans campaign.

Jackson.[5] Eleven hundred men garrisoned the two forts. In the river the Confederates placed obstructions consisting of a chain passed over a line of seven
anchored hulks running from a point abreast Fort Jackson to the opposite
shore. Brig. Gen. Johnson K. Duncan commanded the land defenses.

The River Defense Fleet, a Confederate War Department creation under
the command of Capt. John A. Stephenson, consisted of six small boats with
iron-reinforced prows for ramming. Two vessels from the Louisiana State
Navy, the *Governor Moore* and *General Quitman*, provided additional support.
The Confederate States Navy's contribution to the defense afloat consisted
primarily of the gunboat CSS *McRae* and the thinly ironclad ram *Manassas*.
The ironclad CSS *Louisiana* was potentially the most powerful vessel on the
river, but her unfinished condition and poor design made her almost useless.[6]
The *Mississippi* had not even received her armor.

Cdr. John K. Mitchell, CSN, arrived at Forts Jackson and St. Philip with the

Louisiana on 22 April. The ironclad's guns had yet to be mounted and her power plant was not operational. Mitchell intended to finish the work while at anchor just above Fort St. Philip. Lovell placed all the Confederate vessels at the forts under Mitchell's orders, but Stephenson refused to let his boats fall under the command of the Confederate Navy.[7]

The Union expedition against New Orleans consisted of forty-three armed vessels, including nineteen schooners of Cdr. David Dixon Porter's mortar flotilla. Porter had convinced Secretary of the Navy Gideon Welles that Forts Jackson and St. Philip could be reduced by a long and steady bombardment by the flotilla's 13-inch mortars. The U.S. Army supported the fleet with about twelve thousand men commanded by Maj. Gen. Benjamin F. Butler.[8]

The most important decision Welles made regarding the expedition was the selection of its commander. Although several officers were considered, Welles selected Porter's foster brother, Capt. David Glasgow Farragut. Welles had been greatly impressed upon learning of the circumstances under which Farragut left his home in Norfolk. When the Virginia convention voted to secede, Farragut denounced the act and traveled north, abandoning his home and property, the following day. Fellow officers also spoke well of him.[9]

By the Battle of New Orleans, the sixty-year-old Farragut had served in the U.S. Navy for fifty-one years. He was born the second son to George Farragut and Elizabeth Shine Farragut on 5 July 1801. The Farragut family lived in New Orleans while George was stationed there in the U.S. Navy. They became close friends with another navy family, the Porters. When David Porter Sr. became terminally ill, Mrs. Farragut gently nursed him. She soon fell ill with yellow fever, and both she and David Porter died on 22 June 1808. David Porter Jr. knew firsthand of the Farraguts' kindness to his dying father. He eventually took young David G. Farragut into his home and secured a midshipman's appointment for him on 17 December 1810.[10]

In 1811, David Porter took command of USS *Essex,* and Farragut went with him. The young midshipman served on the frigate throughout the War of 1812, including her disastrous battle with HMS *Phoebe* and *Cherub* off Valparaiso, Chile, on 28 March 1814.

After the war Farragut saw extensive service in the sailing navy. In command of the sloop *Erie* in 1838 he observed the French bombardment and capture of the castle of San Juan de Ulloa at Vera Cruz, Mexico. This victory of ships over a heavily armed fort impressed Farragut greatly, and he proposed a similar operation when the United States went to war with Mexico in 1846. The Navy Department rejected his plan, and he firmly believed that the navy missed its opportunity to cover itself with glory.[11]

Between the Mexican War and the War between the States, Farragut held a variety of positions afloat and ashore. He was sitting on a navy retirement board at New York when the secretary of the navy ordered him to command the West Gulf Atlantic Blockading Squadron in December 1861. Welles recalled that Lincoln believed "there had not been, taken it all in all, so good an appointment in either branch of the service as Farragut."[12] The secretary himself thought that

Farragut has prompt, energetic, excellent qualities, but no fondness for written details or self-laudation. Does but one thing at a time, but does that strong and well. Is better fitted to lead an expedition through danger and difficulty than to command an extensive blockade; is a good officer in a great emergency, will more willingly take great risks in order to obtain great results than any officer in high position in either Navy or Army, and, unlike most of them, prefers that others should tell the story of his well-doing rather than relate it himself.[13]

During the New Orleans campaign, the sexagenarian flag officer left a strong imprint on young men, new to war, as well as on veterans. John Russell Bartlett, a midshipman at the time, recalled, "I was much impressed with his energy and activity and his promptness of decision and action. He had a winning smile and a most charming manner and was jovial and talkative. . . . The officers who had the good fortune to be immediately associated with him seemed to worship him."[14]

The future hero of Manila Bay, George Dewey, was a twenty-four-year-old lieutenant on board the USS *Mississippi* during the campaign. Late in life he declared, "Farragut has always been my ideal of the naval officer, urbane, decisive, indomitable. Whenever I have been in a difficult situation, or in the midst of such a confusion of details that the simple and right thing to do seemed hazy, I have often asked myself, 'What would Farragut do?' . . . Valuable as the training of Annapolis was, it was poor schooling beside that of serving under Farragut in time of war."[15]

Farragut's men grew accustomed to seeing their commander often. He seemed almost ubiquitous, leaving the impression that they were always under his watchful eye. Bartlett remembered, "Farragut was about the fleet from early dawn until dark, and if any officers or men had not spontaneous enthusiasm he certainly infused it into them. I have been on the morning watch, from 4 to 8, when he would row alongside the ship at 6 o'clock, either hailing to ask how we were getting along, or, perhaps, climbing over the side to see for himself."[16]

Nineteenth-century generals had opportunities in battle to ride to the point of danger, encourage their men, and clarify commands. Such opportu-

Flag Officer David Glasgow Farragut still wore a captain's uniform for a photograph made in New Orleans shortly prior to his promotion to rear admiral in July 1862.
U.S. Naval Institute

nities were not available to flag officers. Farragut compensated for this by making himself known to the officers and men of his fleet. He shared with them his ideas, infected them with his enthusiasm, and encouraged them with his determination. During the Battle of New Orleans, each of Farragut's officers had an answer to the question that occurred to George Dewey: "What would Farragut do?"

Porter's mortar schooners began a slow but steady bombardment of Forts Jackson and St. Philip on the evening of 18 April. The Confederates returned fire, striking several vessels and killing and wounding a few men. Farragut's clerk, Bradley Osbon, who had commanded a ship in the Argentine Navy, observed signs of the apprehension felt by so many who had never seen action before. Taking note of the morale on board one of his vessels, Farragut ordered Osbon to go over: "I hear that they are as blue as indigo in that wardroom over there. . . . Tell them some stories of the fights you've been in and come out of alive. It will stir their blood and do them good."[17]

The gunboats *Pinola* and *Itasca* created a gap in the obstructions across the river on the night of 20 April. The Federals planned to blow up one of the bulks with a petard exploded by electric wires. The crew of the *Pinola* threw a petard on board a hulk, but the wires broke when the gunboat backed away. Lt. Charles H. B. Caldwell brought the *Itasca* alongside another hulk, and a boarding party cut the chain with a chisel.[18] Farragut felt that the opening was large enough for his ships to pass through.

Farragut's men spent the next few days preparing for the upcoming battle, arranging cable chains on the outside of the vessels immediately over the engines and boilers; whitewashing the decks so that the guns' tools would stand out in the dark; painting the ships' hulls with a mixture of oil and mud so they would be harder to see; and packing the boilers with bags of ashes, clothing, sand, and whatever was obtainable for the purpose.[19]

Farragut grew impatient with lack of discernible progress by Porter's mortar flotilla. The flag officer met with Porter on 22 April, and stated his intention to run past the forts that evening. Porter pleaded for and received one more day, but the results appeared no more promising. When officers discovered that the vast majority of shots struck outside Fort Jackson, Farragut confronted Porter: "There David, there's the score. I guess we'll go up the river tonight."[20]

Farragut had revealed his plan of attack in a general order on 20 April. The basic idea was simple. "The forts should be run, and when a force is once above the forts to protect the troops, they should be landed at Quarantine

TABLE 7.1 The Battle of New Orleans, 24 April 1862

	Commissioned	Displacement	Speed	Complement	Guns
U.S. NAVY					
Flag Officer D. G. Farragut					
Sloops					
Brooklyn	1859	2,532	11.5	259	26
Hartford (flagship)	1859	2,900	13.5	302	28
Iroquois	1859	1,488	11.5	123	11
Mississippi	1841	3,200	11	229	22
Oneida	1862	1,488	11.5	166	10
Pensacola	1861	3,000	9.5	269	25
Richmond	1860	2,700	9.5	261	22
Varuna	1862	+/−1,600	?	126	10
Gunboats					
Cayuga	1862	691	10	78	4
Itasca	1861	691	10	70	4
Katahdin	1862	691	10	78	4
Kennebec	1862	691	10	78	4
Kineo	1862	691	10	81	4
Pinola	1862	691	10	75	5
Sciota	1861	691	10	65	5
Winona	1861	691	10	93	4
Wissahickon	1861	691	10	80	4
C.S. NAVY					
Cdr. J. K. Mitchell					
Ironclads					
Louisiana	—[a]	1,400	—	+/−250	16
Manassas	1855/61[b]	+/−600	4	35	1
Gunboats					
Jackson	1849/61[b]	297	?	40	2
McRae	?/1861[b]	830	?	119	8
Launches					
Launch No. 3	1861?	?	?	20	1
Launch No. 6	1861?	?	?	20	1
LOUISIANA STATE NAVY					
Gunboats					
General Quitman	1857/62[b]	945	?	90	2
Governor Moore	1854/62[b]	1,215	?	93	2
RIVER DEFENSE FLEET					
Capt. J. A. Stephenson					
Converted tugs					
Defiance	1849/62[b]	544	?	40	1
General Breckinridge	?/1862[b]	?	?	35	1
General Lovell	?/1862[b]	?	?	50	1
Resolute	?/1862[b]	?	?	40	2
Stonewall Jackson	?/1862[b]	?	?	30	1
Warrior	?/1862[b]	?	?	40	1
SHORE FORTIFICATIONS					
Fort Jackson	—	—	—	—	74
Fort St. Philip	—	—	—	—	52

Note: Figures for guns include howitzers
[a] Unfinished
[b] Date completed/date taken into naval service

from the Gulf side by bringing them through the bayou, and then our forces should move up the river, mutually aiding each other, as it can be done to advantage." Farragut retained the option to try to reduce the forts if, during the action, he felt that his fleet held a significant advantage. However, he expected his captains to press on up the river unless ordered to do otherwise.[21]

Farragut divided his ships into three divisions, each formed in a line ahead. The first, commanded by Capt. Theodorus Bailey in the *Cayuga*, included the *Pensacola, Mississippi, Oneida, Varuna, Katahdin, Kineo*, and *Wissahickon*. Farragut commanded the center division, consisting of the *Hartford, Brooklyn*, and *Richmond*. The third division, commanded by Capt. Henry H. Bell in the *Sciota*, also contained the *Iroquois, Kennebec, Pinola, Itasca*, and *Winona*.[22] Farragut planned to send each division through separately, as the opening in the obstructions did not appear to be very large. Porter's flotilla would provide supporting fire.

Between 18–23 April Porter's mortars fired about 16,800 shells, nearly all at Fort Jackson. Although the Confederates suffered few casualties, the constant bombardment left them physically exhausted. Rising water from the Mississippi flooded parts of the forts, adding to the garrisons' misery. General Duncan pleaded with Captain Mitchell to tow the *Louisiana* below the obstructions and drive off the mortar schooners, but Mitchell refused to do so before his engines were operational, convinced that placing the ironclad in such a position was an unnecessary risk.[23] Porter's bombardment has often been dismissed for its lack of physical destruction. Nevertheless, it seriously fatigued the troops at Fort Jackson, which no doubt reduced the effectiveness of their fire on 24 April.

Bradley Osbon recalled the anticipation in Farragut's fleet on the evening of 23 April. "At the usual hour the crews turned in, but I think there was little sleep. The men were cheerful and determined, but wakeful. Most of them had been green hands when we started, and scarcely one of them had been under fire. With a night attack just ahead it was natural that they should be anxious."[24]

Just after midnight on 24 April, the watch roused the crew of the USS *Richmond* from their uneasy sleep. The men moved quietly about, stowing hammocks, clearing the decks, shortening the anchor, and increasing steam pressure in the boilers. The gun crews readied their weapons and themselves for action. Lt. Frederic Stanhope Hill's gunners manned four 9-inch Dahlgrens located amidships. "My men came to their stations stripped for work, some of them without their shirts, their monkey-jackets knotted by the

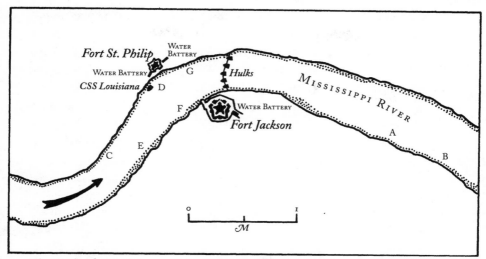

The Battle of New Orleans, 24 April 1862. (A–B) Position of Porter's mortar flotilla. (C–D) and (E–F) Location of southern naval forces immediately before the action. (G) Point at which the *Hartford* grounded.

sleeves, hanging loosely about their shoulders."[25] Similar scenes were enacted throughout the Union fleet.

Anxiety plagued the *Cayuga*'s Lt. George Perkins as he paced the gunboat's forecastle. The vessel's commanding officer, Lt. Napoleon B. Harrison, put the twenty-five-year-old Perkins in charge of piloting the *Cayuga* during the upcoming action.[26] The responsibility may have weighed heavily on his shoulders, but his performance would justify Harrison's faith in his young executive officer.

As hundreds of sailors completed their preparations they turned anxious gazes toward the *Hartford*. At five minutes before 2:00 A.M., on the deck of the flagship, Bradley Osbon hoisted two red lanterns, signaling the fleet to stand up the river. Almost immediately, the leading vessel of Bailey's division, the *Cayuga*, had her anchors up and began to move slowly, leading sixteen other vessels of the Union fleet toward the prize: New Orleans.[27]

Not every ship was ready to get under way when Osbon hoisted the signal. The *Pensacola* appeared to be having trouble hoving up her anchors. Her commanding officer, Capt. Henry W. Morris, was a deliberate man who sometimes annoyed the flag officer with his delays. As precious minutes passed and the fleet remained idle, Farragut's patience gave way. "Damn that fellow! I don't believe he wants to start!" Finally, at three o'clock, the *Pensacola* began to move upriver.[28]

Perkins must have kept only a little steam on the *Cayuga* as she pulled away from the other ships in Bailey's division. At 2:30, before the moon rose, those on the *Hartford* could still see her.[29] It was not until 3:30 that the *Cayuga* passed the opening in the obstructions. Ten minutes later, Perkins experienced the start of his first major action. "Though it was a starlight night we were not discovered until we were well under the forts; then they opened a tremendous fire on us. . . . The *Cayuga* received the first fire, and the air was filled with shells and explosions which almost blinded me as I stood on the forecastle trying to see my way. . . ." Despite the shock of being under heavy fire for the first time, Perkins had the presence of mind to evaluate the tactical situation. "I soon saw that the guns of the forts were all aimed for the mid-stream, so I steered close under the walls of Fort St. Philip, and although our masts and rigging got badly shot through, our hull was but little damaged."[30]

The relief the officers and crew of the *Cayuga* must have felt was short-lived. Perkins recalled, "After passing the last battery and thinking we were clear, I looked back for some of our vessels, and my heart jumped up into my mouth, when I found I could not see a single one. I thought they all must have been sunk by the forts. Then looking ahead I saw eleven of the enemy's gunboats coming down upon us, and it seemed as if we were 'gone' sure."[31]

The deliberate actions of the *Pensacola* resulted in the *Cayuga* temporarily facing the Confederate vessels alone. Morris apparently interpreted his orders differently than Farragut's other captains. He believed they instructed him to *attack* Fort St. Philip and engage the Confederate batteries so that Farragut's division would not have to face the combined fire of both forts.[32]

Morris did not trust his failing eyesight to con his ship through the darkness. He placed his executive officer, Lt. Francis Asbury Roe, in command throughout the battle. Roe recalled that the Confederate fire "was truly terrible. I ran the ship close up to Fort [St.] Philip and engaged in almost a yardarm conflict. The chain was broken only in a small space upon the Fort [St.] Philip side, and, in the darkness, the smoke of burning powder, and the din of battle, my task of guiding the ship through was difficult." Roe admitted that the only bells he rang were "slow" and "stop her."[33]

Nine solid shot struck the *Pensacola* in the hull. Exploding shells cut up the rigging, masts, and gratings and caused serious casualties. Fire from the forts twice swept the bridge. After the sun rose, Roe noticed that shrapnel had cut away the right leg of his trousers at the knee and shredded the skirt of his coat. Miraculously he was unscathed, although the "gun's crews, right under me, were decimated. The groans, shrieks, and wails of the dying and wounded were so horrible that I shudder now at the recollection of it." The

Pensacola lost four men killed and thirty-three others wounded—more casualties than any other Union ship.[34]

The beating the ship and crew took caused some men to break. John McDonald, second captain of no. 6 gun, bolted from his station when an exploding shell seriously wounded the first captain. Lieutenant James H. Stillwell, the division officer, took charge of the gun as McDonald disappeared and could not be found until after the battle. Another seaman on *Pensacola* deserted his station twice. Each time the ship's crew dragged him out from behind the forward bitts and back to his position at no. 2 gun.[35]

The *Mississippi* steamed directly behind the *Pensacola* as Bailey's division got under way. As she passed through the opening in the obstructions, the *Mississippi* paused. Cdr. Samuel P. Lee brought his ship, the *Oneida,* to a halt when he discovered the *Mississippi* blocking the way. Lee proceeded when the current pushed the *Mississippi*'s bow slightly to port, forcing her closer to the Fort Jackson side as she put on steam. The *Varuna* shot past both vessels and steered for Fort St. Philip. As she passed the Confederate batteries, the *Varuna* fired her starboard broadside. The *Oneida* followed close astern, rapidly firing roundshot from her two rifled guns, grape and canister from her 32-pounders, and shrapnel from her two 11-inch pivot guns. The *Oneida,* and probably the *Varuna,* entered an eddy when they neared the shore, accelerating their dash past the forts. Confederate batteries never seemed to find the range, and their casualties were light. Once again, smoke also played a role, obscuring targets and making navigation difficult.[36]

About 4:00 A.M. the Confederate ships entered the fight. The CSS *McRae,* under the command of Lt. Thomas B. Huger, lay anchored near the shore three hundred yards above Fort St. Philip. When her lookouts discovered the *Cayuga* passing the obstructions, the *McRae* slipped her cable and maintained a steady fire with her port battery on the advancing Federal fleet until her 9-inch pivot gun exploded upon firing its tenth round. One of the Union gunboats, probably the *Cayuga,* shot past her. The *McRae* started to turn to give the Union steamer a broadside when two full-rigged ships, probably the *Varuna* and *Oneida,* came into view. They steamed past without firing a shot, evidently mistaking the *McRae* for one of their own gunboats. The Confederate vessel sheered quickly to port, then starboard, delivering two broadsides.[37]

The *Oneida* and *Varuna* sheered briefly to starboard and returned fire. One of the shells exploded in the *McRae*'s sail room and set it ablaze. A thin bulkhead was the only thing between the fire and the shell lockers. The gunboat's executive officer, Lt. Charles W. Read, led the party that eventually managed to extinguish the flames.[38]

Huger's *McRae* was not the only Confederate vessel that engaged the Union fleet under the guns of the forts. The ironclad ram CSS *Manassas* was made fast to the left bank of the river just above Fort St. Philip. Her commander, Lt. Alexander F. Warley, received word that something was going on sometime around three o'clock. "By the time I got on deck, several quick flashes about the chains indicated a movement by the enemy. I instantly cast off . . . and stood down."[39] Warley appears to have been the only Confederate officer who clearly understood that the small squadron's best course of action was a coordinated use of the steam rams and fire rafts to keep the Union vessels under the guns of the forts long enough for the heavier fire to disable them. The captains of the River Defense Fleet were either ignorant of this tactic or else they felt the situation was hopeless. They fled as soon as the action began.[40]

Even if he had to attack alone, Warley was determined to hold the Union fleet in front of the forts' guns. He failed in his first two attempts to ram. The *Resolute* of the River Defense Fleet forced Warley to abandon his first try by steaming into the path of the onrushing ram, and Lieutenant Roe frustrated his second attempt by skillfully maneuvering the *Pensacola*.[41] The tenacious Warley searched for another target. He soon spotted the side-wheel steamer *Mississippi*.

William Waud, an artist for an illustrated weekly, had a position in the foretop of the *Mississippi*. Spying the cigar-shaped *Manassas* heading downriver, he called to Dewey, "Here is a queer-looking customer on our port bow!" Dewey immediately recognized the Confederate ram and decided to engage her. "I called to starboard the helm and turned the *Mississippi's* bow toward the *Manassas,* with the intention of running her down, being confident that our superior tonnage must sink her if we struck her fairly."[42]

However, the ram was more agile, and Warley was an experienced officer. The *Manassas* sheered off to avoid the collision. "But, then," Dewey continued, "sheering in, he managed to strike us a glancing blow just abaft the port paddle-wheel. The effect of the shock was that of running aground. The *Mississippi* trembled and listed and then righted herself. When I saw the big hole that the ram had left in our side I called, 'Sound the pumps!'" Although the *Mississippi* had part of her hull ripped away, she was not leaking. "The impact of the ram, which would have sunk any other ship in the fleet, had taken out a section of solid timber seven feet long, four feet broad, and four inches deep. About fifty copper bolts had been cut as clean as if they were hair under a razor's edge. I remember seeing their bright, gleaming ends when I looked down from the hurricane deck in my first glimpse of that hole in our side."[43]

The vessels from Bailey's division disengaged from the *McRae* and *Manassas* and proceeded past the forts. As they steamed upriver, they passed the *Louisiana,* still moored to the left bank. The ironclad's gun ports were poorly constructed, further limiting the immobile vessel's field of fire. She inflicted little damage.[44]

At the head of the Union line, Lieutenant Perkins's anxiety eased when he discovered that the group of small Confederate vessels he found himself among were actually heading upriver, desperately trying to get away. Many were unarmed and had no choice. A wild melee ensued as the *Cayuga* plowed through the fleeing ships, firing furiously as she went. Three of her targets struck their colors and ran ashore.[45] The *Varuna* and *Oneida* soon came up. As the *Varuna* steamed by, she mistook the *Cayuga* for an enemy vessel and let loose a broadside.

Meanwhile, Farragut grew impatient with the delays caused by the *Pensacola's* slow movements. At 3:25 he ordered the *Hartford* to stand up the river. The smoke obscured Farragut's view, and he ascended the mizzen rigging in order to see over it. Bradley Osbon observed, "With his feet on the ratlines and his back against the shrouds, he stood there as cool and undisturbed as if leaning against a mantel in his own home."[46] Confederate fire concentrated on the *Hartford* as she neared Fort St. Philip.

Shot, shell, grape, and canister filled the air with deadly missiles. It was like the breaking up of the universe, with the moon and all the stars bursting in our midst. As for seeing what the other vessels were doing, or what was going on about us, that was impossible. In that blinding smoke, and night, with everything flying in all directions, the only thing we could see was the flash of guns in our faces and the havoc on our own ship. Ropes were swinging, splinters were flying. . . . At first the enemy's aim had been high, but now they lowered it until their fire began to cut us through.[47]

As Confederate gunfire grew intense, Farragut spotted a raging fire moving swiftly across the water toward the *Hartford's* port side. It was a fire raft pushed along by the unarmed tug *Mosher,* commanded by Horace Sherman. Farragut yelled "Hard-a-port!" The Union sloop quickly turned to starboard, but she was too near the shore, and her bow went hard up on a mud bank. It was 4:15 A.M. Sherman, taking advantage of her predicament, pushed the raft against the *Hartford's* port side. The fire ignited the hull's paint and quickly spread up the rigging. In a letter to Porter, Farragut confessed that at this point he "thought it was all up with us."[48]

Fortunately for the *Hartford,* the gunners in Fort St. Philip could not capitalize on her vulnerable position. The *Hartford* had grounded just above the upper water battery. Federal fire had dismounted one of the fort's Columbi-

An incident of the Battle of New Orleans, 24 April 1862. The Confederate tug
Mosher pushes a fire raft into the grounded *Hartford*. The gun silhouetted in the tug's
bow is an embellishment; she carried no ordnance. *From R. U. Johnson and C. C. Buel, eds.,*
Battles and Leaders of the Civil War, *(New York, 1887)*

ads, and another could not be brought to bear. A 24-pounder bearing directly
on the flagship had been broken in two near the trunions.[49]

Farragut suppressed his own fears and walked up and down the deck,
encouraging the crew. Occasionally, the fire flashed through the gun ports,
causing the men to recoil. The ubiquitous Farragut yelled above the noise,
"Don't flinch from that fire, boys! There's a hotter fire than that for those who
don't do their duty!"[50] The *Hartford*'s gunners blasted the *Mosher,* quickly
sending her to the bottom of the Mississippi.

Osbon carried three shells to the ship's side. After unscrewing the fuses, he
tossed them over the gunwale onto the raft. The ensuing explosions blew
holes in the raft's bottom, drowning the flames at their source.[51]

Captain Richard Wainwright led the *Hartford*'s firefighting teams. They
extinguished the flames on the ship's rigging just as the sloop backed off the
mud bank and away from the sinking fire raft. Lt. Albert Kautz recalled, "The
ship was again free; and a loud, spontaneous cheer rent the air, as the crew
rushed to their guns with renewed energy."[52] The *Hartford* made her way
upriver, out of the deadly space between the forts.

Bailey's division was not entirely through the obstructions when Farragut
ordered the *Hartford* to get under way at 3:25 A.M. At that time, the last three

gunboats of the First Division were still on the starboard beam.[53] This became a problem as the two lines of vessels converged at the narrow opening.

Capt. Thomas T. Craven ordered the sloop *Brooklyn* to follow the flagship. The *Hartford*'s broadside, delivered as she passed the obstructions, completely obscured her and her surroundings from Craven's view. He followed what he supposed was the flagship's fire, sheering to starboard to deliver a broadside of grapeshot at Fort Jackson.[54] The darkness, heavy smoke, and the narrowness of the opening led to two accidents that probably occurred about the same time.

The gunboat *Kineo* of Bailey's division was off the *Brooklyn*'s starboard quarter as the latter sheered. The two ships collided with great force, wrenching the frame of the gunboat out of line. In spite of the shock, the *Kineo*'s commanding officer, Lt. George M. Ransom, backed clear of the *Brooklyn* and pressed on through the forts' fire.[55]

Also about this time, the *Brooklyn* ploughed through a large hulk in the river obstructions. After steaming a little further, the ship suddenly came to a halt. Craven discovered that an anchor "hanging at the starboard quarter, had caught into the wreck of the crushed up hulk, and being torn from its fastenings was way out astern, and the hawser, or small cable which was fast to it, was taut as a bar."[56]

The current pushed the *Brooklyn*'s bow to starboard, placing her under raking fire from Fort St. Philip. While in this precarious position, the vessel was hit several times. One shot tore up the poop deck. Another struck the signal quartermaster, nearly cutting him in two. The Confederate batteries seemed to have found the range when one of the *Brooklyn*'s crewmen rushed up and severed the cable of the fouled anchor.[57]

Craven took his ship close under the guns of Fort St. Philip, giving it three broadsides as he passed. He was assisted by the eddy that greatly reduced the time under fire. The *Brooklyn* nearly grazed the *Louisiana* as she made her way upriver, and the two ships exchanged fire. A 9-inch shell struck the *Brooklyn* about a foot above the waterline, embedding itself three feet into the timbers, but failed to explode. Later her crewmen discovered that the Confederate gunners had failed to remove a lead patch from the fuse.[58]

After the *Brooklyn* passed the Confederate ironclad, Craven found himself enshrouded in smoke from the ships' guns. Unable to see even the banks of the river, he chose a course based on other clues.

Supposing from the direction of the noise and flashes of light that I was steering in the right direction, we went on at full speed. But in a few minutes I found . . . the tide had set us over to the other shore, and all at once I discovered we were almost directly under the fire of Fort Jackson, receiving a raking and terribly scorching fire. . . . At the same time as we grazed the shore, the *Manassas* . . . made her appearance on our starboard beam, steering directly toward our smokestack.[59]

Warley had taken the *Manassas* downriver after ramming the *Mississippi*. He made another attempt at a Union sloop, probably the *Hartford*, which avoided him and proceeded upriver. Union fire had struck the *Manassas* five times in the hull and riddled her smokestack. The damage greatly reduced her speed, ending her hopes of keeping any other vessels from ascending the river. Warley intended to take the ram below the forts and attack Porter's flotilla, but after the Confederate batteries mistakenly fired on the *Manassas*, he decided to go back upriver.[60]

Warley spotted the *Brooklyn* while she was still lying athwart the river, heading toward Fort Jackson. He ordered resin thrown into the furnaces to make more steam. The Federal sloop turned upriver as she neared the shore. The *Manassas* steamed abeam of the Union ship and then turned to port, trapping the *Brooklyn* against the river bank. Warley's vessel was already bearing down on her intended victim when the Union lookouts cried, "The ram, the ram!" Craven quickly called out, "Port the helm, hard!" The blow could not be avoided, only lessened.[61]

A shot fired from the Confederates' 32-pound carronade moments before the collision hit the *Brooklyn* five feet above the waterline and came to rest in the sandbags piled around the steam drum. The *Manassas*'s ram struck the sloop at a slight angle, nearly amidships, crushing in three planks and driving the links of the chain into the side. The blow was so great that at first Craven thought his ship was sinking. However, the chain and a full coal bunker kept the hull intact. Warley backed away from the *Brooklyn* and let the ram slip astern before heading upriver. Smoke still hung thickly in the air, aiding the *Manassas* in disengaging without further damage.[62]

The *Richmond*, under Cdr. James Alden, fell in line behind the *Brooklyn* when she began to steam upriver at 3:35 A.M. As the *Richmond* approached the gap in the obstructions, the guns on ship and shore exchanged fire. Lieutenant Hill recalled:

For the next hour it is all madness: The captain of one of my guns is struck full in the face by a solid shot and his head is severed from his body; as he falls the lockstring in his hand is pulled and his gun is discharged! . . . A young master's mate hurries past me bearing a message to the captain. . . . As he goes up the ladder and touches his cap to his commander a rifle ball from the fort . . . strikes him in the forehead, and the poor boy falls dead, his message not yet delivered! . . . A solid shot passes between two of my men and buries itself in the mainmast not six inches above my head! I am covered with splinters, but unharmed. The early dawn is breaking. . . . The fire upon us slackens, then ceases; I glance through a porthole; we are past the forts. . . .[63]

The steamers of Porter's mortar flotilla got under way about the same time that the *Hartford* moved upriver. The force included the sailing sloop, *Portsmouth,* which was towed into position by tugs. Altogether, these vessels mounted forty-four guns. They came under heavy fire on approaching the Confederate works and dropped anchor about five hundred yards from Fort Jackson. Porter's force did not open fire until 4:20 A.M. and remained in action for no more than thirty minutes, when the last of Farragut's fleet was thought to have passed the forts.[64] Once again, darkness and smoke made it difficult to assess the situation. As Porter's flagship hoisted the signals to cease fire and retire, some of Farragut's vessels were still engaged with the forts.

By now, smoke lay between Forts Jackson and St. Philip like a thick fog. The *Wissahickon,* the last vessel in Bailey's squadron, ran aground, probably after passing the obstructions. Her commander, Lt. Albert N. Smith, lost sight of the other Union ships as he conned his gunboat through the gloom. The Union formation had thoroughly dissolved. As the first rays of sunlight began to illuminate the river just above the forts, Smith found himself close to three vessels of Bell's division (the *Iroquois, Sciota,* and *Pinola*) and the Confederate gunboat *McRae.*[65]

Lieutenant Huger had tried to keep the *McRae* out of action while his executive officer, Lieutenant Read, led the firefighting teams below. With his task completed, Read returned to the main deck and discovered his vessel hotly engaged with the *Iroquois* and the three Union gunboats at a range of three hundred yards. The Confederate steamer closed with the *Iroquois* and let loose a blast of grapeshot and langrage into her stern. The Union sloop returned the favor with shell and canister. Three shots struck the *McRae* near the waterline. Others carried away every stay and three-fourths of her shrouds. One shell passed through the smokestack. Canister and grapeshot riddled her sides. Lieutenant Huger was mortally wounded, three men were killed, and seventeen wounded. The feisty Confederate seemed doomed until the *Manassas* entered the melee.[66]

Lieutenant Warley spotted the *Iroquois* almost immediately after disengaging from the *Brooklyn.* He made for her, but the Union sloop put on steam and forged ahead as if the ram were at anchor. Warley persisted in trying to ram the vessels engaging the *McRae.* The Union captains must have realized the peril they would be in if the ram disabled their vessels above the forts. One by one, they left the *McRae* and stood up the river.[67]

Three gunboats of Farragut's fleet did not make it past the forts. All experienced serious navigational problems. Both the *Kennebec* and the *Itasca* ran afoul of the obstructions, and when the latter attempted to back clear, she collided with the *Winona*. A 42-pound shot through her boiler sent the *Itasca* limping downstream. The *Winona* retired under cover of darkness, and the *Kennebec,* caught between the forts at daybreak, also withdrew.[68]

Fourteen of the seventeen vessels that Farragut ordered toward New Orleans at two o'clock that morning had fought their way past Forts Jackson and St. Philip. The fight was not over, however, and Farragut would lose one more of his ships before it ended.

Lt. Beverly Kennon, in command of the Louisiana state gunboat *Governor Moore,* spied the *Varuna* as she broke out of the pack of Union ships above the forts sometime after 4:00 A.M. To reach her, the southern gunboat had to run past the ships at the front of Bailey's division. Grapeshot, canister, and shell cut her up badly and killed and wounded many of her crewmen. The *Governor Moore* replied with shell. This exchange produced a dense pall of smoke and gave her an opportunity to escape the deadly fire. After sighting the *Varuna,* Kennon took his vessel into the darkness and followed the Union steamer upriver.[69]

The two vessels were faster than those trailing them and soon found themselves almost alone on the Mississippi. Kennon recalled that

both of us held our fire for some minutes, when both opened together. . . . At daybreak we were about 100 yards astern of the *Varuna,* about 600 yards ahead of the rest of the enemy, and quite near the Quarantine Station. . . . The *Varuna* kept up a lively fire with her sternchaser, loaded with grape, shrapnel, case, or canister, and was continually sheering so as to rake us with her broadside guns, but by closely following the motions of her helm we disappointed her.[70]

The Union steamer's fire was devastating, nonetheless. Two-thirds of the men on the *Governor Moore*'s forecastle were killed or wounded. As the ships closed to within forty yards, Kennon felt that the situation called for desperate measures. The *Varuna* was now too close for the Confederate's bow 32-pound rifle to bear on her. Kennon ordered the muzzle depressed and fired a round through his own ship's deck. The exploding shell raked the enemy fore and aft. Kennon stated that

a second shell was fired in like manner with [the] same result. The smoke was now very thick and the ships about 10 feet apart . . . she raked us with her after pivot, sheered so as to give us her starboard broadside, but I was now on top of the hurricane deck and could see her mastheads above the smoke. As quick as lightning our helm was hard aport, and in the twinkling of an eye the crashing noise made by her breaking ribs told how amply we were repaid for all we had lost and suffered.[71]

Kennon backed his vessel away and then rammed his opponent a second time. In the process, the Confederate gunboat received a full broadside from her injured adversary. The *Governor Moore's* decks were swept by canister from four 8-inch Dahlgren guns and two 30-pound rifles. Most of the men on the weather deck were now casualties. At that moment, a new player entered the game. Lt. C. H. Swasey, the *Varuna's* executive officer, recalled, "Hardly had we recovered from the shock of these two blows before we were struck on the port quarter by . . . the *Stonewall Jackson.* . . . We received so much injury from this blow that we made such a quantity of water that it was impossible to keep her afloat, and she was run ashore. . . ."[72] For her temerity, the River Defense boat received two broadsides from the sinking Federal steamer. George W. Phillips, the *Stonewall Jackson's* captain, ordered his vessel run ashore and burned.[73]

As the *Governor Moore* limped away from the fatally injured *Varuna,* Kennon prepared to face the rapidly closing vessels of Bailey's division. Soon realizing the absurdity of the situation, he ordered her to come about and engage the enemy with her stern pivot gun, but she was too badly beat up to escape. "As we came round, the enemy's ships, being near, fired a shower of heavy projectiles which struck the vessel in every part. One gun was dismounted. . . . The wheel-ropes, the head of the rudder, the slide of the engine, and a large piece of the walking-beam was shot away; the latter fell on the cylinder-head and cracked it and filled the engine-room with steam, driving every man out of it." Kennon ran the *Governor Moore* ashore just above the *Varuna,* and set her on fire. Of her ninety-three crewman, fifty-seven were killed and seven wounded.[74]

Farragut's ships assembled off Quarantine Station between 5:30 and 6:00 A.M. Lieutenant Dewey stood on the hurricane deck of the *Mississippi.* "Dawn was breaking and we were just making out the ships around us . . . when we sighted that persistent ram *Manassas* coming up astern in her effort to attack the fleet a second time." Captain Smith returned to the deck with Dewey. Sighting the ram, Smith searched for Farragut to ask permission to attack her. In Dewey's words:

Just then *Hartford,* smoke-blackened from the fire which the fire-craft had caused, and looking a veritable battle-stained and triumphant veteran of war, came steaming by. Farragut was in her rigging, his face eager with victory in the morning light and his eyes snapping. "Run down the ram!" he called. I shall never forget that glimpse of him. He was a very urbane man. But it was plain that if we did not run the *Manassas* down, and promptly, he would not think well of us.[75]

When Lieutenant Warley discovered Farragut's fleet assembled in front of him, he knew his fight was over. The ram's speed was greatly reduced as a result of her riddled smokestack, and her hull had been pierced in a number of places. Warley recalled, "My people had stood gallantly by me, and I owed to them a duty as well as to the country. I cut the delivery pipes, and headed the vessel inshore. . . . I had the opportunity of throwing my men into the swamp and getting them under the cover of the rise in the bank before the enemy commenced to grape us, which they did for an hour and a half."[76]

Battle-scarred and triumphant, Farragut's ships assembled at Quarantine Station to conduct minor repairs and bury the dead before steaming upriver. The actual capture of New Orleans was anticlimactic. Farragut ordered the fleet to get under way about 11:00 A.M. The gunboats *Kineo* and *Wissahickon* remained at Quarantine Station to cover the landing of Butler's troops. After a brief engagement with the Chalmette batteries just below the city, Farragut brought his fleet to anchor off New Orleans shortly after noon on 25 April. An angry crowd met the Union sailors. The Confederate Army had evacuated the city, however, and the civilian authorities announced that they would not resist the conquerors. The wet, tired, and isolated garrison of Fort Jackson mutinied during the early morning hours of 28 April. Later that day, General Duncan surrendered Forts Jackson and St. Philip to Commander Porter. The *Louisiana*, *McRae*, and *Mississippi* were destroyed to prevent capture.

Why did New Orleans fall? Although Confederate mistakes in strategy were decisive, there were tactical reasons for the southern defeat as well. A fractured command structure and a materially weak squadron left the Confederate forces afloat unable either to keep Farragut's ships under the shore batteries or to stop them once they steamed past. The gun crews at Forts Jackson and St. Philip suffered from inexperience and lack of training. This made it less likely that they could solve the firing problems caused by reduced visibility. Exploding shells and burning rafts partially compensated for the darkness, but the dense pall of smoke created by the discharge of so many guns obscured the targets. The forts' officers instructed their gunners to fire at the flashes of the Union guns because the ships' hulls could not be discerned. The change in range further complicated the problem. As Farragut's ships passed through the gap in the obstructions near the middle of the river, they steamed toward one bank or the other. In using the gun flashes as a point of reference, the gunners had not only to lead their targets, but also to adjust for the change in range. Projectiles would overshoot vessels that were much closer than expected. The erratic movement of so many of the Union vessels may have actually helped them avoid being hit.

Another factor in the Union victory was what Farragut believed to be the favor of Providence. Some would call it luck. Fire from the forts disabled only one Union vessel, the *Itasca*. None of the ships grounded for long under Confederate guns. The *Hartford* ran aground in a virtual dead space in Fort St. Philip's field of fire. Farragut was not so fortunate the following year in attempting to pass Port Hudson. There, Confederate fire quickly disabled one vessel and pummeled two others that ran aground under the guns. Only two of seven ships made it past the fortifications.

The fall of New Orleans shifted key advantages from the South to the North in three areas. It delivered a shattering blow to Confederate efforts to gain recognition from France and Great Britain. The South's inability to hold its largest city, the commercial hub of the Mississippi Valley, forestalled the effects of popular agitation for arbitration. Secondly, the city's capture simplified the problems of maintaining the blockade and allowed northern agents to take advantage of the region's rich resources. Finally, Union occupation of New Orleans supported operations along the Gulf of Mexico and up the Mississippi. The opening of a southern front greatly contributed to the eventual failure of Confederate defensive efforts along the Mississippi.

The capture of New Orleans was David Glasgow Farragut's greatest military success. He accomplished it, not by a systematic reduction of the city's defensive network, but, as he predicted, "by audacity." A grateful president and Congress created the rank of rear admiral and made Farragut the first officer in the U.S. Navy to hold it on 30 July 1862. His influence extended far beyond his death in 1870. The midshipmen and lieutenants who served under Farragut during the war became, at the turn of the century, the senior officers of a New Steel Navy that helped a country take its place in the world.

NOTES

1. Mary Boykin Chestnut, *Mary Chestnut's Civil War*, C Vann Woodward, ed. (New Haven, 1981), 330.

2. James M. McPherson, *Battle Cry of Freedom: The Civil War Era* (New York, 1988), 422.

3. Charles L. Dufour, *The Night the War Was Lost* (1960; reprint, Lincoln, Neb., 1994), 339–54.

4. *War of the Rebellion: A Compilation of the Official Records of the Union and Confederate Armies*, 130 vols. (Washington, D.C., 1880–1901), series 1, 6:518 (hereafter ORA).

5. *Battles and Leaders of the Civil War*, 4 vols. (1887; reprint, New York, 1956), 2:30 (hereafter B&L).

6. *Official Records of the Union and Confederate Navies in the War of the Rebellion*, 30 vols. (Washington, D.C., 1894–1922), series 1, 18:346 (hereafter ORN); William N. Still Jr, *Iron Afloat: The Story of the Confederate Armorclads* (Columbia, S C., 1985), 61.

7. *ORN*, 18:328.

8. *B&L*, 2:73–74; *ORA*, 6:707.

9. Gideon Welles, *Diary of Gideon Welles*, Howard K. Beale, ed. (New York, 1960), 3:134.

10. Charles Lee Lewis, *David Glasgow Farragut, Admiral in the Making* (Annapolis, 1941), 17–24.

11. Ibid., 211–15, 243–46.

12. Welles, *Diary*, 1:440.

13. Ibid , 1:230

14. B&L, 2:57–58

15. George Dewey, *Autobiography of George Dewey, Admiral of the Navy* (New York, 1913), 50.

16. B&L, 2:58.

17. Albert Bigelow Paine, *A Sailor of Fortune: Personal Memoirs of Captain B. S. Osbon* (New York, 1906), 185.

18. Frederic Stanhope Hill, *Twenty Years at Sea; or, Leaves from My Old Log-Books* (Boston, 1893), 168–71.

19. Paine, *A Sailor of Fortune,* 179–80

20. Ibid., 184

21. *ORN,* 18:160.

22. Ibid., 166

23 B&L, 2 38; ORA, 6:520–21; ORN, 18 324–30.

24. Paine, *A Sailor of Fortune,* 188

25 Hill, *Twenty Years at Sea,* 174.

26. George Hamilton Perkins, *Letters of Captain George Hamilton Perkins, U.S.N.,* George E Belknap, ed. (Concord, N.H., 1901), 67.

27. Paine, *A Sailor of Fortune,* 190

28. Ibid , 189, 190–91; *ORN,* 18:696, 764, 768

29 *ORN,* 18:696

30. Perkins, *Letters of Captain George Hamilton Perkins,* 67.

31. Ibid , 67–68.

32. *ORN,* 18:201

33 Ibid., 768

34. Ibid , 176–80, 769

35. Ibid., 204–5.

36 Dewey, *Autobiography,* 62–63, ORN, 18:207, 212, 778

37. *ORN,* 18:332.

38 Ibid.

39. Ibid., 336

40. Ibid., 337

41. B&L, 2:90.

42. Dewey, *Autobiography,* 63–64 Orders to the helmsman in this period were given in terms of the position of the tiller rather than the rudder. Thus the ship would actually turn in the opposite direction from the orders given to the helm. See John Harland, *Seamanship in the Age of Sail* (Annapolis, 1984), 175

43. Ibid., 64–65

44. *ORN,* 18:276, 295.

45. Ibid., 754.

46. Paine, *A Sailor of Fortune,* 192

47. Ibid.

48. *ORN,* 18 142, 157, 168; B&L, 64

49. *ORA,* 6:551.

50. Quoted in B&L, 2:45.

51 Paine, *A Sailor of Fortune,* 196–97.

52. B&L, 2.64

53 *ORN,* 18:696

54 Ibid., 182, 197; B&L, 2:62.

55 *ORN,* 18.218.

56. Ibid., 197.

57. B&L, 2:62–63.

58. *ORN,* 18:197, 295–96; B&L, 2:65. Mitchell thought that he was engaging, at this point, the *Hartford.* However, there is no evidence that the Union flagship ever got this close to the ironclad, while the records indicate that the *Brooklyn* did

59. *ORN*, 18:197–98.
60 Ibid., 340.
61. Ibid., 182, 197–98, 340.
62 Ibid., 182, 187, 198, 344; *B&L*, 2:67.
63. Hill, *Twenty Years at Sea*, 176–77.
64 *ORN*, 18:360.
65 Ibid., 220.
66. Ibid., 221, 332, 333.
67. Ibid., 332, 336, 344; *B&L*, 2.90.
68. *ORN*, 18·224–27.
69. *B&L*, 2:80–81.
70. *ORN*, 18:305–6.
71 Ibid., 306.
72. Ibid., 212.
73. Ibid., 213; *B&L*, 2:84.
74. *ORN*, 18·307; *B&L*, 2:84–85.
75. Dewey, *Autobiography*, 68–69.
76. *ORN*, 18:344.

8

The Battle of Mobile Bay

JACK H. FRIEND

In the spring of 1864, as the rebellion entered its fourth year, the heartland of the Confederacy remained unconquered. Mounting Union casualties and a growing belief that the war would continue indefinitely were causing widespread discontent throughout the North. So great was voter unrest that President Lincoln faced the possibility of defeat in the November election. If this should happen, the Democrats, prompted by a strong peace faction, were prepared to end the war by negotiation. Lincoln knew this, his newly appointed general in chief, Ulysses S. Grant, knew it, and the enemy knew it.[1]

Grant was certain that only a succession of quick victories would keep Lincoln in the White House. To achieve this he was convinced that all Union forces must act in concert toward a common objective: the destruction of the Confederacy's two major field armies. His plan entailed: (1) a thrust into the South's heartland via Chattanooga, Tennessee, and Mobile, Alabama, aimed at Gen. Joseph E. Johnston's Army of Tennessee; and (2) continuous, unrelenting pressure on Gen. Robert E. Lee's Army of Northern Virginia. In the west, Union forces would consolidate, go on the defensive, and offer whatever support they could to the two principal operations.

Grant viewed Mobile and its vast inland river system as a natural invasion corridor into the heart of the Confederacy. He had wanted to attack Mobile ever since the capture of Vicksburg in July 1863, but Lincoln and Maj. Gen. Henry Halleck, then general in chief, were always distracted by other priorities. Now that Halleck had been demoted to chief of staff and Grant enjoyed Lincoln's full support, the new general in chief was in a position to dictate strategy. He therefore ordered that an attack on Mobile be linked to Maj. Gen. William T. Sherman's Georgia campaign, which was scheduled to jump off from Chattanooga in May, when the Army of the Potomac moved against Lee.

By thrusting inland from Mobile, a Union army would divert rebel troops from northwestern Georgia and simultaneously give Sherman a secure destination if, after taking Atlanta, he decided to head for the Gulf of Mexico instead of the Atlantic.

Much to Grant's disappointment, on three occasions circumstances intervened to postpone the attack on Mobile. The first occurred when an army of thirty thousand, scheduled to move against the city in May, was mauled by Confederate troops in the Red River campaign in western Louisiana. The defeated commander, Maj. Gen. Nathaniel Banks, one of Lincoln's political appointees, was replaced by Maj. Gen. E. R. S. Canby, a competent, professional soldier. En route to his new headquarters in New Orleans, Canby received a letter from Sherman, dated 4 June, requesting that "a strong feint or real attack be made on Mobile" via Pascagoula, Mississippi, in cooperation with Rear Adm. David G. Farragut.[2] By then, the Union Army was only twenty-five miles from Atlanta, but the Confederate Army remained intact and Sherman wanted something done to keep it from being reinforced. If Mobile were threatened, rebel troops might be sent there rather than to Georgia.

On 17 June, Canby met with Farragut aboard the *Hartford* on the blockade off Mobile to propose an immediate attack on the city. Farragut, elated, agreed to cooperate. As commander of the West Gulf Blockading Squadron, he recognized the strategic importance of Mobile and had been pushing for an attack since the capture of New Orleans. By the time Canby departed, the broad outline of a plan had taken shape: Forts Morgan and Gaines, guarding the gulf entrance to Mobile Bay, would be assaulted by a joint army-navy task force, clearing the way for the army to make an overland advance on Mobile from Pascagoula. Fort Powell, a small earthen fortification in Mississippi Sound, would be the navy's responsibility. Canby anticipated no difficulty furnishing the twenty thousand troops needed for the operation now that he had consolidated his forces and discontinued offensive operations in the West. In contrast, Farragut had a problem: he needed ironclads.

When intelligence reports indicated that the Confederates were building armored rams in Alabama, Farragut requested ironclads to even the scales. Secretary of the Navy Gideon Welles agreed to send him some, but as yet none had arrived. To attack without them would risk the destruction of Farragut's fleet. The South's most formidable warship, the ram *Tennessee,* lay just inside the bay, waiting to engage Farragut's wooden ships as they entered. Measuring 209 feet from stem to stern and 48 feet abeam, the *Tennessee* was armed with six Brooke rifles. Her iron prow and armored shield provided advantages denied to wooden vessels, but her slow speed, sluggish maneuverability, and weakly protected rudder chains were serious defects.

On 1 July, as preparations for the attack were progressing, Canby received a dispatch from Halleck directing him to send all the troops he could spare to Fort Monroe, Virginia. Now that the Army of Northern Virginia had withdrawn into the defenses around Richmond and Petersburg, the possibility of a protracted siege and its impact on the November election cried out for a quick solution. Grant's response was to strengthen his siege lines with more troops, even if it meant weakening the effort against the enemy heartland. Canby promptly informed Farragut that the attack on Mobile had been canceled, but promised to meet in a few days and discuss the situation.[3] Thus for a second time since Grant assumed command of the Union Army, Mobile was spared the rigors of a siege.

Although unhappy that the Mobile operation had been tabled, Farragut was mollified when he learned the monitor *Manhattan* had arrived at Pensacola, Florida, and that Canby was working to put the Mobile attack back on the agenda, in modified form. On 8 July, Canby met with Farragut and told him he had found four thousand troops to invest Forts Morgan and Gaines, but not enough to attack Mobile itself. The admiral again agreed to cooperate and began preparations for landing the army and running past the forts.

Since assuming command in the gulf, Farragut had been pondering how to enter Mobile Bay. On 12 July, he published General Order No. 10, directing all vessels to remove superfluous spars and rigging, and to protect vulnerable machinery with chains, sandbags, sails, and hammocks. Drawing on lessons learned at New Orleans and Port Hudson, he ordered the wooden vessels to be lashed in pairs, with the small gunboats on the side away from Fort Morgan. The monitors would steam in column between the wooden ships and Fort Morgan. In addition, the order prescribed the course to be followed when approaching and moving away from the fort, gave firing instructions, and specified that each vessel go in with low steam. Farragut intended to get as close as possible to the fort, believing that his own broadsides would be the best protection against its fire.[4]

On 18 July, a third setback occurred when Canby informed Farragut that there would be a "delay in collecting the force" to attack the forts. Losing patience, Farragut told him that time was running out; the weather would not hold. The navy would be willing to proceed if the army would scrape up as few as one thousand troops to attack Fort Gaines, on the eastern end of Dauphin Island. Fort Morgan, on Mobile Point, could be invested after Gaines surrendered. The arrival of the *Manhattan* and word that two more monitors would soon join the fleet had emboldened Farragut. He wanted to get on with the attack.

A week later Canby wrote Farragut that he had located two thousand troops to attack Fort Gaines. He was expecting about three thousand more from the evacuation of Union garrisons in Texas and would send them along as reinforcements. Three days later, on 29 July, Canby informed the admiral that twenty-four hundred troops were embarking for Dauphin Island.

Farragut then published General Order No. 11. Anticipating a tough fight, he directed that disabled vessels should drop out of line to the westward and not attempt to reenter until all other vessels had passed. The gunboats were to be cast loose after passing Fort Morgan to prevent the rebel gunboats from escaping up the bay. The order again stressed the need for all vessels to pass to the east of the easternmost buoy, which was clear of all obstructions.

One of Farragut's major concerns was the obstructions and torpedoes—as mines were then called—that had been placed in the channel opposite Fort Morgan. On several occasions his flag lieutenant, John C. Watson, made night reconnaissances to learn more about these obstacles but failed to locate any. Considering the extent of the area and the difficulty of working at night, often close under the fort's guns, Watson's failure was understandable. Refugees and deserters had heard that many of the torpedoes were water-soaked and innocuous, but knew little about the obstructions. Taking no chances, Farragut ordered that vessels with propellers stop their engines and drift past the torpedo field. Their paddle-wheel consorts should maintain headway since they were less likely to be fouled by the enemy's drag ropes.

Meanwhile, Farragut learned that the monitor *Tecumseh* had finally arrived at Pensacola. On 31 July, the double-turreted monitor *Winnebago* steamed in from New Orleans and hove to in Sand Island Channel near the *Manhattan,* reporting that the *Chickasaw* was close behind. With the army aboard transports, and no word concerning the *Tecumseh's* combat readiness, Farragut sent Capt. Thornton Jenkins in the *Richmond* to Pensacola to expedite her departure. Capt. Percival Drayton, Farragut's fleet captain, told Jenkins to stay until the *Tecumseh* left. On 1 August, Maj. Gen. Gordon Granger met with Farragut aboard the flagship and informed him that the army would land on the west end of Dauphin Island in two days. Now that a third monitor, the double-turreted *Chickasaw,* had arrived from New Orleans and the *Tecumseh* was expected momentarily, Farragut finally had the advantage he was seeking and committed the navy to go in on 4 August.[5]

On the third, as Granger's transports steamed up Mississippi Sound toward Dauphin Island, Farragut and his captains met aboard the *Hartford* to discuss final plans for the naval attack the next day. Farragut wanted the *Hartford* to lead but was persuaded that the flagship would be too exposed. His captains argued that the *Brooklyn*, equipped with four bow chasers and a torpedo catcher, would be the best vessel to take the van. The admiral reluctantly agreed, a decision he would regret, but insisted that the *Hartford* be second in line.

Later that afternoon, Farragut was frustrated to learn that the *Tecumseh* would not leave Pensacola in time to arrive the next morning. He wrote a scathing letter to Jenkins, still in Pensacola, telling him that the army was about to go ashore, and he could wait no longer for the *Tecumseh:* "I must go in day after tomorrow morning at daylight or a little after." Farragut then ordered Jenkins to return to the fleet on the fourth with or without the *Tecumseh*, declaring, "I can lose no more days." He also mentioned, somewhat apologetically, that he had consented to let James Alden, captain of the *Brooklyn*, lead in.[6] Late that afternoon a brigade of seventeen hundred Union troops landed unopposed on the west end of Dauphin Island. Though not as many as Canby had promised, this was more men than the thousand Farragut had suggested, and others were on the way.

The next morning, 4 August, skirmishers could be heard popping away at each other on Dauphin Island. Still embarrassed over the navy's failure to attack as scheduled, Farragut was determined to find some way to support the army. Noticing Confederate transports discharging troops and cargo at Fort Gaines, he ordered the *Winnebago* to drive them away. The ironclad steamed within three thousand yards of the fort and fired twenty-four "miserable" shots, receiving several equally "miserable" shots in return.[7] Little was accomplished by this foray except to uphold the navy's honor.

While the *Winnebago* was firing, a contingent of army signalmen was distributed among the vessels that would go in the next morning. These specialists were to open communications with the army once the fleet had entered the bay. They would, however, see action before then.

During the afternoon a final council of war was held aboard the *Hartford*. Farragut emphasized the role of the monitors, explaining that he wanted them to neutralize the fire of the fort as the wooden ships passed and to "look out" for the enemy ram. The *Tecumseh* would lead, followed by the *Manhattan*, *Winnebago*, and *Chickasaw*. The large screw sloops *Brooklyn*, *Hartford*, and *Richmond*, and their side-wheel consorts, the gunboats *Octorara*, *Metacomet*, and *Port Royal*, would comprise the van. The smaller screw sloops *Lackawanna*, *Monongahela*, *Ossipee*, *Oneida*, and *Seminole*, and their consorts, the screw gunboats *Kennebec* and *Itasca* and the screw steamer *Galena*, would follow. The formation would be line ahead in close order, with each pair of ships echeloned to starboard during the final approach so that their bow guns would have a clear field of fire.[8]

Two flotillas would support the battle line with gunfire. The Gulf Flotilla, six gunboats under the command of Lt. Cdr. E. C. Grafton, would shell Fort Morgan from the gulf as the fleet steamed in. The Mississippi Sound Flotilla, five gunboats commanded by Lt. Cdr. J. C. P. De Krafft, would fire on Fort Powell.

About 4:30 P.M., the *Richmond* stood in from Pensacola, followed by the *Tecumseh* in tow of the side-wheel gunboat *Bienville*. At dusk the sloops and gunboats that would form the battle line steamed beyond the bar and anchored in line abreast on either side of the *Brooklyn*. The vessels that would remain outside during the fight moved close to shore to watch for blockade runners.

At 3:00 A.M. all hands were called. Anchor chains were shortened, fires spread, hammocks stowed, and the crews given coffee and sandwiches. Breakfast would be served after the battle. A heavy mist shrouded the gulf as the vessels, with lights up, maneuvered to form pairs. At 5:30 the flagship hoisted General Signal 1218: "Get Underway."[9] Forty-five minutes later, the *Brooklyn* and *Octorara* were crossing the outer bar. As the mist burned off, a scene "worthy of the brush of an Angelo or Raphael" was revealed. From every peak, staff, and masthead fluttered a large national flag, and Farragut's blue pennant floated from the flagship's mizzen.[10]

Conditions on 5 August were ideal for an attack—just what Farragut wanted: a light southwest breeze to blind the forts with smoke, a flood tide to compensate for low steam, and an overcast sky to temper the August heat. The Confederate squadron could nevertheless make the most of its position at the end of the channel by raking the enemy vessels as they approached, unencumbered by their gun smoke or their broadsides—and there were the torpedoes, untested on such a scale, but potentially lethal.

The event now set in motion would be the bloodiest naval battle of the Civil War, a contest between the wills of two great fighting admirals, David Farragut and Franklin Buchanan. Both were American, both had been raised and trained in the same naval tradition, both had fought under the same flag, and each was a hero to the people and government he served. Since the battles of New Orleans and Hampton Roads in the spring of 1862, fate had been bringing these antagonists together.

Adm. Franklin Buchanan was one of the Old Navy's ablest commanders. Entering the navy in 1815, he had made his first cruise under the command of

Commo. Oliver Hazard Perry. As young officers, he and Farragut had served together in the same squadron, chasing pirates and slavers in the Caribbean. Later in the course of a career filled with intriguing assignments, he saw action in the Mexican War, became the first superintendent of the Naval Academy, and served as Commo. Matthew Perry's flag captain in the opening of Japan.

In 1861 Buchanan resigned as a captain in the U.S. Navy and joined the Confederate Navy with the same rank. Six months later, as commander of the ironclad ram *Virginia* on the first day's battle at Hampton Roads, he sank the frigate *Congress* and sloop of war *Cumberland* in one of the most famous naval battles in history.

In August 1862, after recovering from a wound received in that battle, Buchanan was promoted to admiral and became the ranking officer in the Confederate Navy. He was then sent to Mobile to take command of the naval forces there, an assignment that brought him one step closer to his nemesis, David Farragut.[11]

With steel-blue eyes and a clean-shaven face, Buchanan at sixty-two was "strikingly handsome." Of medium height and trim waist, he had the appearance and physique of a much younger man. Although upright in carriage, he walked with a limp acquired at Hampton Roads, a reminder that here was a fighting admiral who had been close enough to the enemy to be shot by a musket. His ruddy complexion and snow-white hair spoke of years on the quarterdeck; his high forehead and aquiline nose, of breeding and intelligence. But it was the set of Old Buck's mouth that best described his resolute character. "When full of fight he had a peculiarity of drawing down the corners of his mouth until the thin line between his lips formed a perfect arch around his mouth."[12]

As the sun rose on 5 August, the Union battle line could be seen moving in from the gulf. At 6:00 A.M. Buchanan was notified that the enemy fleet was crossing the bar. He promptly ordered Cdr. James D. Johnston, the *Tennessee's* captain, to get under way. Within twenty minutes, Buchanan had positioned the Confederate squadron in line ahead across the channel adjacent to the torpedo field, with the wooden gunboats *Morgan, Selma,* and *Gaines* west of the flagship. This would enable him to bring sixteen guns, nearly all rifled, to bear on the approaching enemy.

As the *Tennessee* moved into position, Buchanan came down from the pilothouse to the gun deck and addressed the crew, his snug, grey frock coat, gold braid, and sword imparting a deadly seriousness to his words: "Now men, the enemy is coming, and I want you to do your duty; and you shall not

TABLE 8.1 The Battle of Mobile Bay, 5 August 1864

	Commissioned	Displacement	Speed	Complement	Guns
U.S. NAVY					
Rear Adm. D. G. Farragut					
Turreted ironclads					
Manhattan	1864	2,100	8	106	2
Tecumseh	1864	2,100	8	115	2
Chickasaw	1864	1,300	8	138	4
Winnebago	1864	1,300	8	139	4
Screw sloops					
Brooklyn	1859	2,686	9.5	376	26
Richmond	1860	2,604	9.5	356	22
Hartford	1859	2,550	9.5	404	24
Lackawanna	1863	2,526	11.5	210	14
Monongahela	1863	2,078	11.5	214	11
Ossipee	1862	1,934	11.5	171	13
Oneida	1862	1,488	11.5	183	11
Seminole	1860	1,235	11	138	9
Side-wheel gunboats[a]					
Metacomet	1864	1,173	13	171	8
Port Royal	1862	1,163	11	158	8
Octorara	1862	981	11	146	10
Screw gunboats					
Kennebec	1862	691	10	83	5
Itasca	1861	691	10	97	6
Screw steamer					
Galena	1862	950	8	157	11
TOTAL		29,550		3,362	190
C.S. NAVY					
Rear Adm. F. Buchanan					
Casemate ironclad					
Tennessee	1864	1,914	6	169	6
Side-wheel gunboats					
Gaines	1862	977	10	131	6
Morgan	1862	977	10	145	6
Selma	1861[b]	643	9	102	4
TOTAL		4,511		547	22
SHORE FORTIFICATIONS					
Fort Morgan					46
Bearing south on channel					7
Bearing west on channel					17
Bearing south and west on channel					1

[a] Double-ended
[b] Acquired

Franklin Buchanan in Confederate uniform. *U.S. Naval Institute*

have it to say when you leave this vessel that you were not near enough to the enemy, for I will meet them, and then you can fight alongside of their own ships; and if I fall, lay me on one side and go on with the fight, and never mind me—but whip and sink the Yankees or fight until you sink yourselves, but do not surrender."[13]

Ashore, while the admiral spoke, hundreds of soldiers were rushing to man the batteries of Fort Morgan. While passing the fort, the Union fleet would be subjected to the fire of thirty-four guns: Buchanan's sixteen and eighteen more from the fort.

In the channel opposite Fort Morgan, 180 torpedoes had been laid in three parallel lines, arranged in quincuncial order.[14] The timber obstructions had washed away, a fact the Confederate authorities had managed to keep secret. Directly opposite the fort, a safe-lane 150 yards wide between the beach and a large red buoy had been left clear of torpedoes. This corridor allowed blockade runners to enter and leave the bay, and permitted the Confederate squadron to threaten the blockade with sorties.

By 6:45 the leading Union monitor, the *Tecumseh,* had crossed in front of the column of wooden ships and headed up the channel, her guns loaded with shells. Once fired, the guns would be reloaded with 440-pound solid shot for use against the rebel ram. Two minutes later the gunners on Fort Morgan's ramparts saw a puff of white smoke erupt from the monitor's turret. The projectile became visible within seconds, growing larger and larger as it howled toward the fort. A moment later, a bright flash and an ear-splitting crack sent 350 pounds of iron smashing into the dunes to the south. A second shell burst over the fort. Maj. James T. Gee, an artillery officer, wanted to return the fire, but the fort's commander, Brig. Gen. Richard L. Page, considered the range still too great and would not give the order.

At 7:05, the *Tecumseh* was about two thousand yards from the fort; the van of the wooden column, nearly three thousand. Accuracy at these ranges was problematical, especially when the target was moving, but the morale of the garrison had to be considered. Ignoring for the moment the ironclads, the general turned his attention to the more vulnerable wooden vessels. When Page gave the command to fire, a "soul-stirring cheer" burst forth.[15] The first gun to open was a Brooke rifle in the southwest bastion. It sent a 100-pound shell screaming toward the lead pair of wooden vessels. The projectile fell short, kicking up a geyser of white water. Acknowledging the challenge, the *Brooklyn* sent a 100-pound shell screaming back.

The *Tecumseh*'s captain, Cdr. Tunis A. M. Craven, although an experienced seaman, was unfamiliar with the currents and shoals of Mobile Bay. His pilot, John Collins, knew the bay like the palm of his hand, but he knew little about the handling of a sluggish, 2,100-ton ironclad. Nevertheless, Collins found himself acting as both pilot and helmsman aboard a vessel he had never conned.

As the ironclads approached the fort, Farragut had been busy keeping the wooden vessels closed up and moving. At low steam, the fleet's advance was barely faster than the incoming tide. The wooden column had been gaining on the ironclads, however, and would soon be abreast of the rear vessel. Farragut had climbed the *Hartford*'s port main rigging to avoid the dense smoke enveloping the deck. Fearing that the admiral might fall, Drayton ordered Quartermaster John Knowles to go up and tie him to the futtock shrouds. Farragut mildly protested but allowed Knowles to comply with Drayton's order.[16] The firing had now become more intense, and casualties were beginning to trickle down to the cockpit where the surgeons were stationed. At 7:24, as the *Brooklyn* came abreast of the rear monitor, Captain Alden slowed his rate of advance. Farragut noticed this and ordered his flag lieutenant to hoist General Signal 665: "Go Ahead."

Through the narrow observation slits in the *Tecumseh's* pilothouse, Commander Craven could see the enemy ram—six hundred yards ahead—bucking the current, the *Manhattan* following in his wake, and the *Brooklyn,* five hundred yards astern, bearing down on his port quarter. He and Cdr. James Nicholson, captain of the *Manhattan,* had been ordered to keep the ram away from the wooden ships—but here was the *Brooklyn* threatening to overtake the monitors and enter the bay. In the *Brooklyn,* Alden realized that a serious problem was developing: the *Tecumseh* and *Manhattan* had been ordered to destroy the *Tennessee,* and the *Winnebago* and *Chickasaw* to suppress the fire of Fort Morgan's water battery as the wooden vessels passed. During their approach, however, the ironclads had strayed too far to the west to allow the wooden column to steer east of the buoy. If the admiral did not change his plan, Alden had no alternative but to stop.

Alden needed to communicate with the flagship as quickly as possible. Summoning Capt. E. A. Denicke, an army signalman, to the poop deck, he ordered him to flag the *Hartford:* "The Monitors are right ahead. We cannot go on without passing them. What shall we do?"[17] When lookouts aboard the flagship saw Denicke waving his red-and-white flag, a messenger was sent to the cockpit to request that an army flagman come on deck to take the message. Within minutes, Lt. John C. Kinney was on the forecastle reading Alden's message, which he promptly sent to Farragut by an aide, Lt. Arthur Yates.

Five minutes later Kinney signaled the admiral's reply to Alden: "Go ahead."[18] Finding the *Hartford's* forecastle suddenly shrouded in smoke, Kinney climbed to the foretop, but visibility was no better. It was not until he reached the crosstrees, ninety-six feet above the deck, that he could see the *Brooklyn's* poop, where Denicke was standing with the flag.

By now, the *Brooklyn* had passed the *Winnebago,* the third monitor in line, and was abreast of the *Manhattan;* astern the *Hartford* and *Richmond* were closing fast. Noticing the confusion ahead, the other wooden vessels had begun to lag behind and had yet to come under heavy fire. From the rear of the column the van appeared to be "enveloped in dense white smoke with nothing visible but the red flash of guns and bursting shells."[19]

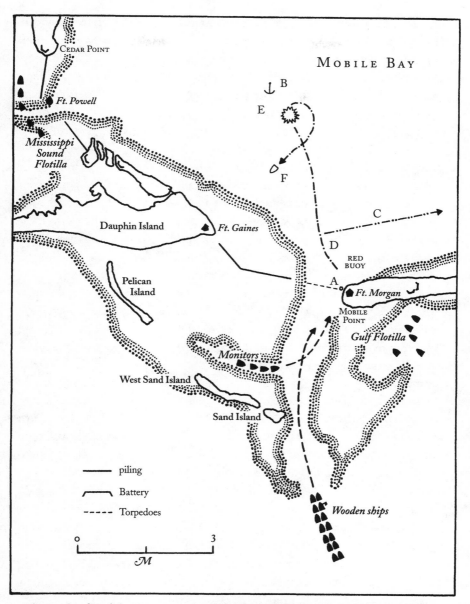

The Battle of Mobile Bay, 5 August 1864. Following the loss of the *Tecumseh* (A), the Union fleet fights its way past the forts and anchors in Mobile Bay (B), while the USS *Metacomet* and three other gunboats pursue the CSS *Selma* (C). The *Tennessee* then advances to the attack (D) and rams the *Hartford* (E), but is forced to surrender (F) after a fierce melee.

As the *Tecumseh* approached the torpedo field, Craven began to doubt that he could pass to the east of the red buoy and turn in time to engage the enemy ram before it attacked the wooden ships. He told pilot Collins, "It is impossible that the admiral means us to go inside that buoy; I cannot turn my ship."[20] Meanwhile, the *Tennessee* had moved a short distance to the west, apparently jockeying for a better position from which to ram the first vessel that passed into the bay. This movement, together with Craven's perception that he could not pass east of the buoy, prompted him to order the *Tecumseh's* helm to starboard and head for the *Tennessee.*

On the far side of the torpedo field, Buchanan was indeed waiting to ram the first enemy vessel that entered the bay. If he could sink one of the big sloops in the narrow passage between the buoy and the beach, the other vessels might give up and retire to the gulf. The leading monitor was now about 250 yards away, with her bow pointing toward the *Tennessee,* as if to cross the torpedo field.

In the *Tennessee,* Lt. A. D. Wharton sighted the ship's bow pivot gun, a 7-inch Brooke rifle loaded with a 140-pound bolt, at the monitor's turret. He had orders to wait until the two vessels touched before firing. Suddenly, the monitor rolled to port, her bow knifing below the surface, her large screw revolving wildly as the stern lifted above the water. The *Tecumseh* had struck a torpedo.

In the *Tecumseh's* pilothouse, Craven and Collins felt the shock of the explosion and no doubt heard shouts of alarm as water surged across the deck and entered the turret. Realizing that his vessel was sinking, Craven may have ordered "abandon ship" as he descended from the pilothouse, but it would have been a futile command, for twenty of the *Tecumseh's* twenty-one survivors had already left the doomed vessel.

On reaching the gun deck, Craven and Collins met at the foot of the ladder leading to the turret roof hatch. Struggling in water up to his chest, Craven pushed back and said to Collins, "After you, pilot." Collins later recalled those last moments: "There was nothing after me, for when I reached the top rung of the ladder the vessel seemed to drop from under me."[21] It had taken less than four minutes for the *Tecumseh* to disappear.

Through the *Tennessee's* forward gunport Wharton could see bodies thrashing in the water but, oddly, noticed very little turbulence. Some of the survivors managed to climb aboard a boat that had been cut loose as the ironclad sank. Others were picked up by a small cutter flying a large U.S. flag, apparently sent by one of the sloops. Four swam ashore and were taken prisoner.[22]

At 7:40 still perched on the *Hartford's* crosstrees, Kinney received a second message from the *Brooklyn:* "Our best monitor has been sunk."[23] He promptly gave the message to Yates for delivery to Farragut. Within minutes Yates returned with the admiral's reply, which Kinney flagged to Alden: "Tell the monitors to go ahead and then take your place."[24]

The *Hartford's* bowsprit was now dangerously close to the *Brooklyn's* stern, both vessels angling across the channel toward the fort. The *Richmond,* a hundred yards behind, had also stopped, her bow swinging to port, her stern just off the beach.

From atop Fort Morgan's ramparts, General Page noticed that the Union vessels were not moving. Apparently they had intended to pass between the red buoy and the beach but now had second thoughts. The general walked back and forth, encouraging the gun crews, pointing out targets, receiving and sending messages. The noise was deafening; commands had to be shouted; smoke obscured both friend and foe. The battle was reaching a climax; a Confederate victory was in sight.

To Lieutenant Kinney, high above the *Hartford's* deck, the sight was "sickening beyond the power of words to portray. Shot after shot came through the side, mowing down the men, deluging the decks with blood, and scattering mangled fragments of humanity so thickly that it was difficult to stand on the deck, so slippery was it."[25]

When Alden failed to advance, despite three orders to go ahead, Farragut decided to act. The din of the battle made conversation impossible except at close range. From his position in the shrouds, the admiral reached up through the lubber's hold and tapped Pilot Martin Freeman on the foot to get his attention. Farragut then asked if there was enough water to pass the *Brooklyn* on her port side. Freeman said yes, but asked about the torpedoes. He would later write that the admiral "told me to pick my way and go into the bay or blow up, so I started the ship ahead."[26]

Freeman was now in virtual command of the *Hartford;* the fate of the flagship and the fleet depended on his actions. Within seconds, he would have shouted into the speaking tube connected to the deck: "*Hartford,* starboard your helm hard and go ahead full!" or possibly: "Hard a-starboard, four bells!" followed by: "*Metacomet,* back full!" The officer monitoring the deck end of the speaking tube, after repeating the order, would have transmitted it to the helmsmen and bell-pull officers of the two vessels. As soon as the *Hartford* cleared the *Brooklyn's* stern, Freeman would have commanded: "*Metacomet,* stop your engine!" then to the *Hartford:* "Meet her!" (meaning stop turning), and to the *Metacomet:* "Ahead full!" When on course he would have said: "Steady!" or "Steady as she goes!"[27] All this took perhaps ten minutes.

On the other side of the torpedo field, Buchanan noticed the *Hartford* swinging to port. Anticipating the enemy's intention, he moved the *Tennessee* still further to the west. At 7:50 A.M., having swung clear of the *Brooklyn's* stern, the *Hartford* and her consort crossed the torpedo field. Despite the loss of the *Tecumseh,* Farragut's belief that most of the torpedoes had been rendered harmless by corrosion or seepage proved to be true.

Determined to maintain the advantage of position, the Confederate gunboats hauled around and headed up the bay, their stern and port-quarter guns raking the Union flagship's deck. Buchanan attempted to ram the *Hartford* as she passed, but failed because of the *Tennessee's* slow speed. For a short while he gave chase, then in frustration swung around and headed toward the enemy sloops now following in Farragut's wake. With limited room for maneuver, these vessels would be forced to do battle on Buchanan's terms. Although the torpedo field had been breached, the old admiral was still full of fight. Before the *Tennessee* turned, Lieutenant Wharton got off a parting shot from his pivot gun that exploded over the *Hartford's* forecastle.

As the *Hartford* steamed up the channel, the three Confederate gunboats maintained their raking positions off her starboard bow. Midshipman George Waterman, who commanded the *Gaines's* after-battery, fired his guns at near point-blank range, seven hundred yards. After directing his aim at the *Hartford's* bow, he concentrated on her decks with devastating effect.

Soon, however, the *Hartford* managed to bring her broadsides to bear on the Confederate gunboats, causing them to break off the fight. By then the *Gaines* was firing five guns in broadside. The *Selma* headed east for shallow water, and the *Gaines,* hulled below the waterline, returned to Fort Morgan, where she sank. The *Morgan* disengaged relatively undamaged and ran aground on a sand spit near the fort. That night she would escape to Mobile.

Meanwhile, Buchanan had passed down the column of advancing Union ships. Except for a brush with the *Monongahela,* the *Tennessee's* sluggishness frustrated her attempts to ram, but her guns inflicted numerous casualties. After exchanging shots with the last pair of vessels, Buchanan turned to port and brought the ram to a stop near Fort Morgan. To the northeast, several miles away, sporadic gunfire could be heard, indicating that the *Selma* was still in the fight. Farragut would later write that the *Tennessee* and the Confederate gunboats accounted for the loss of more men than the fire from Fort Morgan's batteries.

A half hour earlier, Farragut had cut loose the *Metacomet* and ordered her

The Battle of Mobile Bay, 5 August 1864. This view by Union naval officer and artist Henry Walke shows the *Hartford* leading the column of wooden ships into the bay after passing the *Brooklyn*. From left to right, looking south: Buchanan's squadron, the CSS *Gaines, Tennessee, Morgan,* and *Selma;* the monitors *Manhattan, Chickasaw,* and *Winnebago,* with the sunken *Tecumseh*'s boat between the first two and Fort Morgan looming in the background; Farragut's wooden ships, the *Hartford* with the *Metacomet,* the *Brooklyn* with the *Octorara,* the *Richmond* with the *Port Royal,* the *Lackawanna* with the *Seminole,* the *Monongahela* with the *Kennebec,* the *Ossipee* with the *Itasca,* and the *Oneida* with the *Galena;* Union transports; and the Sand Island Light. Walke was not present at the battle, and his composition contains some errors. The walls of Fort Morgan are too high; proportionally to the *Hartford,* the *Metacomet* is too small; the Confederate gunboats *Gaines, Morgan,* and *Selma* were not casemated, and by this stage of the action they had begun retiring up the bay ahead of the wooden ships. *U.S. Naval Institute*

to pursue the *Selma.* By 8:20, three more Union gunboats had joined the chase, but it was the *Metacomet* that finally gained the laurels. A fast, double-ended side-wheeler, the *Metacomet* was more than a match for the *Selma.* When Lt. P. U. Murphy hauled down his ship's flag, he and six crewmen had been wounded, and two officers and six crewmen killed. The other three Union gunboats contributed little, if anything, to the chase. Farragut was furious over the escape of the *Morgan* and *Gaines,* even though the *Gaines* was now a helpless wreck.

Having watched the battle line enter the bay from his station in the gulf, Master's Mate James T. Seaver, captain of the little dispatch boat *Philippi,* could not resist the urge to share in the glory. Seaver had asked to accompany the battle line but was refused. Now, as the fleet was beginning to anchor inside the bay, he defied orders and steamed into the channel, hugging the far side, two thousand yards from Fort Morgan. His excuse was to render assistance to any vessel that might have been disabled. No sooner had the *Philippi* started forward than she ran aground and was sunk by gunfire from the fort, her crew escaping in such haste that a dead seaman was left on board. Farragut, occupied with directing the battle, was unaware of this misfortune.

For twenty minutes the *Tennessee* had remained stationary off Fort Morgan, her large screw turning just enough to offset the incoming tide. An inspection revealed that, although damaged, she was still battleworthy. After a breakfast of coffee and hardtack, officers and crewmen emerged to gulp fresh air, the crew on the afterdeck, the officers on top of the shield.

Four miles to the north, the enemy fleet was coming to anchor near the *Hartford*. Now that the battle was over, Buchanan's officers agreed that the Confederate squadron had courageously defended its honor. It was, therefore, with astonishment and disbelief that they heard Buchanan say to the *Tennessee*'s captain, "Follow them up, Johnston; we can't let them off that way."

Fleet Surgeon D. B. Conrad, standing near the admiral, asked if he intended to take on the entire Union fleet. Buchanan replied that he did. When Conrad remarked, "Well, we'll never come out of there whole," the admiral answered, "That's my lookout, sir!"[28]

As the *Tennessee* steamed toward the Yankee fleet, hundreds of soldiers crowded the ramparts of Fort Morgan, their cheers resounding across the water in the *Tennessee*'s wake. A Confederate marine at Fort Gaines described the scene: "The skirmishing on land ceases by tacit agreement. Now comes a sight that throws all others in the shade."[29]

Buchanan's decision to attack the entire Union fleet was based on a careful assessment of the situation. He believed that "an unexpected dash into the fleet" would be the best way to inflict maximum damage on the enemy. When he had consumed most of his coal, he would "retire under the guns of the fort, and being without motive power" would "assist in repulsing the attacks and assaults on the fort." He did not want to repeat what happened to the *Virginia* when she was eventually blown up in the James River by "her own officers without a fight."[30]

As the *Tennessee* approached the Union anchorage, now about two miles ahead, Wharton fired a bolt at the cluster of ships. It missed, but later he would write, "It was the beginning of a naval combat the like of which history has not seen."[31] The battle of wills between the two American admirals was now entering its last phase. The time was 8:50.

The lookouts in the *Hartford*'s top spotted the *Tennessee* when she began to move. The southwest wind blew her black funnel smoke to the northeast, giving the impression she was going out to attack the vessels that had remained in the gulf, so fleet captain Drayton thought. Farragut disagreed: "No, Buck is coming here. Get underway at once. We must be ready for him!"[32]

Again Kinney's extraordinary communication skills were in need, and he was summoned to the poop. In a matter of minutes he had flagged messages to the *Monongahela* and *Lackawanna,* two of the fleet's fastest sloops, to "run down the ram." At the same time, signal flags were hoisted to the *Hartford's* mizzenpeak, ordering all vessels to attack.

Cdr. James H. Strong, captain of the *Monongahela,* had just dropped anchor when Kinney's message was received. Without waiting to raise the anchor, he slipped the cable and got under way. Earlier, the *Monongahela* and her consort, the gunboat *Kennebec,* had scraped hulls with the *Tennessee* as they passed, but none of the three had suffered serious damage. This time Strong would try to do better.

A few minutes later, the *Lackawanna,* commanded by Capt. John B. Marchand, also headed for the ram. At six knots, it would take Buchanan nearly thirty-five minutes to reach the anchorage, ample time for the fleet to slip anchor and get under way.

There was, however, a problem: Mobile Bay's shallow depths restricted the movement of the larger sloops, those best suited to contend with the *Tennessee.* The monitors, intended to perform this mission, had so far done little damage to her and were somewhat discredited. As the *Monongahela* steamed toward the *Tennessee,* Lt. Oliver Batcheller, the vessel's executive officer, believed "there was no chance for maneuverability, whilst with so many vessels fighting, they were quite as likely to injure their friends as the enemy" and "the experience of the *Merrimac* in Hampton Roads would be repeated, only on a larger scale."[33]

Strong and Marchand chose to ram the *Tennessee* on opposite sides. Making a wide sweep to the east and turning back, the *Monongahela* struck the *Tennessee* on her starboard quarter at full speed. The *Tennessee* spun around to starboard, and the *Monongahela* sheered off to port, losing the iron prow attached to her stem. During contact, both vessels fired, the sloop's balls bouncing harmlessly off the ram's sloping sides, and the *Tennessee's* Brooke bolts crashing into the wooden ship's hull, wounding an officer and two landsmen. Five minutes later, the *Lackawanna* struck the ram on the other side. The two vessels slid bow to stern, exchanging shots as they passed. Again, the Union vessel was worsted: she managed to get off only one shot and came away with her stem crushed, a leak in the forward compartment, and numerous casualties in the powder division and surgeon's cockpit.

Twice the *Tennessee* had been rammed, and still on she steamed, heading for the *Hartford,* fifteen hundred yards ahead. In the meanwhile, however, the monitor *Manhattan* had maneuvered between the *Hartford* and the *Tennessee* and was approaching the ram head on. The *Manhattan's* slow speed greatly impaired her effectiveness. She failed to ram the *Tennessee* and was able to fire only two shots, neither of which did any damage.

Leaving the *Manhattan* astern, the ram was now less than a thousand yards from the *Hartford.* Convinced that Buchanan was after him, Farragut accepted the challenge and ordered the flagship ahead fast. At 9:35 the two vessels struck, their port sides scraping and rasping. The *Hartford* fired a broadside at eight feet; the *Tennessee,* with only two guns in broadside, fired a single shot that exploded inside her opponent's berth deck, killing and wounding a number of men. The other gun misfired.

The collision pushed the *Tennessee's* bow to starboard, away from the *Hartford.* Intending to make a full circle and reenter the melee, Johnston put the ram's helm to port. As the *Tennessee* swung around, she met the double-turreted monitor *Chickasaw* coming in from the east. When the ram had passed, the *Chickasaw* circled around and followed in her wake. The monitor would stay there, pounding away at the *Tennessee's* after gunport shutter until the battle ended.

By 9:45 the *Chickasaw* had been joined by the *Manhattan;* and for the first time, the *Tennessee* sustained serious damage. Her stack was knocked down, and her weakly protected tiller chains jammed, necessitating the use of relieving tackle. Soon the tiller arm was shot away, rendering the relieving tackle useless and steering impossible. As the *Tennessee* circled helplessly in a wide sweep to the southwest, her stern gunport shutter was jammed by a shot from one of the trailing ironclads. While Buchanan was supervising efforts to unjam the shutter, a shot struck it, wounding him in his bad leg and killing two seamen.[34]

In the meantime the *Hartford* had made a 360-degree turn and again was heading for the crippled ram, several hundred yards to the southwest, black smoke trailing from her severed stack. This brought the flagship on a collision course with the *Lackawanna,* which also had made a full circle in hopes of ramming the *Tennessee* again. Neither could change course before the *Lackawanna* struck the *Hartford's* starboard quarter, cutting her down almost to the water's edge.

Farragut, who was on the poop, rushed to the port railing. Finding that the

Hartford was not sinking, he ordered Drayton to continue at full speed. Before giving the order, Drayton noticed that the sloop *Ossipee* was about to cross the *Hartford*'s bow and ram the *Tennessee*. Anxious to avoid another embarrassing incident, Drayton let the *Ossipee* pass.

Aboard the *Tennessee* the situation was becoming intolerable. When Johnston learned that Buchanan had been wounded, he immediately left the pilot-house and went to him for orders. By then the admiral had been taken below to the cockpit, where Fleet Surgeon Conrad was ministering to his wound.

Johnston informed Buchanan that the *Tennessee* was almost dead in the water, and that her bow and stern gunport shutters were both jammed, as well as one in her broadside, so she could not effectively return the enemy's fire. The admiral replied, "Well, Johnston, if you cannot do them any further damage, you had better surrender." Johnston then decided "with an almost bursting heart" to hoist the white flag.[35] On his way to the shield, where the *Tennessee*'s tattered flag was still flying, he gave the order to cease fire. Reaching the shield top amid a hail of shot and shell, Johnston replaced the Confederate battle flag with a white handkerchief, at the same time observing that an enemy sloop was bearing down at full speed on his starboard beam.

Upon learning that the *Tennessee* had hoisted a white flag, Cdr. William E. LeRoy, captain of the *Ossipee,* ordered his ship's engines reversed and attempted to steer clear but could not avoid striking the ram a hard glancing blow. Noticing an officer standing on the shield, LeRoy recognized Johnston and identified himself and his vessel. The time was 10:00 A.M.

LeRoy and Johnston had been in the Old Navy together and were friends. When Johnston came aboard the *Ossipee* to arrange for the *Tennessee*'s formal surrender, LeRoy treated him to a bottle of "navy sherry." Since Johnston had surrendered to the *Ossipee,* LeRoy sent Acting Lt. Pierre Giraud aboard the *Tennessee* to receive Buchanan's sword.

Before Giraud arrived, Acting Lt. Robert Ely, the executive officer of the *Manhattan,* managed to board the *Tennessee* and take her colors. For years the *Manhattan*'s captain, Cdr. James W. Nicholson, would argue that the *Tennessee* struck to his ship.

As Giraud boarded the *Tennessee,* a souvenir-hunting sailor from the *Manhattan* mounted the shield where Buchanan had been moved and was asking for his sword. The admiral's aide, Master's Mate W. S. Forrest, refused, explaining that "it would only be given to Admiral Farragut or his authorized representative."[36] When the man reached down to grab it, Forrest knocked him off the shield, thus striking the last blow of the battle.

Learning that Johnston was on the *Ossipee,* Farragut asked for him to be brought aboard the *Hartford*. When Johnston reached the deck, Farragut expressed regret at meeting him under such circumstances. Johnston replied that the admiral was not half as sorry to see him as he was to see the admiral. Drayton then remarked, "You have one consolation, Johnston; no one can say that you have not nobly defended the honor of the Confederate flag to-day." Johnston thanked him, but gave all the honor to Buchanan, "who was the true hero of the battle."[37] Confederate Secretary of the Navy Stephen Mallory likewise praised Buchanan's heroism, declaring that, "Naval history records few contests between forces so unequal in ships, guns, and men but few in which the weaker party displayed equal heroism."

Thus ended what Farragut described as "the most desperate battle I ever fought."[38] Without the fire support of Buchanan's squadron, Forts Powell, Gaines, and Morgan were untenable. Fort Powell was blown up and evacuated during the night of 5 August, Gaines surrendered on the eighth, and Morgan on the twenty-second.

The Battle of Mobile Bay was a clear victory for the Union. It gave the North an important psychological boost at a time when the outcome of the war was far from certain. But, apart from ending the blockade trade, the battle achieved little of military value since Mobile remained in Confederate hands until April 1865, the last month of the war. Farragut also paid dearly for his victory. With an advantage of 18 to 4 in ships and an overwhelming superiority in firepower, the Union navy suffered 9 times as many casualties as the Confederate: 315 killed and wounded to 35. The only advantages the Confederates possessed were the torpedoes and the "narrow and direct character of the approach by the main ship channel," which permitted the Confederate squadron to rake the enemy ships for a full hour before receiving their broadsides.[39] The contest of wills between Farragut and Buchanan had been settled—but at a terrible price.

Although the Battle of Mobile Bay did little to hasten the end of the Civil War, it influenced the course of naval history for the next eighty years. The astute and perceptive Mallory wrote in a report to Jefferson Davis that, ". . . apart from graver considerations[,] this contest possesses peculiar interest for all who are watchful of the progress of naval affairs, it being the first in which the modern and improved means of naval warfare, offensive and defensive, have been tested."[40] He was, of course, alluding to those emerging technologies that would dominate ship design and naval tactics in the years ahead: iron construction, steam propulsion, revolving turrets, sloping armor, multiple propellers, rifled guns, explosive shells, and mines.

After Farragut's victory at Mobile Bay and Sherman's capture of Atlanta less than a month later, Lincoln's spirits soared. The prospect that he would be reelected had greatly improved. The *Army and Navy Journal* echoed northern sentiment when it praised Farragut for one of the "proudest and most daring achievements of our own or any other navy;"[41] the *Richmond Examiner* expressed the feelings of southerners when it wrote, "It was a most unequal contest in which our gallant little navy was engaged, and we lost the battle; but our ensign went down in a blaze of glory."[42]

NOTES

1. Ulysses S. Grant, *Personal Memoirs* (New York, 1894), 543.

2. Sherman to Canby, 4 June 1864, *The War of the Rebellion: A Compilation of the Official Records of the Union and Confederate Armies,* 130 vols. (Washington, D.C., 1880–1901), series 1, vol. 34, pt. 4, 212. Hereafter ORA.

3. Canby to Farragut, 1 July 1864, *Official Records of the Union and Confederate Navies in the War of the Rebellion,* 30 vols. (Washington, D.C., 1894–1922), series 1, vol. 21, 357. Hereafter ORN.

4. General Order No. 10, 12 July 1864, ORN 1, 21:397–98.

5. Farragut to Welles, 12 August 1864, ibid., 416.

6. Farragut to Jenkins, 3 August 1864, ibid., 403.

7. Robert Ely, "This Filthy Ironpot," *American Heritage* 19, no. 2 (February 1968): 109.

8. Farragut to Stevens, 4 August 1864, ORN 1, 21:404.

9 *Hartford* Deck Log, 5 August 1864, Records of the Bureau of Naval Personnel, Record Group 24, National Archives.

10. Charles L. Lewis, *Our First Admiral,* vol. 2 of *David Glasgow Farragut* (Annapolis, 1943), 264.

11. "Buchanan, Franklin (1800–1874)," *Webster's American Military Biographies* (Springfield, Mass., 1978), 44.

12. D. B. Conrad, "What the Fleet Surgeon Saw of the Fight in Mobile Bay," *The United Service, A Monthly Review of Military and Naval Affairs* 8 (1892): 269.

13. J. Thomas Scharf, *History of the Confederate States Navy* (New York, 1887), 560.

14. Operations Report for July 1864, ORA 1, 39, 2:739–40.

15. Henry St. Paul, "The Attack on Mobile," *The Times Picayune,* 14 August 1864.

16. Lewis, *Our First Admiral,* 265.

17. Alden to Farragut, 5 August 1864, ORN 1, 21:508

18. Farragut to Alden, 5 August 1864, ibid.

19. Oliver Batcheller, "The Battle of Mobile Bay, August 5, 1864," *The Magazine of History* 14, no. 6 (December 1911): 226.

20. A. T. Mahan, *The Gulf and Inland Waters* (New York, 1883; reprint, Freeport, N.Y., 1970), 231.

21. Loyall Farragut, *The Life of David Glasgow Farragut, First Admiral of the U.S. Navy* (New York, 1879), 425.

22. A. D. Wharton, "Battle of Mobile Bay as Witnessed From the Deck of the Ironclad 'Tennessee,'" *Nashville Daily American,* 13 September 1877.

23. Alden to Farragut, 5 August 1864, ORN, 1, 21:508.

24. Farragut to Alden, 5 August 1864, ibid.

25. John C. Kinney, "An August Morning with Farragut," *Scribner's Monthly Illustrated Magazine* 22 (June 1881): 199–208.

26. Newspaper article with no date and no other identification, Farragut Papers, seen at the Naval Historical Foundation, Washington, D.C., now in possession of the Farragut Folklife Museum, Farragut, Tennessee.

27. When Farragut ordered the *Hartford* to cross the torpedo field, the din of battle would have drowned out any order yelled from the futtock shrouds to the deck, sixty feet below. See Kinney's remark concerning noise in Robert U. Johnson and Clarence C. Buel, eds., *Battles and Leaders of the Civil War* (1884–87; reprint, New York, 1956), vol. 4, 391.

28 Conrad, "What the Fleet Surgeon Saw," 263.

29 John L Rapier to Tom Rapier, 5 September 1864 In possession of Mrs E. M. Trigg, Mobile, Alabama.

30 Lewis, *Our First Admiral,* 273–74.

31 Wharton, *Nashville Daily American,* 13 September 1877.

32. Lewis, *Our First Admiral,* 274

33 Batcheller, "The Battle of Mobile Bay," 228

34 James D Johnston, "The Ram *Tennessee* at Mobile Bay," in Johnson and Buel, eds., *Battles and Leaders of the Civil War,* 4:403–4.

35 Ibid , 404.

36. Conrad, "What the Fleet Surgeon Saw," 266–67

37 Johnston, *Battles and Leaders,* 4 405

38. Lewis, *Our First Admiral,* 280

39. A. T. Mahan, *Admiral Farragut* (1892; reprint, St Clair Shores, Mich., 1970), 265

40. Mallory to Davis, 30 August 1864, *ORN* 2, 2, 632–33

41 Rev P C Headley, *Life and Naval Career of Vice-Admiral David Glascoe [sic] Farragut* (New York, 1865), 274.

42 Edward A. Pollard, *The Lost Cause* (New York, 1867), 547.

9

The Battle of Manila Bay

JOHN B. HATTENDORF

Among the battles fought by the U.S. Navy, Manila Bay stands out as exceptional. The first battle in American naval history that involved contingency planning, it was also the navy's first overseas fleet action, and it ended in a dramatic success that brought the navy some unexpected, long-range benefits.

Moreover the Spanish-American War, of which Manila Bay was the opening act, marked a turning point in American history. Its defeat of Spain not only led the United States to be universally recognized as a great power but resulted in the acquisition of colonies in the Caribbean and the Pacific, the defense of which, especially the latter, would occupy future contingency planners for the next forty years.

Although Manila Bay was the first battle of the war, the conflict arose out of a situation in the Caribbean, not the Far East. Americans had been concerned about Spain's repressive colonial policies in Cuba since the mid-1860s. The settlement of the revolt called the Ten Years War in 1878 had left promises for reform that remained unfulfilled more than sixteen years later. In February 1895 a group of dissidents in eastern Cuba launched an armed uprising. That summer, to the disappointment of would-be interventionists, President Grover Cleveland went so far as to recognize the insurgency but declared U.S. neutrality.[1]

By coincidence, during this same period a number of navy officers first began to think about planning for future contingencies. Since its founding in 1884, the Naval War College in Newport, Rhode Island, had promoted this approach. In 1894 the college's president, Capt. Henry C. Taylor, initiated a revised curriculum. Through it, the college planned to educate student officers by studying history as well as using war games to examine hypothetical and potential war situations. With faculty guidance and information from the

Office of Naval Intelligence, Taylor believed that War College students could demonstrate the functions of a naval general staff in a way that eventually would cause staff work to become a permanent fixture within the navy.

As part of the War College program in 1894, Taylor assigned three students to consider the question of strategy in the event of war with Spain. The students examined two different scenarios. The first postulated a conflict in which Spain and Britain allied against France and the United States. In the second the United States fought Spain alone. The following year, Taylor instructed the class of 1895 to address two situations: a general problem devoted to the defense of New England in a war with Britain, and a special problem dedicated to a conflict with Spain. After the class had finished its work, the faculty refined the student's effort, developing a more advanced study that considered three options for war with Spain: (1) a direct attack on Spain; (2) an attack on Spain's Pacific possessions: the Philippines and Guam; or (3) an attack on Spain's American colonies: Cuba and Puerto Rico.[2] Regarding the Pacific option, the college concluded "this would require fewer men and less money, and the issue of a resolute campaign against the Philippines might be regarded as reasonably certain to be successful. Success there, however, would not be of great value to us, as it would not certainly bring the enemy to terms."[3]

These early ideas about a war with Spain were forwarded to Washington, where they may have influenced thinking in the Navy Department. The next major initiative came from Lt. William W. Kimball, an officer from the Office of Naval Intelligence stationed at the Naval War College, who prepared a study that called for a purely naval war centering upon a blockade of Cuba. Kimball reasoned that, by isolating the island from Spain, a blockade would enable Cubans to win their independence while avoiding the commitment of U.S. ground forces. Kimball also considered two secondary campaigns. One was designed to pin the Spanish fleet in home waters by attacking Spanish seaports and coastal trade. The other was an attack on the Philippines "for the purpose of reducing and holding Manila, of harassing trade, of cutting off revenue (especially that due to sugar and tobacco) from Spain, of occupying or at least blockading the Philippines principal ports so that the release of our hold on them may be used as an inducement to Spain to make peace after the liberation of Cuba."[4]

The Naval War College evaluated Kimball's plan during the 1896 summer course. Deeply influenced by studying the experience of the American Civil War as well as recent writings by Alfred Thayer Mahan, the college criticized the plan, arguing that while the Philippine operations could be useful, they could not be decisive; the blockade of Cuba could not be effective until the Spanish fleet had been defeated; and that operations in Spanish home waters should be avoided until after the Cuban operations were completed.

Meanwhile, on 6 April 1896, Congress passed a joint resolution calling for President Cleveland to act more vigorously by recognizing the Cuban insurgency as a revolution and offering direct American aid. Despite such prodding Cleveland remained unmoved. Disassociating himself from the congressional initiative, he delivered a note to the Spanish government asking for some specific reforms to end the insurrection and implying that, if these reforms were undertaken, the United States would support continued Spanish rule in Cuba. Madrid took its time in replying; it was not until June that it rejected Cleveland's suggestions and issued an intransigent defense of Spanish colonial policy in Cuba.

Somewhat to the Democratic administration's surprise, Cuba did not become a major issue in the presidential election of 1896. Although the Republican platform declared the party's interest in American intervention to give Cuba her independence, political-military affairs were not the issues that gave William McKinley his overwhelming victory. While some prominent Republicans, such as Theodore Roosevelt, were keen to intervene, McKinley preferred to concentrate on the serious economic issues facing the country. Furthermore, he sensed that the European powers might not be willing to accept U.S. intervention in Cuba.

The next phase in American planning occurred in December 1896. At that point Secretary of the Navy Hilary Herbert was a lame duck with less than three months left in office. Herbert had not been satisfied with either Kimball's or the Naval War College's plans. To reexamine the matter, he appointed a board consisting of the chiefs of the Bureau of Navigation and the Bureau of Ordnance; the commander of the North Atlantic Squadron; Capt. Henry Taylor, who had just left Newport to take command of the battleship *Indiana;* and Lt. Cdr. Richard Wainwright, who was leaving the Office of Naval Intelligence to become the executive officer of the battleship *Maine.*

This board discarded the idea of an attack on the Philippines and, instead, laid out a plan for the Asiatic Squadron to sail westward to join the U.S. European Squadron and seize the Canary Islands as a base from which to attack Spanish commerce. Reflecting the War College's views, Taylor strongly dissented on a number of points, arguing in particular that naval forces should be concentrated in Cuban waters.

Following the inauguration of the new administration in March 1897, Secretary of the Navy John D. Long and his assistant secretary, Theodore Roosevelt, decided to review the problem of war with Spain and reconvened the strategy board in July. None of its members except Lieutenant Commander Wainwright had served on its forerunner, but they headed the same commands. The new board revised many aspects of its predecessor's plan, dropping the idea of operations in European waters, stressing the central importance of joint operations in Cuba, and adding the idea of capturing Puerto Rico. In regard to operations in the Far East, it concluded:

For the purpose of further engaging the attention of the Spanish Navy and more particularly to improve our position when the time came for negotiations with a view to peace, the Board thinks it would be well to make an attempt to assist the insurgents in the Philippine Islands. It is understood that the insurgents have possession of considerable areas in the islands including some important points in the neighborhood of Manila, and it is thought that if the Asiatic Squadron should go down and show itself in that neighborhood, and manage to arrange for an attack upon that city in conjunction with the insurgents, the place might fall and as a consequence the insurgent cause in these islands might be successful, in which case we should probably have a controlling voice as to what should become of the islands, when the final settlement was made. Certain reinforcements might be necessary from the Pacific Station.[5]

At the time the board submitted its report early in the summer of 1897, the prospects for peace looked good. Following the death of a prominent insurgent leader, Spanish Prime Minister Antonio Cánovas del Castillo announced that the colonial government would introduce reforms in the areas of Cuba that submitted to Spanish rule. Yet unbeknownst to Americans, the new policy encountered powerful internal opposition. In Spain the Cuban issue was a highly emotional one that threatened to shake the foundations of the monarchy itself, and Cánovas faced strong challenges from within his own Conservative party, from the army, and from the Queen Regent, María Cristina. Walking a narrow line, the prime minister tried to avoid conflict with the United States, while at the same time he moved slowly to implement a policy of Cuban home rule.

To the discomfit of both Madrid and Washington, the insurgents remained intransigent. Faced with his own critics in Congress, McKinley advised Madrid of his views and dispatched a new minister, Gen. Stewart Lyndon Woodward, with instructions to press for a rapid end to Spanish military operations against the insurgency and a new political arrangement with Cuba. After a long delay, Cánovas rejected these demands, creating a serious threat of war between Spain and the United States. In that event, it seemed distinctly possible that other European states might come to Spain's assistance.[6]

The possibility of European intervention to aid Spain faded quickly with the first inkling that the impasse over Cuba might be broken. In August, Cánovas was assassinated, opening the way for a new government under the Liberal Party of Práxedes Mateo Sagasta. The U.S. minister, Woodward, continued to press for immediate reforms in Cuba. Apparently reacting to American pressure, Sagasta announced that Spain would grant Cuba autonomy and redress her many grievances.

Meanwhile, in Washington officials began to worry that continued unrest in Cuba would threaten Americans and American investments. As early as October, the Navy Department ordered Capt. Charles S. Sigsbee, commanding the second-class battleship *Maine,* to be ready to sail for Havana should an emergency arise. At the same time, the department looked toward the wider aspects of a possible war. Assistant Secretary Roosevelt, in particular, began making preparations for a short war, perhaps of only six weeks, with the North Atlantic Fleet operating in Cuban waters, the Asiatic Squadron blockading or taking Manila, and a flying squadron harassing Spain itself.[7] At the end of the month, the department ordered Commo. George Dewey to proceed to the Far East and take command of the Asiatic Squadron.

Dewey was an unlikely choice for the job. For nearly five years, he had been president of the Board of Inspection and Survey. Ten years before he had commanded the pre–Civil War steamer *Pensacola* when she served as flagship of the European Station in 1885–89. During the Civil War, Dewey had been praised for his conduct as executive officer of the *Mississippi* during the Battle of New Orleans in 1862. He was still on the *Mississippi* a year later when she ran aground under the Confederate batteries at Port Hudson and had to be burned to prevent her capture. Since then his career had been routine. He had never served at sea in a modern warship and had never commanded a squadron.[8]

On the basis of his sea or command experience, there was no clear reason why the sixty-year-old Dewey should have received the Asiatic assignment. He had played no leading role in the recent growth of the navy and was completely unknown as either a strategist or tactician. However, long experience in Washington gave Dewey the political connections that brought his appointment about. Among these connections was Theodore Roosevelt. Alarmed to learn that the Bureau of Navigation favored another officer, Roosevelt encouraged Dewey to make use of his long-time family connections with Vermont senator Redfield Proctor, a Republican representing Dewey's home state, to influence Secretary Long and President McKinley. While Long initially disapproved, Proctor was successful with McKinley.[9]

In January 1898 Dewey relieved Rear Adm. F. V. McNair at Nagasaki,

George Dewey as Admiral of the Navy, the rank created for him following the Battle of Manila Bay. *U.S. Naval Institute*

Japan, and took command of the six-ship Asiatic Squadron. In an official letter transmitting information about the station, McNair advised Dewey: "The newspapers have contained accounts, for some time past, of a rebellion in progress in the Philippine Islands. No official information has been received in relation thereto, and no information of any sort that shows American interests to be affected."[10]

There is no evidence that McNair gave Dewey a plan of action against the Philippines. However, the Navy Department, anticipating the possible outbreak of war, soon ordered Dewey to hold up the discharge of crewmen whose enlistments had expired.[11]

On the other side of the world, the government in Madrid inaugurated new policies for Cuban autonomy and halted military operations. The new Spanish policies only encouraged the insurrection, suggesting to Cubans that, with perseverance, independence was not far away. In mid-January, Havana was beset with riots and civil violence. Under the circumstances, Secretary Long concluded that a goodwill visit by the battleship *Maine* to Havana would help diffuse tensions by demonstrating that peaceful, routine relations prevailed between the United States and Spain. The *Maine* would also be on hand should violence threaten American lives and property. To those who argued such a visit might be misinterpreted, he replied that it would be better for the ship to be available during a crisis than after one.

Despite the qualms of American diplomats in Havana, the *Maine* arrived on 25 January and lay peacefully at anchor in the harbor for three weeks. To many the ship's presence was neither reassuring nor indicative of routine relations; it suggested an American attempt to intimidate Spain. On the other hand, Captain Sigsbee reported that, in his opinion, it allowed the United States to dominate the situation and reduced the threat of violence.

Early in February American newspapers obtained a highly indiscreet private letter from the Spanish ambassador in Washington complaining that President McKinley was merely a pawn of public opinion. This trivial sensation exacerbated the tensions of the moment. Less than a week later, on the evening of 15 February, the *Maine* exploded in Havana Harbor, killing 260 of her 350 officers and men. In the United States, the tragedy plunged the fine points of foreign policy and delicate diplomatic issues into the cauldron of public outrage. Spanish authorities immediately provided all possible aid to the survivors and showed deep respect for those who had lost their lives. Although the yellow press trumpeted that the ship had been blown up by a Spanish mine, President McKinley concluded from an official U.S. naval enquiry held in March 1898 that "no evidence has been obtainable fixing the responsibility for the destruction of the *Maine* upon any person or persons."[12] The situation remained extremely tense and war seemed more and more probable.

In the Far East, the U.S. Asiatic Squadron was scattered from Aden to Japan. Entering port at Hong Kong in the flagship *Olympia* on 17 February, Dewey learned of the *Maine* disaster and promptly wired the U.S. consul in Manila, Oscar F. Williams, to request an immediate, confidential report on the defenses of the city. In succeeding days Dewey carried out orders for a period of national mourning, ordering flags to half staff and canceling social engagements for officers and men ashore. Yet he refrained from calling his squadron together or committing any other overtly belligerent act.

On 25 February, the Acting Secretary of the Navy, Theodore Roosevelt, following the department's general war plan, telegraphed Dewey to concentrate his ships: "Order the Squadron, except *Monocacy,* to Hong Kong. Keep full of coal. In the event of declaration of war Spain, your duty will be to see that the Spanish Squadron does not leave the Asiatic coast, and then offensive operations in Philippine Islands. . . ."[13]

A day later, Secretary Long emphasized in a telegram, "Keep full of coal— the best that can be had."[14] It was clear that logistical support would be critical for the success of future operations, especially as no prior arrangements had been made to provide such support in the West Pacific in the event of war. In mid-March, Dewey telegraphed Washington requesting that the Navy Department send ammunition and coal from San Francisco immediately. Secretary Long ordered the cruiser *Baltimore* to sail from Honolulu with ammunition for the squadron and authorized Dewey to contract for five thousand tons of coal, directly from England, if necessary, to be delivered wherever he wished to receive it.[15] Two weeks after Dewey received this message, the British steamer *Nanshan* arrived at Hong Kong from Cardiff with three thousand tons of Welsh coal for which he had previously contracted. Foreseeing the difficulties that a state of war would create, on 4 April Dewey requested and received authority to purchase the vessel before the outbreak of hostilities, along with another supply ship, the *Zafiro.* Through the captain of the old gunboat *Monocacy* at Shanghai, he made sub rosa arrangements with "an efficient Chinese comprador" to have the squadron resupplied in case of need at an isolated location in Chinese waters, confident that "so loosely organized a national entity as the Chinese Empire could not enforce the neutrality laws."[16]

By the end of March, Dewey was confident that he could carry out his instructions, and reported to Washington:

I believe that I am not over-confident in stating that with the squadron now under my command the [Spanish] vessels could be taken and the defense of Manila reduced in one day.

There is every reason to believe that with Manila taken or even blockaded, the rest of the islands would fall either to the insurgents or ourselves, as they are now held through the support of the [Spanish] Navy and are dependent upon Manila for supplies.[17]

In the weeks following the sinking of the *Maine,* American diplomats attempted to negotiate a settlement with Spain for Cuban independence. In a final effort to reach a peaceful solution, Spain agreed on 10 April to settle all points of dispute with the United States and proclaimed an armistice in Cuba. Spain coupled these concessions with a request to Russia, France, Germany, Austria-Hungary, and Britain to use their good offices to persuade the United States to withdraw the warships then blockading the Cuban coast. At the same time, Pope Leo XIII offered to mediate the dispute, and the European ambassadors in Washington, acting in secret cooperation with the U.S. State Department, issued a note calling for negotiations. All these measures back-fired, for the American public, misinterpreting them as foreign interference, raised an even stronger call for war.[18] Finally, on 11 April, McKinley reported to Congress that he had "exhausted every effort to relieve the intolerable condition of affairs which is at our doors" in Cuba.

As these events were taking place, the new U.S. revenue cutter *McCulloch* arrived at Singapore en route from the east coast of the United States via the Suez Canal to her new station on the California coast. The Treasury Department telegraphed orders to her immediately to join Dewey at Hong Kong. She arrived there on 17 April. From this point events moved swiftly. On 19 April, the same day that Congress passed a resolution demanding that Spain withdraw from Cuba and authorizing McKinley to use the armed forces of the United States to achieve this objective, Dewey ordered his squadron of white ships painted wartime grey. On 21 April, Secretary Long telegraphed, "War not declared. War may be declared at any moment. I will inform you. Await orders."[19] The very next day, the *Baltimore* arrived with ammunition. Finally and in the nick of time, Dewey had his squadron ready for battle: the cruisers *Olympia, Boston, Baltimore,* and *Raleigh*; the gunboats *Concord* and *Petrel,* plus the *McCulloch*; and the supply ships *Nanshan* and *Zafiro.*

In Hong Kong British authorities watched benevolently, allowing the U.S. squadron to use the Royal Navy's dock and repair facilities before asserting neutrality. Work on the American ships was complete before Maj. Gen. Wilsone Black, acting governor of Hong Kong, advised Dewey on 23 April that the war had begun, issued a proclamation declaring British neutrality, and ordered Dewey's squadron to leave Hong Kong and its territorial waters by 4:00 P.M. the following day.[20]

In Washington Navy Department officials urged President McKinley to order Dewey to implement the plan to attack Manila. At a conference at the White House on Sunday morning, 25 April, however, at least one advisor opposed the idea. On Sunday afternoon, Dewey's cable reporting his departure from Hong Kong reached the Navy Department. The watch officer on duty tried unsuccessfully to contact both Secretary Long and Rear Adm.

Ardent Crowninshield, the chief of the Bureau of Navigation. Eventually Crowninshield came to the bureau, received the message, and took it to the White House, observing that since it was received after the time Dewey was required to leave Hong Kong, the president had no choice but to send Dewey to Manila, as no alternative plan was available. At the White House, members of the cabinet joined in drafting a message. Long carried the rough draft across the street to the Navy Department. Clerks there prepared and encrypted the final message, which Long took to the White House for approval. Returning after dark, he ordered it sent to Dewey[21]: "War has commenced between the United States and Spain. Proceed at once to the Philippine Islands. Commence operations at once, particularly against the Spanish fleet. You must capture vessels or destroy. Use utmost endeavors."[22]

Upon receipt of the Hong Kong government's directive, the *Boston, Concord, Petrel, McCulloch, Nanshan,* and *Zafiro* immediately moved to Mirs Bay, a nearby anchorage in Chinese territorial waters. Two days later, on 25 April, their repairs completed, the remaining ships, the *Olympia, Baltimore,* and *Raleigh,* set out for Mirs Bay. As the *Raleigh* got under way to leave Hong Kong harbor, she smashed a circulating pump. The colony again demonstrated its benevolence, and the Kowloon Dockyard Company had the part ready on the morning of the twenty-seventh. Meanwhile, at Mirs Bay the squadron sent heavy articles, such as side ladders and Dewey's barge, for storage on board the *Nanshan,* and waited for Consul Williams to arrive from Manila with the latest information. Already under threat for his life, he had departed the city on 23 April.

Williams reached Mirs Bay about 1:00 P.M. on the 27 April, and briefed Dewey and his commanders in council on board the *Olympia.* An hour later Dewey ordered the squadron to weigh anchor and shaped a southeasterly coast for the 620 miles to Luzon.[23] The squadron did not darken ship en route but took the opportunity to prepare for battle. Shell hoists were protected with spare cables, woodwork thrown overboard, boats slung and covered with canvas, hoses coupled to plugs, and rails unshipped. On Dewey's order, a bombastic proclamation by the Captain-General of the Philippines, Don Basilio Austin Davila, brought by Consul Williams from Manila, was read to all hands. Its fulsome castigation of everything from the American people ("constituted of all social excresences") to the squadron's personnel ("possessing neither instruction nor discipline") roused the seamen's indignation.[24]

At daylight on Saturday, 30 April, the squadron made landfall at Cape Bolineau on Luzon. Dewey detached the *Boston* and *Concord* to "proceed with

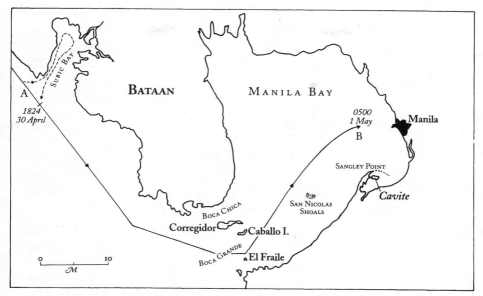

The approach to Manila Bay. After sending the *Boston* and *Concord* to reconnoiter Subic Bay (A), Dewey proceeds to enter Manila Bay, where he discovers and engages the Spanish squadron at anchor off Sangley Point (B).

all speed" to reconnoiter Subic Bay, thirty miles north of Manila, where Williams had heard that the Spanish squadron intended to make a stand under cover of fortifications on Isla Grande at the mouth of the bay.

Williams's information had been correct. On 25 April, Rear Adm. Don Patricio Montojo, commanding Spanish naval forces in the Philippines, had led his squadron from Manila to Subic. Upon arriving there, he had been appalled to find that the guns had not been mounted in a battery he had ordered built on Isla Grande six weeks earlier, and on 28 April intelligence of Dewey's departure from Hong Kong convinced him that they could not be emplaced before the Americans appeared. The council of captains he then convened advocated returning to Manila Bay, where the squadron would have the support of coastal fortifications. The retrograde movement was made the next day. Thus Dewey's scouts, reinforced with the *Baltimore* after someone imagined the sound of firing, returned to report that the bay was empty, though its entrances might have been mined. Dewey welcomed the news with the words, "Now we have them."[25]

Once the three ships had rejoined, Dewey halted the squadron and ordered all commanding officers to repair on board the *Olympia,* where he announced his plans to run past the fortifications guarding the mouth of Manila Bay that night, proceed to the bay's northern end, and anchor until daybreak. In earlier conferences, all had agreed there was little to fear from the possibility that the channel Dewey intended to use had been mined; the Spanish forces at Manila probably did not include the experts needed to plant mines effectively in such deep waters, and mines would not last long in the tropics, in any event. For entering the bay and in all future operations, the squadron was to steam in column formation in the order: *Olympia, Baltimore, Raleigh, Petrel, Concord,* and *Boston.* The *McCulloch* and the two supply ships were to follow into the bay and take up a position out of range of the enemy warships and coastal batteries. All ships were to be darkened except for a single, screened stern-light for the next vessel in line to follow.

The *Olympia's* navigator, Lt. C. G. Calkins, laid out the track and piloted the squadron into the bay.[26] The column proceeded toward the southern entrance, keeping well offshore and steering past Corrigedor Island. At 9:42 on the evening of the thirtieth, the crews went to general quarters, prepared for fire from the Spanish batteries. The lighthouses and navigational beacons along the coast had all been extinguished. At 11:10, a rocket soared into the sky from Corrigedor and a light began flashing at intervals, but nothing further occurred. The squadron continued its southerly course to the latitude of El Fraile rock. At that point it turned east and followed the *Olympia* until she passed El Fraile close aboard and abeam, about three-and-a-half miles south of Caballo Island. At 11:30, still at general quarters, the squadron entered the Boca Grande channel into Manila Bay and turned north-northeast, steaming at 8 knots, to pass clear of St. Nicholas Shoal and bear directly for the city of Manila. "The moon was now hidden in the western clouds," recalled Joseph L. Stickney, a naval officer turned newsman whom Dewey had appointed his aide, "and the solemn stillness . . . as we steamed along in the complete darkness, made the passage of the entrance probably the most oppressive time of our whole operations."[27]

Up to this time, there had been no sign of activity from the Spanish fortifications, but just as the four leading ships had straightened out on their NNE course, soot in the *McCulloch's* stack caught fire and burned brightly for a few moments. A signal flare flashed up from El Fraile, and a battery there fired three shots. One passed between the *Petrel* and the *Raleigh,* while the *Concord* heard another scream overhead between her main and mizzen masts. The *Raleigh, Concord, Boston,* and *McCulloch* returned fire, and the battery fell silent. More than an hour later, at 12:45 A.M. on 1 May, a moving light observed on the *Concord's* starboard quarter disappeared when she reopened fire.

Following these alarms, the squadron proceeded quietly up the bay, and after Dewey reconsidered his original plan to anchor, gradually slowed down. During the still hours of the night, the crews were allowed to sleep, by watches, at their stations. The lights of Manila became visible at 3:00, and at 4:00 the men were served hot coffee, beans, and bread. At dawn, the squadron was directly off the city. Sixteen merchantmen could be seen in the anchorage, but no warships were present. Within moments, however, sharp eyes decried "a line of dark grey objects on the water" to the right, beyond the low point on which stood the Cavite Naval Arsenal.[28] It was the Spanish squadron.

Dewey had expected to find the Spanish ships off Manila, where they could be supported by the city's batteries, but Montojo had chosen his position on the basis of humanitarian rather than tactical concerns. Convinced that his squadron faced certain destruction in any case, he wished to spare the city the bombardment it would receive from American "overs" were the battle to take place off its waterfront. His decision to fight in shoal waters close to shore was also influenced by the thought that this would increase his men's chances of survival after their ships had been sunk.

The Spanish line of battle consisted of seven ships headed by its only two sizeable units, the cruisers *Reina Cristina* (Montojo's flagship) and *Castilla*, both displacing upward of 3,000 tons, followed by the sisterships *Don Juan de Austria* and *Don Antonio de Ulloa*, very small cruisers of 1,152 tons; two even smaller cruisers, also sisterships, the *Isla de Luzon* and *Isla de Cuba*; and the gunboat *Marqués del Duero*. Four other vessels undergoing repair, the small cruiser *Velasco* and the gunboats *Argos*, *El Cano* (sometimes called *Correo*), and *General Lezo*, lay to the rear and took no part in the action.

Though superior in numbers, the Spanish line was significantly inferior to the enemy steaming toward it in displacement, condition, and, most important of all, firepower. There was not an 8-inch gun in the Spanish squadron, whereas its adversary mounted ten, and the largest Spanish guns, eleven 6.2- and 5.9-inchers, were opposed by twenty-three 6-inch guns. Furthermore, unlike their American counterparts, neither of the big Spanish cruisers was "protected" by a steel deck above her engine spaces. The largest, the *Castilla*, was undoubtedly the last wooden ship assigned a place in a line of battle. On the voyage to Subic the opening for her propeller shaft had shipped so much water that it had to be stuffed with cement, reducing her to the status of a floating battery. Barges loaded with sand were anchored beside her to shield her waterline. A second vessel, the *Don Antonio de Ulloa*, was immobilized by defective machinery.

Immediately upon the discovery of the Spanish squadron, two signals fluttered up the *Olympia's* halyards: "Prepare for general action!" and "Follow the

TABLE 9.1   The Battle of Manila Bay, 1 May 1898

	Commissioned	Displacement	Speed	Complement	Main Battery			Torpedo Tubes
U.S. NAVY Asiatic Squadron[a] Commo. G. Dewey					8 in.	6 in.	5 in.	
Protected cruisers								
Olympia (F)	1895	5,870	21.6	381	4	—	10	6
Baltimore	1890	4,413	20	328	4	6	—	5
Boston	1887	3,000	15.6	230	2	6	—	—
Raleigh	1894	3,213	19 1	252	—	1	10	4
Gunboats								
Concord	1891	1,710	16.7	155	—	6	—	—
Petrel	1889	892	13.5	110	—	4	—	—
TOTAL MAIN ARMAMENT					10	23	20	15
SPANISH NAVY Philippine Squadron[b] Rear Adm. P Montojo					6.2 in.	5.9 in.	4.7 in.	
Cruisers								
Reina Cristina (F)	1887	3,042	16.9	370	6	—	—	5
Castilla	1881	3,289	14	392	—	4	2	—
Don Antonio de Ulloa	1887	1,152	13	173	—	—	4	2
Don Juan de Austria	1887	1,152	13	173	—	—	4	2
Protected cruisers								
Isla de Cuba	1886	1,030	15.9	164	—	—	6	3
Isla de Luzon	1886	1,030	15 9	164	—	—	6	3
Gunboat								
Marqués del Duero	1875	492	10	98	1	—	2	—
TOTAL MAIN ARMAMENT					7	4	24	15

Notes: For complement, U S figures refer to those actually on board, while Spanish figures reflect nominal strength, (F) = flagship
[a] Excludes the revenue cutter McCulloch, which was not engaged
[b] Excludes the cruiser Velasco and the gunboats Argos, El Cano, and General Lezo, which were not engaged

movements of the flagship!" Circling toward the city on a large arc, the column moved SSW in formation with about four hundred yards between ships. Shortly after 5:00, when it was between two and three miles of shore, the batteries at Manila opened fire, but their shot fell short. Nevertheless, the Concord and Boston returned an equally futile fire. Dewey made the signal "Close up!" and kept it flying throughout the action. The six ships closed up to take station at two-hundred-yard intervals astern of the Olympia and prepared to engage the Spanish fleet, which lay nearly motionless in a long line east-west between Sangley Point and the shore, athwart the American line of approach. As the U.S. column continued southward, the batteries at Sangley Point and the Spanish ships opened fire, but their shells were also short. At 5:40, the range having fallen to approximately five thousand yards, Dewey gave flag captain Charles V. Gridley the most famous command in American naval history: "You may fire when you are ready, Gridley." An instant later, an 8-inch shell from the *Olympia*'s forward turret signified that battle had been joined.

Standing on for another fifteen hundred yards and then turning westward to open all batteries, the squadron commenced a general fire. During the approach, two Spanish mines exploded harmlessly far ahead of the *Olympia*, and shortly afterward a small launch put out from shore. Assuming that it carried torpedoes, the U.S. vessels opened fire and forced it to beach. On subsequent investigation, it proved to be a market boat that an English family had sent on a domestic errand. Remaining outside the five-fathom curve to avoid any danger of grounding the *Olympia*, which drew twenty-four feet of water, the squadron continued to fire until it passed the battery of two 5.9-inch guns on Sangley Point. It then turned to starboard in column formation and away from the shore to avoid masking the fire of the rear ships while making a firing run to the east. Upon reaching the five-fathom line in that direction, a distance of about two-and-a-half miles, the squadron again turned, this time to port, and made another firing run to the west. In all the squadron made five passes (three to the west and two to the east) at six knots, paralleling the Spanish line at a gradually decreasing range from five thousand to two thousand yards.

Lt. Bradley Fiske viewed the action from a platform on the *Petrel*'s foremast, where he was finding the range to the Spanish ships with a device of his own invention. "To me, in my elevated perch," he wrote,

the whole thing looked like a performance that had been very carefully rehearsed. The ships went slowly and regularly, seldom or never getting out of their relative positions, and ceased firing at intervals only when the smoke became too thick. For a long while I could not form an opinion as to which way fortune was going to decide. I could see that the Spanish ships were hit many times, especially the *Cristina* and *Castilla*; but then it seemed to me that our ships were hit many times also. . . .[29]

In fact the damage was almost entirely one-sided. Both of Montojo's big cruisers had taken considerable punishment, while Dewey's ships remained virtually untouched. Yet American gunnery was far from unerring, and the Spanish maintained a heavy fire. Reporting only a few days later, an English observer commented that, "The firing was inaccurate on both sides. . . . The American ship *Concord*, at short range, was observed to fire nine successive shots before she struck her opponent."[30]

After the second pass, Dewey, irritated that the squadron's fire had not

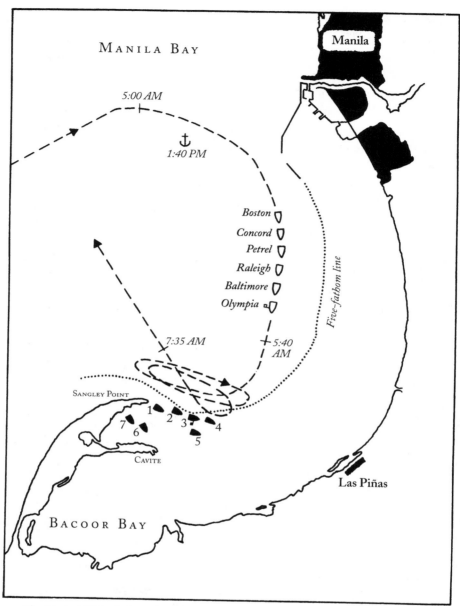

The Battle of Manila Bay, 1 May 1898. (1) *Castilla.* (2) *Isla de Cuba.* (3) *Reina Cristina.* (4) *Isla de Luzon.* (5) *Marqués del Duero.* (6) *Don Antonio de Ulloa.* (7) *Don Juan de Austria.*

made a greater impact on the enemy, decided to try a new tactic and anchor close in. Accordingly, he ordered the *Petrel* to prepare to leave the formation and pass around the eastern end of the Spanish line, while the rest of the squadron followed the *Olympia* to anchor well inside the five-fathom curve within two thousand yards of the Spanish. Completing the third pass at 7:00 A.M., the *Olympia* had just made a 60-degree turn to head southeast and move closer inshore when the *Reina Cristina* started toward her. Dewey immediately canceled his plan to anchor and concentrated fire on the Spanish flagship. Smothered by a hail of projectiles that riddled her superstructure, disabled her engines and steering gear, and set fires raging fore and aft, the *Cristina* suddenly slowed, fell away, and began drifting toward Cavite. Montojo ordered her to be scuttled and signaled the *Isla de Cuba* and *Isla de Luzon* to pick up the survivors. More than half the crew had been killed or wounded. The admiral, himself hit in the leg by a shell splinter, transferred his flag to the *Cuba*.

At the end of the fifth pass at 7:35, the *Olympia* was abreast of Sangley Point when Dewey received a report that his flagship had only fifteen rounds remaining for each of her ten 5-inch guns. On this information he signaled to the squadron, "Withdraw from action," and proceeded to lead his ships out into the bay, to a point four or five miles north of Sangley Point. There the U.S. cruisers stopped engines and lay motionless in several groups. To conceal the real reason for interrupting the action, Dewey adopted a suggestion by Stickney and announced that it was to give the crews time to have breakfast. Three of the Manila batteries continued to fire at the squadron without scoring any hits, although an occasional shell splashed within a hundred yards.

Dewey was disappointed that in two-and-a-half hours the squadron had apparently failed to destroy the enemy. When at 8:40 the ships' captains obeyed a signal to come on board the flagship, he was pleased to learn that there had been no serious casualties, morale on all ships was extremely high, and that the report he had received about the *Olympia*'s ammunition supply was erroneous. She had consumed 350 of her 5-inch shells, but that was only 40 percent of the ammunition on board. Overall only two-fifths of the squadron's ammunition had been expended.

Meanwhile, Montojo had been taking stock of a much less encouraging situation. At the time he shifted his flag, the wooden *Castilla*, though heavily damaged, had remained in action. The fires with which she had contended throughout the battle soon grew out of control, however, and she, too, was scuttled, her crew being rescued by boats from Cavite. Understandably concluding that enough had been done for honor, the admiral ordered his surviving ships to take refuge deep in Bacoor Bay, the body of water behind Cavite. Only the immobile *Don Antonio de Ulloa* remained in her original position near the battery on Sangley Point.

Concerned about the capacity of the Spanish to continue the action, Dewey's officers initially suggested that it might be wiser to blockade Manila from Mariveles at the entrance to the bay. While they were pondering the situation, the visible dissolution of the Spanish squadron led them to change their minds and decide that a determined attack on Cavite might meet little resistance. At 10:30 Dewey ordered the squadron to return to action.

The U.S. ships got under way toward Cavite in column formation at 11:16. Minutes later a merchant vessel was sighted standing up the bay, and Dewey sent the *Baltimore* to investigate. Steaming ahead about two miles, she soon reported that the vessel was a British merchantman. Given the *Baltimore's* advanced position and a lingering concern about the *Olympia's* 5-inch ammunition, Dewey directed the *Baltimore* to take the lead, with the *Olympia* followed in a ragged line by the *Raleigh, Boston, Concord,* and *Petrel* closing up from astern.

As they moved toward Cavite, Dewey signaled, "Attack the enemy's batteries and earthworks!" The *Baltimore* came within range first and engaged the Sangley Point battery at about 2,800 yards, slowing and stopping her engines to deliver rapid and accurate fire. Together with Dewey's other cruisers, she also engaged the *Don Antonio de Ulloa,* whose gallant crew fought her until every gun had been disabled before abandoning ship. Battered by at least thirty-three hits, the little cruiser sank with colors flying. The light-draft *Petrel* then proceeded into the shoal water off the arsenal and took the inner defenses and the smaller vessels under fire, prompting Montojo to give the order: "Scuttle and abandon your ships."[31] Meanwhile, Dewey signaled the *Concord* to destroy the armed merchantman *Isla de Mindanao,* aground near Las Piñas. On the way she shelled the Sangley Point battery and took the *Mindanao* under fire. The latter's crew fled ashore and she burst into flame as two of the *Concord's* boats approached.

At 12:30 P.M. the *Petrel* signaled that the Spanish had surrendered. The Spanish colors flying at Cavite were replaced by a white flag, and the firing ceased. The Spanish ships in Bacoor Bay lay in shallow water where they had been scuttled. To complete their destruction, Lt. E. M. Hughes, the *Petrel's* executive officer, took a whaleboat with seven men and set fire to the abandoned cruisers *Don Juan de Austria, Isla de Cuba,* and *Isla de Luzon,* and the gunboats *Marqués del Duero, General Lezo,* and *El Cano.* Dewey had carried out the secretary of the navy's instructions of 24 April; no Spanish vessel remained afloat. The casualty count proved as one-sided as the action itself. On the American side, not a single man was killed and only eight wounded. The Spanish had lost 167 dead and 214 wounded, all but ten aboard ship.

At 2:00 P.M., while the *Concord* and *Petrel* continued tidying up the situation at Cavite, the U.S. cruisers anchored off Manila. The batteries there had ceased fire, and Dewey sent a message to Captain-General Davila warning that if they resumed fire, "we should destroy the city." The Battle of Manila Bay was over.[32]

In the days and months that followed, the American press electrified the country with reports, many misleading, of the Battle of Manila Bay. Dewey was catapulted into fame, and the navy found broader political support at home, stirring domestic forces that used the action at Manila Bay for broader political purposes. The actual events that had taken place and the naval issues at hand were quickly submerged in the euphoria of the moment and soon stretched into the myth and legend of the New Steel Navy.

While the public saw the battle as a decisive victory along the lines of Nelson's at the Nile or Copenhagen, more sophisticated observers drew a parallel to Tegetthoff's triumph at the Battle of Lissa in 1866, comparing the conduct of the Italian fleet in that action with the Spanish failure to use their considerable defensive resources effectively at Manila. As an English naval officer reported after visiting the wrecked ships and the Cavite arsenal in June 1898: "The only conclusion that could be drawn . . . is that the ships under Admiral Montojo were indifferently fought and that he and his commanding officers were too ready to run their ships on shore, scuttle and burn them while their crews deserted to the beach."[33]

While Dewey had the naval force available to take Manila, he hesitated to occupy the city until he had enough troops to police it. In the interval awaiting these reinforcements, Dewey instituted a naval blockade, bringing a halt to all trade with Manila. He also arranged for the exiled insurgent leader Emilio Aguinaldo to return to the Philippines. The latter proclaimed a provisional Filipino government on 12 June.

Even as of that date, no one knew exactly what American intentions were concerning the islands. It was not clear to Dewey or anyone else whether or not the United States would seek to retain the Philippines or merely use them as a bargaining chip at the peace table. In these uncertain circumstances, a number of foreign powers sent warships to Manila Bay "to observe" American actions. In mid-July 1898, there were four British, three German, two French, one Japanese, and one Austrian as well as Dewey's eight American warships at Manila.[34] As the leading maritime power, Britain allowed the

United States to carry out its blockade activities without interference. Commenting on a report from Commo. Swinton C. Holland, the Royal Navy's commander in chief on the China Station, an admiralty official in London noted that while it was a breach of neutrality for U.S. naval vessels in the Philippines to receive coal from British ships, he did not see that Her Majesty's Government was bound to place any restraint on it.[35]

Vice Adm. Otto von Diederichs, commanding the German Far East Squadron took quite a different view, noting that the blockade was neither legitimate under international law nor officially declared through diplomatic channels.[36] In mid-May the German consul in Manila had informed Berlin that the Filipinos seemed to be inclined to declare their independence under German protection, with a German prince as king. His report raised the question of a partition of the Philippines, but this possibility was quickly dismissed in discussions among British, German, and American officials.[37] Nevertheless, Germany remained concerned about the interests of the eleven German firms doing business in the Philippines and those belonging to the nationals of several other European countries that Germany had formally agreed to represent. Rumors and tendentious newspaper reports suggested that Germany intended to support Spain and establish a German protectorate in the islands. Tensions increased when Admiral von Diederichs arrived off Manila on 12 June in the cruiser *Kaiserin Augusta,* followed by his flagship *Kaiser* and the cruiser *Prinzessin Wilhelm* on 19–20 June. Although the sole purpose of the visit was to carry out a long-planned exchange of fourteen hundred of the squadron's crewmen with men coming out from Germany in the transport *Darmstadt,* its timing made it appear threatening. The arrival of the Kaiser's brother, Adm. Prince Heinrich of Prussia, at the German base at Kiaochow, China, with three more cruisers, and a rumor that a Spanish squadron had sailed from Spain for the Philippines created further concern. There was also a serious disagreement about the propriety of American methods in dealing with neutral warships during the blockade.

Tensions flared when the USS *Raleigh,* detailed to identify vessels entering Manila Bay during the blockade, stopped the German cruiser *Cormoran* by firing a shot across her bow and sent an American officer on board. Von Diederichs initially took little notice of this, but when Dewey dispatched his flag lieutenant to von Diederichs to complain about other German violations of the blockade, the German admiral took the incident more seriously, rejecting Dewey's view that the U.S. Navy had the right to board a neutral warship in order to identify her. In the ensuing exchanges, von Diederichs gained the impression that Dewey reacted in an unfriendly manner, further increasing tensions. No serious political consequences resulted immediately from these incidents, yet, in the long term, they became the most destructive event in German-American relations prior to World War I.[38] Combined with the larger international and domestic issues of the day, it helped push Germany toward building a stronger navy and stimulated German contingency planning for a war against the United States.[39]

Dewey maintained the blockade throughout the more than three-and-a-half months it took to achieve the ultimate goal that U.S. planners had laid out. Finally, on 25 July 1898, Maj. Gen. Wesley Merritt arrived in the Philippines with a U.S. Army expeditionary force of sufficient size to control Manila. Following joint landing operations, the city surrendered on 13 August 1898, and Merritt declared the military occupation of the islands. Up until the time that U.S. commissioners met at Paris in October 1898 to conclude a peace with Spain, American policy on the Philippines was vague and divided. During the month that followed, economic, strategic, and humanitarian considerations led President McKinley into demanding that Spain cede the islands to the United States. Aguinaldo responded by calling upon Filipinos to declare their independence from the United States, and by February 1899, the U.S. army of occupation faced an insurrection that continued until mid-1902.

Manila Bay has long been recognized as one of the great battles in American naval history, "marking the emergence of the United States as a world power,"[40] but an examination of its aftermath shows that it also brought unexpected consequences that included the acquisition of a colony, a native revolt, and a significant increase in tension in German-American relations in the years leading up to World War I.

NOTES

1. Except where noted, this section is based on David Trask, *The War with Spain in 1898* (New York, 1981), chap. 1.

2. John B. Hattendorf et al., *Sailors and Scholars: The Centennial History of the Naval War College* (Newport, 1984), 45–46. See also Trask, *The War with Spain*, chap. 4; Ronald Spector, "Who Planned the Attack on Manila Bay?," *Mid America* 53 (April 1971): 94–102; and Ronald Spector, *Professors of War: The Naval War College and the Development of the Naval Profession* (Newport, 1977), 89–95.

3. Record Group (RG) 8, Series 1, Box 44, UNOpB: War with Spain, 1896–97, Naval War College, Naval Historical Collection.

4. Kimball, "War with Spain," 4, loc. cit.

5. UNOpB, July 1897, Navy Department. Rough draft of the Official Plan in Event of Operations against Spain, 4, loc. cit.

6. William R. Braisted, *The United States Navy in the Pacific, 1897–1909* (Austin, 1958), 18; Ivo Nikolai Lambi, *The Navy and German Power Politics, 1862–1914* (Boston, 1984), 129; J. A. S. Grenville, *Lord Salisbury and Foreign Policy: The Close of the Nineteenth Century* (London, 1974), 201.

7. Elting E. Morison, ed., *The Letters of Theodore Roosevelt* (Cambridge, 1951–54), 1:690: Roosevelt to Henry Cabot Lodge, 21 September 1897, and 716–17: Roosevelt to W. W. Kimball, 19 November 1897.

8. For the most recent full biography, see Ronald Spector, *Admiral of the New Empire: The Life and Career of George Dewey* (New Orleans, 1974, reprint, Columbia, S C , 1988)

9 William N. Still Jr , *American Sea Power in the Old World: The United States Navy in European and Near Eastern Waters, 1865–1917* (Westport, Conn., 1980), 133–34; Spector, *Admiral of the New Empire*, 36–39, differs in some details relating to Howell.

10. Microfilm M-625, RG 45, Area File of the Naval Records Collection: McNair to Dewey, 31 December 1897, National Archives (hereafter NA)

11. Navy Department, *Annual Reports of the Navy Department for the Year 1898. Appendix to the Report of the Bureau of Navigation* (Washington, D C., 1899), 65

12 *Message from the President of the United States Transmitting the Report of the Naval Court of Enquiry upon the destruction of the United States battleship Maine in Havana Harbor, February 15, 1898, Together with the Testimony Taken Before the Court* (Washington, D.C., 1898) Subsequent research shows that the ship was destroyed by an internal explosion; see H G. Rickover, *How the Battleship Maine was Destroyed* (Washington, D C., 1976)

13 Navy Department, *Annual Reports . . . Bureau of Navigation:* Roosevelt to Dewey, 25 February 1898, 65

14 Ibid , Long to Dewey, 26 February 1898

15. Nathan Sargent, *Admiral Dewey and the Manila Campaign* (Washington, D.C., 1947), fnn. 4 and 5, 16

16 Admiral of the Navy George Dewey, *Autobiography*, Eric McAllister Smith, ed. (Annapolis, 1987), 168–69

17 Microfilm M-625, RG 45, Area File of the Naval Records Collection Dewey to Secretary of the Navy, 31 March 1898, NA

18 Grenville, *Lord Salisbury*, 210

19 Sargent, *Admiral Dewey*, fnn 12, 19. Long to Dewey, 21 April 1898

20 Admiralty (ADM) 1 / 7371: Commo Swinton C. Holland, C-in-C China, to Admiralty, 29 April 1898, Public Record Office; Microfilm M-625, RG 45, Area File of the Naval Records Collection: Wilsone Black to Dewey, 23 April 1898, NA, *The Hong Kong Government Gazette.* Extraordinary. 44, 19 (23 April 1898)· 1–2.

21 Microfilm M-625, RG 45, Area File of the Naval Records Collection: Lt. H. H Whittlesey to Long, 22 August 1901, NA, Samuel C Hudnell to H. A. Baldridge, Curator, Naval Academy Museum, 22 August 1940

22 Navy Department, *Annual Reports . . . Bureau of Navigation*, 67, Long to Dewey, 24 April 1898.

23 Microfilm M-625, RG 45, Area File of the Naval Records Collection Williams to Secretary of State Day, 19 April and Special Report [post 1 May] 1898, NA

24. The full Spanish text and an English translation appear in Joseph L Stickney, *War in the Philippines and Life and Glorious Deeds of Admiral Dewey* (Chicago, 1899).

25. Dewey, *Autobiography*, 182

26 The following is based on Capt Asa Walker, USN [Commanding *Concord* at] "The Battle of Manila Bay," Naval War College, Naval Historical Collection, RG 14, Staff Studies; and Navy Department, *Annual Reports . . . Bureau of Navigation*, Reports of Commanding Officers of vessels at the Battle of Manila Bay, 73–93, Lt Carlos Gilman Calkins, "Historical and Professional Notes on the Naval Campaign of Manila Bay in 1898," U.S. Naval Institute *Proceedings* 25 (June 1899). 267–321; and Dewey, *Autobiography*, 174–98 and 266–72, the latter being a translation of Admiral Montojo's official report

27. Stickney, *War in the Philippines*, 36

28 Lt John M Ellicott, "The Naval Battle of Manila Bay," U S. Naval Institute *Proceedings* 26 (September 1900): 501.

29 Bradley A Fiske, *From Midshipman to Rear Admiral* (New York, 1919), 247.

30. Report of commander, HMS *Linnet*, 5 May, 1898, quoted in Arthur J Marder, *The Anatomy of British Sea Power: A History of British Naval Policy in the Pre-Dreadnought Era, 1880–1905* (New York, 1940; reprint, London, 1972), 387

31. John R. Spears, *The History of Our Navy: From its Origin to the End of the War with Spain*, 5 vols (New York, 1899), 5:290, quoting an interview with Admiral Montojo in the London *Mail.*

32 Dewey, *Autobiography*, 196–97.

33 ADM 1/7371: Lt. Cdr. George A. Hardinge, RN, to Vice Adm. Sir Edward Seymour, 1 September 1898, Report on the visit of HMS *Rattler* to the Philippines, Public Record Office.

34. ADM 116/891: Report from Hong Kong, 13 July 1898, loc cit.

35. ADM 116/891· Minute on Report of 30 July 1898, loc. cit

36. German activities are detailed in Otto von Diederichs, "A Statement of Events in Manila, May–October 1898," *Journal of the Royal United Services Institution* 59 (1914): 421–46 Further information appears in Diederichs's review of Dewey's *Autobiography*, published in *Marine Rundschau* 42 (März 1914): 253–59; and Kapitänleutnant Pohl, "Die Thätigkeit S.M.S. *Irene* in der Gewässern der Philippinen 1896 bis 1899," *Marine Rundschau* 30 (1902): 759–66 (especially 763–64).

37. Von Bülow to von Hartzfeldt, 18 May 1898, Document no. 4146 in *Die Grosse Politik der Europäische Kabinette* 15: 39.

38. Walther Hubatsch, *Die Ara Tirpitz: Studien zur Deutschen Marinepolitik, 1890–1918*. Gottinger Bausteine zur Geschichtswissenschaft, vol 21 (Gottingen, 1955), 40 ff; Holger Herwig, *The Politics of Frustration: The United States in German Naval Planning, 1889–1941* (Boston, 1976), 30–36.

39 Lambi, *The Navy and German Power Politics*, 129–30, 226–31.

40 Charles Lee Lewis, *Famous American Naval Officers* (Boston, 1924), 325.

10

The Battle of Santiago

DAVID F. TRASK

The outcome of the naval action off Santiago de Cuba on Sunday, 3 July 1898, reflected sound naval strategy on the part of the United States. President William McKinley and his advisors, relying on several years of prewar planning, adopted a design based on an accurate estimate of the belligerents' naval capabilities. Spain was less fortunate. The defective assumptions Premier Práxedes Mateo Sagasta and his advisors made about the strength of the opposing navies prevented them from devising an intelligent strategy. Most important, the U.S. Navy was asked to impose a realistic political outcome, the independence of Cuba, whereas its adversary pursued an unattainable goal, upholding Spanish domination of Cuba.

The operations of naval forces depend on the feasibility of the political objective, that is, the possession of strength sufficient to impose the nation's political will on the enemy. If other circumstances obtain, only some unlikely combination of operational skill, good luck, and egregious error on the part of the enemy fleet can lead to victory. The United States clearly had sufficient strength to accomplish its policy—independence for Cuba. Spain did not and was forced to rely on mistakes by the opposition, the last resort of a weaker belligerent.

The participation of the United States in the War with Spain constituted the final phase of a Cuban insurgency that began in 1895. Spain's unsuccessful attempts to suppress the uprising led to adverse publicity in the United States, particularly after Gen. Valeriano Weyler inaugurated a program of reconcentration that caused widespread suffering. President McKinley inherited the Cuban question from his predecessor, President Grover Cleveland. Hoping to avoid armed intervention, McKinley tried to arrange some form of autonomy for Cuba, a step short of full sovereignty. Spain eventually agreed to this course, but nothing came of the offer because the insurgents refused to accept it, preferring to continue their quest for independence. When the battleship *Maine* went to the bottom of Havana harbor in February 1898, the victim of an internal explosion, opinion in the United States immediately hardened in favor of the Cubans, and the president was forced to abandon his call for home rule and instead to demand independence.[1]

Despite its willingness to grant Cuba home rule, the Spanish government could not take the final step and free the "Pearl of the Antilles." Sagasta accepted war with the United States not because he anticipated victory, but because he believed that failure to do so would precipitate a revolution at home. Domestic stability seemed preferable to the political chaos that might result from a refusal to accept a war, however hopeless. McKinley, never in favor of war, came to believe that he could not hope to maintain himself and the Republican Party in power unless he bowed to the will of the people. This insoluble dilemma led to the U.S. declaration of war, which took effect on 21 April 1898.[2]

Although its army was unprepared for war, the United States was so much the stronger nation that Spain could not hope to win, barring a complete breakdown of the American war effort. The U.S. Regular Army, only twenty-eight thousand strong, could not conduct major operations until volunteers were mobilized and trained, a matter of at least six months. The U.S. Navy, although modest in size, was prepared to deal with the Spanish fleet without significant augmentation other than the addition of auxiliary vessels. President McKinley now sought to end the war he had hoped to avoid as quickly as he could with the minimum expenditure of blood and treasure. He had been elected to pursue a domestic agenda, not a foreign war; he wanted to resume his efforts to reform the currency and the tariff at the earliest practical moment. The readiness of the fleet and the desire to wage the most limited warfare possible led the United States to develop a strategy for accomplishing its political purpose—the independence of Cuba—by conducting the opening operations at sea in theaters distant from Spain, where U.S. forces could establish early superiority.

U.S. prewar planning reflected this preoccupation with naval power. At all junctures, the United States concentrated on preparations to attack Spanish overseas possessions in the Caribbean and the western Pacific, rather than Spain itself. An assault on the Iberian peninsula would take place only if operations elsewhere did not force an end to the war. The idea of striking principally at Cuba and the Philippine Islands by itself presumed that the navy would take basic responsibility for operations. Planners in the Navy Department and the Naval War College from the first designated the Caribbean as the principal theater of war. A naval attack on Manila Bay, the principal port of the Philippines, was included as a secondary effort, principally to neutralize Spanish naval power that might otherwise harass American maritime commerce in the Pacific. U.S. planners also thought that early operations in the western Pacific would demonstrate the determination of the United States and correspondingly discourage Spain. They did not contemplate the annexation of the Philippines; no consideration was given to land operations in connection with a naval attack.

The main decision was to establish a blockade of Cuba as soon as war began to interdict the reinforcement and resupply of the large Spanish army deployed there to suppress the insurgents. In the event Spain chose to contest this blockade, it would have to dispatch naval forces across the Atlantic, for it had no significant vessels in the Caribbean. If naval engagements ensued in the Antilles, the United States would enjoy a considerable advantage, not only because it possessed a stronger fleet but because its ships would benefit from their proximity to bases. Spain's closest base was in the Canary Islands. Should the United States establish general and lasting command of the sea in the principal theater, Spain must soon sue for peace.

When diplomatic efforts to avoid war came to nothing, the U.S. Navy's North Atlantic Squadron was placed under the command of Commo. William T. Sampson, who was immediately elevated to the rank of rear admiral. Most of his ships were concentrated at Key West, less than a hundred miles from the Cuban capital at Havana, but a significant portion was detached as a "Flying Squadron" under the command of Commo. Winfield Scott Schley and sent to Hampton Roads at the mouth of the Chesapeake Bay as a means of countering possible Spanish naval raids on the eastern seaboard. Meanwhile, Commo. George Dewey, commander of the Asiatic Squadron, then visiting Japan, was ordered to move his ships to Hong Kong. From there he could quickly attack the weak Spanish squadron at Manila Bay commanded by Adm. Patricio Montojo.

Sampson was a highly experienced and talented officer. After compiling a distinguished record at the Naval Academy, from which he graduated in 1861, he served during the Civil War on the blockade of the Confederate Atlantic coast. Thereafter he alternated between sea duty and billets ashore. After several tours of duty at the Naval Academy he became its superintendent in 1886. Recognizing the unprecedented importance of science and technology for navies, Sampson interested himself particularly in these subjects, especially naval weapons, becoming the head of the Bureau of Ordnance between

William T. Sampson in 1899. *U.S. Naval Institute*

1893 and 1897. He then undertook his most important command at sea before the break with Spain, commanding the battleship *Iowa*. After the sinking of the *Maine* in February 1898, he served as president of the board of inquiry into the accident. The board reached the erroneous conclusion that an external explosion had destroyed the vessel, an inadvertent contribution to the public hysteria that forced a reluctant President McKinley to call for a war with Spain. A dignified and reserved man, Sampson shunned the limelight and adhered to the strictest standards of naval professionalism as such standards were understood in the late nineteenth century. He lacked the extroverted personality that occasionally made public idols of such fellow officers as Commodore Schley. Unfortunately, even before assuming command of the North Atlantic Squadron, he had shown signs of declining health. He probably suffered from multiple infarct dementia, the result of a succession of small strokes that progressively diminish the victim's mental acuity, but, unlike Alzheimer's disease, do not affect the personality. Whatever his affliction, it influenced his activities on occasion but did not preclude him from providing sound leadership in the Caribbean theater during the struggle for Cuban independence.[3]

The war began auspiciously for the United States. On 22 April, only four hours after learning that war had been declared, Sampson took his squadron from Key West to Cuba. He quickly blockaded Havana and then closed other Cuban ports on the north coast. Eventually the blockade was extended to the south coast. This operation quickly achieved its goal, preventing significant reinforcement and resupply of the Spanish garrison in Cuba. Much more dramatic events soon ensued in the Philippines. Dewey entered Manila Bay on 1 May and immediately engaged Montojo's ships, which were anchored off Cavite. He easily destroyed the Spanish squadron, but without troops to conduct land operations, he could only lie off the city of Manila and await further developments.[4] As early as 4 May, President McKinley ordered army units to concentrate at San Francisco, the first troops of a modest expeditionary force to be sent to seize Manila.

Meanwhile, the Spanish government decided to dispatch a squadron to Cuba under the command of Adm. Pascual Cervera, hoping by this measure to counter Sampson's blockade. Cervera strongly opposed the idea, arguing that his squadron lacked the strength to engage Sampson's command, but his superiors in Madrid overrode his objections. On 29 April he set out from St. Vincent in the Portuguese Cape Verde Islands for San Juan, Puerto Rico. His squadron consisted of four armored cruisers and three torpedo-boat destroyers. The newest of these vessels, the armored cruiser *Cristóbal Colón*, would have been a formidable opponent had she been fully prepared for battle. Unfortunately for Spain, the *Colón* was missing her main armament of 10-inch guns and could not hope to engage U.S. capital ships successfully. The other three armored cruisers—the *Infanta María Teresa, Vizcaya,* and *Almirante Oquendo*—were in poor repair, especially the foul-bottomed *Vizcaya*. Her low speed lengthened the voyage across the Atlantic, as did the poor sea-keeping qualities of the destroyer flotilla (*Plutón, Furor,* and *Terror*). Furthermore, the older cruisers had wholly wooden upper decks, which guaranteed that hits by high explosives would give rise to serious fires. An American officer aptly described the pathetic condition of Cervera's squadron: as it prepared to engage Sampson it found itself "without guns, without ammunition, without engineers, without coal, and even with the ships short of bread."[5]

Plans for U.S. activity in the Caribbean theater were clarified when, after three weeks of mystery, Cervera's location became known. The distraught Spaniard originally intended to make landfall at San Juan, Puerto Rico, but subsequently he changed his mind. His afterthought proved wise, as Sampson decided to take several strong ships to that port in the hope of intercepting his adversary. Arriving off San Juan on 12 May, he ascertained that Cervera was not there, and, after a brief bombardment, began his return voyage to Key West. That same day, Cervera appeared off Martinique, where he left one of his destroyers, the *Terror*, which was too unseaworthy to continue farther. The captain of another destroyer he had sent ahead reported that the French authorities at Fort de France would not permit him to coal, a misfortune that took him to Curaçao on 14 May, where he expected to find a collier that did not appear. The Dutch allowed him a stay of only forty-eight hours and only six hundred tons of coal. Cervera now decided to proceed to Santiago de Cuba, rejecting San Juan as too dangerous and avoiding Cienfuegos and Havana because the Americans could easily mass their vessels at either location. This choice had serious disadvantages. Few supplies were available at Santiago, and it was almost at the opposite end of the island from Havana, the center of Spanish strength.

Sampson reached Key West on 18 May, just after the arrival of Commodore Schley. The Flying Squadron had been ordered to Charleston on 13 May; while off that port it was directed to Key West. This move by the Navy Department finally united the naval power available in the North Atlantic and further increased the odds against Cervera. As Cervera had expected, Sampson immediately ordered Schley to blockade the port of Cienfuegos on the south coast of Cuba. On 19 May, the same day that Schley left for Cienfuegos, Cervera entered the harbor of Santiago. This fact was immediately reported to the Navy Department through an intelligence network established at Key West. The cable office there was in contact with a Cuban insurgent agent employed as a telegrapher at Spanish headquarters in Havana. This operative quickly reported Cervera's appearance at Santiago. Sampson at first hesitated to accept the Navy Department's belief that the report was genuine, but after a brief delay he directed Schley, en route to Cienfuegos, to blockade Santiago. Schley received these orders on 23 May.[6]

There ensued a strange interlude that still mystifies students of the War with Spain. It took Schley six days to establish himself at Santiago and to ascertain that Cervera was there. He was supposed to have blockaded Santi-

The search for Cervera. The Spanish squadron appears off Martinique on 12 May (A), the same day on which Sampson hopes to find it at San Juan, Puerto Rico (A'). Denied permission to coal at Martinique, Cervera continues on to Curaçao (B), where the Dutch allow him to do so (14–15 May), and enters port at Santiago on 19 May (C). En route back to his base at Key West, Sampson learns of Cervera's presence in the Caribbean. Both Sampson's squadron and Schley's Flying Squadron arrive at Key West on 18 May (D). The next day, Schley is sent to blockade Cienfuegos (E); Sampson then joins the blockade of Havana. When it is learned that Cervera is not at Cienfuegos, Schley is ordered to Santiago, where, after a day's controversial retrograde, he sights the Spanish squadron on 29 May (F). Upon receipt of this intelligence, Sampson returns to Key West (movement not shown) to telegraph Washington, collects the *Oregon* and two smaller vessels off Havana, and reaches Santiago on 1 June (G).

ago on 24 May. The commodore delayed his departure from Cienfuegos to Santiago in the mistaken belief that Cervera had left that port and run into Cienfuegos. He finally steamed eastward toward Santiago on the twenty-fourth after one of his commanders determined that Cervera was not at Cienfuegos. Finally arriving off Santiago on 26 May, he withdrew almost immediately without reconnoitering the harbor, steaming westward briefly but halting on 27 May and drifting for a day. Schley claimed that he left Santiago because he could not coal his vessels in the rough waters off southern Cuba, a statement that both Sampson and Secretary of the Navy John D. Long found hard to credit. The latter termed 28 May the worst day of the war, noting the disappointment President McKinley felt upon learning of Schley's dilatory behavior on that date.

Cervera had ample opportunity to leave Santiago, but no logical destination was available to him. He could not remain in the Caribbean without eventually having to deal with Sampson. He could not return to Spanish waters because some of his ships were in poor repair, notably the *Vizcaya*, and he lacked the coal necessary for a long voyage. Governor-General Ramón Blanco at Havana recognized that Cervera was in great difficulty. Given its modest size, his squadron "must elude encounter and confine itself to maneuvers which will not compromise it and which can not have great results."[7] Escape became impossible without serious risk when Schley finally took station off Santiago on 28 May and observed some of Cervera's ships in the harbor the next day. On the same day, Sampson left Key West for Santiago, sailing eastward and then through the Windward Passage to the south coast of Cuba. He arrived on 1 June, an event that concentrated all the principal vessels of the North Atlantic Squadron. Sampson's blockade now included five battleships (the *Oregon*, *Indiana*, *Massachusetts*, *Iowa*, and *Texas*), two armored cruisers (the *Brooklyn*, Schley's flagship, and the *New York*, Sampson's flagship), and a variety of cruisers and auxiliary vessels.[8] A battalion of marines soon seized Guantánamo Bay, a good harbor east of Santiago, for use as a coaling station. This action eased Sampson's task of resting and resupplying the blockading vessels.

Sampson now set himself the task of maintaining a close watch on Cervera's squadron. His principal chore was to preclude a successful sortie from the harbor through the narrow channel leading to the open sea.[9] Sampson first attempted to block the channel by sinking the collier *Merrimac* in it. A young officer, Naval Constructor Richmond Pearson Hobson, undertook this task, which entailed steaming through mine fields, evading the fire of several batteries located at or near the channel's mouth, and exploding the charges designed to sink the collier at the correct location. Hobson made his attempt on the night of 3 June. Unfortunately, a Spanish shell cut the *Merrimac*'s steering mechanism, and the ship came to rest without blocking the channel sufficiently to prevent Cervera's squadron from departing. Hobson and his seven crewmen were rescued and imprisoned in the Morro Castle, which commanded the height at the east side of the channel entrance.

Thereafter, Sampson depended on a semicircle of ships standing about four miles off the entrance to contain the Spanish squadron. The several obsolete batteries at the entrance posed no serious threat, but he ruled out an attempt to storm the channel because of two lines of electrical mines that could be detonated from stations ashore. After nightfall, some blockading ships closed to about two miles of the channel and directed their powerful searchlights up its mouth. This innovative measure strengthened the likelihood that Cervera would not attempt a sortie at night.[10] The difficulties of the blockade, however, were sufficient to prompt Sampson to suggest that the United States send a land force to Santiago as soon as possible. Its mission would be to force the surrender of the Spanish squadron.

As soon as Cervera was bottled up at Santiago, President McKinley spearheaded a number of significant decisions. He decided to dispatch a modest expedition composed mainly of regular army regiments that had been concentrated at Tampa to southeastern Cuba. The volunteers needed to provide a large force were not yet trained, but an advance on Santiago would not require them. The area was poorly garrisoned and far from the main Spanish force at Havana, which could do nothing to reinforce the troops there. The Cuban insurgents around Santiago, commanded by Gen. Calixto García, were capable of preventing a concentration of the small Spanish garrisons scattered in the vicinity. McKinley also decided to prepare an expedition to attack Puerto Rico as soon as the issue had been decided at Santiago. These small expeditions, along with the corps ordered to Manila, would exert prompt and impressive pressure on the principal Spanish possessions in the Caribbean and Pacific theaters.[11]

In accordance with his fixed intent, McKinley hoped that these enterprises would hasten a Spanish decision to end the war. In this connection, early in June he signaled to Spain through European intermediaries his terms of peace. These included, above all, independence for Cuba, but also the annexation of Puerto Rico in lieu of a monetary indemnity and the acquisition of one of the Mariana Islands, presumably Guam, which would strengthen the maritime line of communications between the United States and eastern Asia. Finally, McKinley specified his desire for a port in the Philippines but said nothing about the ultimate disposition of the archipelago. Spain was informed that delay in coming to terms would lead to additional requirements. This diplomatic initiative did not immediately succeed, but it guided decisions about the future behavior of U.S. armed forces, including the North Atlantic Fleet at Santiago.[12]

The need for haste vastly complicated the preparation of the army's expedition to Cuba, but, after various misadventures, its commander, Maj. Gen. William R. Shafter, finally arranged for its transports to leave Tampa on 14 June. Arriving off Santiago on 20 June, Shafter attempted to coordinate his activities with those of the Cuban insurgents and Admiral Sampson. He landed his force, the Fifth Corps of about seventeen thousand troops, at coastal locations east of Santiago, notably Daiquiri and Siboney. Sampson wanted Shafter, supported by the blockading squadron's gunfire, to seize the heights of the Morro and the Socapa at the entrance to the channel, an operation that would permit the Spanish mines to be swept. Sampson's ships then could enter the harbor without difficulty and deal with Cervera's squadron. This plan accorded well with the view that the principal mission at Santiago was to defeat Cervera. Shafter had a different view. He wished to defeat the Spanish garrison and capture the city. To achieve this purpose, Shafter planned to attack along a line several miles from the coast, a route that would preclude naval gunfire support. Interservice rivalry influenced the attitudes of the armed forces at Santiago. Both the army and the navy sought to make major contributions to the campaign, but the navy had dominated events during the opening weeks of war, a fact that unsettled army leadership. Army-navy differences persisted despite attempts from Washington to resolve them, leading to wartime misunderstanding and postwar recriminations.

As the army and navy positioned themselves for the Santiago campaign, the Navy Department took note of a Spanish attempt to relieve the garrison in the Philippines. A squadron commanded by Adm. Manuel de la Cámara left Spain on 16 June. It included the battleship *Pelayo* and the armored cruiser *Carlos V,* along with several auxiliaries and transports. De la Cámara was ordered to proceed eastward through the Mediterranean and the Suez Canal to the Philippines, which he could reach late in August. To counter this threat, the Navy Department ordered two seagoing monitors with considerable firepower to proceed to Manila. It also began the organization of an "eastern squadron" that, if necessary, could steam to Spanish waters and then pursue de la Cámara. This development did not please Sampson, who wished to retain all his vessels off the Cuban coast.[13]

During the last days of June General Shafter moved into position for an assault on Santiago. His troops marched westward along a poor road that passed through a small settlement called Las Guásimas and crossed the San Juan heights, a line of hills just outside the city. Shafter wished to attack as soon as possible, fearful that tropical diseases might weaken his command and that the Spanish might succeed in reinforcing their weak garrison. The enemy commander, Gen. Arsenio Linares, decided not to offer serious resistance until the Fifth Corps neared Santiago. By 1 July Shafter's troops were organized for an assault intended to overwhelm the defenders on the San Juan heights and then press on to storm the city.[14]

The connected battles of El Caney and the San Juan heights on 1 July placed the Fifth Corps on the hills overlooking Santiago, but inefficient American tactics and stiff Spanish resistance prevented the capture of the city.[15] After some indecision Shafter settled down to a siege, hoping to starve out the defenders. This outcome irritated Sampson, who was not asked to provide more than minimal aid, although his guns could have lent important support to the attack. The difficulties of maintaining a close-in blockade were becoming more and more apparent, especially with the Navy Department contemplating the formation of the Eastern Squadron to follow de la Cámara.

Fortunately for the navy, the actions of 1 July led the authorities in Havana to order Cervera to leave Santiago. Before the U.S. advance on the city, Cervera faced a choice between flight, which would force an engagement with the blockading fleet, or participation in the defense of the city, perhaps by emplacing naval guns in positions around the perimeter manned by Spanish troops. After Shafter's qualified gains of 1 July, Cervera's superior in Havana, Governor-General Blanco, decided the issue. He took the position that Cervera should exit immediately; "the situation in that harbor is, in my judgment, the most dangerous of all." He feared that failure to come out would have a devastating psychological effect at home and abroad. To Cervera's repeated plaint that the squadron faced certain destruction, he responded: "This is an additional reason for attempting the sortie, since it is preferable for the honor of arms to succumb in battle, where there may be many chances of safety."

Blanco and the minister of marine in Madrid, Captain Ramón Auñón, favored a nocturnal sortie. Some authorities agree, arguing that the ships should have departed at night, steamed in different directions, and rendezvoused at a previously specified location.[16] Cervera thought differently, noting the adverse consequences of the U.S. use of searchlights during the hours of darkness. "It was absolutely impossible to go out at night, because in this narrow channel, illuminated by a dazzling light, we could not have followed the channel and would have lost the ships, some by running aground, others by colliding with their companions." If the batteries at the channel entrance had possessed modern artillery, they might have forced the blockade line back to a distance of five or six miles, which would have eased the difficulties of exiting after dark.

On 2 July Blanco informed Cervera that only three U.S. ships were off Cienfuegos and no more than nine off Havana. Later in the day he issued a definite order: "In view of the exhausted and serious condition of Santiago . . . your excellency will reembark landing troops of squadron as fast as possible and go out immediately." At 7:00 P.M. Cervera issued orders for a sortie to take place about 9:00 A.M. on 3 July. After the squadron cleared the channel, it was to head for either Cienfuegos or Havana. The *Infanta María Teresa* would lead, and the *Vizcaya, Cristóbal Colón,* and *Almirante Oquendo* would follow, in that order. The destroyers *Furor* and *Plutón* would go out last. Cervera realized that her combination of speed and firepower made Schley's flagship, the armored cruiser *Brooklyn,* the most dangerous American vessel. His armored cruisers were to concentrate their fire on her while the destroyers fled.

On Sunday morning, 3 July, Sampson's blockading line found itself short of its usual numbers. At full strength it had 102 big guns (5-inch and larger) to the Spanish total of 46, and its vessels, auxiliaries excluded, displaced 73,742 tons to 28,280 tons for Cervera's ships. However, one battleship, the *Massachusetts,* had gone to Guantánamo Bay to coal, accompanied by the cruisers *New Orleans* and *Newark.* More important, the armored cruiser *New York,* with Sampson aboard, had left the line a little before 9:00 A.M. to steam eastward to Siboney. The admiral was to land there and confer with General Shafter in an attempt to satisfy Washington's desire for enhanced army-navy cooperation. The armed yacht *Hist* and torpedo boat *Ericsson* served as escorts. As the *New York* left the blockade line, she signaled: "Disregard the movements of the commander in chief." According to a leading authority, this message meant only that Sampson "had not relinquished or transferred command but merely left his blockade station."[17] The seven remaining vessels formed a semicircle about eight miles in length some three to four miles off the entrance to the channel and its batteries, the Morro and the Socapa. The converted yacht *Gloucester* was farthest east and the converted yacht *Vixen* farthest west. Between these auxiliaries from east to west lay the battleships *Indiana, Oregon, Iowa,* and *Texas,* and the armored cruiser *Brooklyn.* Sampson's departure made Commodore Schley the senior officer present on the blockade.

Although on 3 July the U.S. blockade included only one more big ship than Cervera's squadron, it was much the stronger force, throwing three times the weight of broadside—18,847 to 6,014 pounds. Moreover many of Cervera's batteries were in poor repair and lacked reliable ammunition; and as noted earlier, the *Cristóbal Colón* had sailed without her main battery of 10-inch guns.[18] The tactical circumstances at Santiago vastly increased this disparity. All or most of the blockaders could engage each of the Spanish vessels as they emerged, because the channel was too narrow for more than one ship at a time to pass through it.

At 8:00 A.M. Cervera ordered his squadron to clear for action and then to navigate the channel. Earlier, Capt. Victor Concas had reconnoitered the blockade from a gunboat, the *Alvarado,* an activity that was observed from the

TABLE 10.1 The Battle of Santiago, 3 July 1898

	Commissioned	Displacement	Speed	Complement	Main Battery				Torpedo Tubes
U.S. NAVY North Atlantic Fleet Rear Adm. W. T. Sampson					13 in.	12 in.	8 in.	6 in.	
Battleships									
Indiana	1895	10,288	15	571	4	—	8	4	6
Iowa	1897	11,346	17	587	—	4	8	—	4
Oregon	1896	10,288	16	524	4	—	8	4	6
Texas	1895	6,315	17	433	—	2	—	6	4
Armored cruisers									
Brooklyn	1896	9,215	22	552	—	—	8	—	5
New York (F)	1893	8,150	21	652	—	—	6	—	3
Auxiliaries									
Gloucester	1891/98 [a]	786	17	93	—	—	—	—	—
Hist	1895/98 [a]	?	?	56	—	—	—	—	—
Vixen	1896/98 [a]	806	16	82	—	—	—	—	—
Torpedo boat									
Ericsson	1897	120	24	22	—	—	—	—	3
TOTAL MAIN ARMAMENT					8	6	38	14	31
SPANISH NAVY Cruiser Squadron Rear Adm. P. Cervera					11 in.	6 in.	5.5 in.	4.7 in.	
Armored cruisers									
Almirante Oquendo	1891	6,890	20	487	2	—	10	—	8
Cristóbal Colón	1896	6,840	20	567	—	10	—	6	5
Infanta María Teresa (F)	1890	6,890	20	556	2	—	10	—	8
Vizcaya	1891	6,890	20	491	2	—	10	—	8
Destroyers									
Furor	1896	370	28	80	—	—	—	—	2
Plutón	1897	400	30	80	—	—	—	—	2
TOTAL MAIN ARMAMENT					6	10	30	6	33

Notes: For Spanish ships, the years given are launch dates; for U.S ships, note that crews were reinforced above normal manning levels at the outbreak of war; (F) = flagship

[a] Date completed/date taken into naval service

Brooklyn.[19] His report on the blockaders' disposition led Cervera to order flight westward to Cienfuegos. The flagship *Infanta María Teresa,* with Concas in command, was instructed to ram the *Brooklyn.* If successful, this maneuver might create an opportunity for other ships to escape. Concas's vessel mounted only two big guns, leaving him with no alternative except to ram. It would take the Spanish ships, six to eight hundred yards apart and making way at 8 to 10 knots, about an hour to clear the channel. The *Brooklyn*'s position near the western end of the blockade line would give her an early opportunity to engage the enemy. The *New York* had reached a point about nine miles from the mouth of the channel when the first Spanish vessel exited. There was little chance that the commander in chief would be able to overtake the engagement.

At about 9:30 A.M. the blockaders first spied the smoke of the emerging Spanish vessels. Cervera achieved tactical surprise. Although a sortie had been expected at some point, it did not seem probable that it would come in broad daylight on a relatively calm day. The Sunday routine of the U.S. ships, which included divine services, had proceeded normally. As the *Infanta María Teresa* passed the Morro Castle, the principal blockaders immediately responded. In accordance with Sampson's plan, the *Iowa* raised Signal 250, "The enemy is attempting to escape," and all vessels went to general quarters as the battleship fired the first shot of the engagement.

More than one U.S. observer was struck by the contrast between the blockading ships, weather-beaten and rust-streaked after weeks at sea, and Cervera's smart-looking cruisers, red-and-yellow battle flags streaming from their masts. To the *Texas*'s Capt. John W. (Jack) Philip, it seemed as though "[t]he Spanish ships came out as gaily as brides to the altar." The atmosphere on the bridges of those ships was far from gay, however. In the blare of the bugles he ordered to herald the action's opening, Captain Concas heard "the last echo of those which history tells us were sounded at the capture of Granada. It was the signal that the history of four centuries of grandeur was at an end. . . ."[20]

The most interesting single event of the battle occurred almost at the outset. Concas steered the *Infanta María Teresa* directly toward the *Brooklyn*, attempting to carry out his admiral's orders to ram. Cervera later explained that "it was the utmost importance for us to place this ship in a condition where she could not make use of her superior speed." The *Brooklyn*, with Capt. Francis A. Cook in command, was then heading west-northwest. Cook ordered a turn east, away from the approaching *Infanta María Teresa* and the Spanish destination, Cienfuegos. Commodore Schley concurred in his decision. This eccentric action almost led to a collision with the *Texas*, which had to back her engines. The *Brooklyn* continued the turn until she had completed a 360-degree loop and found herself running parallel to the fleeing Spanish ships, which were closer to shore and steaming westward. Cook's maneuver increased the initial distance between the *Brooklyn* and the enemy, especially the speedy *Cristóbal Colón*. The *Infanta María Teresa*, exposed to the fire of the

The battleship *Oregon,* showing the signs of nearly four months at sea, was photographed shortly after becoming the "Bulldog of the Fleet" at the Battle of Santiago. *U.S. Naval Institute*

entire American line, could not reach the *Brooklyn* and turned toward Cienfuegos.

Among the foremost of the *Infanta María Teresa*'s pursuers was Capt. Charles E. Clark's *Oregon,* whose outstanding performance throughout the battle would be recognized by the sobriquet the "Bulldog of the Fleet." The only battleship to have all her boilers lit that morning, she quickly worked up to full power and amazed everyone except her engineers by keeping pace with the *Brooklyn.* From her forward 13-inch turret, Lt. (j.g.) Edward W. Eberle saw that

[t]he *Teresa* was farther offshore than the other three vessels and was being passed by them. We brought her sharp on our starboard bow, and as we gained on her our forward guns engaged her at two thousand yards' range, when (about ten minutes past ten) we discovered her to be on fire. The *Teresa* was soon left behind by the other vessels. Smoke and flames were pouring from her upper works, and the sight of her hopeless condition seemed to double the energy of our ships, for their fire became more rapid and deadly than ever.[21]

Cervera assumed direct command of his flagship when Concas fell wounded. The admiral ran toward shore and beached the battered vessel near Punta Cabrera at 10:35, an hour after she had left the channel.

The next Spanish ship put out of action was the *Almirante Oquendo,* the fourth to exit the harbor. The second and third, the *Vizcaya* and *Cristóbal*

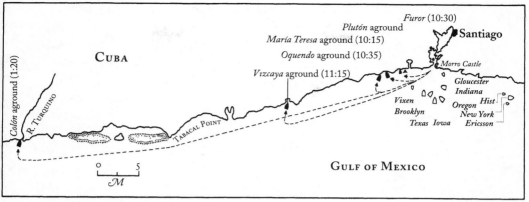

The Battle of Santiago, 3 July 1898.

Colón, initially avoided the blockaders' full fire because the U.S. gunners were concentrating on the *Infanta María Teresa.* When the guns first brought to bear on the Spanish flagship became available for other tasks, the *Almirante Oquendo* came under an intense bombardment. The effect, noted the *Iowa's* Capt. Robley D. Evans, "was most destructive. . . . I could see the shot holes come in her sides and our shells explode inside her, but she pluckily held her course. . . ."[22] Within minutes, however, fires that leaped as high as her fighting tops broke out on the cruiser's decks, and she turned toward shore. She was beached at 10:40 a little west of the flagship. In the *Texas,* men shouted in triumph when an explosion shook the burning wreck. Jack Philip silenced those around him with the words, "Don't cheer, boys; the poor devils are dying." (Afterward, the ship's chaplain insisted he must have said "poor fellows.")[23]

The destroyers *Plutón* and *Furor* were the next victims. All four American battleships fired on them, inflicting extensive damage, but the executioner was the unprotected yacht *Gloucester,* mounting four 6-pounders, whose commander, Lt. Cdr. Richard Wainwright, had survived the destruction of the *Maine.* The *Plutón* was driven onto the beach at 10:45 somewhat west of Cabañas. The *Furor* went down in deep water off Cabañas shortly thereafter. It had taken little more than an hour to destroy all but two of Cervera's ships.

The remaining Spanish vessels, the *Vizcaya* and *Cristóbal Colón,* were able to clear the channel and commence the run to Cienfuegos, with the American battleships and the *Brooklyn* in hot pursuit. In passing the *Iowa,* the *Colón* scored hits with her two 5.5-inch guns, neither of which did much harm. Eventually the *New York,* having reversed course, joined the chase, but Sampson's flagship contributed little, firing only three shots. At first the *Vizcaya* led the cavalcade of the pursued and the pursuing, but she soon came under fierce attack. At 11:15, with all her guns silenced and a serious fire burning forward, she turned toward shore and struck a reef off Aserraderos.

Concluding that the consequences of seventeen months out of dry dock made the *Iowa* too slow to be useful in the chase after the *Colón*, Evans decided that his duty lay in rescuing the *Vizcaya's* survivors, and signaled the *Ericsson* and *Hist* to join in the effort. Miles down the coast, the *Indiana* and the *Gloucester* had already begun picking up the crews of the *María Teresa*, the *Oquendo*, and the torpedo boats. In both locales the Americans were disgusted to see Cuban insurgents ashore firing at the Spaniards in the water. Among the prisoners her boats brought to the *Iowa* was the *Vizcaya's* wounded commander, Capt. Don Antonio Eulate. Piped aboard with all the honors due an officer of his rank, he reenacted one of the ancient rituals of the sea, unbuckling his sword, kissing his hilt, and presenting it to Evans—who promptly handed it back: "I never felt so sorry for a man in all my life."[24]

The dispatch of the *Vizcaya* left only one of Cervera's ships afloat, the modern armored cruiser *Cristóbal Colón*, which must outsteam the *New York*, *Brooklyn*, *Texas*, and *Oregon*. Flight was the only option available to the virtually unarmed Spanish vessel. The *Colón* was able to make about 14.5 knots at top speed, faster than her pursuers, but a chase of about two hours exhausted the small supply of good coal still on hand. With only a low grade of coal taken on at Santiago, the *Colón* lost speed. When the *Oregon* with her mighty 13-inch guns came within range, the doomed ship turned toward shore, hauling down her flag, and struck the beach near the mouth of the Turquino River, some fifty miles from Santiago, at about 1:15 P.M. The engineers then opened the ship's sea valves, and she filled with salt water. This act, a violation of the laws of war for a surrendered vessel, was intended to deny the Americans a valuable prize. That she would be lost did not become known until a prize crew boarded her late that afternoon. At the end of the battle nothing dampened the jubilation aboard the U.S. ships. Commodore Schley summed up the general sentiment when he hailed the *Texas* with the words, "It was a nice fight, Jack, wasn't it?"[25]

An accounting of the damage to the opposing forces underlines the definitive character of the U.S. victory. The entire Spanish squadron of six ships was destroyed. Three U.S. ships—the *Brooklyn*, *Texas*, and *Iowa*—suffered minor punishment. The disparity in casualties was as considerable. Only two U.S. seamen were hit, both on the *Brooklyn*, of whom one perished. Spanish casualties were 323 killed and 151 wounded. A large number of prisoners were taken, 1,720 men, including Admiral Cervera. About 150 others escaped to Santiago. The Cuban insurgents killed perhaps 260. Total casualties might have been much larger; the beaching of five ships mercifully held down the losses. Cervera and his captains had anticipated a hecatomb. Their actions during the battle indicate an attempt to minimize casualties while upholding the honor of the navy, as Montojo had done at Manila Bay.

Sampson hurriedly informed the U.S. government of his victory; too hurriedly, as it turned out. An aide composed a cable, which was insufficiently revised and sent without appropriate consideration. Its brief text aptly summarized the result:

The fleet under my command offers the nation as a Fourth of July present the whole of Cervera's fleet. It attempted to escape at 9:30 this morning. At 2 the last ship, the *Cristóbal Colón*, had run ashore 75 miles west of Santiago and hauled down her colors. The *Infanta María Teresa, Oquendo,* and *Vizcaya* were forced ashore, burned, and blown up within 20 miles of Santiago. The *Furor* and *Plutón* were destroyed within 4 miles of the port.[26]

This message mimed General Sherman's telegram announcing the fall of Savannah during the Civil War. Its principal weakness was its failure to mention the contribution of Commodore Schley, who as senior oYcer present had automatically assumed command of the blockading vessels until Admiral Sampson's return. Sampson and his staV were justifiably angered by Schley's peculiar behavior while attempting to establish the blockade of Santiago. They were naturally chagrined that the admiral should have been absent when Cervera made his sortie. They later made much of Schley's loop at the beginning of the engagement, which temporarily lengthened the distance between the Brooklyn and the enemy squadron. Sampson's adherents also noted that Schley did not exercise command prerogatives very much during the battle. The captains of the individual ships simply followed the plans the admiral had made in the event of a Spanish sortie. The battle was surely "a captain's fight," fought just as it would have been had Sampson been present.

The sea victory at Santiago proved decisive. Soon thereafter, the Spanish government decided to end the war. It recalled Admiral de la Cámara's squadron, recently sent to the Mediterranean, and authorized the capitulation of Santiago after Shafter had conducted a two weeks' siege. When the process of negotiating peace was delayed, the United States dispatched an expedition to Puerto Rico and attacked Manila with the army corps ordered to the Philippines after Dewey's victory. These measures sustained constant pressure on locations at the periphery of Spanish power as a means of guaranteeing an early cessation of hostilities, in line with the president's wishes.

As part of this effort the Navy Department continued preparations to send the Eastern Squadron to Spanish waters, but the war came to an end before it was ordered abroad. Although the army proved successful in capturing Santiago, Manila, and most of Puerto Rico, the destruction of the Spanish squadrons at Manila and especially at Santiago was more important in forcing an end to the war on 12 August.[27]

The navy emerged from the Spanish War with its image much enhanced, the strategic role assigned to it having been executed successfully in two major operations without the loss of a ship. The fleet's exploits confirmed the national impression that the navy must be the first line of defense and the most important guarantor of national security. The triumph of 1898 contributed to the circumstances that led to the enlargement of the fleet during the early twentieth century. Ironically some of the consequences of the war, especially the tendency of the United States thereafter to think of itself as one of the great powers and to act accordingly, would eventually require a huge army and air force as well as a great navy. As long as the United States avoided involvement in Eurasian politics by following an isolationist foreign policy and a defensive military strategy, the fleet would remain the principal means of ensuring national security. If the United States became actively involved in world politics, it would require powerful armed forces of all types. The little War with Spain was a large step toward an interventionist foreign policy and its military requirements.

The specific effect of the sea battle on the future development of navies is less important. Dewey's victory at Manila Bay and Sampson's at Santiago were won without significant opposition. The naval side of the war helped to popularize Capt. Alfred Thayer Mahan's conceptions of the significance of seapower, which also exercised important influence overseas, notably in Germany and Japan. Yet the United States remained implicitly committed to the defensive naval policies of the nineteenth century until the onset of World War I, and President Woodrow Wilson's adoption of the slogan, "a navy second to none," reflected in the Naval Act of 1916. This legislation for the first time scheduled construction of a comprehensive Mahanian battle fleet capable of establishing general and lasting command of the sea. That goal was not achieved until World War II. Nevertheless, the victories of 1898 live on in the lore of the U.S. Navy. Visitors to the U.S. Naval Academy in Annapolis and the National War College in Washington, D.C., encounter Spanish ordnance captured at Santiago in 1898, a tribute to the officers and men who served in the blockade and sea battle.

The only jarring note was a lengthy and destructive dispute between

Sampson and Schley, turning on credit for the victory at Santiago. Sampson and his adherents, including Secretary of the Navy Long and Captain Mahan, claimed the honor for Sampson despite his absence from the concluding combat because he had prepared the meticulous arrangements for the blockade, which included appropriate instructions to counter Cervera's sortie on 3 July. Sampson also drew attention to Schley's inexplicable dilatoriness in establishing the blockade at Santiago and his approval of the odd order that turned the *Brooklyn* temporarily away from the fleeing Spanish vessels during the battle. This controversy led to a formal court of inquiry. The court condemned Schley, although its presiding officer, Admiral Dewey, dissented from the majority. For many years, the division of opinion concerning the merits of Sampson and Schley agitated the naval officer corps, a needless legacy of the sea battle at Santiago that blemished an otherwise admirable naval record during the Spanish-American War.[28]

NOTES

1. For a thorough account of the *Maine* disaster, see Hyman G. Rickover, *How the Battleship Maine Was Destroyed* (Washington, D C , 1976). For the effect of the disaster on public opinion in the United States, see Ernest R. May, *Imperial Democracy: The Emergence of America as a Great Power* (New York, 1959).

2 For discussion of the president's behavior during the War with Spain, see the differing views expressed in Margaret Leech, *In the Days of McKinley* (New York, 1959), May, *Imperial Democracy*; Lewis L. Gould, *The Spanish-American War and William McKinley* (Lawrence, Kans., 1986); and David F. Trask, *The War with Spain in 1898* (New York, 1981)

3. For a recent short biography of Admiral Sampson, see Joseph Dawson's excellent contribution, "William T. Sampson· Progressive Technologist as Naval Commander," in James C. Bradford, ed., *Admirals of the New Steel Navy: Makers of the American Naval Tradition 1889–1930* (Annapolis, 1990), 149–79 Dawson examines Sampson's behavior in 1898 in depth in "William T. Sampson and Santiago. Blockade, Victory, and Controversy," in James C. Bradford, ed., *Crucible of Empire* (Annapolis, 1993), 47–68. For his medical problems, see Martin G. Netsky, M D., and Capt. Edward L. Beach, USN (Ret.), "The Trouble with Admiral Sampson," *Naval History* 9 (November–December 1995): 8–17.

4. For the Battle of Manila Bay, see Ronald Spector, *Admiral of the New Empire: The Life and Career of George Dewey* (Baton Rouge, 1974), 40–63

5. Capt. French Ensor Chadwick, the commander of Sampson's flagship, the armored cruiser *New York*, made this observation in *The Relations of the United States and Spain: The Spanish-American War* (New York, 1911), 1:46. This two-volume work is an excellent account See also H W. Wilson, *Battleships in Action* (reprint, Annapolis, 1995), 1:139.

6. For various American intelligence operations, including the watch on Cervera, see David F. Trask, "American Intelligence During the Spanish-American War," in Bradford, ed., *Crucible of Empire*, 23–46. See also G. J. A. O'Toole, *The Spanish War: An American Epic—1898* (New York, 1984).

7. Blanco to Correa, 20 May 1898, Pascual Cervera, *The Spanish-American War* (Washington, D.C., 1899), 81.

8. The *Oregon*, stationed on the Pacific coast when the emergency occurred, was ordered to the Atlantic. This requirement necessitated a long voyage around Cape Horn. The ship arrived at Key West in time to join Sampson's movement to Santiago.

9. A dangerous obstruction at the mouth of the channel, the Diamond Shoal, restricted the width of the navigable exit to about seventy-five yards.

10. In July 1994 the author had an opportunity to visit the channel of Santiago de Cuba and other

prominent sites in the region connected with the campaign of 1898 This inspection confirmed the established judgment that the channel was difficult for an attacking force to storm, but also difficult for an exiting squadron to transit in the face of an enemy force. I am indebted to Eugene B. Bigler, who visited Santiago with me

11. For information about the three army expeditions, see Graham A. Cosmas, *An Army for Empire: The United States Army in the Spanish-American War* (Columbia, Mo., 1971), passim.

12. The North Atlantic Squadron and the Flying Squadron were formally consolidated on 17 June. Sampson's command thereafter was designated the North Atlantic Fleet.

13. For the history of the Eastern Squadron, see Trask, *The War with Spain in 1898*, chap. 12

14. Ibid., chap. 9.

15. For an authoritative account of this battle, see Graham A. Cosmas, "San Juan Hill and El Caney, 1–2 July 1898," in Charles E. Heller and William A. Stofft, eds., *America's First Battles: 1776–1965* (Lawrence, Kans , 1986), 109–48.

16. See the views of a European observer, Commander Jacobsen, in U.S. Navy Department, *Sketches from the Spanish-American War by Commander J* . . . (Washington, D.C., 1899).

17. Paolo Coletta, *French Ensor Chadwick: Scholarly Warrior* (Lanham, Md., 1980), 89 Some of Schley's supporters thought differently, arguing that this message transferred command of the blockading ships to the commodore

18. Wilson, *Battleships in Action*, 2.148, 135, 141–42

19. Michael Blow, *A Ship to Remember: The Maine and the Spanish-American War* (New York, 1992), 332.

20. Capt. John W. Philip, "The 'Texas' at Santiago," *Century* 57 (May 1899): 90; Capt. Victor M. Concas y Palau, *The Squadron of Admiral Cervera* (Washington, D.C., 1900), 74

21. Lt. Edward W Eberle, "The 'Oregon' at Santiago," *Century* 57 (May 1899): 107.

22. Rear Adm Robley D. Evans, *A Sailor's Log: Recollections of Forty Years of Naval Life*, Benjamin Franklin Cooling, ed. (Annapolis, 1994), 466.

23. Henry F. Keenan, *The Conflict with Spain* (Philadelphia, 1898), 208; cf. Edgar Stanton Maclay, ed., *Life and Adventures of "Jack" Philip, Rear Admiral, USN* (New York, 1903), 104.

24 Evans, *A Sailor's Log*, 470

25. Keenan, *The Conflict with Spain*, 208.

26. Quoted in Trask, *The War with Spain in 1898*, 266. Schley attempted to send a separate report of the battle, but his flag lieutenant was kept from doing so when it was deemed to violate regulations. See also Blow, *A Ship to Remember*, 361.

27. For these matters, see John L Offner, *An Unwanted War: The Diplomacy of United States over Cuba, 1895–1898* (Chapel Hill, 1992), chaps. 12–13.

28. Most historians have supported Sampson despite the vigorous defense that Schley offered in his autobiography, *Forty-five Years under the Flag* (New York, 1904) Recently the distinguished naval historian Harold D. Langley has defended Schley in two articles, one a short biography entitled "Winfield Scott Schley: The Confident Commander," in Bradford, ed., *Admirals of the New Steel Navy*, 180–221, and the other a more detailed examination of Schley's actions in 1898, "Winfield S. Schley and Santiago: Blockade, Victory, and Controversy," in Bradford, ed., *Crucible of Empire*, 69–101. Langley suggests that I did not give sufficient attention to Schley's autobiography in evaluating the Sampson-Schley controversy in *The War with Spain in 1898*. Given the tendentious character of Schley's account, I relied heavily on the testimony at the postwar court of inquiry. Perhaps too much attention has been paid to this controversy. Future historians should reach reasonable evaluations on the basis of the authoritative scholarship of Langley and Dawson cited above.

II

The Attack on Pearl Harbor

E DWARD L. B EACH

As is well known, Japan's attack on the U.S. naval base at Pearl Harbor pre-cipitated the United States' entry into the most terrible war yet fought on earth. Historians now say this was the worst error old Imperial Japan could have made, in that its final cost was astronomical in lives and treasure. For vic-tory, the samurai-proud leaders of old Japan were willing to pay this price—might even have anticipated how heavy it might be. They would not have been willing to pay the added cost of a national defeat that changed Japan's entire future.

Yet now, only half a century after incurring America's absolute and total abomination, and only a century and a half since their nation was wrested out of its self-imposed time capsule, the people of modern Japan recognize that awful outcome, the overwhelming destruction of the fabric of their old, still-medieval society, to have been beneficial to those who survived. Measured in mankind's always resurgent search for betterment, in the largest sense it has also been beneficial to the world at large. Those who gave their lives to pre-serve the old Japan might not agree, frozen in time as they are; but were those uselessly sacrificed warriors able to evaluate today's Japan against the feudal tyranny that so callously requisitioned their lives, they, too, would almost cer-tainly agree that Japan's new society better represents its people than the old. By and large, Japan's citizenry today looks on World War II as the biggest step in the modernization that began with Matthew Calbraith Perry and his great black ships. Their only real regret is its colossal cost in life. Beside this, the cost in treasure, great as that may have been, is simply of no account.

The United States has yet to come to grips with what actually happened on that terrible Sunday morning at Pearl Harbor. We were caught by sur-prise, lost our outmoded fleet of old, slow battleships, and suffered the untimely deaths of 2,335 of our young servicemen and 68 civilians (many times fewer, however, than we willingly sacrificed in Normandy two-and-a-half years later). By Pearl Harbor we were propelled unwillingly into World War II. Given the stakes, this was an inevitability that a large proportion of our citizenry knew could not be long avoided, but which an even larger percentage, dreading war, holding to a futile hope that somehow the problem would go away of its own accord, simply refused to face. The "European War" against the Axis that included already nearly all the Atlantic Ocean, instantly expanded into a two-ocean war involving most of the civilized world.

In the days of whalers and hard-driven clipper ships, the name "Pearl" seems to have become something of a favorite. Many of our seacoast cities boast a "Pearl Street" with antecedents pretty much lost to the residents. Pearl Harbor, a large landlocked bay in the island of Oahu, Hawaii, was known for many years by that very ordinary name. On 7 December 1941, however, courtesy of Japan, it took on a new dimension it will never lose. Never to be forgotten is the surprise attack delivered on our base there by Japan that fateful Sunday morning. To us it was an abominable crime, a "sneak attack" perpetuated in total surprise during a time of peace by a nation that thereby outlawed itself. Japan still has trouble understanding the extraordinary rage into which that cynical act sent the entire population of the United States, nor why it made the atomic bombs inevitable.

A measure of the deterioration of world affairs during recent years: today we think the most likely way in which a major war will begin will be by a "sneak attack" with nuclear weapons. This is part of Japan's ill-considered legacy. Her surprise strike, made with all weapons available at the time, demonstrated conclusively that, could the Japan of 1941 have employed nuclear weapons without fear of immediate retaliation in kind, she would have done so.

But because of its "doomsday" nature, a surprise attack with nuclear weapons must at once, by all possible measurement, be utterly and completely successful. The mind of man boggles at the idea. The total elimination of an entire society is the only thing that can fit this apocalyptic requirement. No one's imagination, or vocabulary, is adequate to encompass this concept. Should a surprise nuclear attack upon a nuclear-armed adversary not instantly destroy that nation's ability to respond in kind, the end result might well be the destruction of humanity. But even this is only part of Japan's legacy, for the surprise assault with nuclear weapons, which Japan foreshadowed at Pearl Harbor, can be said to have truly eliminated traditional warfare (i.e., using all available weapons). No nation, unless supremely confident of total and

Husband E. Kimmel as Commander in Chief of the Pacific Fleet. *U.S. Naval Institute*

instant victory, or possibly suicidal, would dare launch such an attack, and the result, since 1945, has been to push conflict to a lower level.

War has not, of course, been eliminated. It has simply reduced in scope as its weapons become more all-encompassing. Similarly those who plan it, who may be only a tiny group of malcontents able to dispose of weapons of great power and versatility—which almost certainly can only mean secret government involvement—seek to strike terrible blows from places of conventional safety.

Until that fateful morning in Hawaii, the entire experience of our stunned nation had been of the "traditional"—that is to say, orderly—procedures of the western world. These included formalities concerning a declaration of war, absence of which, by the laws of nations, constituted capital offenses on the parts of their leaders. Our commanders at Pearl Harbor, Adm. Husband E. Kimmel and Lt. Gen. Walter C. Short, were nonetheless vilified for not having been ready for the type of attack they received. Their steadily increasing defenders have countered with allegations that the principal blame lay with our national leadership in Washington, for not having been more alert to the warnings that, through code-breaking, were available only to them. It is now clear that they held the key information in their hands but failed to recognize it or act on it. The only impediment to the complete rehabilitation of Admiral Kimmel and General Short is the unease such action might create in political circles.[1]

But because any such analysis inevitably points back to the revered president who sacrificed his life to lead our nation at that parlous time, the majority of our citizenry will not accept it, and in the process of denial denies also the probability that he, or someone acting for him, may have misinterpreted, or misunderstood, warning signals of supreme importance that only they received. Yet today we know it was vital, late in 1941, that the United States enter as soon as possible into the war against the Hitler-dominated Axis powers. With a very small margin of flexibility left in our timing, had we not got in World War II when we did there is no doubt Britain (all that was left of Western Europe still at war with Hitler, except for the governments-in-exile it hosted) would have been engulfed, and so would the Soviet Union, by then unsupportable except by the United States. We would not then have been up to the task in face of all the pressures. Hitler, with his execrable tyranny, would have become the ruler of all Eurasia. His next target would almost surely have been the Western Hemisphere, most likely in South America, where conquest would have been bloodless—until occupation began. Later in the 1940s, perhaps as early as 1945, would have come the turn of the North American continent, and except for the certainty that it would not have been pleasant, there can be little prediction of how all this might have turned out.

Franklin Roosevelt, with far better sources of information than anyone else in the United States, had to make a terrible decision, probably the greatest, and most awful, faced by any president in our history except Lincoln. Had the United States gone in the direction Lincoln's predecessor, Buchanan, was leading—toward accommodation with the proslavery forces—the Civil War might not have taken place at the time it did. What, in that case, would have been our condition now? We were fortunate to have had a president of Abraham Lincoln's caliber in 1861 and fortunate to have had Franklin D. Roosevelt in 1941. Both led us into war; one to save the Union, the other to preserve the free world of which the United States was a part.

Our country has grown up with several myths, one of them being that in our island continent we can somehow avoid the hard choices. Neither in 1861, nor eighty years afterward, would our population have chosen war, could it have known the cost in snuffed-out lives. Yet, if we had not paid that cost, can anyone predict a better condition of the world today? As all our presidents have known—FDR better than most but Lincoln, too—a direct voice in one's own government, combined with greater intercommunication among those so governed and a huge media eager to exploit all it can of the situation, creates a tremendous force that can only infrequently be manipulated. FDR dealt with it very carefully, in full appreciation that a false move would be fatal to his purpose. War, even to save the free world, was the hardest of all choices, and he knew well that the people of America, safe for the present on their side of the Atlantic, could not see the danger as he saw it.

To force Japan to initiate war in the Pacific and decisively align itself with Hitler's Axis became his strategy. FDR and his closest advisors, able to intercept and read the most secret of Japan's messages to its ambassadors in Washington, could not but have seen the approach of the critical moment. Their only miscalculation—a big one—was Pearl Harbor.

In attempting to cut through all the data now available and understand the thread that underlay the events of November and December 1941, the essential element is "Magic": the top-secret code word standing for our ability to intercept and decipher the diplomatic messages flowing in what we called the "Purple" code (another top-secret code word) between Japan and its ambassadors in Washington. Magic was at the absolute top classification level. Through Magic, President Roosevelt was secretly privy to nearly everything known to the Japanese Foreign Office. (Through overzealous concentration on this capability, the White House preempted Magic's budding effort to break JN-25, the equally important Japanese naval operational code, which our code-breakers had to abandon; but Purple opened Japan's intentions to us all the same.[2])

Without Magic, FDR could not have had the sure touch he displayed throughout the war, all the while suffering from an insidiously debilitating illness for which there was no cure. As the probability of Britain's defeat began to seem ominously sure, and Prime Minister Winston Churchill's entreaties became more desperate, it enabled FDR to play a winning hand in the biggest game history has ever seen. Japan signed the Tripartite Treaty of alliance with the Axis in September of 1940, and by the end of the year the United States was seriously tightening the economic screws on her. To any student of U.S. diplomatic policy in 1941, the pressures we began to use on Japan during that year had to end in a cave-in by one side or the other or in active hostilities—in other words, war. As Roosevelt set this course, he could not but have known this must be the result, while at the same time Magic enabled him virtually to read in advance Japan's reactions to every move he made.

Roosevelt and Churchill, the charismatic and determined leaders of their respective nations, talked frequently by secure transatlantic telephone. Most of these conversations are now public property, but of the two held on 26 November 1941, the second remains impounded under the British Official Secrets Act until the year 2025. There have been persistent rumors about this particular conversation, and in 1995 there appeared a book purporting to reproduce it verbatim, *Gestapo Chief: The 1948 Interrogation of Heinrich Müller.* Müller, who supposedly died in Berlin in 1945, is said to have lived under CIA protection until 1977. As the story goes, the Germans, no slouches themselves at code-breaking, intercepted the Roosevelt-Churchill phone calls and were able to defeat the scrambler system. Historians, remembering the embarrassment over the fictitious Hitler diaries in the 1980s, are still extremely skeptical. If the *Interrogation* is to be believed, in that still-secret telephone conversation of 26 November Churchill informed Roosevelt of the approach of the Japanese Pearl Harbor task force, which had, in fact, departed two days earlier, on 25 November, east longitude time.[3]

In Washington, 26 November was a critically important date, for that was the day FDR directed the sending of what amounted to an ultimatum to Japan to withdraw from China. This served to confirm Japan's decision to resort to war, and to begin it in her traditional way, with a surprise attack. From that moment the tension in Washington mounted rapidly, and we read every word exchanged between Japan and her ambassadors in the United States before even the principals, to whom they were addressed, received them. Information of any sort sent to our two top commanders at Pearl Harbor, Admiral Kimmel (Pacific Fleet) and Lieutenant General Short (Department of Hawaii), however, was from that same moment only pro forma. Their defenders asserted they were obviously "set up," while their accusers claim the generally worded "war warning" messages both received on the twenty-seventh should have caused them put their forces on maximum alert for the ensuing ten days.

Adm. Isoroku Yamamoto, commander in chief of the Japanese Combined Fleet, had spent the past year, beginning before Admiral Kimmel took command of our Pacific Fleet, in highly secret preparation for the surprise attack that would eliminate the principal threat to Japan's ambitions in the Far East. His plans were most carefully laid; although he had to force them through the cabinet and the emperor's top advisors by threat of his own resignation, he succeeded there, too. Nothing was left to chance. Secrecy was paramount; Yamamoto was said to have ordered removal of radio telegraph keys from all the ships in his Pearl Harbor task force, so that not even an inadvertent transmission could reveal their presence in the far north Pacific.[4]

On 5 November in Washington, Magic produced a message from the Japanese Foreign Office to the not one but two ambassadors it had accredited to the United States, telling them that "it is absolutely necessary" for an accommodation to be reached by 25 November. The ambassadors, Kichisaburo Nomura (a retired admiral) and Saburo Kurusu (a career diplomat), were enjoined to "tackle the problem. . . . with unstinted effort."[5]

On 26 November, as noted, Roosevelt directed Secretary of State Cordell Hull to call the ambassadors to the State Department and officially "hand them" the ultimatum he had drafted that morning. Hull recorded their genuinely distressed reaction as he did so, and it seems clear he believed they were honestly ignorant of Japan's top-level plans.

Four days earlier, on the twenty-second, through Magic we had read a message from Tokyo to its ambassadors here that, in response to their urgent remonstrance, the deadline date of 25 November (in Washington 24 November)—after which "things are automatically going to happen"—had been delayed to the twenty-ninth, but that this was absolutely the limit. No further delay after that date could be accepted because of reasons "beyond your ability to guess."[6] On 2 December, "Climb Mount Niitaka" (the highest mountain in Japan), the order to attack Pearl Harbor on 7 December, was received by Vice Adm. Chuichi Nagumo, commanding the Japanese task force.[7]

On 27 November, differently worded "war warning" messages, carefully avoiding any possible reference to Magic, were sent to the army and navy commanders in the Pacific. Fairly strongly worded in the original drafts, as transmitted these messages were so restrained (the army's included an injunction against alarming the civil population) that whatever sense of urgency they might once have held cannot be seen in their text. The two commanders responded routinely, Kimmel by mere acknowledgment of receipt, and the messages went into the files.[8]

On 1 December Magic produced a message reading, "The date set in my [earlier message] has come and gone, and the situation continues to be increasingly critical. However, to prevent the United States from becoming unduly suspicious, [we wish you to behave as if] negotiations are continuing."

"The above is only for your information," the message went on to say.[9] If Gen. Douglas MacArthur and his staff received a copy of this communication from the "Purple machine" the navy had sent to the Philippines in April, they would have had the same Magic decode Washington had; but there has never been any indication of this.[10] Possibly Adm. Thomas C. Hart, commander of the Philippines-based Asiatic Fleet, saw it; for his dispositions of forces cannot be faulted. The Purple machine originally designated for Pearl Harbor, however, had been diverted to Bletchley Park, Britain's famous code-breaking headquarters; by consequence, neither Kimmel nor Short, nor anyone on either of their staffs, had ever even heard the term. No one in either Hawaii or the Philippines was informed of this extraordinarily portentous communication. Contrary to the situation of Hart and MacArthur, there was no way they could have known of it on their own.[11]

On this same day, a few hours after breaking the "date has come and gone" message, Magic broke another one, this time directing Japan's embassies and consular offices, worldwide, to destroy their classified libraries and secret coding systems. No information regarding this development was sent to any of the Pacific commanders, although MacArthur and Hart, in the Philippines, should have got the raw message from their own code-breakers.[12]

During the many Pearl Harbor hearings, much was made of a so-called "winds code" message we had discovered Japan would supposedly insert into an innocuous weather broadcast if it became necessary for its overseas offices to destroy secret material in anticipation of hostilities. A tremendous preemptive effort to intercept such a message was instituted, but in spite of numerous reports that one positively was found, no record of it exists. However, after we broke the second 1 December message, officially directing destruction of secret materials, no further need existed for the "winds code." It might as well have been forgotten, and one wonders why the search for it was not called off. Instead, our listening stations and code-breakers spent hundreds of vitally important man hours fruitlessly looking for it, and so did all the Pearl Harbor investigations—all without conclusive result, except for greatly worsening an already confused situation.[13]

Two days after breaking the "code destruction message," in other words on 3 December, the navy sent Kimmel two messages paraphrasing Japan's 1 December order to destroy secret materials. Short received no such information, and Kimmel's failure to check this item with him was a serious mistake, for it might, just possibly, have triggered increased alertness to the rapidly worsening relations with Japan. One of the navy's most astute and professional code-breakers, Cdr. Laurance F. Safford, composed one of the messages sent to Kimmel, and according to his later statement, he deliberately, and in excess of his authority, twice included the word "Purple" in the text in order to alert Kimmel and his staff. Although Kimmel's intelligence officer,

Lt. Cdr. Edwin T. Layton, did question the word "Purple" and got a guarded but accurate answer from a newly arrived intelligence officer from Washington, he was not astute enough—as he frankly admitted in his posthumously published book, *"And I Was There"*—to investigate further. Had he done so, he would have realized there was secret information in Washington to which the Pearl Harbor commanders were not privy.[14]

Although General Short received no similar information on that day, the head of Army intelligence, Brig. Gen. Sherman Miles, two days later attempted to alert him by sending a message to Short's intelligence officer, Lt. Col. Kendall Fielder, directing him to "[c]ontact Commander Rochefort immediately . . . regarding broadcasts from Tokyo reference weather."[15] Joe Rochefort, a close friend of Layton, was himself under direct control of Washington-based intelligence officers, but he was also well known to the entire military intelligence community. Miles evidently hoped a full discussion between two highly cleared intelligence officers might result in some sort of special alert for Short. In this, as with Safford with his calculatedly injudicious use of the word "Purple," Miles was doomed to disappointment. Fielder, an obvious failure in common sense as well as intelligence, made no attempt to contact Rochefort. Possibly he expected to do so on Monday, 8 December.

There was, however, an unlooked-for result of the Safford and Miles efforts. Both men found their careers summarily destroyed, their credibility in their respective services ruined. Miles was put out to pasture in South America, unable even to influence the army detailing office. Safford, once the navy's most highly regarded intelligence officer, who had built up the code-breaking system essentially from scratch, discovered he was now being blamed for being temperamentally unstable, subject to obsessions, and given to peculiar work habits. Undoubtedly, he did have peculiar work habits: who could have carried on a heroic schedule of eighty- or ninety-hour work weeks indefinitely without some sort of innovations? For that matter, nearly all the intelligence officers in either service who might have been characterized as "in the know," or "active in the business," found advancement blocked, their basic judgment and capability under internal service criticism. Pearl Harbor, in short, destroyed more than only old battleships and some twenty-three hundred servicemen. It also destroyed reputations—very publicly in the case of the two top commanders, subtly for the more junior officers involved. Except for Colonel Fielder. He was promoted.

On Saturday, 6 December, came the climax of the diplomatic maneuvering. Magic produced a message alerting Japan's ambassadors that a "very long" reply to the U.S. ultimatum of 26 November was being transmitted in fourteen parts. The embassy in Washington was to put it in "nicely drafted form" and prepare to deliver it when further instructed. The embassy was warned (for the second time that week) that although Japan considered all negotiations to have been ruptured, it should take care to avoid giving that impression.[16] Through Magic, U.S. officials were actually able to read this message and contemplate its possible meaning before the Japanese officials to whom it was addressed could do so. Naturally we instantly set up a special watch for this fourteen-part reply, and by 9:15 P.M. on 6 December FDR was called from his dinner table in the White House and given the first thirteen parts, along with the pilot message stating there would be fourteen parts in all. Roosevelt's comment, after reading the lengthy document, was, in substance, "This means war!"[17] He then returned to the dinner table and is reputed there to have said that war would break out the next day.[18]

As the code-breakers eagerly grabbed for the terribly important documents they were to decode, it was noted that the documents did not come in the expected regular order, and furthermore, that when "broken," the text came out in impeccable English, not in the circumlocutious Japanese they had found in all previous messages. All the code-breakers commented on this, but compartmentalized as they were, trained to do their jobs and ask no questions, they nevertheless, as directed, sent all the messages through the translation section, where they were logged in and logged out almost simultaneously. No provision existed for noting this unusual bit of information on the transmission forms, and the high officials to whom they were routed for information were thereby deprived of this important bit of insight. The motive for sending the messages in English was obvious. Japan wanted to be absolutely sure that this important transmission would be delivered exactly as composed in Tokyo, and take no chance of inexact translation by some embassy flunkey![19]

There were rumors of an after-midnight meeting in the White House during the early morning of 7 December, but of this there is only hearsay evidence.[20] The Secretaries of War and the Navy, Henry L. Stimson and Frank Knox, and the two service chiefs, Gen. George C. Marshall and Adm. Harold R. Stark, were supposedly in attendance along with Roosevelt and his special assistant, Harry Hopkins. Given the circumstances, it would have been surprising had such a meeting not been called to await the fourteenth part of the fourteen-part message and decide what should be done in light of whatever its contents might be. Doubtless those present expected a declaration of war, or at least to be able to read some idea of Japan's intentions into whatever text came from the code-breakers.

Whatever their expectations, they were disappointed; for the fourteenth part, actually received from the code-breakers around midnight, was seen only by a tired and unbriefed watch officer who, noting nothing special in the wording, did not bring it to any official's notice until 7:00 A.M. of that morning, long after the White House meeting, if it did take place, must have broken up.[21]

General Miles's second in command in army intelligence, Col. Rufus Bratton, arriving for work at 7:30 A.M., also interpreted the fourteenth part as essentially innocuous—not the declaration of war many expected. But at about 8:00 or 8:30, when he saw the "delivery message" specifying delivery to the secretary of state in person at precisely 1:00 P.M. that same afternoon, he was suddenly triggered into strenuous action. He and most high-ranking military persons were well acquainted with Japan's propensity for beginning wars with surprise attacks. She had done this against China in 1894, Russia in 1904, China in 1931, and China once again, at the Marco Polo Bridge, in 1937. Bratton went urgently looking for General Marshall, who alone held authority for transmitting important messages to such outlying posts as Pearl Harbor, the Philippines, and the Canal Zone. But General Marshall was nowhere to be found. He was neither in his office nor in his quarters at Fort Myer, Virginia. It was guessed he might be out horseback riding, as was his habit on leisurely Sundays, but he had left no information on where he might go. Finally he was located about two hours later, and, refusing Bratton's offer to seek him in his quarters, announced he would arrive at his office around 11:00 that morning, which he did.[22]

Though historians disagree over the details, the story from the navy side was equally inept. About 8:30 A.M., Lt. Cdr. Alwin P. Kramer, the chief of Safford's translating section, reached the Navy Department with the fourteenth part, which he delivered to Cdr. Arthur H. McCollum, the head of the Far Eastern Division of the Office of Naval Intelligence (ONI). Capt. Theodore S. Wilkinson, the director of ONI, was also present, and the three men took the message to Admiral Stark, the chief of naval operations (CNO). Although McCollum believed the wording presaged war, the CNO did not consider it necessary to send another warning.

About two hours later, Lieutenant Commander Kramer, who had been on duty all night, except for the time between midnight and 5:00 A.M. when he was home in exhausted sleep, arrived with his second delivery of that morning, the "delivery message." Both pilot and delivery messages were short and had required translation from the original Japanese. The fourteen parts of the main message, each very much longer, were in perfect English. Kramer, like Bratton of the army, might have picked up on that point had he had time to think about it. This he did not have, for urgency was the order of that day, of all days. Like Bratton, however, he saw something dangerous in the strange timing specified: 1:00 P.M. on a Sunday afternoon. Quickly he made a time chart of the Pacific, noticing that 1:00 P.M. in Washington would be 7:30 A.M. in Hawaii, and that the battleships would be finishing Sunday morning breakfast. Their normal Sunday schedule would call for morning colors at 8:00, followed by quarters for muster, and, depending on each ship's particular routine, regular church services at about 9:00.[23]

The delivery message was clearly important, relating directly as it did to the fourteen-part message that all hands in the code-breaking hierarchy had been working on for the past twenty-four hours. Kramer decided it should be seen immediately by someone in authority, and returned to the Navy Department. In the doorway of the CNO's office he met Commander McCollum and pointed out the significance of the time difference to him. McCollum and Wilkinson presented the message to Stark. Wilkinson urged the CNO to use his secure telephone to alert Admiral Kimmel at his quarters in Pearl Harbor. This would have wakened Kimmel about 5:00 A.M. Hawaiian time and given him two-and-a-half precious hours to consider what action he should take with this intelligence. Testimony differs on the exact sequence of the next minutes. Apparently Stark picked up the telephone, hesitated for a moment, then dialed the White House and asked to speak with Roosevelt. The White House operator was unable to put through the call. Then Stark tried General Marshall's office, but he was not there. All sources agree that the senior officer in the navy, holding in his hands information that Japan was almost certainly going to attack U.S. forces somewhere at 1:00 P.M. Washington time, sat in his office from 10:30 A.M. until noon when he was at last able to speak with Marshall, and during that entire critical last-minute period did not a single thing about it![24]

Critics have savaged Kimmel for not having been able to take more decisive action between the USS *Ward*'s report of having sunk a submarine in the Pearl Harbor entrance channel and the beginning of the air attack, just an hour later. By contrast, not a word of criticism surfaced over Stark's far more egregious failure.

When Marshall finally answered Stark's call, having already spent half to

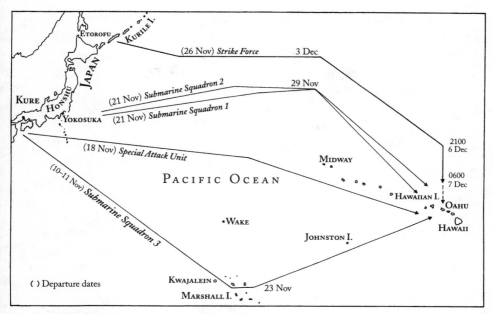

The Japanese advance on Pearl Harbor.

three-quarters of an hour driving the army's number two intelligence officer crazy as he deliberately read the entire sixteen-page group of Japanese messages, then finally composed a tepid warning to be sent routinely to General Short. Stark's only input was the equally weak request that the navy also be informed. And so went this last-ditch message, logged out of army headquarters thirty-eight minutes before the attack actually began, but because of low precedence not delivered until long after the whole business was over.[25]

This was the only notice sent to Pearl Harbor bearing directly on the climactic event of that year—indeed of the century—and it arrived routinely, via a Western Union motorcycle messenger, several hours after both waves of Japanese attack planes had completed their job and returned to their carriers. Navy Secretary Knox, arriving at Pearl Harbor two days afterward, on being met by Admiral Kimmel asked, "Did you get . . . the dispatch the Navy Department sent out" Saturday night? When Admiral Kimmel replied that he had not received any such message, Knox exclaimed, "Well, we sent you one."[26] The early morning White House meeting—if it took place—might have generated such a message, but even the reported meeting cannot be confirmed. The only known message Knox could have been referring to was the one sent by General Marshall shortly after noon Sunday, logged out at 12:17 to be exact, but there has never been any explanation how he could have known of it, nor why he referred to it as the message "*we* sent" when he had had nothing to do with it.

Admiral Nagumo had brought his Kido Butai attack force in total blackout, without detection, from its final staging port in the Kurile Islands, Hitokappu Bay, across the North Pacific to a point two hundred miles due north of Pearl Harbor—our biggest Pacific naval base—exactly on schedule in twelve days. Preceding him were three squadrons of long-range submarines, twenty-seven boats altogether, that had departed the home islands between 10 and 21 November and were now several days on station. Five of these, the so-called Special Attack Force, carried piggyback secretly built two-man submarines: battery-powered, cigar-shaped, about sixty feet long, armed with two 18-inch diameter torpedoes. All five of these were launched well before the time of the planned attack with the mission to penetrate into the harbor, and three of them succeeded. One, its compass awry, could not find the harbor entrance, finally beached itself outside, and its skipper became our much-publicized Prisoner-of-War Number One (Sakamaki by name, he survived the war and lived many years in South America, where he became a wealthy business-man). One, apparently heading for the entrance, was detected at 3:42 A.M. by the minesweeper *Condor* and was unsuccessfully searched for by USS *Ward,* a World War I "four-piper" destroyer. At 6:30, a PBY patrol plane detected another tiny submarine headed for the entrance, dropped smoke flares and depth charges on it, and alerted the *Ward,* which sent it to the bottom with a 4-inch shell through the clearly visible conning tower at very close range.[27]

This sinking occurred at 6:45 A.M., and both patrol plane and destroyer promptly reported it by radio. Critics of the Pearl Harbor command, neither aware of nor caring about realities, believe the news should have had any fleet, except one commanded by an incompetent, at battle stations within minutes. They should ask themselves how long it would take them to encode a secret operational message, and how long they would expect it to take to get through the operational chain of command above them.

The situation of Army 2d Lt. Kermit Tyler might also be considered. Two days after reporting for duty he drew his very first assignment, supervising new radar trainees before daybreak on a Sunday morning in December on an Oahu mountain top, the sort of assignment to which shavetails are subject. One of his men, who had become interested in the radar device and had not yet turned it off in anticipation of arrival of the breakfast "chow wagon," saw something unusual on his cathode-ray screen. It was to the north and looked like a large flight of airplanes, he reported. "Well," said Tyler, recalling that some B-17s were flying in from the West Coast, "don't worry about it."[28] To its credit, possibly realizing that putting Tyler in the spotlight might become embarrassing, the army did not court-martial the inexperienced young officer for this monumental misjudgment.

Had Tyler immediately made the right report and had everyone in the chain been ready instantly to do exactly the right thing, the ships on Battleship Row might have had half an hour to get ready for war. Had the reports that actually were made by the PBY and the *Ward* likewise, instantly and ungarbled, gotten all the way through the chain of command watch officers, the fleet might have had nearly an hour. But such ideas are not logical to anyone who has experienced military service, where the first thing you learn is that if things can go wrong, they will. It took time to encode and decode the two reports and sort out the claims of the patrol plane and the destroyer, each reporting having sunk a submarine in the prohibited zone (the Pacific Fleet command duty officer correctly evaluated it was the same sub, but he could not be sure it had truly been sunk). Telephones in the base began jangling madly, the several duty officers in the various base commands had to wait precious minutes to make their obligatory reports to each other, and Kimmel's own command duty officer had to preempt a busy line finally to notify him, which he did as the admiral was dressing for a golf date with General Short. Directing Short's office be informed that something had come up and he would call him later, Kimmel put on his uniform instead of his golf outfit and had just walked out of the house to the front yard of his quarters at Makalapa, when noise of the Japanese attack, and clouds of smoke beginning to rise from Battleship Row, told him the disaster of his life had begun.[29]

For the highly trained fliers in the Japanese task force and all the crewmen in all the ships, none of the foregoing considerations figured. They had been preparing for the mission of their lives for a year, and their enthusiasm was at its highest possible pitch. Now they had driven their ships for twelve days through the cold and sometimes stormy northern Pacific Ocean, and the moment they'd been waiting for, the culmination of all the effort and privation, was to hand. Who knew what their fliers might find at Pearl Harbor! Had there been a security leak, even a small one, the American fleet might be at sea readying a deadly ambush! True, it had fewer carriers, but if they were at sea in attack position, they might be able to catch the Japanese carriers denuded of combat aircraft, all of them far away in a fruitless search for a fleet that was expecting them and had made its own plans!

It was a sobering thought that had occupied many of them since departure from Hitokappu Bay on 25 November, particularly the staff officers surrounding Admiral Nagumo who knew the details of the expedition. But everyone in the task force, all hands aboard every ship, knew something very special was to happen, an extraordinary event fit to take its place with the most glorious of Imperial Japan's two thousand years of history. Crew members who could be spared from below decks came topside in large numbers to cheer their intrepid compatriots as they manned their planes, took off around first light, formed up, and headed south. They had about a two-hour flight ahead of them, and they planned to arrive over their target at 8:00 A.M.[30] It would be Sunday in Hawaii, morning colors would take place just as the first bombs fell, church services, regularly held aboard the battleships, would be thoroughly disrupted, and the time in Washington would be 1:30 P.M., exactly half an hour after Ambassadors Kurusu and Nomura were to deliver their portentous fourteen-part message to Secretary of State Hull.

Probably Admiral Nagumo had been briefed that some sort of a breaking of diplomatic relations with the United States would take place at 1:00 P.M. in Washington, and that it was important no bombs be dropped before then. The time for the attack to begin had been very carefully set for half an hour after official notification to Hull. Were Hull prescient beyond belief, he might conceivably instantly realize something drastic was about to happen, would so inform the president and the service chiefs, they would react just as fast, and the sailors and airmen in Hawaii would have perhaps fifteen minutes to get ready for war. By any stretch this would be a ridiculous hypothesis, but technically Japan would have terminated diplomatic negotiations *before* breaking the peace. Of recent years, Robert J. C. Butow, Professor Emeritus of the University of Washington in Seattle and one of our country's foremost Japanese scholars, has discovered, buried in our own Library of Congress, microfilms of two papers of surpassing interest to this subject. The first, couched in similar language—therefore obviously written by the same man, or men, who composed the famous "fourteen-part" message—was only half as long, and in the end became far more specific, stating that "Japan has girt on the sword." The second, less than a page long, worded as though written by Nomura himself despite the well-known fact that his command of English was not up to it, addressed to "Your Excellency," presumably Hull, has only three paragraphs, the first of which ends, "there now exists a state of war between the two countries."[31]

Neither of these two stronger documents was used. Both are merely interesting footnotes that illustrate some of the machinations that must have been

TABLE 11.1   The Attack on Pearl Harbor, 7 December 1941

	CV	BB	CA	CL	DD	PG	CM	MS	SS	Aux.
U.S. NAVY										
Pacific Fleet[a]										
Adm. H. E. Kimmel	—	8	2	6	29	1	9	10	5	24
Sunk	—	5[b]	—	—	2[b]	—	1[b]	—	—	1
Damaged	—	3	—	3	1	—	—	—	—	3
TOTAL HIT	—	8	—	3	3	—	1	—	—	4
IMPERIAL JAPANESE NAVY										
Advanced Expeditionary Force										
Vice Adm. M. Shimizu									27[c]	
Pearl Harbor Striking Force [d]										
Vice Adm. C. Nagumo										
First Air Fleet										
Vice Adm. C. Nagumo	6	—	—	1	9				—	
Support Force										
Vice Adm. G. Mikawa	—	2	2	—	—				—	
Sea Lane Reconnaissance Unit										
Capt. K. Imaizumi	—	—	—	—	—				3	
Midway Neutralization Unit										
Capt. K. Konishi	—	—	—	—	2				—	

Notes: CV = carrier; BB = battleship, CA = heavy cruiser; CL = light cruiser, DD = destroyer; PG = gunboat; CM = minelayer, MS = minesweeper; SS = submarine, Aux. = auxiliary

[a] Ships actually in harbor

[b] Three of the sunken battleships, both destroyers, and the minelayer were salvaged and rejoined the fleet; damaged ships were, of course, repaired

[c] Including a Special Attack Force of five conventional submarines carrying the same number of midget submarines

[d] Excluding a fleet train of eight oilers and cargo ships

taking place in Japan's highest circles. Had either been used in place of the longer fourteen-part message, Japan might have been able to claim it had fulfilled the laws of civilized nations regarding war, instead of failing in this obligation by more than an hour.

As it was, a small inadvertence on the part of the attacking planes caused the attack actually to begin at 7:55 A.M. in Hawaii, instead of on the dot of 8:00; so it was 1:25 P.M. in Washington instead of 1:30, but the message was in fact not delivered to Hull until an hour and fifteen minutes after the attack started its grisly business. But any contention over the specifics of time, in a context such as this, is specious balderdash. Even had the one-page "declaration of war" been delivered exactly on time, by then the planes had been on their attack run for a couple of hours, the Kido Butai had been at sea en route to its target for nearly two weeks, and three of the midget submarines were already inside Pearl Harbor. To argue legality over the technical juxtaposition of a few moments of time is ridiculous.

The Japanese embassy had had difficulties decoding and then making smooth copies of the fourteen-part message, as a consequence of which it had to ask for an extension of the delivery time. The paper was actually given to Hull an hour and forty minutes late. Hull had not only read it carefully hours before, courtesy of Magic, he had already received notification that the attack was actually taking place![32]

There were two flights in all. The first, encompassing all the planes that could be spotted on the deck for takeoff, amounted to 183 aircraft: a mixed bag of torpedo planes, horizontal bombers, dive bombers, and fighter planes sent along for defense. The second flight, brought up from below immediately, was able to take off an hour after the first. It consisted of 168 planes, similarly mixed, and they were on their way as soon as the deck could be arranged for their launch.[33] Altogether, it was believed, about half of them would probably not return—a heavy price, but one Japan's navy had been trained for. When they did return, with reports of a complete surprise on the American forces and only minimal losses to their own, Japanese joy, and pride, knew no bounds. They had proved themselves worthy of their greatest heritage. Admiral Togo, their navy's idol, would now be joined by another, just as great: Yamamoto! And they were part of that historic action.

The Pacific Fleet's three carriers escaped destruction for the simple reason that none of them happened to be in port, but the attackers had dealt a devastating blow to the American battle line. Off Ford Island, the *Arizona* was destroyed by a bomb that detonated her forward magazine and killed 1,103 of her men. The *Oklahoma*, next hardest hit, capsized with the loss of 415 lives. Thanks to counter-flooding, the *West Virginia* settled to the bottom on an even keel, leaving her superstructure above water. The *California* did the same. The *Maryland* and the *Tennessee*, though damaged, remained afloat. The *Nevada*, the only battleship to sortie, received heavy damage and was ordered to run aground for fear she would sink in the channel. The drydocked fleet flagship *Pennsylvania*, a sister ship to the *Arizona*, got off lightly. Of the sixty-two other warships and twenty-four auxiliaries present, seven warships and four auxiliaries were damaged or sunk. Close to three-quarters of the roughly five hundred U.S. Navy, Marine Corps, and Army Air Corps planes on Oahu were damaged or destroyed.[34]

Cdr. Mitsuo Fuchida, in overall command of the attacking fliers, vainly urged Admiral Nagumo to mount yet a third wave of attackers to destroy the fuel oil tanks so visible on the hills within the base boundaries. Were they to be destroyed, the American fleet would be bound to its own waters for many months, if not years. But Nagumo had accomplished his mission. Trying to take too much, he felt, might jeopardize his task force, which it was his duty to preserve now that the main objective had been accomplished, the U.S. Pacific Fleet crippled.[35]

Although Kermit Tyler's report, when he made it, was correctly evaluated as putting the attack force directly to the north of Oahu, such was the plethora of conflicting material that this bit of quickly obsolete information was not received by our authorities in time to be of use. Most of the U.S. commanders thought the attack force must have come from the Marshall Islands area because that was the nearest Japanese-held base, and the immediate search for the enemy was therefore in the wrong direction. The Japanese, in short, got away scot-free, having lost only twenty-nine aircraft and five two-man submarines.[36]

The midget subs, being powered by a large battery without provision for recharge except from the mother submarine, had been directed to return when their charge was low. The dedicated and enthusiastic crews of these craft had determined, however, to greatly extend their range and endurance by converting their assignment into a suicide mission. None of them expected to return, but sadly, from their point of view, they apparently (with a single possible exception, not yet proved) inflicted no damage. One ran aground outside the Pearl Harbor entrance channel. One, as described, was sunk by the destroyer *Ward* an hour before the attack began. Three, apparently, got into the harbor. Of late years William G. (Burl) Burlingame, who has made a life hobby of researching these little boats, has begun to put together possible evidence that, contrary to earlier belief, one of them, at least, may have been able to put one of its two torpedoes into the *West Virginia* and the other into the *Oklahoma*. If so, it was an outstanding success that ought to be recognized, even if accomplished by an enemy submarine.[37]

Burlingame's case rests mainly on a photograph taken by a Japanese plane during the attack that shows a V of torpedo wakes emanating from a dark object that computer enhancement seemingly reveals to be a midget submarine. These two torpedoes were not the only ones these unlucky ships received, but from the picture, and since the submarine must have been lying "doggo" for some time waiting for the moment to strike, they may have been among the first. The *West Virginia*'s port side, when seen in drydock, was an absolute shambles, showing some twenty torpedo hits by my own personal

The attack on Pearl Harbor, 7 December 1941. This photograph, taken from a Japanese aircraft over Ford Island, shows from lower left to upper right (and from astern) the battleships *Nevada, Arizona, West Virginia* (outboard), *Tennessee* (inboard), *Oklahoma* (outboard), and *Maryland* (inboard), the oiler *Neosho,* and the battleship *California.* The "V" of wakes that appears to emanate from a small object in the water to the right of the splashes at left center have caused a recent researcher to conclude that at least one Japanese midget submarine fulfilled its mission. *U.S. Naval Institute*

count, so many that some could not be distinguished one from another, and there was no way that a hit by a smaller torpedo could be told off from among the many 21-inch warheads that also exploded against her side. Some of them were in fact high above the waterline, where no torpedo had a right to be (but before the attack was over the "Wee Vee" was nearly fully submerged, only her upper decks being out of water).

The reader will note that there has been very little of the usual description of brave deeds and death-defying action in the foregoing account. The entire "Battle of Pearl Harbor" took place, actually, within minutes—more specifically in two waves, each attack lasting less than an hour, the two attacks separated by approximately an hour. There is very little to tell about the "battle" as such, except to emphasize the distinction that it was not a battle but a surprise attack. Nor was it lost by an "unready" fleet. True, that fleet was unprepared in the material sense because it did not have any of the anti-aircraft ordnance all navies of 1941 knew they must have and for which the fleet commanders had been begging. Our ships in Pearl Harbor were shooting back within minutes, but they did not have much to shoot back with. The *West Virginia,* for example, one of the best ships in the fleet, winner of the "Iron Man" athletic trophy more than any other, had been built to give a good account of herself at the 1916 Battle of Jutland. She had virtually no anti-aircraft battery; though scheduled for improvement, she could not have defended herself much better than she did even if everything intended for her had been installed. Having had two years to study the needs of warships in the air age, Congress had completely failed in its duty to "provide for the common defense." The battleships—and all the other ships in Pearl Harbor as well— simply were not armed for the problems they were to face. They were indeed unready, but not in the sense of being untrained or unprepared to use the tools they had. They could and did use them, but what they had was far from enough for the problems they faced in the air age.

The fact was that our country had not given them the tools they needed, nor the information they had a right to have; and for this these magnificent, if aged, ships, and 2,335 American servicemen, paid with their lives.

NOTES

1. For recent developments in the effort to rehabilitate these officers, see Michael Gannon, "Reopen the Kimmel Case," *U.S Naval Institute Proceedings* 120 (December 1994): 51–56; Capt. Edward L. Beach, USN (Ret.), *Scapegoats: A Defense of Kimmel and Short at Pearl Harbor* (Annapolis, 1995), 176–85; Fred L. Schultz, "Resurrecting the Kimmel Case," *Naval History* 9 (July–August 1995)· 43–46; and Capt. Edward L. Beach, USN (Ret.), "More than Half a Loaf," *Naval History* 10 (May–June 1996): 16

2. Frederick D. Parker, *Pearl Harbor Revisited: United States Navy Communications Intelligence, 1924–1941.* U.S. Cryptologic History, ser. 4, World War II, vol. 6 (Fort George C. Meade, Md., 1994).

3. Gregory Douglas, ed., *Gestapo Chief: The 1948 Interrogation of Heinrich Müller* (San Jose, 1995), 45–50.

4. For Yamamoto's role, see Hiroyuki Agawa, John Bester, trans., *The Reluctant Admiral* (New York, 1979).

5. The full text appears in Henry C. Clausen and Bruce Lee, *Pearl Harbor: Final Judgement* (New York, 1992), 318.

6. The full text appears in ibid., 324.

7 Gordon W. Prange, with Donald M. Goldstein and Katherine V. Dillon, *At Dawn We Slept: The Untold Story of Pearl Harbor* (New York, 1981), 445.

8. Rear Adm. Husband E. Kimmel, USN (Ret.), *Admiral Kimmel's Story* (Chicago, 1955), 43–48; Rear Adm Edwin T. Layton, USN (Ret.), with Capt. Roger Pineau, USNR (Ret.), and John Costello, *"And I Was There": Pearl Harbor and Midway—Breaking the Secrets* (New York, 1985), 215–18.

9. The full text appears in Clausen and Lee, *Pearl Harbor,* 337.

10. Prange, *At Dawn We Slept*, 81–82, John Costello, *Days of Infamy: MacArthur, Roosevelt, Churchill—The Shocking Truth Revealed* (New York, 1994), 260–61

11. Prange, *At Dawn We Slept*, 82

12. Layton, *"And I Was There,"* 238–39

13. For a detailed account, see Gordon W. Prange, with Donald M. Goldstein and Katherine V Dillon, *Pearl Harbor: The Verdict of History* (New York, 1986), 312–30

14. Layton, *"And I Was There,"* 250–52. The full texts of the messages appear in Roberta Wohlstetter, *Pearl Harbor: Warning and Decision* (Stanford, 1962), 49–50

15. Prange, *At Dawn We Slept*, 459.

16 Clausen and Lee, *Pearl Harbor*, 341.

17 *Hearings before the Joint Committee on the Investigation of the Pearl Harbor Attack*, 79th Congress, 39 vols (Washington, D C , 1946), part 10, 4661ff.

18 John Toland, *Infamy!* (2d ed , New York, 1992), 332 (Postscript)

19. Prange, *At Dawn We Slept*, 474

20. Costello, *Days of Infamy*, 209–10, cf the letter from James R. Stahlman to Rear Adm. Kemp Tolley, USN (Ret), 26 November 1973, quoted in Beach, *Scapegoats*, 202–3

21 Prange, *At Dawn We Slept*, 485

22. Ibid., 486, 493

23. Ibid., 488–89.

24 Ibid., 485, 488–89; Layton, *"And I Was There,"* 300–301, 303–4; Wohlstetter, *Pearl Harbor*, 334–35; Beach, *Scapegoats*, 95–96

25 Prange, *At Dawn We Slept*, 494–95

26 Ibid , 586–87

27 For a detailed account of the midget subs' operations, see Burl Burlingame, *Advanced Force Pearl Harbor: The Imperial Navy's Underwater Assault on America* (Kailua, Hawaii, 1992).

28. Walter Lord, *Day of Infamy* (New York, 1957), 44–49.

29. Prange, *At Dawn We Slept*, 497, 505–7

30 Ibid , 488–87, 490–92

31. Robert J. C. Butow, "Marching Off to War on the Wrong Foot· The Final Note Tokyo Did *Not* Send to Washington," *Pacific Historical Review* 63(1): 67–79.

32 Prange, *At Dawn We Slept*, 466, 554

33 Ibid., 491–92

34 For a concise account of the attack, see Samuel Eliot Morison, *History of United States Naval Operations in World War II*, vol. 3· *The Rising Sun in the Pacific* (Boston, 1975), 98–125

35. Mitsuo Fuchida, "The Air Attack on Pearl Harbor," in David C Evans, ed and trans., *The Japanese Navy in World War II: In the Words of Former Japanese Naval Officers* (2d ed , Annapolis, 1986), 69–70.

36. Morison, *The Rising Sun*, 213–14

37. Burlingame, *Advance Force Pearl Harbor*, 198–99

12

The Battle of the Coral Sea

E. B. POTTER

Following the Japanese air raid on Pearl Harbor, President Roosevelt appointed Adm. Chester W. Nimitz to relieve Adm. Husband E. Kimmel as commander in chief of the Pacific Fleet (CinCPac). Nimitz, offered the use of an airplane to convey him to Pearl Harbor, begged off. For his new duty he had been plucked from his post as Chief of the Bureau of Navigation, in which capacity he had been overwhelmed by emergency duties stemming from the raid. He and his assistants had been obliged to make provision for thousands of officers and men left stranded and stripped of everything by the sinking of their ships. They had to notify the next-of-kin of the dead, ensure that bodies were brought home, and, in many cases arrange for funerals. The sustained effort had left Nimitz exhausted. He chose to go to the West Coast by rail in order to regain his strength and read the reports of damages inflicted on the base. Pending Nimitz's arrival at Pearl, the president appointed as interim CinCPac Vice Adm. William S. Pye, commander of the shattered Battle Fleet, which had been the Japanese raiders' chief target.[1]

For the Japanese, the Pearl Harbor raid had been mainly a diversion—to dislodge a threat to their drive to the East Indies and its oil wells. When they landed troops in Malaya for an advance on Singapore, the British intervened by rushing in the battleship *Prince of Wales* and the battle cruiser *Repulse,* only to have both ships sunk by enemy planes out of Indochina.

The Japanese seemed to be everywhere. They had seized Guam, overrun Thailand, invaded the Philippines, Borneo, and Hong Kong, and shelled Midway Atoll and Johnston Island. They made a grab for Wake Island, an American outpost halfway between Hawaii and Japan, but U.S. marines on the island repulsed the invasion force, sinking two destroyers and damaging sev-

The Pacific Theater, 1941–45.

eral other ships. From this objective the Japanese force limped away, having put not a man ashore.

Admiral Kimmel, as almost his last official act before being relieved, had devised a stratagem, using his three available carrier forces to safeguard embattled Wake. With a little luck he might also win a victory at sea. The *Saratoga* force (headed by Rear Adm. Frank Jack Fletcher) would carry in supplies, ammunition, and a squadron of fighter planes to supplement those already on the island and bring away the wounded and as many civilians as possible. The *Lexington* force (Vice Adm. Wilson Brown) would raid the Marshall Islands, source of bombers attacking Wake. The *Enterprise* force (Vice Adm. William F. Halsey) would take position to support either of the other two as needed. Hopefully, the Japanese would employ no forces the U.S. carriers could not handle.[2]

Nimitz, on his westbound railroad train, read in the newspaper that Adm. Ernest J. King had been confirmed as the navy's commander in chief (CominCh). That would make him Nimitz's immediate superior. King had the reputation of a brilliant, aloof, and very hard taskmaster. Nimitz suspected that he would soon have battles to fight against Washington as well as against the Japanese.

On 23 December, Nimitz reached San Diego, but his flight from there was delayed by a southeast gale. Next morning's newspapers reported that Japanese troops were ashore on Wake but the island's garrison was still holding out. Nimitz wondered why the relief expedition had not reached the scene by then. No further word had reached him when his Catalina was airborne at 1600 that afternoon. He told the crew he was sorry to take them away from home on Christmas Eve.

The flight took all night. At dawn, Christmas 1941, Nimitz arrived over Pearl Harbor. When the admiral's plane had set down in the water, he smelled the stench of floating fuel oil, scorched paint, and decomposing corpses. A whaleboat came alongside carrying the welcoming committee—the commander of the navy patrol air wing in Hawaii and the chiefs of staff of Admirals Kimmel and Pye.

The trip ashore was grim. In the early morning light, Nimitz could make out across the oil-covered water vaguely familiar contours among the wreckage along Battleship Row. With a pang he recognized what had been the *Arizona,* his old flagship. She was sunk now, only a crumpled mast and a fragment of her fire-blacked bow left protruding from the water. It was a chilling scene, and Nimitz knew that he had thus far seen only a fraction of the damage inflicted on American ships, planes, and structures.

"This is a terrible sight," said Nimitz, "seeing all these ships down." Then he put the question that had been weighing on his mind: "What news of the relief of Wake?" Informed that the expedition had been withdrawn and the island had fallen, he made no comment.

At the submarine-base wharf Admiral Pye was waiting to conduct the new CinCPac to his quarters. At Nimitz's insistence, Pye remained with him through breakfast. The conversation got around to the loss of Wake. The Japanese, for their second grab at the island, had been considerably strengthened. This time they were supported also by two carriers, detached from what the Japanese called Kido Butai, their six-carrier striking force, then returning to Japan from its raid on Pearl Harbor.

At that time, Pye told Nimitz, he and his staff had soberly discussed the situation at Wake and concluded that the Americans had no more than a 50 percent prospect of victory. Had he been permanent CinCPac, Pye explained, he might have taken the chance, but he could not bring himself to risk presenting the incoming commander in chief another defeat. With a heavy heart, he had recalled the relief expedition.

Nimitz decided to have a look around and size up his task before taking command. He soon drew the disappointing conclusion that he would never be able accompany the fleet to sea. The navy's complex communications network would require his presence ashore at Pearl Harbor.

As Nimitz moved about Pearl Harbor, he found that its morale was sinking. The fleet had responded to the Japanese attack with a spirit of defiance. In the intervening weeks that spirit had been depressed by inaction, by relentlessly bad news, and, most of all, by the failure to support Wake—attributable, most believed, to fumbling and ineptitude of the outgoing high command. Soon, Nimitz became sharply aware that he could delay no longer to assume his new responsibilities. The Americans at Pearl Harbor and those back at home in the States were looking to him for prompt offensive operations. At 1000 on the last day of 1941, Nimitz formally took command of the Pacific Fleet. The simple ceremony was performed on the deck of the submarine *Grayling* because no other suitable undamaged man-of-war happened to be at Pearl Harbor.[3]

Admiral King had lost no time reminding Nimitz that as CinCPac his primary responsibilities were to defend the Hawaiian Islands and to safeguard the flow of shipping between those islands and the United States and the United States and Australia. That much was implied by geography and the historic function of sea power, but it was also generally understood that Nimitz at the earliest opportunity was to take offensive action to halt, or at least retard, Japan's expansion in the Pacific.

Proposed as opening offensive moves by U.S. forces were carrier raids on the Japanese-occupied Gilbert, Marshall, and Wake Islands. The raid on Wake, Nimitz reluctantly had to cancel. Enemy submarines had fired torpedoes into the carrier *Saratoga*, which was to have executed that task, and into the *Neches*, one of Nimitz's scarce oilers. The *Neches* sank; the *Saratoga* had to retreat to a West Coast shipyard for extensive repairs.

At dawn 1 February 1942 the *Enterprise* force, commanded by Vice Adm. Halsey, the Pacific Fleet's senior carrier officer, and the carrier *Yorktown* force, commanded by Rear Admiral Fletcher, began their brief raids on the Gilberts and Marshalls. These islands turned out to be less heavily fortified than the Americans had assumed. Halsey suffered lighter losses than he feared and inflicted less destruction than he counted on, but his aviators grossly overestimated the extent of their victory. They thereby provided a terrific lift to American morale and made a national hero of Halsey. Fletcher's force, hampered by bad weather and lack of military targets in his assigned area, had nothing to report except the loss of seven planes.

Meanwhile, Japanese bombers had been hammering away at the advanced Australian outpost of Rabaul in the Bismarcks. On 23 January, a Japanese amphibious force, supported by the aircraft carriers of Kido Butai, landed at Rabaul troops who quickly overcame the slender Australian garrison. Rabaul in Japanese hands would serve as a defensive barrier between Australia and Japan's major island base of Truk in the Carolines.

When word reached the Japanese fleet that U.S. forces were raiding in the Gilberts and Marshalls, Vice Adm. Chuichi Nagumo, at Truk with Kido Butai, sped east with his carrier force to counterattack. But on learning that the Americans had withdrawn, Nagumo assessed the raid as a simple hit-and-run affair not worth his attention. He turned disdainfully away and headed Kido Butai toward the Indian Ocean to carry out his next assignment—putting the British Eastern Fleet out of action.[4]

Meanwhile, Vice Adm. Wilson Brown, intent on raiding Rabaul, was in the big carrier *Lexington* approaching the newly captured Japanese stronghold. Discovered and attacked by Rabaul-based aircraft, Brown concluded that the proposed raid was too risky. He returned to Pearl Harbor, where King relieved him of his command, and Nimitz appointed Rear Adm. Aubrey Fitch to replace him at the head of the *Lexington* force.

Admiral King, alarmed by a Japanese stepped-up offensive in the southwest, fired off dispatches to Nimitz demanding more action, using all available forces, including the half-dozen battleships on the West Coast. Somehow it had not yet dawned on King that all the existing battleships in the U.S. Navy were obsolescent. None had been added to the fleet since 1923 and none even in their heyday could make better than 21 knots. They were too vulnerable to go to sea without air cover and too slow to move with the 34-knot carriers.

To King Nimitz replied: "Pacific Fleet markedly inferior in all types to enemy. Cannot conduct aggressive action Pacific except raids of hit-and-run character which are unlikely to relieve pressure Southwest Pacific."

To which King fired back: "Pacific Fleet not, repeat *not*, markedly inferior to forces enemy can bring to bear within operating radius of Hawaii while he is committed to extensive operations in Southwest Pacific. . . . Review situation in above premises and consider operations against mandates and Wake."

In response to this challenge, Nimitz sent Halsey westward with the *Enterprise* force to raid first Wake and then Marcus, the latter a Japanese island base just a thousand miles from Tokyo. Halsey's aviators dropped their bombs, but all hands recognized that there was nothing important to destroy on either island. One officer dismissed the raids with the remark, "The Japanese didn't mind them any more than a dog minds a flea."[5]

Certainly the American operations had no discernible effect on the enemy campaigns in the southwest. The Japanese concluded their conquest of Hong Kong, Burma, and Malaya, including Singapore. A Japanese surface fleet moving down the east coast of Borneo met and shattered an Allied fleet in the Java Sea and then supported troops in an invasion of Java, the conquest of which would complete the subjugation of the East Indies.

Kido Butai, on entering the Indian Ocean, raided the Australian port of Darwin, provided air support for the final Japanese conquest of Java, and then steamed twenty-five hundred miles to Ceylon (Sri Lanka), where it raided the British naval bases at Colombo and Trincomalee and sank two destroyers, two cruisers, and a carrier. The British, thus scourged, withdrew to Africa what was left of their Eastern Fleet.

In five months of operations, extending a third of the way around the world, not one of Kido Butai's ships had been sunk or even damaged. It had, however, lost many trained aviators, and for that Japan would pay a price.[6]

In contrast to the American depression, the Japanese were exultant. They had captured the East Indies oil wells and the other products of what they called their "Southern Resources Area," all within ninety days, less than half the time even the most sanguine had predicted. The result was what thoughtful Japanese later called "victory disease," a general feeling of invincibility, overlooking the fact that the United States within a few months could utterly outbuild Japan in ships, planes, and guns.

Of the several proposals advanced for further Japanese conquests, invasions of India and Australia were turned down by the army as demanding too much manpower. Already thinly distributed by Japan's invasions to date, troops had to be held in reserve to meet a possible threat from the Soviet Union. The Naval General Staff therefore developed plans for a southeastward advance around the Coral Sea via the Solomons and New Hebrides. The ultimate aim was to capture the islands of New Caledonia, Fiji, and Samoa. From these the Japanese would operate ships, submarines, and aircraft to block the U.S. buildup of troops and munitions in Australia for an advance on the Philippines.

On 13 March, Imperial General Headquarters approved this program. Within days, however, Adm. Isoroku Yamamoto's Combined Fleet Staff submitted a radically different plan of its own, calling for a return to the Central Pacific with the aim of seizing Midway Atoll and thereby compelling the

Pacific Fleet to accept a battle in which the carriers that had eluded Kido Butai at Pearl Harbor could be destroyed. When the Naval General Staff resisted the change Yamamoto threatened to resign, and on 5 April a dangerous compromise was reached. The Central Pacific offensive, Operation MI, would be launched in late May; but in the meantime limited resources would be allocated to carry out the first phase of the South Pacific advance, the seizure of Port Moresby, New Guinea, and the small Solomon island of Tulagi, both held by the Australians, early that same month.[7] From Moresby, Japanese aircraft could command eastern New Guinea, northern Australia, and the Coral Sea. A base at Tulagi could operate long-range seaplanes to assist in controlling the Coral Sea but mainly for observation and warning. This undertaking was designated Operation MO. By crowding both operations into so short a period, the Japanese left themselves no margin for error.

While the Imperial Navy haggled over strategy, President Roosevelt introduced a new element that had to be taken into consideration by Japanese and American planners. Gen. Douglas MacArthur, commanding the Filipino-American army in the Philippines, obviously could not hold out much longer against the invading troops from Japan. The president, determined not to lose the services of his most senior and most experienced general, ordered MacArthur to escape. The general, his family, and members of his staff made good their getaway by PT boat and plane. On arriving in Australia, MacArthur announced to the press: "I came through and I shall return."

The Allied governments assigned to the general as his theater of operations the Southwest Pacific Area, which included Australia, New Guinea, the Philippines, and the Bismarck and Solomon Islands. He was shocked, however, to learn there was no army waiting to enforce his authority. Most of Australia's soldiers were in North Africa with the British defending Egypt and the Suez Canal. The bulk of American troops were in England or en route there preparing to invade Europe. The Australian and U.S. governments now applied themselves to enlisting, training, and transporting troops for the general, who had his eye on Port Moresby as the jumping off place for his return to the Philippines.[8]

Thus a small settlement on the southeastern coast of New Guinea became briefly the focal point of the Pacific War. By mid-April, Japanese preparations for Operation MO were well under way. Kido Butai, en route back to Japan from its foray into the Indian Ocean, detached the big carriers *Shokaku* and *Zuikaku*, together with two heavy cruisers and six destroyers. These took station at Truk. At Rabaul the Japanese began assembling troop-laden transports and supporting forces, including the light carrier *Shoho*.

CinCPac headquarters at Pearl Harbor had general knowledge of these preparations, mainly through a study of enemy ship movements and communications picked up by radio listening stations in the Pacific. Occasionally there would be a dead giveaway, such as Japanese use of the term Operation MO, a fairly obvious reference to Port Moresby. Useful information was more often the product of brain-wracking traffic analysis and code-breaking.

Now that the *Shokaku* and the *Zuikaku* were separated from Kido Butai, U.S. forces resolved to make a mighty effort to destroy them or at least fairly strip them of planes and aviators. Not for another year would enough new U.S. aircraft carriers with fully trained fliers arrive in the Pacific to take on the six-carrier Kido Butai. Meanwhile, the Americans must seize opportunities to destroy it piecemeal. Such an occasion had offered in January, when two of Kido Butai's carriers detached themselves to assist in the capture of Wake. The Americans had flunked that opportunity. Such a shortfall must not happen twice.

American means for saving Port Moresby and Tulagi were slim. MacArthur had several hundred U.S. Army Air Force and Australian planes, but their pilots were not trained to operate against ships at sea. If the Japanese invasion was to be frustrated, it would have to be by means of carrier planes.

The United States had in fact six fleet carriers, but the *Wasp* was in the Mediterranean Sea ferrying planes to Malta. The *Saratoga* was still undergoing repair at the Bremerton Navy Yard. The *Enterprise* and the new *Hornet* groups were at sea together on an extraordinarily dangerous and unprecedented mission—to drop bombs on Tokyo and other Japanese cities.

Commanding the Tokyo expedition was Halsey, his *Enterprise* providing air cover. Lashed to the *Hornet*'s flight deck were sixteen long-range army B-25s, capable of taking off but not of landing on so short a runway. On 18 April, unexpectedly encountering picket boats 620 miles east of the Japanese coast, Halsey ordered the B-25s launched at once. That done, the *Hornet* and *Enterprise* reversed course and raced back toward Pearl Harbor. The volunteer pilots dropped their bombs as planned and most of the men subsequently landed in or parachuted into China. This was King's project, which both he and Nimitz now had reason to regret. It would give a lift to American morale and a blow to Japanese morale but had little military significance.

What Nimitz had left to combat Operation MO were Fletcher's *Yorktown* force, Task Force (TF) 17, in the Coral Sea, and Fitch's *Lexington* group, at Pearl Harbor. Nimitz directed Fletcher to proceed to Tongatabu for such upkeep and replenishment as that minor base could provide and to return to the Coral Sea before the end of the month. And he ordered Fitch to take his

Frank Jack Fletcher. *U.S. Naval Institute*

Lexington group to the Coral Sea by 1 May and join it to TF 17. In Halsey's absence, Fletcher would command.

Just turned fifty-seven at the end of April, Frank Jack Fletcher was a graduate of the Naval Academy class of 1906. In 1914 he had won one of the fifty-five Medals of Honor awarded for the seizure of Veracruz, Mexico, and his performance as captain of the destroyer *Benham* in World War I brought him a Navy Cross. His interwar assignments included tours as chief of staff of the

Asiatic Fleet, aide to the secretary of the navy, and assistant chief of the Bureau of Navigation, attendance at both the army and navy war colleges, and command of several vessels, including the battleship *New Mexico*. In 1928 he applied for flight training at the age of forty-two. The timing of his request was not as unusual then as it would be now; King qualified for his wings at forty-eight, Halsey at fifty-two. Unlike them, however, Fletcher failed his flight physical.[9] The aviation community deplored the appointment of outsiders to head carrier forces, and its view of Fletcher was summed up by the CinCPac staff officer who called him "a big, nice, wonderful guy who didn't know his butt from third base"[10]; yet forces under his command won the first three carrier battles ever fought—Coral Sea, Midway, and the Eastern Solomons. A genial, outgoing man, he had been a great favorite of the midshipmen while stationed at the Naval Academy on the eve of World War I. Decades later, historian Gordon Prange found him as "sympathetic, warm, and understanding as some of the old friends of my father that I might meet on the streets of my hometown."[11]

Halsey, with TF 16, arrived at Pearl Harbor on 25 April. The *Enterprise,* the *Hornet,* and their escorts required an absolute minimum of five days for upkeep. With the invasion of Tulagi scheduled for early May in the Coral Sea some thirty-five hundred miles away, Halsey was unlikely to arrive in time to take command of the U.S. forces opposing it, but there was always a chance the battle might shape up more slowly than expected. At about 0800, 30 April, TF 16 put to sea.

The elements of Operation MO, commanded by Vice Adm. Shigeyoshi Inouye, were already on the move, carrying out a typically complex strategic plan. In the last days of April, Rear Adm. Kiyohide Shima's Tulagi Invasion Force from Rabaul and Rear Adm. Aritomo Goto's Covering Force from Truk with the light carrier *Shoho* headed for the Solomons. After providing air support for Shima's Tulagi invasion, the Covering Force would turn back and support the invasion of Port Moresby. On 1 May Vice Adm. Takeo Takagi's Striking Force, with carriers *Shokaku* and *Zuikaku,* left Truk and headed toward the Eastern Solomons. The small Australian garrison on Tulagi, warned by coast watchers of Shima's approach, hastily demolished the island's military installations and, with permission from headquarters, cleared out.[12]

Meanwhile, American ships were assembling. In the morning of 1 May, Fitch's *Lexington* force from Pearl Harbor, Fletcher's *Yorktown* force from refit at Tongatabu, and the *Chicago* and a destroyer from Norméa made rendezvous in the Coral Sea some 350 miles northwest of New Caledonia and

TABLE 12.1 The Battle of the Coral Sea, 4–8 May 1942

	CV	CVL	CA	CL	DD	AV	AO	AP
U.S. NAVY								
Task Force 17 [a]								
Rear Adm. F. J. Fletcher								
Task Group 17.2—Attack Group								
Rear Adm. T. C. Kinkaid	—	—	5	—	5	—	—	—
Task Group 17.3—Support Group								
Rear Adm. J. G. Crace, RN	—	—	2	1	2	—	—	—
Task Group 17.5—Carrier Group								
Rear Adm. A. W. Fitch	2	—	—	—	4	—	—	—
Task Group 17.6—Fueling Group								
Capt. J. S. Phillips	—	—	—	—	2	—	2	—
TOTAL	2	—	7	1	13	—	2	—
IMPERIAL JAPANESE NAVY								
Task Force "MO"								
Vice Adm. S. Inouye								
Carrier Striking Force								
Vice Adm. T. Takagi	2	—	2	—	6	—	1	—
Invasion Forces,								
Rear Adm. A. Goto								
Tulagi Invasion Force								
Rear Adm. K. Shima	—	—	—	—	2	—	—	1 [b]
Transport Force (Port Moresby)								
Rear Adm. K. Abe	—	—	—	—	—	—	2	12 [b]
Attack Force (Port Moresby)								
Rear Adm. S. Kajioka	—	—	—	1	6 [b]	—	—	—
Covering Forces								
Rear Adm. A. Goto	—	1	4	—	1	—	1	—
Support Force								
Rear Adm. K. Marumo	—	—	—	2	—	1 [c]	—	—
TOTAL	2	1	6	3	15	1	4	13

Notes: CV = fleet carrier, CVL = light carrier; CA = heavy cruiser; CL = light cruiser; DD = destroyer; AV = seaplane tender; AO = oiler, AP = transport

[a] Excluding Task Group 17.9, a search group of seaplanes based on New Caledonia

[b] Plus assorted auxiliaries

[c] Plus three gunboats

came under Fletcher's tactical command. The ships began fueling from the oilers *Neosho* and *Tippecanoe*.

The *Lexington* and the *Yorktown* were an interesting combination. The former, 37,000 tons and converted from a battle cruiser, had been commissioned in December 1927. Still on board were "plankowners," members of her original ship's company. Among these and many later crew members, the *Lexington* was accorded heartfelt devotion. They called her the "Lex" and in more sentimental moments "Lady Lex." The *Yorktown*, 19,800 tons, was commissioned ten years later. She had acquired less of the fondness accorded the *Lex,* being known, rather, by the sportive title "Waltzing Matilda," perhaps in tribute to her maneuverability, which was exceptional.

MacArthur's aviators, based on Australia, were trying to make sense out of the Japanese forces they observed. At 1900, 3 May, Southwest Pacific headquarters reported that its aircraft had seen two Japanese transports disembarking troops at Tulagi. This, said Fletcher excitedly, was the kind of report he "had been waiting two months to receive." Fitch's force presumably had not finished fueling, and that was to be regretted, but Fletcher thought his *Yorktown* force could handle the situation. He signaled Fitch a new meeting time and place and then, with Waltzing Matilda headed north through the night, stepping up his speed to 27 knots. This was the first offensive Allied move in the series of naval operations between 4 and 8 May 1942 that became known collectively as the Battle of the Coral Sea.

The situation was shaping up favorably for Fletcher. Goto with the MO Covering Force, having seen Shima safely ashore, assumed that the Japanese, once established on Tulagi, could defend themselves. Hence he turned back west to carry out his other mission, that of protecting the Port Moresby invasion.

In the absence of Goto, Shima had counted on Takagi's Carrier Striking Force for support, as needed. But Takagi, assigned an additional duty of delivering fighter planes to Rabaul, had been delayed by stormy weather in making his delivery. He was now refueling, too far away to the northwest to lend support before 5 May.

The stormy weather that had delayed Takagi had concealed Fletcher's approach. At first light, 4 May, the *Yorktown* was directly south of Guadalcanal. Beginning at 0630 Fletcher launched three attacks by Dauntless dive-bombers and Devastator torpedo planes. The attacking aircraft soared over the Guadalcanal mountains and across brightly sunlit Savo Sound to pounce on little Tulagi and nearby naval craft. The pilots returned with electrifying accounts of having sunk cruisers, destroyers, and transports. In reality, they had sunk two minesweepers and a transport, forced a destroyer to be beached, and set five float planes afire. By 1632 all the U.S. aircraft had returned to their carrier, and the "Battle of Tulagi" was over.

Some of Fletcher's sailors, impressed by their fliers' grandiose reports, thought the main battle, against major Japanese forces, had been fought, with the Americans victorious. There was talk of liberty in Sydney. Fletcher himself, of course, knew better. With the *Yorktown* and her escorts, he now headed back south and rendezvoused with the *Lexington* at 0816, 5 May.[13]

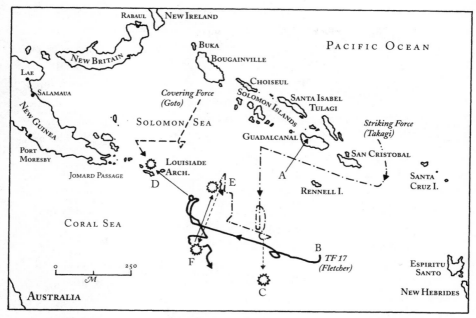

The Battle of the Coral Sea, 4–8 May 1942. U.S. forces commence action on 4 May, when the *Yorktown*'s aircraft attack Japanese vessels off Tulagi (A). The *Yorktown* rejoins the *Lexington* a day later (B). On 7 May, aircraft from the *Shokaku* and *Zuikaku* sink the destroyer *Sims* and terminally damage the oiler *Neosho* (C), while a strike by both U.S. carriers sinks the light carrier *Shoho* (D). The next day, in a virtually simultaneous exchange of attacks, the *Shokaku* is disabled (E) and the *Lexington* suffers damage (F) to which she soon succumbs. In the interest of clarity, the tracks of Japanese occupation and support forces are not shown.

By this time British Rear Adm. J. G. Crace had joined, bringing the Australian cruisers *Australia* and *Hobart* and a destroyer. Fletcher devoted much of the day to refueling. At 0700, 6 May, he integrated Fitch's and Crace's groups into his own TF 17, and the joint force assumed circular formation. The two carriers at the center with 136 aircraft, were surrounded by 7 heavy cruisers, 1 light cruiser, and 13 destroyers. TF 17 was now entering General MacArthur's Southwest Pacific Area, but by prior agreement, because the general had had no naval experience, the task force would remain under Nimitz's strategic command.

Fletcher was heading northwest to intercept the Port Moresby Invasion Force, which he correctly assumed had now left Rabaul and was steering for Jomard Passage, a major doorway into the Coral Sea. Jomard Passage consisted of a break in the Louisiade Archipelago, a chain of reef-surrounded islands extending eastward of the New Guinea bird tail. The sea route from Rabaul around east of the Louisiades would add seven hundred miles.

What Fletcher did not suspect was that Takagi's Striking Force with the two big carriers had rounded the eastern end of the Solomons chain at noon the preceding day. It had then entered the Coral Sea on a northwest course closely parallel to his own but slightly ahead and some three hundred and fifty miles to the north. Operating under an overcast sky, the Striking Force was not discovered by TF 17 search planes. Hence, Fletcher for some time was unaware he had company.

Takagi, however, knew that Fletcher was somewhere in the Coral Sea, and, with the help of land-based Japanese planes, was actively searching for him. At 0930, 6 May, his Striking Force changed from course northeast to due south, and thus he hoped was placing himself in position for an attack on TF 17.

At 1100 a search plane out of Rabaul sighted and reported Fletcher's ships, steaming northwestward in bright sunlight, now almost due south of the oncoming Japanese Striking Force. The sighting, rebroadcast by the Rabaul transmitter, was picked up by several Allied radio listening stations and passed on to Fletcher. An attack by aircraft from the *Shokaku* and *Zuikaku* was now to be expected. TF 17 launched fighters and waited tensely, but no attack arrived. Incredibly Takagi's Striking Force had failed to pick up the contact report. At 1600, still heading south, it was only seventy miles from TF 17. Then, all unaware of this grand opportunity, it reversed course to northward to refuel, while Fletcher continued on course northwest.[14]

At about this time Fletcher detached his oiler *Neosho.* Escorted by the destroyer *Sims,* she headed south, where she presumably would be safer than if attached to the combat formation. In these southern waters she would adopt a cruising pattern that would place her, when needed for refueling, at a position called Point Rye.

The Striking Force maintained its northward course until 0200, 7 May. At that time Rear Adm. Tadaichi Hara, commanding the *Shokaku* and *Zuikaku,* proposed to Admiral Takagi another reversal of course. This would permit Hara's aviators to penetrate beyond the cloud cover and make a thorough search southward.

What followed during the next twenty-four hours has been called the "Battle of the Blunders." Each participant committed errors that might have proved disastrous had not their effects been canceled by equally absurd boners perpetrated by the other.

At 0600 Hara launched his search planes, and one of these at 0736 reported sighting a carrier and a cruiser at a considerable distance due south of his position. Much gratified at the contact, Hara promptly launched his full strike force of seventy-eight planes against the supposed enemy carrier.

Hardly had these aircraft departed when Hara received from a land-based Japanese plane a sighting report correctly placing TF 17 off to the west. Hara, puzzled, decided to let his air attack proceed against the warships reported in the south before heading west to deal with Fletcher. The planes of Hara's southbound attack force found and correctly identified the carrier and cruiser as an oiler and a destroyer. They thereafter spent two hours searching the area for the reported carrier. Finding nothing of the sort, their fuel running low, they settled for the oiler and destroyer, which were, in fact, the detached *Neosho* and *Sims*. The Japanese aircraft gave these ships a thorough working over. They hit the *Sims* with three 500-pound bombs, two of which, exploding in her engine room, broke her keel, and she sank by the stern. Dive-bombers meanwhile had scored seven direct hits and eight near-misses on the *Neosho* and left her a barely-floating derelict.

TF 17, unaware of these Japanese activities, continued on its northwesterly course. A little before 0700, Fletcher, warned by reconnaissance planes that the Port Moresby Invasion Force was approaching Jomard Passage from the north, seriously weakened his own force by detaching three cruisers and two destroyers as a Support Group under Admiral Crace. He ordered Crace to continue on to the northwest so as to be in position to block the advance of the invaders.

Fletcher himself, with the rest of TF 17, including the *Yorktown* and the *Lexington,* headed north to place himself on the invader's flank. His plan was that, should TF 17 and its carriers be defeated in the forthcoming contact, Crace's Support Group would still be on hand to bar the way to Port Moresby—a fallacious assumption since any force capable of defeating two carriers could readily chew up five surface ships.

Early that afternoon a dozen single-engine land-based enemy aircraft attacked Crace's task group south and slightly west of Jomard Passage. These were followed by an equal number of twin-engine land-based navy torpedo bombers and then by nineteen high-flying bombers. The Japanese claimed to have sunk two battleships and a cruiser. In fact, their pilots had hit nothing and had lost several planes, the ships of the Support Group having saved themselves by means of well-aimed gunfire and radical maneuvers. A little later, three U.S. Army B-17s from Australia discovered the Support Group and identified it as the Japanese fleet about to stage an invasion of Port Moresby. They dropped three bombs, hit nothing, and returned to base, convinced they had saved Moresby.[15]

After detaching Crace, Fletcher sent out an air search, one of whose pilots at 0815 reported "two carriers and two heavy cruisers" some 250 miles to the northwest. Fletcher promptly launched ninety-three planes toward the reported contact, which he naturally supposed to be Takagi's Carrier Striking Force. At the same time TF 17 entered a cold front, with cloud cover that could conceal it from enemy planes.

This nearly perfect setup was proved fruitless by the return of the pilot of the reporting scout plane. He discovered that he had misaligned the message and its coded equivalent in his cipher book. His 0815 report should have read not "two carriers and two heavy cruisers" but "two heavy cruisers and two destroyers."

Admiral Fletcher exploded. "Young man, do you know what you have done?" he shouted. "You have just cost the United States two carriers!"

Fletcher's strike force found itself under clearing skies over a sea devoid of anything resembling a carrier. Then, by a stroke of luck, at 1022 MacArthur's headquarters passed on a report from a B-17 that had observed an enemy carrier about to enter Jomard Passage from the north. What the bomber's crew had seen was the light carrier *Shoho*, part of Goto's Covering Force. Apprised of this opportunity, the ninety-three planes from the *Yorktown* and *Lexington* swung a few degrees to starboard and raced toward the new target.

Hardly had this gladsome change of outlook come to pass when a shocker arrived by radio from back eastward. The U.S. oiler *Neosho* and her escorting destroyer were under attack by enemy bombers. Since they were beyond range of any Japanese air base, it became apparent that TF 17 was now confronted by Japanese carrier forces both ahead and astern.

It was a critical situation, but for most of the men in TF 17 the overwhelming concern was the challenge that lay ahead. Those whose duties permitted, anxious for news, crowded around radio rooms. After a long silence, snatches of pilot chatter began penetrating the heavy static. Suddenly the static died down, and the voice of Lt. Cdr. R. E. Dixon came through loud and clear: "Scratch one flattop! Dixon to Carrier, Scratch one flattop!"

History had been made. This was the first attack on an enemy carrier by U.S. carrier planes. A pair of Zero fighters had made a fruitless attempt to intercept. Two 1,000-pound bombs wrecked the *Shoho*'s flight deck and set her afire. Thereafter she took uncounted hit after hit by bombs and torpedoes. At 1131, "Abandon Ship" was ordered, but it was scarcely necessary; the carrier was sinking rapidly. Within five minutes she disappeared beneath the surface.

When word of the sinking of the *Shoho* reached Takagi and Hara, they

The Japanese light carrier *Shoho* under attack on 7 May 1942, the fourth day of the Battle of the Coral Sea. Two of the aircraft that would soon sink her are visible in the photograph: one clearly silhouetted by the smoke she is trailing and a second just below her waterline amidships. *U.S. Naval Institute*

were exasperated. They had been sent to the Coral Sea to destroy the American task force and protect the Japanese invasion forces. Now the Port Moresby Invasion Force had turned back toward Rabaul and, while aircraft from the *Shokaku* and the *Zuikaku* were expending themselves against an oiler and a destroyer, the *Yorktown* and the *Lexington* were destroying the *Shoho*. The situation, declared Hara, caused him "much chagrin."

Grimly determined to retrieve his bad judgment, at 1630 Hara launched twelve bombers and fifteen torpedo planes from the *Shokaku* and *Zuikaku* with orders to search out the U.S. task force and attack it at dusk. Heavy rainfall frustrated the search, and when the Japanese aircraft headed back toward their own carriers, fighters from the *Yorktown* and *Lexington* intercepted them and shot down nine at the cost of two of their own. The Japanese remnant, again seeking in the growing darkness to return to their carriers, unwittingly headed for the American carriers instead. Three tried to join the *Yorktown's* landing circle, and one was shot down. In endeavoring at last to make night landings on their own carriers, eleven more were lost.

Fletcher, Inouye, and Takagi each independently considered launching a night attack on the enemy main force with cruisers and destroyers. Each canceled the project, partly out of sheer exhaustion and partly because none could make a dependable guess whither his enemy was moving during the hours of darkness.

The MO Striking Force headed north during the night; TF 17, southeast. Thus they drew apart but not beyond reach of their aircraft. Dawn found Takagi's ships partially concealed by a heavy overcast with occasional rain squalls. The U.S. ships were exposed under a cloudless sky.[16]

For two-and-a-half days the two forces had been together in the Coral Sea without making contact. The U.S. carriers had sunk an uncertain number of vessels off Tulagi and a light carrier near the Louisiades. Fletcher and Fitch were now eager to top off their success by taking on the *Shokaku* and *Zuikaku*. Takagi and Hara, having failed to support the Tulagi invasion and then expended much of their air power on an oiler and a destroyer, felt disgraced and were fiercely resolved to salvage their reputations by sinking the U.S. carriers.

The opponents were well matched. The Americans had 121 planes, the Japanese 122. The American carriers had air-search radar and homing beacons; the Japanese had none. The Japanese air groups included a higher share of fighters and torpedo bombers, both of excellent quality. The carriers in both forces lacked adequate cruiser and destroyer escorts—the Americans, because Fletcher had detached Crace's Support Group; the Japanese, because of their habit of breaking their naval forces into several segments. The aviators in both forces were top men, very well trained. The Japanese carriers, however, had been working together since December, whereas the *Lexington* and *Yorktown* were in their first joint operation. By prior arrangement, Admiral Fletcher, who had had little experience with carriers, turned tactical command over to the more-experienced Admiral Fitch.

Both the Americans and the Japanese launched early morning searches. A scout from the *Lexington* sighted the MO Striking Force at 0815. By 0838 he had reported its composition, course, speed, and location, 175 miles northeast of TF 17. By 0915 the *Yorktown* had launched a strike of thirty-nine planes. Ten minutes later the *Lexington* launched a forty-nine-plane strike. A Japanese scout meanwhile had located the Americans, and the *Shokaku* and *Zuikaku* launched strikes of thirty-five and thirty-nine planes minutes after the departure of the U.S. aircraft.

Here was another historical first. Never before in the annals of naval warfare had ships engaged in battle without ever catching sight of each other. As the *Yorktown* planes approached the reported location of the enemy, her dive-bombers climbed to seventeen thousand feet and orbited while awaiting the attack far below by the slower torpedo planes. Suddenly a break in the cloud cover revealed to the American aviators both Japanese carriers and most of their escorts. One of the carriers ducked into a rain squall. The other, the *Shokaku,* was caught in the open, launching Zero fighters, which the attacking Wildcats engaged hotly. Down below, the American torpedo planes approached, fired, and turned away without achieving a single hit. From their approach altitude twenty-four bombers dived on the carrier and scored two hits, one well aft that wrecked a repair compartment, the other well forward. The forward hit started gasoline fires and so damaged the flight deck that the *Shokaku* could no longer launch planes.

Most of the *Lexington*'s planes failed to find the enemy. Of twenty-one that did, three Wildcats were promptly shot down by Zeros. The *Shokaku* easily sidestepped the slow torpedoes, which the American torpedo planes fired at long range. Four dive-bombers dived at the carrier and achieved one hit that further battered her crumpled flight deck. The *Shokaku* had lost 148 men killed and wounded, her flight deck was in shambles, but none of the hits she took were below the waterline, and her fires were soon under control.

The Japanese attack on TF 17 was almost simultaneous with the American attack on the *Shokaku.* It was far more professionally conducted, a superiority partly attributable to bright sunshine and almost cloudless skies but a consequence also of six months' combat experience with Kido Butai against every sort of target, moving and stationary.

No more than five Wildcats got into the fight over their own carriers, and the Zeros saw to it that none ever got low enough to interfere with the Japanese torpedo planes or high enough to impede the Japanese dive-bombers. The former employed the tricky anvil technique—separating on the approach and then launching torpedoes simultaneously toward the ship's starboard and port bows—impossible to dodge. The *Lexington* thus took two torpedoes on her port side. At the same time, the Japanese dive-bombers released their charges, two of which penetrated her flight deck. Both started fires. Near-misses, meanwhile, had ruptured some of the carrier's plates and threw up great geysers of black water. The vibration set off by these explosions triggered the ship's siren, which added an unearthly wail to the general pandemonium.

Waltzing Matilda, thanks to her superior maneuverability and the fact that against this target the Japanese did not employ the anvil technique, was able to dodge all torpedoes. She was victim of a couple of bomb near-misses, but the only serious damage she suffered was inflicted by an 800-pounder hurled by a dive-bomber. The bomb struck her flight deck fifteen feet inboard the island and, exploding, penetrated three decks, inflicting widespread destruction and killing or seriously injuring sixty-six men but not impairing the carrier's flight operations.

Japanese fliers, heading back toward their own force, saw behind them such clouds of smoke that they can perhaps be excused for overestimating their achievements. To Hara they reported that they had sunk one large and one medium carrier and left a battleship or cruiser in flames. In fact, only the carriers had fires on board, and these were of a minor magnitude that in later battles would prove readily extinguishable.

Admiral Takagi, accepting his aviators' report, had few qualms about detaching the *Shokaku*. With an unusable flight deck, she was of no use in combat. He transferred as many as possible of her planes to the *Zuikaku* and sent her back home to Japan. Here she was found to require extensive repair.[17]

The battle had left the *Lexington* listing 7 degrees to port, with her plane elevators jammed and several boiler rooms partly flooded. Damage control and engine and fireroom personnel went quickly to work and within an hour the carrier had resumed flight operations. At 1247, however, a deafening thunderclap deep below the *Lexington*'s decks jolted the carrier from stem to stern. A generator someone left running had ignited the fumes from gasoline tanks ruptured by a torpedo hit.

For a while the ship continued flight operations, but as additional explosions jarred her, the communications system disintegrated, and this became impossible. The *Yorktown* was ordered to recover all planes in the air. A destroyer came alongside the *Lexington* and passed fire hoses, but the fire was soon obviously beyond control and threatening the bomb storage. The wounded, some 150 men, were lowered into whaleboats.

At length, a little at 1700, Admiral Fitch decided the situation was hopeless. From his bridge he called down to the captain that he had better "get the men off." In calm seas, it was a most orderly abandonment. The captain and the executive officer made a personal inspection to be sure that none of the wounded had been overlooked. Now flames began towering from the ship's decks. Two destroyers moved slowly around her blazing hulk to see that nobody was left in the water.

Finally, at 1915, Admiral Fletcher, on board the *Yorktown*, signaled for the fleet to resume formation and continue on its southerly course. It was high time. The ships had been waiting there, almost motionless, in dangerous waters. Nor could the *Lexington* be left behind. Exploding and blazing ever higher as flames reached her ammunition, she would serve as a beacon indicating the American location to any enemy, ship, plane, or submarine within many miles.[18]

Fletcher ordered one destroyer to remain behind to deliver the coup de grâce. This it did with four torpedoes fired into the *Lexington*'s heat-reddened hull. From the receding fleet men who had been with her since she was commissioned in 1927, and many who had joined her since, now watched her last plunge with tears in their eyes. As a witness recorded, "dipping neither bow nor stern," she slipped upright beneath the surface. "There she goes," murmured one of her officers. "She didn't turn over. She is going down with her head up. Dear old *Lex.* A lady to the last!"[19]

Judged in the usual way, by weight of shipping sunk, the Japanese could claim the victory in this Battle of the Coral Sea, but Americans could take heart in that for the first time in six months of warfare a Japanese advance was stopped and turned back. It was thus an American strategic victory. Furthermore, the outcome in the Coral Sea did much to even the odds in the forthcoming campaign in the Central Pacific, temporarily depriving the Imperial Navy of the services of one-third of its fleet carriers. The damaged *Shokaku* could not be repaired in time for the operation, and the Indian Ocean cruise and the Battle of the Coral Sea had left the *Zuikaku* virtually stripped of aircraft. Thus Japan's carrier force, Kido Butai, would be reduced to four carriers. To counter this force, the U.S. Navy had surely only Halsey's *Enterprise* and *Hornet*. Fitch estimated it would take about ninety days to repair the *Yorktown*, but Nimitz, who in his youth had had experience in marine engineering, believed Waltzing Matilda might be rendered seaworthy and battleworthy in no more than three. Luckily Nimitz proved to be right.

NOTES

1. E. B. Potter, *Nimitz* (Annapolis, 1976), 8–11.

2. E. B. Potter, ed., *Sea Power: A Naval History* (2d ed., Annapolis, 1981), 289–90; Samuel Eliot Morison, *History of United States Naval Operations in World War II*, vol. 3, *The Rising Sun in the Pacific, 1931–April 1942* (Boston, 1948), 230–37.

3. Potter, *Nimitz*, 14–21, 35; Morison, *Rising Sun*, 107–8, 250–53.

4. Stephen D. Regan, *In Bitter Tempest: The Biography of Frank Jack Fletcher* (Ames, Iowa, 1994), 87–93; Morison, *Rising Sun*, 26–65; Mitsuo Fuchida and Masatake Okumiya, *Midway: The Battle That Doomed Japan*, Clarke H. Kawakami and Roger Pineau, eds. (Annapolis, 1955), 37–39; Potter, *Nimitz*, 33–39.

5. Regan, *In Bitter Tempest*, 101–2; Potter, *Nimitz*, 40–49.

6. Potter, *Sea Power*, 292–93.

7. H. P. Willmott, *The Barrier and the Javelin: Japanese and Allied Pacific Strategies, February to June 1942* (Annapolis, 1983), 51–53, 66–76.

8. William Manchester, *American Caesar* (Boston, 1978), 252–71; Fuchida and Okumiya, *Midway*, 55; Samuel Eliot Morison, *History of United States Naval Operations in World War II*, vol. 4, *Coral Sea, Midway, and Submarine Actions, May 1942–August 1942* (Boston, 1949), 4–5.

9. Regan, *In Bitter Tempest*, 48, 63.

10 Gordon W Prange, with Donald M Goldstein and Katherine V Dillon, *Miracle at Midway* (New York, 1982), 97 Most historians, accepting the less than laudatory evaluation of Fletcher's conduct in Morison's hugely influential *History of United States Naval Operations in World War II*, have at least implicitly endorsed that verdict, but it has recently been challenged by Regan, *In Bitter Tempest*, and John B Lundstrom, "Frank Jack Fletcher Got a Bum Rap," *Naval History* 6 (Summer–Fall 1992): 2–3, 22–27, 22–28.

11 Regan, *In Bitter Tempest*, 251

12. Fuchida and Okumiya, *Midway*, 66–71; Morison, *Coral Sea*, 12–16; E. B. Potter, *Bull Halsey* (Annapolis, 1985), 57–67; Edwin T. Layton, with Roger Pineau and John Costello, *"And I Was There"*: *Pearl Harbor and Midway—Breaking the Secrets* (New York, 1985), 382–85; Ronald Lewin, *The American Magic: Codes, Ciphers, and the Defeat of Japan* (New York, 1982), 91–92

13 Morison, *Coral Sea*, 21–28, John B Lundstrom, *The First South Pacific Campaign: Pacific Fleet Strategy, December 1941–June 1942* (Annapolis, 1976), 102; Layton, *"And I Was There,"* 396; Stanley Johnston, *Queen of the Flat-Tops* (New York, 1942), 143–52

14 Layton, *"And I Was There,"* 397–98, Lundstrom, *The First South Pacific Campaign*, 105–6; Morison, *Coral Sea*, 29–32

15 Morison, *Coral Sea*, 33–39

16. Layton, *"And I Was There,"* 398–400; Morison, *Coral Sea*, 39–45

17. Morison, *Coral Sea*, 46–56; Layton, *"And I Was There,"* 399–402, Johnston, *Queen of the Flat-Tops*, 213–34, Lundstrom, *The First South Pacific Campaign*, 110–11, Regan, *In Bitter Tempest*, 137–42.

18. Morison, *Coral Sea*, 57–59, Johnston, *Queen of the Flat-Tops*, 255–64; Layton, *"And I Was There,"* 402–3

19 Johnston, *Queen of the Flat-Tops*, 265–69

13

The Battle of Midway

BARRETT TILLMAN

The Battle of Midway sealed the fate of the Japanese Empire and made an American lake of the Pacific Ocean for the balance of the century. The conduct of that decisive engagement confirmed the aircraft carrier as *the* major naval combatant—a trend that continues into the 1990s.

Midway—or something much like it—had been the subject of conjecture, debate, and planning for decades. The United States and Japan, recognizing an impending war, both expected a decisive battle in the mid-Pacific. The American "Plan Orange" evolved over more than three decades, anticipating a major fleet engagement near Wake Island. However, Orange's evolution was inconsistent. Joint army-navy planning did not begin until 1903, and President Woodrow Wilson refused to sanction any war plan against Japan at all.[1] While U.S. planners eventually allowed for the use of aircraft carriers, few expected the battle to be decided by such fragile warships. Pearl Harbor changed all that in one December morning.

Militarist and expansionist, with the emperor no more than a figurehead, Japan's role in the twentieth century was determined by the army. Accustomed to easy victories—not only on the Asian mainland but also against Czarist Russia in 1905—Imperial Japan looked ever outward. At length her depredations in China brought economic sanctions by the United States, leading to an oil embargo in 1940. Tokyo's warlords faced a harsh dilemma: submit to foreign extortion or settle the matter by force of arms.

The cabinet of Prime Minister Hideki Tojo chose the latter. Consequently the surprise attack on U.S. military bases in the Territory of Hawaii represented a calculated risk—a roll of the geopolitical dice. Japanese leaders banked on martial ardor and temporary advantage, hoping that a decadent

America would sue for peace. Ironically the man who had sponsored the attack on Pearl Harbor was among the least optimistic. Adm. Isoroku Yamamoto, commander of the Combined Fleet, had served in naval-diplomatic posts, including the 1935 London Naval Conference. Like most naval leaders, Yamamoto possessed greater knowledge of the Western world than his army counterparts. He correctly concluded that, despite her alliance with Germany and Italy, Japan had merely provoked America and "awakened a sleeping giant."

Yet the army hard-liners seemingly were validated early on. Following hard upon the triumph at Pearl Harbor, Allied plumbs fell ripely into Tokyo's waiting hands: Hong Kong, Singapore and Malaya, Burma, the Philippines, and the oil-rich Dutch East Indies, among others. Thus was established the Greater East Asia Co-Prosperity Sphere, ostensibly a "new order" devoted to Asia for Asians.

Japan's victory string stretched into May 1942. At that point it was broken by the Battle of the Coral Sea.

Operation MO was aimed at seizure of Port Moresby, New Guinea, and Tulagi in the Solomons as a means of securing bases for a subsequent advance across the Southeastern Pacific, culminating in the occupation of the Samoan islands, to interdict communications between the United States and Australia. U.S. radio intelligence quickly learned of MO, and Pacific Fleet commander Chester Nimitz positioned his two available carriers, the *Lexington* and *Yorktown*, to intercept the Port Moresby invasion force.

The world's first carrier battle lasted two days, 7–8 May, and resulted in the loss of one flattop for each side. The Japanese light carrier *Shoho* was overwhelmed on the seventh, but the next day Pearl Harbor veterans *Shokaku* and *Zuikaku* terminally injured the *Lexington*. Both forces then withdrew to lick their wounds. Nevertheless, Coral Sea constituted an American victory. Not only was Port Moresby saved from invasion, but the *Shokaku* and *Zuikaku* lost heavily among their air groups and the former also suffered bomb damage, temporarily eliminating them from the Japanese order of battle.

A month before Coral Sea, Admiral Yamamoto had bullied the Naval General Staff into accepting the Combined Fleet's plan to force the issue in the Pacific, and the Halsey-Doolittle raid on Tokyo and other Japanese cities on 18 April had silenced its lingering opposition. Prudence dictated postponing so fateful an operation until the *Shokaku* and *Zuikaku* could rejoin the fleet, but Yamamoto, obsessed with the need to bring the United States to the bargaining table before the output of its industry tipped the scales against Japan, would brook no delay. The fleet movements intended to provoke his decisive battle began on schedule late in May.

Midway Atoll, eleven hundred miles northwest of Honolulu, was a logical target. Japanese occupation of Midway could not be tolerated, as it would pose a dagger at the heart of Hawaii. Tokyo knew as well as Washington that the remnants of the Pacific Fleet would be forced to battle in defense of Midway—and the course of the war hung in the balance.

Operation MI contained a fatal contradiction: overwhelming power diluted by wide dispersal. Not content with the awesome local superiority possible at the decisive point, Admiral Yamamoto sought further to reduce American presence. Therefore a deception plan called for landings in the Aleutian Islands, which were expected to draw U.S. strength away from Midway. Attacks on Dutch Harbor, Attu, and Kiska did in fact draw American attention, but Admiral Nimitz held a trump card in his hand—detailed knowledge of enemy intentions.

In a sense, the Battle of Midway was won before the first shot was fired. The Fleet Reconnaissance Unit (Pacific)—FruPac in navalese—worked round the clock deciphering Japanese naval codes. Under the ceaseless attention of Lt. Cdr. Joseph J. Rochefort, FruPac's analysts seldom saw daylight, and their work was never easy. Often decisions were made as much on intuition as evidence, but by mid-May Rochefort was convinced that Operation MI's objective—code-named AF—was Midway, with a diversion in Alaska. Any lingering doubt was removed when Rochefort had Midway send a message stating that the atoll's water-distillation plant was inoperative. Two days later a decrypted Japanese message showed that "AF" was short of fresh water. AF was Midway!

At that point events accelerated. The *Enterprise* and *Hornet* were put on immediate readiness and the *Yorktown* hastily returned from the Coral Sea. She reached Pearl on 27 May and went directly into drydock for repair of her bomb damage. Meanwhile, her fatigued air group was largely replaced by *Saratoga* squadrons, as "Sara" had received torpedo damage in January.

Nimitz heavily reinforced Capt. Cyril T. Simard's Midway garrison. Elements of seven Consolidated Catalina patrol squadrons crammed onto the atoll: PBY-5 seaplanes at Sand Island and PBY-5A amphibians on Eastern. The two resident U.S. Marine Corps squadrons received extra dive-bombers and fighters. Army Air Force bombers—long-ranged Boeing B-17s and speedy Martin B-26s—also went to Midway. At the last moment, a six-plane detachment of new Grumman TBF Avengers arrived, having "missed the boat"

TABLE 13.1 The Battle of Midway, 4–6 June 1942

	CV	CVL	BB	CA	CL	DD	SS	AV	AO	AP	AK
U.S. NAVY											
Carrier Striking Force											
Rear Adm. F. J. Fletcher											
Task Force 17											
Rear Adm. F. J. Fletcher	1	—	—	2	—	6	—	—	—	—	—
Task Force 16											
Rear Adm. R. A. Spruance	2	—	—	5	1	9	—	—	—	—	—
Oiler Group	—	—	—	—	—	2	—	—	2	—	—
Midway Patrol Group (Task Group 7.1)											
Rear Adm. R.H. English	—	—	—	—	—	—	12	—	—	—	—
TOTAL	3	—	—	7	1	17[a]	12	—	2	—	—
IMPERIAL JAPANESE NAVY											
Advanced Expeditionary Force											
Vice Adm. T. Komatsu	—	—	—	—	—	—	15	—	—	—	—
First Fleet (Main Body)											
Adm. I. Yamamoto	—	1	3	—	1	9	—	—	—	—	—
Guard (Aleutians Screening) Force											
Vice Adm. S. Takasu	—	—	4	—	2	—	—	—	4	—	—
First Mobile Force (Carrier Striking Force)											
Vice Adm. C. Nagumo	4	—	2	2	1	12	—	—	4	—	—
Second Fleet, Strike Force Support Force (Main Body)											
Vice Adm. N. Kondo	—	1	2	4	1	8	—	—	4	—	—
Second Fleet Escort Force											
Rear Adm. R. Tanaka	—	—	—	—	1	10	—	—	1	15	—[b]
Second Fleet Occupation Support Force											
Rear Adm. T. Kurita	—	—	—	4	—	3	—	2	—	—	—
Special Duty Force	—	—	—	—	—	—	—	2[c]	—	—	—
First Supply Force	—	—	—	—	—	1	—	—	—	—	2
TOTAL	4	2	11	10	6	43	15	4	13	15	2

Notes: CV = fleet carrier, CVL = light carrier, BB = battleship; CA = heavy cruiser; CL = light cruiser; DD = destroyer, SS = submarine, AV = seaplane tender, AO = oiler, AP = transport, AK = cargo ship

[a] Two additional destroyers were assigned to escort an oiler from Pearl Harbor to Midway, which they reached on 6 June, a third was stationed at French Frigate Shoals, roughly one-third of the way from Oahu to Midway, where in March Japanese flying boats had been refueled by submarine

[b] Plus a minesweeping group consisting of four minesweepers and several auxiliaries

[c] Tasked with carrying midget submarines

TABLE 13.2 The Aleutian Sideshow

	CV	CVL	BB	CA	CL	DD	YP	SS	AV	AO	AP
U.S. NAVY											
Task Force 8											
Rear Adm. R. A.											
Theobald	—	—	—	2	3	13	20[a]	6	3	3	—
IMPERIAL JAPANESE NAVY											
Northern Area Force											
Vice Adm. B.											
Hosogawa	—	2	—	3	2	12	—	6	1	3	8

Notes: CV = fleet carrier, CVL = light carrier, BB = battleship; CA = heavy cruiser; CL = light cruiser; DD = destroyer; YP = patrol craft, SS = submarine; AV = seaplane tender; AO = oiler, AP = transport

[a] Including a gunboat and five Coast Guard cutters

when *Hornet* departed the East Coast. In all Midway somehow found room for 115 navy, marine, and army aircraft.

Then, on 27 May, Vice Adm. Chuichi Nagumo's Kido Butai—the Carrier Striking Force—sortied from home waters: four carriers, two battleships, three cruisers, and a dozen destroyers. Yamamoto himself sailed in the Main Body, which included three battleships and a light carrier, while the invasion force and the Alaskan diversion force also departed. In all, the Imperial Navy committed seventy warships (plus fifteen submarines) and twenty-six auxiliaries to the Midway assault. Another twenty warships went to the Aleutians.

The Pacific Fleet committed three carriers, twenty-eight cruisers or destroyers, and twelve submarines to the defense of Midway. The carriers represented the culmination of two decades of design and operating experience. The *Yorktown* and *Enterprise* were sisters, commissioned in 1937 and 1938, respectively. The *Hornet,* the newest carrier in the fleet, was a near-sister, which had first flown her commissioning pennant in October 1941. Each displaced approximately 19,800 tons and embarked about 80 aircraft.

At the time of Midway, U.S. carrier aircraft were still in transition. Grumman's Wildcat fighter had just been upgraded from four to six .50 calibers with folding wings in the F4F-4 but had reduced speed and climb compared to the F4F-3 model. The Douglas SBD Dauntless was, like the F4F, a design in the fleet only since 1940. In combat, the SBD-3 serving at Midway proved spectacularly effective—arguably the best dive-bomber of World War II. Oldest carrier plane in the inventory was Douglas's TBD-1 Devastator, soon to be replaced by the TBF-1 Avenger. Though consigned by conventional wisdom to the trash heap of aviation history, the TBD was much maligned. It had been the first carrier monoplane in 1937 and suffered no aerial losses to enemy action until 4 June 1942. Its faults were glacial speed and erratic torpedoes.

Japan's four carriers were older and, generally, larger. The *Akagi*, like both *Lexingtons*, was laid down as a battle cruiser but completed as a carrier in 1927. She became Nagumo's flagship in Kido Butai for her entire wartime career. The *Kaga*, at 38,200 tons, was larger, owing to her origin as a battleship. Converted under provision of the 1922 Washington Naval Treaty, she joined the fleet in 1930. Both carriers were modernized during the 1930s in order to operate more aircraft—upward of eighty each.

Regarded as sisters, the *Soryu* and *Hiryu* were more look-alikes than relatives. Completed in 1937 and 1939, they displaced 15,900 and 17,300 tons, respectively, and comprised Carrier Division Two. Their architecture reflected the Japanese practice of different island placement—*Soryu*'s to starboard, *Hiryu*'s to port. This was consistent with doctrine, permitting simultaneous flight operations without overlapping traffic patterns for their seventy aircraft.

All four carriers flew the same three types of planes: Mitsubishi A6M2 fighters, Aichi D3A2 dive-bombers, and Nakajima B5N2 attack planes. The Type Zero fighter was unlike anything else flying on earth, possessed of good speed, superior maneuverability, and phenomenal range. The Aichi, later called "Val" by Allied airmen, was built along the lines of Germany's Junkers 87: a big aircraft with fixed landing gear and under-wing dive brakes. "Kate" proved versatile as a level bomber and torpedo plane, possessed of surprising speed.

Ironically, in the world's most important carrier battle, none of the on-scene commanders in either fleet were aviators. In 1942 carrier aviation was merely twenty years old in both the U.S. and Japanese navies. Consequently, career paths had not evolved to the point that fliers were senior enough to command task forces. The Americans recognized that fact in the 1930s and provided accelerated flight training for air-minded senior officers, such as Ernest J. King and William F. Halsey. They were then designated naval aviators because in the U.S. Navy—unlike those of Britain and Japan—only pilots could command aircraft carriers.

The ability of such aviation latecomers to fly an airplane was largely irrelevant. In fact ample talent was available among "genuine" aviators, such as Capt. Marc A. Mitscher of the *Hornet*, who had learned to fly in 1916. Combined with experienced staff officers, the carrier skippers provided task force commanders with all the technical expertise necessary. What mattered at the top was institutional awareness of the critical nature of aviation in 1942 naval

Raymond A. Spruance later in the war, wearing the four stars of a full admiral. *U.S. Naval Institute*

warfare. Thus, when Halsey was beached with dermatitis just before Task Force (TF) 16 sailed for Midway, his knowledge was not lost. Asked by Nimitz to designate a successor, Halsey was insistent: Rear Adm. Raymond A. Spruance.

Spruance, twenty-fifth in the Annapolis Class of 1907, was already recognized as one of the finest minds in the U.S. Navy. Aged fifty-five, he had led Halsey's cruisers since the earliest days of the war. Therefore, when he broke his flag in the *Enterprise* he inherited not only TF 16's air staff, but a personal knowledge of task force operations. Samuel Eliot Morison considered his strengths to be "attention to detail, poise, and power of intelligent decision."[2]

Commanding TF 17 was Rear Adm. Frank Jack Fletcher, another "black-shoe." Senior to Spruance by one year, he possessed invaluable experience in carrier warfare. Cautious in combat—some insisted overly so—he had ridden the *Yorktown* during the early hit-and-run raids, then through the Coral Sea battle. To Yorktowners, Fletcher looked "leather-tough and spare," his face creased from "a thousand nights and days on the bridges of warships."[3]

Leadership of the Japanese Carrier Striking Force similarly was long on practical knowledge and short on flight time. A fifty-five-year-old torpedo authority, Vice Adm. Chuichi Nagumo had come up through cruisers but competently directed carrier operations from Pearl Harbor to the Indian Ocean and beyond. Although only one of his carrier captains was an aviator, his staff included some of Japan's most experienced airmen: the likes of Commanders Minoru Genda, a gifted planner, and Mitsuo Fuchida, a well-regarded strike leader. When Fuchida came down with appendicitis the first day at sea, he was ably replaced by Lt. Joichi Tomonaga, a *Hiryu* pilot who had missed Pearl Harbor.

Despite its depth of leadership, the striking force had problems. Nagumo judged that his aircrews needed time ashore after almost nonstop operations since December. Others complained of the command structure, insisting that Nagumo merely rubber-stamped Genda's plans. If so, it was wise policy. Kido Butai had ravaged the Anglo-Americans for six months without a scratch in return.

At the theater level, the antagonists were a Japanese aviator and an American submariner. Though Isoroku Yamamoto rose to prominence on his advocacy of aviation, he still relied heavily on the world's greatest warships. Chester Nimitz, however, was deprived of a battle line and recognized that submarines were properly directed against the enemy merchant marine. He had no choice but to rely upon his carrier aircrews. They repaid his trust with triumph.

By Wednesday, 3 June, the Japanese Northern Area Force was positioned to initiate the Alaskan deception plan. The two light carriers of Rear Adm. Kakuji Kakuta's Second Mobile Force launched air strikes against Dutch Harbor, inflicting notable damage. Then, unimpeded by an American cruiser-destroyer force deployed too far east to intercept, the *Ryujo* and *Junyo* returned the next day. Their efforts deceived no one. Japanese troops occupied Attu and Kiska in the western Aleutians four days later, but it counted for naught. Midway absorbed the knowledge that Yamamoto's grand strategy was under way, then stood by to repel boarders.

As Kakuta's aviators were pounding Dutch Harbor, the Midway occupation force appeared. On the morning of the third, a PBY came across two Japanese minesweepers 470 miles west-southwest of the atoll. Shortly thereafter another Catalina flushed bigger game.

Piloting the latter was Ens. J. H. Reid, whose radioman monitored Japanese communications. Continuing beyond the scheduled turn point, Reid's patience was rewarded.

"We were flying 270 degrees at 1,000 feet. At the end of 730 miles, just before I was to turn on a north heading, I spotted what at first appeared to be specks on the horizon or dirty spots on the windshield. After a second look, I shouted, 'Enemy ships thirty miles dead ahead!' [Copilot] Hardeman snatched the binoculars and, after looking, shouted, 'You're damn right, they're enemy ships!' "[4]

After shadowing the "main body" for more than ninety minutes, Reid broke contact while another PBY headed for the contact to relieve him. It was none too soon. Upon landing in Midway's lagoon, he had logged more than fourteen hours in the air.[5]

Reid's discovery immediately set in motion a flurry of activity. Lurking some three hundred miles northeast of Midway, Rear Admiral Fletcher monitored the PatRon frequency. Deciding on a prudent look around, he launched scouts in a sector search. The SBDs turned up nothing, but Midway's air force leapt into action.

A B-17E with long-range fuel tanks left Midway at noon with orders to broadcast the location of the enemy transport force. It was followed by six other Flying Fortresses under Lt. Col. Walter Sweeney, which arrived overhead the target that afternoon. Swinging around to the west, approaching from upsun, the Boeings surprised their quarry and attacked from altitudes between 8,000 and 12,000 feet. However, none of the twenty-four bombs struck closer than one hundred yards from a Japanese ship.

Results improved after dark. Lt. W. L. Richards, executive officer of VP-44, gathered a mixed formation of three VP-24 Catalinas and another from VP-21. Newly arrived on Midway, the crews learned that they had been selected for a nocturnal attack mission following a ten-hour flight from Hawaii.

Hunting through the clouds and darkness, three of the flying boats found their target. Attacking after 0100 on the fourth, they pressed in, and Richards torpedoed the oiler *Akebono Maru*. The PBYs then headed for Midway, more than ready to turn in.

About that same time, reveille sounded in TF 16 and TF 17. It was the beginning of a long, long day.

Sunrise revealed superb flying weather over the combat arena. A light southeasterly breeze favored Nagumo's carriers, which could advance on Midway without turning out of the wind, while Fletcher and Spruance had to reverse course for flight operations. But at 0430 the U.S. carriers launched the dawn combat air patrol (CAP), and the *Yorktown*'s scouts (actually Lt. Wallace C. Short's redesignated VB-5) began probing their search sectors.

Kido Butai also was stirring. By 0445 Nagumo's four flattops had 107 bombers and fighters winging southeasterly toward Midway, 240 miles away. Once the strike group had set course, scouts were fired off the cruisers *Tone* and *Chikuma* as well as the battleship *Haruna*. All departed on schedule except one of the *Tone*'s Aichi E13Ks, which was delayed with catapult problems. Even as the scouts dispersed to their wedge-shaped sectors, Nagumo's deck crews began spotting a second strike: thirty-six each Vals and torpedo-armed Kates, plus twenty-five Zeros.

On Midway itself the day's first CAP had been launched while twenty-two PBYs began their tedious searches and sixteen B-17s sought the Japanese transports. In the hour before 0600, whatever lethargy existed on Midway evaporated in an adrenalin rush. A VP-23 Catalina sighted two of Nagumo's carriers and immediately radioed "Main body." Minutes later, another PatRon 23 crew encountered a large formation of unidentified aircraft one hundred miles out. The word crackled over the radio channel: "Many planes heading Midway."

That message was monitored by one of the obscure players in the unfolding drama. Northwest of the atoll, the submarine USS *Nautilus* scoured her patrol area in compliance with the overall operations plan. Her skipper, Lt. Cdr. W. H. Brockman Jr., determined that the carriers that launched those "many planes" had to be farther along his patrol route and set course accordingly. One of only two in her class, the *Nautilus* was among the largest submarines in the world. She had been commissioned in 1930, making her one of the oldest subs in the fleet, but she would be heard from.

Meanwhile, Midway's radar station began tracking the inbound intruders. By 0556 the garrison had gone to Condition One, and a mad scramble began on Eastern Island. With the raiders steadily closing the range, VMF-221's twenty-five Brewster F2A-3s and Grumman F4F-3s took off by sections and divisions, somehow missing one another on the two intersecting runways. Next off were the ten torpedo planes: VT-8's six TBF-1s, followed by four Martin B-26s. Finally twenty-eight SB2U-3s and SBD-2s of VMSB-241 lifted off, armed with 500-pound bombs and the approximate location of Kido Butai.

Maj. Floyd Parks's untried fighter squadron found the Japanese strike group about forty miles out, flying an impeccable V-of-V formation. Capt. John F. Carey, leading VMF-221's F4Fs, made initial contact. He radioed "Tally

Ho! Hawks at angels 12," then rolled into an overhead pass on the lead bombers.

A few Buffalos and Wildcats made unopposed gunnery passes on the Nakajima level bombers from 14,000 feet. The *Hiryu*'s bombers absorbed the brunt of the marine attack, with two B5Ns shot down in the first rush and another that ditched. The Nakajima of Lt. Joichi Tomonaga received .50-caliber holes in its wings—damage that would haunt the strike leader later in the day. A *Soryu* bomber also failed to return, but then the worst was over—for the Japanese. It was the beginning of the worst for VMF-221.

Once the escorting Zeros descended on the U.S. fighters, the combat turned to hash. Neither Major Parks nor thirteen of his pilots returned to Midway. Another Buffalo pilot bailed out but was the only one recovered. Said one Brewster survivor, Capt. Philip R. White: "It is my belief that any commander who orders pilots out for combat in an F2A should consider the pilot as lost before leaving the ground."[6] However with the marine fighters committed piecemeal and caught at an altitude disadvantage, it only could have gone one way.

Flying a Wildcat in Carey's division was another newly minted captain, Marion E. Carl. Unlike most other fighter pilots, Carl found little to choose between the Brewster and the Grumman. With more than one thousand hours flight time, he was more experienced than most of his squadronmates, and he put his experience to good use. After a pass at the bombers he dueled briefly with a Zero, took some hits in his airframe, and evaded with an uncoordinated skid that caused his pursuer to overshoot.

Carl took stock of the situation and, with one machine gun inoperative, he noted three widely separated Zeros in the area. Taking advantage of the Japanese lack of mutual support, he began stalking one of them:

Completely unaware of me, he probably was looking down when I dived on him from above and behind.

I waited until the Zero's wingspan filled the mil rings of my gunsight. Then, at boresight range, I began firing. Despite the asymmetrical recoil resulting from only three guns, I managed to keep my sight on target and closed in. The fighter took a concentrated cluster of .50 caliber hits and dropped into a spin. It never recovered, and neither of the two nearby Japanese pilots noticed the event.[7]

Carl had no trouble finding home. The atoll sent thick, black smoke billowing hundreds of feet into the sky—testimony to the accuracy of the Japanese bombers. Fires burned everywhere, debris was strewn about, and several hangars or other buildings were flattened. Only nine other pilots had returned, and eight of the planes had battle damage—including his own. Four surviving pilots were wounded, and few others were inclined toward additional combat. As a unit, VMF-221 was finished.

Lieutenant Tomonaga's bombers had been thorough. On Eastern Island hangars were destroyed with the power plant and command post, while fuel tanks were set afire. Damage was not as severe on Sand Island, but just as extensive, including the destruction of three oil tanks, the dispensary, mess hall, and an armament building. Nearly thirty men were killed or wounded on the ground.

Pulling away from the wrecked atoll, Lieutenant Tomanaga assessed his handiwork. The primary targets had all been struck, and fires blazed satisfactorily. However Midway's strength had been surprising. The Japanese estimated they had been intercepted by more than forty Grummans, and the anti-aircraft fire was alarming. In fact the gunners of the Sixth Defense Battalion had downed about six planes but damaged many more. Tomanaga radioed: "There is need for a second attack."[8]

Meanwhile, Midway's own attack group was straggling outbound to the northwest. Devoid of fighter escort, Marine Dauntlesses and Vindicators trailed the Navy Avengers and Army Marauders in a triservice version of 1940s "jointness." However, in the press of events there was almost no chance for a coordinated attack. None of the disparate elements had ever trained together, and varying aircraft performance and aircrew proficiency compounded the problem. Most of the Marine Corps dive-bomber pilots were so green that they were limited to shallow glide attacks rather than the 70-degree dives of their carrier-based counterparts.

Typical of the aircrews facing combat for the first time were Lt. Langdon K. Fieberling's Torpedo Eight detachment. Flying 8-T-1 was Ens. Albert K. Earnest:

At approximately 0700 we sighted the enemy force about fifteen miles away. . . . Just as we sighted the enemy fleet we were attacked by a large force of enemy fighters. We immediately started a dive at full throttle through clouds to within 150 feet of the water and headed directly for the carriers. The enemy fighters . . . continued to attack us and on the second burst hit my turret gunner, AMM3/c J. D. Manning, putting him out of action and eventually killing him. At the same time my hydraulic system was shot away, causing my tail wheel to drop and blank out my tunnel gun.

Soon after this my tunnel gunner, RM3/c H. H. Ferrier, was hit on the head and although dazed and bleeding, was not seriously injured. I received a small cut on my right cheek, apparently by shrapnel from an explosive shell.

When we were still several miles from the Japanese carriers, my elevator wires were shot away. I released my torpedo at the nearest ship, a light cruiser, as I thought I was out of control, but regained control with the elevator tab. . . . I could not see whether or not my torpedo hit the cruiser.

Two enemy fighters chased me for about ten minutes . . . and although they made runs on me as well, no vital parts of the plane were hit and it continued to perform very well.[9]

Earnest managed a one-wheel landing back at Midway, the only one of TorpRon Eight's detachment to return. Similarly twelve of the twenty-seven marine dive-bombers were lost in the attack on Kido Butai, as were two of the four B-26s.

At least the sixteen SBDs of VMSB-241 had a shot at Japanese carriers. Maj. Lofton R. Henderson went after the *Hiryu* but was killed by Zeros, which splashed seven other Dauntlesses. Maj. Benjamin W. Norris's eleven SB2Us, slower than the SBDs, arrived next. Faced with overwhelming odds, they diverted from the carriers and went for Nagumo's two battleships. Four planes were shot down or ditched without compensating damage to the enemy.

It had been a gallant, futile effort: thirty-seven aircraft against four carriers, two battleships, three cruisers, and a dozen destroyers—plus at least twenty-seven CAP fighters. Many of Midway's surviving planes would not fly again in the battle, but other U.S. forces were near at hand—above and below.

The latter was the *Nautilus*, which had found Nagumo after eavesdropping on the morning PBY reports. Depth-charged by circling destroyers, the big submarine remained in the area, as Commander Brockman hoped for a shot at something important. One quick look convinced him of the risk: "The picture presented on raising the periscope was one never experienced in peacetime practice. Ships were on all sides moving across the field at high speed and circling away to avoid the submarine's position."[10] Brockman fired at a large warship, missed, then went deep to await events. He had patience, time, and courage.

As if combined dive-bombing and submarine attacks were not enough, Nagumo next was harried by high-level bombers. Fourteen of Lt. Col. Sweeney's B-17s attacked in five groups at about 20,000 feet, claiming hits on three flattops and two Zeros destroyed. In fact none of the bombs came close, as the targets—*Akagi* and *Kaga*—were not even dented. The big Boeings returned to base with insignificant damage.

As the Americans limped off toward Midway, Nagumo took stock. He had repulsed a fairly large but uncoordinated air and submarine attack, had all his ships intact, and was prepared to receive his inbound attack force. Thus far, things had progressed much as Yamamoto had expected. Then the *Tone*'s number four scout, delayed a half-hour in launching, radioed that a small American force was "accompanied by what appears to be a carrier."

While Midway expended its strength against Kido Butai, the two U.S. carrier task forces considered their options. Both Fletcher and Spruance followed the PBY reports and calculated the earliest moment to launch deckload strikes. Fletcher, ring-wise from Coral Sea, knew the importance of getting in the first punch. But he had to recover his scouts before launching against the enemy's expected position. Therefore Spruance's TF 16 had first chance at Nagumo. The *Enterprise* and *Hornet* commenced launch at 0700—about the time the TBFs spotted enemy carriers.

The *Hornet*'s Capt. Marc A. Mitscher had been selected for rear admiral, but neither his ship or air group were yet up to speed. Unaccountably, VF-8's ten Wildcats were the first strike aircraft off the deck, followed by the longer-ranged SBDs and finally the TBDs of Torpedo Eight. By the time the rest of the formation was ready to set course, the F4Fs had been airborne an hour.

It was not much better on the "Big E." Lt. Cdr. C. Wade McClusky, previously skipper of Fighting Six, was the new air group commander (CAG). Circling overhead with thirty-three SBDs, he wondered at the delay in launching the fighters and "torpeckers" but could not break radio silence to inquire. Finally, at 0745, Spruance ordered Bombing and Scouting Six to "proceed on mission assigned." The F4Fs and TBDs would have to make up the deficit as best they could.

Thus was set the stage for confusion and tragedy. Following respot of the deck, the *Enterprise* got off ten fighters and fourteen torpedo planes. But in the strung-out procession leading southwesterly toward Nagumo, formations became separated. Lt. James S. Gray, leading VF-6, unknowingly attached himself to Lt. Cdr. John C. Waldron's Torpedo Eight, while Torpedo Six, under the injured Lt. Cdr. Eugene Lindsey, proceeded alone.

The rest of the Hornet Air Group took itself out of the battle. Cdr. Stanhope C. Ring led his SBDs and F4Fs well north of the actual track and, insisting on tight formation, ran short on fuel. The VF-8 CO ignored his declining fuel state until too late. Refusing to heed his more knowledgeable junior officers, he missed the task force and all ten Wildcats went in the water, with two pilots lost. Most of the SBDs landed at Midway or squeaked back to the *Hornet*, but the air group missed its chance to effect the outcome of the battle.

Not so VT-8; just before 0900 Waldron led his fifteen TBDs almost directly to the target. Without time to await help, he took his Devastators straight into the attack, tragically unaware that Gray and VF-6 circled high overhead. Gray, expecting to coordinate with Lindsey, heard nothing from VT-6 and reluctantly turned for home. The Zeros and flak chopped Torpedo Eight to pieces, leaving one survivor in the water.

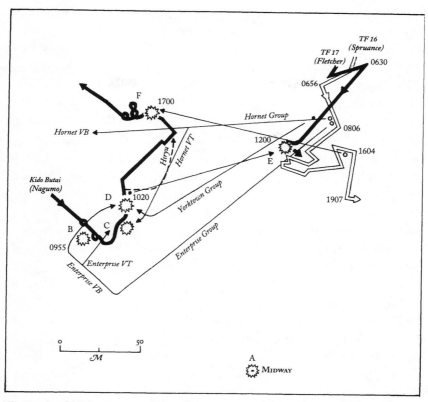

The Battle of Midway, 4 June 1942. The action opens at 0634 with a Japanese air strike on Midway (A). Between 0705 and 0900 the Kido Butai beats off counter-attacks by Midway-based aircraft (B), recovers its strike force, and emerges unscathed from a succession of virtually suicidal runs (C) by three U.S. torpedo-bomber squadrons (VT). Before it can launch against the U.S. carriers, however, dive-bomber squadrons (VB) from the *Enterprise* and *Yorktown* deliver an attack (D) that reduces the *Akagi, Kaga,* and *Soryu* to flaming wrecks. The remaining Japanese carrier, the *Hiryu,* then gets off a strike that damages the *Yorktown* (E). The *Hiryu* hits the *York-town* with a second strike (not shown) at 1445, but a little more than two hours later the *Enterprise*'s dive-bombers bring her operations to an end (F).

Forty minutes behind was Torpedo Six, which also attacked alone. Ten of Lindsey's fourteen planes went down, including the CO. No hits were scored on any Japanese ship, and of the four aircraft that returned to the *Enterprise,* two were jettisoned with battle damage. The morning of 4 June ended an eye-watering string of good fortune for the TBD. In the previous six months, not one Devastator had fallen to enemy flak or fighters. Now, in less than an hour, two squadrons had been destroyed.

Meanwhile, the *Enterprise*'s SBDs continued their patient hunt. Lt. Cdr.

McClusky led his formation to the expected contact point only to find empty sea and a cloud-flecked sky. Double-checking his navigation, he felt confident that he had reached the area projected by Spruance's staff—150 miles southwest of TF 16. McClusky was faced with the battle's crucial decision: continue searching southwesterly or look elsewhere. It was as if a major had decided the course of Waterloo.

With impeccable logic, McClusky had allowed Nagumo a maximum rate of advance, meaning that Kido Butai had not reached the briefed position. Therefore the CAG reasoned that his prey lay somewhere to the north. He eased into a starboard turn, beginning the first leg of a box search.

Thirty-five minutes later, McClusky's decision was rewarded. From 19,000 feet he spotted the wake of the destroyer *Arashi*, speeding to catch Nagumo after pummeling the *Nautilus*. Concluding that the "cruiser" was liaison between the transports and carriers, McClusky altered course to match the lone Japanese—to the northeast. Barely five minutes after that, his binoculars showed the pale wakes of Kido Butai. He radioed a report, then began his approach.

It took a quarter hour to close the distance, but in those fifteen minutes Nagumo was unknowingly caught in an aerial vise. While McClusky's squadrons approached from the southwest, the *Yorktown*'s strike appeared in the southeast. Launching later than TF 16, Fletcher's aircrews benefited from better intelligence and steered a straighter course to the enemy. Now, Lt. Cdrs. Maxwell F. Leslie, Lance E. Massey, and John S. Thach arrived over the target with seventeen Dauntlesses, twelve Devastators, and six Wildcats.

Closest to the Japanese was VT-3, which had been navigating for the others. Massey took his squadron down toward the water, but drew heavy attention from swarming Zeros. Thach's half-dozen F4Fs fought for their lives, forcing the Devastators to rely on their rear gunners. It wasn't nearly enough. Massey's plane was among the first to splash, leaving an enlisted pilot, W. G. Esders, in the lead. With a mortally wounded gunner, Esders had seconds to evaluate the situation: "I felt I should continue the approach the skipper had started. I had a moment to look around and we must have had at least twenty to twenty-five Zeros after us. I decided I couldn't afford to lose even a few seconds in making the attack, as I then saw only four aircraft, plus my own. I took the lead, proceeded to the proper point and gave the attack signal."[11]

Only Esders's and one other plane survived the attack, both ditching near the task force. TorpRon Three had gone the way of VT-6 and VT-8, but gleeful Zero pilots were drawn to the low-level shootout. High overhead three SBD squadrons approached unseen.

"Battle of Midway," by war artist Commander Griffith Bailey Coale, USNR, shows the successful attack on the Japanese fleet carrier *Kaga* on the morning of 4 June 1942. *U.S. Naval Institute*

Unaware of the Yorktowners, McClusky quickly assigned targets to his *Enterprise* pilots. Aborts had reduced him to thirty SBDs so, without further delay, he opened his dive brakes and pushed over on the nearest carrier—and nearly collided with his bombing skipper.

Lt. Richard H. Best had taken his division below the rest of the formation, concerned about faulty oxygen systems. Doctrine called for the trailing squadron to attack the closest ship, but McClusky—a fighter pilot by trade—eagerly jumped on the more vulnerable carrier. Best's division quickly regrouped and proceeded to the next visible flattop.

In Kido Butai the second strike group was turning up, ready to launch. Belated word of U.S. carriers at sea had forced Nagumo into a painful decision—download bombs and upload torpedoes. Consequently flight decks and catwalks were crowded with ordnance. Then the lookouts all were shouting at once, screaming a belated warning: "Helldivers!"

Dauntless pilots still argue about which squadron sank what carrier. Most of the fliers insisted they hit "a big one," but in history's ledger it mattered not. There was plenty for all.

McClusky, with Scouting Six and most of the bombers, undoubtedly put four bombs on the *Akagi*. Best's VB-6 division likely attacked the *Kaga*, batting three for five. Leslie, like three of his pilots, was deprived of a bomb owing to the maddening malfunction. However, he took his squadron down on the *Soryu* and left her ablaze. The course of the Pacific War had shifted in five minutes.[12]

While VB-3 made a clean getaway, outraged Zeros pursued McClusky's planes, wounding him in the process. Of thirty-two SBDs that departed the *Enterprise*, only sixteen returned, but the funeral pyres blazing in their slipstream proved a landmark on the road to Tokyo. Bombing and Scouting Six both had been caught in the Sunday surprise on 7 December, and Dick Best spoke for all when he summarized the morning off Midway as "Revenge, sweet revenge. The Italians say it's a dish best served cold, and by June it was six months cold."[13]

As Vice Admiral Nagumo's stunned staff transferred the emperor's portrait from the burning flagship, the remaining Japanese carrier was still in the fight. Capt. Tomeo Kaku in the Hiryu quickly adjusted to the appalling turn of events and sent off a retaliatory strike at 1045. Eighteen Vals launched with six Zeros, two of which aborted after tangling with homing SBDs. But the others knew where to find the Americans, and at 1152 they interrupted the Yorktown's recovery. The SBDs in the traffic pattern were told to stand clear, and, just after the stroke of noon, a gunfight erupted over TF 17.

"Jimmy" Thach's VF-3 had a very high order of experience among the twelve airborne Wildcats. Reinforced with a division each from VF-6 and VF-8, in the next several minutes they shot at least eleven Vals from the sky. Three each fell to VF-42 veterans, Lts. (j.g.) E. S. McCuskey and A. J. Brassfield.

But then the Hiryu's bomber squadron was overhead the Yorktown, ignoring the flak that splashed two more Aichis. The five survivors hit "Old Yorky" three times, snuffing out most of her boilers and bringing her to a stop. Forced off his flagship, Admiral Fletcher shifted to the light cruiser Astoria and awaited events.

Of the twenty-two Japanese planes that reached TF 17, only six returned to the Hiryu, but by then her hard-working air department had a second strike ready to go. Despite damage to his plane's fuel tank, Joichi Tomonaga prepared to lead ten Kates and six Zeros on a mission from which he could not possibly return. His orders: attack an undamaged American carrier.

Meanwhile, rescue efforts proceeded with Nagumo's three stricken flattops. Worst off was the flagship, which obviously was doomed. But other forces were at work, not least of which was the Nautilus's tireless skipper, Bill Brockman. After chasing the carriers again, he maneuvered into position on the still-burning Akagi at 1400 and fired three torpedoes. One connected but failed to explode. The Nautilus slipped away, having played a bigger role in the battle than any other U.S. submarine.

By this same time, a minor miracle had been worked in the Yorktown. Her superb engineering and damage-control team not only subdued the fires but had worked back up to 19 knots in barely two hours. It was cruel irony: when Tomonaga's strike group arrived at 1430, the first target was an "undamaged" Yorktown-class carrier. TF 16 lay forty miles beyond.

Protected by her own fighters and a few from VF-6, the *Yorktown* made a fight of it. The CAP splashed five Kates and a Zero, losing two Wildcats with both pilots recovered. Lieutenant Commander Thach, who had flamed three Zeros over the enemy fleet that morning, added a Kate that afternoon—probably Tomonaga's. But the *Hiryu's* determined aircrews pressed the attack, and they slammed two torpedoes into her. Capt. Elliott Buckmaster reached a painful decision and reluctantly ordered abandon ship.

By mid-afternoon all the *Yorktown's* surviving planes were aboard the *Enterprise,* awaiting word on the enemy's elusive fourth carrier. That information was supplied by another orphaned Yorktowner, Lt. Samuel Adams, whose scout team found the *Hiryu.* Armed with that crucial knowledge, TF 16 launched a maximum-effort strike: fourteen displaced VB-3 Dauntlesses plus ten remaining VB- and VS-6 planes, followed by sixteen of the *Hornet's* regrouped SBDs. Spruance then queried Fletcher in the *Astoria,* who passed the conn, adding, "Will conform to your movements."[14]

Without fighter escort, Lt. Earl Gallaher's *Enterprise* strike attacked the *Hiryu* at 1700. Diving out of the westering sun, the SBDs were met by fourteen Zeros. Fighting to preserve their last flight deck, they shot three Dauntlesses into the water. As the first bombs splashed close aboard the *Hiryu,* Lt. D. W. Shumway of VB-3 astutely shifted from the battleship he had been ordered to attack. Between them, Shumway's squadron and Lieutenant Best's VB-6 division did the job. The *Hiryu* absorbed four bombs, gushed smoke and flames, and began sinking. The *Hornet's* strike arrived in time to harass some destroyers, then it was over. The *Akagi* had already sunk; *Kaga* and *Soryu* followed that evening. The *Hiryu* lingered until morning. Flying eastward toward TF 16, the SBD crews watched a sight rich in symbolism—a red sun setting.

At dawn on 5 June, Spruance was the victor of Midway. However many aviators felt differently. During the night he had turned his force easterly—away from the retreating Japanese fleet. Ill-concealed resentment smoldered in ready rooms, where proud-tired pilots marveled at a blackshoe admiral who would retire from a beaten enemy.

But that controversial decision sealed the stamp of Spruance's greatness. His orders were clear: protect Midway by employing attrition tactics against a superior force. He had done that. Then, by refusing to be drawn under the huge guns of Yamamoto's battleships, Spruance coolly deprived Japan any chance of recouping her severe losses. It is doubtful that the combative Bull Halsey could have resisted the temptation to pursue his enemy to complete destruction. Raymond Ames Spruance was the right admiral in the right place at the right time.

Action did resume, however, both from the carriers and from ashore. Marine dive-bombers attacked the Japanese cruisers *Mogami* and *Mikuma*, resulting in a posthumous Medal of Honor for Capt. Richard E. Fleming. Later that day, pursuing another contact report, fifty-eight SBDs found only the destroyer *Tanikaze*. Her capable captain evaded damage, and her anti-aircraft guns shot down the *Yorktown's* Lieutenant Adams, who had found the *Hiryu*.

On 6 June the carrier squadrons finished with the *Mogami* and *Mikuma*, which had intended to bombard Midway. Between them, *Hornet* and *Enterprise* SBDs put the *Mikuma* on the bottom. It was the Americans' last offensive action of the battle.

Though the *Saratoga* was rushing from the West Coast, all that remained was to determine whether the *Yorktown* could be saved. Abandoned on 4 June, she stubbornly remained afloat. Therefore, at dawn on the sixth, the destroyer *Hammann* was lashed alongside while other destroyers stood guard. A hand-picked repair crew went aboard the *Yorktown*, making slow progress throughout the day. By jettisoning heavy gear and pumping water and oil, her port list slowly improved.

At 1336 lookouts sounded an alarm. The Japanese submarine *I-168* had penetrated the screen and fired four torpedoes. One missed astern. Another broke the *Hammann's* back, sinking her immediately. The other pair struck the *Yorktown's* exposed starboard flank, detonating with awful finality. Her 20,000 tons shuddered, settled lower, and began to die.

Lt. Cdr. Yahachi Tanabe eluded the vengeful American destroyers and escaped without damage to the *I-168*. His victim lasted until dawn the next day. When the *Yorktown* sank at 0500 on 7 June, the Battle of Midway was over.

It had cost the lives of 307 American fliers, sailors, and marines. It cost Imperial Japan 3,500 men—and the war.

In his superb campaign history, *Guadalcanal,* Richard B. Frank cites a Japanese naval officer's assessment of the Pacific War. "There were many famous battles," said Capt. Y. Tomagawa, "but after the war we talked only about two—Midway and Guadalcanal."[15]

That concise appraisal summarizes the collective attitude of U.S. naval historians as well. But which proved the greater victory—Midway or Guadalcanal? Perhaps the most balanced assessment holds that Midway meant that Japan could not win, while Guadalcanal guaranteed that America would not lose. It is no simple equation, for the outcome at Midway was directly linked to events at Coral Sea, just as Midway influenced Guadalcanal.

In Churchillian terms, Midway marked "the end of the beginning." Following Yamamoto's promised six months of uninterrupted victories, Japan had lost the initiative, never to regain it. Her subsequent offensive actions in the Solomons and Marianas were reactive. Strategically defensive in nature, they attempted to preserve what had already been won before Midway.

For the United States, Midway was the last purely defensive operation of the war. The crippling losses inflicted on Kido Butai deprived the Imperial Navy of the ships and aircrews necessary for further conquest, whereas American production of weapons and warriors spiraled ever upward to Olympian heights.

While Midway did not create the primacy of the aircraft carrier, the battle certainly confirmed what had gone before: Taranto, Pearl Harbor, and Coral Sea. American battleships fought two surface engagements during the Second World War—one at Guadalcanal, another in the Philippines—but carriers were engaged almost daily. So too were submarines, which played a major role in strangling Japan's war industry.

Though ballistic missile submarines remain part of America's strategic deterrent, as a fighting tool submarines have been almost irrelevant since 1945. The cruise missiles launched during Operation Desert Storm marked the first time that U.S. Navy submarines had "shot for record" in forty-six years. Undoubtedly submarines have performed covert missions, such as surveillance and special-operations transport, but carrier aviation remains America's geopolitical trump card. Korea, Vietnam, Desert Storm, and hundreds of lesser events have continued the pattern unbroken since Midway: when crisis looms, presidents still ask, "Where are the carriers?"

NOTES

1. Edward S. Miller, *War Plan Orange: The U.S. Strategy to Defeat Japan* (Annapolis, 1991), passim.

2. Samuel Eliot Morison, *The Two-Ocean War* (Boston, 1963), 334.

3. Pat Frank and J. D. Harrington, *Rendezvous at Midway* (New York, 1972), 34.

4. Roscoe Creed, *PBY: The Catalina Flying Boat* (Annapolis, 1986), 106.

5. Ibid., 107.

6. Robert Sherrod, *History of Marine Corps Aviation in World War II* (Washington, D.C., 1952), 57.

7. Marion E. Carl and Barrett Tillman, *Pushing the Envelope: The Career of Fighter Ace and Test Pilot Marion Carl* (Annapolis, 1994), 24.

8. Walter Lord, *Incredible Victory* (New York, 1967), 100–110.

9. Barrett Tillman, *TBF-TBM Avenger at War* (New York, 1980), 20–21.

10. Robert J. Cressman, et al., *"A Glorious Page in Our History": The Battle of Midway* (Missoula, Mont., 1990), 77.

11. Wilhelm G. Esders, "Torpedo Three and the Devastator," *The Hook* (August 1990): 35.

12. Lord, *Incredible Victory*, 164–66.

13. Richard S. Best, interview, October 1993.

14. Lord, *Incredible Victory*, 230–31.

15. Richard B. Frank, *Guadalcanal* (New York, 1990), 618.

14

The Naval Battle of Guadalcanal
The Battleship Night Action

PAUL STILLWELL

For the first five months of war, the Japanese offensive that broke over the Pacific in December 1941 had been a virtually complete success. Not only had Japanese forces secured their every objective, for the most part they had done so well ahead of schedule. But in mid-1942 their great offensive faltered. In May, an attempted advance deeper into the Southwest Pacific was checked at the Battle of the Coral Sea, and a month later a new thrust into the Central Pacific culminated in the disaster at Midway.

In the wider context of the war, U.S. strategy aimed primarily at aiding Great Britain and the Soviet Union in order to defeat Germany and liberate the rest of Europe. In the meantime, President Franklin D. Roosevelt and the Joint Chiefs of Staff intended to conduct a holding action in the Pacific so the bulk of the war resources could go to the European theater. The speed and overwhelming nature of the Japanese advance had been dramatic testimony to the weakness of the Allied effort in the Pacific in the opening of the conflict.

As the losses mounted in the war against Japan, two particularly strong-willed officers sought to change America's defensive stance. Gen. Douglas MacArthur had been evacuated from the Philippines to Australia, where he began spinning corncob pipe dreams about an offensive toward the Japanese stronghold at Rabaul on the island of New Britain. In Washington Adm. Ernest J. King was both Chief of Naval Operations and Commander in Chief of the U.S. Fleet. King chafed under the Europe-first restrictions. At the end of March 1942, he directed Adm. Chester Nimitz, Commander in Chief Pacific Fleet, to begin planning for a counteroffensive in the South Pacific.

Included in the objectives put forth by King were the occupation of the Santa Cruz Islands, Tulagi, Guadalcanal, and Florida islands in the Eastern

Solomons, and the reinforcement of Espiritu Santo in the New Hebrides. These islands would provide a springboard from which to launch a northward campaign toward Japanese-held territory. With no support from the rest of the joint chiefs, King moved ahead on his own, finally receiving acquiescence from Army Chief of Staff Gen. George Marshall. To avoid command squabbles in the Pacific, the two chiefs agreed to move the dividing line between the command areas of Nimitz and MacArthur to the west of the Solomons, thus ensuring that the capture of those islands would be a Navy–Marine Corps effort.[1]

Plans for the invasion of the Solomons were given a new sense of urgency in early July, just a month after Midway, when an Allied reconnaissance plane observed that the Japanese were beginning to build an airfield on the island of Guadalcanal. Perhaps more than anything else, the first six months of the Pacific War had demonstrated the new importance of air power in naval conflict. If the Japanese could operate planes from Guadalcanal, they could control the waters throughout the Solomons chain, which stretched northward toward the base at Rabaul.

The Americans invaded Guadalcanal and nearby Tulagi on 7 August. In the initial landings, the marines on Tulagi ran into greater opposition than those at Guadalcanal. Resistance was light on the latter so the marines were able to capture the still-unfinished airfield easily. In the long run, though, Guadalcanal proved to be a difficult prize to hold. Because of the island's strategic importance, the Japanese fought tenaciously in their efforts to retake it. Indeed, for the next six months Allied and Japanese forces waged a bitter contest—on the ground, on the sea, and in the air—for the prize.

An early indication of the importance the Japanese gave to recapturing the airstrip came on the night of 8–9 August. Late on the day of the invasion, Vice Adm. Gunichi Mikawa formed a task force of seven cruisers and one destroyer to steam from Rabaul in order to disrupt the Allied occupation of Guadalcanal. Although the Japanese ships were spotted by Allied aircraft, the warnings went unheeded by the inexperienced American forces then in process of unloading transports to supply the marines ashore. The Japanese chose to make their approach at night because they had practiced night tactics, and because they would be unmolested by the Americans' daylight-only aviation forces. The result, which came to be known as the Battle of Savo Island, was a slaughter and an embarrassment for the Americans. At no cost to itself, Mikawa's force sank four heavy cruisers: the U.S. *Astoria, Vincennes,* and *Quincy,* and the Australian *Canberra.* Fortuitously Mikawa did not follow up on his advantage, and the transports remained unharmed.

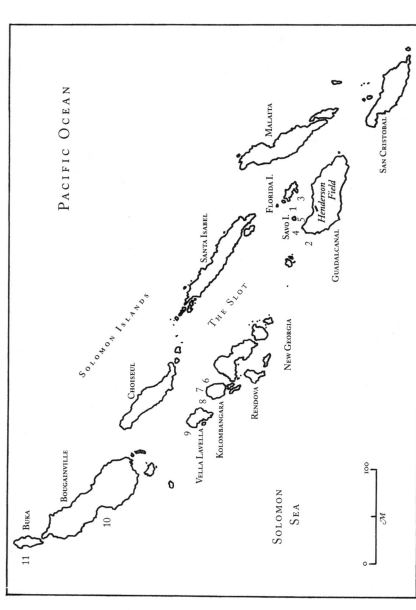

Sea battles in the Solomons: (1) Savo Island, 8–9 August 1942. (2) Cape Esperance, 12 October 1942. (3) The Naval Battle of Guadalcanal: The Cruiser Night Action, 12–13 November 1942, and (4) The Battleship Night Action, 14–15 November 1942. (5) Tassafaronga, 30 November 1942. (6) Kula Gulf, 6 July 1943. (7) Kolombangara, 13 July 1943. (8) Vella Gulf, 6–7 August 1943. (9) Vella Lavella, 6–7 October 1943. (10) Empress Augusta Bay, 2 November 1943. (11) Cape St. George, 25 November 1943.

As the struggle continued through the following weeks, a number of patterns developed. Ashore, the marines distinguished themselves in fierce fighting against Japanese troops. Their efforts were all the more remarkable in that they suffered from jungle disease and had to endure shortages of weapons, supplies, and food. The Japanese frequently sent air attacks against Guadalcanal and nearby ships. Allied coast watchers provided a valuable service in sending advance warning by radio when Japanese air raids were en route. That enabled the plucky pilots of Navy and Marine F4F Wildcat fighters to get airborne and achieve an altitude advantage from which to attack incoming raids. The pilots and ground crews slept in tents and often had to repair to slit trenches for protection against attacks.

Later in the war, the U.S. Navy forged a highly effective team from carrier planes and amphibious assault forces. In late 1942, however, the navy was still in a groping-and-learning stage as it sought the best means to use aircraft carriers in support of a campaign ashore. The learning was an expensive process, and the carriers became an increasingly scarce resource, particularly after the loss of the *Lexington* at Coral Sea and *Yorktown* at Midway. The fleet carriers of the time were all holdovers from the prewar period; it would be another year before the war-built carriers started emerging in strength.

The first big carrier encounter after the invasion of Guadalcanal was the Battle of the Eastern Solomons on 24 August. The *Enterprise* suffered three bomb hits and had to withdraw for repairs. On 31 August a Japanese submarine torpedoed the old *Saratoga* and put her out of action as well. On 15 September, another submarine torpedoed the *Wasp*, which had to be sunk by American torpedoes to keep her from falling into enemy hands. On 26 October, at the Battle of Santa Cruz Islands, Japanese aerial bombing inflicted fatal blows on the *Hornet*. By then the *Enterprise* had been repaired and returned to action. She was again damaged at Santa Cruz; for a time there was no operational U.S. aircraft carrier in the theater.

The Japanese were also employing naval surface forces in their effort to retake the vital airfield, which had been named Henderson Field in honor of a marine aviator killed in the Battle of Midway. Imperial Navy task groups appeared off Guadalcanal so frequently that the marines dubbed them the "Tokyo Express." The Americans, with their mastery of the air, controlled the area by day. Unable to fly after dark, they often ceded the sea space at night to Japanese ships, which steamed south down the Solomons chain; landed reinforcements and supplies; bombarded the marine positions; and then escaped northward under cover of darkness.

The Americans at times attempted to counter these nocturnal incursions.

Their first notable success occurred on the night of 11–12 October in the Battle of Cape Esperance, which took its name from the point of land at the northwest "corner" of Guadalcanal. The Japanese forces included a bombardment group and a transport group ordered to land men and material on the island. Facing them was Task Force (TF) 64, comprised of two heavy cruisers, two light cruisers, and five destroyers. The commander was Rear Adm. Norman Scott in the heavy cruiser *San Francisco*. The Americans were still not polished in night fighting but did have the advantage of surface-search radar, notably the new SG type on board the light cruiser *Helena*. Thanks to the initiative of her skipper, Capt. Gilbert Hoover, the *Helena* got off the first shots at her unsuspecting enemies. The ensuing clash included the classic maneuver in which the Americans capped the Japanese T. Though the destroyer *Duncan* was sunk in the action, the Japanese fared worse. The heavy cruiser *Furutaka* and destroyer *Fubuki* were lost, and the cruiser *Aoba* badly damaged. A few nights later, however, the Japanese succeeded in landing more than four thousand troops.

In overall command of the U.S. Navy–Marine Corps effort during these early months of the Guadalcanal campaign was Vice Adm. Robert Ghormley, Commander South Pacific Force. He had headquarters in Nouméa, New Caledonia, where he was isolated physically from the action and, to a degree, psychologically as well. He had been hesitant about executing Admiral King's order for an offensive in the Solomons, and the grinding weeks of combat had not improved his frame of mind. His pessimism was reinforced by shortages of food, fuel, ammunition, ships, planes, and other naval and military requirements. The Guadalcanal operation acquired the sardonic nickname of "Operation Shoestring." Further adding to Ghormley's miseries were painfully infected teeth. Believing that Ghormley projected an air of defeatism to his forces, Admiral Nimitz reluctantly decided in mid-October to relieve the commander who had not been able to turn the offensive into victory. In his place came the aggressive, inspiring Vice Adm. William F. Halsey, a carrier admiral who did much in the ensuing weeks to energize American forces.

In mid-November, the Japanese, under Vice Adm. Nobutake Kondo, set out to reinforce Guadalcanal still further. On 12 November eleven transports, filled with eleven thousand Japanese soldiers, set out for Guadalcanal. They headed south down "the Slot," the name given to the ocean passageway between the two chains of islands comprising the Solomons. Accompanying the transports was a heavy bombardment force. Commanded by Vice Adm. Hiroaki Abe, the formation included the battleships *Hiei* and *Kirishima*, cruiser *Nagara*, and eleven destroyers. They would cover the approach of the transports and also deliver a heavy-duty pounding to the dug-in Americans on Guadalcanal.

To interfere with the intended night work of the Japanese, Rear Adm. Kelly Turner sent a surface force of five cruisers and eight destroyers. In command was Rear Adm. Daniel J. Callaghan in the *San Francisco.* Ahead of the flagship in the column formation was the light cruiser *Atlanta;* embarked in her was Rear Admiral Scott, victor at Cape Esperance a month earlier. The battle was joined early on the morning of Friday the thirteenth. It was the last day of life for both American admirals. In the changing ways of a war then less than a year old, air power had already made a dramatic impact. Radar would also have an important effect, but it took flag officers longer to grasp the significance of this new electronic tool. At the time of his fatal battle, Admiral Callaghan had an incomplete appreciation of its value and uses.

Three of the thirteen ships in the formation were equipped with the newest type of SG surface-search radar. Its PPI scope provided a maplike picture, in which it appeared as if an aerial observer were looking down on the scene. Individual ships showed up as glowing "blips." The less sophisticated scopes in other ships merely showed blips on a horizontal electronic line that extended in the direction of the antenna at a given moment. The *Helena,* whose SG set had contributed significantly to the victory at Cape Esperance, was buried in the center of the long U.S. column. The brand-new destroyer *Fletcher* was also equipped with the SG; she was the thirteenth and last in the line of ships. Both could have been better placed in the column to give early warning, as could the SG-equipped destroyer *O'Bannon.* Moreover Admirals Callaghan and Scott would have done better to be on board SG-equipped ships.

The battle itself was a concoction of searchlights, confusing orders, inadequate communication among U.S. ships, jumbled formations on both sides, rapid course changes, torpedoes in the water, and major-caliber gunfire at point-blank range. During the course of the melee, the *San Francisco* mistakenly sent two salvos of 8-inch shells screaming into the *Atlanta.* They set the light cruiser afire and killed Admiral Scott and most of his staff. Soon afterward gunfire from the Japanese battleship *Hiei* found the mark on the *San Francisco's* bridge, killing Admiral Callaghan and fatally wounding her skipper, Capt. Cassin Young.

The U.S. ships dished out so much gunfire that they dissuaded Admiral Abe from conducting his planned bombardment of Henderson Field. But the price was high. Lost as a result of the engagement were the destroyers *Barton,* *Monssen,* *Laffey,* and *Cushing,* and the cruiser *Atlanta.* The cruiser *Juneau* was torpedoed and sank the following day with the loss of nearly her entire crew, including five brothers of the Sullivan family. The Japanese lost the destroyers *Akatsuki* and *Yudachi* during the battle. The battleship *Hiei* took such a beating that she was essentially immobile at dawn on 13 November. American dive-bombers and torpedo planes made a series of attacks that eventually put her beyond salvage. The Japanese crew scuttled her and abandoned ship.[2]

The stakes at Guadalcanal were so high and the fighting so desperate that Admiral Halsey was about to add one more ingredient to the South Pacific stew—fast battleships. During the first part of the war, the navy's newest battleships, commissioned in 1941, had operated in the Atlantic, in part as a force in readiness to aid the British in the event of a breakout by German capital ships. In the summer of 1942 that changed in recognition of the ascendancy of aircraft carriers. In the Battle of the Eastern Solomons in late August, the *North Carolina* was in the screen of the *Enterprise*. In mid-September, the *North Carolina* was escorting the *Wasp* when a spread of torpedoes hit both them and the destroyer *O'Brien*. The *North Carolina* steamed away for repairs that put her out of action until 1943.

In August 1942, the recently commissioned *South Dakota* left Philadelphia for the far Pacific. Shortly before her departure, she received the first occupant in her flag quarters. He was Rear Adm. Willis A. Lee Jr., who had become Commander Battleship Division Six through unusual circumstances. His predecessor, Rear Adm. John W. Wilcox, had disappeared in March from the *North Carolina*'s sister ship, the *Washington,* which was then en route to the British Isles. No convincing evidence has ever been found to indicate whether he jumped overboard, fell accidentally, or perhaps was the victim of foul play. Whatever the reason, the billet was open when Admiral Lee came to the end of a long shore tour in Washington, D.C., and prepared to embark on his first shipboard assignment of the war.

Born in the village of Natlee, Kentucky, on 11 May 1888, Willis Lee was the son of a local judge. For years the boy was known as Mose, because his mother had been fishing in a nearby stream shortly before his birth. That conjured up visions of the biblical Moses and bulrushes, thus leading to the nickname.[3] Young Lee grew up in Owenton, the seat of government in Owen County, a rural area in the rolling terrain of north central Kentucky.

Even as a youngster, Lee displayed the sense of humor that caused many who knew him to observe that he frequently had a twinkle in his eye. In school, for example, he once came to class with a sack of Bull Durham tobacco in his shirt pocket. The teacher saw the drawstring dangling from the pocket, confiscated the tobacco, and threw it into the schoolroom stove. The next day Lee came back with another sack and another drawstring. When the teacher also took this sack and threw it into the stove, it exploded, for Lee had puckishly loaded this sack with gunpowder.[4] One lasting result of Lee's youth was chronically poor eyesight that resulted from a botched experiment with gunpowder and a tin can.

Only twenty years old when he graduated from the Naval Academy in 1908, Lee stood 106th in a class of 201. Though possessed of a brilliant mind, particularly apt in mathematics, he manifested during his academy years what would be a lifelong trait: he applied himself only to things that interested him. One was marksmanship; in 1907 he became the only person ever to win both the national rifle and pistol championships in the same year.

Lee early developed a fondness for China, growing in part from his service in the U.S. Asiatic Fleet gunboat *Helena*, 1910–13. Throughout his career he was known widely in the navy as "Ching" or "Chink." As a member of the battleship *New Hampshire*'s landing party, he went ashore during the U.S. landing at Veracruz, Mexico, in 1914. He spent World War I as a naval ordnance inspector in Illinois and didn't reach Europe until shortly after the close of hostilities. In 1920 as a member of the U.S. rifle team at the Olympic Games in Antwerp, Belgium, he was awarded five gold medals, one silver, and one bronze for his participation in events won by the U.S. team.

Throughout the 1920s, Lee mostly alternated between rifle team duty and command of destroyers. As a destroyer skipper, he was skillful at shiphandling and gunnery but devoted little attention to administrative matters or the appearance of his ships. His inveterate interest in mechanical devices manifested itself in an invention for the wardroom of the four-stack destroyer *William B. Preston*, which he commanded on the China Station. The ship was plagued by rats that, among other things, scurried along the I-beams near the wardroom's overhead. Lee rigged up a remotely controlled electric guillotine. The game among Lee and his officers was to close the solenoid-operated switch at just the right moment to decapitate a rat.

Lee's shore duty during the 1930s comprised three separate tours in Washington as a member of the Division of Fleet Training, on the extended staff of the Chief of Naval Operations. His specialties were gunnery and tactics. The division's mission was the administration of competitive exercises as a means of promoting readiness and training among the ships of the fleet. Though Lee had a good deal of knowledge of gunnery, he was considered even more valuable in tactical development—thus the assignments to Fleet Training.

From 1931 to 1933, Lee was navigator, then executive officer, of the U.S. Fleet flagship *Pennsylvania*. After another tour in Washington, Captain Lee commanded the light cruiser *Concord* from 1936 to 1938. Since Lee and his wife, Mabelle, were childless, he often took a fatherly interest in the enlisted men and junior officers of his crews. He was inclined to be lenient when administering discipline. Shipmates remember the *Concord* as a happy ship, and they remember as well the skipper's consuming professional interests. For instance, when Lee was in his shipboard cabin on Sundays, the large morning paper often lay unread because he was working out calculations to improve the fleet's woeful anti-aircraft capability.

Lee's professional competence and unflappable demeanor attracted the attention of Rear Adm. Harold R. Stark, who had his cruiser division flag in the *Concord*. After being relieved as commanding officer, Lee joined Stark's staff. When Stark was chosen Chief of Naval Operations in 1939, Lee accompanied him to Washington as assistant director of the Division of Fleet Training. Lee became director of the division in early 1941, by which time it was actively preparing the fleet for war. Shortly after the attack on Pearl Harbor, he was appointed head of the Readiness Division on Admiral King's U.S. Fleet staff. Major concerns during the period were equipping as many warships as possible with radar and anti-aircraft guns. Lee was promoted to rear admiral early in 1942, a few months before taking command of Battleship Division Six. He thus became the first officer to command a division of the new, 35,000-ton fast battleships in the South Pacific.

Willis Lee was a quiet man with a keenly analytical mind and the capacity for working long hours. He read voraciously and had an intense curiosity about what made mechanical devices work. For instance, when an officer messenger brought to the South Pacific a sample of the radio proximity fuze for 5-inch antiaircraft projectiles, Lee sent for a hacksaw. He wanted the fuze cut open so he could see the innards.[5] Gunnery was a lifelong interest for Lee; even as a senior officer wearing thick-lensed glasses, he enjoyed practicing small-arms marksmanship.

An officer who avoided ceremony and the spit-and-polish style of a number of admirals, Lee was casual, even sloppy, in his personal appearance. He had an unpretentious give-and-take manner with juniors, dealing man-to-man rather than standing on superior rank. In issuing reprimands and teaching lessons, he was gentle rather than harsh. Lee had something of a paunch, smoked steadily, and slept little. He had a fascination with the electronic images that appeared on radar scopes, sometimes sitting alongside and watching for hours at a time. On occasion during these vigils, Lee dozed off, still holding a burning cigarette between his fingers. Someone on watch with him then gently removed the smoldering cigarette with its lengthening cylinder of gray ash.[6]

Willis A. ("Ching") Lee, shown following his promotion to vice admiral in March 1944. *Courtesy Mr. Donald Siders*

At the outset of their employment in the Pacific, the fast battleships seemed snakebit. On 4 September, with Lee on board, the *South Dakota* arrived at her first South Pacific destination, Tongatabu in the Tonga Islands. Two days later, as she was undergoing training to form a division with the *North Carolina*, the *South Dakota* struck an uncharted underwater pinnacle and suffered considerable damage to her hull. She left for Pearl Harbor and repairs on 12 September. Two days later the *Washington* arrived at Tongatabu, and Lee moved aboard with his small staff. The next day the *North Carolina* was torpedoed and put out of action.

Not until the *South Dakota*'s return in late October did the U.S. Navy have two fast battleships in the region. The damage to the *South Dakota* had been a disguised blessing. While at Pearl Harbor, her anti-aircraft capability had been improved considerably by the installation of 40mm guns. She used those and her 5-inch secondary battery to good advantage in shooting down a number of Japanese aircraft while protecting the *Enterprise* at Santa Cruz on 26 October. In that battle she was hit atop turret one by a bomb; flying fragments nearly killed the *South Dakota*'s skipper, Capt. Thomas Gatch.

Although the Japanese had been deterred from their planned bombardment on the night of 12–13 November, the Tokyo Express ran again the following night. Halsey directed TF 64 to be formed with Lee's battleships and an escort of four destroyers. Detached from a carrier task force commanded by Rear Adm. Thomas Kinkaid in the *Enterprise,* they were to rush north to Guadalcanal and try to prevent a bombardment. But Halsey's message didn't get out soon enough for Lee's ships to reach Guadalcanal in time. Thus, on the night of 13 November, no U.S. ships opposed the Japanese, who sent three heavy cruisers with a strong screen to wreak havoc on Henderson Field.

A reinforcement group—eleven transports escorted by eleven destroyers—had set out for Guadalcanal under the command of Rear Adm. Raizo Tanaka late that afternoon. The next morning planes from the *Enterprise* were aloft to take them on. They destroyed seven of the transports, but the indomitable Tanaka pressed ahead. The Japanese also persevered in their plan to bombard Henderson Field, and that same morning Vice Admiral Kondo headed south toward Guadalcanal with an emergency force consisting of a battleship, two heavy cruisers, two light cruisers, and nine destroyers.

Opposing them would be Lee's TF 64, which was strictly an ad hoc organization. Its use was a measure of American desperation in the continuing effort to stave off Japanese thrusts toward the island. The waters around Savo Island were really too narrow to risk battleships, but Admiral Halsey had little else. The ships had not had an opportunity to work and train together; they just happened to be the ones available. Lee had no chance to put out a formal operation order; instead, he sent out directions by visual signal.[7]

As he had for the previous two months, Lee flew his flag in the *Washington.* The other heavy gun ship in the task force was Gatch's *South Dakota.* The latter still bore scars from the bomb hit she had taken on 26 October. In fact only seven of her nine 16-inch guns would be available for the coming action. Fragments from the bomb that hit turret one had damaged two guns of turret two.[8] The escort ships did not make up a destroyer division experienced at operating together. It just happened that the destroyers of TF 64 were the four in the *Enterprise* screen that had the most fuel on board. There was no embarked destroyer division or squadron commander to coordinate their actions.[9]

TABLE 14.1 The Naval Battle of Guadalcanal: The Battleship Night Action, 14–15 November 1942

	Battleship	Heavy Cruiser	Light Cruiser	Destroyer
U.S. NAVY				
Task Force 64				
Rear Adm. W. A. Lee	2	—	—	4
IMPERIAL JAPANESE NAVY				
Bombardment Unit				
Rear Adm. N. Kondo	1	2	1	6
Sweeping Unit				
Rear Adm. S. Hashimoto	—	—	1	3
Late reinforcements	—	—	—	2 [a]
TOTAL OF JAPANESE FORCES	1	2	2	11

[a] Detached from Rear Adm. Raizo Tanaka's escort force

TABLE 14.2 The Naval Battle of Guadalcanal: Armament Comparisons

	16 in.	14 in.	8 in.	6 in.	5.5 and 5 in.	3.9 in.	TT
Task Force 64	18	—	—	—	59	—	46
Japanese forces	—	8	20	14	95	8	139

Notes: Excludes guns smaller than 40mm; TT = torpedo tubes

Lee's attempts to obtain recent reports on the Japanese provided another symptom of the makeshift nature of his venture that night. He didn't have a voice radio call sign to use when calling the forces on Guadalcanal. Thus, he used plain language: "Cactus, this is Lee. Tell your big boss Ching Lee is here and wants the latest information." Before the boss, Maj. Gen. Archer Vandegrift, could be summoned, the radio receivers on the *Washington's* bridge were alive with discussions among the crews of American PT boats, speculating on the identity of Lee's ships.

Rather than risk the danger that the PTs would confuse his force with that of the enemy, Lee put out another radio transmission. The wording was later reconstructed by historian Samuel Eliot Morison, who visited the *Washington* a few weeks after the battle. As Morison had it, Lee said, "Refer your big boss about Ching Lee; Chinese, catchee? Call off your boys!" The PTs said they knew who Lee was, and then the marine headquarters on Guadalcanal reported that it had no update on the Japanese.[10]

The U.S. ships formed a column in the order: *Walke, Benham, Preston, Gwin, Washington,* and *South Dakota.* They traced a boxlike series of courses around Savo Island—heading initially northeast, then east, then southeast. Meanwhile, the Japanese were approaching the island from the north. Kondo's bombardment unit comprised the battleship *Kirishima*, heavy cruisers *Atago* and *Takao*, the light cruiser *Nagara,* and six destroyers. A distant screen commanded by Rear Adm. Shintaro Hashimoto was made up of the light cruiser *Sendai* and three destroyers. Kondo intended to synchronize his bombardment of Henderson Field with the arrival of Tanaka's transports.

As they neared Guadalcanal, the Japanese put the night vision ability of their lookouts to use. At 2310 men in the *Sendai* spotted the U.S. warships but misidentified them as two cruisers and four destroyers.[11] It was an understandable mistake in view of the American use of cruisers to counter previous runnings of the Tokyo Express. Hashimoto thereupon decided to investigate both sides of Savo, sending two destroyers to the west of the island and taking his flagship and remaining destroyer to the east. Kondo also divided his force, detaching the *Nagara* and four destroyers under Rear Adm. Masanori Kimura to make a sweep south of Savo while his main body lay in wait to the west.

Still unaware that they had company, the U.S. ships completed their southeasterly leg. At 2352, as the moon was setting, they turned to head westward. This would complete the clockwise circumnavigation of Savo and take them between that island and Guadalcanal. The *Washington*'s radar and then her optical range finders picked up the easternmost Japanese ships around midnight and began tracking them. At 0015 the *Washington* opened up with her 16-inch rifles at the light cruiser *Sendai.* The *South Dakota* followed moments afterward. This was the first time an American battleship had fired her main battery in anger during the Pacific War.

Radar was still such a novelty that the *Washington*'s only screen for the SG was in a compartment on the flag bridge level. There were no repeaters elsewhere in the ship. After using the radar to familiarize himself with the tactical situation of divergent Japanese forces, Admiral Lee had gone to the navigation bridge so he could see the battle visually. Thereafter he had to rely on oral reports of radar data, a condition he found less than completely satisfactory. During the engagement, he stood on the starboard wing of the bridge with Capt. Glenn Davis, the flagship skipper; Lt. Ray Thompson, flag lieutenant; and Lt. (j.g.) Al Church, radar officer. When the opening salvo burst forth from the 16-inch guns, the concussion was so intense that it ripped Lee's thick glasses from his head. He was helpless without them, and he and Church groped on the deck until Lee found his glasses in the darkness.[12]

Forward of the *Washington,* on board the destroyer *Preston,* Ensign Bob Reed had an excellent vantage point for the battle. He had brought along a movie camera, so the destroyer's skipper had relieved him from his normal

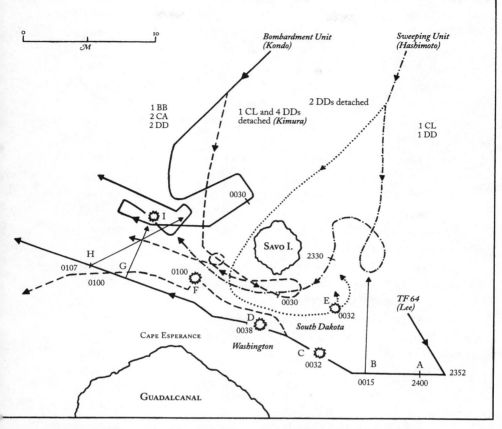

The Naval Battle of Guadalcanal: The Battleship Night Action, 14–15 November 1942. U.S. radar detects the Japanese Sweeping Unit (A) and the U.S. battleships open fire (B). In less than ten minutes, all four U.S. destroyers are disabled (C–D); the *Preston* and *Walke* sink at 0036 and 0043, respectively, and the *Benham* and *Gwin* retire to the west. The Japanese destroyer *Ayanami*, hit at 0032 (E), sinks shortly thereafter. To the west, the *South Dakota* is heavily damaged in action with the Japanese Bombardment Unit (F) and the *Kirishima* is taken under fire by both the *Washington* (G–H) and *South Dakota*. Shattered in this exchange, the Japanese battleship is scuttled at 0425 (I). The track of the Japanese late reinforcement, which did not affect the course of the battle, is not shown.

battle station in the engine room and put him on deck to photograph the action. Reed was facing aft as the *Washington* and *South Dakota* fired their 16-inch guns. He saw the blinding flash of yellow-orange flame as the guns erupted. Then he watched with fascination as the after ends of the shells traced cherry-red arcs through the night sky. He saw the projectiles head into low-hanging clouds, disappear for a time, and then emerge at the downward end of their trajectories.[13] His observation was consistent with that of Lieutenant Church, who described that night's battle as being "like a red snowball fight."

Up ahead, the U.S. and Japanese destroyers were spewing out smokescreens and 5-inch shells. The Japanese were firing both guns and torpedoes. The U.S. battleships also used their 5-inch secondary batteries in successful attempts to shoot out Japanese searchlights. Without fire control radar, the Japanese had to depend on optical range finders so it was important to have their targets illuminated. It was just as important for the Americans to prevent that illumination.

The four destroyers took a fearful pounding.[14] Within five minutes after the Japanese started shooting at her at 0022, the *Preston's* superstructure was on fire, providing a bright beacon of flame that Japanese gunners could range on. They fired at virtually point-blank range; by 0036 she was sinking. At 0032 Japanese heavy shells, probably from the cruiser *Nagara,* ripped into the van destroyer *Walke.* Shortly afterward a torpedo exploded against her side, practically tearing off her forecastle all the way back to the bridge. When her fantail sank at 0043, the depth charges there exploded underwater and killed a number of the men who abandoned the ship and—until then—survived her.

The *Benham,* which had been second in the column, caught a torpedo at 0038. With her bow badly damaged, she limped toward the *Preston* and *Walke* with the intention of rescuing the men in the water. Japanese shells continued to rain down around the stricken vessels, however, and the *Benham's* skipper steamed away in an attempt to save his own ship, which was experiencing progressive flooding from the bow. Admiral Lee then ordered the *Benham* out of the battle. Later, accompanied by the *Gwin,* which had also been hit, the *Benham* was directed to proceed to Espiritu Santo and safety. She never made it, finally breaking up and sinking off the south coast of Guadalcanal on the midafternoon of the following day. Of the four American destroyers that entered the battle, only the *Gwin* survived to make a contribution to the classic gun duel between the Japanese and American dreadnoughts. On the Japanese side, the destroyer *Ayanami* had been fatally wounded by gunfire at 0032; she sank eight minutes later.

While the U.S. destroyers were running the gauntlet of gunfire and torpedoes, the U.S. battleships continued their westward march. With so many enemy ships swarming around, the U.S. radar screens were pockmarked with blips. The Japanese had less cause for confusion because the American ships were grouped together. Then at 0033, the electrical circuit breakers on board the *South Dakota* tripped out. The malfunction deprived her of lights, communications, and of the electronic sensors that her officers had come to rely on.

As the battleships reached the burning *Preston* and *Walke* at 0035, the *Washington*'s conning officer, Lt. Ray Hunter, ordered a course change to port to avoid them. The *South Dakota*, blind without electrical power, turned to starboard to avoid the damaged *Benham*. She regained her electricity at 0036, but the turn to starboard had put her between the flaming wrecks and the Japanese guns. The U.S. battleship's silhouette was distinctly outlined for the Japanese range finders. Moreover, with her radar picture incomplete, she was steaming toward the Japanese ships, which illuminated her with their searchlights. They launched thirty-four torpedoes at the *South Dakota*; all missed. She was not so fortunate when the Japanese gunners proceeded to shower her with major-caliber shells.

During the trip past the shattered destroyers, the *Washington*'s fire control team had been tracking a large Japanese ship on its narrow-beam fire control radar. Down in main battery plot, Lt. Cdr. Ed Hooper called the bridge and urged Admiral Lee to open fire on the looming target off the starboard beam. However, because of the position of the SG radar antenna on the front of the *Washington*'s foremast, there was a blind spot that extended about 30 degrees in either direction from directly astern. Concerned that Hooper might be tracking the *South Dakota*, which was on the flagship's starboard quarter, and unable to distinguish the target visually in darkness, Lee ordered the *Washington* to hold her fire. After the battle, Hooper had a chance to compare models of the *South Dakota* and *Kirishima*; from some angles they were so similar that he concluded that Lee had made the right decision.[15] Only two nights earlier, Admiral Scott in the *Atlanta* had succumbed to a lethal dose of "friendly fire." Lee didn't want to repeat the mistake.

Once the *South Dakota* was illuminated by the destroyer pyres and Japanese searchlights, of course, all doubt as to her identity vanished. At 0100 Lee gave Hooper his head, and the *Washington* began sending off salvos of both 16-inch and 5-inch shells toward the *Kirishima*. The American ship's 16-inch/45-caliber guns had a maximum range of about 37,000 yards when firing armor-piercing projectiles at an elevation of 45 degrees. The Japanese battleship was only 8,400 yards away when the *Washington* took her under fire; the gun bar-

"U.S. Battleship *Washington* in Night Battle, Guadalcanal," by Cdr. Dwight D. Shepler, USNR, a navy war artist. *Official U.S. Navy photograph*

rels were almost horizontal. The Japanese hammered away at the *South Dakota,* perforating her superstructure with shell fire from 14-inch to 5-inch and jamming her after turret in train.

The *Washington* was not illuminated and not hit. Her gunnery struck the *Kirishima* with nine of seventy-five 16-inch projectiles and about forty of the 5-inch. After she had absorbed considerable punishment, the Japanese ship began steaming in circles, her steering gear out of action. Flames leapt up in her superstructure. The two U.S. battleships also inflicted damage on the heavy cruisers *Takao* and *Atago.* In the early hours of the following morning, Sunday, 15 November, fires continued to ravage the battered *Kirishima.* Her crew flooded magazines to prevent their explosion, and the big ship listed farther to starboard as more water entered her damaged hull. Finally the Japanese conceded defeat, removed the emperor's portrait, and abandoned ship. The *Kirishima* sank northwest of Savo Island at 0425.[16] The Imperial Japanese Navy had lost no battleships at all prior to the night action against Admiral Callaghan's force. Now the Americans had sunk two of them in two days.

Of the six U.S. warships in the fight, only the *Washington* remained unscathed. She steamed to the west, toward the Russell Islands, hoping to draw the enemy away from her damaged cohorts. The Japanese ships did indeed head in her direction, but Admiral Kondo decided not to risk further salvos and called off the chase after about fifteen minutes. Two destroyers

Admiral Tanaka had sent ahead from his escort force did likewise after firing torpedoes at the *Washington* at 0139. The battleship's lookouts saw them coming in time for her to get out of their way.

Her radios and radars disrupted by the beating she had taken, the *South Dakota* was unable to communicate with Lee. Instead she left for a pre-arranged rendezvous; the two battleships met up at 1000 the following morning. The *South Dakota* had received forty-two large-caliber hits. When Ens. Paul Backus, turret officer in turret two, went out to survey the scene, he found two half-moon cutouts on the coaming surrounding a topside hatch. Both were fourteen inches in diameter, and both were the same height off the deck. The flatness of the *Kirishima*'s projectiles provided vivid evidence of the close range at which the battle was fought.[17]

Of the *South Dakota*'s crew, thirty-nine men were killed and another fifty-nine wounded. During the night, some of the able-bodied had gone into the damaged fire control tower, groping in the darkness for wounded among the corpses and parts of bodies. A boatswain's mate who was in the working party suffered from nightmares for several years afterward. He was cured only when hypnosis revealed the cause of the torment inflicted by his subconscious as a result of that terrible night.[18]

In the months immediately after the battle, a number of the *South Dakota*'s men harbored ill will toward the crew of the *Washington*. Instead of viewing Lee's withdrawal as a feint to protect the rest of the force, the *South Dakota* crew believed they had been abandoned. Gradually wiser council prevailed.

Remarkably, the number of deaths on both sides was almost identical: 242 for the Americans and about 250 for the Japanese.[19] Even though three of its six ships were sunk and two others damaged and Tanaka succeeded in landing his transports, TF 64 was the winner on the night of 14–15 November 1942. Lee's command had staved off the planned bombardment of Henderson Field and demonstrated American resolve to hold the line on Guadalcanal. Part of that resolve was indicated by Admiral Halsey's willingness to commit battleships in an environment for which they were not well suited. As Lee put it in his after-action report, "Our battleships are neither designed nor armed for close range night actions with enemy light forces. A few minutes intense fire, at short range, from secondary battery guns can, and did, render one of our newest battleships deaf, dumb, blind, and impotent through destruction of radar, radio, and fire control circuits."[20]

There would be one more, anticlimactic cruiser action, off Tassafaronga, on the night of 30 November–1 December. In that one the heavy cruiser *Northampton* was sunk, and the heavy cruisers *Minneapolis* and *New Orleans* lost their bows. But the victory had essentially been achieved two weeks earlier when Lee's force routed the bombardment group under Admiral Kondo. On 12 December the Japanese Navy, unable to support the attrition to which it was being subjected, advised abandoning Guadalcanal, and at year's end Imperial General Headquarters concurred. The Tokyo Express adroitly extracted the surviving defenders in February 1943.

The night battle of 14–15 November was the only engagement of the entire war in which U.S. fast battleships fought against an enemy battleship at sea. The fast battleships had been designed and built with just this purpose in mind—to fire their big guns against the enemy's biggest and best-armed ships. Prewar doctrine and war planning had envisioned a great fleet action in the open seas with one battle line confronting the other somewhere around the Marshall Islands or the Philippines. The Japanese and American war plans were almost mirror images of each other, but in both cases the mirrors were cloudy. The great gunnery action never took place.

Necessity had dictated that the battleships be used almost in the fashion of cruisers and destroyers during the close-in fighting around Guadalcanal. As the Japanese conceded the loss of the island, they no longer sent their big ships into those troubled waters, nor did the Americans have to send theirs to stop them. In the ensuing months, the campaign for the Solomons moved north. The Americans invaded more islands, and the Japanese again came out to contest them with the guns and torpedoes of their night-capable ships. The main American naval weapons in the fighting at such places as Kula Gulf, Vella Gulf, Rendova, Kolombangara, Cape St. George, and Empress Augusta Bay were light cruisers and the new destroyers of the *Fletcher* class.

Meanwhile, the fast battleships spent part of the year 1943 in less frantic activities than those of late 1942. The *North Carolina, Washington, Indiana,* and *Massachusetts* escorted convoys and supported carriers. The *Alabama* and *South Dakota* were dispatched to the Atlantic to aid the British. The *Iowa* and *New Jersey* stood watch on the East Coast against a possible outbreak by the German *Tirpitz*. All went through various stages of training and waiting for the action to come. When it did come—with the Central Pacific offensive that began in late 1943—the fast battleships had been cemented into the role that developed from the autumn of 1942 onward. They had become basically anti-aircraft cruisers and well-armed replenishment oilers to accompany the fast carrier task groups. Occasionally they took stints at shore bombardment, but—studded with dozens of anti-aircraft guns apiece—they spent most of their time steaming in the carrier screens.

Willis Lee was elevated to vice admiral in the spring of 1944. Administratively he was Commander Battleships Pacific Fleet, but he no longer had an independent operational role. His main job was riding in a carrier task group and remaining ready in the event the Japanese surface fleet ventured out to do battle. It did so in June 1944 when the Americans invaded the Marianas. Lee was offered the opportunity for a night surface engagement. He declined, in part because he hadn't had a chance to exercise his ships together and in part because the Japanese were heading away from the Saipan beachhead and didn't constitute a strategic threat.

In October of that year, during the invasion of Leyte in the Philippines, Lee was deprived of the chance to fight a surface action. Adm. William Halsey, Commander Third Fleet, insisted in taking Lee's battleships north—as part of the fast carrier task force—when chasing after a force of largely empty Japanese carriers intended as a decoy. Lee felt considerable frustration at not being able to use his capable new ships for the purpose intended. Halsey's maneuver left San Bernardino Strait unguarded. Had Lee and at least some of his battleships been left behind, they would have been in the enviable position of crossing the enemy's T as the Japanese emerged from the mouth of the strait on 25 October 1944.

In early 1945, as the fast carriers began striking the Japanese home islands and supporting the invasion of Iwo Jima and Okinawa, Lee's battleships were still on a short leash. By then they had opportunities to practice surface tactics together, but by then the Japanese surface fleet was no longer a factor. In late June of that year, because of his considerable analytical capability Lee was dispatched to Casco Bay, Maine. His temporary new job was to devise weapons and procedures to defeat the Japanese kamikazes, suicide planes that were inflicting great damage on the U.S. fleet. They were expected to be even more troublesome in the planned invasion of the Japanese home islands that autumn. Lee was scheduled to return to the western Pacific to take part in that invasion in late 1945. In early August, his wife Mabelle wrote to her sisters about her husband: "He is anxious to get back to his battleships—you'd think they were his toys and [he's] afraid someone will damage them while he's away."[21]

That return trip never came to pass. On 14 August, Lee learned that Japan had surrendered. The great Pacific War had come to a successful conclusion, and he wasn't there to see its end. Mary Aertsen, wife of Lee's long-time flag lieutenant Gil Aertsen, observed that Lee seemed depressed over the way things had turned out. The war had been won, and the battleships had experienced few opportunities to do what they were intended to do.[22] With the Japanese swept from the seas, the future prospects of the battleships did not look promising. Lee had been an enthusiastic member of the Gun Club, and now its day appeared to be passing.

As a flag officer, Willis Lee had been in or near the combat zone for nearly the entire period from September 1942 to June 1945. The stressful days and nights, short sleep, responsibility, chain smoking, and little exercise caught up with him. On the morning of 25 August 1945, the Aertsens drove away to return to civilian life. For the first time in a long while, Lee set off to work by himself—without the aide whom he had regarded almost as a surrogate son. As his barge headed for his office, Admiral Lee suffered a fatal heart attack. The former battleship commander was dead at the age of fifty-seven.[23]

NOTES

1. An excellent review of King's forcing the Solomons onto the strategic agenda is in Thomas B. Buell, *Master of Sea Power: A Biography of Fleet Admiral Ernest J. King* (Boston, 1980), 214–25.

2. The descriptions of this battle are drawn largely from Samuel Eliot Morison, *History of United States Naval Operations in World War II*, vol 5. *The Struggle for Guadalcanal* (Boston, 1949); Paul S. Dull, *A Battle History of the Imperial Japanese Navy (1941–1945)* (Annapolis, 1978); and Richard B Frank, *Guadalcanal: The Definitive Account of the Landmark Battle* (New York, 1990)

3. Ruth Williamson, letter to Evan E. Smith, 12 February 1962. This letter and some of the other sources for this chapter were among papers donated to the author by Mrs. Smith after the death of her husband, who had started work on a biography of Lee in the early 1960s

4. Owen F. Cammack, letter to Evan E. Smith, 9 February 1962; Smith papers.

5. The messenger was Lt (j.g.) James Van Allen, who had helped develop the fuze. In later years he became world-famous for his discovery of the Van Allen belts of radiation circling the earth. Van Allen, letter to author, 26 April 1976

6. Capt. Albert T. Church Jr., USN (Ret), interview with author, 23 December 1979.

7. Morison, *Struggle for Guadalcanal*, 271–72.

8. Cdr Paul H. Backus, USN (Ret), Naval Institute oral history interview with author, 28 October 1981

9. Morison, *Struggle for Guadalcanal*, 271

10 Ibid., 272–73.

11. The times used in this account are from the clocks of the American task force. Morison's history places the times in all cases an hour earlier, arbitrarily establishing an artificial time as a compromise between that observed on board the ships of the opposing forces

12. Church interview

13. Robert Reed, interview with author, 6 May 1995.

14. For ship-by-ship details and excellent diagrams of the battle, see Theodore Roscoe, *United States Destroyer Operations in World War II* (Annapolis, 1953), 200–204.

15. Rear Adm. Harvey T Walsh, USN (Ret.), letter to Evan Smith, 30 July 1962; Vice Adm. Edwin B. Hooper, USN (Ret.), Naval Institute oral history interview with John T. Mason, 26 June 1970.

16. Frank, *Guadalcanal*, 484

17. Backus interview.

18. Backus interview

19. A ship-by-ship breakdown of casualties appears in Frank, *Guadalcanal*, 486.

20 Commander Battleship Division Six, action report A5/A16-3, serial 0010, dated 18 February 1943.

21. Mabelle Lee to Margaret Allen, et al , 4 August 1945

22. Mary Aertsen, interview with author, 10 October 1976.

23 Guilliaem Aertsen III, interview with author, 10 October 1976

15

The Battle of the Atlantic

WILLIAM T. Y'BLOOD

Dictionaries usually define a battle as "a large-scale combat between two armed forces" or "any intense or extended struggle."[1] The latter definition fits many people's conceptions of land warfare as exemplified by such actions as the Battle of the Bulge or, say, the Battle for Okinawa. In contrast most people envision a naval battle as an intense fight of just a few days', or, more likely, just a few hours' duration. Needless to say the Battle of the Atlantic does not fit these conceptions, for, although intense at times, it extended over a period of years.

The Battle of the Atlantic should not be viewed as a battle but as a war within a war. It began on 3 September 1939, two days after Germany invaded Poland, when the *U-30* torpedoed and sank the passenger liner *Athenia,* and ended only on 8 May 1945, when Germany surrendered. Between these dates were numerous instances of great heroism, along with examples of cowardice; extreme brutality as well as compassion; intense moments of action and days of excruciating boredom.

A major problem for the German Navy (*Kriegsmarine*) in 1939 was that it was unprepared for the war. Naval rearmament had begun in 1935, and in 1938 an ambitious construction program to build a powerful fleet able to take on the Royal Navy was initiated.[2] Such construction takes time, but Grand Adm. Erich Raeder, the Kriegsmarine's commander in chief, had been assured repeatedly by Hitler that a war with Britain would not take place until 1944 at the earliest. Thus, September of 1939 found the navy with only eight major surface vessels operational and the great battleships *Bismarck* and *Tirpitz* a year or more from completion. Even then-commodore Karl Dönitz's U-boat fleet was not a particularly strong force at that time; forty-seven of his fifty-seven submarines were operational, but of these forty-seven, only twenty-two were capable of extended operations. This was a far cry from the three hundred U-boats Dönitz believed necessary to defeat the enemy.

Nonetheless the Battle of the Atlantic has long been considered a U-boat war. It is true that the German submarines played a far greater role and did more damage than their surface compatriots, but the surface vessels did their part by acting as the ubiquitous "fleet in being," holding in place their opposite numbers at a time when they could have been used more profitably elsewhere. The sortie of the *Bismarck* and her sinking in May 1941 by a goodly portion of the British Home Fleet shows just how effective was this supposed threat.

Dönitz's theory of U-boat warfare was based on the "tonnage doctrine" of sinking the maximum number of enemy vessels (primarily merchantmen) for the minimum number of U-boat losses. Although the doctrine proved painful to the Allies, it was flawed. To Dönitz a ship was a ship was a ship, even if this meant sinking vessels in areas well away from the critical convoy routes. By underestimating the Allied (particularly the American) ability to build ships rapidly and refusing to recognize that a merchant vessel sunk off Brazil really did not impede the Allies' efforts to get war material to the primary war zones, Dönitz eventually played into his enemies' hands.[3]

The Battle of the Atlantic began auspiciously enough for the Kriegsmarine, with almost one hundred ships sunk (including thirty-seven in the North Atlantic) during September and October 1939. Only seven U-boats were lost in this same period. From November 1939 through May 1940, however, the number of sinkings and total tonnage in the North Atlantic shrank considerably, while U-boat losses rose to seventeen. This lack of success was primarily because of the diversion of boats to support the invasion of Norway.[4] With the fall of France in June 1940 and the almost immediate utilization of French Atlantic ports, the U-boats were able to make longer patrols, and sinkings grew markedly. Also, the number of U-boats at sea at any one time began to grow.

At the outbreak of war, the British initiated a convoy system. For several months this system was successful; most of the ships sunk were stragglers from the convoys or sailing independently. But in June 1940 Dönitz initiated *Rudeltaktik*—wolf-pack tactics—and ship losses and tonnage figures soared. There were never enough escorts to go around and, too often, if a strong escort became available, it was poorly managed. For the U-boat sailors, this was the "Happy Time." Allied losses would have been even greater had not Hitler sent many U-boats to the Mediterranean or back to Norwegian waters.

From the start of the war, the United States was engaged (however indirectly) in the Battle of the Atlantic. A series of mutual defense pacts, the Neutrality Patrol, the establishment of a "protectorate" over Greenland, the destroyers-for-naval-bases deal with Britain, and Lend-Lease were but steps toward full involvement. In the mid-summer of 1941, the United States increased its activities with the occupation of Iceland, followed by the commencement of convoy escort in September 1941.

The probability that these enterprises would lead to clashes between U.S. and German forces became a reality on 4 September 1941, when the *U-652* attacked the destroyer *Greer.* If not officially the U.S. Navy was in reality now at war with Kriegsmarine in the North Atlantic. No one was hurt in this attack, but it was only a matter of time before blood would be spilled. On 17 October, the destroyer *Kearny* was helping protect a convoy under attack by a wolf pack. A torpedo from the *U-568* lanced the *Kearny*'s side, killing eleven men. Fortunately the destroyer managed to limp back to port. Unfortunately the next American warship attacked was not as lucky.

The *Reuben James* was one of five U.S. destroyers escorting a convoy on 31 October. At dawn, while the "tin can" was investigating a possible contact, a torpedo slammed into her side. The ensuing explosion obliterated the ship's forward section. Only 45 of her crew of about 160 survived.

Pearl Harbor caught both the Germans and Italians by surprise, but they recovered quickly. Prior to the U.S. entry into the war, Hitler had restricted U-boat operations in American waters, even though the United States was acting more like a belligerent than a neutral country. Now these restrictions were lifted, and German submariners found themselves enjoying a second "Happy Time" as they launched Operation *Paukenschlag* (Drumbeat).

The Germans benefited immensely from the fact that the U.S. Navy was not yet the force it would become. Resources were slim, and most of those available went to the Pacific. Because of a lack both of escort vessels and a real understanding of the benefits of the convoy system, merchant ships usually sailed independently in American waters. The U-boats quickly exploited this situation and a "merry massacre" ensued.[5] Surprisingly, for all the damage they caused in the first months of 1942—82 merchantmen sunk totaling more than 490,000 tons—seldom were there more than 12 U-boats operating off North America. Obviously these were more than enough.[6]

The Navy's slow response in instituting the convoy system; the generally poor showing of U.S. forces against the U-boats; and what role, if any, Admiral King's Anglophobia played in these matters has generated considerable controversy over the years. It is beyond the scope of this study to go into detail concerning these subjects; however, it should be noted that King was not adverse to convoys. Viewing troopship movements to the United Kingdom as more important than sailings along the U.S. coast, he provided strong escort forces for these transports.[7]

Eventually—because of the institution of convoys, increased numbers of escorts with better coordination of their efforts, assumption of responsibility by Anglo-Canadian escort forces for convoys sailing between Boston and Halifax, and the invaluable contributions from Ultra—sinkings diminished and the Americans reestablished some measure of control over coastal waters.[8]

Seeing the "Happy Time" ending off North America, Dönitz terminated *Paukenschlag* in July 1942 and shifted emphasis back to the North Atlantic. *Paukenschlag*'s conclusion did not mean the U-boats pulled out of the Caribbean or other parts of the Atlantic. Dönitz now had more submarines available, and their effectiveness increased with the appearance of big supply submarines, the "milch cows," which enabled the U-boats to remain on patrol for longer periods and in more areas.

July 1942 also saw the destruction of Convoy PQ-17, en route to Archangel. Although German surface units never contacted the convoy, the threat posed by these forces prompted the Admiralty to scatter PQ-17. The merchantmen then fell easy prey to U-boats and Luftwaffe aircraft, which sank two-thirds of them—one of the worst loss rates suffered by a convoy during the war. Such battles raged throughout the last part of 1942 and early 1943 as one side, then the other, gained the advantage. But for both sides these successes were merely tactical not strategic.

Then came the big convoy battles of March 1943. During the first twenty days of March four eastbound convoys—SC-121, HX-228, SC-122, and HX-229—with 202 ships were set upon and savaged by wolf packs totaling 77 submarines. In these brutal battles thirty-nine merchantmen were sunk against the loss of only three U-boats. This was in addition to the more than forty other vessels that U-boats bagged elsewhere in the Atlantic. For a time it appeared to the Allies that the Germans were close to winning the Battle of the Atlantic.[9] The following month, though, resulted in a virtual stand-off. Then the appearance of long-range, land-based aircraft with airborne radar, along with escort carriers, finally closed the Atlantic Air Gap, giving the submariners no respite from attack. With more surface escorts becoming available, U-boat sinkings climbed, and the battle shifted in favor of the Allies.

Most historians now consider the March battles, followed by the terrible losses suffered by the U-boats in May, during which no fewer than forty-one submarines were sunk, as the turning points in the Battle of the Atlantic. On

24 May, shaken by the loss of so many boats in such a short time, Grand Adm. Dönitz, who had replaced Raeder as commander in chief of the Kriegsmarine, withdrew his subs from the North Atlantic. Although neither side realized it, that was the day the Allies began to win the Battle of the Atlantic.

When Dönitz withdrew his boats he shifted them primarily to the Central Atlantic, a position in which they could attack convoys between the United States and North Africa. Unknowingly he placed his submarines in a dangerous area where American escort carriers would be operating under better weather conditions and with the invaluable advantage of Ultra intelligence.

Although the British escort carrier *Audacity*, a converted German merchant vessel that carried only six aircraft, which greatly limited her usefulness, enjoyed some success before being sunk by a U-boat on 22 December 1941, the March convoy battles saw the introduction of the escort carrier, or CVE in navy parlance, as a major player in the fight against the U-boats. Neither the USS *Bogue* (the first U.S. escort carrier to be used in support of convoys) nor HMS *Biter* (an American-built vessel converted from a merchantman) accomplished much during those actions.[10] Nonetheless a great deal of operational knowledge was gleaned, knowledge that would be put to good use later. Drawing from the experience gathered in these operations, the *Bogue* began to obtain results. Between 22 May and 12 June 1943, her planes sank three U-boats.[11] This pioneering flattop was joined during the summer by the *Card, Core, Croatan,* and one of the larger *Sangamon*-class vessels, the *Santee*, in the continuing fight to protect the convoys and to render the U-boats impotent, preferably by sinking them, but also by forcing them to dive to depths from which they were unable to attack the convoys. While all these new carriers enjoyed success against the U-boats in the last half of 1943, the big scorer was "Buster" Isbell's *Card*, which destroyed ten boats.

Capt. Arnold Jay "Buster" Isbell graduated from the U.S. Naval Academy in 1920. After being designated a naval aviator in January 1924, he served aboard the *Lexington, Ranger,* and *Saratoga*. His career was typical of naval officers of the era: shipboard service, interspersed with duty ashore, and a steady, slow climb in rank. Gradually Isbell's leadership qualities resulted in his being given greater responsibilities and more demanding tasks. Between 1936 and 1942, he was deeply involved in patrol aviation, moving up the ladder from executive officer and commander of several patrol squadrons to duty on the staff of the Commander, Patrol Wings, Atlantic Fleet. Isbell then went to Alaska, where he was Commanding Officer, Naval Air Station, Sitka, from 5 July 1942 until 31 March 1943.

But like any ambitious naval officer, Isbell was not content with a shore-

Arnold J. ("Buster") Isbell in December 1943. *U.S. Naval Institute*

based desk job; he wanted command of a combat ship. In April 1943 he got his chance. The *Bogue*-class escort carrier *Card* was fitting out and Isbell assumed command of the little flattop. As it turned out, this was a fortuitous melding of man and ship. Isbell and *Card,* along with their usual escorts, the old flush-deck destroyers *Goff, Borie,* and *Barry,* and Composite Squadrons (VCs) 1 and 9, became the Navy's second highest–scoring CVE hunter-killer group. In the process, the *Card's* unit, Task Group (TG) 21.14, received the Presidential Unit Citation for its aggressive and successful operations against the U-boats.

Additionally Isbell was awarded the Distinguished Service Medal for his leadership of TG 21.14. His citation reads in part,

For exceptionally meritorious and distinguished service to the Government of the United States . . . as Commanding Officer of the USS *Card* and as Anti-submarine Task Group Commander from July 27 to November 9, 1943. Operating in the Atlantic, the planes and escort destroyers under Captain Isbell's intrepid leadership developed into a powerful combat force, seeking out the enemy with relentless determination and striking with superbly coordinated action in a sustained drive. . . .

Isbell was relieved of command of the *Card* and TG 21.14 in March 1944 and assigned to duty with Tenth Fleet in Washington, where his experience as a hunter-killer group commander was invaluable in preparing further assaults against the U-boats. He remained in Washington for almost a year, but once again shore duty chafed and he sought a return to the sea.

In late February 1945, Isbell received a choice assignment, command of the *Essex*-class carrier *Yorktown* in the Pacific. He quickly flew to the war zone, where he was posted to the *Franklin* as an observer prior to taking over the *Yorktown*. Sadly, Isbell never got the chance to command "The Fighting Lady." On 19 March 1945, a kamikaze turned the *Franklin* into a raging inferno. Although the horribly mangled *Franklin* was eventually saved, Capt. Arnold J. "Buster" Isbell was among the more than 720 men killed.[12]

Despite having his career cut tragically short, Isbell left his mark on the Atlantic (and Pacific) antisubmarine war. The hard training he had put the men and ships under his command through paid off many times over for the remainder of the war. The tactics and theories of antisubmarine warfare he helped develop were disseminated widely throughout the antisubmarine warfare community and used to great effect against the enemy.

The summer of 1943 saw a dramatic change in Allied antisubmarine operations. In May Admiral King established Tenth Fleet as an integrated antisubmarine command within his headquarters. Though Tenth Fleet came under King's personal direction, its everyday operations were conducted by Rear Adm. Francis S. Low. Additionally, more carriers and escorts were on hand. Also, as the Allies learned to decipher and disseminate Ultra information more quickly and to provide better analysis of high frequency direction finding (HF/DF or "Huff-Duff") fixes on the U-boats, the tethering to the convoys was loosened and the antisubmarine groups won more freedom of action.

Eventually the Americans decided to exploit the break-in to the U-boat codes and use the information offensively. Hunter-killer groups were formed, with or without escort carriers as their cores, and were directed against specific U-boat concentrations, particularly meetings of combat U-boats with their supply submarines. The British looked askance at the use of Ultra information for offensive purposes, apprehensive that such initiatives might tip off the Germans that their codes were being broken. Fortunately for the Allies, although the Germans suspected possible compromises in their cipher systems, "knowledgeable" officials continued to claim that was impossible. Long after the war, when the Ultra secret became known, Dönitz apparently still refused to believe his ciphers had been compromised.[13]

Meanwhile, the loss of so many of its submarines in May caused U-boat Command to revise its tactics. Now, as the U-boats returned home, they strengthened their anti-aircraft armament considerably by adding a 20mm quadruple mount, and U-boat Command directed them to remain on the surface and, if surprised, fight back. The U-boats were to travel in groups to increase the effectiveness of their guns, particularly through the Bay of Biscay, where British aircraft and ships were enjoying great success.[14] This "Fight back" directive remained in force just ninety-four days. During that time U-boats shot down fifty-seven aircraft, but aircraft sank twenty-eight submarines and damaged twenty-two more.[15]

Following an uneventful first cruise, the *Card*'s aircraft ran into several U-boats willing to "fight back" on the surface.[16] Isbell had received Ultra information that U-boats were operating west-southwest of the Azores, and, after departing Hampton Roads on 27 July, led TG 21.14 in that direction.[17] His mission—to protect the convoys and seek out and destroy U-boats—was indicative of the changing nature of the war against the U-boats. Previously the escort carriers remained tethered closely to the convoys. In essence this had been a defensive tactic (let the U-boats come to the convoys) rather than an offensive one (let the "jeeps" go after the U-boats).

It was not long before the *Card*'s planes came upon the enemy. The *U-66* was heading home following a relatively unproductive patrol, having sunk only two ships. On 3 August, the U-boat was cruising slowly on the surface when it was surprised by a VC-1 Avenger/Wildcat search team. The two planes pounced on the U-boat, damaging it and wounding its captain. Despite these attacks the *U-66* submerged and escaped. In serious trouble, however, it surfaced that evening to radio a request for assistance to U-boat Command, which directed the closest milch cow, the *U-117*, to rendezvous with the *U-66*.

Listening in with great interest to these messages was Tenth Fleet. Though the eavesdroppers could not determine the rendezvous point, they identified the area. Quickly, Tenth Fleet ordered the *Card* to find the submarines. On the morning of 7 August, one of the *Card*'s Avengers sighted both the *U-66* and

The *Card*. A wartime photograph in which her radar antennas have been scratched out for security reasons. She measured 495'8" overall, displaced 13,891 tons full load, and was designed to carry 28 aircraft. Her complement numbered 890. *U.S. Naval Institute*

U-117. Once again the submariners were caught napping, and the bomber was almost upon the boats before their crews reacted. The big milch cow had been fitted with additional armament and its crew, thoroughly indoctrinated in the new tactic of "fighting back," opened a heavy but inaccurate fire. The Avenger was untouched. Two depth bombs that exploded close aboard prevented the U-boat from submerging. In the meantime the *U-66* dove and escaped again.

The *U-117* was not as lucky. Responding to calls for help from the first attacker, more planes from the *Card* showed up and began pummeling the helpless submarine. Pounded by depth bombs and holed by machine-gun fire, the *U-117* wallowed on the surface, then its bow lifted up and the boat slipped backward into the sea. At this moment two Avengers planted a pair of Mk.24 mines (homing torpedoes called "Fidos") on each side of the swirl of water left by the disappearing vessel. Minutes later a patch of light-blue water bubbled up to mark the *U-117*'s last dive.

For U-boat Command the loss was a serious setback. Due to the sinking of another milch cow off Iceland, the *U-117* had been supposed to refuel fourteen homebound U-boats. Now other U-boats would have to be called off patrol to act as tankers or curtail their patrols because of a lack of fuel. The escort carriers were already having an impact on Atlantic operations.

The next morning *Card* planes came upon the *U-664* and *U-262* idling on the surface. The fliers raced in to attack but discovered the Germans were ready. Heavy anti-aircraft fire brought down both planes, killing the Wildcat pilot and one of the Avenger's crew, but not before depth bombs damaged the *U-262* so severely that it was forced to head for home. Informed of this development, U-boat Command directed the *U-262* to transfer any superfluous fuel and provisions to the *U-664* and *U-760*. The latter two would then continue their patrols. But once again the *Card* threw a monkey wrench into German plans.

That evening, reflecting on the loss of his two aircraft against the U-boats, Isbell and his squadron commander decided to combine two Avengers and a Wildcat as an attack team. One Avenger would carry two instantaneously fuzed 500-pound bombs; the other, depth bombs and Fidos. The new tactic would be tested the next day.

While the two men made their plans, neither they (nor anyone else on the carrier) were aware that the *U-664*, still in the neighborhood, had fired three torpedoes at the *Card*, which the sub's captain identified as a large tanker. All three missed, and the *Card* steamed off into the darkness.

The *U-664*'s failure to leave the area proved fatal. On the afternoon of the ninth, one of the new three-plane attack teams sighted the submarine, decks awash. One bomber and the fighter attacked simultaneously, raking the boat with machine-gun fire and dropping a 500-pounder that hit some twenty feet off the U-boat's port bow. The second Avenger then released two depth bombs that exploded beneath the diving sub and drove it back to the surface.

A few sailors who panicked and tried to abandon ship were killed as the fighter made another strafing gun. The *U-664* again attempted to dive, but another bomb effectively stopped that. Helpless on the surface and gushing oil, the U-boat came under increased attack as three more Avengers and another Wildcat showed up. The submariners swarmed out of their boat and into the water as the *U-664* slipped backward into the oily sea. Hours later the *Borie* picked up forty-four survivors.

The *Card* was not yet finished deleting submarines from U-boat Command's roster. On the afternoon of 11 August, an Avenger/Wildcat team sighted the big supply submarine *U-525* leaving a tell-tale white wake as it cruised on the surface. A combined strafing and bombing attack damaged the

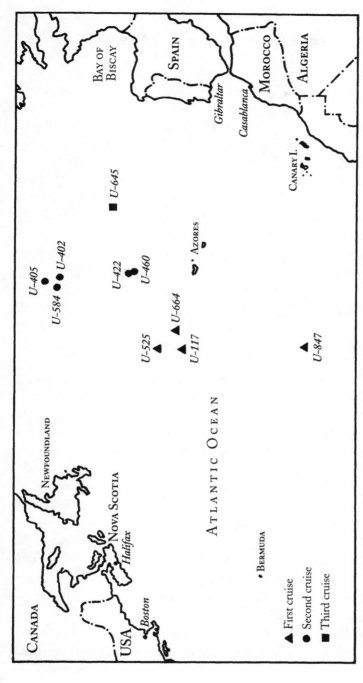

The *Card*'s score, 27 July 1943–2 January 1944. First cruise: *U-117*, 7 August; *U-664*, 9 August; *U-525*, 11 August; *U-847*, 27 August. Second cruise: *U-460* and *U-422*, 4 October; *U-402*, 13 October; *U-584*, 31 October; *U-405*, 1 November. Third cruise: *U-645*, 25 December.

U-boat, and it started to dive. As the submarine went under, the Avenger pilot darted in to drop a Fido. The Wildcat pilot, meanwhile, got a good look at a Fido in action.

Although the U-525 was losing oil, the water was clear enough for the pilot to see well below the surface. The Fido entered the sea slightly ahead and about twenty feet to the right of the sub's swirl. Then the Fido veered left and struck the U-boat midway between its stern and conning tower. A plume of brownish water shooting 150 feet into the air, followed by a large air bubble and a spreading oil slick, marked the U-525's grave site.

Three U-boats to the Card's and VC-1's credit so far on this one mission and they were still not done. After putting into Casablanca for replenishment, TG 21.14 was back at sea. Ultra again signaled a planned rendezvous of a supply submarine with operational U-boats.[18] On 27 August, VC-1 fliers spotted the U-508, which was attacked by a single Avenger but got away. Next was the U-847, a big boat that belonged to a unit, the 1st Monsoon Group, bound for operations in the Indian Ocean and then on to Penang, Malaya, for replenishment. However the loss of two milch cows forced U-boat Command to keep the U-847 in the Atlantic as a supply submarine. The sub had performed this duty admirably since the nineteenth and had already supplied five boats on the twenty-seventh.

While cruising on the surface, the U-847 was jumped by a three-plane team. Strafing attacks by the Wildcats scythed down several Germans before the U-boat submerged. At this point the Avenger roared in to drop a Fido. A dark mound of oil bubbled to the surface, followed by an intense flash that extended for hundreds of feet through the water. Miles away the U-508's crew heard and felt the explosion.

The U-847 was the sixteenth submarine sunk by U.S. escort carriers since the Bogue's first kill on 22 May. This averaged out to a U-boat a week. Significantly, eight of these boats were Dönitz's vital milch cows. One postwar history stated, "In concentrating on refueling R/V's [refueller vessels] in the summer of 1943, Allied air power was in truth striking at the heart of Dönitz's system. For without refuellers, neither prolonged independent cruise nor extended convoy operations were possible to the [smaller boats] that made up the vast majority of the U-boat fleet."[19]

By the end of August, only three of the twelve milch cows that had been in U-boat Command's inventory in May still survived. Consequently Dönitz was compelled to recall his boats from the Central Atlantic much sooner than he had intended. The hunter-killer groups had proved their worth.

The rich pickings the escort carriers had enjoyed in August petered out the following month, when Dönitz redeployed his subs to attack the North Atlantic convoys with the new *Zaunkönig* (acoustic torpedo). This vaunted weapon did not prove especially productive, sinking six merchantmen and three escorts. Its lack of success prompted Dönitz to return his boats to the eastern Atlantic and southward to the Azores and Gibraltar, where convoys to North Africa were plentiful.[20]

While Dönitz attempted to unleash his submarines in the *Zaunkönig* assault against the convoys, Buster Isbell and TG 21.14 were back at sea seeking more U-boats. On the morning of 4 October, they uncovered a nest of U-boats. A patrolling VC-9 Avenger (the squadron transferred from the *Bogue* while the *Card* was in port) found four submarines clustered in the open area. This sighting was not accidental. Two days earlier Adm. Sir Andrew Cunningham, the First Sea Lord, relying on Ultra information, asked the U.S. Navy to intercept this refueling operation.[21] The milch cow *U-460* had just fueled the *U-264* and was preparing to fuel the *U-422*. Awaiting its turn was the *U-455*. This was the largest number of U-boats yet encountered by the "jeep" fliers. There may have been even more subs nearby, for the Avenger pilot thought he saw another group a few miles farther ahead.

Immediately upon sighting this congregation, the pilot sent a contact report but his message was garbled in transmission and Isbell remained unaware that four U-boats had been located. So, instead of a major attack group, only one bomber and two fighters were dispatched. In the meantime the first plane began its attack.

The attacker was helped by the fact that the *U-460*'s and *U-264*'s commanders wasted time arguing over who should dive first. (Dönitz's specific orders were for the milch cows to dive immediately when attacked.) Instead all four subs loosed a hail of flak at the Avenger. The Avenger's 500-pound bomb fell between two of the boats, damaging neither. Left with one Fido, the attacker decided to await reinforcements.

When these arrived they radioed for more planes. Isbell quickly sent eight Avengers and two Wildcats. With the appearance of more aircraft, first the *U-455*, then the *U-422*, dove for safety. The remaining pair of U-boats were then attacked by one bomber each. In his excitement one Avenger pilot pressed the wrong button and released all his depth bombs well short of the *U-264*, which submerged and escaped; *U-460* did not. The big supply submarine was slow to submerge and a Fido caught the *U-460* while it was barely under water.

Believing more milch cows were nearby, Isbell kept his planes combing the area. That afternoon their perseverance was rewarded when the *U-422*, perhaps damaged during the earlier encounter, surfaced just a few miles from its site. Unfortunately for the U-boat, an Avenger/Wildcat team was directly overhead. A Fido ended the *U-422*'s career.

Ultra now revealed another area where several U-boats would be resupplied, and on 9 October, Admiral Cunningham again requested assistance in finding them. The *Card* was closest to the suspected refueling point, and the VC-9 fliers exerted great effort in seeking out these submarines.[22] Soon U-boats began popping up all over the place. First, the *U-488* was attacked by a pair of Avengers on 12 October. Their attacks were ineffectual, and the submarine escaped. Then the *U-731* was discovered. It too, survived an attack, but sustained enough damage to cause it to return home.

VC-9 did better the following day. The *U-378* managed to evade the *Card*'s planes only to succumb one week later to aircraft from the *Core*. This attack, however, drew more VC-9 aircraft to the area and about noon yet another sub was seen. The *U-402* remained surfaced too long and drew the attention of a pair of Avengers. When the U-boat's captain finally decided to dive, the bombers were on his boat like vultures and brought the *U-402*'s patrol to a deadly end.

Still another U-boat was encountered before the *Card* put in to Casablanca for supplies on 18 October. This boat, however, was full of fight and managed to severely damage its assailant before diving and getting away. Although most of the U-boats had eluded their attackers during this period, the VC-9 fliers had severely hampered the Germans' supply operations.

Meanwhile, the *Card* and the *Core* had ceased to be the only American escort carriers in the Central Atlantic. A brand-new CVE, the *Block Island,* was at sea, and on 28 October, her planes sank the big minelayer *U-220*. With the appearance of more carriers and escort vessels, the Central Atlantic was becoming very dangerous for the U-boats.

Back at sea on 30 October, the *Card*'s task group arrived in the area where the *U-220* had been sunk. Ultra information had revealed that more U-boats were nearby and Buster Isbell hoped to catch them. One sub was found that afternoon, but its captain, obeying Dönitz's new orders not to fight back, "pulled the plug" and escaped.

The following afternoon the *U-91* and the *U-584* were discovered just eighteen miles ahead of TG 21.14. Conforming to Isbell's new procedures, the Avenger pilot sent a contact report, but did not attack. Instead he shadowed the boats while awaiting reinforcements. When two more bombers showed up, the *U-91* quickly went under, but once again a U-boat skipper made the fatal mistake of dawdling on the surface. Two Fidos sank the *U-584* about 580 miles north of the Azores.

Isbell was determined to sink the *U-91*, which he mistakenly believed to be a milch cow. At dusk he signaled the *Borie* to go after it. This order initiated one of the most dramatic episodes in the Battle of the Atlantic. Lt. Charles H. Hutchins's ship was older than some of his crewmen, but all were well trained and eager for action. And action they got!

At the scene of the afternoon attack, the *Borie* made a radar contact at a range of 6,500 yards. This was the *U-256*, surfaced and unaware that an enemy was nearby. When star shells suddenly blossomed over his boat, the sub's skipper took her down, and radar contact was lost. Sound contact was swiftly acquired, and the *Borie* made three depth charge runs, damaging her quarry. The *U-256* broached briefly then settled by the stern. Convinced that his ship had killed the U-boat, Hutchins radioed the *Card*, "Scratch one pig boat. Am searching for more." The submarine, however, lived to fight another day.

About five hours later, Hutchins found the *U-405*. Bucking waves fifteen to twenty feet high, the *Borie* closed with her quarry. Before the "tin can" could open fire with her 4-inch guns, the U-boat submerged. Sonar then pinpointed the enemy's position, and Hutchins prepared to drop a standard depth charge pattern. But the release mechanism malfunctioned, and all the ready depth charges plopped overboard. The shower of charges brought the *U-405* bobbing to the surface off the *Borie*'s port quarter.

In the bright glare of a searchlight, the Germans popped out of the conning tower to man their guns. As they did so, accurate 4-inch and machine-gun fire from the *Borie* swept their vessel, blowing its deck gun from the sub. Despite the hail of gunfire, the Germans continued to defend their boat.

Hutchins decided to ram, but as the *Borie* was about to hit, the *U-405* went hard left. At the same time, a big wave heaved the destroyer up and over the U-boat and gently deposited her across its forecastle about thirty feet aft of its bow. The shock was so slight that men below decks in the destroyer did not realize what had happened. Those topside were startled to see the submarine's hull protruding from below the sides of their ship at an angle of about 30 degrees.

Firing with everything they had, the *Borie*'s crew raked the pinioned U-boat's deck. Men threw knives, cans, and whatever else they could get their hands on at the enemy. One German was knocked overboard by a well-aimed 4-inch shell casing.

This close combat continued for about ten minutes until the vessels broke apart. Both the *U-405* and the *Borie* were in serious straits. Although his ship's worn plating began to separate and water rushed into her engine spaces, Hutchins was not about to let the U-boat escape. More 4-inch fire slammed into the submarine, slowing but not stopping it.

About this time the U-boat's captain decided to ram and circled toward the destroyer. He almost succeeded, but the *Borie* turned to present her stern to the sub and Hutchins dropped a three depth charge pattern that bracketed the *U-405*'s conning tower. The impact lifted the boat in the water and brought it briefly to a stop. Amazingly the sub continued to move, but its time was running out. Another shell hit slowed the boat even more, and, at last, the submariners began to abandon ship. Moments after a 4-inch shell blew away most of its conning tower, the *U-405* reared up by the bow, slid quickly under, and exploded.

When they came topside the *U-405*'s crew had fired star shells that were answered by a signal to the southwest. As the *Borie* approached to pick up approximately fifteen survivors, a torpedo was seen coming from that direction. In maneuvering to avoid the torpedo, the *Borie* steamed through the Germans in the water; none were rescued. By now Hutchins's ship was in a bad way. The ramming had left her port side in ruins, and her forward engine room was completely flooded. A volunteer, MM1c Irving R. Saum Jr., worked for some time in and under the frigid water and debris closing valves so that all pumps could be used to stem flooding in the after engine room. For his courageous actions, Saum received the Navy Cross.

Hutchins signaled the *Card* that his ship might have to be abandoned. Unfortunately the transmission was unclear, and Isbell did not learn of the *Borie*'s situation for some time. At 0900, the "flush-decker" lost power, and her crew redoubled their efforts to keep her afloat. Although the *Card* had sent planes looking for the destroyer, they were frustrated by mist and clouds.

Then at 1100 Isbell received a grim message from the *Borie*: "Commenced sinking." This time the *Card* managed to get a fix on her signal, and half an hour later an Avenger discovered the destroyer only fourteen miles away. The task group soon reached the scene and found the *Borie* dead in the water and down by the stern. Attempts to pass over pumping gear were thwarted by forty-foot swells.

Isbell finally told Hutchins to abandon the *Borie* while it was still light. Hutchins reluctantly relayed the order, and his men went over the side into the rough and very cold—about 44°F—water. The turbulent seas made it extremely difficult for the boats and rafts to come alongside the rescue vessels, and some men tried their luck swimming. Although none of the destroyer's crew had been killed in the action, three officers and twenty-four men perished trying to get to the *Barry* and the *Goff*.

Receipt of what turned out to be exaggerated reports placing fifty U-boats within three hundred miles of the task group led Isbell to rule out further efforts to save the *Borie*. On the morning of 2 November, the *Barry* was ordered to put her down. The destroyer's three torpedoes missed, and it took four depth bombs from an Avenger to send a brave ship to the bottom. With only two escorts left, Isbell set course for Norfolk, and on 9 November, the *Card* reached port. Lieutenant Hutchins was awarded the Navy Cross for his leadership during the battle.

The *Card* set out on her third hunter-killer cruise with a new escort group, the destroyers *Decatur, Leary, Schenck,* and *Babbitt,* on 24 November. The *Babbitt* had been detached because of engine problems when, two days before Christmas, TG 21.14 made contact with five of a group of thirteen U-boats positioned to screen a blockade runner returning from Japan. This time the honors were even. Depth charges from the *Schenck* destroyed the *U-645,* but torpedoes from the *U-275* and *U-382* sank the *Leary,* with the loss of more than half her company. The *Decatur* having developed engine problems, the *Card* was left with only one fully operational escort, and on 3 January 1944 she returned to port.

In the nine months since the *Bogue* had led them into battle, the CVE groups had demonstrated outstanding effectiveness in offensive antisubmarine warfare. The *Card* was top scorer, with ten U-boats to her credit. Next came the *Bogue* with eight, then the *Core* with five, the *Santee* with three, and the *Block Island* with one. The British carriers *Tracker* and *Biter* both had accounted for two U-boats.

Ironically as World War II progressed into its final stages, Dönitz found himself with a much larger, more technologically advanced submarine fleet than ever.[23] Allied air attacks on the submarine pens and yards hardly slowed U-boat construction. In 1944 387 submarines, including midgets, were built, a 43 percent increase in production over the previous year. However only 237 of this number were commissioned that year.[24] Yet this larger fleet accomplished little. It faced just as technologically advanced an antisubmarine force that had grown in numbers as well.

The U-boats enjoyed some successes in 1944–45, but these were few and far between. Dönitz, clinging to his tonnage doctrine, shifted his boats constantly in the Atlantic and Indian Oceans in futile attempts to find Allied weak points. These attacks seldom achieved the results desired, for they were usually in areas distant from the primary convoy routes. Too, the U-boats were often unable to continue their attacks because of the intense response elicited from the defenders.

From mid-1943 until the end of the war, German submariners found the Atlantic a terribly dangerous place. Once the hunters, U-boat crews had become the hunted. As the battle wore on, the U-boat arm became "less bold when pressing an attack which was sure to reveal their presence."[25] U-boat operations, "once so boldly offensive, [came to take] on increasingly the character of makeshift and evasion, the search for counter measures and counter tactics."[26]

What did the Battle of the Atlantic cost in lives and matériel? Estimates of U-boat losses vary widely, but a reasonable number is 785 lost of 1,162 built. Scuttlings accounted for another 220, and more than 150 were surrendered. Figures for personnel losses among the U-boat force also differ. Dan van der Vat's *The Atlantic Campaign* gives 25,870 killed and 5,000 captured. The highest casualty estimate is 32,000 dead.[27]

The cost to the Allies was horrific also. Merchant vessels suffered the most, with 2,452 ships of 12.8 million tons going to the bottom. In addition 175 warships were sunk. More than 110,000 people perished in the Atlantic. The Battle of the Atlantic was an exceedingly bloody affair.

The exploits of TG 21.14, as described above, should not be construed to signify that the CVE groups won the Battle of the Atlantic. They were but one element of the victory. But if the CVE groups did not win the battle, the same is true of land-based aircraft, close support groups, and even the convoy system. A postwar U.S. Navy analysis states, "Superior leadership and tactics, quick initial action, and well-coordinated attack and defense played as much of a part in the defeat of the U-boats as did concentration of forces at the decisive points and weapon superiority."[28]

The authors of this analysis were either unaware or could not then reveal that most often the "concentration of forces at the decisive points" was the result of Ultra information and the increasingly effective use of HF/DF fixes from both land- and ship-based stations. Probably the most important factor in the winning (and losing) of the Battle of the Atlantic was Ultra. Without Ultra the Allies might still have won, but their victory would have been far more expensive.

NOTES

1. These definitions come specifically from *The American Heritage Dictionary of the English Language* (New York, 1976), but other dictionaries define the terms similarly.

2 Jürgen Rohwer, "Codes and Ciphers Radio Communication and Intelligence," in Timothy R. J. Runyan and Jan M Copes, eds , *To Die Gallantly* (Boulder, Colo., 1994), 39

3. Sönke Neitzel, "The Deployment of the U-boats," in Stephen Howarth and Derek Law, *The Battle of the Atlantic 1939–1945* (London/Annapolis, 1994), 296; Werner Rahn, "The Campaign: The German Perspective," in Howarth and Law, *The Battle of the Atlantic,* 539.

4. John Terraine, *The U-boat Wars 1916–1945* (New York, 1989), 767; Neitzel, "Deployment of the U-boats," 277.

5. Samuel Eliot Morison, *History of United States Naval Operations in World War II,* vol. 1: *The Battle of the Atlantic, 1939–1943* (Boston, 1947), 128.

6. Philip Lundeberg, "Allied Co-operation," in Howarth and Law, *The Battle of the Atlantic,* 355.

7. Ibid., 356; Dan van der Vat, *The Atlantic Campaign* (New York, 1988), 243.

8. Lundeberg, "Allied Co-operation," 356–57.

9. Van der Vat, *The Atlantic Campaign,* 322–25; Morison, *The Battle of the Atlantic,* 342–44.

10. Another British innovation, MAC-ships (converted from grain ships and tankers) were developed as an interim measure when it appeared that CVEs would be late in entering service. Only able to carry two or three Swordfish, however, they too were quite limited in their effectiveness. Ironically by the time the first of these conversions began operations in May 1943, increasing numbers of CVEs were becoming available, making the MAC-ships somewhat redundant. Nevertheless the MAC-ships provided exemplary service during their rather short careers. (David Hobbs, "Ship-borne Air Anti-Submarine Warfare," in Howarth and Law, *The Battle of the Atlantic,* 392–93.)

11. William T. Y'Blood, *Hunter-Killer: U.S. Escort Carriers in the Battle of the Atlantic* (Annapolis, 1983), 282.

12. Capt. Arnold J. Isbell Official Biography, no date; Capt. Arnold J. Isbell Officer Service Record, 27 March 1945. Copies in Naval Historical Center files.

13. Jürgen Rohwer, "Codes and Ciphers," in Runyand and Copes, eds., *To Die Gallantly,* 52–54; Jürgen Rohwer, "The Wireless War," in Howarth and Law, *The Battle of the Atlantic,* 408–17; Graham Rhys-Jones, "The German System: A Staff Perspective," in Howarth and Law, *The Battle of the Atlantic,* 143–55.

14. F. H. Hinsley, et al., *British Intelligence in the Second World War* (London, 1984), vol. 3, pt. 1, 215.

15. Y'Blood, *Hunter-Killer,* 55.

16. Unless otherwise noted, the following section on the activities of the *Card* and other CVEs is based on the author's *Hunter-Killer,* 40–129.

17. Hinsley, *British Intelligence,* 214. Hunter-killer group commanders remained unaware of just how the information supplied them about the U-boats was obtained.

18. Ibid.

19. Tenth Fleet/Op-20-G, *Allied Communications Intelligence and the Battle of the Atlantic* (n.d.), vol. 2:114.

20. Neitzel, "Deployment of the U-boats," 295.

21. Hinsley, *British Intelligence,* 226.

22. Ibid.

23. Examples of this technology include the schnorkel and the Type XXI "electroboat." The very advanced Walther U-boat design was delayed so long that, except for a couple of experimental vessels, none were built.

24. Samuel Eliot Morison, *History of United States Naval Operations in World War II,* vol. 10, *The Atlantic Battle Won: May 1943–May 1945* (Boston, 1956), 62.

25. *Allied Communications Intelligence,* 1:55.

26. Ibid, 2:101–2.

27. Van der Vat, *The Atlantic Campaign,* 382; see Y'Blood, *Hunter-Killer,* 272, for figures compiled from other sources.

28. C. M. Sternhell and A. M. Thorndike, *Antisubmarine Warfare in World War II* (Washington, D.C., 1946), 37.

16

The Battle of the Philippine Sea

H. P. WILLMOTT

When did the Japanese cause pass recall? All great failures provoke the usually unanswerable question; Japan's defeat in World War II is no exception. A number of events present themselves for consideration for this dubious distinction, most obviously the air raid on Pearl Harbor. With this attack Japan initiated a war with the only power that could defeat her, and substantial evidence exists to support the view that her ruination was assured from the time her carrier aircraft struck the Pacific Fleet at its moorings. The date can be pushed back by the most determined of determinists: to the fall of France in May 1940 that offered temptation and opportunity; the China Incident in summer 1937 that proved a quicksand for Japanese ambitions; the Manchurian Incident of September 1931, from which the Japanese date the Greater East Asia War. The Great Depression, the assassinations that ended democratic government in Japan . . . the list can be extended. But the problem associated with the identification of any of these as the event that marked the moment when Japan's defeat was assured is that they predate the outbreak of the Pacific War. They suggest that Japan's defeat was inevitable from the outset, and nothing is more difficult to explain than an inevitable defeat. Convenience thus suggests a place and time after the Day of Infamy, and a combination of circumstances identify November 1943 as the point when Japan's cause passed recall.

Our understanding of naval warfare comes primarily from an Age of Sail that is all but synonymous with British naval mastery. That mastery was primarily based on a superiority of geographical position, numbers, personnel, and morale that brought victories: victories did not bring supremacy other than in the most limited sense. The Pacific War began with Japanese victories that were the product of supremacy, but in its middle and latter years victory and supremacy provided for one another in turn. Between May 1942 and February 1943 two prewar navies fought for the initiative, and in the victories that were won by the U.S. Navy lay supremacy. After 1943 a wartime navy fought a prewar navy, and in the former's growing numbers, power, and effectiveness was the supremacy that provided victory. November 1943 was the watershed between victory and supremacy. In this month, and thereafter, the Americans moved forward in such strength that the issue of individual campaigns, of the war itself, was never in doubt. The only questions that remained unanswered were when final victory would be won, its form, and its cost.[1]

But if in the third quarter of 1943 the war had taken a turn "not necessarily to Japan's advantage," to the Japanese, defeat seemed impossible. Although reverses in the Southwest Pacific pointed to the fact that Japan was fighting a defensive war, the vast swathes of conquest that remained offered space in which Imperial General Headquarters proposed to conduct operations in depth. The New Operational Policy inaugurated in September 1943 set out "an absolute national defense sphere" bound by the Kuriles, Bonins, Marianas and Carolines, western New Guinea, and the Malay Barrier, beyond which the Japanese would fight "strong delaying actions" to buy time to strengthen the Inner Zone extending from Saipan through Truk to Timor.[2]

The change was both belated and doomed. The resources and shipping needed to implement it were beyond Japan's means. Furthermore, the Japanese leadership did not follow its own policy consistently. The New Operational Policy effectively wrote off the forces beyond the Inner Zone: indeed, their only value was if they were abandoned. But as pressure along the perimeter mounted in late 1943 the Japanese Navy committed its carrier air groups and cruiser squadrons to reinforce the fleet and air base at Rabaul, thus depriving itself of formations needed for the defense of the Saipan-Truk-Timor line.[3]

Still more important, the New Operational Policy was doomed because it could not bridge the widening disparity between the opposing navies. Mid-1943 saw the U.S. Navy with only one operational carrier in the Pacific, but within months it acquired the means whereby it was to shatter Japanese designs. Very slowly at first and then with irresistible speed and strength, U.S. forces rendered Rabaul impotent and smashed through the outer defenses in the Gilberts. With the new year came the Japanese loss of Majuro, Kwajalein, and Eniwetok in the Marshalls and more reverses on New Guinea and around Rabaul. As the outer defenses crumbled the fleet, unable to stem a U.S. advance in either the Southwest or Central Pacific, abandoned Truk. Forced to withdraw to the Palaus and then to Singapore, it was powerless to prevent the American rampage throughout the Central Pacific in March and April 1944. But while the Imperial Navy lost its fleet commander, Adm. Mineichi Koga, in an aircraft accident during the evacuation of the Palaus, his 8 March 1944 campaign plan designed to check the Americans in the Central Pacific survived. Given the need for six months to reconstitute the air groups devastated in the Rabaul raids in November 1943, Plan Z envisaged offering battle in mid-1944 on the Saipan-Palaus-Vogelkopf line. Koga assumed prior warning of enemy moves and time to deploy strong air formations, his intention being to use his carriers to support air groups in the islands if the Americans assaulted the Marianas and air groups in the islands to support his carriers if they moved against the Palaus.[4]

By any standard Plan Z reflected a baseless optimism. Nothing in the war to date suggested that effective coordination of Japanese land-based and carrier-borne air power was possible. Yet if under the circumstances Koga's design was perhaps the best available to the Imperial Navy, the events of April belied Japanese hopes. The Americans, informed by signals intelligence of Japanese strength around Madang and Wewak and weakness in the Hollandia-Aitape area, attacked the latter with overwhelming force. Hollandia and Aitape were lost, their garrisons able to offer but minimal resistance and the fleet impotent to intervene. Their fall evidenced the two terrible problems with which Japan had to contend: the conduct of a strategic defense against an enemy with the choice of where, when, and with what strength to attack, aggravated by a dispersal of resources along extended fronts that rendered each individual base vulnerable to defeat before it could be supported.[5]

In reality the Japanese position was worse than these considerations suggest. Between the outbreak of war and 31 March 1944, the Japanese commissioned three fleet and four light carriers compared to the U.S. totals of eight and nine, respectively. Of the Japanese additions, only one fleet carrier was purpose-built. The others were conversions, too slow, too weak in size of air group, or too fragile to be considered frontline units. The converted light carriers were too small to operate the latest aircraft and thus obliged to embark obsolescent models. Moreover, because of the failure to insist upon the minimum possible unfolded wingspan for aircraft, Japanese carrier groups could not embark a full aircraft complement.

Numerically and qualitatively, therefore, the Japanese Navy became increasingly outclassed as the war lengthened. Yet the most profound element in its weakness relative to the U.S. Navy resulted from the latter's having attained a strength that transformed its strategic capabilities. In early 1944 individual U.S. carriers still attacked single targets, but such forays were dated. In the Gilberts campaign the Americans deployed eleven carriers, in the raid on Truk nine. By mid-1944, U.S. carrier groups had the means to conduct sustained operations in massive strength. A new generation of fleet carriers built for sixteen days' high-speed steaming and ten days' operations was joining the fleet. With their arrival the Americans acquired the ability to move into enemy-controlled sea areas and secure command of the air preparatory to deeper penetration of the Japanese defense zones. By mid-1944, when the Japanese believed they would be able to offer battle, the Pacific Fleet had achieved a numerical strength and technical proficiency that ensured the Japanese could never again engage it with any realistic hope of success. And by spring 1944 the U.S. high command, after much dispute, had settled plans for an advance across the Central Pacific and assembled the team of commanders who were to direct it.

American strategy in the Pacific was shaped by choice and necessity. The disastrous opening phase of the struggle left the United States with a commitment in the Southwest Pacific, where in mid-1942 the U.S. high command chose to make its initial offensive effort after the victories at Coral Sea and Midway. The subsequent campaign in the Solomons witnessed two navies fight one another to exhaustion, but after November 1942 a combination of successes in the battle for Guadalcanal, plus the greater resources and industrial potential of the United States, ensured an American victory. It also ensured that for the greater part of 1943 the U.S. initiative would be exercised in the Southwest Pacific. The Americans and their Australasian allies developed a dual offensive, on New Guinea and in the Solomons, that was to form the Southwest Pacific element of a two-pronged assault across the Pacific commencing in November 1943. Supposedly the Southwest and Central Pacific offensives were complementary. In fact they were rivals. For all the evidence that the Pacific was and had to be a naval theater, the Southwest Pacific was under army command. For institutional and other reasons, not unconnected with the distance of Gen. Douglas MacArthur from Washington and the desire that this distance should not be decreased, the army refused to cede the navy direction of the war against Japan. For his part MacArthur sought to promote the primacy of his Southwest Pacific theater and endorsement of his plan to mount an offensive toward the Philippines. For Adm. Ernest J. King, Commander in Chief, U.S. Fleet, and Chief of Naval Operations, the proposed advance inside the line of the Carolines was nonsensical: a drive through the Marshalls, Carolines, and Marianas had to take priority over operations in the Southwest Pacific. After fall 1943 he was supported by the Army Air Force, for the Marianas offered air bases from which the Japanese home islands might be taken under attack. But another factor of greater significance was at work in King's calculations: the capture of Saipan would place U.S. forces in a position to sever enemy lines of communication between Japan and southeast Asia. Not all his subordinates shared King's view of the importance of Saipan, and in the wake of the sanguinary assault on Tarawa in November 1943 the Pacific Fleet command, headed by Adm. Chester W. Nimitz, gave its support for the MacArthur thesis. His hand strengthened by the less costly capture of Kwajalein in February 1944, King ensured that the Marianas' priority remained intact and with a mid-year timetable. In so doing he also ensured that fleet action would be joined because the Imperial Navy had no alternative but to give battle for the Marianas.[6]

The team that was to lead the Central Pacific offensive was headed by Nimitz, returned to the paths of naval righteousness by King, but the demands of his theater precluded his exercising command at sea. For most of 1943 Nimitz groomed his chief of staff, Vice Adm. Raymond A. Spruance, to fill that role. A quiet man with a reputation as a thinker, Spruance had commanded one of the carrier groups at Midway in the enforced absence of Vice Adm. William F. Halsey Jr., with whom his name will be forever linked and with whom he was unfavorably compared. Halsey possessed aggression and drive and was prepared to improvise and leave something to chance; Spruance was noted for his powers of reasoning and logic, a painstaking attention to detail, and commitment to order and organization. Halsey, with a brawler's pug face, was flamboyant and made for the media; the handsome Spruance was remote and distant. No less important in an organization increasingly built around the carrier, Halsey wore wings, and Spruance did not. This would be held against him by the naval air lobby after the Battle of the Philippine Sea.

Below Spruance in his role as commander of the Fifth Fleet were Vice Adms. Marc A. Mitscher, commander of the carrier element Task Force (TF) 58, and Richmond Kelly Turner, commander of the Joint Expeditionary Force (TF 51) assigned to carry out amphibious operations in the Marianas. Relations between Spruance and Mitscher had been difficult as a result of the latter's less than satisfactory performance at Midway, but after June 1942 Mitscher had reestablished his credentials. For the Marianas invasion (Operation FORAGER), he was to have one battleship and four carrier task groups, with 904 carrier aircraft, under his command. Turner would exercise overall

TABLE 16.1 The Carrier Forces at the Battle of the Philippine Sea, 19–20 June 1944

	CV	CVL	BB	CA	CL	DD	AO	AC
U.S. NAVY								
Fifth Fleet								
Adm. R. A. Spruance								
Fast Carrier Task Force (TF 58)								
Vice Adm. M. A. Mitscher								
Task Group 58.1								
Rear Adm. J. J. Clark	2	2	—	3	1	14	—	267
Task Group 58.2								
Rear Adm. A. E. Montgomery	2	2	—	—	4	12	—	244
Task Group 58.3								
Rear Adm. J. W. Reeves	2	2	—	1	4	13	—	228
Task Group 58.4								
Rear Adm. W. K. Harrill	2	1	—	—	4	14	—	163
Task Group 58.7								
Vice Adm. W. A. Lee	—	—	7	4	—	14	—	—
TOTAL	8	7	7	8	13	67	—	902
IMPERIAL JAPANESE NAVY								
First Mobile Fleet,								
Vice Adm. J. Ozawa								
Force A								
Vice Adm. J. Ozawa	3	—	—	2	1	9	—	225
Force B								
Rear Adm. T. Joshima	2	1	1	1	—	10	—	135
Force C								
Vice Adm. T. Kurita	—	3	4	8	1	8	—	90
Supply Forces	—	—	—	—	—	6	6	—
TOTAL	5	4	5	11	2	33	6	450

Notes: CV = fleet carrier; CVL = light carrier, BB = battleship; CA = heavy cruiser, CL = light cruiser, DD = destroyer, AO = oiler; AC = aircraft

command of landings on Saipan, Tinian, and Guam. Tinian was the main objective, but because of tactical considerations Saipan had been selected as the first objective. The landing there was scheduled for 15 June. Guam was to be assaulted on the eighteenth. Turner's subordinate commands included three marine and two army divisions, one of the latter held at Pearl Harbor for want of shipping. In total some 600 ships and 128,000 troops were committed to taking the southern Marianas in June 1944.

TF 58 sailed from Majuro Atoll in the Marshalls on the day that Allied forces landed in Normandy, but other developments, critical to the course and outcome of FORAGER, predated its departure. MacArthur's Southwest Pacific offensive had survived the confirmation of the Saipan priority, and following the capture of Hollandia and Aitape his forces extended their operations into western New Guinea, specifically against Wakde, the Arare-Toem area, and Biak Island. On 2 May, the Imperial Navy determined to make Biak and Manokwari its centers of resistance in western New Guinea. The loss of troops bound for this area forced the navy to substitute Sorong and Halmahera, but upon the U.S. landing on Biak on 27 May the navy, discarding its own policy, convinced itself of the opportunity to implement Plan Z and force "a decisive battle" off the island. The immediate problem was that only one air formation with just eighteen aircraft was within range of Biak. In order to mount a counterattack about 170 land-based aircraft, roughly one-third of the number so carefully horded in readiness for battle, were committed to New Guinea. Accidents and tropical diseases destroyed the effectiveness of the air units involved within a matter of days. Their collapse and the debacle that attended attempts to ferry troops to the battle zone early in June only hardened Japanese resolve to see matters through to the bitter end.

Accordingly Adm. Jisaburo Ozawa, commander of the First Mobile Fleet, the Japanese carrier force, decided to make another attempt to relieve Biak on 15 June and to do so in strength. He therefore detached a force consisting of the superbattleships *Yamato* and *Musashi,* one heavy and two light cruisers, and eight destroyers under Vice Adm. Matome Ugaki for Operation KON. This formation left Tawi-Tawi on 10 June, but by the time it reached Batjan the following day the irrelevance of Biak had become evident. On 11 and 12 June, U.S. carrier forces struck by Guam, Tinian, and Saipan. On 13 June the fast battleships entered action, and the next day two fire-support task groups joined in the bombardment of Saipan.[7] These developments showed the Japanese where "the decisive battle" would have to be fought. Operation KON was suspended on the twelfth and Ugaki ordered to rejoin Ozawa in the Philippine Sea.[8]

Ozawa's carrier force sailed having been taken by surprise strategically, but, in fact, its position had been compromised even earlier on three other counts. First, the storm that accounted for Koga's aircraft in March also accounted for the one carrying his senior staff, and documents recovered for the Americans from the crash by Filipino guerrillas laid bare the details of Plan Z. This, plus the knowledge derived from Allied code-breaking, provided the Americans with knowledge of Japanese plans and intentions long before TF 58 departed Majuro.[9]

Second, by the time the Japanese carriers sailed on the thirteenth, no fewer than eleven U.S. submarines were covering the exits from Tawi-Tawi, seventeen were off the Bonins and the Japanese home islands, and another fifteen were in the Philippines, the Philippine Sea, and the western Carolines. Thus the initial movement of the carrier force and its subsequent passage through San Bernardino Strait into the Philippine Sea was noted and reported to Pearl Harbor. At almost the same time, the *Seahorse* found Ugaki coming north from Batjan.[10] From the outset, therefore, any Japanese hope of achieving strategic or tactical surprise was compromised.

Third, and arguably even more important, the initial American operations in the Marianas possessed a singular significance. In the hope of securing tactical surprise, U.S. air groups attacked the islands in late afternoon on 11 June, and thereafter struck at the Jimas on 15 and 16 June, and at Guam and Rota on 16 and 17 June. These raids were not attacks on single bases: by June 1944 the Pacific Fleet had a strength that enabled it to move not against a single part of a linear defense but simultaneously against an area defense. Destroying 150 Japanese aircraft in the process, TF 58 broke the back of the air formations that had to be available to support the carrier force, and safeguarded itself against attack by enemy shore-based aircraft during the forthcoming campaign. With TF 58 having secured air supremacy, U.S. forces began landing on Saipan at about 0843 on 15 June. By nightfall twenty thousand troops were ashore and had consolidated positions more or less on the line of first-day objectives. A Japanese counterattack after dusk was defeated with the help of naval gunfire, leaving U.S. commanders sufficiently confident of success on Saipan to order the landings on Guam to proceed as planned on the eighteenth.[11]

By the following morning, however, the knowledge that the Japanese carriers were coming out caused a change of the plan. To begin a second landing with a fleet action in the offing clearly involved unacceptable risk, one enhanced by the fact that the prevailing easterly wind meant that the assault beaches and amphibious shipping lay on the west coast of Saipan, in the path of the Japanese approach. Very aware that the Fifth Fleet stood on the threshold of not just a battle but a long and arduous campaign intended to lead to the shores of Japan, Spruance was convinced that the Japanese would make the transport and amphibious forces their primary targets. Accordingly, he ordered the support shipping to haul off to the east after sunset on the seventeenth to place Saipan between itself and the Japanese fleet. His months at Pearl Harbor had made Spruance familiar with Japanese tactics of fighting in dispersed formations and offering bait to draw enemy main forces out of position in an attempt to fall upon unprotected flanks and rear. Therefore he directed the old battleships to loan destroyers to Task Group (TG) 58.7 and take station some twenty-five miles west of Saipan, where they could counter the Japanese attempt to work around the flank of TF 58. The carrier groups would continue to strike Guam and Rota that day, but were to be reconcentrated, refueled, and readied for a fleet action the next morning. Patrol aircraft were to be flown to Saipan in order to search to the west for the approaching Japanese fleet.

Although by the eighteenth the patrol aircraft were operational and the threat of being outmaneuvered thus reduced, Spruance did not reconsider his decisions. At midnight on 18–19 June he turned his force toward the east and Saipan. A false radio report indicating that the Japanese might be attempting to work their way behind TF 58 served to confirm Spruance's views and his intention to keep between the enemy and the beachhead. Given the prevailing wind, by standing to the west and launching and recovering aircraft while steaming east his carrier groups could cover and remain within range of the amphibious forces. By so defining his priorities, Spruance ensured that TF 58 could not close the enemy carriers and that the air battle would be fought overhead—the Japanese having selected the U.S. carriers, not the transports, as their main target.[12] The Japanese, moreover, were concentrated and had neither a decoy nor a flanking force. With scouts that could search to a range of 560 miles compared to the 350 miles of U.S. reconnaissance aircraft and bombers that could strike at 300 miles compared to the 200 miles of their U.S. counterparts, the Japanese could launch and recover aircraft without having to close. Ozawa would seek to preserve this advantage by declining a short-range action and by shuttle-bombing with his aircraft using bases in the Marianas to refuel and rearm. Possessing the advantage of wind and range, he could take as much or as little of the battle as he chose.

What Spruance hoped to achieve in the Marianas was, in effect, to bring to success a plan of campaign remarkably similar to the one the Japanese had implemented with disastrous results at Midway: namely, to strike successively against an island target and enemy fleet but to do so with margins of superiority and time denied the Japanese in 1942 and to a very different result. He depended upon Mitscher's five-hundred-plus fighters, backed by the massed guns of TF 58, to break up whatever attacks the Japanese might launch. But by refusing Mitscher's proposals to move westward to close with the Japanese on the nights of the 17–18 and 18–19 June, Spruance was to bring bitter criticism upon himself after the battle by a carrier air lobby that claimed it had been denied the opportunity to destroy the enemy fleet—and denied the opportunity despite its own proposals.

The battle was slow to develop. On 16 June the two main Japanese formations—the three carrier divisions and the KON battle force—rendezvoused
some three hundred miles east of Samar. They spent most of the seventeenth
refueling before moving northeast to locate TF 58. Late on the eighteenth
contact was established with a reconcentrated U.S. carrier force some two
hundred miles west of Saipan and at a distance of about four hundred miles—
an ideal range for Japanese aircraft at the start of the battle. Force C's three
light carriers, each embarking six fighters, fifteen dive-bombers, and nine torpedo-bombers, promptly began launching a strike. This operation was canceled upon receipt of a message from Ozawa making clear his intention to
decline battle until the following day. Whatever advantage might be gained by
an attack at sunset had to be balanced against the hazards of a night recovery,
while aircraft that went to fields in the Marianas would be limited to a single
mission after returning to their carriers on the morning of 19 June. Unsuspecting the odds against his airmen surviving a single encounter with the U.S.
combat air patrol, Ozawa believed he could not limit himself to just one strike
mission on 19 June. Thus in the late afternoon he turned away before dou-
bling back under cover of dark. In the meanwhile he issued orders for land-
based air formations to proceed to the southern Marianas to join the battle.
At the same time, he deployed his forces into battle formation, with Force C
in the van and the two main carrier groups about one hundred miles astern.
Ozawa hoped that the heavy units of Force C could attract and absorb enemy
attention while its numerous seaplanes would be able to conduct effective
reconnaissance.[13]

The battle seemed to begin well for the Japanese when all three of the
scouting units launched between 0445 and 0530 made contact with U.S.
forces. The earliest contact was obtained around 0730, and first the light carriers of the vanguard and then Ozawa's task group committed aircraft to the
attack. The first strike, consisting of eight Jills armed with torpedoes, forty-
five Zeke dive-bombers, and sixteen fighters was launched at about 0826. The
second, consisting of twenty-seven Jill torpedo-bombers, fifty-three Judy dive-
bombers, and forty-eight Zeke fighters began to become airborne at 0856. In
the course of these operations the Japanese suffered their first serious
reverse.[14]

The obvious weakness of the Japanese in the air has served to obscure a
second weakness that was no less important. By mid-1944 the Imperial Navy
had lost so many destroyers that its capital ships could not be screened properly, a problem exacerbated by the concentration in the vanguard of seaplanes

that could have conducted antisubmarine patrols. Even as the *Taiho* launched her strike, the *Albacore,* threading her way through the screen, fired six torpedoes at Ozawa's flagship. Only one hit but more than six hours later an explosion in the *Taiho's* upper hangar, directed downward by the armored flight deck, blew out the hangar walls, devastated the engine and boiler rooms, and blasted its way through the bottom of the ship. With the carrier on fire throughout her length, Ozawa and his staff transferred to a cruiser. The *Taiho* settled very quickly and soon after 1700 she capsized and sank, taking with her most of her crew and thirteen aircraft.[15]

Although the *Taiho* was the first Japanese carrier damaged at the Battle of the Philippine Sea, she was not the first to be lost. After chasing the Japanese for more than two days, the *Cavalla* put four torpedoes into the *Shokaku* shortly after midday when the carrier was some sixty miles southeast of the position where the *Taiho* had been hit. The detonations set off a series of fires and explosions that blew the carrier to pieces shortly after 1500.[16]

The course and shape of the air battle on 19 June was largely fashioned by Mitscher's deployment of his task groups into a reversed F that lost its textbook symmetry as its formations chased the wind at the expense of station-keeping. But one aspect of his deployment remained constant throughout the day. In unconscious imitation of Ozawa, Mitscher placed his battleships and the smallest of his carrier groups between the enemy and the others, employing TG 58.7 to draw attacks upon itself. With their massive armor and fire

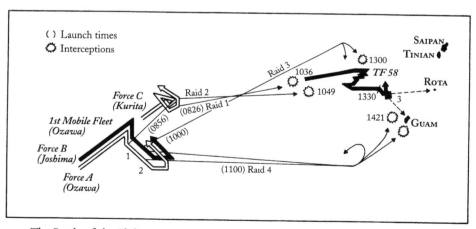

The Battle of the Philippine Sea. Situation as of midafternoon, 19 June 1944. (1) The *Albacore* torpedoes the *Taiho* at 0920. (2) The *Cavalla* torpedoes the *Shokaku* at 1220. (3) U.S. aircraft keep the airfields on Rota and Guam under attack.

The Battle of the Philippine Sea. One of Fighting Squadron (VF) 1's F6F Grumman Hellcats prepares to take off from the *Yorktown* to join in the "Marianas Turkey Shoot" of 19 June 1944. The canister underneath the fighter's fuselage is a drop-tank.
U.S. Naval Institute

power, the battleships were deemed able to look after themselves; TG 58.4 would furnish close support. The backbone of the fleet's defensive effort would be provided by the three carrier groups deployed behind these formations.

After launching two unsuccessful searches before and at dawn, the U.S. effort opened with fighters from TG 58.1 and TG 58.3 carrying out a series of sweeps over Guam and Rota. With Japanese carriers to the west, this commitment did not recommend itself to certain commanders, and it was brought to an end when radar detected the approach of Japanese aircraft about 1000. While the Hellcats over the Marianas were recalled and concentrated for the air battle, a number of carriers flew off strike aircraft simply to clear their decks and facilitate handling the fighters. Many of the bombers chose to attack Japanese installations on Guam and Rota rather than circle aimlessly waiting for a lull or an end to the fighter battle. Moreover some Hellcats engaged in "hot pursuit" of enemy aircraft making their way to airfields ashore after their missions against the U.S. task groups. In the course of actions that lasted throughout the daylight hours, the Americans destroyed roughly eighty aircraft that were either on the islands or being flown into them from Truk or the Bonin and Volcano Islands. In this manner TF 58 achieved the extraordinary feat of keeping Guam and Rota neutralized even as it annihilated Japanese carrier air power.[17]

At sea, the battle developed along lines that the U.S. command could not have foreseen in its most optimistic assessments. The Japanese first wave attacked the first target it encountered, the radar picket line and battleships of TG 58.7. Between 1036 and 1057 it lost eight fighters, thirty-two dive-bombers, and two torpedo-bombers—two-thirds of its strength—in return for a single bomb hit on the battleship *South Dakota,* a near-miss on a cruiser, and the destruction of a solitary Hellcat. To all intents and purposes, this attack ended Force C's active involvement in the battle.[18]

The second wave, from Ozawa's own carriers, fared no better than the first. Even without the *Taiho*'s misfortune, the attack began inauspiciously: nineteen aircraft were lost or forced to turn back before reaching the enemy. Despite a successful diversion that drew off Hellcats from TG 58.1 by the use of "window"—radar-deflecting foil—95 of the 109 aircraft that reached TG 58.3 and TG 58.7 were destroyed in return for very minor damage inflicted on the carriers *Wasp* and *Bunker Hill.* Overall the Japanese lost twenty-three Jills, thirty-two Zekes, and forty-two Judys in the course of an attack that lasted from 1139 to 1202.[19]

Even before the first two attacks were delivered, Ozawa mounted a third strike, launching fifteen Zeke fighters, twenty-five Zeke dive-bombers, and seven Jills from Force B between 1000 and 1015. He made his final move between 1100 and 1130, when he launched thirty fighters, forty-six Judy, Val, and Zeke dive-bombers, and six Jills from Joshima's carriers and the *Zuikaku* in a fourth strike. With this attack, Ozawa committed his reserve before being able to verify the results of his initial attacks. By so doing he left himself with barely enough fighters for a combat air patrol and no means to mount a follow-up strike.[20]

By midday Ozawa's hopes for success rested with his third and fourth waves. The third, sent too far to the north, had only a glancing encounter with TG 58.4 and TG 58.7. Hellcats from TG 58.1 attempted an interception, but contacts were fleeting. No U.S. ship was hit, and only seven of forty-seven

Japanese aircraft were shot down. The fourth raid fared disastrously. Directed too far to the south, most of its eighty-two aircraft failed to locate the U.S. task groups. One detachment found and attacked TG 58.2 with flair but no luck. The others, proceeding on to Guam, were detected by carrier radar, with the result that Hellcats shot down or severely damaged every plane trying to reach Orote airfield. All but nine of the aircraft committed to this attack were lost.[21]

In the course of the day the Japanese had lost more than 80 aircraft in the Marianas and at least 260 from their carriers. By dawn on 20 June they had just a hundred fit for operations, which must mean that another seventy or eighty were lost, damaged, or became unserviceable on 19 June. On the American side, seventeen aircraft were destroyed in combat over TF 58. Another eight went down over Guam, and five more were written off after operations over the island. Thus on 19 June U.S. forces lost eighteen Hellcats and a dozen other aircraft while accounting for perhaps 350 Japanese planes. There have been few such one-sided victories as the Battle of the Philippine Sea on 19 June. It was small wonder that the victors dubbed the day's proceedings "the Great Marianas Turkey Shoot."[22]

Ozawa had no inkling of the enormity of his defeat. Even though very few planes had returned to their carriers, the assumption that missing aircraft had made their way to Guam hid the extent of Japanese losses. Moreover the handful that did return reported staggering U.S. losses of both ships and aircraft. To add to the confusion, Vice Adm. Kakuji Kakuta, commander of shore-based aviation with headquarters on Tinian, informed Ozawa that carrier aircraft had been recovered on the airfields but failed to add that very few remained serviceable. He also claimed that his forces were continuing to inflict heavy losses on the enemy. In a sense Kakuji's disinformation did not make much difference to the battle, but candor might have prompted Ozawa to clear the combat zone as quickly as possible. As it was he resolved to refuel his ships on 20 June and resume the battle on the twenty-first.[23]

By the middle of the afternoon of 19 June, Japanese offensive power had been broken, and, with no threat against which to guard, TF 58 was freed for offensive action. It had to turn back to the west in any event because it was fast running out of searoom. By 1500 some units were within visual or radar range of Guam and Rota, leaving Spruance and Mitscher no option but to bring their forces back to the west.

Seeking out the enemy was not without problems. TF 58 could not turn west immediately because of the need to recover aircraft. With the approach of night the process was slow, and it was not until about 2000 that the last air-craft were aboard and TF 58 was able to head west. Even then it did not make full speed. The demands of the day had been heavy, and if battle resumed the following morning needs were unlikely to be any less onerous. Destroyers could not indulge in prolonged high-speed steaming, and a speed of 23 knots was selected as a compromise between haste and economical cruising. More-over TG 58.4 was detached. Low on fuel, it was ordered to remain off Saipan to refuel and keep the enemy airfields under attack.

In addition, Spruance and Mitscher had no clear idea of the whereabouts of the enemy, and they made very little attempt to redress this situation. The Japanese trail was cold by the time TF 58 turned west, but the U.S. carriers did not conduct long-range searches either during the night of 19–20 June or the following morning. TF 58 did not mount a deep reconnaissance until noon, and then only on a very restricted search sector, and did not launch a deep reconnaissance in strength before 1330.

An Avenger from this mission secured the all-important contact with Ozawa's force at about 1540. The initial report, more confusing than enlight-ening, was clarified over the next twenty-five minutes by a number of amplifi-cations. These announced the presence of three enemy task groups steaming slowly west, apparently refueling. The latter observation was erroneous. Such was Japanese confusion that not one warship refueled on 20 June; when found, the Japanese were preparing to refuel the next day.

The U.S. sighting reports were eavesdropped. This, combined with sight-ing reports of TF 58 by Japanese scouts, belatedly convinced Ozawa that his only hope lay in flight. The Japanese ships turned northwest and began to work up speed, but their chance to escape had gone. The Avenger had located the nearest Japanese task group at a position 275 miles from TF 58. This was extreme range for U.S. strike aircraft, but what made American decision-making difficult was the lateness of the hour. An attack could not be made much before dusk and would necessitate a night recovery, which no com-mander undertook lightly. Spruance and Mitscher, however, had little choice: it was inconceivable that TF 58 should pass up the chance to attack when the opportunity finally presented itself. Thus the hazards of a night recovery were accepted, and eighty-five fighters, seventy-seven dive-bombers, and fifty-four torpedo-bombers were launched by eleven carriers in just fifteen minutes.[24]

A two-hour flight brought the first U.S. aircraft into contact with the scat-tering Japanese task groups at about 1840. The carrier groups had separated and left the oiler group trailing as they tried to put themselves beyond the range of U.S. bombers. In the course of a wildly confused action fought as the sun set, the Japanese combat air patrol was swept aside. Some of the attackers went for the first target they encountered, with the result that two of six oilers were crippled and subsequently scuttled. Of the carriers, the *Zuikaku* was hit and suffered a serious fire in her upper hangar. At one time the flames appeared unmanageable and the order was given to abandon ship, but at length the fire was brought under control, and she returned to Kure under her own power. In Force C only the *Chiyoda* was attacked. Her hangar empty and her fuel lines drained, she survived the damage caused by a single hit aft.

All three of Force B's carriers underwent attack. The *Ryuho,* on her first and last operation, was slightly damaged by near-misses. The *Junyo* emerged with minor damage, despite being hit twice on her flight deck abaft her island. Her sister ship, the *Hiyo,* was not so fortunate. The only fleet carrier ever to be sunk solely by aerial torpedo attack, she was lost as a result of a series of explosions set off by a single hit by an Avenger from the *Belleau Wood.*[25]

Amongst the Japanese escorts, one battleship and one heavy cruiser sustained slight damage. More serious were the losses incurred by the already hopelessly depleted air groups. Eighty carrier aircraft and seaplanes were lost, just thirty-five aircraft, all but ten of them Zeke fighters, being left to the six surviving carriers. This time, however, the U.S. air groups paid a high price for their success. Only seventeen aircraft were shot down in the attack, but another eighty-two either ditched or had to be written off in trying to return to their carriers. Of the 209 aircrew involved, all but 49 were saved. Losses would have been still higher had not Mitscher courageously ordered his carriers to turn on their searchlights to guide his weary pilots home.[26]

The U.S. attack was not the end of the battle. On 21 and 22 June, TF 58 sought in vain to renew contact with the enemy, and, when his escape was conceded, consoled itself with strikes by TG 58.1 against Pagan on 23 June and the Jimas the next day. Just as the earlier raids on the islands formed part of the overture to battle, these raids were the finale. On 24 June the Americans destroyed a minimum of 60 of the 122 aircraft on Iwo Jima. Thus perhaps 200 Japanese land-based aircraft were destroyed in the Bonins, Volcanos, and Marianas before and after the Battle of the Philippine Sea, in addition to about 450 aircraft and seaplanes from the First Mobile Fleet.[27]

For a U.S. Navy reared on the expectation of "decisive battle" as prescribed by Mahan, the action's outcome was a grievous disappointment, and for a long time the conduct—or alleged misconduct—of operations was a subject of fierce controversy. Much of the disappointment and frustration felt in the immediate aftermath of the battle stemmed from the fact that, the sinking of the *Taiho* and *Shokaku* being unknown, the Americans did not realize the extent of their success. More seriously, much of the controversy was personal and institutional, the by-product of the struggle by the naval air lobby for supremacy within the navy. Within this context Spruance, and hence the Gun Club, was accused of having allowed the opportunity to win an annihilating victory to slip away for want of an understanding of naval air power. The bitterness of such criticism obscured reality. Despite possession of the weather gage, Spruance could not have imposed battle on the enemy; even if he had done what Mitscher proposed, there is no certainty that the results would have been greater than those that were attained. Admittedly one aspect of his conduct of the battle was questionable: failure to mount deep reconnaissance until the afternoon of twentieth was, at best, somewhat unfortunate. Had timely reconnaissance contacted the enemy early on 20 June, perhaps two strikes could have been mounted and some of the ships that escaped to fight in October sunk; but this is by no means certain. The need to steam to the east to launch and recover aircraft might well have limited TF 58 to a single strike no more successful than the one that took place.[28]

Much of the controversy that surrounded the battle was also the product of failure to understand both the nature of naval warfare and what TF 58 achieved. The "decisive battle" so beloved by Mahan was largely the product of a misreading of history. In modern times fleet actions have been few, and fleet actions fought to a finish still fewer. The importance attached to such battles of annihilation as the Nile, Trafalgar, and Tsushima lies in the fact that they were very exceptional. Even such clear victories as Quiberon Bay, the First of June, and Cape St. Vincent were limited. Most battles proved indecisive in terms of both losses and results. By World War II, the concept of "decisive battle" had lost whatever relevance it ever possessed. Navies were too large and diverse for any single victory to be truly decisive because no single action could encompass the destruction of more than one part of an enemy navy. Of course not all parts were of equal value, but the result of battle is not determined simply by the balance of losses. Herein lies the significance of the Battle of the Philippine Sea.

The victory in the Philippine Sea is properly measured in terms of losses, position, time, and organization. Victory in the Philippine Sea left the U.S. Navy free to complete the conquest of the southern Marianas and thereby place an American thumb on the Japanese windpipe. Victory in the Philippine Sea bared the Western Pacific to an American advance in a manner and at a time of American choosing. Conversely defeat in the Philippine Sea cost the

Imperial Navy months of preparation in the raising of carrier air groups; never again could it put a balanced fleet to sea. Recourse to the use of *kamikazes* was acknowledgment of a naval defeat much greater than just the Philippine Sea, but it was defeat in the Philippine Sea that brought the Imperial Navy to the realization that the war was lost—and within a month of the battle, the hard-line Tojo cabinet fell. By ensuring the security of its amphibious shipping and the subsequent conquest of the Marianas, and by breaking Japanese naval aviation, TF 58 won one of the greatest victories in the history of naval warfare.

NOTES

1. This argument is developed at some length in the introductory chapter of the author's *Grave of a Dozen Schemes: British Naval Planning and the War against Japan, 1943–1945* (Annapolis, 1996).

2. Louis Morton, *United States Army in World War II: Strategy and Command, The First Two Years* (Washington, D.C., 1962, reprint, 1989), 543–58.

3. Philip A. Crowl and Edmund G. Love, *United States Army in World War II: Seizure of the Gilberts and Marshalls* (Washington, D.C., 1955; reprint, 1989), 70.

4. Samuel Eliot Morison, *History of United States Naval Operations in World War II* (Boston, 1947–62); vol. 6: *Breaking the Bismarcks Barrier, 22 July 1942–1 May 1944,* 323–36 for the strikes in November 1943 on Rabaul; vol. 7: *Aleutians, Gilberts and Marshalls, June 1942–April 1944,* and vol. 8: *New Guinea and the Marianas, March 1943–August 1944* for the relevant operations.

5. For the Hollandia-Aitape operation, see chap. 4 in Edward J Dres, *MacArthur's ULTRA: Codebreaking and the War against Japan* (Topeka, 1992), and the relevant volumes of Morison, *History of United States Naval Operations in World War II* and the Army's official history.

6. For the meeting of 27 January 1944 at Pearl Harbor and the subsequent exchanges involving King's defense of the Central Pacific offensive, see E. B. Potter, *Nimitz* (Annapolis, 1976), 280–86, and Thomas B. Buell, *Master of Sea Power: A Biography of Fleet Admiral Ernest J. King* (Boston, 1980), 440–44. Grace Person Hayes, *The History of the Joint Chiefs of Staff in World War II: The War against Japan* (Annapolis, 1982), chap. 21, "The Months of Critical Decision," presents the most authoritative account of the general planning process at this time.

7. William T. Y'Blood, *Red Sun Setting: The Battle of the Philippine Sea* (Annapolis, 1981), 37–62.

8. Ibid., 25–29.

9. Rear Adm. Edwin T Layton, USN (Ret.), with Capt. Roger Pineau, USNR (Ret.), and John Costello, *"And I Was There": Pearl Harbor and Midway—Breaking the Secrets* (New York, 1985), 484–85; John Prados, *Combined Fleet Decoded: The Secret History of American Intelligence and the Japanese Navy in World War II* (New York, 1995), 549–61

10. Y'Blood, *Red Sun Setting,* 66.

11. See, for example, Philip A Crowl, *United States Army in World War II: The War in the Pacific, Campaign in the Marianas* (Washington, D.C., 1960; reprint, 1989), chap. 5, for the events of the first day, and Louis Morton's chapter, "The Marianas 1944," in Lt. Col. Merrill L. Bartlett, ed., *Assault from the Sea: Essays on the History of Amphibious Warfare* (Annapolis, 1983), for a general view of the campaign in the Marianas.

12. Vice Adm. Emmet P. Forrestel, *Admiral Raymond A. Spruance, USN: A Study in Command* (Washington, D.C., 1966), 137–38; and Thomas B. Buell, *The Quiet Warrior: A Biography of Admiral Raymond A. Spruance* (Boston, 1974), 268–72.

13. Y'Blood, *Red Sun Setting,* 85–88.

14. Ibid., 95–103. Accounts of the battle appear in numerous works, but *Red Sun Setting* is considered the authoritative treatment

15. Ibid., 115, 127–29.

16. The official account of the submarines' role in the battle is given in Theodore Roscoe, *United States Submarine Operations in World War II* (Annapolis, 1949), 379–83

17. Y'Blood, *Red Sun Setting,* 131–38.

18. Ibid., 102–12.

19. Ibid., 116–26.

20. Ibid., 132.

21. Ibid., 130, 132–37.

22. George Baer, *One Hundred Years of Sea Power: The U.S. Navy, 1890–1990* (Stanford, 1994), 249, states that the Japanese carriers lost 297 aircraft on this single day, plus another 100 land-based aircraft, for the loss of 25 American aircraft, and gives total Japanese losses, presumably only from the Mobile Fleet, as 476 aircraft and 445 pilots

23. Y'Blood, *Red Sun Setting,* 143; Kiyoshi Ikeda, "Vice Admiral Jisaburo Ozawa," in Stephen Howarth, ed., *Men of War: Great Naval Leaders of World War II* (New York, 1992), 287.

24. Y'Blood, *Red Sun Setting,* 148–51.

25. Ibid., 153–76.

26. In his chapter on Ozawa in Howarth, ed., *Men of War,* 287, Ikeda states that Japanese fighters shot down twenty American aircraft.

27. Y'Blood, *Red Sun Setting,* 199–200.

28. Perhaps the best summary of the various arguments is provided by Clark G. Reynolds in the sixth section of chap. 6 in *The Fast Carriers: The Forging of an Air Navy* (New York, 1968; reprint, Annapolis, 1992), 204–10.

17

The Battle of Leyte Gulf

Thomas J. Cutler

On the morning of 25 October 1944, there occurred an act of heroism rarely equaled in the annals of American naval history. Three U.S. destroyers and four destroyer escorts charged headlong toward a Japanese formation consisting of four battleships—including one of the two largest ever built—and a great array of cruisers and destroyers. The action was among the most one-sided engagements in history—the Japanese 8-, 14-, and 18-inch guns arrayed against the 3- and 5-inch guns of the Americans; the Japanese ship tonnage outweighing the American by a ratio of more than 20 to 1. Although sustaining serious losses themselves, these intrepid American destroyermen were able to prevent the powerful Japanese force from devastating a group of helpless carriers and to frustrate the Japanese attempt to disrupt the invasion of the Philippines.

This battle—known today as the Battle off Samar and but one of several engagements comprising the Battle of Leyte Gulf—was the result of blunders on a grand scale. A foolhardy venture in a purely tactical sense, it was carried out in the midst of almost total chaos with little or no plan or design. But it was one of those grand moments in military history when reason succumbs to spontaneity, when courage reigns supreme, when noble sacrifice is the foremost tactic. Certain defeat and strategic disaster were warded off by the courage of a few men who faced death with a fortitude that can barely be imagined.

The Battle of Leyte Gulf was actually a series of battles, spanning several days and occurring in the various waters that surround and penetrate the Philippine archipelago. The stage for this great action was set in late October 1944 when the Allies moved to recapture the Philippines from the Japanese.

In retrospect, an assault on the Philippines seems a logical step in the dual thrust of the U.S. Pacific War strategy. Adm. Chester Nimitz's Central Pacific and Gen. Douglas MacArthur's Southwest Pacific campaigns had led each of them, by different routes, to the vicinity of the Philippine Islands. But as the two drives converged in the Western Pacific in mid-1944, there was a division of thought as to where they should meet. To MacArthur there could be no other decision than to strike at the Philippines. Two years earlier, after President Roosevelt ordered him to escape the islands' fall, he had vowed, with much fanfare, "I shall return." Chief of Naval Operations Ernest J. King and other U.S. planners favored bypassing the Philippines and invading Formosa instead. The matter eventually came before Roosevelt when the president met with MacArthur and Nimitz at Pearl Harbor to discuss future Pacific strategy. MacArthur carried the day, convincing Roosevelt of the political necessity of recapturing the Philippines by arguing that the United States would lose face among the Asian nations in the postwar world if an Asian ally were allowed to suffer under Japanese domination any longer than was absolutely necessary. With the president supporting MacArthur and several strategic setbacks in the China campaign causing King to back off his Formosa preference, the Philippines became the point of convergence.

Once the decision had been made, a timetable was drawn up that would have brought the Allies back to the Philippines in late December 1944. This schedule might have held had it not been for the pugnacious tenacity of an admiral the press had taken to calling "Bull."

In the latter part of 1944, Nimitz had given command of the Third Fleet—the most powerful naval force the world had ever seen—to Adm. William F. "Bull" Halsey. A "johnnie-come-lately" to the aviation community—he had earned his wings in 1935 at the age of fifty-two—Halsey had commanded some of the earliest carrier raids of the war, including the daring strike on Tokyo itself in April 1942. Six months later he had been sent to command the South Pacific theater when less than spectacular battle results and flagging morale had threatened the Allied position there; and as much by the force of his personality as by any strategic or tactical decisions, he was able to revive the struggle for Guadalcanal and eject the Japanese from the Solomons. His pugnacity and outspokenness earned him the reputation of an aggressive fighter and made him the best known of America's World War II admirals. The press loved him because he provided good copy, whether by calling the enemy "lousy yellow rat monkey bastards" or offering to send the Japanese his current position so they could come fight him.[1]

Despite his colorful image and his wartime successes, Halsey had been frustrated by his inability to meet the enemy in a full-scale carrier battle. Bad

William F. ("Bull") Halsey. *U.S. Naval Institute*

luck had kept him from arriving in time for the Battle of the Coral Sea, a debilitating skin rash had hospitalized him just before the carrier clash at Midway, his responsibilities as theater commander in the South Pacific had kept him out of the carrier battles around the Solomons, and the rotational command system that Nimitz had set up in 1944 left Halsey ashore while Adm. Raymond Spruance led U.S. forces to the stunning victory in the Battle of the Philippine Sea. Halsey was spoiling for a fight, especially for one with enemy carriers.[2]

As Commander Third Fleet, Halsey was certainly prepared for a major engagement. At Leyte Gulf Task Force (TF) 38, the fleet's offensive element, would include sixteen carriers with more than a thousand aircraft, six battleships, six heavy cruisers, nine light cruisers, and fifty-seven destroyers. In regular cruising formation, this force stretched over an area forty miles long and nine miles wide.[3]

On 12 September 1944, just weeks after Halsey had assumed command, Task Force 38 arrived off the west coast of the Philippines to launch strikes against Japanese forces there. A downed American flyer who was returned by friendly Filipinos reported that he had seen no Japanese on the island of Leyte. This, coupled with the rather desultory Japanese response to the U.S. attacks, caused Halsey to send out a series of reconnaissance flights. The only signs they saw of the Japanese were a number of seemingly abandoned airstrips.[4]

Reflecting on these discoveries, Halsey decided to "stick [his] neck out" and sent a recommendation to the Joint Chiefs of Staff via Admiral Nimitz that several interim targets be bypassed and the invasion date of the Philippines be moved up.[5] As later events would prove, his description of Leyte as "wide open" was overly optimistic, but his characteristic aggressiveness caused the schedule to be accelerated, forcing the Japanese to react before they were adequately prepared. All this would have a significant effect on the forthcoming battle.[6]

The Joint Chiefs accepted Halsey's recommendation and the invasion of the Philippines was set for late October. The plan for the invasion, codenamed "King Two," brought together a powerful but disparate array of forces. MacArthur's Southwest Pacific command would spearhead the amphibious assault, while Halsey's powerful Third Fleet would be present to meet the Japanese fleet should the latter choose to challenge the operation. Halsey's amphibious assets were transferred to MacArthur's control, leaving the Third Fleet with the striking capability of Task Force 38 as a mobile force ready to respond to any Japanese threats.

MacArthur's naval forces, designated the Seventh Fleet, were under the command of Vice Adm. Thomas C. Kinkaid, an experienced commander who had been described in the 1908 Naval Academy yearbook as "a black-eyed, rosy-cheeked, noisy Irishman who loves a rough-house." Kinkaid had gotten his share of rough-houses in the Pacific War. Although his training and experience had been primarily in gunnery and in big-gun ships, he had proven himself a capable carrier force commander in the Solomons campaign. After solidifying his reputation in the North Pacific where his Task Force 8 had engaged the Japanese in Alaskan waters, he was sent in June of 1943 to the Southwest Pacific to take over the Seventh Fleet. He and MacArthur got on well, and Kinkaid remained in command of a much-improved Seventh Fleet when MacArthur was ready to return to the Philippines.

Leyte Gulf was chosen as the invasion site because its position on the eastern side of the Philippines would force Japanese naval forces—then concentrated in the Inland Sea of Japan and in Lingga Roads near Singapore—to come around or through the archipelago should they choose to contest the landings. The assault would be the first landing to involve two U.S. fleets, and it was the first that would not have the benefit of a unified command. Kinkaid answered to MacArthur, who would be present at the landing, and Halsey answered to Nimitz, who would remain at his headquarters in Pearl Harbor. MacArthur and Nimitz had no common commander closer than Washington, D.C.

Kinkaid's forces, augmented by the amphibious components of the Third Fleet, were to mount the assault on Leyte. His orders, the result of meticulous planning, were clear and unambiguous. Halsey's guidance from Nimitz was less so. The Third Fleet, now essentially Task Force 38, was ordered to "cover and support forces of Southwest Pacific in order to assist the seizure and occupation of objectives in the Central Philippines." Halsey was also directed to "destroy enemy naval and air forces in or threatening the Philippine Area." Unfortunately these unequivocal instructions were clouded by a qualification that had not figured in any of Nimitz's previous directives: "In case opportunity for destruction of major portion of the enemy fleet offer [*sic*] or can be created, such destruction becomes the primary task."[7]

Ever since their defeat at the Battle of the Philippine Sea in June, the Japanese had been frantically trying to recover from their devastating losses of aircraft and pilots in what had been dubbed the "Marianas Turkey Shoot." They also were planning a last-ditch defense against the next major American thrust. Not sure where that thrust might come, they devised a number of contingency plans and designated them with the optimistic sobriquet *Sho*, meaning "victory." *Sho 1* applied to the defense of the Philippines and *Sho 2* through 4 covered other areas, including Formosa and the home islands. When U.S. forces arrived off Leyte and began their assault, the Japanese activated *Sho 1*. This complicated plan called for bringing essentially all remaining Japanese naval forces together at Leyte from several different directions.

Vice Adm. Jisaburo Ozawa had been operating his carriers among the home islands, trying desperately to train new pilots in time to counter the next U.S. move. When *Sho 1* was activated, he headed south with the heavy carrier *Zuikaku,* three light carriers, two hybrid battleship-carriers, three cruisers, and nine destroyers. Earlier the Americans had turned the tide of war at Midway with a force smaller than this, but there was a crucial difference. Though there were only three U.S. carriers at Midway, they had been filled with aircraft and well-trained pilots. But by 1944, the Japanese naval air arm had taken such heavy losses that Ozawa's force had a total of only 116 aircraft embarked as it steamed toward Leyte Gulf. Worse for the Japanese, the pilots available to fly these pitifully few planes were barely trained and without combat experience. Recognizing their carriers' virtual impotence, the Japanese had decided to use them as a decoy, hoping that some part of the American armada might be lured away from Leyte Gulf, thereby giving the other Japanese forces a chance of success.

Those other forces included most of Japan's remaining surface formations. The strongest, commanded by Vice Adm. Takeo Kurita, consisted of five battleships, twelve cruisers, and fifteen destroyers. Two of Kurita's battleships were the super dreadnoughts *Yamato* and *Musashi.* With full load displacements of 70,000 tons and overall lengths of 862 feet, these giant sister ships were considerably bigger than any U.S. battleship, and their 18.1-inch guns were the largest ever mounted on a naval vessel. Each of their three triple turrets weighed 2,774 tons, more than a large destroyer displaced. The blast from these guns tore the clothing from crew members exposed on the weatherdecks and, in some cases, knocked them unconscious. Special housings had to be designed to protect the ships' boats from blast damage, and anti-aircraft guns could be placed only in areas where they would not be disabled by the firing of the main batteries. A single shell weighed 3,200 pounds—a third more than the 16-inch shells fired by the U.S. *Iowa*-class battleships.[8]

The Japanese plan called for Admiral Kurita to depart from his anchorage in Lingga Roads near Singapore, proceed to Brunei for refueling, cut through the Philippine archipelago via the Sibuyan Sea, and emerge through San Bernardino Strait to the north of Leyte Gulf. Meanwhile, another surface-action force was to approach from the south of Leyte Gulf through Surigao Strait after crossing the Sulu Sea. This element, for reasons not entirely clear but probably related to the personalities involved, was to advance in two echelons. The first, commanded by Vice Adm. Shoji Nishimura, would sortie from Lingga Roads; the second, under Vice Adm. Kiyohide Shima, would steam south from the Ryukyus.

This pincer attack on the U.S. amphibious units at Leyte Gulf by Kurita's, Nishimura's, and Shima's combined forces had a very real chance of success provided that the timing was impeccable and, more important, provided that

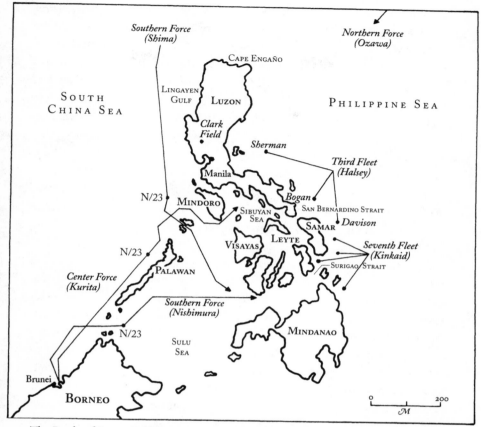

The Battle of Leyte Gulf. Situation as of noon, 24 October 1944. The notation N/23 indicates positions at noon the preceding day.

Ozawa could lure Admiral Halsey's Third Fleet to the north. The latter expectation might have seemed far-fetched except for two factors. While the Americans were certainly aware that they had inflicted grievous harm upon the Japanese in earlier battles, they had no way of knowing just how serious the damage had been to the Japanese naval air component. This meant that a carrier force approaching from the north might seem an important enough target to warrant the commitment of at least part of the Third Fleet. The other factor centered on Halsey's pugnacious personality. The grizzled old admiral's aggressive spirit was well-known and gave reasonable grounds to expect that he might be decoyed away when presented with the opportunity of engaging enemy carriers.

Shortly after midnight on 23 October, the U.S. submarines *Darter* and *Dace* surfaced on the eastern side of the Philippines in a relatively narrow water-way flanked by shoal water known as Palawan Passage. The subs had rendezvoused to exchange message traffic in case one or the other had missed any important communications. While still alongside, the *Darter* picked up a radar contact to the southwest. At first the radar operator believed he had detected nothing more than a rain squall, but when the *Dace's* radarman reported the same contact and both operators began to make out details in the fuzzy phosphorescent image, the subs' skippers were convinced they had detected a large formation of ships.

The two subs separated and increased speed to close the new targets. Because the night was very dark, they ran surfaced until the approach of dawn. At 0510 both submarines took to the depths and continued to jockey for position. By then it was clear that they had indeed intercepted a sizable enemy force. It was, in fact, Kurita's force, bound for the Sibuyan Sea.

Twenty-two minutes passed before the *Darter* opened fire on the lead ship in the formation with six torpedoes from her bow tubes. Turning about she fired four more torpedoes from her stern tubes at the second ship in the column. The sound of multiple explosions soon confirmed that the *Darter's* torpedoes had found their target. The *Dace*, meanwhile, opened fire on yet another Japanese ship, and as the two American submarines went deep to evade retribution, two enemy cruisers succumbed and a third, badly damaged, turned back to Brunei with a pair of destroyers as escorts.

Beside deleting three heavy cruisers from the Japanese order of battle and giving the Americans at Leyte a warning of Kurita's approach, this encounter would prove significant for other reasons. One of the cruisers sunk was Kurita's flagship, the *Atago*. The admiral had to be rescued from the sea and resume command from the battleship *Yamato*. This cannot have been without some physical and psychological effects on the Japanese commander just hours before the big battle, and it forced him and his staff to work in an unfamiliar environment. Furthermore, some members of his staff had been picked up by a different vessel and were not reunited with Kurita before combat commenced. How much these events influenced those that followed is impossible to assess, but during the next two days, Kurita would face great challenges and be called upon to make some critical decisions. Losing his flagship and part of his staff cannot have helped.[9]

SIBUYAN SEA

As the sun rose from the waters of the Philippine Sea on the morning of 24 October 1944, four different Japanese forces were converging on Leyte Gulf.

Admiral Ozawa's carrier force was approaching from the north. Admiral Nishimura's battleships *Yamashiro* and *Fuso,* accompanied by one cruiser and four destroyers, were crossing the Sulu Sea headed toward Surigao Strait, followed by Vice Admiral Shima's three cruisers and seven destroyers. And Admiral Kurita was crossing the Sibuyan Sea, headed for San Bernardino Strait with his five battleships—*Yamato, Musashi, Nagato, Kongo,* and *Haruna*—his remaining nine cruisers, and thirteen destroyers. In the course of the ensuing action, the Americans called Ozawa's formation Northern Force; Kurita's, Center Force; and Nishimura's and Shima's, Southern Force.

Admiral Kinkaid's battleships, cruisers and their escorts were operating inside Leyte Gulf, providing gunfire support to the amphibious shipping whose job it was to put the huge landing force ashore. The little escort carriers (CVEs) assigned to the Seventh Fleet to provide antisubmarine and ground support steamed just outside the gulf. They were accompanied by a number of destroyers and destroyer escorts to guard them against enemy aircraft and submarines. This force was assigned to the Seventh Fleet as Task Group (TG) 77.4 under Rear Adm. Thomas L. Sprague. The eighteen carriers and twenty-three escorts that composed the group had been subdivided into three task units, officially designated TU 77.4.1, TU 77.4.2, and TU 77.4.3, but generally known by their radio call signs as Taffy 1, 2, and 3. The task group commander doubled as commander of Taffy 1. Taffy 2 was commanded by Rear Adm. Felix B. Stump and Taffy 3 by Rear Adm. Clifton A. F. "Ziggy" Sprague (no relation to Thomas L.).

Almost due east of Leyte Gulf was one of Halsey's Third Fleet task groups, TG 38.4, under Rear Adm. Ralph E. Davison. North of Davison's force was TG 38.2, commanded by Rear Adm. Gerald F. Bogan, and still further north, off the east coast of the main Philippine island of Luzon, was Rear Adm. Frederick C. Sherman's TG 38.3. Each of these formations included from three to four big carriers, two fast battleships, and from sixteen to twenty-three cruisers and destroyers. Because there had been no sign of a Japanese reaction to the invasion at Leyte prior to the engagement in Palawan Passage, Halsey had detached Vice Adm. John S. McCain's TG 38.1, the fourth and final element of the Third Fleet/Task Force 38, for resupply and some much needed rest at Ulithi.

Warned the night before of Kurita's approach by the submarines *Darter* and *Dace,* Halsey ordered the three task groups east of the Philippines to converge and directed McCain to abort his rest and resupply mission and to rejoin the fleet. Just before dawn he also sent out search groups from several carriers to locate the oncoming Japanese. Before long the American aircraft had

TABLE 17.1 Surface Forces Engaged at the Battle of Leyte Gulf, 24–25 October 1944

	CV	CVL	CVE (USN) or BB/CV (IJN)	BB	CA	CL	DD	DE	PT	AO
U.S. NAVY										
Third Fleet										
Adm. W. F. Halsey										
Task Group 38—										
Fast Carrier Force										
Vice Adm. M A. Mitscher										
Task Group 38.1										
Vice Adm. J. S. McCain	3	2	—	—	4	2	14	—	—	—
Task Group 38.2										
Rear Adm. G. F Bogan	1	2	—	2	—	3	18	—	—	—
Task Group 38 3										
Rear Adm F. C. Sherman	2	2	—	2	—	4	13	—	—	—
Task Group 38.4										
Rear Adm. R. E. Davison	2	2	—	2	2	—	12	—	—	—
TOTAL FOR TASK GROUP 38	8	8	—	6	6	9	57	—	—	—
Seventh Fleet										
Vice Adm. T C Kinkaid										
Battle Line										
Rear Adm. J. C. Oldendorf	—	—	—	6	4	4	28	—	39	—
Task Group 77.4—Escort Carrier Group,										
Rear Adm. T. L. Sprague										
Task Unit 77.4.1										
Rear Adm. T. L. Sprague	—	—	6	—	—	—	3	5	—	—
Task Unit 77.4.2										
Rear Adm F. B. Stump	—	—	6	—	—	—	3	5	—	—
Task Unit 77.4.3										
Rear Adm. C. A. F. Sprague	—	—	6	—	—	—	3	4	—	—
TOTAL FOR SEVENTH FLEET	—	—	18	6	4	4	37	14	39	—
TOTAL FOR U.S. NAVY	8	8	18	12	10	13	94	14	39	—
IMPERIAL JAPANESE NAVY[a]										
Northern Force										
Vice Adm. J. Ozawa	1	3	2	—	—	3	8	—	—	—
Northern Force Supply Unit	—	—	—	—	—	—	1	6	—	2
Center Force										
Vice Adm T. Kurita	—	—	—	5	10[b]	2	15[b]	—	—	—
Southern Force / 1st Echelon										
Vice Adm. S. Nishimura	—	—	—	2	1	—	4	—	—	—
Southern Force / 2d Echelon										
Vice Adm. K. Shima	—	—	—	—	2	1	7	—	—	—
TOTAL	1	3	2	7	13	6	35	6	—	2

Notes: CV = fleet carrier, CVL = light carrier, CVE = escort carrier, BB/CV = hybrid battleship-carrier, BB = battleship, CA = heavy cruiser, CL = light cruiser, DD = destroyer, DE = destroyer escort, PT = torpedo boat, AO = oiler

[a] Excluding a transport force consisting of a heavy cruiser, a light cruiser, a destroyer, and four destroyer-transports that landed two thousand reinforcements on the west coast of Leyte on 26 October

[b] Including three cruisers and two destroyers eliminated from the Japanese order of battle as a result of the encounter in Palawan Passage early on 23 October

sighted not only Center Force in the Sibuyan Sea, but Nishimura's in the Sulu Sea as well. Halsey immediately ordered a strike, concentrating on Kurita's larger formation. As American planes rolled in on Center Force at approximately 1025, the fire of Japanese anti-aircraft (AA) batteries announced the opening of the Battle of the Sibuyan Sea.

Kurita's ships, aware that they had little hope of air cover, had increased their AA armament while at Lingga Roads, and the effect was significant. Several U.S. aircraft were shot down at the beginning of the twenty-four-minute engagement, but others pressed home their attack. Several near-misses sent geysers leaping skyward near Kurita's flagship, the super-battleship *Yamato*. A direct hit on her forecastle failed to penetrate the deck's armor. Her sister ship, the *Musashi*, was struck by a torpedo, but the steel blisters along her sides kept it from reaching her inner hull. Both ships steamed on, undaunted by the attacks.

The heavy cruiser *Myoko*, flagship of Cruiser Division Five, did not fare so well. She did not enjoy the same blister protection as her gargantuan consorts, and a torpedo hit reduced her speed to 15 knots. As she began to lag behind, the division commander and his staff shifted to the cruiser *Haguro*. The *Myoko* came about and headed for Brunei as the last American planes returned to their carriers. Kurita had lost his fourth cruiser, and the day was young.

At about 1240, Kurita's lookouts spotted a second wave of planes winging their way from Halsey's carriers. When this wave broke off, the *Musashi* had sustained three more torpedo hits.

A third wave soon followed. It, too, converged on the *Musashi*, hitting her with several bombs and a fifth torpedo. With no opposing aircraft to occupy them, U.S. fighters swooped in and sprayed the ship's decks with machine-gun fire.

The huge protective plates that shielded the *Musashi*'s inner hull had stopped the first torpedoes, but their explosions had holed it. When one struck in the vicinity of an earlier hit outside no. 4 engine room, it penetrated the inner hull, flooding the engine room. The flooding and loss of power reduced the *Musashi*'s stability and slowed her speed. Other hits affected some of the ship's damage control equipment and impaired her internal communications.

Now listing to port, the *Musashi* braced for more as a fourth wave of American aircraft appeared on the horizon a little after 1400. In a desperate attempt to turn the tide, the captain gave permission to fire special AA rounds from the *Musashi*'s 18.1-inch guns. A great shock convulsed through the battleship's hull as her main batteries fired for the first time in battle, but the sixty-five American aircraft were untouched. Within minutes they were adding to the huge ship's misery.[10]

Despite the claims of her invincibility by her builders, the great *Musashi* began to succumb to her wounds. Smoke was pouring from holes in her deck, she had lost electrical power, her list to port was growing worse, and hits to her bridge had taken her captain out of the battle.

Halsey's fifth wave struck about an hour later. Concentrating on the *Musashi*, it put ten more torpedoes into her ravaged hull. Too late, Kurita ordered the *Musashi* to retire, escorted by two destroyers and the cruiser *Tone*. At 1530, with aircraft still filling the skies overhead, Kurita turned his whole formation around and headed back across the Sibuyan Sea. Up to that moment, Center Force had been attacked by 259 planes, of which it had shot down 18.

To Kurita's surprise, the attacks subsided almost immediately once he had come about. He continued westward for about an hour, passing the dying *Musashi* along the way. Her steering gear had been destroyed, and she was slowly steaming in circles, trying desperately to stay afloat. At 1714, Kurita again ordered a course change and soon Center Force was once more heading eastward toward San Bernardino Strait.

By 1900, Center Force was again approaching the *Musashi*. The cruiser *Tone* rejoined the formation as it passed, leaving only the destroyers *Hamakaze* and *Kiyoshima* to keep the deathwatch. They did not have long to wait. Not long after Kurita's ships had disappeared over the eastern horizon, the *Musashi* rolled over and then plunged bow-first into the depths of the Sibuyan Sea, taking half of her 2,200-man crew with her.[11]

Information from U.S. submarines and aircraft had alerted Halsey and Kinkaid to all the Japanese forces en route to Leyte Gulf with the exception of one. Ironically the exception was Northern Force, which was doing its best to be detected. For much of the transit from Japanese home waters, Ozawa had been deliberately but unsuccessfully trying to attract Halsey's attention in hopes of luring him away from Leyte Gulf. Late on the twenty-fourth, Third Fleet air searches at last discovered Ozawa's force off Cape Engaño, the northeastern tip of Luzon, some four hundred miles from Leyte Gulf.

Beside the sentence in Nimitz's orders to Halsey that read, "In case opportunity for destruction of major portion of the enemy fleet offer [sic] or can be created, such destruction becomes the primary task," a letter sent to Halsey by Nimitz just twelve days before the Leyte landing made it clear that Halsey had the authority to make unanticipated tactical decisions "because of local situations which may develop quickly and in light of information which has come to you and which may not be available to me."[12] The discovery of Ozawa's carriers seemed to fit this definition, and the aggressive Halsey, unaware of the pathetic state of Ozawa's air groups and convinced that Kurita's force had been rendered impotent by the air strikes in the Sibuyan Sea, took the bait and went north.

Another factor that probably influenced Halsey's decision to go after Ozawa was the knowledge that Admiral Spruance had been the subject of considerable criticism for his decision *not* to close the Japanese carriers on the eve of the Battle of the Philippine Sea. Coupled with his own frustration over missing all the big carrier battles in the war to date, it is not difficult to see why Halsey would jump at the chance to attack Northern Force.

What is less understandable is Halsey's decision to take his entire force with him. To make matters worse, Halsey sent several confusing messages that led Kinkaid and others to believe he had detached a surface-action group of four fast battleships with appropriate escorts as Task Force 34 to stay behind and guard San Bernardino Strait. Upon learning from aerial reconnaissance that Kurita had turned back to the east, two of Halsey's subordinates suggested that a force should indeed be left to cover the strait, but their recommendations were ignored.[13]

As darkness settled over the Philippines, Halsey's Third Fleet steamed northward in pursuit of Ozawa's decoys, while the bloodied but by no means crippled Kurita continued toward a now unguarded San Bernardino Strait and Leyte Gulf beyond.

SURIGAO STRAIT

Nishimura's Southern Force had been discovered and attacked earlier that morning in the Sulu Sea by Third Fleet aircraft from the *Enterprise* and *Franklin*. Damage was slight, however, and the Americans soon devoted their full attention to Center Force. Unlike Kurita's ordeal in crossing the Sibuyan Sea, Nishimura's passage through the Sulu Sea was almost tranquil. Still on schedule, he would enter Surigao Strait at about 0130.

Even though the Seventh Fleet obtained no more intelligence about either echelon of Southern Force after midday, Admiral Kinkaid foresaw that the Japanese meant to penetrate Leyte Gulf through Surigao Strait and began laying plans accordingly. The coming clash was shaping up to be a night surface engagement in which aircraft would play no role. There was a certain irony in this because the Pacific War had turned out to be a test of air power rather than the big surface fleet action that so many had predicted in the years leading up to the war. Only at Guadalcanal, where the nature of that bitter struggle had temporarily altered the newly emerging rules, had surface forces—indeed, battleships—engaged in the kind of shoot-outs that naval strategists had mistakenly foreseen. Now guns and torpedoes would again have the final say.

There was another—perhaps even greater—irony. Five of the six battleships that Kinkaid's subordinate, Rear Adm. Jesse Oldendorf, would bring to the battle that night were survivors of the attack on Pearl Harbor. The *Mississippi* alone had been absent. The *Tennessee, Maryland,* and *Pennsylvania* had all been damaged in the attack, and the *West Virginia* and *California* had actually been sunk and later raised. This night would give them a chance for revenge.

But more than battleships would be waiting for the Japanese at Surigao Strait. A considerable number of cruisers and destroyers had been allocated to the Seventh Fleet for the Leyte invasion, and Kinkaid had lent many of these ships, plus some three dozen PT boats, to Oldendorf to reinforce the reception he was preparing for Southern Force.

A combination of favorable geography and tactical acumen gave Oldendorf the advantage of being able to "cap the T," a classic maneuver of naval warfare that all but guaranteed success. Because ships are elongated in shape, more weapons can be placed along their sides than at their bows and sterns. It is therefore a distinct advantage if a captain can maneuver his ship into a position so that her side is facing her opponent's bow or stern—forming the shape of a "T." The same applies to columns of ships, giving the column that has the capping position the ability to mass its fire on the head of the other. Oldendorf positioned his battleships and cruisers at the north end of the strait, ordering them to steam back and forth along an east-west axis so that their broadsides could be brought to bear on the Japanese, who would be forced by the narrow strait to approach in a column head on.

Oldendorf's preparations were not limited to exploiting this geographical advantage. He organized his destroyers into several groups that would enter the strait and strike at the Japanese flanks, and he sent his PTs down into the strait to serve as early warning pickets.

About 2300 Nishimura's force steamed into the gauntlet set by Oldendorf. The waves of PT boats that initiated the attack did little to impede the Japanese advance but their sighting reports kept Oldendorf informed of the enemy's progress. The destroyers coming down the strait fired their torpedoes into the Japanese column, doing considerable damage. Nishimura nevertheless ploughed ahead to oblivion at the end of the strait, where gunfire from the waiting battleships and cruisers sank both of his battleships and three of his destroyers. The admiral went down with his flagship. Shima, following with his separate echelon, prudently reversed course after encountering the battered remains of Nishimura's force and retired. This devastating American victory eliminated the southern arm of the Japanese pincer.

BATTLE OFF SAMAR

The jubilation over the one-sided victory in Surigao Strait was soon to be offset. Even though Japanese hopes of a pincer attack had been ruined by Oldendorf's elimination of Southern Force, Ozawa's decoys had succeeded in drawing off not just a portion of Halsey's Third Fleet but *all* of it. The door was wide open for Kurita to steam through San Bernardino Strait and approach Leyte Gulf from the north. Because Kinkaid mistakenly assumed Halsey had detached Task Force 34 to guard against this possibility, he had sent all his heavy firepower south to do battle with Nishimura and Shima. This left the invasion site vulnerable to attack—especially since many of the supplies that had been landed remained on the beaches where they could easily be destroyed by fire from ships offshore. The potential for a disaster was very real as Kurita emerged from San Bernardino Strait an hour before midnight to find an empty sea.

Just outside the gulf steamed the only obstacle between Kurita and the beachhead—Adm. T. L. Sprague's three Taffies. These did not represent much of an obstacle—at least on paper. The CVEs were, after all, small and inexpensive imitations of larger and far more potent CVs and CVLs. There was a grim joke that their letter designators stood for "combustible, vulnerable, expendable." Useful as they had proved as aircraft ferries, as antisubmarine platforms and as a source of limited air support for amphibious landings, they were not designed to tangle with battleships and cruisers. The two dozen or so aircraft they each carried had very little armor-piercing ammunition, being equipped with munitions appropriate to the softer targets ashore.

When the masts of Kurita's force first pierced the horizon at about 0650, lookouts in the escort carriers and destroyer screen of Ziggy Sprague's Taffy 3, the northernmost Seventh Fleet unit, did not realize what they were seeing. Even after their tell-tale, pagodalike structures revealed that these were Japanese masts, many believed them to be remnants of the force that had been defeated in Surigao Strait. When Japanese shells began raining down, reality at last took hold, and the U.S. ships turned south in a mad dash to escape. Unfortunately there was no way the CVEs, with a maximum speed of 18 knots, could outrun Japanese battleships.

As the jeep carriers dodged the salvos from Kurita's big guns, flyers from all three Taffies attacked the Japanese ships despite their inappropriate ammunition. Some pilots swooped down on the Japanese with *no* ammunition, hoping to distract them.

The destroyers and destroyer escorts assigned to protect the CVEs were primarily tasked with defending against submarines and aircraft. No one ever anticipated that they would find themselves taking on the most powerful elements of the Japanese surface fleet. But that is exactly what transpired on the morning of 25 October 1944.

In an act of courage that rivals anything ever done by John Paul Jones or Stephen Decatur, the seven small escorts of Taffy 3 charged headlong at Kurita's overwhelming force, firing what torpedoes and guns they had in a charge as desperate as that immortalized by Tennyson's famous poem, *The Charge of the Light Brigade*. In an incredible irony, that long-ago charge of light cavalry in the Crimean War had also taken place on 25 October!

The confusion these recklessly brave Americans created prevented the Japanese from accurately evaluating the situation and organizing a coordinated attack. At times the diminutive American ships were so close to their larger enemies that the latter were unable to depress their guns enough to bring them to bear. While the U.S. escorts and aircraft were able to inflict some damage on Kurita's cruisers, their effect on his battleships was negligible. After a time three of the U.S. ships (the destroyers *Johnston* and *Hoel* and destroyer escort *Samuel B. Roberts*) paid the only price imaginable in such a one-sided encounter. All three were gradually pounded into submission and their mangled remains plunged to the ocean floor. In a tribute that even the passions of war could not suppress, a Japanese officer was seen by many of the survivors to render a salute to the *Johnston* as she disappeared beneath the waves.[14]

The best efforts of these gallant ships notwithstanding, one of the CVEs, the *Gambier Bay,* was also dispatched by Kurita's big guns. The loss of these four ships is lamentable, but it was a relatively small price to pay in light of what might—perhaps *should*—have happened under the circumstances.

Kurita and his staff, probably suffering from nervous and physical exhaustion, seemed confused by what was happening. Many of his staff erroneously reported the small U.S. carriers as full-sized CVs and their escorts as cruisers and even battleships, giving Kurita reason to believe that he was engaging all or part of Halsey's Third Fleet. The behavior of the American ships certainly did little to dispel these assumptions. The attacks by the Taffies' aircraft and escort vessels had left three more of his heavy cruisers sinking or sunk.

"Battle off Samar," by Commander Dwight C. Shepler, USNR, depicts a moment in the desperate charge of Taffy 3's escorts. From left to right: the battleships *Nagato* and *Haruna;* the destroyers *Heermann* and *Hoel,* the latter sinking; and, on the horizon, the heavy cruisers *Tone* and *Chikuma.* The geysers leaping up in front of the *Heermann* are from the battleship *Yamato's* 18-inch guns. *U.S. Naval Institute*

Yet what Kurita did not know was that the Americans were on the ropes. The CVEs were losing ground to the pursuing Japanese ships, the escorts were all sunk or disabled, and the aircraft had expended their ammunition. Before long victory would be his—a devastating victory that could not affect the ultimate outcome of the war but might have serious consequences on its course. But at this crucial moment, fortune smiled on the Americans. Kurita did not recognize his advantage, and at 0911 he ordered his ships to come about.

By leaving the beachhead at Leyte in his wake and the Seventh Fleet to lick its relatively minor wounds, Kurita had fumbled a great opportunity. The last hope of the Imperial Japanese Navy to achieve a major victory was gone forever. That night Center Force wound its way back through San Bernardino Strait.

CAPE ENGAÑO

While the Battle off Samar was raging, Kinkaid, still under the impression that Halsey had left Task Force 34 behind, was sending him urgent messages asking for help. At first Halsey was more perplexed than alarmed. To him it seemed that Kinkaid should be able to handle the Japanese with the forces at his disposal. But when the appeals became increasingly strident, Halsey ordered Vice Admiral McCain's TG 38.1 to head for Leyte Gulf. Unfortunately, McCain was too far from the scene to be of immediate help.

Halsey himself was also too far from Leyte Gulf to have any hope of intervening in the disaster taking shape off Samar. In hindsight, it is clear that at this point he would have done better to have continued after Ozawa. But about 1000, before anyone knew that the crisis had passed, a message arrived from Nimitz, who had been monitoring the battle from his headquarters at Pearl Harbor. With information copies to King and Kinkaid, it read: "Where is rpt where is Task Force Thirty-four xx The world wonders." Halsey interpreted this a public rebuke, though Nimitz had not intended it as such. The seemingly sarcastic "world wonders" was security padding that was intended as nonsense to confuse enemy traffic analysts and should have been stripped from the message before it reached Halsey. The "rpt" had not been in Nimitz's original draft but had been inserted by a yeoman processing the message and the information addressees added by a staff officer.[15] Angry and hurt Halsey reacted by dividing his forces and heading south with all six battleships and TG 38.2 in a futile attempt to retrieve the situation off Samar. By then his battle line had closed to forty-two miles of Northern Force.

The remaining Third Fleet forces, now under Vice Adm. Marc Mitscher, attacked Ozawa, sinking the *Zuikaku*—the last of the Pearl Harbor carriers—the light carriers *Chitose* and *Zuiho*, and the destroyer *Akitsuki*, and damaging the cruiser *Tama* and light carrier *Chiyoda*. Both battleship-carriers and nine cruisers and destroyers escaped essentially unharmed. Because Ozawa's sacrificial success in luring Halsey north was not exploited, and because the Americans, with their overwhelming advantage, failed to completely destroy Northern Force, this final phase of the Battle of Leyte Gulf, known to posterity as the Battle of Cape Engaño, is somewhat anticlimactic. Ensuring that anticlimax was Halsey's decision to take his battleships south, eliminating any possibility of a great daylight surface engagement—something that would have captured the imagination of future generations. Not only did this countermarch take the dreadnoughts out of the Cape Engaño action, it took them out of any action whatsoever, condemning them to a kind of purgatory between the battles taking place north and south of them. Halsey never admitted any misjudgment in heading after Ozawa, but he regretted his decision to turn away in response to Nimitz's misunderstood message. After the war, he conceded, "I am in agreement that I made a mistake in bowing to pressure and turning south. I consider this the gravest error I committed during the Battle of Leyte Gulf."[16]

So the Battle of Leyte Gulf came to an end. In the intervening years it has come to be described by such superlative terms as "the greatest naval battle in history," and well it should be. It encompassed a geographical area in excess of a hundred thousand square miles. More ships—216 American, 2 Australian, and 64 Japanese—participated than in the great Battle of Jutland, and nearly two hundred thousand men could rightly call themselves veterans of this gargantuan engagement. Literally thousands of those veterans went to the bottom with the dozens of ships that were forever lost.[17] The largest guns ever used in naval battle fired here, and it proved to be the last time that battleships confronted one another, as well as the first and only time that a U.S. aircraft carrier was sunk by gunfire.

Yet despite all these facts and the legitimacy of the description of this battle as the "greatest," it is not well known outside historical circles. Most Americans have heard of Midway and everyone knows about Pearl Harbor, but not many will recognize the name of Leyte Gulf. The reasons for this lie in timing. The battle took place during the last year of the war, four months after the D-day landings in Normandy. The end was in sight, and such great victories as Leyte Gulf had come to seem almost a matter of course.

Yet it was this very attitude that made Leyte important, not just as a tactical triumph that sounded as the death knell of the Imperial Japanese Navy, but as a strategic necessity that might have had serious consequences had it not yielded the expected American victory. A setback at Leyte—which, as it happened, was narrowly averted—might have depressed American morale and given the Japanese the bargaining power to negotiate something other than the unconditional surrender insisted upon by the Allies.

Because this battle was tied to the liberation of the Philippines, its importance to the Filipino people and the thousands of prisoners of war who languished there in horrid conditions cannot be overemphasized. Had Kurita, Nishimura, and Shima succeeded in disrupting the landing at Leyte, the suffering of those under Japanese domination in the Philippines might have lasted even longer.

All these potential consequences could have been averted in any number of ways had other decisions been made by the commanders on both sides. And the outcome of this battle unquestionably owes to the planning, diligence, and courage of the many men who manned the guns, fired the boilers, flew the aircraft, and performed the countless other tasks that brought these powerful fleets across great expanses of ocean to do battle in distant waters. But the moment of truth, the instant when victory was indeed snatched from the jaws of defeat, occurred when Taffy 3's escorts and all three Taffies' aircraft threw themselves headlong into harm's way, upholding the finest traditions of the United States Navy in a selfless act of courage that has sometimes been equaled, but never surpassed.

NOTES

1. Ralph B. Jordan, *Born to Fight: The Life of Admiral Halsey* (Philadelphia, 1946), ix–x.

2. E B Potter, *Bull Halsey* (Annapolis, 1985), 133–297.

3. C Vann Woodward, *The Battle for Leyte Gulf* (New York, 1947), 27

4. Ernest J. King and Walter Muir Whitehill, *Fleet Admiral King: A Naval Record* (reprint, New York, 1987), 571

5. Potter, *Halsey*, 277

6 Samuel E Morison, *History of United States Naval Operations in World War II*, vol 12: *Leyte* (Boston, 1958), 13–14

7 Potter, *Halsey*, 279, 402

8 L Matsumoto and M Chihaya, "Design and Construction of *Yamato* and *Musashi*," U.S. Naval Institute *Proceedings* 79:10 (October 1953): 1103–7

9. R C. Benitez, "Battle Stations Submerged," U.S Naval Institute *Proceedings* 74:1 (January 1948): 25–32, and Theodore Roscoe, *United States Submarine Operations in World War II* (Annapolis, 1953), 390–95.

10 John Toland, *The Rising Sun: The Decline and Fall of the Japanese Empire* (New York, 1971), 623–24.

11 Ibid , 633–34.

12. William F Halsey and J. Bryan III, *Admiral Halsey's Story* (New York, 1947), 223–24.

13. Gerald F Bogan, oral history transcript (Annapolis, 1969), 109, and Ivan Musicant, *Battleship at War: The Epic Story of the USS Washington* (New York, 1986), 290–94

14 Morison, *Leyte*, 274, and William E. Mercer, *The Fighting and Sinking of the USS Johnston, DD-557 as Told By Her Crew* (Euless, Tex., 1991), 14, 88, 100, and 138.

15. Bernard Brodie, "The Battle for Leyte Gulf," *Virginia Quarterly Review* (Summer 1947) 459–60, and William F Halsey, "The Battle for Leyte Gulf," U.S Naval Institute *Proceedings* 78:5 (May 1952): 492

16 Hanson W. Baldwin, "The Battle for Leyte Gulf," in Don Congdon, ed., *Combat WWII: Pacific Theater Operations* (New York, 1983), 658.

17 The light cruiser *Princeton* and the escort carrier *St. Lo*, sunk on 25 October by aircraft based on Luzon, raised the U.S. Navy's losses to six ships displacing 33,118 tons (standard load). Including retiring vessels sunk by air strikes on 26–27 October, the Imperial Japanese Navy lost three battleships, one fleet and three light carriers, six heavy and four light cruisers, and eleven destroyers for a total of twenty-eight ships displacing 310,922 tons. About 1,500 U S. naval personnel were killed or missing in action. Japanese dead numbered approximately 10,500.

18

The Battle for Okinawa

JEFFREY G. BARLOW

By mid-March 1945, U.S. forces were firmly established in the southern Bonins, the archipelago that stretches south for some seven hundred miles from the Japanese home island of Honshu.[1] The two marine divisions ashore on Iwo Jima since 19 February had begun mopping up the last pockets of resistance. American air and naval bases in the Marshalls, the Marianas, Luzon, and now the Bonins were drawing an ever-tightening ring around the remains of the Japanese Empire.

U.S. Navy operations in waters bordering Japan in early 1945 were the culmination of the Central Pacific offensive conducted by Fleet Adm. Chester W. Nimitz, Commander in Chief Pacific Fleet and Pacific Ocean Areas (CinCPac/CinCPoa). The drive had begun in November 1943 with invasions of Makin and Tarawa in the Gilberts. From the Gilberts, the Central Pacific Force had moved westward toward Japan. By the end of February 1944 the Marshalls were secured. In June, the Fifth Fleet invaded Saipan in the Marianas. The islands of Tinian and Guam were assaulted in late July, and by mid-August the Marianas were in American hands. The capture of Iwo Jima set the stage for the next major advance.

The Nansei Shoto (or the Ryukyus, as they are known in the West) are a series of volcanic islands that dot the Pacific in a line stretching southwest from Kyushu, the southernmost of the Japanese home islands, for almost eight hundred miles. The 140-some islands of which they consist are divided into three major groupings—the Amami Gunto in the north, the Okinawa Gunto in the center, and the Sakishima Gunto in the south. Together they mark the eastern boundary of the East China Sea.[2]

If the Allies were to invade Japan, they first would have to establish a jumping-off point, either on Formosa or in the Ryukyus. Thus when the U.S. Joint Chiefs of Staff (JCS) ruled out an invasion of Formosa in September 1944, the Ryukyus became the focus of the planners' efforts. Okinawa, the largest island in the chain and located just 360 miles from Kyushu, was quickly selected as the principal target.

The leader of the Allied naval forces for the Okinawa operation was Adm. Raymond A. Spruance, Commander Fifth Fleet. The fifty-eight-year-old Spruance was a cautious, painstaking, surface officer known for his meticulous planning and the explicit trust he placed in his immediate subordinates to do their jobs with a minimum of supervision. He was a firm believer in employing all available force in his battles in order to increase the chances of success.[3]

Initial planning for the invasion, designated Operation ICEBERG, began with a CinCPoa joint staff study issued on 25 October 1944. In line with a JCS directive to Nimitz to occupy one or more positions in the Nansei Shoto beginning on 1 March 1945, the ICEBERG study called for accomplishing two tasks. The first was to "[c]apture, occupy, defend, and develop OKINAWA Island and establish control of the sea and air in the NANSEI SHOTO area." The second was to extend control of the archipelago by capturing and developing other islands. In addition to providing a staging base for an invasion of the Home Islands, such an operation would sever communications between Japan and its southeast Asian conquests and secure Allied sea and air communications through the East China Sea to the coast of China and the Yangtze Valley.[4]

During November and December 1944, the Fifth Fleet staff conducted thorough planning for the assault on Okinawa, using the CinCPoa study as a guide. On 3 January 1945, Admiral Spruance issued his Operation Plan 1-45, which set the date for the invasion of Okinawa (LOVE-Day) as 1 April 1945. This document was supplemented just over a month later by a detailed plan covering the amphibious aspects of ICEBERG issued by Vice Adm. Richmond Kelly Turner, Commander Amphibious Forces Pacific Fleet and Commander Task Force (TF) 51 (Joint Expeditionary Force) for the operation.

The attack on Okinawa and its dependencies was to begin with a naval bombardment commencing eight days prior to the landings. The gunfire support ships were part of the Amphibious Support Force (TF 52) under the command of Rear Adm. William H. P. Blandy, which on L-Day minus 6 was scheduled to seize a circular group of small islands called Kerama Retto, twenty miles off Okinawa's southwest coast. Control of these islands would enable the Allies to establish a logistics anchorage and a seaplane base close to the main objective.[5]

The landings on Okinawa itself were to occur over a five-mile expanse of the so-called "Hagushi beaches" on the southwest coast of the island. The Northern Attack Force (TF 53) under Rear Adm. Lawrence F. Reifsnider would land two marine divisions north of the town of Hagushi, while the Southern Attack Force (TF 55) under Rear Adm. John L. Hall landed two infantry divisions to the south. In addition, the Demonstration Group (Task Group [TG] 51.2), under Rear Adm. Jerauld R. Wright, with a marine division embarked, was to stage simulated landings on the southeast coast as a diversion on L-Day and the day after. All expeditionary troops were part of the Tenth Army, commanded by Lt. Gen. Simon Bolivar Buckner, USA.

Once ashore, the marines were to thrust to the east and north, while the army troops attacked to the east and south. Important initial objectives included two major airfields located less than a mile from the island's coast—Yontan, behind the marine beaches, and Kadena, to the rear of the army's landing area.[6]

In late 1944, Japanese planners expected the United States to pursue a three-step strategy in 1945, thrusting superior air and surface forces ever closer to Japan's final defensive perimeter, completing the country's encirclement by cutting seaborne communications to the west and south, and, finally, invading the Home Islands. From a variety of possible targets for Allied attack, Japanese officers pinpointed Formosa, the Nansei Shoto, and the Bonins as the most likely. Seizure of one or more of these positions would allow the United States to build airfields from which its heavy bombers could operate even more effectively over Kyushu and Honshu and would furnish advanced bases for the expected invasion of the Home Islands.

The "Outline of Army and Navy Operations" issued on 20 January 1945 called for waging a campaign of attrition in defense of these citadels. Army aircraft were to attack enemy troop transports, while navy planes hit aircraft carriers and other important combatants. The most powerful weapons left in the Japanese arsenal were the *kamikaze* (Divine Wind) special attack forces. Kamikaze (suicide) attacks by navy aircraft, first used in the Battle of Leyte Gulf in October 1944, had been employed with increasing frequency against U.S. vessels in subsequent months. The new plan called for enlarging and reinforcing the navy and army air forces by increasing the output of special attack planes and personnel to fly them.

On 6 February 1945, the Imperial Japanese Army and Navy determined to concentrate all formations in the Home Islands at bases around the periphery of the East China Sea and to accentuate kamikaze training. At about the same time, preparations were begun for the TEN-Go Operation—massed air assaults by all available air power designed to repulse enemy invasions of any of the key strong points. It was hoped that two thousand planes could be assembled for combined kamikaze and conventional bombing attacks by 1 April. The plan to be used in the event of enemy landings in the Nansei Shoto was designated the TEN-Go No. 1 Operation. When Iwo Jima was invaded on 19 February, Japanese planners quickly issued a revised estimate of the situation, predicting that Okinawa would be invaded in late March or early April.[7]

Although the fighting on Iwo Jima was still grinding on at the end of February, Spruance's attention was already oriented toward Operation ICEBERG. On 2 March, he directed Vice Adm. Marc Mitscher, commanding the seventeen fast carriers of TF 58, to prepare plans to support the invasion by striking the airfields on Kyushu. He hoped that by achieving surprise Mitscher could destroy a high percentage of the planes that would otherwise be used against the fleet off Okinawa.

The four carrier task groups of TF 58 sortied from Ulithi lagoon at dawn on 14 March. Three days earlier, Mitscher's men had received a preview of the danger they would face off Okinawa. Several long-range kamikazes attacked Ulithi after sunset. One plane struck the carrier *Randolph*, crash-diving into the starboard edge of the after end of her flight deck. The ensuing fires and explosion put a forty-foot wide hole in the flight deck and wrecked a portion of the hangar deck underneath, destroying fourteen aircraft and damaging ten more.

On 16 March, Admiral Nimitz advised Spruance that the carrier task group commanded by Vice Adm. Sir Bernard Rawlings from the recently formed British Pacific Fleet was to participate in the Nansei Shoto offensive. Spruance replied that the British carriers would be directed to operate against enemy airfields in the Sakishima Gunto. They entered action on 26 March.

At approximately 0545 on 18 March, Mitscher's carriers launched the first fighter sweeps and combat air patrols at a position one hundred miles off the southern tip of Kyushu. Since Japanese aerial reconnaissance had alerted the forces on Kyushu to TF 58's approach, the first flights found few enemy planes, either in the air or on airfields near the coast. Mitscher therefore directed that the afternoon strikes attack targets farther inland, which were to have been hit on the nineteenth. This change in targeting proved successful and resulted in the destruction of a substantial number of Japanese planes. The bombing raids on enemy airfields proved an even greater success, causing heavy damage to hangars, machine shops, and other installations.

Only some fifty Japanese aircraft undertook to challenge the intrusion with conventional bombing attacks. Less than half returned to base, but they succeeded in hitting three carriers. Fortunately the damage was not serious.

Beginning at dawn the next day, sweeps and strikes were launched against naval targets that photoreconnaissance had revealed in the Inland Sea. Despite the Japanese curtain of fire, the American planes pressed home their attacks to obtain a number of hits. The only major ship seriously damaged, however, was the carrier *Ryuho* at Kure.[8]

Again on the nineteenth, Japanese defenders reacted by seeking out the U.S. carriers. The *Franklin* was halfway through launching her second strike, with planes on the flight and hangar decks gassed and armed, when she was attacked at 0708 by a single Japanese bomber that took her by surprise. It dropped two bombs that penetrated the flight deck and exploded in the hangar, setting off fires that were fed by gasoline from aircraft fuel tanks. Additional blasts from her own exploding ordnance soon staggered the ship; observers some distance from the scene noted six enormous explosions on the skyline. In all the *Franklin* lost 724 men killed or missing and 265 wounded. No other carrier ever sustained such damage and remained afloat.

At about the same time, the *Wasp* was hit by another lone aircraft that also arrived unannounced. This one dropped a semi–armor piercing bomb that exploded in the living compartment on her third deck and started substantial gasoline fires. Efficient fire-fighting put them out within fifteen minutes, enabling the ship to begin recovering aircraft by 0800, but 101 of her crewmen were killed or died of wounds and another 269 were wounded. That afternoon TF 58 retired, covering the crippled *Franklin* and launching additional strikes against the Kyushu airfields.

Trickles of enemy aircraft appeared again on 20 March. A kamikaze knocked the destroyer *Halsey Powell* out of the war, but the only serious damage to a carrier occurred when the *Enterprise* was hit by two 5-inch rounds of friendly anti-aircraft fire.

The next day Mitscher directed the three badly damaged carriers to proceed to Ulithi with TG 58.2, while the other three task groups moved toward Okinawa. That afternoon the Japanese unleased their new suicide weapon—the piloted *Oka* (cherry blossom) bomb. Oka, which the Americans soon nicknamed the *Baka* (foolish) bomb, was a glider powered by a short-range rocket engine that carried a 2,645-pound warhead. Designed to glide at speeds up to 230 miles per hour for up to 53 miles following high-altitude release from its mother ship, the bomb's rocket engine would be started by the pilot when it was within three miles of its target. Then, with luck, it would slam into its victim with devastating impact after reaching a top speed of 535 miles per hour.

A group of eighteen Betty twin-engine navy bombers, sixteen carrying Okas under their fuselages, took off with an escort of about thirty fighters that afternoon and headed toward the U.S. task force, then some 320 miles from Kyushu. The raid was picked up on radar at 1400, when still one hundred miles to the northwest. Mitscher scrambled extra fighters to deal with it. Within a few minutes, all of the heavily laden Bettys and fifteen of their escorts were destroyed, at a loss of only two U.S. planes. It was days before the Americans realized that the strike they annihilated had been the first combat appearance of the Baka.[9]

Having refueled on the twenty-second, TF 58 headed northwestward toward its launching positions for the scheduled attack on Okinawa. Its first fighter sweeps and air strikes took off at dawn on 23 March. On the twenty-fourth Rear Adm. Alexander Sharp's Mine Flotilla (TG 52.2) started sweeping the approaches to the landing sites, and a surface-action group detached from TF 58 shelled the Southeastern Demonstration Beaches. Underwater demolition teams (UDTs) began operating off the beaches the next day, and commencing at dawn on the twenty-sixth, Rear Adm. Morton L. Deyo's Covering and Gunfire Support Force (TF 54) subjected Okinawa to the first of six days' continuous pre-invasion bombardment.

At the same time, units of TF 52 began landing troops from the 77th Infantry Division on five islands in the Kerama Retto. Hardly had the movement commenced than some eight kamikazes attacked. Several were quickly shot down. One crash-dived into the 2,100-ton destroyer *Kimberly*, doing little damage, and another grazed the high-speed transport *Gilmer*.[10]

Later that day Japan's Combined Fleet ordered all forces to execute the TEN-Go Operation. To unify operational command of all homeland naval air forces, the Third and Tenth Air Fleets were placed under the orders of Vice Adm. Matome Ugaki's Fifth Air Fleet.

The next morning turned out to be a hectic one for the Gunfire and Covering Force off Okinawa. Shortly after 0500, its ships were attacked by a group of ten army kamikazes. Unfortunately there was no combat air patrol (CAP) overhead. One suicide plane struck the high-speed minesweeper *Dorsey*, causing superficial damage. Another, already ablaze from anti-aircraft fire, crashed into the starboard side of the battleship *Nevada*'s main deck just behind turret no. 3. A third slammed into the port side of the light cruiser *Biloxi*. Ships in the patrol line off Okinawa and at Kerama Retto were also hit.

Despite these attacks the landings against the last three of the Kerama islands were carried out as scheduled, and the entire group was declared secure on the twenty-eighth. On two of the islands troops discovered several hundred one-man, plywood suicide boats hidden in caves. Each boat was about eighteen feet long and seemed to be designed to carry two depth charges.[11]

L-Day minus one provided some unanticipated excitement for Admiral Spruance and his staff. At 0710 his flagship was struck by a kamikaze. The bomb-carrying Oscar army fighter came out of the clouds and dived into the deck on the *Indianapolis*'s port side before falling overboard. Its bomb passed through the main, first, and second platform decks and straight through the heavy cruiser's hull before detonating off the port side, beneath the turn of her bilge. The mining effect of the explosion ruptured her no. 4 shaft, and she began taking on water. After the crew extinguished her fires, the seriously wounded cruiser limped into the anchorage at Kerama Retto. An inspection by divers revealed that she would have to be sent to the United States for repairs. Spruance shifted his flag to the old battleship *New Mexico*, which was in turn hit by a kamikaze on 12 May. Searching for the admiral immediately after the crash, his staff found him helping man a fire hose.

The UDTs and gunfire support ships completed their missions against the Hagushi beaches on 31 March, and the assault waves began landing at 0830 on Easter Sunday, 1 April. Soldiers and marines pushed quickly inland, and by 1230 both Yontan and Kadena airfields had been captured with minimal losses. Before dark the Tenth Army had some 65,000 troops ashore in a beach-head 4,000 to 5,000 yards deep.

Things did not got as smoothly for the Demonstration Group off the southeastern beaches. At about 0545, the attack transport *Hinsdale* was hit by a kamikaze that holed the hull in three places, flooding her engine rooms. Several minutes later another suicide plane crashed into the *LST-884*, starting a fire that exploded her ammunition. Both ships were towed into Kerama Retto after transferring their troops and casualties to nearby vessels.[12]

For more than a week, U.S. commanders had been receiving intelligence based on decryption of Japanese messages that large-scale kamikaze attacks would be made on the invading forces. Yet L-Day passed with relatively little evidence of the dreaded kamikazes. A principal reason for this inactivity was the disruption produced by TF 58's attacks on the Kyushu airfields in the last part of March. Unfortunately Mitscher's carriers were now almost continually occupied providing air support around Okinawa, and although on occasion Maj. Gen. Curtis E. LeMay's Marianas-based B-29 bombers were employed against Kyushu's air bases, their attacks could not produce the same effects as the navy's more sustained targeting.

Luckily, Admiral Turner had made extensive preparations for the expected onslaught by Japan's suicide legions. His plans to screen the transport areas included two measures specifically oriented against suicide attacks—a radar picket screen and an anti–small craft screen.

The anti–small craft (or "flycatcher") screen was established to protect the transport area, primarily at night, against attacks by suicide boats and motor torpedo boats and to prevent the movement of enemy barges and small craft. It consisted of stations of one or more landing craft, infantry (LCIs), each with a destroyer in support, operating about a mile offshore and patrolling two-by-three-mile areas of the coastline. These arrangements proved effective. During the battle for Okinawa only one vessel, the *LCI(G)-92*, was sunk by a suicide boat and only three others seriously damaged.

The radar picket screen consisted of up to sixteen picket stations situated from twenty-one to nearly ninety-six miles from a cape (Zampa Misaki) just north of the Hagushi beaches, designated for reference purposes as Point Bolo. The line of picket stations looked something like a horseshoe, with the greatest number of stations situated to the north and west of Okinawa—the directions from which most kamikazes were expected to come. At the height of the battle, nine stations (1–4, 7, 9, 10, 12, and 14) were actually manned; on 16 May, by which date radar stations had been established at Hedo Saki, the northern tip of Okinawa, and on the island of Ie Shima, this number was reduced to five (5, 7, 9, 15, and 16).

Each occupied station was manned initially by a destroyer or high-speed minesweeper and two landing craft, support (LCS) vessels. They were to patrol a circular area 5,000 yards in radius at a normal speed of 15 knots. The destroyers were equipped with air-search radars and had fighter director teams embarked to provide early warning and vectoring information to the fleet on incoming raids. They were to report all contacts at once and to open fire on all unidentified aircraft that approached within 12,000 yards. For their protection, each of the picket ships was to have four to six CAP fighters operating overhead during the day.

For the first few days after L-day, kamikaze activity continued at a moderate level, with dawn and dusk attacks by a few aircraft at a time, mainly on ships in the transport areas or on radar picket duty. On 5 April, Turner reported that as of 1800 that day, sixty-five Japanese aircraft had been destroyed in TF 51's area since the invasion. This relative calm was suddenly about to end.[13]

On 3 April, Japan's Combined Fleet had issued the outline order for the *Kikusui* (floating chrysanthemums) No. 1 Operation, the first of the mass kamikaze attacks envisioned under the TEN-Go plans. The participating

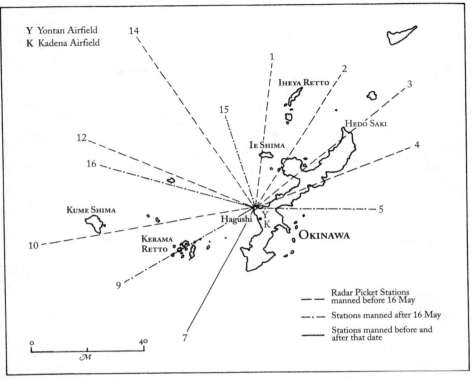

Y Yontan Airfield
K Kadena Airfield

IHEYA RETTO

HEDO SAKI

IE SHIMA

KUME SHIMA

Hagushi

KERAMA
RETTO

OKINAWA

— — Radar Picket Stations
          manned before 16 May

—.— Stations manned after 16 May

——— Stations manned before and
          after that date

0   40
M

The Battle for Okinawa, 1 April–21 June 1945.

units included the Fifth Air Fleet (which encompassed elements of the Third and Tenth Air Fleets) and Sixth Air Army in the Home Islands and the First Air Fleet and 8th Air Division on Formosa. In addition to the aerial onslaught, Adm. Koshiro Oikawa, the chief of the Naval General Staff, ordered a sacrificial attack by the super-battleship *Yamato* and her escorts, principally because the Imperial Navy's surface forces must not be seen by the emperor to be idle during Okinawa's great trial. The plan called for this Surface Special Attack Force to sortie from the Inland Sea on 6 April and charge down to Okinawa by dawn on the eighth.

The first few of the 699 aircraft, including 355 kamikazes, involved in Kikusui No. 1 took off in the early morning of 6 April, shadowed the gunfire support ships of TF 54, and then raided the transport area. During the morning others shadowed the carriers of TF 58. At 1245, an intermittent but ineffective attack developed against TG 58.1 and TG 58.3 northeast of Okinawa and lasted the rest of the afternoon.

The ships on radar picket patrol and in the transport area were not as lucky. At about 1500, while Mitscher's carriers were busy to the north, some 110 Japanese navy planes that had deceptively detoured to the west began striking the ships off Okinawa. Around the same time, ninety Japanese Army aircraft attacked the transport area. The destroyer *Bush*, which had radar picket station (RP) 1, directly north of Point Bolo, was hit at 1530 by a kamikaze that struck the starboard side of her main deck amidships. The bomb it carried detonated in her forward engine room. About two-and-a-half hours later, a second suicide plane crashed into the *Bush*'s main deck, setting her ablaze. A third kamikaze slammed into her a quarter-hour thereafter, and within a few minutes she jackknifed and sank.

The destroyer *Colhoun*, on RP 2, just to the east, was heading to the *Bush*'s aid when she herself was attacked. At about 1700 a Zeke struck her port side near her after fireroom, causing severe fires. Within minutes direct hits from two more kamikazes left her dead in the water. Late that night she was sunk by U.S. gunfire after an attempt to tow her had failed. Other suicide attacks that day sank a high-speed minesweeper, a landing ship, tank (LST), and two ammunition ships, and caused major damage to ten more ships, including eight destroyer types, a destroyer escort, and a minelayer. This was a frightful loss of ships and men, but a far smaller one than the Japanese believed they had inflicted. At a cost of more than three hundred pilots and their aircraft, most of them shot down by combat air patrol fighters, the Divine Wind had managed to make twenty-two successful crashes.[14]

In mid-afternoon on 6 April, the *Yamato* and her escorts headed south on their one-way mission. The Special Attack Force, commanded by Vice Adm. Seiichi Ito, consisted of the 18.1-inch-gunned *Yamato*, the light cruiser *Yahagi*, and eight destroyers. The Japanese hoped that they would arrive off the Hagushi beaches and attack the shipping there. Eventually the *Yamato* would ground herself off Okinawa and fire her remaining rounds in support of the forces ashore.

Intelligence indications had already alerted U.S. forces to the possibility of a Japanese sortie. Thus, as Ito's ships emerged from the Bungo Suido, the submarine *Threadfin*, which was patrolling that strait, quickly picked them up on radar and sent off a contact report. Minutes later they were spotted by the submarine *Hackelback*. By nightfall Spruance and Mitscher were fully informed of the Japanese advance.

Shortly after midnight on the seventh, Spruance directed Mitscher to allow the enemy task force to continue south toward Okinawa, leaving the battleships and cruisers of Deyo's TF 54 to destroy it, while readying TF 58's aircraft to handle the strong enemy air strikes that were expected to accompany the battleship's approach. Mitscher had ordered all his task groups to concentrate northeast of Okinawa when the submarines' reports first had been received, and he did not countermand his order upon receiving Spruance's directive.

At dawn TF 58 sent out ten groups of fighters to search for the Japanese ships, which were discovered off Kyushu at 0822. Mitscher launched a tracking and covering force of fighters at 0915, and at 1000, while Deyo's staff was still drawing up a battle plan, sent off strikes from TG 58.1 and TG 58.3.

Following the launch Spruance ordered Mitscher to attack the Japanese ships after all, concerned that the Japanese might be moving out of range of Deyo's force. Despite poor visibility the *Yamato* and her escorts were spotted again at 1030, still several hundred miles north of Okinawa, by PBMs that shadowed them for the next five hours.

Mitscher's planes finally homed in on Ito's force at 1230. The *Yamato* began throwing up heavy but inaccurate anti-aircraft fire. At 1241 two medium bombs hit her aft. Four minutes later, she was struck on her port side forward by a torpedo. At 1337 she took three torpedoes portside amidships, damaging her auxiliary steering gear. Seven minutes later, she was struck in about the same spot by another two torpedoes. Following additional hits by bombs and four more torpedoes, the *Yamato* developed an increasing list to port, and at 1423 she slid under the waves. With her she carried 2,498 men, including Admiral Ito.

The *Yamato*'s escort fared little better. The *Yahagi* and four of the eight destroyers were sunk in the attack or subsequently scuttled. The other four, damaged to varying degrees, managed to make it back to Sasebo. The cost to Mitscher's air groups for destroying this remnant of the once-vaunted Imperial Japanese Navy was ten aircraft and twelve men.[15]

The sinking of the *Yamato* provided no respite for the weary Fifth Fleet sailors off Okinawa. Ashore, as the army troops (and later the marines) began pushing up against the heavily fortified, inland positions of Gen. Mitsuru Ushijima's 100,000-man strong Thirty-second Army, the going got much tougher. The ground forces needed all the naval air and fire support they could get, which meant that the navy's ships were forced to remain off Okinawa, tethered to the island almost like sacrificial goats for the waiting kamikazes.

As April wore on, each new day seemingly brought with it a series of suicide attacks. Most raids were small scale, but even these took their toll. On the tenth, with losses in sunk and damaged radar pickets mounting, Admiral

Turner ordered the strength on each picket station increased to two destroyers and four "pallbearers," as destroyermen began referring to the LCSs.

The Japanese continued to mount mass Kikusui attacks as often as they could. The second of these occurred on 12 April and involved some 380 planes, 185 of them kamikazes. Heavy attacks by groups of kamikazes coming in from the north began just after 1300 and continued off and on until about 1720. For the Japanese, Kikusui No. 2 was notable for including the first successful use of the Baka bomb.

The destroyer *Mannert L. Abele* was patrolling in RP 14, seventy-two miles north-northwest of Point Bolo, when kamikazes attacked her. At about 1445 she was struck on the starboard side just below the main deck and immediately behind the after engine room by a plane carrying a large bomb. Seconds later a Baka bomb hit her on the same side at the waterline, behind the forward fireroom. The effect of the two nearly simultaneous explosions knocked out her power and broke her keel. Three minutes after the second hit, she split in two and sank. Other Baka bombs launched that afternoon near-missed the destroyers *Jeffers* and *Stanly.*

The twelfth proved to be a costly day for Spruance's forces. Although some three hundred Japanese aircraft were shot down, enough got through to sink the *LCS(L)(3)-33* in addition to the *Mannert L. Abele* and to damage seventeen other vessels, five of them severely.[16]

The following day Turner pointed out in a message to Spruance that since the beginning of ICEBERG six escort vessels had been sunk, twenty-two had been seriously damaged, and sixteen more had been sufficiently damaged to require them to return to the forward area for overhaul. He stressed that, because TF 51 had been assigned an insufficient number of escorts to begin with, the situation was now critical.

On 15 April, in an attempt to reduce the weight of the expected third Kikusui attack, Spruance directed Mitscher to hit the southern Kyushu airfields that same day or the next morning. Accordingly TF 58 launched 125 fighters in a special sweep at 1315 that afternoon. The raid caught the Japanese with numerous planes on the ground. About eighty were destroyed and a like number damaged. Another sweep was carried out the following morning, with comparable results. Nonetheless the Japanese were able to stage a large kamikaze raid that day.

Kikusui No. 3, staged by 165 planes, commenced about an hour-and-a-half after sunrise. The destroyer *Laffey* was on picket duty in RP 1 when her eighty-minute ordeal began. The first four incoming Val dive-bombers were quickly shot down by her gunfire. Two Judy dive-bombers were also splashed

The destroyer-minelayer *Aaron Ward* was hit by five kamikazes during a hellish hour off Okinawa early on the evening of 3 May 1945. *U.S. Naval Institute*

before another Val grazed the top of her aft 5-inch mount and plunged over the side of the ship. From that point on, the *Laffey* began absorbing serious damage from suicide crashes. In the course of twenty-two separate attacks, she was struck by six kamikazes and hit by two bombs. Yet she miraculously survived to be towed into the harbor at Kerama Retto.

The destroyer *Pringle,* on station in RP 14 with two other ships, had still worse luck. At about 0910 the group was attacked by three Vals. Dodging through heavy anti-aircraft fire, a kamikaze grazed the starboard wing of *Pringle's* bridge and crashed through her main deck just forward of her no. 1 stack and onto the forward fireroom, where the bomb it was carrying exploded. The ship jackknifed, began breaking in two at the forward fireroom, and sank within five minutes, taking sixty-two of her crew with her.

Later that day Spruance reported to Nimitz that "the skill and effectiveness of enemy suicide air attacks and the rate of loss and damage to ships" necessitated employing "all available means to prevent further attacks."[17] Nimitz had become concerned that the prolonged struggle for Okinawa was leaving his naval forces open to heavy casualties from kamikaze assaults. Deciding to take a first-hand look, he flew to Okinawa on 22 April with a party that included Marine Commandant Alexander Vandegrift. Arriving that evening at Yontan field, Nimitz was greeted by the sight of a kamikaze crashing into a nearby cargo ship.

The next morning, accompanied by Spruance, Nimitz visited the frontline commanders. In a meeting with General Buckner, Nimitz declared that the troops would have to speed up their advance in order to free the Fifth Fleet from its role of supporting the fighting ashore. The Tenth Army's commander responded by pointing out that this was a ground operation, clearly implying that the question of how to fight it was best left to the army. An angry but composed Chester Nimitz retorted, "Yes, but ground though it may be, I'm losing a ship and a half a day. So if this line isn't moving within five days, we'll get someone here to move it so we can all get out from under these stupid air attacks." By the time Nimitz left Okinawa the following morning, everyone had become aware of how serious he was about the need to complete the conquest of the island as quickly as possible. Nevertheless a month would pass before the Tenth Army broke through the enemy's main line of resistance and almost another before it breached his final defenses.[18]

In part because Marianas-based B-29s began sustained bombing of Kyushu airfields on 17 April, the fourth Kikusui attack did not arrive until just before midnight on the twenty-seventh. Despite the participation of some 115 aircraft, it proved a disappointment for the suicide forces. The light minelayer *Aaron Ward* and destroyer *Mustin* in RP 1 came under attack ten times without being hit. Similarly the destroyers *Daly* and *Twiggs,* in RP 2 to the east, were under heavy attack late that afternoon but sustained damage only from near-misses, while in RP 12 the *Wadsworth* lost only her gig and life float when she was grazed by a kamikaze that night.[19]

The picket destroyers' luck was too good to last. Kikusui No. 5, which began on 3 May and continued into the fourth, was a bloody one for them. Approximately 165 aircraft took part. RP 10, located some 73.5 miles west of Point Bolo, became the scene of much carnage. At about 1830 on the evening of the third, the *Aaron Ward* was struck on the fantail by a suicider. During the next hour, she was hit by four more. Burning furiously and taking on water, she was towed into Kerama Retto. The destroyer *Little,* also in RP 10, was even less fortunate. The fourth of a group of Vals that had been diving on *Aaron Ward* suddenly turned and crashed into her abaft the no. 2 stack. Three more kamikazes slammed into her in quick succession, and she jackknifed and sank within fourteen minutes of the first hit.

The next day, 4 May, proved still more grueling for the pickets. The destroyer *Luce* was patrolling in RP 12, sixty-one miles northwest of Point Bolo, at about 0805 when a near-miss kamikaze crashed on her starboard beam. The shock caused a loss of power to her guns and radars. A second suicide plane crashed into her after deckhouse about a minute later. The bomb it carried detonated in her after engine room, causing severe damage. Following rapid, progressive flooding, she rolled over on her beam ends and plunged by the stern only four minutes after being hit, taking with her 149 of her crew. Shortly after the *Luce* went down, the destroyer *Morrison* in RP 1 was struck by a kamikaze that crashed into the starboard side of her main deck abreast the forward stack. Three other planes hit her within minutes. Flooding rapidly and burning from oil fires, the *Morrison* rolled to starboard on her beam ends before sinking by the stern with 153 of her crew still on board.[20]

Before the battle for Okinawa ended, a further five Kikusui attacks took place. Even though after the seventh raid the number of aircraft involved in each succeeding attack was smaller than the one before it, some planes continued to get past the defending fighters and through the anti-aircraft fire to hit U.S. ships. Sporadic kamikaze and conventional attacks also continued, and on 16 June a torpedo bomber sank the destroyer *Twiggs,* killing or wounding every one of her twenty-two officers. She was the twelfth and last ship of her type lost during the conquest of Okinawa. Despite the attention the kamikazes paid to the picket destroyers, the aircraft carriers of TF 58 suffered increasing damage as the campaign wore on. In all, five fleet carriers and an escort carrier were put out of action by suicide crashes. These included Admiral Mitscher's flagship, the *Bunker Hill,* hit on 11 May, and the repaired *Enterprise,* to which he transferred his flag, disabled on the fourteenth. The American carriers' experience was in stark contrast to that of the British carriers, which, because of their armored flight decks, were able to shake off the majority of hits and continue operating.

Although it was not customary to change commands in the midst of an operation, Admiral Nimitz decided that after four months in combat, the last two under kamikaze attack, the Fifth Fleet team should have a rest. Accordingly, Spruance, who would have preferred to stay on, turned over command of the fleet to Adm. William F. Halsey on 27 May. The weary and ailing Marc Mitscher was relieved by John McCain two days later. Vice Adm. Harry W. Hill had already taken over the amphibious forces from Kelly Turner.

Anxious to resume offensive operations with what now became the Third Fleet, Halsey urged Buckner to accelerate the construction of additional radar stations and airfields ashore and appealed to Nimitz to send another marine air group to Okinawa to furnish the close support the carriers had been providing. He also reduced the number of manned picket stations to four and reinforced their complements.

On 2 and 3 June, TG 38.4 launched long-range fighter sweeps against airfields on Kyushu. These proved only moderately successful since the Japanese were alert to the threat. The following day, Halsey and McCain had the bad luck to let two of their task groups blunder into the path of a typhoon, resulting in considerable damage to ships in both groups. This was the second time in six months that the Third Fleet had failed to outmaneuver a typhoon, and Secretary of the Navy James V. Forrestal seriously considered relieving Halsey of command.

By then the struggle for Okinawa was entering its final phase. The ninth Kikusui attack, which extended over 3–7 June, involved only about fifty aircraft, less than half as many as its predecessor of 25–27 May. On 10 June TF 38 was finally released from duty off Okinawa after eighty-nine days at sea. Ashore, U.S. forces penetrated the last Japanese line of resistance four days later, and on the twenty-first the island was declared secure. Ironically the final Kikusui attack began that afternoon. No more than forty-five aircraft participated.

The bloody contest off Okinawa proved the most expensive American naval campaign of the war. During twelve weeks of combat, the U.S. Navy lost thirty-six ships and craft sunk and 243 damaged, most of them by kamikaze attacks. The picket destroyers bore the brunt, accounting for 31 percent of the ships hit while constituting less than 11 percent of those present. More than 4,900 men were killed or missing in action, and another 4,824 were wounded. For its part Japan lost more than eighteen hundred pilots and crewmen. It was a horrendous butcher's bill.[21]

Okinawa provided a sobering lesson to the Allies of what could be expected when the Home Islands were invaded. The massive casualties, afloat and ashore, that could be produced by fanatical Japanese resistance and suicidal sacrifice had become all too apparent well before the end of the fighting for the Nansei Shoto. By mid-1945 planning had already begun for Operation OLYMPIC—the invasion of Kyushu—scheduled to begin in November, and the follow-on invasion of Honshu set for 1946 loomed ominously close.

Fortunately for all concerned, the dropping of atomic bombs on Hiroshima and Nagasaki in early August and the sudden entrance of the Soviet Union into the war provided Japan's emperor and its cabinet with an opening to sue for peace, despite the vehement objections of some military leaders. Thus, in the end, Okinawa proved to be the last great battle of the war.

NOTES

1. Technically, the Bonin Islands make up only the central group of the archipelago the Japanese call the Nanpo Shoto, while the southern group (which includes Iwo Jima) constitutes the Volcano Islands. The term Bonins, however, is frequently used to refer to the entire island chain

2. Geographical details on the Ryukyu Archipelago are drawn from Samuel Eliot Morison, *History*

of *United States Naval Operations in World War II*, vol. 14, *Victory in the Pacific, 1945* (Boston, 1960), 79–80; and Jeter A. Isely and Philip A. Crowl, *The U.S. Marines and Amphibious War: Its Theory, and Its Practice in the Pacific* (Princeton, 1951), 532.

3. For an excellent biography of Spruance, see Thomas B. Buell, *The Quiet Warrior: A Biography of Admiral Raymond A. Spruance* (Boston, 1974; reprint, Annapolis, 1987).

4 *Commander-in-Chief Pacific Ocean Areas Joint Staff Study ICEBERG*, PACFLT/POA Serial 000131, 25 October 1944, 1-2, 4; Box 52, World War II Plans Records (hereafter Plans), Operational Archives, Naval Historical Center (hereafter OA)

5. Commander Fifth Fleet War Diary, January 1945, 1, enclosure to memo from COMFIFTH-FLT to COMINCH, serial 00144, 30 May 1945, Box 32, World War II War Diaries Records (hereafter War Diaries), OA; and Commander Task Force Fifty-One and Commander Amphibious Forces U.S. Pacific Fleet Operation Plan No. A1–45, serial 000120, 9 February 1945, 24, 35, Box 137, Plans, OA.

6. "Commander Task Force Fifty-One [and] Commander Amphibious Forces U.S. Pacific Fleet Report on Okinawa Gunto Operation from 17 February to 17 May, 1945 ("L" Day 1 April, 1945)," (I)–1, enclosure to memo from COMPHIBSPAC to COMINCH, serial 01400, 25 July 1945, Box 9, Harry W. Hill Papers, OA.

7. *Imperial General Headquarters Army High Command Record Mid-1941–August 1945*, Japanese Monograph 45 (Tokyo), 172–76, 198–200; *Okinawa Operations Record*, rev. ed., Japanese Monograph 135 (Tokyo, 1949), book 1, 2, 45–46; and *Reports of General MacArthur*, vol. 2, pt. 2, *Japanese Operations in the Southwest Pacific Area* (Washington, 1966), 584–96.

8. Entries for 12 and 14–18 March 1945, COMFIFTHFLT War Diary, March 1945, 10, 12–16; report from Commander Task Force Fifty-Eight to Commander in Chief, U.S Fleet, Subj: "Report of Operations of Task Force FIFTY-EIGHT in Support of Landings at OKINAWA, 14 March through 28 May (East Longitude Dates), including Actions against KYUSHU, NANSEI SHOTO, Japanese Fleet at KURE, the YAMATO, and Operations in Direct Support of Landings at OKINAWA," serial 00222, 18 June 1945, 3–5, Enclosure A-1, Enclosure B-2, and Appendix Two to Part 2, Box 216, World War II Action Reports (hereafter Reports), OA; Morison, *Victory in the Pacific*, 94; and *The Campaigns of the Pacific War* (Washington, D.C., 1946), 340–63.

9. CTF 58 Report for 14 March–28 May 1945, 4–6, Enclosure A-1, Enclosure B-2; entries for 18–21 March 1945, COMFIFTHFLT War Diary, March 1945, 16–22; NavShips A-4 (424), *Summary of War Damage to U.S. Battleships, Carriers, Cruisers, Destroyers and Destroyer Escorts, 8 December 1944 to 9 October 1945* (Washington, D.C., 1946), 28, Box 456, World War II Command File, OA; Morison, *Victory in the Pacific*, 95–100; Rikihei Inoguchi and Tadashi Nakajima, "The Kamikaze Attack Corps," in *The Japanese Navy in World War II: In the Words of Former Japanese Naval Officers*, David C. Evans, ed. (2d ed., Annapolis, 1986), 436–37; Jeffrey G. Barlow, "The U.S Navy's Fight against the Kamikazes," in *New Interpretations in Naval History: Selected Papers from the Tenth Naval History Symposium Held at the United States Naval Academy, 11–13 September 1991*, Jack Sweetman et al., eds. (Annapolis, 1993), 409; and Masatake Okumiya and Jiro Horikoshi, with Martin Caidin, *Zero* (New York, 1956), 342–43.

10. Report from Commander Task Group 58.4 to COMINCH, Subj: "Action Report—14 March 1945 to 14 May 1945," serial 0300, 25 May 1945, 7–8, Box 231, Reports, OA; Report from Commander Task Unit 58.4.3 (COMDESRON 47) to COMINCH, Subj: "Action Report— Carrier Operations in Kyushu-Ryukyus Area, 14 March to 23 March 1945," serial 019, 1 April 1945, 13, Box 231, Reports, OA; Entries for 23–26 March 1945, COMFIFTHFLT War Diary, March 1945, 24–29; CTF 58 Report for 14 March to 28 May 1945, 7, Enclosure A-2; CTF 51 and COMPHIBSPAC Report on Okinawa Gunto Operation (II)—14, 20; Morison, *Victory in the Pacific*, 113–17; Report from Commander Fifth Fleet to COMINCH, Subj: "Action Report, RYUKYUS Operation through 27 May 1945," serial 0333, 21 June 1945, V-3–V-4, Box 43, Reports, OA; *Japanese Operations in the Southwest Pacific Area*, 2–2:598; and *Summary of War Damage—8 December 1944 to 9 October 1945*, 54.

11. Entries for 26–31 March 1945, COMFIFTHFLT War Diary, March 1945, 29–40; *Summary of War Damage—8 December 1944 to 9 October 1945*, 8, 17, 42, and 55; *Japanese Operations in the Southwest Pacific Area*, 2–2:598; entry for 27 March 1945, in Donald M. Goldstein and Katherine V. Dillon, *Fading Victory: The Diary of Admiral Matome Ugaki*, Masataka Chihaya, trans. (Pittsburgh, 1991), 562; Morison, *Victory in the Pacific*, 115–16, 133–34, 136–37; and CTF 51 and COMPHIBSPAC Report on Okinawa Gunto Operation (IV)—66.

12. Entry for 31 March 1945, COMFIFTHFLT War Diary, March 1945, 38–40; entry for 1 April 1945, COMFIFTHFLT War Diary, April 1945, 3, enclosure to memo from COMFIFTHFLT to COM-INCH, serial 00224, 30 June 1945, Box 32, War Diaries, OA; *Summary of War Damage—8 December 1944 to 9 October 1945*, 40; CTF 51 and COMPHIBSPAC Report on Okinawa Gunto Operation (III)—9–10; and Morison, *Victory in the Pacific*, 154–55

13. See Barlow, "The U.S. Navy's Fight against the Kamikazes," 409–11; CTF 51 and COMPHIB-SPAC OpPlan A1–45, Annex K, Appendix 2—1–2, 6–10; CTF 51 and COMPHIBSPAC Report on Okinawa Gunto Operation (III)—11–19, and entries for 2–5 April 1945, COMFIFTHFLT War Diary, April 1945, 5–10.

14. Ugaki Diary entry for 6 April 1945 in Goldstein and Dillon, *Fading Victory*, 572–73; *Japanese Operations in the Southwest Pacific Area*, 2–2:600; CTF 58 Report for 14 March–28 May 1945, 7–8; entry for 6 April 1945, COMFIFTHFLT War Diary, April 1945, 11–12; and Morison, *Victory in the Pacific*, 179–97.

15. Ugaki Diary entries for 6–9 April 1945 in Goldstein and Dillon, *Fading Victory*, 572–79; *Japanese Operations in the Southwest Pacific Area*, 2–2:599–600; and "YAMATO's Battle Chronology April 6–7, 1945," 1–4, WDC 160463, Group 25, Item 25 I, Box 37, Records of Japanese Navy & Related Documents 1940–1960, OA; CTF 58 Report for 14 March–28 May 1945, 7–9, CTF 51 and COMPHIBSPAC Report on Okinawa Gunto Operation (III)—20–22; entries for 6 and 7 April 1945, COMFIFTHFLT War Diary, April 1945, 11–13; *Summary of War Damage—8 December 1944 to 9 October 1945*, 9; Barlow, "The U.S. Navy's Fight against the Kamikazes," 411; Buell, *The Quiet Warrior*, 383–84; Theodore Taylor, *The Magnificent Mitscher* (2d ed., Annapolis, 1991), 281–85; and Morison, *Victory in the Pacific*, 179–97, 199–209.

16. Ugaki Diary entry for 12 April 1945 in Goldstein and Dillon, *Fading Victory*, 581–83; CTF 51 and COMPHIBSPAC Report on Okinawa Gunto Operation (III)—33–36; *Summary of War Damage—8 December 1944 to 9 October 1945*, 10; and entry for 12 April 1945, COMFIFTHFLT War Diary, April 1945, 22–23.

17. Entries for 13–16 April 1945, COMFIFTHFLT War Diary, April 1945, 26–30; CTF 51 and COMPHIBSPAC Report on Okinawa Gunto Operation (III)—40–45; Rear Adm. F Julian Becton, USN (Ret), with Joseph Morschauser III, *The Ship That Would Not Die* (Englewood Cliffs, N.J., 1980), 237–63; *Summary of War Damage—8 December 1944 to 9 October 1945*, 10, 65; Morison, *Victory in the Pacific*, 236–38, and Ugaki Diary entry for 16 April 1945, in Goldstein and Dillon, *Fading Victory*, 587–88.

18 Quoted in E B. Potter, *Nimitz* (Annapolis, 1976), 375. See also entries for 22–24 April 1945, COMFIFTHFLT War Diary, April 1945, 42–46.

19 CTF 51 and COMPHIBSPAC Report on Okinawa Gunto Operation (III) 66–67; *Summary of War Damage—8 December 1944 to 9 October 1945*, 69; and Morison, *Victory in the Pacific*, 239.

20. CTF 51 and COMPHIBSPAC Report on Okinawa Gunto Operation (III)—75, 77; *Summary of War Damage—8 December 1944 to 9 October 1945*, 11–12; copy of memo from Lt. Harold X. McGowan, USNR, to Intelligence Officer, Task Group 51.15 (Commander Amphibious Group Seven), Subj: "Suicide Attack on LITTLE (DD-803)," n d., part of enclosure S to report from Commander Amphibious Forces, U.S. Pacific Fleet to COMINCH, Subj: "Information on and Comments Concerning Suicide Plane Attacks," serial 00406, 25 June 1945, Box 330, World War II Command File, OA; and Morison, *Victory in the Pacific*, 253–55.

21. Entry for 15 April 1945, COMFIFTHFLT War Diary, April 1945, 28; CTF 58 Report for 14 March–28 May 1945, 12–13; *Summary of War Damage—8 December 1944 to 9 October 1945*, 29–31; entries for 27–31 May 1945, Commander Third Fleet War Diary, February–May 1945, 5–16, enclosure to memo from COMTHIRDFLT to COMINCH, serial 00204, 22 June 1945; Box 30, War Diaries, OA; COMTHIRDFLT War Diary, June 1945, 1–39, enclosure to memo from COMTHIRDFLT to COM-INCH, serial 00246, 28 July 1945, Box 30, War Diaries, OA; Barlow, "The Navy's Fight Against the Kamikazes," 412–13; Morison, *Victory in the Pacific*, 282; and memo for the Secretary of the Navy, subject: "U.S Naval Losses from Enemy Action in Okinawa Campaign," Op 33-P serial 624P33, n.d. [6 May 1946], "GENERAL INTEREST, 1947–48" Folder, series 3, Chester W. Nimitz Papers, OA.

19

Operation Praying Mantis

MICHAEL A. PALMER

Since the end of World War II, the West's need for Persian Gulf oil, the impact of the region's politics on the Arab-Israeli crisis, and, until 1989, Cold War antagonisms have combined to make the gulf an intractable trouble spot for the United States.[1] For decades policy makers sought to safeguard Western interests there without committing major U.S. forces to the defense of the region. From 1945 to 1971, the British bore the principal part of that burden. Following their withdrawal from "East of Suez," the administration of President Richard M. Nixon turned to Iran and Saudi Arabia (the latter being a very junior partner) as "Twin Pillars" to secure Western interests in the gulf. The application of the Nixon Doctrine to Southwest Asia was a Hobson's choice for an administration, already heavily engaged in Indochina, that lacked the domestic support to shoulder new international commitments.[2]

In 1979 the U.S. policy of eschewing commitments to the defense of the Middle East collapsed along with the regime of Mohammed Reza Shah Pahlavi. His fall, combined with the Soviet invasion of Afghanistan, left President Jimmy Carter facing a dilemma. None of America's allies, nor any of the local pro-Western powers, had either the strength or the will to ensure the security of the region. Carter recognized that if Western interests were to be protected, the United States would have to assume the role long played by Great Britain in the Persian Gulf.

The Carter administration, at work since 1977 reassessing American Middle East policy, responded promptly to the new situation.[3] While Carter muddled through the Iran hostage crisis, his administration sure-handedly built up the Rapid Deployment Joint Task Force for possible deployment to Southwest Asia; undertook an extensive, long-term expansion of base and port facilities in the Arabian peninsula; began prepositioning equipment and sup-

381

plies closer to the scene of possible action; and initiated the routine deployment of major U.S. naval forces to the Indian Ocean basin, including aircraft carrier battlegroups. Carter also proclaimed a new doctrine, bearing his name, in which he announced that the United States would not allow any external power to threaten the security of a region so critical to the West.

While Carter aimed his doctrine primarily at the external threat posed by the Soviet Union, he did not ignore the possibility of an internal threat. Because of the often tortuous relationship between the United States and the gulf Arabs, as Secretary of Defense Harold Brown later admitted, the administration considered "an explicitly declared policy on defense against local threats unwise."[4] But in October 1980, when the Iran-Iraq War created new internal threats to the stability of the region, Secretary of State Edmund Muskie announced, "We have pledged to do what is necessary to protect free shipping in the Strait of Hormuz from any interference."[5]

The administrations of Ronald Reagan and George Bush built upon the Persian Gulf policies initiated under Carter. In a 1981 press conference President Reagan announced his Corollary to the Carter Doctrine, noting that "there is no way . . . that we could stand by and see [Saudi Arabia] taken over by anyone that would shut off the oil."[6] Reagan's remarks were aimed not at the Soviets, but at internal forces unleashed by Iran, then at work in the gulf. His administration continued the development of the Rapid Deployment Force and in 1983 established a new unified command—United States Central Command. Reagan oversaw the continued expansion of port and base facilities as well as the prepositioning of equipment and supplies in the region, particularly at Diego Garcia.

In 1987 the long-feared spillover of the Iran-Iraq War into the waters of the Persian Gulf became a reality. As the war escalated, President Saddam Hussein's Iraq struck at Iran's oil exports by attacking its tanker traffic. The Iranians, despite their superior geographic position fronting the gulf, could not respond in kind since the Iraqis exported most of their oil via pipelines that ran through Turkey and Saudi Arabia. In an effort to strike at Iraq, if only indirectly, the frustrated Iranians turned their wrath against Kuwait, a major supporter of Saddam and an entrepôt for the Iraqis, who controlled no major gulf port of their own.

The Kuwaitis were the weak link in the Arab gulf. Their country was small, vulnerable, and within fairly easy striking distance of the Iranians entrenched in the Faw Peninsula. Aware that their tankers had been singled out by Iran, the Kuwaitis sought help. In accordance with their traditional policy of trying to avoid becoming too reliant on the West, they turned to both the United States and the Soviet Union to provide protection for Kuwait's tanker fleet.

The sudden turn of events of late 1986 and early 1987 in the Persian Gulf alarmed the Reagan administration, and the president decided to accede to the Kuwaiti reflagging request.[7] Intelligence sources indicated that the Iranians were not only trying to isolate Kuwait but also planning an invasion of the islands off the country's northeastern coast. Furthermore, U.S. leaders were loath to see the Soviet Union become the protector of a major source of the West's petroleum.

The administration pursued its policy despite strong domestic political opposition. Revelations about the Iran-Contra scandal, involving a secret U.S. approach to the Iranians, weakened Reagan politically while simultaneously making a positive response to Kuwait's reflagging request imperative. Then, in May 1987, an Iraqi Mirage fighter-bomber mistakenly fired a pair of Exocet antiship missiles at the U.S. Navy frigate *Stark,* killing thirty-seven sailors and driving home to the American people the potential cost of involvement in the gulf.

Indeed, the Reagan gulf policy was not without risks. The president, notwithstanding his oft-stated determination to avoid another Vietnam-like conflict, had involved the United States in an eight-year-old, seemingly endless struggle, in which U.S. military forces would be forced to fight with limited resources while seeking limited objectives. That is not to say that the policy was faulty, but simply that Reagan, despite his best intentions, found himself, as had so many of his predecessors, compelled to fight yet another twilight war.

In an effort to avoid deeper entanglement, the administration anticipated, or hoped, that a minimal show of force would deter Iran from its continued attacks against Kuwaiti shipping. Government officials assured Congress that the Iranians had heretofore "consistently avoided" attacking American-flagged ships and would likely do so in the future. If Iran did strike, the administration expected the Iranians to use the Chinese-made Silkworm antiship missiles deployed in the approaches to the Strait of Hormuz. U.S. military experts considered this threat limited, believing that the missile could be countered. When asked by Sen. Dan Quayle about the possibility that the Iranians might undertake a minelaying campaign in the gulf, Undersecretary of State Michael H. Armacost assured him that the chairman of the Joint Chiefs of Staff, Adm. William J. Crowe Jr., considered the risk "very small."[8] As Crowe himself later wrote, "I did not believe the Iranians were going to challenge us seriously."[9]

Unfortunately the Iranians who, in fact, ought to have been deterred, ignored the overwhelming military power of the United States, issued a "challenge," and did so with the naval weapon the U.S. Navy was least able to counter directly—the mine. On 24 July 1987, during the first escorted transit one of the reflagged Kuwaiti ships, the tanker *Bridgeton,* struck an Iranian-laid mine in the gulf. As the stricken vessel made its way toward Kuwait City, the "escorting" U.S. frigates steamed for safety in the tanker's wake.

Rather than run the risk of broadening the war by striking at Iran with U.S. air power, the administration chose to meet the mine threat with a limited countermine effort in the international waters of the Persian Gulf. Crowe rushed the navy's meager minesweeping assets to the gulf; but he was well aware that mine warfare was the navy's Achilles heel and understood just how "vulnerable" U.S. forces would be in the gulf.[10] "Vietnam was hovering over everyone's shoulder," he wrote.[11]

Crowe also recognized that a flawed command structure threatened to exacerbate an already difficult campaign.[12] The war would be waged along the boundary between two unified commands—United States Pacific Command, which controlled naval forces in the Arabian Sea, and United States Central Command, which controlled forces inside the Persian Gulf. Command boundaries are notoriously weak links in military hierarchies, and the U.S. command setup in and around the gulf was especially so. Coordination of U.S. operations would depend heavily on the cooperation of the commanders of the Middle East Force, inside the gulf, and the carrier battlegroup in the Arabian Sea. Such coordination was not forthcoming, and Crowe ultimately decided that control had to be vested in a single commander.[13] In February 1988, Rear Adm. Anthony A. Less was selected to pick up the reins.

Less was a fifty-year-old native of Salem, Ohio, who entered the U.S. Navy via the Naval Aviation Officer Candidate Program at Heidelberg College in Tiffin, Ohio. Commissioned an ensign in April 1960, he gained promotion to lieutenant (j.g.) in 1961 and augmented to the regular navy three years later. In 1968–69 he served in the Vietnam War, flying A-7 Corsair IIs from the *Kitty Hawk.* In 1973 he was chosen to command the navy's flight demonstration team, the Blue Angels, a testament to both his flying and leadership skills. His climb into the higher ranks of the navy began with his assignment as commanding officer of Carrier Air Wing 9 in 1976. Later that year Less became executive assistant to the Deputy Chief of Naval Operations (Air) in the Pentagon, serving in that capacity until 1979, when he took command of the oiler *Wichita* in the Indian Ocean. In 1982 following a year as executive assistant to the commander in chief, Pacific, he was given command of the carrier *Ranger,*

Anthony A. Less shortly before his assignment to command Joint Task Force Middle East. *U.S. Naval Institute*

again in the Indian Ocean. In 1983 he became chief of staff to the commander, Seventh Fleet, gaining promotion to rear admiral in 1985.

As a flag officer, Less continued his rapid and steady rise. He served as the deputy director for politico-military affairs in the Strategic Plans and Policy Directorate in 1987 and before the year was out became commander, Carrier Group One/Battle Group Echo, in the Indian Ocean. On 3 February 1988 Less took over the Persian Gulf command, wearing two hats as a commander, Joint Task Force Middle East (JTFME), and commander, Middle East Force.[14]

"Tony" Less appeared to be the perfect man for the job. He was a young, bright, junior admiral who impressed all who met him. His amiable personality made him a good choice for an assignment that required extensive diplomatic skills, soon to be exercised in the capitals of the Arab gulf states, including Baghdad. His previous experience gave him the combat, logistics, policy, and joint know-how necessary for the difficult duty he was about to undertake. Of his assumption of command, Less wrote:

In order to streamline location, command and control functions, it was decided to consolidate the two geographically separated staffs and install a single commander who would be responsible for the region. . . . My job was to plan, coordinate and direct joint and combined operations in the Arabian Gulf, the Gulf of Oman, and the Northern Arabian Sea. This included protecting U.S. flagged ships, and others as directed, providing a military presence in the region and coordinating operations and training with allied and friendly forces. We were tasked to operate a regional joint force.[15]

When Less shifted his flag to the command ship *Coronado*, moored at Mina Sulman Pier in Manama, Bahrain,[16] he inherited a fairly well-developed concept of operations. Based on excellent intelligence, it recognized that the best method of mine countermeasures was to prevent the Iranians from laying mines in the first place. The United States hoped to deter attacks, be they from Iranian minelayers, small boats, aircraft, or naval assets by establishing a military presence throughout the gulf and through threat of retaliation. If such measures failed, U.S. commanders expected that intelligence and surveillance would reveal, and permit the defeat of, Iranian efforts, whatever their nature.

Established in August 1987, JTFME had quickly begun to monitor events throughout the gulf region. Aerial reconnaissance was performed by U.S. Air Force and Saudi Arabian E-3A Sentry airborne warning and control system (AWACS) aircraft, U.S. Navy P-3C Orion patrol planes flying from Saudi airfields, and E-2C Hawkeyes from the carrier battlegroup maintained in the Arabian Sea. The gulf itself had been divided into sectors, in all of which a destroyer or frigate was routinely on patrol. Mk III patrol boats and army helicopters operating from two mobile sea bases—a Vietnam War innovation—carried out additional surveillance activities in the northern gulf. A frigate and two or more ocean minesweepers were attached to each base. Guided-missile cruisers coordinated air defense procedures, and frigates not assigned to patrols escorted reflagged Kuwaiti tankers and other merchant vessels in the 127 convoy missions that comprised Operation Earnest Will.[17]

Less recognized, as had his predecessor, that good intelligence was central to U.S. operations and, in fact, had led to the most significant success achieved in the first few months of the tanker war. Iran had ascribed the mining of the gulf to "the hand of God." To prove who was really doing the mining and to discourage the Iranians from persevering in it, the United States resolved to catch them red handed. Using a variety of intelligence assets, on the night of 21 September 1987 an army MH-6 helicopter gunship based on the frigate *Jarrett* ambushed the Iranian landing craft *Iran Ajr* laying mines in the tanker anchorage fifty miles northeast of Bahrain. Attacking with rockets and machine-gun fire, the helicopter disabled the vessel, which was boarded by navy SEALs the next morning. Still on board were ten mines of a type that had previously been found floating in the gulf. Photographs of this cargo were widely publicized.[18]

More mundane surveillance and presence operations had also yielded results. On 8 October 1987, army MH-6 helicopters flying from frigates intercepted four Iranian speedboats fifteen miles southwest of Farsi Island.[19] When the boats opened fire, the helicopters replied, sinking one and damaging three others, two of which were later captured.

Despite these U.S. successes, the Iranians refused to be deterred. In mid-April 1988 they eluded U.S. forces and laid a string of mines in the shipping channel fifty-five miles northeast of Qatar. On 14 April the U.S. frigate *Samuel B. Roberts* struck one of the mines. The explosion blew a 690-square-foot hole in the ship's port side, knocked her engines off her mountings, almost broke her in two, and injured ten of her crewmen. It took extraordinary damage control measures to save the vessel.

The Reagan administration responded by instructing U.S. Marine Corps Gen. George B. Crist, Commander-in-Chief, U.S. Central Command, to undertake a retaliatory action. At Bahrain Admiral Less's staff immediately identified several options for the consideration of Central Command and Washington policy makers.

Personnel serving in the gulf naturally favored an attack on Iranian installations, such as mine storage depots, directly involved in the minelaying campaign. Aerial strikes against Iranian shore facilities posed no military problem. The Iraqis flew with near impunity through Iranian airspace, and U.S. Navy attack aircraft could certainly do the same. But many government leaders viewed attacks against Iranian territory as an escalatory step to be avoided.

Nine months earlier the Reagan administration had debated, and rejected, proposed vigorous retaliatory strikes. On 15 and 16 October 1987 the Iranians fired Silkworm antiship missiles from launching sites in the Faw Peninsula

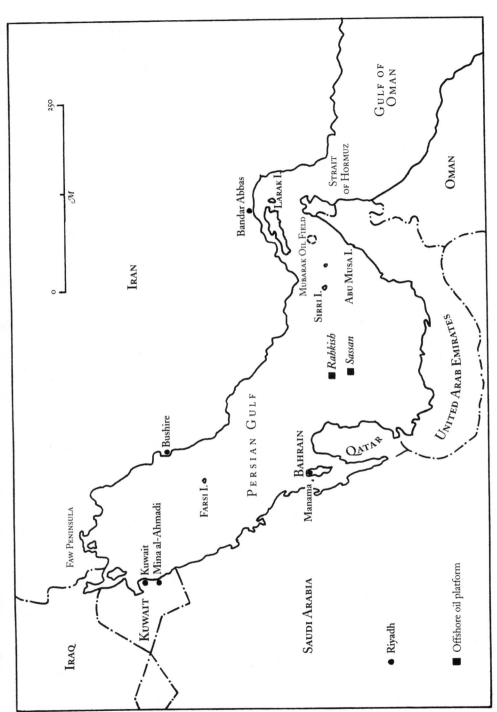

Operation Praying Mantis, 18 April 1988.

against tankers at Kuwait's Mina al-Ahmadi terminal. One of the missiles struck the reflagged Kuwaiti Oil Tanker Company vessel *Sea Isle City*. The administration considered but ruled out direct strikes against the missile sites, unless the Iranians launched Silkworms at U.S. naval forces. A recommendation by Admiral Crowe for a retaliatory strike against an Iranian warship was also rejected. Instead policy makers instructed naval surface units to destroy two old Iranian gas/oil separation platforms that were serving as control and support centers in the war on shipping.[20]

Following the mining of the *Samuel B. Roberts,* Crowe and Less pushed for a more forceful reply. But the administration continued to call for a Vietnam-like "proportionate" response, fearful that direct attacks against Iranian territory would escalate the confrontation. In the event JTFME was directed to eliminate another two offshore oil platforms. Thanks to Admiral Crowe's persistence, however, an Iranian warship would also be targeted.[21] If Less's forces could not locate a suitable warship, they would destroy a third platform instead.

Central Command and JTFME planners selected for destruction the Sassan platform in the central gulf and Sirri in the south. The latter was an active oil platform yielding about 180,000 barrels a day, but like the former, it was being used as an outpost for attacks on merchant ships. Both were garrisoned by Iranian forces and mounted ZSU-23mm automatic guns on their roofs. The naval target of choice was the *Sabalan,* one of four 1,540-ton, British-built Vosper Mark 5 ("Saam")–class frigates left over from the Shah's regime.[22] Since the start of the tanker war this vessel had gained an unsavory reputation and her commander the sobriquet "Captain Nasty" for firing at merchant ships' crew quarters.

Planning for the operation, which was code-named Praying Mantis, was completed on the *Coronado* early on 17 April. In the gulf three Surface Action Groups (SAGs), each consisting of three ships, were organized to carry out the action, while in the Arabian Sea the carrier *Enterprise* battlegroup advanced to within 120 nautical miles of the Strait of Hormuz. SAG Bravo was assigned the task of destroying the Sassan platform. In the event no naval target could be found, it would demolish the Rahkish platform as well. SAG Charlie was to deal with the Sirri platform, and SAG Delta to engage the *Sabalan.* The *Enterprise* would furnish a SUCAP (surface combat air patrol) of four F-14A Tomcats, two A-6E Intruders, and two EA-6B Prowlers, and keep a war-at-sea strike group on alert-15 (minutes) status in case additional air power was required. A continuous in-flight refuelling capability would be provided by U.S. Air Force KC-10 tankers flying from Saudi Arabia. Air Force

TABLE 19.1 Operation Praying Mantis, 18 April 1988

	Comm.	Displ.	Speed	Cmpl.	Guns	SAM	SSM
U.S. NAVY							
SAG Bravo							
Merrill (DD)	1978	7,810	33	319	2 5-in., 2 20mm	Yes	Yes
Lynde McCormick (DDG)	1961	4,500	30	360	2 5-in.	Yes	Yes
Trenton (LPD)	1971	17,000	21	420	2 3-in.	No	No
SAG Charlie							
Wainwright (CG)	1966	8,200	32.5	479	1 5-in., 2 20mm	Yes	Yes
Bagley (FF)	1972	3,877	27	288	1 5-in., 1 20mm	Yes	Yes
Simpson (FFG)	1985	3,585	29	206	1 76mm, 1 20mm	Yes	Yes
SAG Delta							
Jack Williams (FFG)	1981	3,585	29	206	1 76mm, 1 20mm	Yes	Yes
O'Brien (DD)	1977	7,810	33	319	2 5-in., 2 20mm	Yes	Yes
Joseph Strauss (DDG)	1963	4,500	30	360	2 5-in.	Yes	Yes
IRANIAN NAVY							
Sabalan (FF)	1972	1,540	39	125	1 4.5-in., 2 35mm	Yes	No[a]
Sahand (FF)	1972	1,540	39	125	1 4.5-in., 2 35mm	Yes	No[a]
Joshan (PTF)	1978	275	36	31	1 76mm, 1 40mm	Yes	Yes
Boghammar boats	1987[b]	5.5	45	5–6	Variable[c]	No	No

Notes: Comm = commissioned, Displ = displacement (full load, in tons), Cmpl = complement, SAM = surface-to-air missile, SSM = surface-to-surface missile, CG = guided missile cruiser, DD = destroyer; DDG = guided missile destroyer, FF = frigate, FFG = guided missile frigate, LPD = amphibious transport dock, PTF = fast attack craft

[a] Equipped with launchers but lacking missiles

[b] Ordered in 1984, twenty-nine had been delivered by July 1987

[c] 1 106mm recoilless rifle and/or rocket-propelled grenade launcher, plus machine guns

E-3A Sentry AWACS, also based in Saudi Arabia, and E-2C Hawkeyes from the *Enterprise* would maintain constant radar surveillance of the area of operations.

In keeping with the nonescalatory nature of the action, the platforms' occupants would be allowed five minutes to evacuate before the attacks. Any resistance offered would be overcome by ships' fire. Both platforms would then be seized, searched, and destroyed, Sassan by a navy-marine team, Sirri by navy SEALs.

SAG Bravo opened Operation Praying Mantis at approximately 0755 on 18 April by broadcasting warnings to withdraw in both English and Farsi to the personnel on the Sassan platform. The Iranians predictably requested an extension of the five-minute deadline, and JTFME servicemen monitoring their radio transmissions heard panicky appeals for instructions from headquarters ashore. After a brief delay, about half the facility's roughly sixty occupants scrambled on board two tugs. The others chose to remain, and when the destroyer *Merrill* took the platform under fire at 0804 they replied with its ZSU-23mm gun. Air bursts from the *Merrill* and frigate *Lynde McCormick* quickly silenced this weapon, leaving the Iranians to endure the bombardment until another tug asked for permission to take them off. SAG Bravo ceased fire, and in the words of an American observer, "a large crowd of converted martyrs" happily embarked. Once they had departed, the installation was boarded by an assault element of Marine Air-Ground Task Force 2-88, a navy explosive ordnance disposal detachment, and an intelligence-gathering team fast-roping down from navy and marine helicopters. Inside, the boarding party discovered anti-aircraft weapons and stores of rocket-propelled grenades and ammunition as well as communications equipment. After rigging demolitions charges that allowed the platform to be destroyed by remote control, the Americans withdrew.

Leaving the ruins of the platform in its wake, SAG Bravo steamed north to be in position to attack the Rahkish platform in the event an Iranian vessel could not be engaged. On two occasions it encountered unidentified, possibly Iranian warships, but both proved to be false alarms. The first was a United Arab Emirates patrol boat. The other was a Soviet destroyer whose captain was taking photographs "for history."

Matters got off to a slightly slower start at the Sirri platform, where SAG Charlie gave the Iranians until 0815 to depart. Once more a number refused to do so. The ensuing unpleasantness was briefly interrupted when SAG Charlie suspended fire to permit an Iranian vessel to evacuate some defenders who had undergone a change of heart and a U.S. helicopter dropped a life raft to six men in the water. Finally one of the ship's shells ignited a compressed gas tank, transforming the platform into a raging inferno that eliminated both its remaining defenders and any possibility that it could be boarded by the waiting SEALs.

While these actions were in progress, SAG Delta entered the Strait of Hormuz in search of the *Sabalan*. But the frigate declined to depart Bandar Abbas, where she was ensconced between two civilian tankers that sheltered her from U.S. Harpoon antiship missiles. Even the *Enterprise*'s aircraft could not attack the *Sabalan* without endangering the adjacent ships.

The Iranian failure to respond promptly, and as expected (or hoped) by the Americans, had many causes. The Iranian command structure was far less coherent than the U.S., involving regular military forces—the navy and air force—and the Islamic Revolutionary Guards (*Pasdaran e-Inqilal e-Islami*). A coordinated response necessitated centralized direction from Tehran, but on the morning of 18 April 1988 the focus of the Iranian government was elsewhere. About three hours before JTFME initiated Operation Praying Mantis, the Iraqi army began its "Blessed Ramadan" offensive against Iranian forces deployed in the Faw Peninsula. The Iraqi counteroffensive was preceded by month-long deception measures that convinced the Iranians the blow would fall further north. The assault, which began at 0500 on 18 April, caught the Iranian command off balance, and in the process of sending troops home for the Ramadan holy days that began at sunset on 17 April. Iraqi Republican Guard spearheads, supported by heavy artillery firing both conventional and chemical munitions, quickly shattered the Iranian front and made rapid progress. To the Iranian leadership, the naval events transpiring in the Persian Gulf on the morning of the eighteenth were little more than a distraction.[23]

It was late morning before the Iranians began to react. About 1100 five Swedish-built Boghammar speedboats based on Abu Musa Island and other Iranian small craft sped into the southern gulf, striking at Arab oil installations and merchant shipping. In the following hour, they fired on the U.S.-flagged supply ship *Willie Tide,* the Panamanian-flagged jack-up barge *Scan Bay,* which had fifteen Americans in her crew, and the British-flagged tanker *York Marine.* Admiral Less authorized the combat air patrol's Intruders to intervene, and the SAG Delta frigate *Jack Williams* directed them to the rampaging Boghammars. The aircraft sank the leading boat with a string of Rockeye Mk II cluster bombs, each spreading a shower of 247 bomblets. The remaining Boghammars raced ashore on Abu Musa.

Meanwhile, at about 1130, the Iranian fast attack craft *Joshan,* a French-built vessel of the Combattante II class, sortied from Bushire. In addition to her 76mm gun, the *Joshan* carried an American-built Harpoon missile. In the gulf she headed south toward SAG Charlie.

The *Joshan's* sortie, along with the activity of the small boats, demonstrated that the Iranians had decided to respond to the U.S. attacks. It also posed a dilemma for Admiral Less. Intelligence reports indicated that the Iranian frigates were preparing to steam out of Bandar Abbas.[24] JTFME had been authorized to attack a single Iranian warship. Sinking the 275-ton *Joshan* might well let Captain Nasty's 1,540-ton *Sabalan* off the hook. But the *Joshan* carried a functional Harpoon—in fact, as the Americans knew, the only such Harpoon in the entire Iranian naval arsenal. In that sense the small attack craft represented, if not the only, certainly the most serious threat to U.S. naval forces operating in the gulf on 18 April.

The impact of the twilight war atmosphere now came to the fore. In a purely military operation, Admiral Less's decision would have been simple. Intelligence provided the JTFME staff with information that kept its commander well-informed about the comings and goings of the Iranian units deployed against him. Less commanded an overwhelmingly powerful force, well able to destroy the *Joshan, Sabalan, Sahand,* and any other Iranian ship afloat or in harbor that day. But, because of the political restrictions imposed by Washington, Less had to play by an artificially restrictive set of rules. Preferring to sink one of the larger frigates, he chose not to preempt the approach of the *Joshan.* He ordered the *Enterprise* to launch elements of her war-at-sea strike group in preparation to strike the *Sabalan* and *Sahand* when they finally sortied and directed the commander of SAG Charlie to warn off the approaching fast attack craft.

As the *Joshan* continued to close on SAG Charlie, the Americans issued four distinct warnings for her to turn back. The Iranians ignored them all. When the *Joshan* closed to within thirteen nautical miles, Admiral Less gave the U.S. ships "weapons free" permission to engage—that is, to fire at will with any or all weapons in their batteries. The *Wainwright's* captain signaled the *Joshan:* "Stop your engines and abandon ship; I intend to sink you."

The scene was reminiscent of earlier actions by U.S. naval commanders. For example, in February 1800 Capt. Thomas Truxtun, commanding the frigate *Constellation,* intercepted the French frigate *la Vengeance* in the Caribbean. As the two men-of-war closed, Truxtun grabbed a speaking trumpet and demanded "the surrender" of the French frigate "to the United States of America."[25] The French answered Truxtun's heroics not by surrender but with gunfire.

The commanding officer of the *Joshan,* having ignored the warnings, not surprisingly disregarded the demand for surrender and fired his Harpoon at the cruiser. Admiral Less later described this as the "most tense moment" of his Middle East command.[26] To the Americans' relief, the Harpoon sped past the *Wainwright* close aboard her starboard side. Either the missile had malfunctioned or at such close range it passed its target before reaching its homing radar's programmed activation point. In a literal sense, the *Wainwright* had "dodged a bullet."

SAG Charlie now unleased its wrath against the *Joshan.* Over the course of the next few minutes, the *Wainwright* and the frigate *Simpson* fired five SM-1 Standard missiles in surface-to-surface mode at the 147-feet-long attack craft. The frigate *Bagley* contributed a Harpoon. All five SM-1s slammed into the *Joshan,* reducing her to a blazing derelict that the *Bagley's* Harpoon ignored. The *Wainright* and the *Simpson* finished her off with gunfire.

As SAG Charlie dueled with the *Joshan,* an American-built Iranian F-4 Phantom II fighter-bomber sortied from Bandar Abbas, apparently in what was supposed to have been a coordinated air-surface strike. Though the *Joshan* was already a flaming wreck by the time the Phantom reached the scene, it continued toward the *Wainwright*. After the aircraft disregarded the by-now-standard American warnings, the cruiser fired a pair of SM-2 surface-to-air missiles (SAMs). The F-4 was damaged and returned to base.

Having easily countered the small boats of the Revolutionary Guard and destroyed or damaged the regular air and naval assets sent against SAG Charlie, JTFME now prepared for the third round of Iranian responses. As expected, at 1459 one of the frigates emerged from Bandar Abbas to engage SAG Delta. The *Enterprise*'s war-at-sea strike group was nearby, operating with the SAG Delta frigate *Joseph Strauss* near the Strait of Hormuz. The strike leader spotted a ship off Larak Island that he identified as a "Saam"-class frigate, possibly the *Sabalan*, steaming southwest at a speed of twenty-five knots. In fact he had sighted one of the *Sabalan*'s sisters, the *Sahand*.

Three U.S. aircraft—two A-6E Intruders and an F-14A Tomcat—approached and circled the ship. Even though the aviators were certain that she was an Iranian frigate, the rules of engagement in force required an Intruder to fly low over the vessel to "VID" (visually identify) her before they were free to attack. The *Sahand*, of course, put up a barrage of anti-aircraft fire and several heat-seeking SAMs. Launching flares to distract the missiles, the Intruder maneuvered away from the fire. Now that they had VIDed the frigate, the Americans could attack. The Intruders launched two Harpoons, four Skipper infrared homing rockets, and several laser-guided bombs. To this fusillade the *Strauss* added a third Harpoon. Within seconds the *Sahand* was hit by two of the Harpoons, three of the Skippers, a Walleye laser-guided bomb, and several 1,000-pound bombs. They left her dead in the water, with fires raging from stem to stern. The shock from the ensuing explosion of her magazine was felt on board the *Strauss*. By nightfall the *Sahand* had become one of the few blue-water combatants to be sunk in battle since World War II.

In the meantime the *Sabalan* had finally emerged from Bandar Abbas. The Intruders that had neutralized the Boghammars were still on hand, having refueled from a KC-10. Admiral Less instructed them to intercept the newcomer south of Larak Island. Once again, the mandatory VID obliged an Intruder to make a low-level pass over the ship. The *Sabalan* acknowledged its presence with a flurry of fire and three SAMs that the aircraft evaded. The other Intruder promptly dropped a 500-pound Mk-82 laser-guided bomb. Penetrating the frigate's superstructure amidships, the bomb detonated inside her hull, knocking out her engines and breaking her back. As a second strike group headed toward the helpless vessel, a request for permission to attack went all the way up the chain of command to Washington. Secretary of Defense Frank Carlucci and Chairman Crowe considered the request, but the

The ruins of the Iranian frigate *Sahand*. *U.S. Naval Institute*

latter decided against it and advised Carlucci: "We've shed enough blood today."[27] U.S. forces looked on as Iranian tugs began towing the *Sabalan* back to port.

Operation Praying Mantis was a complete success. JTFME planning and intelligence was first class. Jointness—the cooperation and coordination of U.S. Navy, Marine Corps, Army, and Air Force units—worked smoothly. American personnel, weapons, and equipment had performed extremely well. JTFME assets annihilated half of Iran's operational navy, destroying two oil platforms and sinking a frigate, a fast attack craft, and several Bogham-mars. U.S. naval surface and air strikes badly damaged the *Sabalan*, probably beyond repair. U.S. losses were limited to two Marines killed when their AH-IT Sea Cobra helicopter crashed into the gulf for what remain unknown reasons during a reconnaissance flight that evening.[28]

While Praying Mantis was a clear operational success, especially for the U.S. Navy, the battle had a minimal impact on the course of the Iran-Iraq War.

The prolonged conflict came to an end in July 1988, but the cease-fire had less to do with U.S. naval successes in the Persian Gulf than it did with the ground victories won by Saddam Hussein's army.

Nevertheless Praying Mantis was part of a larger, successful U.S. operational concept that sought to prevent the Iranians from breaking the stalemate ashore, at sea. The U.S. naval effort in the Persian Gulf kept the Iranians isolated and helped to ensure their eventual defeat. Had Iran been able to intimidate Kuwait, threaten the other gulf Arabs, and force them to cut their support for Iraq, the war might well have reached a different outcome.

If the battle of 18 April 1988 had little direct impact on the minds of policy makers in Tehran, what of Praying Mantis's importance to American military leaders, especially those in the U.S. Navy? Despite the advanced technological weaponry involved, as two author-participants later wrote, "The war-at-sea strikes executed on 18 April were not a demonstration of sophisticated tactics against a formidable threat."[29] The contest in the gulf between the Americans and the woefully inept Iranians was so one-sided that the outcome of the battle was almost predetermined. The Libyan raid of 14 April 1986—Eldorado Canyon—had been a far more challenging operation for U.S. naval aviators. What made Operation Praying Mantis noteworthy was that it marked the first occasion since Leyte Gulf in 1944 that U.S. naval surface forces had engaged their enemy counterparts.

However the only "true" surface action was that between SAG Charlie and the *Joshan,* and the small Iranian missile boat stood little chance against a U.S. surface-action group consisting of a cruiser and a pair of frigates. Had it not been for the existence of rules of engagement restricted by political considerations, the *Joshan* probably would have been destroyed by an air strike before it ever closed to within Harpoon range. Even under the existing rules, SAG Charlie's men-of-war could have subjected the vessel to missile attack long before she closed to under thirteen nautical miles and fired her lone Harpoon.

Nonetheless as the two participants quoted above also noted, Praying Mantis "clearly demonstrated the substantial force and capability of the U.S. Navy."[30] In the midst of the Cold War, the United States was able to deploy an overwhelming force halfway around the world. No other navy possessed such a capability. The operational excellence of the assets deployed in and around the gulf indicated that the military buildup of the 1980s had produced substantial improvements in readiness and capabilities. And from the operation itself, the personnel involved drew myriad lessons regarding the impact of the fog of war on the modern naval battle, problems of time management, the need for better contingency planning, the importance of sound tactical strike

organization, the centrality of intelligence, the need for clear rules of engagement, the requirement for simple planning, and the functionality of the SM-1
Standard missile in surface-to-surface mode.[31] While Eldorado Canyon had
established that naval aviators had mastered the weapons and techniques of
the modern electronic battlefield, Praying Mantis demonstrated that the
navy's surface community had done so as well.

Nevertheless despite the good showing during Praying Mantis and the
many valuable lessons learned, the one-day operation did not provide an adequate test of the U.S. Navy's capabilities. During Operation Desert Storm
(January–February 1991), naval aviators would have to learn new lessons
about joint planning and operations in a modern warfare environment. While
U.S. naval surface forces would not play a major role in the war against Iraq,
the weaknesses of the navy's mine countermeasures remained all too evident.

There were also two other lessons that might have been drawn from Praying Mantis or, more broadly speaking, from the U.S. naval experience in the
Persian Gulf in 1987–88. The first was that the United States was willing to
use military force to defend Kuwait; the second was that third-world states
have difficulty employing first-world military technology against first-world
military powers. Had Saddam Hussein noted these lessons, he might well
have chosen a different course in August 1990 and have avoided a disastrous
war.

NOTES

1. For the background of the U.S. relationship with the Persian Gulf, see Michael A. Palmer,
Guardians of the Gulf: A History of America's Expanding Role in the Persian Gulf, 1833–1992 (New York,
1992); and for the U.S. Navy and the gulf, see Michael A. Palmer, *On Course to Desert Storm: The United
States Navy and the Persian Gulf* (Washington, D.C., 1992).

2. The Nixon Doctrine envisioned increasing reliance of local states for regional security. In
Indochina the Nixon Doctrine meant "Vietnamization." In Southwest Asia the doctrine implied
reliance on Saudi Arabia and, especially, Iran.

3. In Presidential Directive (PD)-18 of 24 August 1977, well before the fall of the Shah, the Carter
administration anticipated a broader U.S. security role in the region. PD-18 called for the development of a force of "light divisions with strategic mobility" that could be employed in a variety of
trouble spots, particularly the Korean peninsula and the Persian Gulf. See Zbigniew Brzezinski, *Power
and Principle: Memoirs of the National Security Adviser, 1977–1981* (New York, 1985), 177.

4. Harold Brown, *Thinking about National Security: Defense and Foreign Policy in a Dangerous World*
(Boulder, Colo., 1983), 157.

5. 14 October 1980 address by Secretary of State Edmund Muskie, U.S. Department of State,
American Foreign Policy: Basic Documents, 1977–1980 (Washington, D.C., 1983), 258.

6. Presidential press conference, 1 October 1981, U.S. State Department, *American Foreign Policy:
Current Documents* (Washington, D.C., 1982), 405.

7. Casper Weinberger, *Fighting for Peace: Seven Critical Years in the Pentagon* (New York, 1990),
387–94.

8. U.S. Senate, Committee on Armed Services, *U.S. Military Forces to Protect "Reflagged" Kuwaiti Oil
Tankers*, S. Hrg. 100–269, 100th Cong. 1st sess., 5, 11, 16 June 1987, 29, 60.

9. William J Crowe Jr , with David Chanoff, *The Line of Fire: From Washington to the Gulf, the Politics and Battles of the New Military* (New York, 1993), 189.

10. For a discussion of the U.S. Navy's mine-clearing efforts in the Persian Gulf and a broader perspective on the history of the navy's inattention to mine warfare, see Tamara Moser Melia, *"Damn the Torpedoes": A Short History of U.S. Naval Mine Countermeasures, 1777–1991* (Washington, D.C., 1991), 118–27.

11 Crowe, *The Line of Fire*, 193.

12. Ibid., 187–89.

13 Ibid., 188–89n.

14. After his return from the gulf, Less served as Assistant Deputy Chief of Naval Operations (Plans, Policy, and Operations) in 1989, OP-06B in 1990, became a vice admiral in July 1991, and served as ComAirLant until his retirement in the summer of 1994. As a pilot Less logged 6,000 carrier air hours with 890 traps. Biographical information on Vice Admiral Less was drawn from his official biography maintained along with those of other retired flag officers by the Operational Archives Branch of the Naval History Center in Washington, D.C.

15. Interview with Anthony A. Less, "Mideast Perspective," *Wings of Gold* 15 (Spring 1990): 50–52.

16. Manama, Bahrain, had been the "home port" of the U.S. Navy's Middle East Force (MEF) since the early 1950s But technically, for political reasons, neither the *Coronado* nor MEF's usual flagship, the *LaSalle*, was actually "homeported" in Manama. The navy's official roster listed both ships as being homeported in a U.S port, although the *LaSalle* had not been back to the United States for years Likewise all but a few of MEF's personnel were on short—six to twelve months—unaccompanied temporary duty hours

17 Ronald O'Rourke, "Gulf Ops," *United States Naval Institute Proceedings* 115 (May 1989): 49

18. Anthony H Cordesman and Abraham R. Wagner, *The Lessons of Modern War*, vol. 2: *The Iran-Iraq War* (Boulder, Colo., 1991), 318, reports that the operation was planned by Rear Adm Harold Bernsen, Commander Middle East Force, and Admiral Crowe during the latter's tour of the gulf earlier in September. Robin Wright, *In the Name of God: The Khomeini Decade* (New York, c. 1989), 168, notes that the *Iran Ajr* "had been tracked for several days after intelligence indicated that it had loaded 'suspect devices' at an Iranian port " Weinberger, *Fighting for Peace*, 414, asserts: "That we caught the ship was no accident." Crowe, *The Line of Fire*, 197, also portrays the operation as an intelligence coup.

19. Ronald O'Rourke, "The Tanker War," *United States Naval Institute Proceedings* 114 (May 1988): 33.

20 *Wall Street Journal*, 8 February 1988, 1, Wright, *In the Name of God*, 170

21 The following account of the action is drawn from O'Rourke, "Gulf Ops," 44–47; Bud Langston and Don Bringle, "Operation Praying Mantis: The Air View," *United States Naval Institute Proceedings* 115 (May 1989): 54–65; J B. Perkins III, "Operation Praying Mantis: The Surface View," ibid , 66–70, John H. Admire, "A Report on the Gulf," *Marine Corps Gazette* 72 (December 1988) 56–61; William M Rakow, "Marines in the Gulf—1988," ibid., 62–68, Hans S. Pawlisch, "Operation Praying Mantis," *VFW Magazine* (January 1989): 34–37; Palmer, *On Course to Desert Storm*, appendix A, "Operation Praying Mantis," by Hans S. Pawlisch, 141–46; Palmer, *Guardians of the Gulf*, 138–44, and the author's discussions with U.S. participants.

22. The *Saam* was the lead Iranian ship in the class

23. Officially the United States has always denied that it coordinated the start of Operation Praying Mantis with the opening of the Iraqi offensive. The chronology of the development of the retaliatory plan between 14 and 18 April 1988 supports that view. Nevertheless, given the capabilities of the intelligence assets the United States had deployed to and over the region, it is hard to believe that those at the highest levels of the U.S. military did not know that the Iraqis were about to strike and that the two operations might well coincide

24. According to Crowe, "we had intercepted their [the Iranians'] attack orders." See Crowe, *The Line of Fire*, 202

25 See Michael A. Palmer, *Stoddert's War: Naval Operations during the Quasi-War with France, 1709–1801* (Columbia, S.C , 1987), 186

26. Less, "Mideast Perspective," 50–52

27. Crowe, *The Line of Fire,* 202.

28. Subsequently Iran claimed to have downed the Sea Cobra during the afternoon's action. Wreckage recovered by U.S forces showed no sign of having been hit, although the possibility remains that the helicopter may have crashed while trying to evade an Iranian surface-to-air missile.

29. Langston and Bringle, "Operation Praying Mantis," 59.

30. Ibid.

31. See ibid., 60–65; and Perkins, "Operation Praying Mantis," 70 The SM-1 Standard missile can be fired as either a surface-to-air or surface-to-surface missile. In the engagement all five SM-1s hit their mark. One participant wrote of the missile: "With its high speed, it should be the weapon of choice in a line-of-sight engagement." See Perkins, "Operation Praying Mantis," 70.

Index

Vessels and forces for which no nationality is shown are American Other nationalities are abbreviated as follows: A=Australia; CS=Confederate States of America; F=France; G=Germany; GB=Great Britain; I=Iran; J=Japan; P=Panama; S=Spain

A-6E Intruder, 389, 392, 394
Aaron Ward, 376
Abe, Hiroaki, Rear Adm., 251, 288, 289
Abebono Maru (J), 271
Adams, 68
Adams, Samuel, Lt., 281, 282
Aertsen, Gil, Lt. 303–4
Aertsen, Mary, 303–4
Africa (GB), 60
Aguinaldo, Emilio, 193, 195
Aichi D3A2. *See* D3A2 ("Val")
Akagi (J), 268, 275, 279, 280, 281
Akatsuki (J), 290
Akitsuki (J), 360
Alabama, 302
Albacore, 334
Alden, James, Capt , 144, 156, 162
Alfred, 29, 31
Allen, 96, 97
Allen, Ethan, 3, 8
Alliance; in squadron commanded by John Paul Jones, 34, 35; in Battle of Flamborough Head, 36, 39, 40, 41; Jones takes command of, 43
Almirante Oquendo (S). statistics, 210, description of, 202, in Battle of Santiago, 209, 213, 214, 215
Almy, Thomas, 71, 73
Alvarado (S), 209
Alwyn, 96, 97
Amelia, 69
Anaconda Plan, 108
Aoba (J), 288
Arashi (J), 278
Argos (S), 187
Argus, 50
Ariel, 70, 73, 75, 76, 78
Arizona, 236, 243
Armacost, Michael H., 383
Armstrong, John Jr., 85, 90, 91
Army of the North West, 72, 82
Arnold, Benedict, Brig. Gen.: profile of, 6–8; in capture of Fort Ticonderoga, 3, and invasion of Canada, 4–5; opening operations on Lake Champlain, 9, 11–12, 13, 14; in first day's Battle of Valcour Island, 15, 16, 18, 19; in second day's battle, 20, 21, 22; conduct of campaign assessed, 23–24, 25; mentioned, 27

Asiatic Fleet, 226
Asiatic Squadron, 177, 179, 180, 200
Astoria, 280, 285
Atago (J), 296, 300, 350
Athenia (GB), 305
Atlanta, 289, 299
Atlantic, Battle of the: opening of, 305–6; German strategy in, 306, 321; German success in, 306–8; crisis of, 308–9; elements of Allied victory in, 308, 322; activities of hunter-killer groups in, 309–21; losses in, 322
Audacity (GB), 309
Auñon, Ramón, Capt., 208
Australia (A), 253
Avenger. *See* TBF Avenger
Avenger (GB), 53
Axis Powers, 220, 222, 223
Ayanami (J), 298
Aylwin, John, Lt., 61

B5N2 ("Kate"), 268, 272, 273, 280, 281
B-17 Flying fortress: in Battle of the Coral Sea, 255, 256; in Battle of Midway, 265, 271, 272, 275; mentioned, 233
B-26 Marauder, 265, 272, 274, 275
B-29 Superfortress, 369, 376
Babbitt, 321
Backus, Paul, Ens., 301
Bagley, 390, 393
Bailey, Theodorus, Capt.: commands Farragut's first division in Battle of New Orleans, 136, his division gets under way, 137, 139; its passage of the forts, 141, 142, 143, 145, 146; it overtakes the *Governor Moore,* 147
Bainbridge, Williams, Commo., 52, 60, 61
Baka bomb, 367–68, 374
Ballard, 96, 97
Baltimore: statistics, 188; joins Dewey, 182, 183; departs Hong Kong, 184; scouts Subic Bay, 185; in Battle of Manila Bay, 186, 192
Banks, Nathaniel, Maj. Gen., 153
Barclay, Robert Heriot, Lt.: assigned to command British forces on the upper Great Lakes, 69; logistical problems of, 70, 72; forces of, 73, 75; tactics of, 74, 76; in Battle of Lake Erie, 76, 77, 78, 80, 82
Barry, 310, 321

The Naval Institute Press is the book-publishing arm of the U.S. Naval Institute, a private, nonprofit, membership society for sea service professionals and others who share an interest in naval and maritime affairs. Established in 1873 at the U.S. Naval Academy in Annapolis, Maryland, where its offices remain today, the Naval Institute has members worldwide.

Members of the Naval Institute support the education programs of the society and receive the influential monthly magazine *Proceedings* and discounts on fine nautical prints and on ship and aircraft photos. They also have access to the transcripts of the Institute's Oral History Program and get discounted admission to any of the Institute-sponsored seminars offered around the country.

The Naval Institute also publishes *Naval History* magazine. This colorful bimonthly is filled with entertaining and thought-provoking articles, first-person reminiscences, and dramatic art and photography. Members receive a discount on *Naval History* subscriptions.

The Naval Institute's book-publishing program, begun in 1898 with basic guides to naval practices, has broadened its scope in recent years to include books of more general interest. Now the Naval Institute Press publishes about 100 titles each year, ranging from how-to books on boating and navigation to battle histories, biographies, ship and aircraft guides, and novels. Institute members receive discounts of 20 to 50 percent on the Press's nearly 600 books in print.

Full-time students are eligible for special half-price membership rates. Life memberships are also available.

For a free catalog describing Naval Institute Press books currently available, and for further information about subscribing to *Naval History* magazine or about joining the U.S. Naval Institute, please write to:

Membership Department
U.S. Naval Institute
118 Maryland Avenue
Annapolis, MD 21402-5035
Telephone: (800) 233-8764
Fax: (410) 269-7940
Web address: www.usni.org